FRANCE
ON THE MEKONG

*A History of the Protectorate in Cambodia,
1863-1953*

John Tully

University Press of America,® Inc.
Lanham · New York · Oxford

Copyright © 2002 by
University Press of America,® Inc.
4720 Boston Way
Lanham, Maryland 20706
UPA Acquisitions Department (301) 459-3366

PO Box 317
Oxford
OX2 9RU, UK

Library of Congress Cataloging-in-Publication Data

Tully, John A. (John Andrew)
France on the Mekong : a history of the Protectorate in Cambodia,
1863-1953 / John Tully.
p.   cm
Includes bibliographical references and index.
1. Cambodia—History—1863-1953.
DS554.7 .T85 2003
959.6'03—dc21   2002040830 CIP

ISBN 0-7618-2431-6 (paperback : alk. ppr.)

♾™ The paper used in this publication meets the minimum
requirements of American National Standard for Information
Sciences—Permanence of Paper for Printed Library Materials,
ANSI Z39.48—1984

For my children, Seán, Alex and Kieran.

Contents

Foreword

John Tully's masterful, fine grained study of the French colonial era in Cambodia fills a wide lacuna in Cambodian historiography and is also a marvelous read. Drawing on a wide range of unexploited archival materials, Tully weaves a story filled with skullduggery, high ideals, and low shenanigans and marked by tragedy, polemics, and farce. In the process he provides one of the fairest and most nuanced pictures of the French *geste* that I have encountered in over forty years of immersion in the subject.

—Professor David Chandler, Washington DC, June 2002.

Author's Preface

This book aims to fill a gap. For the longest part of her modern history Cambodia was a *de facto* colony of France, but the ninety-year period between 1863 and 1953 has never been the subject of a full-length study. This book is the first attempt in any language to provide an integrated social and political history of the period.

Until the 1980s, most Westerners outside of a tiny group of academic specialists were only dimly aware of the existence of Cambodia. If they knew of it at all, it was as an exotic principality, ruled by an eccentric prince, and home to the fabulous ruins of Angkor. Sadly, it took the horrors of war and genocide to put the country on the map. There has been a flood of books about the Pol Pot period—some of them well-written works of scholarship, others more derivative—but the literature on earlier periods of Cambodian history is comparatively sparse: it as if the last twenty to thirty years have been lit by arc lights, beyond which dark shadows crowd in.

Historians have not completely ignored the colonial period. The French historian Alain Forest published an important work on the Protectorate in the first twenty years of the twentieth century and the Australian writer Milton Osborne's book *The French Presence in Cochinchina and Cambodia. Rule and Response (1859-1905)* was groundbreaking. The Indian historian V.M. Reddi examined the growth of the independence movement from the perspective of an Asian nationalist. Osborne and David Chandler have examined specific phenomena: the former in a study of the so-called 1916 Affair, the latter in studies of the Bardez Affair, and "Independent Kingdom of Kampuchea" of 1945. Chandler's *History of Cambodia* also made use of archival sources and provides a valuable framework for study. To this list, we must add the present author's *Cambodia Under the Tricolour*, which examines the French *mission civilisatrice* in the country during the reign of King Sisowath. Mention must also be made of Ben Kiernan's classic study of the origins of Cambodian Communism.

The reader will see from the bibliography and the endnotes to the present work that numerous writers, including historians, geographers, journalists and anthropologists, have contributed to our knowledge of the period. The present author freely concedes his intellectual debt to all of these. However, this work is the only book to examine the entire colonial period in detail and this should lend it a depth and coherence that is missing in more fragmentary, general, or shorter studies.

Almost all of the published works on Cambodian history have been written by foreigners. When the French arrived, there were no printed books in the Khmer vernacular; such "books" as existed were written by hand on pieces of palm leaves glued together and secured with string in the corner or along the "spine". These works were generally in Pali, a sacred language similar in function to Latin in the Catholic liturgy. Practically the only Khmer sources dealing with Khmer history and society were the "Royal Chronicles". These are curious documents, written to describe events rather than to analyze them and, as David Chandler, has written, to act as bulwarks against the chaos that threatened to engulf Khmer society. Magazines, books and newspapers in the Khmer language did not appear until the 1920s and 1930s and these did not enjoy a mass circulation in what remained a largely pre-literate peasant society. Another reason for the dearth of Cambodian historians has been that Khmers have traditionally viewed life differently than westerners. As the French scholar Serge Thion observed "explaining Cambodia is typically a foreigner's business" and "Khmers themselves are not prone to explanations. They believe in fate and fate is a powerful explanation." [Serge Thion, (1994), *Explaining Cambodia: A Review Essay*, ANU Research School of Pacific and International Relations, Canberra, p.1.] Today, there are few Khmer historians, although Sorn Samnang has written an unpublished study of Cambodian society between the two world wars for his doctorate at the University of Paris and Khy Phanra has written about the Caodai sect in his country. As the country rebuilds and recovers from the tragedies of recent decades, perhaps Khmers will be able to devote the time and resources to the study of their history.

Acknowledgments

More people helped during the writing and research for this book than it is possible to list. Some provided documents or clues as to where information might be found. Some read drafts of the manuscript. A number of publishers gave permission to quote from the works of other authors. Other people, sometimes in the course of apparently unrelated matters, corrected errors of judgment or fact. Some provided me with a roof over my head in foreign cities. Others showed kindness in simple, but telling ways to a bewildered foreigner. I am grateful to Professor Robert Pascoe, Dean of the Faculty of Arts at Victoria University in Melbourne, for his help in making publication of the book possible.

In London, thanks to Anna and Phillip Turner, who made me welcome in their house during my visits to archives and libraries in their city. Thanks also to the staffs of the Public Record Office at Kew, West London; the British Library newspaper archives at Colindale; and the library of the School of Oriental and African Studies. In Paris, the staff of the futuristic new Bibliothèque Nationale were always helpful, as they were previously at the old newspaper annex at Versailles and at in the old library premises on the Right Bank. Thanks also to the staffs of the French Foreign Office archives at the Quai d'Orsay and the overseas army archives (CMIDOM) at the Château de Vincennes. Much of my primary information came from the French Overseas Archives (AOM) at Aix-en-Provence, near Marseilles, where the staff were patiently cooperative, not the least with my outlandish French. I must also thank the young American Ph.D. student from Duke University who was researching the history of Martinique at Aix. She took pains to provide me with information about Washington D.C. and I feel very guilty about forgetting her name.

Thanks also to the staffs of the Library of Congress at Washington D.C. and the Canadian National Archives at Ottawa. I owe a special debt of gratitude to the ever-helpful staff of the Cambodian National Archives at Phnom Penh, in particular to Peter Arfanis, Chhem Neang, Y Dari, Mam Chhien and Lok Sophea. Thanks to Peter for the clay tiger from Preak Leap, which helped placate my youngest child for yet another absence. Thanks also to Mathieu Guérin and his wife Lakhena for their help and friendship during my visits to Phnom Penh. Mathieu drew my attention to interesting documents he had unearthed in the archives in Phnom Penh and provided me with other very relevant material.

Thanks also to the efficient and friendly staff at the Australian Archives in Canberra, Sydney and Melbourne. Thanks are also due to the staffs of the Australian National Library and the State Library of Victoria. Thanks also to Professor John McKay for appointing me as an honorary research associate of the Monash Asia Institute during 1998. I cannot overlook, either, the patient assistance of the staff of the Monash University library, particularly in the microfilm, rare books and Asian Research departments. Thanks also to Mme. Aude Sowerwine of the Victoria University library at St. Albans in Melbourne for tracking down long out-of-print French language books. Thanks to Brian and Christine Hearn for keeping the rain and frost off my head during winter visits to archives and libraries in Canberra. I owe a debt of gratitude to my former teacher, Professor David Chandler, formerly of Monash University, and now Adjunct Professor of Asian Studies at Georgetown University at Washington D.C., and Senior Advisor to the Khmer Studies Center at Siem Reap. David kindly read drafts of the manuscript and made invaluable suggestions. David also contributed a generous foreword to the book, for which I am grateful. He was always willing to share his vast knowledge of Cambodia and brought his keen historical insight to bear on matters I had fudged or misinterpreted. Also, I cannot overlook my native francophone friend Regina Zajusch, of Launceston in Tasmania, for her translations of a poem by Prince Monireth and a Khmer song. I would also like to thank Mr. A. C. Smith, of Toronto, for permission to access his late father's papers in the Canadian National Archives.

Nor can I neglect to thank my family. My eldest son Seán and his partner Vicky helped make my visits to London happy and fruitful. My younger sons Alex and Kieran were always encouraging and never made me feel guilty for leaving them for extended periods on overseas research trips, although they would have been justified in doing so. My wife, Professor Dorothy Bruck, has helped me more than she could ever know. She encouraged me when the work seemed in the doldrums and never flinched at the cost of yet another overseas journey. An academic in her own field, she was always willing to discuss the project and was able to bring the point of view of an intelligent non-specialist when reading drafts of the manuscript.

Regardless of any of the above, any errors are of course, my own responsibility. All translations are my own, unless otherwise stated. I have adopted US spelling of English words except where quoting from sources that use British orthography.

Finally, I must acknowledge the permission to quote from other writers kindly given by a number of publishers and writers. Thanks to the Karen Fisher Nguyen for permission to quote a number of her translations of Khmer proverbs. These are reprinted from Mary M. Ebihara, Carol A. Mortland, and Judy Ledgerwood (eds.): *Cambodian Culture Since 1975: Homeland and Exile*. Copyright © 1994 by Cornell University. Used by permission of the publisher, Cornell University Press. Thanks also to Éditions du Seuil for permission to quote from Norodom Sihanouk's *L'Indochine vue de Pékin*. Copyright © 1972 Éditions du Seuil. Used by permission of the publisher. I must also thank the Perseus Project at Tufts University, Boston, Massachusetts, for permission to quote from Hilary Binda's edition of Christopher Marlowe's *The Tragical History of Doctor Faustus,* (1604 A Text) in *The Complete Works of Christopher Marlowe: An Electronic Edition* at http://www.perseus.tufts.edu Copyright © 2000 Perseus Project, Tufts University. Used by permission of the publisher. Thanks to Eleanor Mordaunt, for quotes from her book *Purely for Pleasure*. Copyright © 1932 Eleanor Mordaunt. Thanks to the Curtis Brown group for their help in this latter matter. Thanks are also due to David Chandler for permission to quote from his translation of a Cambodian normative poem (*chbap*), which appeared in the *Journal of South East Asian Studies*, Vol. XV, No.2. Copyright © 1984 David Chandler. Used by permission of the author. Finally, thanks to Wordsworth Editions for permission to quote from Joseph Conrad's *Heart of Darkness and Other Stories*. Copyright © 1999 Wordsworth Editions. Used by permission of the publisher.

Introduction

A Faustian Bargain

Go beare those tidings to great Lucifer
. . . .
Say, he surrenders vp to him his soule,
Letting him liue in voluptuousnesse,
Hauing thee euer to attend on me,
. . . .
To slay mine enemies, and ayde my friends...
—Christopher Marlowe, *The Tragical History of Doctor Faustus*

The French Protectorate in Cambodia lasted ninety years, from 1863 until 1953; short by the standards of older empires, but long enough to disturb the foundations of a traditional society. When the Protectorate was set up in 1863, France was approaching the zenith of her imperial power, but once-powerful Cambodia had already become a helpless principality. That empires rise, decline and fall is a truism of history, and thus it was with France and Cambodia. When the first Hindu kingdoms of Funan, Chenla-of-the-Water and Chenla-of-the-Land emerged between roughly AD 500 and 650 in what is today Cambodia, it was the beginning of the Dark Ages in Europe and France did not exist. The Romans had divided the geographical space later controlled by the modern French state into a number of Imperial provinces. Barbarians sacked Rome in AD 410 and again in 455. Flourishing cities fell into serious decline and after rallying under Justinian (AD

527-565), Roman power perished for good. While the Hindu rulers were building the city of Vyadhapura on the banks of the Mekong, Eurasian tribes were carving up the Roman Empire, some settling in the valleys of the Seine, Loire, Rhône, and other French rivers. As the Roman Empire perished in Europe, the Khmer empire was rising in the Far East.

The Khmer empire[1] reached its apogee between c.1000 and c.1220. A dynamic, centralized power, it stretched from the shores of the Andaman Sea on the Isthmus of Kra in the southwest, eastwards to the South China sea coast of what are now the Vietnamese regions of Annam and Cochinchina, and northwards up the Mekong and over the Dangrek Mountains, deep into what is today Laos and Thailand. The vast lowlands of the Banam River, which today form the heartland of the Thai nation, were under Khmer rule. The drive towards empire gained impetus during the reigns of Jayavarman II and III, and Yasovarman in the centuries before AD 1000. At the center of the empire stood the fabulous slave-built city of Angkor, an enormous complex of stone and brick temples, mausoleums and palaces, and humbler dwellings of bamboo and thatch, situated just inland from the northwest tip of the Tonlé Sap, the Great Lake of central Cambodia. A vast irrigation system sustained the city. The most characteristic building of the complex, Angkor Wat, dedicated to the Hindu god Vishnu, dates from the reign of Suryavarman II in the 12th century.[2] Today, the ruined city still strikes awe into the hearts of those who see it, thanks to French money and expertise, which restored it after long neglect.

We can trace the origins of the modern French state to the Frankish Empire that sprang up in the ruins of the old Roman provinces of Gaul between AD 714 and 814. In AD 732, the Frankish ruler Charles Martel, soundly defeated an Arab army at Poitiers and assured the sovereignty and territorial integrity of the crystallizing state, whose greatest leader, Charlemagne, later carried Frankish power deep into central Europe. By the time that Angkor commenced its decline, in the second decade of the 13th century, the French monarchy was consolidating its territory and its power. By the early 14th century, the great Khmer Empire remained larger than modern Cambodia, but it had lost the vast sweep of territory across to the Andaman Sea. Its western boundaries lay in the Banam River valley and its northern border had shrunk down the Mekong to what is southern Laos today. Between c.1350 and c.1450, it stabilized at roughly its present size, plus the Mekong delta, where a Khmer seaport, Prey Nokor, stood where the Vietnamese city of Saigon/Ho Chi Minh City is today. In about 1450, the Khmer kings shifted their capital from Angkor to Phnom Penh. This turning point coincided with the dawn of the era of European sea power.

The rise of European power

From the late 15th century onwards, impelled by the desire for trade and assisted by revolutions in shipbuilding technology and navigational science, Europeans sailed to the far corners of the Earth. Iberian mariners sailed up the Mekong delta to Prey Nokor (today's Ho Chi Minh City) in the early 16th century and in the same era, Iberian Catholic missionaries penetrated deep into the hinterland in what proved a vain quest for souls. France herself colonized the coasts of Acadia and Nova Scotia in North America early in the 17th century, although it was to be some time before her sailors appeared off the coasts of Asia. Earlier, at the same time as the Khmer capital shifted from Angkor, King Charles VII (r.1422-1461) was re-conquering French territory from the English, reducing them to an enclave around Calais. The reign of Louis XIV in the 17th and early 18th centuries established France as the leading land power in Europe. King Louis presided over an era in which agricultural productivity grew and major state-run public works schemes were completed. Industry and trade expanded. France's "triangular trade" with the African coast and the West Indies was worth some 5.3 million pounds sterling by the late 18th century; more than the Caribbean trade of Britain and the Netherlands combined. During the same period, Khmer power continued to decline. By the 17th and 18th centuries, the Vietnamese were pushing down the coast from their homeland of Dai Viet in the Red River basin. They annexed Prey Nokor and the surrounding districts in 1674, followed by the Ha Tien littoral in 1714 and the Cape of Camau in 1780.

By the late 18th century, European power dominated much of the globe, although France itself suffered reversals in North America following Montcalm's defeat at Quebec in 1763, and in Europe after Napoleon's downfall at Waterloo in 1815. Nevertheless, France shared in the general industrial and scientific progress of the age. In the 17th and 18th centuries, a scientific and technological revolution swept Europe in a huge wave of discoveries and inventions, including the calculating machine (1673), three color printing (1711), the casting of steel in 1735, the breech-loading rifle in 1751, the spinning jenny in 1767, James Watt's steam engine in 1769, and the mechanical power loom in 1785. By the 19th century, the Industrial Revolution had spread

to France. Invention followed invention. Iron steamships appeared
from about 1805. The inventions of the revolver in 1835 and the needle
gun in 1836 further revolutionized warfare. The electric motor,
developed in 1834, presaged a later phase of the Industrial
Revolution.[3] By 1850, France was home to a large industrial area on
the coalfields around Lille, there were iron mines in the foothills of the
Pyrenees, and the Lorraine ironmasters had established their trade as
the basis for a growing engineering and armaments industry. Paris,
Bordeaux and Lyons had developed as major industrial centers. The
French Revolution of 1789 had spread legal, administrative and other
reforms across much of continental Europe. All of this was set against
the general intellectual background of the Enlightenment, which built
on the achievements of the Age of Reason and the Renaissance and
ushered in the era of modernity. As her intellectual, industrial and
military confidence grew and the memory of previous colonial losses
faded, France began new overseas conquests, annexing Algeria in
stages after 1830 and turning her eyes to South East Asia, "Black"
Africa and the Pacific.

   In contrast, Cambodia had entered into its own Dark Ages. By the
first half of the 19th century, Cambodia was racked by internal revolts
and threatened by external enemies. In 1794-95, Siam annexed the
northwest provinces of Battambang and Siem Reap, followed by
Melouprey in the north in 1814. Vietnam had permanently annexed the
Mekong delta lands, along with whole swathe of the Gulf littoral
including Kampot, although she returned that town in 1848. In the
1850s, Ang Duong, the Khmer king, desperate for allies, turned to the
French Emperor Napoleon III, asking him to set up a Protectorate over
Cambodia. The destinies of two very different countries were about to
converge, but it was not a meeting of equals. The French were about to
acquire a distant oriental curio, but the Cambodians were about to
embrace the dynamic, restless West. The French took over in
Cambodia in 1863 as part of their larger colonization project in
Indochina. This was an ambitious undertaking. In these days of
intercontinental air travel, we tend to forget how vast distances were at
the end of the age of sail. In 1863, de Lesseps' laborers had not yet dug
the Suez Canal and access to the Far East was still via the Cape of
Good Hope, a journey of over ten thousand miles. Even when travelers
bound for Cambodia entered the Mekong delta, the old capital at
Udong still lay over 200 miles upstream from Saigon and the
hinterland was a remote, mysterious place. This book tells the story of
how the French set up, administered and exploited their protectorate on
the lower middle Mekong.

A discrete period of history

The period studied covers no more than ninety years, brief in comparison with the history of human society in general and Cambodian civilization in particular. Although French power triumphed, it did so for only a (long) human lifespan. Moreover, it ended just less than fifty years ago. This, the reader might reflect, is insufficient time for us to be able to determine its significance. However, the Protectorate is dead; it perished in the great wave of decolonization that swept the globe after World War II. It will not reappear and although western imperial power now manifests itself in a different form, France has little sway over its former colony. ("Colony" is the correct word, for the Protectorate was a legal fiction for the reality of imperial power.) French colonialism in Cambodia forms a discrete period and we have access to many of the archival and other sources from it. We can, with some confidence, expect to be able to lay bare its sinews and bones, although not perhaps with the same precision as the anatomist. Our material is scattered and sometimes deals with more intangible matters than flesh and blood, yet we know enough to reconstruct the period and to reflect on how it affected the subsequent history of the country.

The ninety years of the Protectorate form a distinct era in Cambodian history and can be sub-divided without undo distortion or artifice into three shorter periods. The first period, which we might call the "heroic" years—at least from the French point of view—lasted from the inception of the Protectorate in 1863 until the death of King Norodom in 1904. The adjective "heroic" is especially true of the earliest years when adventurous French naval officers carved out an Asian Empire for their emperor. Regardless of their subjective intentions, there can be little doubt that these sailors saved Cambodia from absorption by its two powerful neighbors, Siam and Annam—today's Thailand and Vietnam. Exhausted by civil strife and foreign meddling, Cambodia might well have suffered the same fate as the old empire of Champa, its sons and daughters relegated to the status of a national minority.[4] The dark side of this period was the gradual reduction of Norodom into a French puppet. After Norodom helped to end the Great Rebellion of 1885-86, the French took away his power piece by piece. He died a broken man. The Faustian bargain he had struck with France assured the integrity of his country and allowed him a "voluptuous" life, but it came at great cost.

The second period opened in 1904, when the French put King Norodom's successor and half-brother Sisowath on the throne according to the terms of a secret agreement. These were the halcyon days of the Protectorate. They ended in 1940-41, after the ignominious fall of France to Hitler, and the subsequent loss of Cambodian territory to Thailand. The provinces of Battambang and Siem Reap had reverted to Cambodia in 1907, after forming part of Siam for some one-hundred-and-twelve years. Now they were lost again. These two events—the retrocession of 1907 and the amputation of 1941—are as distinct a set of historical markers as a pair of bookends. Following Sisowath's death in 1927, the French put his son, Monivong, on the throne. He reigned until 1941, just after the Japanese-brokered settlement of the Franco-Thai War. He died just before the hand-over of the western territories to Thailand, but he knew the loss was inevitable and it shattered his faith in France. France was unable "to slay his enemies" and "aid his friends". Between them, Sisowath and Monivong ruled for over forty years and for most of that time the kingdom enjoyed relative peace and prosperity, disturbed only by the Great War, the Great Depression of the 1930s and some enigmatic events such as the vast rural strike of 1916 and the murder of *Résident* Bardez in Kompong Chhnang province in 1925.

Sihanouk on the throne

With Monivong's death, Cambodia moved into a new and more turbulent phase of its history. The third period opens with the loss of the western provinces and ends with the granting of independence following King Sihanouk's "royal crusade" of 1953. In October 1941, *Résident Supérieur* Thibaudeau crowned Norodom Sihanouk, who still reigns as an octogenarian today. The war years were a dark period for France. Although the French still governed Indochina, they did so by grace of Japan, whose garrisons and warships were the real power in the land. The humiliations inflicted on France by Japan and her ally, Thailand, were a powerful blow to French prestige but they encouraged the growth of Khmer nationalism: in Faustian terms, it was the beginning of Cambodia's redemption. In late 1945, the Japanese put paid to the sorry interlude of Vichy rule: a time of privations, repression, fascist salutes and anti-Semitism. By 1945, however, Governor General Jean Decoux had woken up to the approaching defeat of Germany and Japan and was preparing to turn his coat. The Japanese forestalled this with a *coup d'état*, locking up French soldiers and civilians alike and declaring an "independent" Kingdom of Kampuchea with Sihanouk as head of state. The life of this state was cut short by the capitulation of Japan in August 1945 and the arrival afterwards of General Gracey's British troops, with the "Free French" in their baggage. Limited as it was, the brief period of quasi-independence made many Cambodians thirst for authentic sovereignty. The return of the French to Saigon and Hanoi triggered off the First Indochina War, in which the Viet Minh forces battled against a French Expeditionary Force. In Cambodia, Khmer Issarak or "Free Khmer" guerrillas waged armed struggle against the French and their nominally autonomous royalist allies. However, although some of the leaders of the Japanese-installed Kingdom of Kampuchea were punished with prison and exile, Sihanouk remained on the throne and the French were forced to allow the development of political parties and semi-autonomous governmental institutions in Cambodia. The Protectorate itself was formally abolished in 1946 and a measure of self-rule allowed as the French tacked before what were later described by Harold Macmillan as "the winds of change". To the Issarak insurgents, Sihanouk was a French puppet and traitor, but this was a one-sided view. Sihanouk puts his own "spin" on events in order to denigrate the contributions of his rivals, but he *did* help secure his country's independence. Whether he could have achieved independence without the military struggle of the Viet Minh in neighboring Vietnam, and the pressure of the Issarak guerrillas in his own country is a moot point. Certainly, he is wrong to claim all the credit for it. By the 1950s, French power in Indochina was seriously weakened and not even the Cold War and the injection of massive US military aid could save it. In 1953, the ever-astute Sihanouk realized that the hour had struck for full independence.

France's reluctant departure

The French left Indochina reluctantly, forced out of Vietnam and Laos by General Giap's pith-helmeted soldiers and out-maneuvered by Sihanouk in Cambodia. The tricolor was pulled from the mast and a new flag emblazoned with the towers of Angkor fluttered in its place. Ninety years earlier, Admiral de Lagrandière had sailed up the broad Mekong to treat with Sihanouk's great-grandfather. He offered that king a loaded bargain: maintain your crown and territorial integrity against Siam's claims, but at the high price of allowing in a much more powerful foreign power. France's aims were contradictory: the desire for power and glory mingled with the venality of the profit motive. Priests were anxious to convert the "heathens" to Christianity. The Saigon Admirals were concerned to block possible British expansion eastwards from Siam. All of this was mixed up with the *mission civilisatrice*—the self-appointed duty of Europeans to bring the supposed benefits of white civilization to the brown Caliban.[5] In the event, Caliban was "ungrateful", preferring his own civilization to the European version. Inevitably, the two civilizations collided, sometimes sharply, as during the Great Rebellion of the mid-1880s, but more often as part of a slower and more subtle process. By the turn of the nineteenth century, on the face of it, the French had emerged on top, determined to force upon Cambodians the kind of society they believed they should have. It was an unequal struggle between societies based, without too much hyperbole, on steel and straw respectively. We should never forget, however, the well-known Asian adage that there is strength in the grass, which bends with the wind in order to spring back upright when the storm passes. How much the French changed Cambodian society is a point for debate and one to which we will return throughout this study. Was colonialism a contradictory force with a "double mission", as Marx believed?[6] Was it both creator and destroyer? Did it lay the basis, whatever the subjective intentions of the colonizers, for a modern society, state and economy? Did "the industrially more developed country...[show] the less developed only the image of its own future"?[7] How much would the claims of Paul Leroy-Beaulieu and the other apostles of the *mission civilisatrice* be borne out in practice? This book will argue that in many things the French "mission" was weighed and found wanting. Expressed another way, Marx's early predictions that colonialism would transform the colonies in its own image were not fully born out, with unenviable consequences for Cambodia.

There is some evidence that Marx modified his early views on colonialism, although the point is hotly contested. Those who argue that Marx's views definitively changed, include Kenzo Mohri, Suniti Kumar Ghosh, John Bellamy Foster and Horace B. Davis.[8] Other writers such as V.G. Kiernan[9] and Anthony Brewer[10] are not convinced. Part of the problem is, as Kiernan notes, that Marx had no systematic view of imperialism[11] and that "no philosopher ever gave his system to the world in so unsystematic a fashion."[12] However, as Kiernan further notes, Marx's later "sympathy with the Narodnik dream of a direct transition from *mir* or village community in Russia to socialism can be interpreted, as [Eric] Hobsbawm suggests, as a shrinking from the price in human suffering implied in any overwhelming of an old rural society by capitalism. The spectacle of India, as well as of Russia, may well have influenced him."[13] Ghosh, however, suggests that Marx's well-known condemnation of British colonialism's exploitative role in Ireland[14] can be generalized to what we call today call the Third World. This is dubious. As Brewer has argued, Marx was pessimistic about the potential for revolutionary anti-colonial movements in India and China, but "In Ireland, by contrast," he discerned "a modern nationalist movement" in a country "at a different stage of development". Brewer concludes by noting "Marx's political analysis was always based on analysis of particular situations."[15] Probably the most that can be said is that as his early optimistic zeal cooled, Marx became less convinced of the regenerative side of the colonial dialectic. Regardless of who is correct—or more correct—in a complex debate, Marx's idea of the "double mission" of colonialism provides us with a useful heuristic tool with which to analyze and evaluate France's *mission civilisatrice* in Cambodia.

Notes

[1] See David P. Chandler, (1993), *A History of Cambodia,* Second Edition, Allen and Unwin, St. Leonards, NSW, Ch.2, "The beginnings of Cambodian History". Another handy reference work is Jan M. Pluvier, (1995), *Historical Atlas of South-East Asia*, E.J. Brill, Leiden.

[2] For an account of the Angkorean period, see Chandler, op.cit. Chapters 3 and 4.

[3] These details are taken from Hermann Kinder and Werner Hiligemann, (trans. Ernest A. Menze), (1974), *The Anchor Atlas of World History*, Two Vols. Anchor Books, New York.

[4] There are today large Khmer minorities still living in Thailand and Vietnam.

[5] Caliban was the dark "savage" in Shakespeare's play, *The Tempest.*

[6] Marx set out his early views on the "double mission" of colonialism in such essays as "The Future Results of British Rule in India" and "The British Rule in India". See Shlomo Averini, (ed.), (1969), *Karl Marx on Colonialism and Modernization: His Dispatches and Other Writings on China, India, Mexico, the Middle East and North Africa*, Anchor Books, New York. See also Karl Marx and Friedrich Engels, (1959), *On Colonialism*, Foreign Languages Publishing House, Moscow.

[7] Marx, cited in Leon Trotsky, (trans. Max Eastman), (1967), *The History of the Russian Revolution*, (Vol. III), Sphere Books, London, p.9. Marx's later, more critical writings on colonialism were more scattered and it is possible that Trotsky was not aware of them.

[8] Kenzo Mohri, (1979), "Marx and 'Underdevelopment'", *Monthly Review*, Vol. 30, No.11, July; Suniti Kumar Ghosh, (1984), "Marx on India", *Monthly Review*, Vol. 35, January; John Bellamy Foster, (2000), "Marx and Internationalism", *Monthly Review*, Vol. 52, July; and Horace B. Davis, (1967), *Nationalism and Socialism*, Monthly Review Press, New York.

[9] V.G. Kiernan, (1974), *Marxism and Imperialism*, Edward Arnold, London.

[10] Anthony Brewer, (1980), *Marxist Theories of Imperialism. A Critical Survey*, Routledge and Kegan Paul, London and Boston.

[11] Kiernan, op.cit. p.6.

[12] Ibid. p.165.

[13] Ibid, p.175.

[14] Karl Marx and Friedrich Engels, (1971), *On Ireland,* Lawrence and Wishart, London.

[15] Brewer, op.cit. p.60.

Abbreviations

AAc	Australian Archives at Canberra.
AAm	Australian Archives at Melbourne.
AAs	Australian Archives at Sydney.
AF	Ancien Fonds (at AOM, see below).
ANC	Archives Nationales du Cambodge; Cambodian National Archives at Phnom Penh, Cambodia.
AOM	Archives d'outre-mer, French Overseas Archives, at Aix-en-Provence, France.
CMIDOM	Centre militaire d'information de documentation sur l'outre-mer, French overseas military archives, Château de Vincennes, Paris.
CO	Colonial Office files (at PRO - see below)
FO	Foreign Office files (at PRO - see below)
Gougal	Governor General of Indochina
HCC	Haute Commission au Cambodge. AOM files on Cambodia after World War II.

CNA	Canadian National Archives/Archives Nationales du Canada, Ottawa.
NF	Nouveau Fonds (at AOM)
PRO	Public Record Office, Kew, London.
QO	Documents from the archives of the French Ministry of Foreign Affairs at the Quai d'Orsay, Paris.
RSC	Résidence Superiéure du Cambodge (files with the name appear at both ANC and AOM)

Chapter 1

August 1863: Gunboat Diplomacy on the Mekong

The ruler of Cambodia himself placed his kingdom under the French Protectorate without any pressure being put on him...and the Upper Mekong became French without the firing of a single shot, according to an expression that today is famous, this was a 'conquest of hearts'...
— Pierre Pasquier, Governor General of Indochina, 1929.

It was the rainy season and Cambodia was a watery world, steaming under a sun invisible above the clouds. The date was 11 August 1863. On the broad brown river often pock-marked with rain at that time of year, a gunboat lay at anchor off Udong; the tricolor flag limp at the mast. In the monsoon rain, it is often difficult to discern where the river ends and the flat delta lands begin, but the sailors might have made out the palm thatch huts of the town around the wooden bulk of the royal palace. In the distance were two low hills, surmounted by the stone spires of a cluster of *stupas*, which marked the burial grounds of the post-Angkorean Cambodian kings. There, under these fairytale spires, according to Khmer legend, a *Makor* (a sea monster) lived below a giant statue of the Buddha in a tunnel leading to the center of the earth. Ancient Chinese geomancers had believed that if the *Makor* escaped, Cambodian power would eclipse that of the Middle Kingdom.[1] As it happened, the monster remained in its lair and a greater empire than Beijing was about to check Cambodian power.

Admiral Pierre Paul Marie Benoît de Lagrandière—resplendent in the uniform of the Imperial French Navy, gorgeous in gold epaulettes, cuffs and sash, ceremonial sword by his side and cocked hat on his head—had gone ashore from the gunboat in the Tonlé Sap River at Udong.[2] His gunboat had sailed up the turbid Mekong from Saigon, several hundred miles downstream, before entering the Tonlé Sap River, which, by a freak of hydraulics, flows backwards at that time of year into the lake of the same name. Photographs show the admiral to have been an imperious-looking Breton, 56 years-of-age,[3] graying and balding, with an erect military bearing and rows of decorations above his shining brass buttons. This "strong-willed and competent political schemer",[4] was a man on the "cutting edge" of French imperial policy, despite, or perhaps because of, the thousands of miles of sea between Saigon and France. Some writers describe him as a viceroy[5] who often acted without reference to his nominal superiors in Paris. As he walked into the royal palace that day, he was about to present the French Emperor, Louis Bonaparte, with another *fait accompli*. He had come to Cambodia some months earlier, perhaps, as some writers claim, on the orders of M. Prosper Justin Chasseloup-Laubat, the Minister of the Navy and Colonies,[6] but perhaps more on his own initiative, to negotiate a treaty with the man who now sat nearby, ready to sign the document that lay on the table between them. The document committed France to act as Cambodia's "protecting power", arguably without the full knowledge of the French Government.

The other man, small in stature, black-eyed and inclined to corpulence, but with an "expansive, intelligent and mobile"[7] face, was equally resplendent, albeit in silks and oriental finery, and younger than the admiral. Twenty-seven-years old, he had been born Ang Vodey, and had spent such of his life at the Siamese court in Bangkok. After his coronation in 1864, he was to reign for forty years as Norodom I.[8] Three years earlier, his father, King Ang Duong of Cambodia, had died. Chaos had descended on the kingdom and after some hesitation, the Siamese overlords had picked Norodom for the Cambodian throne, overlooking two other contenders, his half-brothers Si Votha and Sisowath.[9] The bitter rivalry between the three half-siblings was never to abate.[10] In desperation, Norodom had turned to France—which had shown at least some interest in his kingdom—as a counterweight to the power of Bangkok.

Norodom must have had a troubled heart as he took the pen, for from his subsequent behavior, we know that he was unsure if signing the Treaty was the correct course. The Treaty, eventually ratified by Napoleon III in February of the following year,[11] was a desperate gamble, but Norodom was anxious to free his country from Siamese[12] and Vietnamese domination and to rule as a sovereign in the full sense of the word. How much coercion, overt or otherwise, de Lagrandière applied is a moot point. The Australian writer Wilfred Burchett claims that the Admiral gave Norodom a four-hour ultimatum, backed up by his warship's guns. He does not give a source, however.[13] Was the Admiral so blunt? One imagines that he was superficially cordial and respectful, yet used to getting his way and determined that Norodom would sign. The Austrian-American historian Joseph Buttinger believes that the Admiral bullied Norodom into signing[14] and Milton Osborne concludes, prudently, that the Treaty was "chiefly the result of French pressure."[15] In truth, the civilized courtesies masked the cruder reality of "gunboat diplomacy". Admiral de Lagrandière had the firepower to level Norodom's humble capital and his marines could easily overwhelm the *Tagal* palace guards.[16] It was not a treaty between equals. De Lagrandière's representative Doudart de Lagrée pulled the smiling mask aside on a number of occasions shortly afterwards, when Norodom attempted to assert a measure of independence in the conduct of his external affairs. The French naval officers at Saigon were waging a bloody campaign to subdue the nearby Vietnamese rebels. Such swashbuckling imperialists were unlikely to tolerate resistance from the ruler of the debilitated Cambodian state. Norodom had little option but to sign. Nevertheless, the French later often claimed the Cambodians had invited them into the kingdom and that there was no bloody or illegitimate seizure of power. It was a "conquest of hearts", a high colonial official later claimed.[17] This was disinguous. As a later generation might say, the bluff, red-faced admiral had made Norodom "an offer he could not refuse", although it was probably the best option for him at the time.

The motives of the French are less clear. Admiral de Lagrandière's relatively autonomous role in the establishment of the protectorate supports the claim of the British historian D.K. Fieldhouse that "imperial expansion during the period [1815-1882] was almost entirely unplanned by Europe: the momentum came from the periphery."[18] Regardless of subsequent mythmaking, France's intervention was far from selfless. Although the imperialist project had multiple causes, it has its origins more in national egoism and greed than in the self-professed altruism of the *mission civilisatrice*. The French Government was initially slow to respond to its opportunities in Cambodia. It was not an obvious jewel compared with Vietnam, and so the French were lukewarm to Ang Duong's initial overtures that began the process that led to the Treaty. Later, they were absorbed with pacifying Vietnam. France was also deeply involved in an invasion of Mexico at the time.[19] Indochina, let alone Cambodia, was a poor competitor for Imperial attention.

Yet, the imperialist impulse ran strong among the naval officers who controlled the new colony at Saigon, far from Paris. They were forceful, "hands-on" types, quite capable of making hard decisions by themselves. As J.A. Hobson, the doyen of the theoreticians of capitalist imperialism observed, "the itch for glory and adventure among military officers on disturbed or uncertain frontiers of the Empire" was "a most prolific source of expansion in India."[20] Arguably, the French naval officers at Saigon were as "imperialist by conviction and professional interest"[21] as their British counterparts in Calcutta and Madras. As we shall see, the apparent persecution of "native" Christians in the disorderly conditions current in Cambodia at the time gave them a pretext for intervention. Further, they had reason to believe that Cambodia held strategic and commercial importance for French interests. The French writer and administrator Jean Moura tells us that when the French Governor of Cochinchina, Admiral Louis Adolphe Bonard, traveled to Cambodia in September 1862, he was interested not just in the politics of the kingdom, and its relations with Siam, but also in "its agricultural and commercial importance".[22] Cambodia also seemed to lie athwart the route to even richer pickings. The country itself might be what one writer later called with some license a "picturesquely useless fragment of oriental medievalism",[23] but Camoens' regal waterway,[24] the Mekong, ran through Cambodia from the faraway Chinese province of Yunnan. It was not until the explorations of Francis Garnier revealed the existence of the Khône falls and other obstacles to navigation that the French realized that the Mekong was not a "river road to China".[25] By then, it was too late and the French were already committed to their protectorate in Cambodia. Perhaps the French admirals might have taken Cambodia even if they had known that it did not lie astride a natural trade route from Saigon to China. The world was close to the edge of an unprecedented "Age of Empire" during which the European powers carved up most of the globe into colonies, protectorates and "spheres of influence".

Colonies could also be important strategically. Cambodia was a relatively small country, with a small population, weakened by war and domestic turmoil, but at the very least, together with Laos, it formed a natural buffer between the new French colony in Cochinchina and the British sphere of influence in Siam. Had France not taken Cambodia, Siam might well have done so, and thus it might have fallen under British influence by default. "Perfidious Albion" would then have been almost within cannon shot of Saigon and potentially able to meddle in the affairs of the Vietnamese lands. Even if the British did not harbor such designs—and there is no proof that they did—the French were naturally suspicious of their old enemies from across the English Channel, despite the relatively cordial relations between the two powers in the wake of the Crimean War.

The allure of the Orient

To these strategic, political and proto-economic considerations, we must add the elements of national prestige and the romantic allure of the Orient for the European public. The Emperor Louis Bonaparte was an ardent imperialist. He yearned to restore France's battered prestige, lost after his uncle's defeat at Waterloo in 1814 and the earlier loss of Quebec and Haiti. He involved France in six aggressive foreign wars during his 18-year reign.[26] If Mexico was proving too tough a nut to crack, Napoleon III might save face in Cambodia, so his wily Colonial Minister, M. Chasseloup-Laubat, de Lagrandière's ally, might have argued. Restoring French prestige would also build up his own personal credibility, for he must have been acutely conscious that he had spent much of his life after Waterloo in 1814 as an exiled pretender across the Rhine, and would always speak French with a German accent. Louis Bonaparte had come to power by dubious means, overthrowing the Second Republic of which he had been president, and he must have craved legitimacy.[27] He must also have been aware of his illustrious uncle's military-cum-scientific mission to Egypt in 1798,[28] so perhaps he believed he could emulate that mission to the pyramids in the land of Angkor. It could raise his prestige no end.[29]

Louis Bonaparte would have been on safe ground here. The European public had long shown great interest in the "mysterious" and "exotic" Orient, and Cambodia was a juicy morsel; an antidote for what Max Weber called "the disenchantment of the world" that came in the wake of the bourgeois and industrial revolutions. Not so very long before, Europeans had thought of Asia as an utterly remote and alien place, populated with remarkable monsters and dotted with fantastic cities. Europeans marveled at books that mixed fact with wild fantasies of cynocephales and cyclopean giants, some of them 65 feet tall. The fabulous kingdom of Prester John awaited discovery in this continent, they thought. There were "vales of enchantment" and "vales of devils", wizards, talking trees, dragons and feathered men.[30] Cambodia was as remote and mysterious as any other part of Asia, and its ancient heart was the irresistibly romantic city of Angkor. Writers claimed that the city had suffered a "green burial" for six hundred years before Henri Mouhot's celebrated visit.[31] Many others, infected by the ubiquitous racism of the 19th century, were certain that the Cambodians could not have built it and cited the ignorance of illiterate Khmer peasants as to its provenance as "proof".[32] All of this made a splendid fireside tale for a wet winter's evening in London, Paris or Boston, but it bore little relationship to reality. The truth was somewhat more prosaic. Marvelous though Angkor is, Khmers built it, and although they abandoned it as the capital in the 15th century, they had never forgotten it.[33] However, romantic tales flourished, regardless of the body of factual knowledge, creating a kind of parallel shadow land to the real Cambodia. Arguably, a major impetus to French intervention came with the posthumous publication of Henri Mouhot's memoirs.[34] Mouhot was a legendary figure, half-French, half-English (and, some thought, half-mad), a naturalist who had perished in the jungles and left a vivid account of his travels. Mouhot never claimed to have discovered the Angkor ruins. He tells us that the *Abbé* E. Silvestre of Battambang "guided me through the thick forest..." to the ruins. Moreover, there were Buddhist *bonzes* there.[35] He was also aware of the visit of the French priest, Father Charles Bouillevaux, ten years earlier.[36] Despite this disavowal, the public steadfastly believed he had discovered a lost city in the jungles. The myth endures to this day, even in mass circulation publications.[37] It was a great stimulus to French designs on the kingdom.

Notes

[1] Bou Saroeun, (2001), "The Buddha of Chinese Deception", *Phnom Penh Post,* 22 June, p.3.

[2] Udong was the post-Angkorean capital of the Khmer kings, and final resting-place of many of them. In 1866, the French transferred the capital to its present site at Phnom Penh. Some accounts give the date as 1865. The French called Udong either Houdon or Oudong. The spelling of de Lagrandière's name varies. It is sometimes rendered as de la Grandière and la Grandière. I have

adopted the form used by the historian Jean Moura, who knew him in the French administration.

³ Born at Quimper in Brittany, in 1807, the Admiral served as Governor of Cochinchina from 1863 until 1868. [Antoine Bréboin, (1910*), Livre d'Or du Cambodge, de la Cochinchine et du Annam, 1625-1910*, Burt Franklin, New York, (reprint 1971).]

⁴ Joseph Buttinger, (1958), *The Smaller Dragon. A Political History of Vietnam*, Atlantic Books, London, p.361.

⁵ Stanley Karnow, (1984), *Vietnam. A History*, Penguin Books, Harmondsworth, p.51.

⁶ A. Bouinais and A. Paulus, (1884), *Le Royaume du Cambodge*, Berger-Lévrault, Paris, p.11.

⁷ Louis de Carné, (1872), *Travels in Indo-China and the Chinese Empire*, Chapman and Hill, London, p.31. Norodom granted Viscount de Carné an audience in early 1866 and the author has left us with a detailed description of him.

⁸ Born in 1836 and reigned 1864-1904. From this point, I have referred to him as Norodom for the sake of convenience.

⁹ Si Votha lived from 1841 until 1891. Sisowath was born in 1840 and died in 1927. After Norodom's death in 1904, the French put Sisowath on the throne.

¹⁰ The rivalry of the three half-siblings began earlier. Born of three different mothers, they were largely reared apart and never formed close family bonds. In 1856, Ang Duong requested that the Siamese make Norodom his successor, or *Obbareach*. Sisowath was made *Prea-Keo-Fea*, or next in line after Norodom. The decision angered both Sisowath and Si Votha. See Milton E. Osborne, (1969), *The French Presence in Cochinchina and Cambodia. Rule and Response (1859-1905)*, Cornell University Press, Ithaca, New York, pp.30-31.

¹¹ PRO FO 881/2395. "Traité d'Amitie, de Commerce, et de Protection Française, entre la France et le Cambodge. - Conclu à Houdong, le 11 août, 1863. [Ratifications échangées à Houdong, le 14 avril, 1864.]" Napoleon III ratified the Treaty in February, but Norodom did not receive a copy of the document until April.

¹² Siam changed its name to Thailand in the 1930s. I refer to the country by its original name up until that time.

¹³ Wilfred Burchett, (1957), *Mekong Upstream*, Red River Publishing House, Hanoi, p.82.

¹⁴ Buttinger, op.cit. p.362.

¹⁵ Osborne, op.cit. p.183.

¹⁶ The *Tagals* were Filipino mercenaries.

¹⁷ Pierre Pasquier, (1929), "Indo-China Today", *The Asiatic Review*, XXV (84), October, p.600. Pasquier was Governor General of French Indo-China when he wrote the article.

¹⁸ D.K. Fieldhouse, (1966), *The Colonial Empires. A Comparative Survey from the Eighteenth Century*, Weidenfeld and Nicolson, London, p.179.

[19] The French Emperor, Napoleon III, tried to foist the Hapsburg Archduke Maximilien onto the Mexicans as emperor, but the adventure was a disaster. The Mexicans routed a French army, and executed the hapless Hapsburg at Querétaro in 1867. The French also ran foul of the USA's Monroe Doctrine.

[20] J.A. Hobson, (1965), *Imperialism: A Study*, Ann Arbor Paperbacks, University of Michigan, p.50. (This work was originally published in 1902.)

[21] Ibid.

[22] Jean Moura, (1883,) *Le Royaume du Cambodge*, Vol. I, Ernest Leroux, Librairie de la Société Asiatique de l'École des Langues Orientales Vivantes, Paris, p.145.

[23] Stephen Roberts, (1929), *The History of French Colonial Policy, 1870-1925*, Frank Cass, London, p.457.

[24] The Mekong was mentioned in the great epic poem of the famous Portuguese poet. See Luis Vas de Camoens, *Lusiads* (trans. William C. Atkinson), (1952), Penguin Books, Harmondsworth, Canto 10, p.243.

[25] The phrase is the title of a book by Milton Osborne, (1975), *River Road to China. The Mekong River Expedition, 1866-1873*, George Allen and Unwin, London. See also Roger Vercel, (1952), *Garnier à l'assault des fleuves*, Paris; and Francis Garnier (translated Walter E.J. Tips), (1996), *Travels in Cambodia and Part of Laos. The Mekong Exploration Commission Report (1866-1868)*, White Lotus, Bangkok.

[26] Buttinger, op.cit. p.398, n.38.

[27] "Legitimacy" in both the personal and political senses of the word. For an entertaining, if racy, account of Louis Napoleon's life, replete with details of his uncertain parentage and other seedy details, see John Bierman, (1990), *Napoleon III and His Carnival Empire*, Sphere Books, London. For an account of the coup d'état that brought Louis Bonaparte to power, see Karl Marx, (1969), *The Eighteenth Brumaire of Louis Bonaparte*, in *Karl Marx and Frederick Engels. Selected Works,* Vol. I, Progress Publishers, Moscow, pp.394-487. Curiously, Norodom also seems to have craved legitimacy. His rivals claimed that he could not be the legitimate king, as his father, Ang Duong, had not been crowned when he was born. See Chapter 3.

[28] For an account of this "cultural" dimension of imperialism, see Edward Said, (1991), *Orientalism*, Penguin Books, Harmondsworth, pp. 42-43 and 80-88, which deal directly with Napoleon's mission to Egypt. Max Weber also commented on the role of intellectuals who wished to see their national culture penetrate the colonial world. [Max Weber, (1978), *Economy and Society*, Vol. 2., University of California Press, Berkeley, pp.920-922.] This is especially relevant to Cambodia, where the restoration of Angkor was both a high point, and justification, of the French presence.

[29] Weber also commented directly on the national prestige accruing to successful imperialist rulers. [Ibid, (Weber).]

[30] See, for instance, *The Travels of Sir John Mandeville, Facsimile of Pynson's Edition of 1496*, Introduction by Michael Seymour, (1980), University of Exeter Press, Exeter; John Keast (ed.), (1984), *The Travels of Peter Mundy,*

1597-1667, Dyllansow Truran, Redruth; and Henry Yule (trans. and ed.), (1903), *The Book of Ser Marco Polo the Venetian concerning the kingdoms and marvels of the East*, Third Edition, 2 Vols. John Murray, London.
[31] Alfred C. Reed, (1939), "The curse of Angkor. Death comes quickly in the tropics", *Scientific Monthly*, March, New York, p.231.
[32] For example, see Frank Vincent, Jnr., (1873), *The Land of the White Elephant. Sights and Scenes in South-Eastern Asia. A personal narrative of travel and adventure in Farther India embracing the countries of Burma, Siam, Cambodia, and Cochin-China (1871-2)*, Sampson, Low, Marston, Low and Searle, London, p.279.
[33] Angkor was partly restored by King Satha I after 1576. [Bernard P. Groslier (avec la collaboration de C.R. Boxer), (1958), *Angkor et le Cambodge au XVI siècle. D'après les sources portugaises et espagnoles*, Presses Universitaires de France, Paris, p.17.] See also Bernard Groslier (trans James Hogarth), (1970), *Indochina*, Barrie and Jenkins, London, p.117. The American scholar Larry Briggs reiterates this and adds that, "Once, during the wars with Siam near the end of the sixteenth century, a Cambodian king moved his capital temporarily to the Angkor region." [L.P. Briggs, (1947), "A sketch of Cambodian history", *Far Eastern Quarterly*, August, pp.356-357.]
[34] Henri Mouhot, (1864), *Travels in the Central Parts of Indo-China (Siam), Cambodia and Laos during the years 1858, 1859 and 1860*, Two Vols. John Murray, London.
[35] Ibid, Vol. I, p.282. The Portuguese friar Antonio de la Magdelena had visited Angkor between 1585 and 1589. See Groslier, op.cit. p.132.
[36] See, for instance, V. Bouillevaux, (1874), *L'Annam et le Cambodge*, V. Palme, Paris and (1850) *Ma visite aux ruines cambodgiennes*, Imprimerie J. Monceau, St. Quentin. Also Georges Taboulet, (1955), "Le Père Bouillevaux à Angkor (1850)," in *La Geste Française en Indochine. Histoire par les textes de la France en Indochine des origines à 1914*, Librairie d'Amérique et d'Orient, Paris, Tome II.
[37] The *World Book Encyclopedia* [1981, Vol. I. World Book-Childcraft International, Chicago] claims that Mouhot discovered Angkor Thom in 1860. Ruth Tooze claims that Mouhot, whom she wrongly describes as an archaeologist, came across the ruins in 1876. [Ruth Tooze, (1962), *Cambodia: Land of Contrasts*, Viking Press, New York, p.46.]

Chapter 2

The Cambodian Dark Ages

Srok Khmer mün del soun: The country of the Khmers will never die.
—Cambodian proverb.[1]

The 1863 Treaty was a desperate attempt by the young as-yet-uncrowned monarch to staunch the hemorrhage of Cambodian sovereignty that had began at least a century earlier. Although it would be naïve to believe all the French propagandists said about the disinterested nature of their "mission" in Cambodia, there can be little doubt that their intervention prevented the political disappearance of the kingdom: a striking example of Marx's early view of imperialism as a "double-edged sword", both destroyer and savior. Parts of the Khmer realm had fallen under the direct control of her neighboring powers in the eighteenth century, with the Vietnamese annexing the fertile lower Mekong delta, and in the 1790s the Siamese seizing the provinces of Battambang and Angkor in the west and Melouprey in the north. By the early 1860s, Cambodia's fortunes were at their lowest ebb. Although Norodom's father, Ang Duong,[2] had attempted to regain political autonomy and restore a measure of probity in government, his death in 1860 was the occasion for a fresh outbreak of civil war that exhausted the country and left it prostrate before predatory neighbors described by the Khmers as "the tiger and the crocodile".

The historian David Chandler originally argued that Norodom was more fearful of the Vietnamese than of the Siamese.[3] The Siamese had been reasonably content to let the old Khmer ways continue in the provinces they annexed,[4] but Vietnamese settlers overran the Mekong delta and turned the local Khmer Krom population into a minority in their own land.[5] There were no natural topographical barriers to Vietnamese expansion between Phnom Penh and Saigon; both cities stand on the delta mud of the Mekong and the land is flat and relatively featureless. Even the annual floods allowed the Vietnamese to attack by boat. Norodom's fears of further encroachment by his dynamic eastern neighbor were realistic.

The decay of a great power

Cambodia had once been a great power in the region, but its glory-days were long gone. The Khmers moved the capital from the great stone city of Angkor to Phnom Penh in the 15th century, probably because of the threat posed by nearby Siam, but perhaps because of shifts in trade away from the west to the east and China. It is also possible that soil salting and/or exhaustion contributed to the move. In relatively recent geological time, what is today the great basin of Cambodia was an arm of the sea. The Angkor farmlands depended on irrigation and this could have raised the water table, triggering the release of salt dating from the period of saline inundation. Chandler has speculated that the vast amounts of water used in the Angkorean hydraulic works might have served as breeding grounds for malarial mosquitoes.[6] Perhaps the irrigation channels also silted up as Bernard Groslier has suggested.[7] Whatever the reasons for it, the move signaled the end of a civilization based on enormous state-run hydraulic works and irrigation. Whether this constituted "decline" or "change" is debatable,[8] but perhaps as early as the 17th, and certainly by the 18th century, Cambodian power had declined relative to that of its neighbors, who increasingly meddled in her internal affairs and sent armies deep into the country, burning and pillaging. The Scottish sea captain, Alexander Hamilton, described a visit to the country three years after a Siamese fleet destroyed the once flourishing seaport of "Ponteamass"[9] in 1717. Hamilton records that the Cambodians, acting on royal orders, employed a scorched earth policy that left the border zones "a meer desart" (*sic*). Although the tactic worked, reducing the fleeing Siamese to eating their own elephants and other "carriage beasts", the effects on Cambodia were melancholy. Both farmland and cities were ruined.[10]

By the mid-18th century, Cambodia had shrunk to its present limits, minus the western provinces and the Khmer coronations took place in Bangkok and their kings' status downgraded to that of "viceroys".[11] At times, the Vietnamese fought with the Siamese on Cambodian territory.[12] The Siamese would attack by land in the dry season and the Vietnamese would send fleets in the wet. The Siamese invaded again in 1808, eleven years after the 17-year-old Ang Chan ascended the throne at Udong. They seized more land, forced the young king to pay tribute and in 1834, they burned Phnom Penh.[13] The capital had been a large, walled town, with a circumference of 20 *li* or ten kilometers; the walls pierced by five large double gates and with broad streets and a number of big bridges.[14] The following year the Vietnamese took the unusual step of putting a woman, Queen Ang Mey, on the Cambodian throne. (Ang Chan died leaving no sons.) They later forced her from the throne and into concubinage in Annam. Thereafter the meddling of the Annamese court intensified, with sanguine disorders and uprisings fomented in the east of the country. In 1841, the Siamese regained the upper hand from their rivals and placed Ang Duong on the throne, but the intrigues and bloody struggles continued. In 1845, the Vietnamese laid siege to the capital at Udong, dashing Ang Duong's dreams of peace.[15] Despite this bloody interference, however, the king introduced much needed reforms to the country's penal code, lowered taxes and even built some roads. He restored a large measure of his country's sovereignty, but he lived in dread of his neighbors.

The darkest days of a dark age

In 1853, acting on the advice of French Catholic missionaries, Ang Duong sent gifts of silk, ivory and *repoussé* work to Napoleon III (Louis Bonaparte, nephew of Napoleon I) and asked him for French protection.[16] The French Emperor did not respond at this stage, and after the king's death the country plunged again into poverty-stricken vassalage and chaos. The British Consul at Bangkok could report that in 1863, "The province [*sic*] of Cambodia is at present of but little value. The population is under four hundred thousand and the inhabitants are very poor".[17] Compared with the splendors of the ancient capital at Angkor, or even with Phnom Penh in happier times, the capital, Udong, and other towns were dreary places. Angkor itself, away to the northwest beyond the Great Lake, or Tonlé Sap, was deep inside Siamese territory. As Chandler observes, "The first sixty years of the nineteenth century form the darkest portion of Cambodia's dark ages before the Armageddon of the 1970s."[18]

Norodom, then in his mid-twenties, fled to Bangkok to escape the bloody civil disorders that erupted around the time of Ang Duong's death in 1859. The Cham people[19] rose in revolt in 1857 and again in 1858, marching on Udong and only falling back after sustaining heavy losses in hand-to-hand fighting. In 1859, Norodom's half-brother, Si Votha and his uncle, Strang So, rose in revolt and in 1861 the unruly Chams joined them. Another half-brother, Prince Sisowath, seems to have tried to run with the hare and chase with the hounds; at times he sided with Norodom against the rebels, yet he led another revolt in following years.[20] The Vietnamese and Siamese were, predictably, active in behind-the-scenes intrigue. Interestingly, although King Mongkut of Siam had appointed Norodom to succeed his father, there were claims that he had reservations about his personal ability and trustworthiness (or perhaps pliability). According to the British Consul at Bangkok, "while here he [Norodom] bore a very indifferent character and there were doubts about appointing him to succeed his father; *but they were removed by the solicitation of the French authorities at Saigon.*"[21] [Emphasis added.] If this is the case, it indicates that the French had already decided to intervene in Cambodian affairs and saw Norodom as either a potential ally or, more probably, as a future puppet. Perhaps they considered his half-brothers too warlike and independent-minded, or pro-Siamese, to advance their ends? If so, this was a sound judgment of the fierce warrior Si Votha, who was to remain implacably opposed to France until the end of his life. However, as we shall see, the French would soon regret favoring Norodom over Sisowath, for the latter would prove himself by far the more reliable Francophile of the two.

Yet, it is easier to make such judgments with the benefit of hindsight. At the time, it must have been difficult for outsiders to make sense of the intra-dynastic struggle, and to evaluate its central actors (although the French priests stationed near Udong must have had their own shrewd opinions). De Lagrandiére's nephew, the Viscount Louis de Carné,[22] who visited Cambodia in early 1866, records that the anti-Norodom revolt led by Sisowath, the *Prea-keo-fea* (or second king), was particularly savage, and that its leader's "hatred of the Siamese gave him a kind of popularity"[23] among the common people.[24] Perhaps the French officers at Saigon reasoned that such popularity and anti-Siamese "patriotism" was dangerous because it could have translated into francophobia when they curbed Siamese influence. Anti-French fervor was to show itself some twenty years later in the Great Rebellion, but it was Si Votha who harnessed it, rather than Sisowath.

Norodom must have seemed insipid in comparison with his two warrior-half-brothers. He played little part in quelling the Cham rebellions and in fighting off Si Votha; indeed, he fled first to Battambang and then to Bangkok, leaving Sisowath to defend the capital at Udong. The French historian Alain Forest has suggested that the Siamese supported Norodom precisely because he *was* unpopular, reasoning that he would be docile because of his dependence on Siam.[25] The French probably agreed with this assessment, but reasoned that he could be made just as dependent on them. Certainly, Norodom appears to have enjoyed little independent support in Cambodia; he seems to have been downright unpopular, at least at this stage in his career. His flight to Bangkok in 1861 must have been a product of desperation, for he had lived in that city until 1858 as a kind of prisoner of the Siamese and must have been loath to go back to potential bondage. The Siamese had held him hostage to ensure the "good behavior" of his father, Ang Duong,[26] although some writers have suggested that Mongkut considered Norodom as his adopted son.[27]

The Siamese court claimed the right to nominate and crown Cambodia's kings; indeed, they regarded Norodom as a puppet "viceroy", not as the ruler of a sovereign country.[28] After his ignominious flight from the rebels, the Siamese brought him back to Cambodia under armed guard in February 1862 and he was "re-established at Udong".[29] Clearly, his position was untenable, menaced as he was by rebels and predatory neighbors. There are claims, probably accurate, that he attempted to appease the Siamese by offering them the provinces of Kompong Svay and Pursat in March 1863.[30]

The coming of the French

Yet, a far more formidable power than Siam had entered the fray, although in a halting and contradictory fashion. The French were observing developments in the kingdom with a view to possible intervention there. In 1858, they had annexed part of Cochinchina (the Mekong delta region of Vietnam adjacent to Cambodia) and because of this, Governor de Lagrandière reasoned that they had inherited Vietnam's "legal" rights in Cambodia.[31] Although the French had been lukewarm when Ang Duong had asked for their protection in 1853, they had sent the Montigny Mission in 1855-56 to meet with him and discuss his request. The Cambodians received M. Louis Charles de Montigny with great honors at Kampot (on the Gulf of Siam littoral), but he was unable to proceed to Udong, perhaps because of the dangerous state of the countryside,[32] but more probably because of Siamese displeasure.[33] By 1860, the French were again seriously considering moving into Cambodia. M. Prosper Chasseloup-Laubat, a leader of the "party of aggressive imperialism",[34] became Minister for the Navy and Colonies and in him the independent-minded naval officers at Saigon, who were enthusiastic expansionists, had found a reliable ally. Cambodia was ripe for intervention, with rival factions fighting each other for the throne and her neighbors backing this or that pretender in pursuit of their own ends. French troops had been dispatched to the border between Cochinchina and Cambodia in August 1861, presumably to guard against insurgency spilling over the border, and if necessary to march in to protect the lives of French citizens and Catholic converts in Cambodia. In the same month, the French sent a steamship up the Mekong to Udong and when the "second prince" of Cambodia asked the ship's officers why they had come, they replied that they were there to protect the French priests and their native flock from the dangers of civil war.[35]

From this point onwards, the French stepped up their intervention. Shortly after the dispatch of the gunboat, they sent the Viscount de Castelnau, their acting consul at Bangkok, aboard a Siamese man-of-war according to the British,[36] "for the purpose of entering into preliminary arrangements for the conclusion of a treaty between Cambodia and France." De Castelnau repeated claims that atrocities had been committed against French citizens and "Annamite" Catholics and blamed the Siamese government for them. In the event, the Siamese must have discovered de Castelnau's objectives, for he returned empty-handed, allegedly because the water in the river was too low to allow the vessel to pass[37] but perhaps really because the Siamese had decided not to allow the treaty to proceed.[38] Still, de Castelnau pursued the matter with the Siamese authorities at Bangkok, submitting a ten-point draft treaty for their perusal in December 1861.

Not surprisingly, the Siamese rejected the draft as it proposed that Norodom was to have "title equal to an independent sovereign" and on a par with the Siamese king. The French also wanted to install a French *Agent* at Udong and demanded punishment for those who had persecuted Catholics, plus payment of an indemnity of $20,000 to the Catholic Church by the Cambodian government.[39] The Siamese commented, "Cambodia is quite a jungle and a poor country. To demand twenty thousand dollars is beyond what it can give."[40] The demand was unreasonable because Norodom was not responsible for the attacks on the priests and their flock, but it did fit into an established pattern in which French gunboats followed the crucifix and the rosary into "heathen" and "barbarous" lands; the most recent being Cochinchina. The American historian John Cady has noted that political intrigue was a "perennial activity" of French Catholic missionaries in far-flung regions of the globe. It is arguable that the

Société des Missions Étrangères[41] saw its role as spreading the French *mission civilisatrice* perhaps as much as Christianity; indeed that the two were inseparable. The Society had sent Pigneau de Behaine, a "missionary statesman" (and later "vicar apostolic to Cochin-China, Cambodia, and Tongking"), to "Siamese Cambodia" in 1765[42] and had maintained a presence in the country thereafter (albeit with a striking lack of success in winning Khmer converts). It is likely that Father (later Monsignor) Jean-Claude Miche,[43] who lived near Udong, suggested the idea of the protectorate to Ang Duong.[44] The same priest was involved in negotiations for the 1863 treaty with Norodom. The persecution of Christians had also served as an excuse for the annexation of Tahiti[45] (1843) and Cochinchina (1858) and was to serve as a pretext for the tightening of French control over Cambodia following the installation of their protectorate.

The Treaty of 11 August 1863

Although Norodom was suspicious of the French, he was anxious to escape from the clutches of the Siamese, who still held the Cambodian royal regalia in Bangkok and who had displaced Vietnam as the main threat to his country's independence. Perhaps wishing to play one side off against the other, he put out feelers to the French. In September 1862, the French Governor at Saigon, Admiral Bonard, traveled up the Mekong to see the country for himself.[46] On 4 August of the next year, his successor as Governor, Admiral de Lagrandière, arrived from Saigon intent on finalizing a treaty with Norodom.[47] The result was the "Treaty of Friendship, Commerce and French Protection", concluded at Udong on 11 August 1863 and consisting of nineteen articles. After ratification, Napoleon III extended his protection to the Cambodian King, and in return gained the right to name a *Résident* who was "authorized under the higher authority of the French Governor of Cochin China to keep watch over the strict implementation of the terms of the protectorate." The *Résident* received the rank of a grand mandarin of the Cambodian court. In return, they authorized Norodom to station a *Résident* at Saigon, although this latter clause appears to have been a dead letter. French citizens were to enjoy free circulation throughout the kingdom, and Cambodians were free to enter any part of the French Empire. French citizens were to be subject to French courts and Norodom granted the Catholic Church freedom of worship and the right to build churches, seminaries, schools, hospitals, convents and other buildings in all parts of the kingdom.[48] This was not too great a concession, as the number of Catholic converts in the kingdom was small, and remained so for the life of the Protectorate. Importantly, the Treaty also gave the French permission to build a fort and naval facilities at the *Quatre Bras*, where the arms of the Tonlé Sap, Mekong and the Bassac rivers intersect, and granted extensive commercial and trading rights to French interests.[49]

The French did not pursue their earlier demands for compensation to the Catholic Church from the Cambodian government. Religion, however, was a strong impetus to colonialism. Although Louis Bonaparte was an agnostic like his uncle, he shared his pragmatic attitude to the Church, which in any case had backed his *coup d'état* in 1852 against the anti-clerical Second Republic. His Spanish-born wife, Eugénie, was also a devout Catholic with a clerico-imperialist bent. Bonaparte also could not but be aware of the value of the Church in paving the way for earthly imperialism in far-flung regions of the world. The Church was a strong advocate of imperialism, hoping to carve out a "Christian empire" in Asia.[50] The recognition of Catholicism as an approved religion in the 1863 Treaty with Norodom would have boosted his standing with France's powerful Catholic congregations, which acted as a counterweight to anti-clerical republicanism.

A de facto French colony

On the face of it, the treaty was innocuous for Norodom and Cambodia. Although it granted the French wide-ranging commercial, territorial and religious rights, it did not seem to give them *carte blanche* to meddle in Cambodia's internal political and administrative affairs. Yet, the truth was that for all the legal window-dressing of the protectorate, Norodom had delivered up his country as a *de facto* colony of France and the new overlords were eventually to prove far more intrusive than Siam had been. Legal documents are subject to interpretation, after all, and the French were adepts at such arts. If challenged, they also could rely on superior force or the threat of it to cow their adversaries. Norodom might have had some premonition of this, or perhaps he was following a plan of playing off his "suitors" against one another, for he almost immediately sought to mollify the outraged Siamese for what they saw as his disloyalty and the flouting of their rights. The Franco-Cambodian treaty caused "a considerable amount of alarm and indignation" on the part of the Siamese king and his officers", who claimed that the treaty was illegal and that the Khmer court could do nothing without their prior approval.[51]

British diplomats suspected that Norodom was "dissimulating" with the French and/or the Siamese, and with reason. Just four days after he had signed the treaty with Admiral de Lagrandière, Norodom wrote to a high Siamese official in Battambang, complaining that the French had bullied him into signing, and asking him to convey the matters raised in his letter to King Mongkut. Norodom complained that de Lagrandière had read the draft of the treaty to him in French, a language he did not properly know. He said that he had protested, "I did not understand it and moreover I had not considered the matter with my nobles." He said that the French priest, Jean-Claude Miche, had only given him a Khmer translation two days before he signed it. Moreover, he claimed to have "stated to Father Miche that as the Treaty was different from the Bangkok one, [presumably de Castelnau's earlier draft] I could not agree to it as Cambodia was tributary to Siam and I feared I would be at fault." He concluded that "whether this treaty is beyond all measure or not, I leave to your Excellency's consideration as you are my refuge in whom hereafter I depend for happiness."[52]

Norodom's vacillations

Norodom must have been in two minds after signing the treaty. He was the Siamese nominee for the throne, and powerless to resist any display of force on their part, yet he had now dealt them a resounding slap in the face. He also lived in dread of revolt by his unruly subjects[53] and owed his earlier survival to Siamese intervention. He must have wondered how much French support he could count on in the event of hostile Siamese action. The French were bogged down in a bloody pacification campaign in Cochinchina and despite displays of saber rattling they would hesitate to begin a war with Siam (and thus possibly with Britain) over Cambodia. Norodom was an astute man, with a more sophisticated knowledge of foreign affairs than his detractors would have us believe. He had an intimate knowledge of Siamese politics and knew of the close alliance between the King Mongkut and the British. It is possible—although not likely—that Norodom knew that de Lagrandière had acted without the express permission of Napoleon III, who was anxious not to offend the British and who in any case was preoccupied with his imperialist project in Mexico at the time. The French Emperor eventually did ratify the Treaty in April of the following year, 1864, but only after intense lobbying by de Lagrandière's ally, M. Chasseloup-Laubat.[54]

The Siamese rulers were furious with Norodom. They feared there might be war with France over the Cambodian provinces ceded to Siam, and demanded equal rights with France in Cambodia, for instance in the investiture of her kings.[55] Norodom continued to try to buy time, for he hastened to assure the suspicious French of his good intentions. According to the French representative at Udong, the aristocratic naval lieutenant Ernest Marc Louis de Gonzague Doudart de Lagrée,[56] Norodom said he was concerned that the Siamese had been pressuring him to sign a treaty with England. The shrewd de Lagrée was aware of Norodom's deceit[57] and according to Forest, he threatened him with exile if he continued with his duplicity.[58] Norodom, however, tried to continue to play off the rival powers. In early March 1864, he set off for Bangkok, intending to stage his coronation there. Doudart de Lagrée moved swiftly to dissuade him. French troops occupied Norodom's palace and ran up the tricolor and a gunboat anchored in the river fired a salvo of shots (probably blanks, but the demonstration of power was clear). Norodom realized he had to abandon his plans.[59] The French, wisely, did not push the Siamese too far. Norodom was crowned at Udong on 3 June 1864, but representatives of France and Siam jointly supervised the ceremony, allowing Mongkut to save face. It was, however, the last time that Siam's claims would be recognized in this way. At the coronation, an "ecstatic" (or perhaps diplomatic) Norodom[60] told Commander Desmoulins, the French representative, "I consider the Emperor Napoleon as my father, the Admiral [de Lagrandière] as my brother. I am happy to see all these French officers, all those who come here are my parents and friends."[61] Within a few years, he felt confident enough to sneer about the Siamese to European visitors. He also called for the return of the "lost provinces" of Angkor and Battambang from Siam.[62] To his chagrin, the French formally agreed three years later to recognize Siamese sovereignty over them.[63]

Norodom's secret treaty with Siam

In the meantime, however, he had continued his machinations (or, perhaps, his vacillations). On August 20 1864, just over two months after the coronation, the French were shocked to see for the first time, in the *Straits Times*, the text of a new treaty between Cambodia and Siam.[64] Norodom and Mongkut had negotiated and ratified the new treaty in secret by 22 January 1864, i.e. *before* the ratification of the treaty with Napoleon III. French sources show that the treaty was signed in December 1863 and point out that "the principle clauses were in flagrant contradiction to those established by the treaty concluded between [Cambodia] and France..."[65] The French Minister at Bangkok, M. Aubaret, said that he "intended to insist on the said articles being expunged..." An article that agreed to the right of the King of Siam to appoint the "kings or viceroys of Cambodia" incensed the French.[66] According to the French writer Charles Meyer, the terms of the treaty also gave away two more Cambodian provinces, Kompong Svay and Pursat, to Siam.[67]

The French got their way, for neither Mongkut nor Norodom were strong enough to resist. The Siamese were unhappy at seeing their vassal slip away, but could do nothing about it. Relations between Britain and France were reasonably friendly and if Napoleon III had been worried about offending his allies from across the English Channel, the concern was reciprocal. The British counseled Siam to accept the French ascendancy over their former vassal as a *fait accompli*. They warned that otherwise the French might "make a demonstration against this country [i.e. Cambodia] even to the extent of one or two gunboats..." They believed "that all they [the French] ask will be granted to them and their influence in this place will be paramount, as the Siamese fully appreciate the strength of European arms and have a considerable respect for those they think likely to make use of them."[68] *Force majeure* had prevailed and the Siamese signed a treaty with France recognizing that their own treaty of December 1863 with Cambodia was invalid.[69] Norodom was forced to make a trip to Saigon in October 1864 with *Résident* Doudart de Lagrée to apologize to Admiral de Lagrandière,[70] as an errant schoolboy is escorted to the headmaster's office for chastisement.

The knowledge that he was powerless to resist his internal enemies without French help rubbed in his humiliation. The country was still in a state of rebellion, with the pretenders and their armed bands still at large. Norodom requested military protection. Forty marines under the command of Captain Herbillon sailed up from Saigon to Udong soon after the coronation.[71] A month or so later, Admiral de Lagrandière sent Lieutenant Doudart de Lagrée back up the Mekong with two gunboats, the rebels were scattered, and order was soon restored.[72] Norodom probably imagined that he had concluded things satisfactorily. The French had broken him out of Siam's stifling embrace and neutralized the power of Annam. The treaty promised to sit lightly on his kingdom, and did not appear to threaten his prerogatives as an absolute ruler. France's intentions were, in any case, unclear at this stage and Napoleon III was distracted from Cambodia's internal affairs by events elsewhere. Yet, although Norodom could not have been completely aware of it, the seeds of the *mission civilisatrice* were sown early on in the Protectorate, although it took some time for the green shoots to emerge.

An "oppressive regime"

In early 1863, Admiral Bonard had sent a young naval officer, Ernest Brière d'Isle,[73] on a mission to explore Cambodia. D'Isle's report was damning and his themes were to recur many times. The Cambodian population, d'Isle claimed, was "subservient to an oppressive regime", a "deplorable state of affairs" in which corrupt mandarins subjected the people to arbitrary exactions, forcing them to live from day to day in a "most precarious state". There was apathy and a general lack of initiative, a lack of public works and enterprise.[74] France could both clean up an incompetent and corrupt administration, and save the souls of the "heathens" who dwelt there. Such a *mission civilisatrice* would mean the end of Cambodian sovereignty. D'Isle's report echoed the words of another Frenchman, Henri Mouhot, who had died in Cambodia some years before the Protectorate. Mouhot was a zealous imperialist; convinced of the benefits France could bring to an allegedly benighted and crumbling land. He had prescribed, "European conquest, abolition of slavery, wise and protecting laws, and experience, fidelity, and scrupulous rectitude in those who administer them..." because these "would alone affect the regeneration of the state."[75] In short, Mouhot wanted to subject the "savage tribes" of Cambodia[76] to Europe's *mission civilisatrice* regardless of their wishes. Mouhot was ahead of his time in this. The French would gradually strip Cambodia of the quasi-sovereignty it had so briefly acquired during the interregnum when Norodom was able to play off the French and Siamese, but the main push for this came under the Third Republic, after the fall of Napoleon III in 1871. In the meantime, so long as Norodom left the conduct of foreign affairs to the French, they would not meddle too much in his internal affairs. Norodom could also congratulate himself on ensuring the survival of his country. Without French intervention, the "country of the Khmers" most probably *would* have perished, at least as a separate political body.

Notes

[1] Cited in Henri Marchal, (19?), *Angkor. La Resurrection de l'Art Khmer et l'Ouevre de l'École Française d'Extrême-Orient*, Office Française d'Edition, Paris, p.32.

[2] Ang Duong reigned from 1841 until 1860.

[3] David P. Chandler, (1993), *A History of Cambodia*, Second Edition, Allen and Unwin, St. Leonards, NSW, p.136. Chandler now thinks it is an open question. (Personal communication to author, 7 February 2001.)

[4] The Siamese even appointed the Apheuyvongs, a Cambodian family, as hereditary viceroys of the annexed region. (See John Tully, (1996), *Cambodia Under the Tricolour. King Sisowath and the 'Mission Civilisatrice' 1904-1927*, Monash Asia Institute, Clayton, Victoria, Ch. Three. See also Chapters Eight and Twenty Two.) The Siamese, however, had once been much more ruthless. According to Virginia Thompson, "The Siamese invasions were the most disastrous, for they forcibly transplanted those Khmers they did not massacre, in order to people their own kingdom." Virginia Thompson, (1968), *French Indo-China*, Octagon Books, New York, p.323.

[5] There is still a Khmer Krom or "lower Khmer" minority in southern Vietnam today. Fear of Vietnam has been a constant theme of Cambodian governments, regardless of their political coloration. There were almost 69,000 Khmers out of nearly 391,000 people in the Transbassac region of Cochinchina in 1886. By 1928, this had risen to 224,452 out of 1,451,064. [Pierre Brocheux, (1972), "Vietnamiens et Minorités en Cochinchine Pendant la Période Coloniale", *Modern Asian Studies*, 6, 4, p.446.]

[6] Chandler, op.cit. p.78.

[7] Bernard Philippe Groslier, (trans. James Hogarth), (1970), *Indochina*, Barrie and Jenkins, London, pp.75-76.

[8] Chandler, op.cit. pp.78-79. Although Marx's theory of the "Asiatic Mode of Production" is too broad to fit the disparate societies of Asia, it does seem to describe Angkorean civilization. See Chapter 3.

[9] Today known as Banteay Méas, a small village near Kampot on the Gulf of Thailand littoral. Another variation is "Pontiamias", shown on a French map in 1819. [Jean Pierre Abel-Rémusat (trans.), (1819), *Description du Royaume de Cambodge, par un voyageur chinois qui a visité cette contrée à la fin du XIIIe siècle; précédée d'une notice chronologique sur le même pays, extraite des annales de la Chine*, Imprimerie J. Smith, Paris, endpaper.]

[10] Captain Alexander Hamilton, (1744), *A New Account of the East Indies*, Vol. II, C. Hitch and A. Millar, London, pp. 195-197.

[11] That is, to the same status as the Apheuyvongs, see note 4 above.

[12] Chandler, op.cit. p.118.

[13] Francis Garnier (translated Walter E.J. Tips), (1996), *Travels in Cambodia and Part of Laos. The Mekong Exploration Commission Report (1866-1868)*, White Lotus, Bangkok, p.48. See also A. Bouinais and A. Paulus, (1884), *Le Royaume du Cambodge*, Berger-Lévrault, Paris, p.29.

[14] Abel-Rémusat, op.cit. pp.39-42. One *li* is about half a kilometer.

[15] This paragraph is mainly based on Edouard Testoin, (1886) *Le Cambodge, Passé, Présent, Avenir*, Ernest Mazereau, Tours, p. 69 and pp.76-77. However, there is no agreement about the dates even of the reigns of the kings and of Queen Ang Mey. Justin Corfield, (1990), *The Royal Family of Cambodia*,

Khmer Language and Cultural Centre, Melbourne, (p.4) gives the following dates: Ang Eng, 1779-1796; Ang Chan II, 1797-1834; Ang Mey, 1785-1847; Ang Duong, 1847-1860. The contradictions perhaps derive from the confused conditions in the country itself in those times, although the Royal Chronicles also give internally contradictory dates.

[16] ANC RSC D35 File 5838 Box 577, "Organisation politique du Cambodge". See also J. Moura, (1883), *Le Royaume du Cambodge,* Vol. II, Librairie de la Société Asiatique de l'École des Langues Orientales Vivantes, Paris, pp.129-130. Also Chandler, op.cit. pp.135-136.

[17] PRO, FO 69/3. British Consul at Bangkok to Foreign Office, 29 September 1863.

[18] Chandler, op.cit. p.117.

[19] The Chams are a large minority ethnic group in Cambodia and Vietnam. Muslim in religion, they are the descendants of the ancient empire of Champa. It is difficult to estimate how numerous they were in Cambodia in the mid-19th century. A.C. Hanna, citing the *Annuaire de Monde Musulman* gives a total of around 200,000 Muslims for all of Indochina in the early 1930s, including 120,000 Chams. [A.C. Hanna, (1931), "The Chams of French Indo-China", *The Moslem World. A Christian Quarterly Review of Current Events, Literature, and Thought among Mohammedans,* Missionary Review Publishing, New York, July, pp.263.] Perhaps half of these lived in Cambodia. In 1999, the Cambodian Ministry of Cults and Religion estimated there were over 400,000 Chams in the country. (Nanaho Sawano, "Cham Revival", *The Cambodia Daily,* Phnom Penh, No. 66, 15 May 1999.)

[20] ANC RSC F451, File 24217, Conseil des Ministres, 37e séance du 8 novembre 1900, réunion spéciale. Letter from Sisowath to the *Résident Supérieur,* 17 November 1900.

[21] PRO, FO 69/39, Consul at Bangkok to Foreign Office, 8 October 1864.

[22] De Carné's personal details are recorded in Antoine Brébion, (1910), *Livre d'Or du Cambodge, de la Cochinchine et de L'Annam, 1625-1920,* Burt Franklin, New York, (reprinted 1971.) p.36.

[23] Louis de Carné, (1872), *Travels in Indo-China and the Chinese Empire,* Chapman and Hill, London, p.15.

[24] Nevertheless, by Sisowath's own admission, he owed his high position to Siam. The Siamese King had named him *Prea-Keo-Fea* at the same time as they named Norodom *Obbareach.* (Letter from Sisowath to the *Résident Supérieur,* 17 November 1900, ANC RSC F451 File 24217 Conseil des Ministres, 37e séance du 8 novembre 1900. Réunion spéciale.)

[25] Alain Forest, (1980), *Le Cambodge et la colonisation française. Histoire d'une colonisation sans heurts (1897-1920),* Éditions L'Harmattan, Paris, p.6.

[26] PRO FO 69/39, British Consul at Bangkok to Foreign Office, 29 September 1863.

[27] Charles Meyer, (1971), *Derrière le Sourire Khmer,* Plon, Paris, p.69.

[28] AOM Indochine AF Carton 10, Dossier A30 (6), Admiral de Lagrandière to Ministry of the Navy and Colonies, 20 October 1864.

[29] Louis de Carné, op.cit. p.12. Sisowath claimed—probably accurately—that he had been forced to take charge of Udong's defenses after Norodom's flight. (ANC RSC F451, File 24217, Conseil des Ministres, 37e séance du 8 novembre 1900, réunion spéciale. Letter from Sisowath to the *Résident Supérieur*, 17 November 1900.)

[30] Meyer, op.cit. Although Meyer is not always reliable, his service at the court of Norodom Sihanouk gave him access to an oral tradition less accessible to most historians. Besides, Norodom did agree to give up extra territory in the abortive treaty he signed with Siam in 1863.

[31] ANC RSC D35 File 5838 Box 577. Documents et Voeux Addressés à la commission d'enquête parlementaire (1937–1938).

[32] Moura, op.cit. Vol. I, p.130. Also John F. Cady, (1954), *The Roots of French Imperialism in Eastern Asia*, Cornell University Press, Ithaca, New York, p.143 and Chandler, op.cit. p.140.

[33] Bouinais and Paulus, op.cit. p.11. See also A. Raquez, (1904), "Norodom. Le Cambodge avant son avènement", *Revue Indochinois*, Hanoi, Deuxième Semestre, pp.150-151. De Montigny was the French Consul at Shanghai.

[34] Joseph Buttinger, (1958), *The Smaller Dragon. A Political History of Vietnam*, Atlantic Books, London, p.349.

[35] PRO FO 69/39 Siamese Government to British Consul at Bangkok, 4 October 1861.

[36] This is curious, given the hostility of the Siamese towards French designs on Cambodia. Perhaps the Siamese were not originally aware of the nature of de Castelnau's business in Cambodia.

[37] PRO FO 69/39,op.cit.

[38] Chandler, op.cit. pp.136 and 140.

[39] PRO FO 69/39, op.cit. The French also wanted free navigation on the Mekong, rights to exploit timber for shipbuilding, extra-territorial rights for French citizens, and concessions of land. See also AOM Fonds Ministeriels Carton 1/AOO (3) Notes sur l'expedition de Cochinchine 1864. De Castelnau to the Minister at Paris.

[40] Ibid (FO 69/39). These were probably silver dollars, and thus a substantial sum.

[41] Established in 1663 to propagate the faith in foreign lands.

[42] Cady, op.cit. p.12. Pigneau de Behaine played a part in the accession of a pretender, Emperor Gia Long, to the throne of Annam at Hué. The meddlesome cleric was killed in 1799 because of his political intrigues.

[43] Miche was the first "vicar apostolique" of Cambodia. A scholar-priest born in the Vosges in 1804, he wrote a Franco-Khmer dictionary and other books. He died at Saigon in 1873. (Brébion, op.cit. p.23.)

[44] Chandler, op.cit. p.140. According to Sisowath, Miche encouraged him to seize power when Norodom fled to Bangkok in 1861. We only have Sisowath's word for this. (Letter from Sisowath to the *Résident Supérieur*, 17 November 1900, op.cit.)

[45] Cady, op.cit. p.30.

[46] Moura, op.cit. p.145.

[47] AOM Indochine AF Carton 10, Dossier A30 (6), letter of Siamese officials, 12 August 1863. Also PRO FO 69/39, op.cit., covering letter by British Consul and letter from Norodom to "His Excellency 'Chow Phraya Kalathorn, Udong, 15 August 1863. (Kalathorn, or Kathathorn, was the Governor of Angkor province, annexed to Siam.) Moura (op.cit. p.146) claims de Lagrandière arrived in July.

[48] Buddhism and Catholicism were thus the only authorized faiths in the kingdom, as later Protestant and Caodai missionaries were to discover. See Chapters 11 and 15.

[49] PRO FO 881/2395, Traité d'Amitié, de Commerce, et de Protection Française, op.cit.

[50] See, for instance, Buttinger, op.cit. p.396, note 31.

[51] PRO FO 69/39, British Consul at Bangkok to Foreign Office, 29 September 1863.

[52] PRO FO 69/39, Letter from Norodom to His Excellency Chow Phraya Kalathorn, [sic] Udong, 15 August 1863.

[53] Bouinais and Paulus, op.cit. p.13.

[54] Buttinger, op.cit. p.415.

[55] AOM Indochine AF Carton 10, Dossier A30 (6), French Commander-in-Chief, Saigon, to the Minister of Colonies, Paris, 27 January 1864.

[56] The lieutenant later had a school and a major Phnom Penh thoroughfare named after him. The details of his remarkable name are from Brébion, op.cit. p.33.

[57] French Commander-in-Chief, Saigon, to the Minister of Colonies, Paris, 27 January 1864, op.cit.

[58] Forest, op.cit. p.7, and Meyer, op.cit. p.70, claim that the French occupied the royal palace at Udong and that Norodom fled to Bangkok. Although Doudart de Lagrée does seem to have threatened to occupy the palace, it is unlikely that Norodom would have fled to the court of his vengeful "allies" at Bangkok.

[59] Milton E. Osborne, (1969), *The French Presence in Cochinchina and Cambodia. Rule and Response (1859-1905)*, Cornell University Press, Ithaca, New York, p.186.

[60] Ibid. p.205.

[61] AOM Indochine AF, Carton 10, Dossier A30 (6), Admiral de Lagrandière to the Minister of Colonies, 1 March 1864.

[62] AOM Indochine AF 11, A 30 (12). Letter from Norodom to the French Governor of Cochinchina, 12 March 1868.

[63] Treaty between France and Siam, signed 15 July 1867. See AOM Indochine AF Carton 20 Dossier A30 (96). Gouvernement Général de l'Indochine, Recueil Générale de la législation et de la réglementation de l'Indochine, à jour au 31 décembre 1925, Tome Premier, Service de législation et d'administration du Gouvernment Général, MCMXXVII. Norodom was never happy with the decision. See, for instance, AOM Indochine AF A30 (12).

Letter from Norodom to the Governor of Cochinchina, 12 March 1868. However, he himself, under pressure, had agreed to the annexation of the provinces.

[64] *The Straits Times*, Singapore, August 20 1864.

[65] AOM Indochine AF Carton 10, Dossier A30 (5), Admiral de Lagrandière to the Minister of the Navy, 29 October 1864.

[66] PRO FO 69/39, British Consul at Bangkok to the Foreign Office, 8 October 1864.

[67] Meyer, op.cit. p.69.

[68] PRO FO 69/39, British Consul at Bangkok to Foreign Office, 8 October 1864.

[69] Ibid, "Treaty between Siam and France re Cambodia, 14 April 1865."

[70] Buttinger, op.cit. p.414.

[71] AOM Indochine AF Carton 10, Dossier A 30 (6), op.cit. Admiral de Lagrandière to the Minister of Colonies, 25 April 1864.

[72] Ibid. De Lagrandière to the Minister, 27 August 1864.

[73] The officer was scarcely 20 years old at the time. (Brébion, op.cit. p.47.)

[74] AOM, Indochine AF Carton 10, Dossier A30 (6). Governor of Cochinchina to the Minister, 27 May 1863.

[75] Henri Mouhot, (1864), *Travels in the Central Parts of Indo-China (Siam), Cambodia and Laos during the years 1858, 1859 and 1860*, Vol. I, John Murray, London, p.275.

[76] Ibid, p.46.

Chapter 3

Take the road traveled by the ancestors

At the time of the establishment of our protectorate, we found it in a lamentable state: a race decimated by foreign invasions, prey to sickness, exposed to famine...the masses of people ignorant, living in a sordid condition and having lost the ability to react against their misery.
—Anonymous French journalist, 1935.[1]

Admiral de Lagrandière's gunboat had steamed the two hundred or so miles up the "Cambodian Nile",[2] the Tonlé Thôm, from Saigon to meet Norodom in a fraction of the time it would have taken a sailing junk, let alone a peasant's pirogue. The capitalist Age of Steam had arrived in a "vegetable kingdom",[3] an industrial civilization based on iron and steel, coal and concrete, glass, macadam and the telegraph had come to a traditional society of paddy, bamboo and palm thatch. The former would begin, ineluctably, to disturb the latter, although traditional Khmer society would prove surprisingly resilient, and the French would not begin to attempt real change until the 1880s. The social underpinnings of this medieval kingdom were absolute monarchy, established religion, slavery, and a highly distinctive land system. It was an *ancien régime*, but one with a very different material base to that which had existed in France before 1789. If it were "feudalism", it was a very idiosyncratic version of it. If there is substance at all to Marx's well-known ideas of the Asiatic Mode of Production and of "oriental despotism"[4] then Cambodia might be a case in point. If so, however, it was a case of the Asiatic Mode of Production *manqué* or *sui generis*, for no large-scale hydraulic works had been built since Angkorean times.

De Lagrandière's crew must have gazed in awe at the immensity of the river that merged into the horizon of the delta lands, flat and dotted with jungle scrub and sugar palms. Although often dismissed as Lilliputian, Cambodia occupies an area a fifth the size of France,[5] and much of it was uncharted at the time. The Cambodian people, while peasants in the main, were the descendants of the builders of Angkor, a fabulous complex of temples, squares and great irrigation works. Cambodia's salient physical features, the Mekong and the Great Lake, are impressively large even by world standards.[6] After the spring thaw in distant Yunnan, the swollen waters pile up and spill over on the flat alluvial plains of Cambodia, bringing with them silt and precious nutrients for the peasants' plots on the *chamcars*.[7] Every year this flood is so vast that it cannot escape quickly enough out through the delta, and so flows *backwards* up the Tonlé Sap River, past Phnom Penh and Udong, over the Véal-phok (the "plain of mud") to the Great Lake of central Cambodia. The floods greatly augment the size of this lake, the Tonlé Sap, which lies almost in the geographical center of the country. The low-lying forests are flooded, and the nutrients released feed an enormous and diverse population of fish and crustaceans, including the giant catfish, which grows to twelve feet or so long.

Stretching in all directions from this lake was a vast, largely trackless plain, covered in tropical forest for the most part. To the north, the plain stops at a rim of high, steep hills, the Dangrek Mountains, beyond which lies the eastern interior of Siam. To the south, the peaks of the Cardamom and Elephant Mountains cut off the plain from the littoral of the Gulf of Siam, although passes allow access. To the east and north of the Mekong delta is the jungle wilderness of the Annamite Chain, avoided for fear of malaria and "demons" by the Khmers. Elsewhere, on the flat lands to the east and west, the frontiers of the kingdom were ill defined, much to the anxiety of the kings, ever fearful of their predatory neighbors.[8] The jungles were home to numerous tigers and elephants, rhinoceroses, crocodiles, bears, wild boar, wild cattle and a variety of poisonous snakes (including the cobra), not to mention the fiercely independent hill tribes who lived there by hunting and swidden agriculture. Sadly, the elephants and tigers are rare today, although the flesh of the former was widely available in the markets at the turn of the nineteenth century and beyond, with the trunk and feet offered first to the King.[9] White, or albino elephants, were always very rare and were always given to the King and treated with great veneration, even eating sugar cane and cakes off silver platters[10] as the Khmers believed them to be close to the incarnation of Buddha.[11] The ferocious Siamese crocodiles, once hunted widely for their meat by the "Annamites", and sold as far away as Saigon—and depicted on the Bayon *bas-reliefs* at Angkor—are practically extinct today.[12] There was also a brisk trade in other wild animal products until well into the twentieth century. The *Résident* of Stung Treng province regularly listed the market prices for various skins, elephant, rhinoceros and tiger bones, ivory, and pangolin (spiny anteater) scales.[13] Still more animals fell victim to the guns of "great white hunters", one of whom was the splendidly eccentric Gilbert Filleau de Sainte-Hillaire, the blue-blooded *Résident* of Takeo during the 1920s. The traveler Harry Hervey describes how Sainte-Hillaire ordered a river steamer into shore so that he could rush off to shoot a tiger in the jungle.[14] Others delighted in blazing away at unwary saurians on mud-banks or birds in trees. It might have seemed like ripping good fun but within a few generations, the once broad species diversity of Cambodia was in peril.[15] The decline in the numbers of "keystone species" led to attempts at environmental protection as early as 1901, when a royal decree forbade the hunting of wild elephants.[16]

The Khmer people

The Khmers themselves had been described by the 18th century visitor Captain Hamilton as being "of a light brown complexion, and very well shap'd, their hair long, their beards thin." The same author wrote, "Their women are very handsome, but not very modest. The men wear a vestment like our nightgowns, but nothing on their heads or feet. The women wear a petticoat reaching below the ancle [*sic*], and on their bodies a frock made close and meet for their bodies and arms, and both sexes dress their hair."[17] The clothing of the common people, as distinct from the nobles, was somber. Except on holidays—which were admittedly quite numerous—the peasants habitually dressed in black, the dye derived from the fruit of the *mackloeu* (or *maclua*) tree, although the *kramah*, or scarf, was in brighter colors.[18]

The juice of the betel nut (a mild narcotic) often stained their mouths and teeth red and even the poorest peasant would own a copper box with compartments for the nuts, leaves and lime. Those of the rich were of gold or silver.[19] They struck the French visitor Dr. Morice in the 1880s as quieter than the "Annamites", even as gloomy and silent. An anonymous writer, basing himself on Morice's observations, described the Khmers as "the morose and untamable denizens of the hills and woods".[20] The words had a splendidly romantic ring, but only tell part of the story.

The population of the kingdom, decimated by perennial wars and revolts, was somewhere between 400,000[21] and one million[22] when de Lagrandière's gunboat anchored at Udong. Such towns as existed were ramshackle affairs of wood and bamboo; even the royal palace at Udong was wooden. The largest town, Phnom Penh, had only one street, the present day *Quai Sisowath*. Henri Mouhot estimated the population of that "long and dirty town" at 10,000 permanent residents in 1859, but there was also a transient population of double that size, living on boats on the Tonlé Sap River.[23] De Carné described the town unflatteringly as "only a crowd of petty wooden and bamboo houses, most of them raised above the ground on posts, round which pigs and chickens live in a familiarity which brings the inhabitants inconvenience of more kinds than one." "The natives", he added, "huddle together in the strangest way."[24] Given the uncertainties of life at the time, one can sympathize with them. Before the endless period of revolts and foreign invasions—indeed until the Siamese burnt the city in 1834—there had been perhaps 50,000 residents in the city. The town was now a shadow of its former self. Even Norodom's palace at Udong was insubstantial, and he seems to have left it without regrets when the French suggested he move to Phnom Penh in 1866.[25]

Cambodia must have seemed an utterly alien, remote place to the marines who came to guard the newly installed king after the signing of the Treaty. They must have cursed the orange dust of the "winter" dry season and the red mud of the endless monsoon rains of "summer"; puzzled that the European seasonal categories did not fit this land of perpetual heat and flies.[26] Even by the straitened standards of an old *marsouin*[27] from the back alleys of Paris or Lyons, the poverty of the population must have been stark and distressing. Even if Europeans had only recently struggled to a scientific understanding of the connection between filth and illness, this place must have seemed straight out of distant medieval times, perhaps even the Dark Ages, with its epidemics of strange disease. To the French mind, the Khmer dwellings were mere "dog kennels", their furnishings unbearably meager. There were sudden reeks of decay amidst the tropical flowers and the pungent aroma of fish sauce and durian in towns without drains. Some European observers put the general misery down to what they saw as the inherent sloth and indolence of the Khmers. Henri Mouhot was one of these. He complained of the "pride, insolence, cheating, cowardice, servility, [and] excessive idleness...[of] this miserable people".[28] Moreover, he opined, they were of "repulsive dirtiness",[29] and lived in squalor amidst vermin.[30] He contrasted them unfavorably with those who had built Angkor Wat and wrote, "All that can be said of the present Cambodians is that they are an agricultural people, among whom a certain taste for art still shows itself in the carved work of boats belonging to the better classes, and their chief characteristic is unbounded conceit."[31] Of all the peoples of Cambodia—Khmers, Chams, "Annamites" and Chinese—he had positive things to say only of the hill tribes, whom he cast in the light of Rousseau's noble savages. Many writers since have repeated this jaundiced point of view. It is in stark contrast with the generally favorable opinions of earlier visitors, including Captain Alexander Hamilton[32] and the Iberian missionaries. From other accounts, the Khmers bathe frequently. They were probably personally much cleaner than their European counterparts under the *ancien régime* were.[33] If so, however, this private cleanliness contrasted with public squalor (and still does today).

Mouhot, and many like him, came to Cambodia full of assumptions of European superiority. The Cambodians were all liars, advised a friend of the traveler in 1859, and they were not to be trusted.[34] Some writers have argued that the French in general were not as virulently racist as other Europeans, pointing out that official colonial policy was to assimilate the "natives" into Gallic civilization as "brown or black Frenchmen". Yet, the strain of racism ran deep. France did not abolish black slavery in the colonies until the Second Republic in 1848,[35] and in the following century, when Khmers brought back white spouses from France, they faced the wrath of racist *colons*.

Mouhot seems to have been blind to the effects of an oppressive social system, and unaware of the detrimental effects of protracted war and instability on the Cambodian people. He claimed that the Cambodians of the port of Kampot were little troubled with taxes,[36] whereas other contemporary writers stress the arbitrary and onerous nature of the traditional tax system. Further, although he "felt deeply" for the oppressed Russian serfs of the time, whom he said were kept in a condition of "slavery",[37] he had little sympathy for their Cambodian counterparts who also lived under despotic quasi-feudal rule. Other

French observers looked deeper for explanations of the melancholy facts of Cambodian life. Perhaps, floating in their gunboats on the Mekong, peering at the alien shore, they reflected that their own Seine and Loire had once been among "the dark places of the earth" [38] and that any claim to superiority on France's part was of recent vintage. Besides, any claim to superiority rested on technological supremacy rather than virtue.

A deeply traditional society

De Lagrandière, like the missionaries such as Father Jean-Claude Miche, would have seen and deplored a society marked by poverty, ignorance and superstition. Compared to the upheavals and restless dynamism of capitalist Europe in the Age of Steam, which by the 1860s had taken root in the cities of peasant France, Cambodia was static, technologically backward and steeped in musty tradition; at least from the European point of view. The socio-economic system assured land to the tiller, and yielded ample taxes to swell the coffers of the mandarin class, yet it kept the country chronically underdeveloped and poor.

Most of population were poor peasants, above whom in an often-predatory relationship, was a thin layer of Chinese merchants and moneylenders. There was a hereditary ruling class of rich mandarins and nobles, at the apex of which was the King himself, the sole landowner in the entire kingdom. Norodom was a monarch whose power was in theory limitless over his subjects;[39] the French emperor, Louis Bonaparte, in contrast, drew his "legitimacy" from a plebiscite, no matter how dubious, and feudal absolutism in France had died under the guillotine during the Revolution after 1789. The French, steeped in the doctrines of the Enlightenment, found much of what they saw deeply disturbing. Battalion Chief Brière d'Isle reported in 1863 that a class of corrupt mandarins milked the peasants in order to live in wasteful opulence. He claimed that the people lived from day to day "in a most precarious state" and painted a picture of exorbitant and arbitrary impositions, of the routine violation of such laws as existed. The Cambodian legal code itself, the *Préa-thomma-sat*, was medieval, and the punishments often barbarous, even if, as Virginia Thompson has observed, in practice "Buddhism… tipped the scales on the side of mercy." In theory, there were twenty-one legally recognized ways of inflicting slow death on malefactors.[40] The Buddhist code, which exhorted believers not to kill, did temper it, however, in practise. The custom was decapitation by sharp sword, with quartering for usurpers and rebels.[41]

The rapacious self-interest of the rulers (including, and especially, the King) effectively stunted private enterprise and (in contrast with Marx's model of the "Asiatic Mode of Production") there were virtually no public works. As opposed to the thrift and industry of the Vietnamese, the Khmers displayed a general lack of initiative that stifled commerce and industry. D'Isle's complaints were to set a pattern.[42] Francis Garnier agreed that the stagnation was the "sad result of system of government that kills this unfortunate country" and waxed indignant about,

> The interference of the mandarins in everything and for everything— [which] by always grabbing the lion's share of the gains—has killed all initiative. The king and a few other big men seem to be the only proprietors and the only businessmen of the kingdom. The extravagant tastes of the king, which have grown even further after his contact with Europeans, leave his treasury constantly empty and he has been obliged to farm out one by one all the taxes or the sources of public revenue. [43]

Garnier believed that French support for the current system could only worsen the plight of the inhabitants.[44] In a report written after a decade of the protectorate, Étienne Aymonier, the French *Résident* at Phnom Penh, was scathing about the bad character of many of the top mandarins. The *Chauféa*, or Prime Minister, "had a great reputation for avarice". The *Véang (Péang)*, or finance minister, was "greedy like the others" and was unpopular because of his ruthless extraction of taxes.[45] Corruption extended down to all levels of the government. Louis de Carné noted that lesser mandarins lived in luxury, despite their low official salaries. They supported their opulent way of life, he surmised, by "pitiless and arbitrary exactions" on the peasantry, restrained only by the fear that too great a rapacity might force the victims into emigration.[46] An 18th century Khmer "normative poem", or *chbap*, had cast Cambodian officials in a rapacious light:

> Officials, civil and military,
> Are comparable to tigers
> Or spotted snakes.
> Whenever the people come to them
> Seeking assistance
> They change immediately into demons
> Without compassion.[47]

Doudart de Lagrée noted that the superabundance of such functionaries also acted as a breeding ground for discontent, with pretenders able to pitch for their support by promising rewards to those willing to change the color of their coats.[48]

There was no landed property in Cambodia before the French; only crown land. The King, the *Maître de la Terre*, owned every square inch of the soil and it could not be bought or sold.[49] As another writer observed, "the king is so completely the owner of his country that the word 'sovereignty' is confounded with that of property. Since it is in his interest that his lands should be worked, he permits his subjects to farm his kingdom and share with him its produce."[50] One of Norodom's sons, the rebel Yukanthor, put a different spin on it. The soil was "God's earth, given into the care of the king...[and] left by him at the disposition of all who had need of it."[51] The very concept of the alienability of land seemed wrong, pointless, even heretical, to the mass of the peasants, although it was some years before the French attempted to introduce so new-fangled a thing, and much longer before they had any success. Whether such "reform" improved the lives of the peasants is open to debate. According to the *Khmers Rouges* leader Hou Yuon, writing in post-colonial Cambodia, the French land program led to a degree of social stratification among the peasantry and therefore to an income gap between rich and poor peasants. Hou Yuon did not assume that the peasants in pre-colonial society were materially better off than under the French. He described their lot under the *ancien régime* as "miserable" and recognized that the land and tax system discouraged industry.[52] Prince Yukanthor argued passionately that the French reforms did not improve the peasants' lives.

The peasants paid no land taxes *(impôt foncier)* and in effect they could occupy a plot of land for as long as they chose to cultivate it, with the stipulation that any land left fallow for three years could be taken over by others, regardless of how long the original incumbents had tilled it. Such a situation would have been unthinkable in the more densely populated parts of Asia, Tonkin or Java, for example, where competition for the life-giving soil was fierce. It could exist in Cambodia because there was very little competition for land, given the relatively small population, even if this was concentrated in the provinces along the Mekong and Tonlé Sap. The King owned all the land, but divided it up into four "fiefs", or *apanages*,[53] each presided over by high-ranking members of the royal family, including the King and the Queen Mother, and these were responsible for the collection of taxes in each. The mandarins levied taxes on crops, livestock, fruit trees and the implements of farming and fishing—a system that was unwieldy and did not lead to a stable tax base, but was lucrative for those who collected the money. Revenues fluctuated markedly due to variations in harvests, and there was a tendency on the part of the peasants to understate their production in order to avoid taxes. The system also bred corruption; it was much easier for the tax collectors (petty officials on small fixed salaries) to falsify records of money collected on crops than on landholdings and to pocket the difference between the official and actual sums.

Such a system positively discouraged industry and enterprise: the more one produced, the more taxes one paid. This was, in Marxist terms, the material basis for such "superstructural" phenomena as the "tendency to nonchalance and insouciance" and the "passivity" of the peasants observed by Kleinpeter.[54] A seventeenth century English trader, Charles Browne, had called the Khmers "dull and lazie" and claimed that "onely necessity inforceth them to worke to clothe the bodye & fill the belly". Browne, however, had added that it was "the custome of the countrey [that] makes them soe careles"[55], blaming in particular the slave system and the absolute monarchy for their condition. [Browne's spelling in the original.] The peasants were not "naturally" lazy; there was simply no point in producing beyond a certain amount because any surplus was liable to expropriation, by legal or illegal means, by those "fated" to hold power. As Doudart de Lagrée observed, there was no indigenous middle class and "all commerce was in the hands of strangers, Chinese, Malays [Chams?] and Annamites."[56]

Nor did the payment of taxes lead to any discernible improvement in the lives of the population. There was no sense of "commonwealth" because there was no tradition of local self-government, as an inducement to produce more and pay more taxes. Public works were almost non-existent, unless they served the direct and most selfish ends of the rulers. When the French arrived, such roads as existed followed the routes of the ancient Khmers. The only substantial ones stretched between Phnom Penh and Udong and between Udong and Kampot.[57] Norodom had little, if any understanding of their importance as things separate from his own needs. Louis de Carné has recorded a revealing anecdote about the King's attitude to a proposed new road: "Despotism shows itself with a naïve candour, and he [Norodom] does not hesitate to reply, when recommended to open or repair a road necessary for commerce, —'There's no use for it—I never went by it.' "[58] Most of the monies collected from the peasants went to support the extravagant lifestyles of the mandarins and the royal family, who were themselves, along with thousands of their retainers, exempt from taxation. The minutes of a meeting of the Council of Ministers in 1899 reveal that although the peasants paid head taxes of 2.50 piastres per annum (in addition to sundry taxes on crops and agricultural and fishing equipment etc), extraordinary numbers of people were exempt. These included not only "deserving cases" such as the aged and the infirm, beggars and those considered incapable of work, *achars* and Cham mosque guardians, but also Khmer nobles, officials and their sons, employees and retainers. *Résident Supérieur* Gustave Ducos was outraged to learn that the majority of the inhabitants of the capital were exempt from the head tax because they were either employees of the government or the palace. Although most "Annamites" paid even higher head taxes than the Khmer peasants, Ducos was astounded that many of the inhabitants of the Catholic (i.e. Vietnamese) quarter of Phnom Penh were excused because they were royal artillerymen. The system was "iniquitous", Ducos fumed, because it exempted those having the easiest lives and penalized those with the hardest.[59]

The Asiatic Mode of Production?

One hesitates to describe such a system as "feudal", because feudalism was a European system based on serfdom and the *private ownership of land* by hereditary nobles. In Cambodia, by contrast, there was no private land ownership in the generally accepted sense: all land was crown land. Marx's theory of the Asiatic Mode of Production has been rightly criticized as "static" and as "a mere geographical terminology", rather than historical or dialectical analysis[60]—and according to some writers, he later quietly dropped it—but it does seem to fit Cambodia in many respects. Central to the theory is the idea of a system based on the lack of private property in land, coupled with despotic government, and with large public works. Marx has summed up his theory (based on James Mill and other second hand sources) thus: "There have been in Asia, generally, from immemorial times, but three departments of Government: that of Finance, or the plunder of the interior; that of War, or the plunder of the exterior; and, finally, the department of Public Works."[61] In Cambodia, as we have seen, all land was owned by the King, who would have agreed with the Bourbons that *"l'état, c'est moi"*.[62] This system had existed since the inception of the Khmer monarchy. The department of Public Works was certainly missing under Norodom, but it *had* existed in the Angkorean period,[63] with its great state-directed hydraulic works, dikes, canals and reservoirs *(Baray)*.

Whether what existed by the 19th century was an evolved or degenerated form of the Angkorean system is point for debate, but it had maintained the plunder of the interior, even if the power of the state had waned in respect to neighboring states. What remained was a unique social system that we cannot conveniently force into the mold of alien, European typologies. However we define it, though, this system of "social being" was the material basis for the backwardness of Cambodian society. Racist "explanations" in fact explained nothing.

In contrast to the conspicuous wealth of the royal family and the mandarins (based on the "plunder of the interior"), the peasants had few possessions apart from sleeping mats, some simple cooking utensils, their clothing and their tools of work. Moura says that they were a people of "extreme frugality" who ate but two meals a day, with little meat, and were abstemious with liquor.[64] They lived as their ancestors had done for thousands of years, in palm-thatched huts, often mounted on piles for ventilation and refuge from floods, snakes and insects. They made a modest living by tilling the soil for their staple crop of rice, supplementing this with fruit and greens from their kitchen gardens, and dried fish, *prahoc,* and *nuoc mam,* or fish sauce, from the teeming life of the waterways. In many respects, this way of life remains little changed even in present times.

In the good times, they had food enough, for the soil was fertile and there was land enough for all who wished to cultivate it. The climate, too, meant, as Kleinpeter put it, that a palm leaf was sufficient shelter from the elements.[65] Unfortunately, bad times—in the form of drought or floods—came often enough and "Rice production oscillated wildly. Some years saw bumper harvests, others saw the spectre of famine stalk the villages."[66] Despite this roller coaster of bounty and famine, the peasants were relatively content with their lot because they could envisage no other life and their fatalism was reinforced by the ubiquitous Buddhist teachings. Central to the Buddhist view was a belief in the reincarnation of souls, the accumulation of merit and the renunciation of all desire. One's station in this life was part of one's *karma*: if this life were a vale of tears, it was one's nemesis for bad deeds in a previous life.[67] Conversely, there was little resentment of the privileges of the despotic nobility, for these were seen as reward for good actions in a previous life. Many years later, in the twilight of French rule, when political parties made their appearance in the kingdom, this doctrine was to justify the abuse of power and the further enrichment of the wealthy at the expense of the poor.[68] Yet, there was always some expectation of *noblesse oblige* in Cambodia, as is evident in the Khmer proverb *Neak mean reaksa khsat dauch samuat poat pi krav;* "The rich should take care of the poor like the cloth which surrounds you".[69] If they neglected to do so, however, then one must be humble and aware of one's place: *Kom yok mehk troap angkuy*, "Don't take the sky to make a seat for yourself".[70] There was no point kicking against Fate; it was best to make the best of it and hope to accrue merit so as to live a more prosperous life the next time round. This was an intensely traditional society, and adults counseled children against change: "Don't reject the crooked road and don't take the straight one; instead, take the road traveled by the ancestors,"[71] exhorts another proverb.

Tradition was intertwined inextricably with religion, and bade the peasants to be content with very little; something the French found difficult to understand. Such social discontent that did boil up was often sidetracked into banditry,[72] although this frequently took on a distinctly "social" and even quasi-political hue.[73] Quacks and pretenders also exploited the misery of the poor. The victims of such ingrained forms of criminality and foolishness were generally other peasants, or Chinese merchants, and seldom the Cambodian ruling class. Such a belief system also nurtured a radical individualism at variance with European notions of collective responsibility and official probity, at least in the public sphere. Notions of the "solidarity of the oppressed" were also foreign to it, at least in the sense of leading to common political action in the interests of the poor and downtrodden. Marx's well-known words about "stagnant" Indian village life are certainly harsh and "orientalist", but they ring *partly* true. They might also have been written about aspects of Cambodian peasant life, which, it can be argued, *did* "restrain... the human mind within the smallest possible compass, making it the unresisting tool of superstition, enslaving it beneath traditional rules, depriving it of all grandeur and historical energies."[74]

We must sharply qualify this one-sided view, however. Another writer (who had the close personal acquaintance with Asia that Marx lacked) saw the Indian villages as resilient "little republics" which "seem to last when nothing else lasts. Dynasty after dynasty tumbles down; revolution succeeds to revolution; Hindu, Pathan, Moghul, Mahratta, Sikh, English, are masters in turn; but the village communities remain the same."[75] As for Bihar or the Punjab, so as for the Khmer villages of Tayninh, Pursat, or Battambang, whether they were under Siamese, Cambodian or Vietnamese rule. From Jean Delvert's sympathetic standpoint, the Cambodian peasants were a tenacious and lively folk who had developed "an original rural civilization."[76] Later in life, Marx himself adopted a more sympathetic view of Asian peasant life and recognized that Asians themselves must transform their own societies.[77] Writing in the early 1930s, Guy de Pourtalès claimed that they were Asia's only authentic peasants,[78] by which he meant that they had clung to their ancient ways longer than peasants in most other parts of the continent had. The geographer Delvert later described an honest and joyful people dedicated to family life, with a good comic sense and a love of singing and story telling that belied their somber clothing. They were devoted to their numerous festivals, for instance the fête of the sacred plough and the festival of *Kathan*,[79] and the *Chol Chhneam*, or New Year's festival, comparable to the Vietnamese *Têt*.[80] They also loved boat racing[81] and their dark clothing contrasted with a passion for flowers.[82] If proverbs distil the wisdom of a people, the pithy sayings of the Khmers reveal a wise people indeed. Kleinpeter has remarked that, among themselves (as opposed to their relations with the ruling class) they were an egalitarian people.[83] This sense of equality did not exclude women, who were not "downtrodden" and might have ambitions separate from those of their husbands, or *for* their husbands.[84] Cambodian law, however, did allow male commoners three wives,[85] and the vast majority of women, like the men, were illiterate.[86] Such restrictions did not apply to the ruling class, and although the commoners viewed incest with horror, the royal family practiced it regularly.[87]

Religiosity and superstition

Superstition and ignorance were deeply embedded in this village society and intermingled inextricably with religious dogma.[88] In one instance, a Buddhist monk dreamed that the Queen Mother had ordered him to drink from a pond inside the grounds of her palace at Udong. The water would cure people of their illnesses, the monk claimed. The pond received large numbers of pilgrims until the French stepped in to stop "this exploitation of public credulity".[89] This was also a pre-literate society, although some males did learn a smattering of letters from their study of the religious texts during their youthful period as monks.[90] Delvert has noted that the Khmer peasants do nothing without first consulting the stars. Houses must point east and the sleeper must repose with his head towards the south: a westerly orientation "is always funereal".[91] Amulets and charms played a big part in the people's lives. They believed that little cylinders of gold, silver or lead worn next to the skin would keep away evil spirits, ghouls and the sicknesses they caused. A favorite charm for other purposes was the *Sne*, or love charm.[92] Bandits also believed that charms and magic waistcoats could ward off bullets;[93] a belief still held in the 1970s by General Lon Nol and his soldiers during the Second Indochina War,[94] and even today.[95] The Khmers generally dreaded the uplands as the abode of demons. Ghosts, generally, were for them as real as the living.

The Buddhist religion was a cornerstone of village life; and the peasants were impervious to the proselytizing efforts of the Catholic missionaries.[96] The Muslim Chams were perhaps even less open to Christian doctrines than their Buddhist neighbors were.[97] Mentally, the peasants lived in a medieval universe and saw no reason why they should change; indeed resistance to change was a virtue because change was itself an illusion that could lead only to pain. Milton Osborne has noted the words of the French priest Jean-Claude Miche, "that the only sure way to advance Christianity was for missionaries to purchase the freedom of slaves, who would then become converts."[98] Delvert has also drawn attention to the economic effects of Buddhist doctrine, particularly the idea of the "noxiousness" of material things, which, he holds, tends to discourage commercial activity and leaves the peasant "badly adapted to the rigorous conditions of modern economic life."[99] A sympathetic French Canadian writer later observed that, the Khmer peasant's "intense Buddhist faith has taught him to be more concerned with the after-life than with worldly goods..."[100] They were "wise", but "resigned", perhaps like peasants the world over,[101] and would have approved the Irish proverb, "contentment is wealth". Nothing good had ever come from attempts at change, they might have believed, and political turmoil underlined the need to hold fast to the conservative virtues that formed a bulwark against chaos.

The problem of slavery

If the peasants were the "pack animals" of Khmer civilization, there were others worse off. From the French point of view, perhaps the most unjust and economically iniquitous institution in this puzzling land was slavery.[102] Although France had only ended slavery in the West Indies little more than a decade previously,[103] the naval officers at Saigon saw its abolition as central to their *mission civilisatrice* in Cambodia. They saw it as morally repugnant and as a barrier to economic development. Slaves are seldom dedicated and efficient workers, since the facts of their servitude do not dispose them towards initiative or acquisition of advanced skills: wage laborers are much more reliable and efficient. Slaves normally acquire only the most rudimentary skills, and close supervision is necessary even of those who do possess advanced skills. Nor can they be trusted with fine tools or intricate machinery.[104] Nor should we ignore the corrupting and dehumanizing effects of slavery on the owners of "thinking property".

Estimates of the size of the slave population in Cambodia vary and it would have been difficult to quantify in any case, given there were no censuses until the establishment of French power. Louis de Carné claimed that there were 40,000 slaves in 1866.[105] Paul Branda claimed that out of a total population of 900,000 in the 1880s, 150,000 were slaves.[106] According to a French official, debt slaves made up one-third of the population of the Siamese-occupied Khmer province of Battambang in 1902, and the number was increasing.[107] There can be no doubt that the Cambodian variant of the "peculiar institution" was deep-rooted and extensive in the kingdom. A Chinese account from the twelfth century mentioned that "wild men from the hills" served as slaves and that the wealthy might own up to one hundred of them. Only the poorest Khmers did not own slaves in those Angkorean times.[108] Moreover, as subsequent resistance to its abolition showed, the population (including some of the slaves themselves) viewed it as "natural" and necessary.[109]

When the French set up their protectorate in Cambodia, there were two broad types of slavery in the kingdom: *khnhom*, or debt slavery, and *neahk ngear*, or hereditary slavery. Prisoners of war, rebels, criminals and *Montagnard* tribes people—*chunchiet* to the Khmers—could become hereditary slaves. As Branda points out, it was common for a child whose grandparent, or even great grandparent had committed a crime, to be born into slavery.[110] Hereditary slaves included Khmers owned by the royal court (generally for political offenses) and pagoda slaves.[111] Hereditary slaves were persons whose ancestors had fallen into slavery because of war, revolt, or capital crimes. Pagoda slaves were most often criminals, perhaps fleeing the death sentence or lengthy imprisonment, who had sought sanctuary in a Buddhist *wat*. Royal slaves had to give three months free service per year to the King; sometimes their fate was perpetual bondage.[112] The most widespread form of slavery, however, was enslavement for non-payment of debts. As Branda remarked, it was possible for a person to fall into the condition for inability to pay a debt of 50 piastres or about 250 francs.[113] Given that legal rates of interest might be anything between 40 to 100 per cent per annum in Cambodia, falling into slavery was not very difficult.[114] Debt slaves generally served as domestic servants in the houses of their creditors, and could buy their freedom if they managed to accumulate the money. Their children were also born into servitude. Masters had to provide them with free board and lodging and they enjoyed certain legal rights, for instance, while they could be whipped for insubordination, the master was forbidden in theory to sexually abuse his slaves or use cruel physical force.[115]

The Stung Treng slave trade

Although such servitude often sat comparatively lightly on the shoulders of the slaves, enslaved hill tribesmen were "slaves in all senses of the word", even thirty years after the arrival of the French.[116] Owners prized the "savages" as "vigorous and intelligent". They cost more than their Khmer or Vietnamese counterparts, but they had to endure the "worst slavery".[117] Slavers captured them in Laos or the adjacent parts of Cambodia and took them in chains to the riverbanks for sale to waiting merchants who took them downstream to Cambodia, Siam, or even Burma.[118] Francis Garnier has left us a vivid account of the Stung Treng slave trade and the subsequent fate of those sold to the slavers. The trade (like that in Africa) could not have existed without the active participation of the tribal chiefs. Garnier claims that "For a little brass work or [gun] powder, for some glass trinkets, the chiefs of the wild tribes...agree to deliver adolescents, often even entire families..." to the slave traders. The trade led to "an almost permanent state of war between the various wild tribes, [and] armed kidnappings and violent outrages on the part of the traders..." It also ensured that the Stung Treng region bordering Laos remained in a permanent state of economic and social backwardness. Chinese traders sold the slaves in the central markets of Phnom Penh at a huge mark-up on what they paid for their "human merchandise" in Attopeu, the center of the trade in the remote border region. A slave who cost 100 or 150 francs in kind at Attopeu would fetch 500 in Phnom Penh.[119] Even if the treatment meted out to the *Montagnard* slaves did not in general compare with the cruelty suffered by the black slaves of France in the West Indies, their loss of freedom, cultural deracination, and the frequent separation of family members was a cruel burden. Garnier witnessed the arrival of a convoy of slaves in Stung Treng and wrote,

I could not help being deeply affected by this spectacle. If the men appear to be generally indifferent to their fate, the women convulsively pressed their young children around them, hid them with their arms, and their eyes gave away their agonising fear each time a bystander approached to examine them.[120]

Most of the French officials would have agreed with Garnier's demand to suppress the trade and close down the slave market in Phnom Penh, as perhaps the most urgent task of the new protectorate.[121]

The Pou Kombo revolt

Yet, regardless of the fatalistic consensus in this tradition-bound society, there was no real social peace in the kingdom. A history of dynastic feuding and endemic banditry retarded development and prosperity. Garnier claimed that competition for the throne "is virtually eternal in Cambodia" and blamed it for the social and political decay of the kingdom.[122] Pretenders to the throne were commonplace, and could generally attract followers from among the more credulous and ignorant (or restless) of the villagers. However, such discontent was fuelled by the personal ambition of the pretenders rather than any wish to overthrow the existing social order in the interests of their gullible followers, who in any case were usually devoid of any egalitarian sentiments themselves.[123] One such pretender was Pou Kombo, who might well have overthrown Norodom but for the presence of the latter's new friends from across the ocean.

The Pou Kombo revolt highlighted both the fragility of the Cambodian state and the personal unpopularity of the newly crowned king. Pretenders to the throne were not in short supply. Norodom's two half-brothers, Si Votha and Sisowath, had already unsuccessfully challenged his right to rule, and had taken up arms against him before the French arrived. Others held that Norodom could not be the legitimate ruler, as his father, Ang Duong, was uncrowned at the time of Norodom's birth.[124] Scarcely had Captain Herbisson's marines restored order after Norodom's coronation in 1866, than the Pou Kombo challenge exploded. Louis de Carné states flatly, "If we had not supported...[Norodom] in 1866, he would certainly have lost his throne".[125] This is an accurate assessment. Pou Kombo had great personal prestige, especially in the eastern part of Cambodia, whereas Norodom was extremely unpopular at the time[126] and the pretender could count on the martial valor of zealous followers.

Pou Kombo, 48-years-old in 1866, was an energetic and capable military commander, easily more than a match for his rival in Phnom Penh. The rebels began the revolt by killing the French administrator in Tayninh, Cochinchina, in early June, before marching on Cambodia-proper.[127] For all of his bloody impact on the country, Pou Kombo's origins are shadowy. Garnier claims that the he was a cousin of

Norodom, who had "raised the standard of rebellion" after escaping from internment in Saigon.[128] Pou Kombo himself claimed to be a son or grandson of King Ang Chan, but the French disputed the claim.[129] It is likely that the pretender was both a commoner and a *Montagnard*, of the *Kui* people, born in the village of Thbong prea Khleang in Kompong Svay province and that his name was an assumed one.[130] The peasants, no matter how credulous, would not support a rebel chieftain unless they believed he was of royal blood. Yet, although he cloaked his uprising in traditional garb, Pou Kombo seems to have been a genuinely charismatic leader who managed to rally ten thousand Khmers in the Tayninh border region to his cause,[131] with whole provinces, such as Baphnom, joining the insurgents. "The entire country is in revolution", Admiral de Lagrandière reported to Paris after he was forced to station 700 French infantrymen at Phnom Penh and to deploy gunboats and artillery against the rebels.[132] Pou Kombo defeated a royal Cambodian army in October 1866[133] and killed the *Kralahom*, or Minister of the Navy, who commanded it.[134] Many of the King's soldiers deserted.[135] In the same period, the rebels surrounded the new capital of Phnom Penh, trapping Norodom in the town and even penetrating into the main fortress. Only the intervention of French troops lifted the siege.[136] In January 1867, the French dealt the pretender a major defeat.[137] De Lagrandière could report with satisfaction that "energetic officers", such as Captain Jean Duclos, had thrown back Pou Kombo's men and "demoralized them by successive defeats".[138]

The revolt sputtered on for a few more months but the French gradually drove Pou Kombo's bands into the wild *Montagnard* country in the north.[139] Pou Kombo fled to Laos before his return and capture in December 1868 following a vain attempt to rekindle the revolt. His captors cut off his head, placed it in a bag filled with salt, and displayed it impaled atop a long pole in Phnom Penh. Moura wrote that, "With Pucombo [i.e. Pou Kombo] the immense revolution was finished." Yet, although the French had snuffed out the flame of rebellion, Pou Kombo's loyal lieutenants, A Nong and A Chreng, kept a spark of it alive in the remote forests[140] and their long guerrilla campaign was to fuse with that of Si Votha in a still greater uprising in the years to come.

The Pou Kombo uprising confirmed the worst fears of the French about the competence of their *protégé*, King Norodom, and they questioned his fitness to continue on the throne. An official at Saigon complained that, "Things aren't going well in Cambodia. We are obliged to occupy and defend this country... [but] we are wasting our time."[141] Shortly afterwards, another exasperated official complained of the proof, "in everything" of Norodom's "insouciance" and "ineptitude".[142] De Lagrandière compared him unfavorably with Prince Sisowath, who had shown "more energy and intelligence" than the King in the suppression of the revolt.[143] Sisowath had returned from Saigon aboard a French warship to command the native Khmer troops in the latter period of the revolt. He himself subsequently claimed that Admiral de Lagrandière had personally charged him with the suppression of the revolt.[144] Even if this is an exaggeration, he performed creditably[145] and the French named him Governor of the eastern provinces for his trouble.[146] He returned to Cambodia for good in June 1868.[147] Just why he should throw his weight into saving his brother is unclear, but perhaps he saw it as a way of ingratiating himself with the French, for he was to prove their most loyal supporter. The French were relieved by the apparent reconciliation between them.[148] Sisowath hovered in the wings as *Obbareach*, or official heir, for the next 37 years before Norodom's death gave him the throne he coveted.[149] The Pou Kombo revolt was the last large-scale anti-dynastic insurrection during the Protectorate, although other pretenders emerged often enough to cause localized strife. The much-larger Si Votha rebellion of 1884-85 was primarily an anti-French insurrection, and only ended when Norodom himself persuaded the rebels to lay down their arms.

Notes

[1] Anonymous, (1935), "Une tournée d'inspection au Cambodge", *L'Illustration*, Paris, 2 February.

[2] The phrase was apparently coined by Paul Collard, (1925), *Cambodge et Cambodgiens*, Société d'Editions Géographiques, Paris.

[3] The geographer Pierre Gourou used the phrase to describe the Sinitic countries of the Far East. It is just as applicable to Cambodia. See Pierre Gourou, (1975), *Man and Land in the Far East*, Longman, London.

[4] See Karl Marx, (1969), (Ed. Shlomo Avineri), "The British Rule in India", in *Karl Marx on Colonialism and Modernization. His Dispatches and Other Writings on China, India, Mexico, the Middle East and North Africa*, Anchor Books, New York.

[5] J. Moura, (1883), *Le Royaume du Cambodge*, Vol. I, Librairie de la Société Asiatique de l'École des Langues Orientales vivants, Paris, p.7. See also Umberto Melotti, (1972), *Marx and the Third World*, Macmillan, London.

[6] The area of present-day Cambodia is 173,000 square kilometers, compared with 550,000 for France. See Roger Kleinpeter, (1935), *Le Problème Foncier au Cambodge*, Editions Domat-Montchrestien, Paris, p.30.

[7] *Chamcars* = fertile river verges. (Khmer.)

[8] AOM, Indochine, AF, Carton 10, Dossier A30 (6). Letter to the Minister of the Navy and Colonies (hereinafter abbreviated to Minister of Navy) from the Governor of Cochin China, 27 May 1863. See also PRO, Kew, FO 69/39 British Consul at Bangkok to Foreign Ministry, 29 September 1863.

[9] B. Marrot, (1894), *Exposition de Lyon 1894. Section Cambodgienne. Notes et souvenirs sur le Cambodge*, Forézienne P. Roustan, Roanne, p.38. The trunk and feet were considered delicacies.

[10] Ibid. pp.40-42.

[11] Moura, op.cit. p.101.

[12] Ibid. p.56. See also Georges Taboulet, (1955), *La Geste Française en Indochine. Histoire par les textes de la France en Indochine des origines à 1914*, Librairie d'Amérique et d'Orient, Paris, Tome II, p.658. The crocodiles, which grew to three meters in length, were trussed and sold alive in the markets. Moura, op.cit. pp.71-72 attests to their ferocity. Mathieu Guérin, a Phnom Penh resident and researcher on the *Montagnards*, told me that he traveled in remote areas of Cambodia by canoe in the late 1990s, without ever seeing one of these animals. (Conversation with the author, Phnom Penh, November 1999.) A former Tonlé Sap fisherman said that he had seen crocodiles in the lake, but they were very rare. (Conversation with the author, Phnom Penh, 3 July 2001.) The crocodiles are also rare in Thailand and Vietnam. However, the rare Siamese crocodile has been sighted recently in the Cardamon Mountains of southern Cambodia.

[13] ANC RSC E 03, File 14992 Box 1246, Résidence de Stung Treng. Rapports politiques et économiques trimestriels, 1914-1919. For example, reports for the fourth trimester 1914, first trimester 1917, and first trimester 1918. Tiger bones cost 60 piastres per picul and ivory 400 per picul in the latter period. Much of this "produce" was exported to other Asian countries for "medicinal" purposes. One picul = 60 kilograms.

[14] Harry Hervey, (1928), *Travels in French Indo-China*, Thornton Butterworth, London, pp.6-8.

[15] This ecological devastation accelerated during post-colonial times with deforestation caused by population pressure and illegal logging, along with carpet-bombing by the US air force in the late 1960s and 1970s.

[16] ANC RSC F451 File 2432, Conseil des Ministres, 52e séance du 5 octobre 1901, item 5, procès-verbal. The minutes note that action was necessary "In order to preserve wild elephants from destruction from hunters…" Offenders would be fined and jailed on the second offense and the proceeds of the hunt would be confiscated.

[17] Capt. Alexander Hamilton, (1754), *A New Account of the East Indies*, Vol. II, C. Hitch and A. Millar, London, p.203. Hamilton (p.198) also records that tigers and elephants were common in the forests.

[18] Jean Delvert, (1961), *Le Paysan Cambodgien*, Mouton, Paris, pp.143-145.

[19] Marrot, op.cit. p.37.

[20] Anonymous, (preface by Dean Meyers), (2000), *The French in Indochina. With a Narrative of Garnier's Explorations in Cochinchina, Annam and*

Tonkin, White Lotus, Bangkok, p.90. The anonymous author based his remarks on the ideas of Dr. Morice, who visited the Khmer Krom lands in the Cochinchinese delta in the early days of French power.

[21] PRO, Kew, FO 69/39. British Consul at Bangkok to the Foreign Office, 29 September 1863. This is probably much too low, although there was no way of making an accurate count at the time.

[22] Louis de Carné, (1872), *Travels in Indo-China and the Chinese Empire,* Chapman and Hill, London, p.10.

[23] Henri Mouhot, (1864), *Travels in the Central Parts of Indo-China (Siam), Cambodia and Laos during the Years 1858, 1859 and 1860,* Vol. I, John Murray, London, p. 225.

[24] De Carné, op.cit. p.6.

[25] The exact date of the move varies. Moura, op.cit. p.245, says 1866.

[26] There are two seasons in Cambodia, the wet monsoon from April to October, and the dry monsoon between October and April.

[27] Figuratively, *Marsouin* = French colonial infantryman. The term is a French corruption of the Danish and Swedish *marsvin;* literally a type of cold water dolphin, white in color. [Dictionnaires Le Robert, (1994), *Le Robert pour tous. Dictionnaire de la langue française,* Paris.]

[28] Mouhot, op. cit. pp.180-181.

[29] Ibid p.236.

[30] He was no more complimentary about the Vietnamese, and he thought the Laotians to be "almost cretins". Ibid. p.236.

[31] Mouhot, op.cit., Vol. II. p.23.

[32] Hamilton, op.cit.

[33] A Chinese visitor noted the bathing habits of the Khmers were noted as long ago as the late thirteenth century. See Jean Pierre Abel-Rémusat, (trans), (1819), *Description du Royaume de Cambodge, par un voyageur Chinois qui a visité cette contrée à la fin du XIIIe siècle; précédée d'une notice chronologique sue le même pays, extraite des annales de la Chine,* Imprimerie de J. Smith, Paris, p.15. These relatively salubrious habits were in part derived from a fear of bodily "pollution" inherited from their ancient Hindu past.

[34] Mouhot, op.cit. Vol. II p.278. (Letter to Mouhot from M. Guilloux, 12 August 1859.)

[35] French officials in Indochina admitted this. See, for example, the discussion of Cambodian slavery in AOM Indochine AF 13 Dossier A30 (22) Krantz, Governor of Cochinchina to Minister of the Navy, 25 August 1874.

[36] Mouhot, op.cit. Vol. I pp.180-181.

[37] Ibid, p.12. (Memoir of Henri Mouhot by J.J. Belinfante, who writes that Mouhot had spent time in Russia and had written an unpublished manuscript, entitled "Slavery in Russia" based on his observations.)

[38] Thus speaks Joseph Conrad's character Marlowe, waiting for the ebb tide to carry his ship from the Thames to the Congo in the story *Heart of Darkness.* [Joseph Conrad, (1999), *Heart of Darkness and other Stories,* (Revised Edition), Wordsworth, Ware, Herts. p.33.]

[39] Moura, op.cit. p.221.

[40] Virginia Thompson, (1968), *French Indo-China*, Octagon Books, New York, p.330. See also Moura, op.cit. pp.281 and 296. For a discussion of the Buddhist religious commandments, see Moura, p.201.

[41] Moura, op.cit. p.296.

[42] AOM Indochine AF, Carton 10, Dossier A30 (6). Governor of Cochin China to Minister of the Navy, 27 May 1863.

[43] Garnier, op.cit. pp.53-54.

[44] Ibid.

[45] AOM Indochine AF 13 Dossier A30 (22) Rapport Confidentiel sur le Cambodge, 24 August 1874.

[46] De Carné, op.cit. p.3.

[47] Cited and translated by David P. Chandler, (1984), "Normative Poems (Chbap) and Pre-Colonial Cambodian Society", *Journal of South East Asian Studies*, Vol. XV, No. 2, p.274.

[48] Cited in A. Bouinais and A. Paulus, (1884), *Le Royaume du Cambodge*, Berger-Lévrault, Paris, p.13.

[49] Kleinpeter, op.cit. p.105 and passim.

[50] Thompson, op.cit. p.340.

[51] Prince Norodom Yukanthor, cited in Thierry de Beaucé, (1967), "Le Cambodge. Bouddhisme et développement", *Ésprit*, Vol. 35, Nr. 9, septembre, p.268. Yukanthor, a famous anti-French rebel, is discussed in Chapter 6.

[52] Hou Yuon, "The Peasants of Kampuchea: Colonialism and Modernization", in Ben Kiernan and Chanthou Boua, (eds.), (1982), *Peasants and Politics in Kampuchea, 1942-1981*, Zed Press, London, pp.34-68. Hou Yuon was murdered during the fall of Phnom Penh in 1975, probably for calling on his erstwhile comrades to have mercy on the inhabitants. In contrast to Pol Pot's zealots, he emerges as a humane and thoughtful man.

[53] *Apanages* were portions of the royal domain or lucrative offices put at the disposition of loyal courtiers in medieval France and England. The term fits for Cambodia. "Fief" has an altogether more European, feudal, and thus imprecise, connotation. Strictly speaking, the *apanages* were part of a system of 57 provinces.

[54] Ibid. p.57. Although many urban Khmers made their living from petty commerce.

[55] D.K. Bassett, (1962), "The trade of the English East India Company in Cambodia," *Journal of the Royal Asiatic Society of Great Britain and Ireland*, London, pp.35-61. Appendix, "A Relacon of the Scituation & Trade of Camboja, alsoe of Syam, Tunkin, Chyna & the Empire of Japan from Q[uarles] B[browne] in Bantam", p.57.

[56] Cited in Bouinais and Paulus, op.cit. p.13.

[57] Ibid. p.73.

[58] De Carné, op.cit. p.32.

[59] ANC RSC F451 File 24210. Conseil des Ministres, 30e séance du 8 novembre 1899.

[60] Shlomo Avineri in the introduction to *Karl Marx on Colonialism* op.cit. pp.5-5. See, also Perry Anderson, (1974), *Lineages of the Absolutist State,* New Left Books, London, Note B, "The 'Asiatic Mode of Production", pp.462-549. Anderson points out that in Turkey, Persia and India did not have private property in land, and lacked the great irrigation projects of China, which did have landed property. (p.491.) Anderson concludes by asking for a "decent burial" for the theory. (p.548.) However, Marx might have unwittingly provided a model for Cambodian society. If so, it might more accurately be termed the Angkorean Mode of Production.

[61] Marx, "the British Rule in India", op.cit. p.90.

[62] "I am the state"; a sentiment that informed the political practise of King/Prince Sihanouk after independence until the Lon Nol *coup d'état* of 1970.

[63] See, for instance, Michael Vickery, (1984), *Cambodia: 1975-1982,* Allen and Unwin, North Sydney, Ch 5. Vickery considers that the period of Democratic Kampuchea from 1975-1978 might be seen as a reversion to the Asiatic Mode of Production of Angkorean times. For other views on the hydraulic systems see Bernard Philippe Groslier, (1974), "Agriculture et religion dans l'empire angkorien", Études Rurales, No 53-56, (Jan-Dec.) and Victor Goloubew, (1940), "L'hydraulique urbaine et agricole à l'époque des rois d'Angkor", *Cahiers de L'École Française d'Extrême-Orient,* No 24, 18.

[64] Moura, op.cit. p.381.

[65] Kleinpeter, op.cit. p.38.

[66] John Tully (1996), *Cambodia Under the Tricolour. King Sisowath and the 'Mission Civilisatrice' 1904-1927,* Monash Asia Institute, Clayton, Victoria, p.65.

[67] For a discussion of the concepts of merit and demerit, see Moura op.cit. p.158.

[68] See Chapter 25.

[69] Cited in Fisher-Nguyen, op.cit. p.99.

[70] Ibid. p.94.

[71] Ibid. p.97.

[72] Banditry seems to have been endemic for centuries. Hamilton (op.cit. p.402) had remarked that bandits "infested" the Cambodian islands.

[73] See Chapter 9.

[74] Marx, "The British Rule in India", op.cit. p.94. The same might be said of life in medieval European villages.

[75] C. Metcalfe, cited in J.A. Hobson, (1965), *Imperialism: A Study,* Ann Arbor Paperbacks, University of Michigan, p.293.

[76] Delvert, op.cit. p.134.

[77] See Suniti Kumar Ghosh, (1984), "Marx on India", *Monthly Review,* Vol. 35, January.

[78] Guy de Pourtalès, (1990, orig. published 1931*), Nous, à qui rien n'appartient. Voyage au Pays Khmer,* Flammarion, Paris, p.109.

[79] Delvert, op.cit. pp.137-138.

[80] Bouinais and Paulus, op.cit. p.46.

[81] Ibid. p.39. This is still seen in the annual Phnom Penh water festival.

[82] Ibid, p.61,

[83] Kleinpeter, op.cit. p.82.

[84] Delvert, op.cit. p.137.

[85] Moura, op.cit. p.268.

[86] Tully, op.cit. p.226. See also Chapter 11.

[87] See, for example, A. Cabaton, (1910), "La vie domestique au Cambodge", *Revue Indochinoise*, Premier Semestre, Hanoi, p.105. The marriage of princes to their half sisters was common, as with Norodom's children Prince Yukanthor and Princess Malika, and Prince Sutharot and Princess Phangangnam. The latter couple were the grandparents of the current king, Sihanouk. (From genealogical chart in PRO Kew FO 474/9.)

[88] Moura, op.cit. p.153.

[89] ANC RSC F451 File 24420 Conseil des Ministres, 240e séance du 27 janvier 1916.

[90] Tully, op.cit. pp.225-226 and Chapter 12.

[91] Delvert, op.cit. p.140.

[92] Ritharasi Norodom, (1929), *L'Évolution de la Médecine au Cambodge*, Librairie Louis Arnette, Paris, pp. 33-35. Such beliefs are widespread even today, even among the country's elites.

[93] Delvert, op.cit. p.141.

[94] See, for example, John Tully, (1990), "Certain and Inevitable Misfortune: War and Politics in Lon Nol's Cambodia, March 1970 – December 1971." Unpublished MA thesis, Institute for Contemporary Asian Studies, Monash University, pp.109-111. The General encouraged his troops to wear "magical" scarves and enlisted wizards to cast spells on the enemy.

[95] Pech Kunthea of Siem Reap, who fought on the Thai border during the 1990s, told the author that he also wore such amulets and that this was common in the Cambodian army at the time. (Conversation with the author at Siem Reap, 17 June 2001.)

[96] This was in contrast to the missionaries' successes elsewhere in the colonized world. Such converts as they made in Cambodia were usually Vietnamese. There were also a few Christian families of Portuguese extraction.

[97] William Augustus Collins, "An investigation into the division of the Chams into two regions", Unpublished MA thesis, University of California, Berkeley, 1966, p.48. Collins cites Father Gabriel Quiroga de S. Antonio on the antipathy of Chams to Christian missionaries.

[98] Milton E. Osborne, (1969), *The French Presence in Cochinchina and Cambodia. Rule and Response (1859-1905)*, Cornell University Press, Ithaca, NY, p.27. A Khmer king who converted to Islam in the mid-17th century "earned himself the epithet 'apostate'..." (Collins, op.cit. p.49).

[99] Delvert, op.cit. p.141.

[100] Charles Bilodeau, (1995), "Compulsory Education in Cambodia", Part One, in Somlith Pathammavong and Lê Quang Hông, *Compulsory Education in Cambodia, Laos and Viet-nam*, UNESCO, Paris, p.15.

[101] Delvert, op.cit. p.142.

[102] For a general discussion of slavery in Cambodia, see Alain Forest (1980), *Le Cambodge et la Colonisation Française. Histoire d'une colonisation sans heurts (1897-1920)*, Editions L'Harmattan, Paris, pp.345-357 and Moura, op.cit. pp.329-334.

[103] The date of abolition, 1848, is significant, given the revolutionary upsurge across Europe.

[104] See Karl Marx (trans. Eden and Cedar Paul), (1972), *Capital*, Vol. I, Everyman's Library, London, p.191n.

[105] De Carné, op.cit. p.122.

[106] "Paul Branda," (1892), *Ça et La. Cochinchine et Cambodge. L'Âme Khmère. Ang-Kor*, Librairie Fischbacher, Paris, p.9. (Paul Branda was the *nom-de-plume* of Rear Admiral Réveillère.) The evident decline in total population shown in Branda and de Carné's figures is due to the effects of the Great Rebellion.

[107] Brien, cited in Tully, (*Cambodia Under the Tricolour*) op.cit. p.102. See also AOM, RSC 229 (23) Letter from M. Breucq to M. Boissonnas, French Chargé d'Affaires at Bangkok, 4 February 1904.

[108] Zhou Daguan (Chou Ta-Kuan), (trans. From Paul Pelliot's French version of the Chinese original by J. Gilman and D'Arcy Paul), (1987), *The Customs of Cambodia*, The Siam Society, Bangkok, p.xii, and Abel-Rémusat, op.cit., pp.59-60

[109] Again, we must ask ourselves if Marx was so wide of the mark when he observed of village life that, "We must not forget that these little communities were contaminated by distinctions of caste and slavery..." ("The British Rule in India", op.cit. p.94.) Caste did not exist in Cambodia, but slavery did.

[110] Branda, op.cit.

[111] Edouard Testoin (1886), *Le Cambodge, Passé, Présent, Avenir*, Ernest Mazereau, Tours, pp.85-86.

[112] AOM, AF, A30 (28) "Esclavage au Cambodge", 1877-1880. Aymonier, French *Résident* at Phnom Penh, to the Governor of Cochinchina, 18 March 1880.

[113] Branda, op.cit. p.10.

[114] De Carné, op.cit. p.125.

[115] Aymonier, op.cit.

[116] Marrot, op.cit. p.13.

[117] AOM AF A30 (28) "Esclavage au Cambodge, 1877-1880", extract from *La Lanterne, Journal Politique*, 14 January 1880, Paris.

[118] Dr. Harmand, cited in Bouinais and Paulus, op.cit. pp. 35-36.

[119] Garnier, op.cit. p.67.

[120] Ibid.

[121] Ibid. p.125.

[122] Garnier, op.cit. Vol. I, p.50.

[123] Cambodian versions of Eric Hobsbawm's "social bandits" became more common as the French tightened their grip on the country. For a general discussion of the phenomenon in other countries, see E.J. Hobsbawm, (1969), *Bandits*, Weidenfeld and Nicolson, London. On Cambodia. See Tully, (*Cambodia Under the Tricolour*) op.cit. Chapter 5. See also Chapter 9 below.

[124] We should not take such claims and counter claims too seriously. Norodom's descendant, Prince Areno Yukanthor, later said that Sisowath's claim to the throne was illegal because his mother was, allegedly, a concubine and not a wife, of Ang Duong. The French themselves stirred the pot of pettifoggery for their own machiavellian ends. See Chapters 6, 8, 11 and 18.

[125] De Carné, op.cit p.32.

[126] Moura, op.cit. Vol. II, p.160.

[127] Ibid. p.159.

[128] Garnier, op.cit. p.50.

[129] Ibid. Moura claims that the Pretender took the identity of the dead child of Ang Chan and his aunt, Princess Pucombo (or Pou Kombo). See also Justin J. Corfield, (1990), *The Royal Family of Cambodia*, Khmer Language and Culture Centre, Melbourne, p.7. Pou Kombo lived from 1818 until 1867.

[130] Moura, op.cit. See also Gerald Cannon Hickey, (1982), *Sons of the Mountains: Ethnohistory of the Vietnamese Central Highlands to 1954*, Yale University Press, New Haven, Connecticut, pp.200-201. Hickey, after Moura, adds the detail that after Pou Kombo's capture and death in 1867, two of his senior lieutenants sought shelter with the *Stieng* tribespeople.

[131] Moura, op.cit. p.159.

[132] AOM Indochine AF Carton 11, A30 (12) Letter from Admiral de Lagrandière to the Ministry of the Navy, 9 January 1867.

[133] PRO FO/371/46308 citing the Chambre de Commerce Internationale, (1945) *La Situation de l'Indochine Française. Vol. I, L'Oeuvre Politique*, Paris. Also ANC RSC F451 File 24217. Conseil des Ministres, 37e séance du 8 novembre 1900.

[134] Moura, op.cit. p.161.

[135] De Lagrandière to the Ministry of the Navy, 9 January 1867 op.cit.

[136] Garnier, op.cit. p.145.

[137] PRO FO/371/46308 op.cit.

[138] AOM Indochine AF Carton 11, A30 (12) Governor of Cochinchina to Ministry of the Navy, 29 January 1867.

[139] AOM Indochine AF Carton 11, A30, (12) Governor of Cochinchina to the Ministry of the Navy and Colonies, 10 and 29 April 1867.

[140] Moura, op.cit. pp.170-175. In Khmer, the prefix "A" means despicable or detestable and is not part of the actual name but rather a kind of infamous title.

[141] AOM Fonds Ministeriels, Indochine, Ancien Série, Carton 1, A00 (7). Letter to the Ministry of the Navy, 12 November 1866.

[142] Ibid. 27 November 1866.

[143] AOM Indochine AF 11 A30 (12) 29 April 1867 op.cit.

[144] ANC RSC F451 File 24217 op.cit.

[145] *Bulletin de l'École Française d'Extrême-Orient*, Tome XXVII, p.519. See also Moura, op.cit. p.171; Milton Osborne, (1969), *The French Presence in Cochinchina and Cambodia. Rule and Response (1859-1905)*, Cornell University Press, Ithaca, New York, p.188 and V.M. Reddi, (1970), *A History of the Cambodian Independence Movement, 1863-1955*, Sri Venkateswara University Press, Tiraputi, pp.36-37.

[146] AOM Indochine AF 11 A30 (12) Letter from the Governor of Cochinchina to the Ministry of the Navy, 27 August 1867.

[147] Moura, op.cit. p.171.

[148] Ibid. Governor of Cochinchina to Ministry of the Navy, 31 January 1868.

[149] Sisowath was promoted to *Obbareach* on 28 May 1870. (Moura, op.cit. p.172.)

Chapter 4

An Unequal Struggle

Despotic and often cruel, unjust and insensitive to the sufferings of his people, he stayed for all the god-king, sacred and inviolable.
—Charles Meyer, *Derrière le Sourire Khmer.*[1]

Norodom did not lack ability, despite his ineffectuality during the Pou Kombo rebellion and his apparent pusillanimity during the siege of Udong in 1861. In the early years of the Protectorate, many observers remarked on his shrewd intelligence, and one commented on his "remarkable energy".[2] Milton Osborne notes "his lively intelligence and his deep sense of the dignity of kingship" and cautions against too ready an acceptance of the official French view of him as an oriental despot.[3] Moreover, although he was said to have been unpopular with the Cambodian people in the early years of his reign, as time wore on, he was accepted as the legitimate ruler, even as a *devaraj*, or semi-divine figure. His word was law in the palace, where 300 pages waited on him. Khmer horsemen would dismount and walk past the palace as a show of respect.[4] Regardless of his personal failings (and as we shall see, he had many), he was the King, a traditional Asian monarch, and he expected, and received, the customary devotion of the people. Moura has recorded an incident that conveys the quasi-religious aura surrounding the King. One day he fell heavily in the street in Phnom

Penh, but no Khmer dared to help him to his feet for fear of defiling the royal person. Eventually, a European passer-by came to his assistance.[5] The Khmer writer Huy Kanthoul relates an amusing, but telling anecdote concerning Norodom's passion for bicycles, which were a novelty during his reign. One day the king went for a ride outside his palace, accompanied by five members of the Council of Ministers, also on bicycles. The royal steed struck a pothole and Norodom fell off into the mud. The five ministers promptly fell off themselves, thus "saving their sovereign from certain loss of face."[6]

A ruler with many faults

Some writers have tended to skirt around the more unsavory aspects of Norodom's rule. There is no doubt that he *was* a despot, even if he was not so bad as the French officials claimed. Many of his courtiers did not inspire confidence; the French considered them "dubious" types, preoccupied with robbing the people.[7] Increasingly, the French viewed Norodom as the biggest robber of the lot, and the greatest obstacle to the changes they wished to bring to the kingdom. As we have seen, some French observers during the early days of the Protectorate were very critical of his rule. Later, especially after the restoration of the French Republic in 1871, the criticisms intensified. Confidential reports from the mid-seventies described him as "arrogant and haughty" and as "a sharp, cunning man", "egotistical and pleasure-bent" and "avaricious", who was incapable of making "a simple, useful expenditure".[8] One of the French Saigon admirals claimed later, under a *nom-de-plume*, that Norodom's court "surpassed the buffooneries of Offenbach".[9] His greed and self-indulgence repelled and fascinated them but, most importantly, it made enormous demands on the revenues of the kingdom (which he did not distinguish from his personal finances) and he had little notion of public duty that might have moderated his expenditure. To the French, he lacked a sense of *noblesse oblige*, and, by many accounts, he held his subjects in contempt. Norodom considered he was born to rule and this would have repelled the new generation of republican politicians and administrators after 1871. He could in any case justify the private wealth and public squalor of his kingdom with the Buddhist doctrine of accumulated merit,[10] whilst conveniently ignoring his religion's prescriptions of humility and abstemiousness in one's current life. A French official considered that "the King governs and administers at his pleasure" and that he took little notice of the five mandarins who made up the Council of Ministers unless it suited him. Such government was "absolute in the full sense of the term",[11] the official believed. Yet, at other times, the French complained of the malign influence of the mandarins over the King. They would have their cake and eat it, too.

The French reform program

Before the political demise of Napoleon III in 1870, the French tended to keep a low profile in Cambodia. This was a step back from the more meddlesome style of de Lagrandière and Doudart de Lagrée in the first years of the French presence in the country. Osborne's opinion that the Great Rebellion of 1884 "came as late as it did was due to the restrained role that the French first assumed in Cambodia"[12] is accurate, if we add the caveat about de Lagrandière's early bullying. A heavy hand, after a light one, is bound to provoke hostility. As one writer, reflecting the views of Governor General J-L de Lanessan put it; "an act of brutality followed a long indifference".[13] Increasingly, after 1871, the French spent their time maneuvering to reduce Norodom's power in order to introduce a program of reform. Foremost among these reforms were the creation of private property in land; the abolition of slavery; legal and administrative restructure; drastic cuts in the conspicuous consumption of Norodom and the nobility (harems in particular) via the creation of a civil list; and the redirection of the savings from such cuts into public expenditure. Norodom was to spend much of the remainder of his life trying to block the reforms, his relationship with the French descending into outright hostility as they pressed their demands. The "protectors" toyed with the idea of forcing him from the throne and into exile in Réunion or Tahiti, but their expectation that his sensual excesses would lead him to an early death restrained them. They were disappointed, however, for his physical constitution proved robust and he lived on for several decades. To their bewilderment, they were to discover that, because of his traditional authority over the people, he was an indispensable partner in their rule. Although he was a despot, once he had established himself on the throne, the Khmer people believed his rule to be legitimate. It was to prove a hard lesson for the colonizers in their attempts to introduce what Max Weber called "legal-rational authority" in place of traditional forms of authority rooted in thousands of years of practice.[14]

Norodom had been born Ang Vodey in Angkor Borey in 1834. Like many other young male Khmers, he spent time as a monk, donning the saffron robes as a thirteen-year-old in 1848 following the *rite de passage* of the traditional hair-cutting ceremony.[15] A year later, he went as a kind of hostage to the Siamese court at Bangkok, and was not to return for ten years.[16] According to Milton Osborne, his upbringing was strict, even brutal, and he was beaten and sometimes kept in chains.[17] It must have been a strict school of despotism, an oriental equivalent of the regimen of pain and humiliation inflicted on upper class English boys in their "public" schools. Norodom learned the lesson that those with power had the right to act as they saw fit. De Carné claimed that Norodom refused to believe that any nation could be great without despotic monarchy,[18] hardly surprising given that ideas of democracy and representative government were recent, European innovations, and that the monarchy had always been absolute in Cambodia. Moreover, the French usurper, Louis Bonaparte, was scarcely a democratic role model and the Third Republic, which succeeded the Second Empire, was not anxious to export democracy to the colonies.

Still, Norodom could be a pleasant and charming host, receiving European visitors graciously at his palace,[19] and often playing billiards with French inhabitants of the capital in the 1860s and early '70s.[20] The French shifted his court from Udong to Phnom Penh in 1866, installing him in a complex of thatched structures in the royal compound, before building the more substantial and palatial residence that still stands today. According to Viscount de Carné, the King was "full of warmth, animation, and spirits."[21] If so, this side of his character was often reserved for his foreign guests. One writer records that although he "presented agreeably" at receptions, he was a "terror" to his wives and ministers,[22] and even had his own mandarins beaten if they displeased him.[23]

Norodom was a diminutive fellow, already running to fat in his mid-twenties. Yet, he had a quick wit and his conversation was graphic and "full of sallies almost Voltairean".[24] An Anglo-Saxon visitor described him in the early 1870s as,

> a pleasant-looking person – thirty-six years of age... a little man with intelligent and expressive features; teeth blackened after the Siamese fashion [from chewing betel, JT], the head shaved excepting a small tuft up on the crown; upon the lip was a thin moustache; and he was dressed in a white linen jacket, with gold buttons, and a silk *panoung*, his feet were bare, and around his neck was a fine gold watch chain, upon which were strung some rings, one or two of them set with very large diamonds.[25]

Although he always remained a Khmer, he quickly acquired the patina of a European gentleman, dressing in elaborate military-style uniforms and developing some contempt for the old Cambodian court etiquette.[26] For instance, he shocked his old retainers by shaking hands with European visitors;[27] such familiarity smacked of *lèse-majesté*. The "correct" approach was a posture of prostration, and his wives awoke the Great Man by gently caressing his feet. Nor was he above mocking the Buddha when the mood took him.[28] He grew increasingly offhand about the Siamese whom he had formerly held in dread[29] and although he had originally feared his own subjects, as his confidence in the French grew, he came to despise the people. Perhaps because of fear of his people, he preferred foreign mercenaries to Khmers as bodyguards, employing chiefly Filipino *Tagals*, between fifty and ninety of them, at the palace.

He loved to dress up and was encouraged in his sartorial excesses by his chief *aide-de-camp*, said to be an English Jew, who himself was fond of wearing uniforms "fit for a field marshal", covered with an enormous amount of gold lace.[30] In the early years at least, he was a dedicated Francophile; the traveler Frank Vincent noted that, "since the King has become a French *protégé* he imitates France in everything".[31] As the old saying goes, "imitation is the sincerest form of flattery" and Norodom clearly did admire French and European culture. He was prouder of his fine English porcelain dishes than of his collection of massive gold vases of local manufacture.[32] He loved his new palace, designed by a French architect and completed in about 1870 by Cambodian workmen. His architectural aim, he freely confessed, was to surpass anything in Bangkok. Although the exterior was Asian, the methods of construction were European and the royal abode was equipped with modern furnishings and fittings. Some time in the early 1880s, it was lit by electricity.[33] Norodom had a fascination with machinery, and owned a collection of European artifacts, including a telegraph machine, water pumps, cameras and electric motors.[34] A French chef supervised the kitchens and the King could relax in his billiards room (decorated with "'rather fast' pictures"), his luxurious French-style parlor, or in his library with its engravings of Napoleon III, a "magnificent bronze clock" on the mantelpiece, and its marble statuettes of Goethe and Schiller. Another sign of Norodom's francophilia was his generous contribution to France's reparation payments to Germany after the war of 1870-71 with Prussia.[35]

Yet, these sentiments contrasted sharply with the traditional behavior of the autocrat. One decidedly un-French feature of the royal palace was the harem at the rear of the main building, with its "saffron-powdered damsels",[36] almost a regiment of them according to a bestseller of the period.[37] But if Frank Vincent considered that Norodom's palace surpassed anything in Bangkok, he also noted that, "The strong contrast between the bamboo huts of the city and the grandeur of the palace is painfully apparent, and for the expenses of beautifying the latter, His Majesty is said to have appropriated private property without indemnification."[38]

A life of ease and excess

If his childhood had been austere, he was determined to compensate for it in adulthood. His indulgence contrasted with the lives of the people. The Khmer peasants were relatively abstemious, monogamous people, and they generally eschewed the vices of their overlords. Although one writer thought they were "generally very dissolute",[39] those who knew them better denied it. They rarely smoked opium,[40] although they consumed great quantities of tobacco.[41] Polygamy, whilst *de rigueur* for the upper classes, was rare among the peasantry or town poor.[42] There was, however, no doubt about Norodom's vices and love of luxury. He smoked "incessantly... now a green-leaved, now a dry native, afterwards a German cigar, then a Manilla..."[43] He was addicted to the pleasures of wines, spirits and the opium pipe, consuming a stunning amount of expensive alcohol and opiates each year.[44] His favorite tipples included sherry and Marsala, which he drank "to excess",[45] and champagne, which he downed by the magnum-bonum.[46] His prodigious consumption worried the French, who believed it was stunting his mental faculties and would lead him to an early grave. Nor was he the only "opium fiend" in the kingdom. "All—kings and princes—are big opium smokers," wrote the French Governor at Saigon. He added that, "The King sometimes spends the night smoking at the house of the Mandarin *Presor* Sauvirong, leaving his carriage parked at the door. I also saw this vehicle, along with those of several mandarins, and with a cavalry escort, stationed all night outside the opium company."[47]

Although his word was law, the King was relatively indifferent to the mundane affairs of the kingdom, leaving such details to his entourage of trusted ministers, so long as they did not try to restrain his expenditures or support the alien reforms of the French. An English visitor described how he found Norodom "stretched out in a nearly nude condition, betel chewing and smoking" during a performance of the royal ballet and remarked that "Truly, the cares of state must sit easily on his royal breast".[48] So long as the taxes flowed in to replenish his coffers, he was satisfied. Having never had to differentiate between the public and the private in his financial affairs, the French considered he lacked a sense of personal honesty. His custom of bribing (or "rewarding") his favorite functionaries with money and gifts repelled them. This, to be fair, derived from the custom of dispensing largesse as a form of insurance against the defection of mandarins to the cause of pretenders. Perhaps he also believed that it was an honor for traders if he graced them with his patronage.

The French were not impressed with such customs; at least in the early years of the Protectorate when Cambodia was a "frontier" posting staffed by zealous naval officers and the days of *Bonjour*, as corruption was known,[49] were yet to come in the French administration. After Pou Kombo's defeat, Norodom offered Doudart de Lagrée a gold bar as a token of thanks. The lieutenant's refusal to accept it astonished him.[50] Despite his considerable wealth, Norodom was not above cheating on his debts and the French often heard complaints from merchants and bankers to whom he owed substantial sums of money. The Saigon branch of a China-based bank complained to the French *Résident* at Phnom Penh that the King had repeatedly ignored requests to settle an outstanding 30,000-piastre loan.[51] A Phnom Penh merchant begged the *Résident* to intervene to secure payment for large quantities of quantities of alcohol and liquid opium.[52] In another instance, a French jeweler lamented that Norodom had owed him large amounts for a long time. He also spent a great deal of his time at the gaming table playing *Ba-Quan*, a kind of roulette.[53]

A city within a city, the royal harem

Such debts as these activities incurred were petty, however, compared with the extraordinary expenditures of the royal harem. From the French point of view, the harem was, after slavery, the most grotesque institution in the kingdom. Norodom spent a large portion of his time in seduction and attending to his harem, to which he made constant addition. If necessary, he kidnapped young girls who took his fancy. In one instance, he abducted a young girl from Chaudoc in Cochinchina, but had to release her and pay her family an indemnity after they complained to the French.[54] Such philandering probably contributed to his early unpopularity with the people, although this might be a misreading of the attitudes of Khmer commoners to the sexual privileges of royalty.[55] His mandarins were just as goatish and there were rumors that they trafficked in young Siamese girls. An

English language Bangkok newspaper claimed in 1882 that a certain "Malabar" had lured a princess and others to Phnom Penh harems. Some French officials believed that "Malabar" was a coded reference to either Norodom or Sisowath, although others dismissed this aspect of the tale as being unlikely.[56]

Norodom's palace was almost a city within a city, and made huge demands on the country's finances. The Hanoi paper *Le Mékong* reported in 1894 that maintaining Norodom cost the public purse 800,000 piastres per year,[57] much of it swallowed up by the harem. This translated into around five million francs, worth many times that amount in today's currency. *Résident* Étienne Aymonier grumbled in a confidential report to his superiors that, "the greatest part of the country's revenue is absorbed by the harem."[58] The French were determined that after Norodom's death, his successor's harem would be much smaller. Estimates of just how many wives, dancers, and concubines lived in it vary. One writer claimed it contained between four and five hundred wives, living in what was in effect "a great village, five hundred meters long by three hundred wide, behind high walls and a strong palisade built of stakes and beams." The wives lived in an assortment of houses, some of stone, some of wattle and daub, others of the more conventional Khmer straw and palm thatch. They shared the compound with their (and Norodom's) children, his sisters, and, at times, the Queen Mother, although the latter generally remained in isolation at Udong. In total, between one thousand and fifteen hundred women and children lived *en sérail*.[59] Norodom soon lost count of how many children he had fathered. One writer estimated the number at sixty in the late 1880s.[60] Another thought there were seventy-two.[61] Another thought Norodom had 30 children when he was in his mid-thirties.[62] The confusion was understandable because Norodom himself was not sure. "After reflection", wrote one visitor, he put the figure at eighty to one hundred, "give or take ten". The following anecdote illustrates Norodom's uncertainty:

> One day, out for a stroll, as was his custom, in the main street of Phnom Penh, he [Norodom] met a mandarin surrounded by little boys. "What beautiful children!" he said to him. "My compliments to you." "But, Your Majesty, these are yours."[63]

Father Guédon and other French priests had tried to convert the King to Christianity, but his attachment to the harem proved an insurmountable obstacle. According to one source, when Guédon suggested that one wife was enough for any man, Norodom had tried to compromise by reducing the number from five hundred to one hundred.[64] Another source was more conservative, avowing that Norodom "begged to be allowed at least ten. Finally, he came down to five, but from five he would not budge..."[65] Even if Guédon had convinced him, it is unlikely that Norodom would have converted to Christianity. The story of the "apostate" Khmer king who "left religion" by converting to Islam in the mid-17th century would have reminded him of the strong link between the monarchy and established religion. In that case, the king, Ram or Rama, scandalized the Khmer population and was eventually driven from the throne and killed after a civil war along religious lines.[66]

Given its considerable size, the harem functioned on strictly hierarchical lines, with Norodom's principal wives at the apex of the pyramid of power, and a division of labor of domestic tasks according to "quality" of birth and age. The senior wives kept order, if necessary, by the use of the *bastinado*, or cane.[67] Entry to the harem was forbidden to non-wives and family, with one category of exceptions. The compound was under strict guard, but not, as in the Middle Eastern *seraglio*, by eunuchs. Instead, "monsters" kept watch over the women. It was the custom in Cambodia to give children born with gross physical deformities to the King for protection at the age of ten to twelve years. The category included those afflicted with albinism, and even twins, regarded by Cambodians as freaks. Such a system was humane in that it provided these unfortunates with food and lodgings, but at the cost of their liberty, as they were, in effect, slaves of the royal household.[68] The less deformed of these slaves were selected as guardians of the harem.[69] Those who believe in the intrinsic superiority of European society might contrast the Cambodian system with the frightful life of John Merrick, the so-called "Elephant Man", in England in the same period. Merrick, a gentle and pensive soul who suffered a grossly disfiguring and incurable disease, was condemned to the workhouse, freak show and constant beatings because of his outward deformity.[70]

Most of the wives and concubines had had little or no choice about their situation. Although they were raised to see their station as an honor, in fact they were slaves, even if pampered ones. Not surprisingly, they were often lonely and homesick, and they frequently sought sexual and emotional solace where they could find it, for it was impossible to seal the compound off hermetically from the outside world. However, if Norodom was unsure of how many children he had, he kept a close track on his wives and any infidelity on their part was seen as treason, *lèse-majesté*, or even *lèse-divinité*. He reacted to it with "a pitiless jealousy" that could only be slaked by the swift and cruel punishment of the offenders.[71] His father, Ang Duong, sometimes sent his unfaithful wives to brothels or put them to death, but Norodom in his jealous rages always demanded the death sentence. In September 1873, he ordered the deaths of four harem women and two of their male lovers. When the *Tagal* guards bravely refused the task, Norodom called in a squad of Cambodian slave-soldiers who messily shot the women and their lovers to death after several volleys. One of those executed was a 17-year-old Vietnamese palace slave girl whose "crime" was to have failed to denounce her mistress. The victims' heads were cut off and impaled on spikes, *pour décourager les autres* and to assuage Norodom's wounded pride.[72]

The incident horrified the French and they stepped in to prevent a similar tragedy seven years later when several young women from the harem were caught with young men and a number of slaves were charged with acting as their accomplices. The French Governor at Saigon categorically ruled out the death sentence, but Norodom was intransigent and a potentially embarrassing incident loomed. The Governor considered kidnapping the prisoners, but the *Résident* at Phnom Penh was able to convince Norodom (who was susceptible to flattery) that his good reputation in Europe would suffer if he proceeded with the executions.[73] In fact, the case came to the attention of the left-wing paper *La Lanterne* in Paris. A scandal erupted, embarrassing the French Government, which no doubt felt guilt by association, despite its disapproval of the harem.[74]

Norodom's cuckolds often lived inside the palace itself, although his male offspring only lived in the harem until the ceremony of hair cutting around puberty. In one instance, the King discovered that one of his sons, Prince Phatavong, was involved in an affair with one of his Siamese wives, Mévang. Norodom flew into a violent rage, declaring that he would have the woman put to death. As for Phatavong, he wanted him tied to a horse's tail and dragged around the town as an adulterer. Phatavong took flight to Chaudoc in nearby Cochinchina, and although the French prevented Norodom from killing Mévang, she received one hundred lashes. The King's rage caused general panic in the palace. The French believed that several other sons, including Prince Mayura, were "ready to flee to Cochinchina at the first alert", adding that only Prince Duong Chakr was calm "because he only has relations with his own sister".[75] Another son received 100 strokes of the cane and two years incarceration for illicit relations with his father's current favorite.[76] A more poignant case was that of a young palace dancer who fell in love with a "monster" of the palace guard (a twin) and fled with him to Cochinchina, with Norodom's guards in pursuit. *Montagnards* betrayed the unfortunate lovers for four buffaloes and a bag of salt and they were taken back to the capital where Norodom was eager to have them decapitated,[77] although it is probable that the French prevented the executions.

Increasing French impatience

The existence of so bizarre an institution as the royal harem (and those of other members of the nobility) highlights the despotism of the Cambodian political system. The King's power was absolute and unlimited and that of the nobility scarcely less so over the common people. Yet, the French were determined to force something like the rule of law on the kingdom. Privately, they had contempt for many of the nobles, whom they regarded as lazy parasites, not without reason in many cases. When Norodom's favorite brother died aged 40 in July 1883, the Governor of Cochinchina told the Colonial Minister at Paris that, "His Highness Serivong will not be regretted…" Serivong's short life was one of prodigious abuse of alcohol and opium,[78] much of it in Norodom's company. By the mid-1870s, the French were determined to ram through reforms, regardless of the King's opinion. Norodom's health had suffered greatly by this time, and although he was scarcely into his forties, the French considered his death imminent.[79] They were already sketching out a program of reforms and plotting to engineer the elevation of a more pliable successor. A new revolt in Kompong Svay province in June 1874 stiffened their resolve. Although the revolt was "smothered" within a few weeks, it absorbed the energies of up to 5000 Cambodian soldiers and much of the population of the province fled to Laos at the call of the rebel leaders. The French sheeted the blame for the uprising directly to the corrupt and incompetent rule of the mandarins. Admiral Krantz wrote to Paris expressing the fear that more uprisings would break out unless he received permission to tackle what he saw as the appalling maladministration of the country.[80] So extreme was the people's misery, he wrote, that many of them were emigrating to Siamese-controlled Battambang province, where taxes had been reduced comparative to those in Cambodia-proper following the Franco-Siamese Treaty of 1867.[81] Shortly afterwards, his forecast appeared confirmed when a fresh revolt broke out in 1875 in the northeast, led by the veteran insurrectionist Prince Si Votha,[82] and continued into 1877. Jean Moura blamed it on "general discontent" arising from the bad administration of the King and the mandarins. The situation was so serious that the French sent gunboats and troops up the Mekong to assist the King's forces.[83] If we are to believe a later report in the *Siam Free Press*, Norodom's role in this military campaign was anything but distinguished. "Despite his *képi* his functions were humble," the paper claimed, "and he was to be seen holding a candle while the French General read his dispatches in his tent before turning in for the night." The paper also claimed that Norodom had joined the French column because he did not feel safe from the rebels in Phnom Penh.[84]

Squeezing the peasants for taxes

To the French, the Cambodian administration was ramshackle, unjust, wasteful, and labyrinthine. There were no less than 57 provinces in the country, each of which was the personal *apanage*, or "fief", of a member of the royal family or of a high mandarin. It should be remembered that with the Siamese control of much of the west and northwest of the country, it was significantly smaller than today. Some 41 of these bailiwicks fell under the direct or indirect authority of the King; a further twelve were the direct or indirect *apanages* of the *Obbareach*, or Second King; the Queen Mother directly controlled three; and one was under the direct control of the Prime Minister.[85] Even under a more benign administration, there would have been unnecessary duplication of functions with such a bewildering number of provinces.

There was little, if any, distinction between public treasuries and the private finances of their masters. The French chafed because they had little say on how taxes were collected or spent. Levels of taxation varied from province "according to the needs or whims of the master".[86] *Résident* Étienne Aymonier claimed that taxes were constantly increasing, with new taxes on silk and even on drums and gongs. The most onerous tax, he wrote, was the *rachat des corvées*, introduced six years previously. This provided that people could buy themselves out of performing *corvée* labor, but at a steep cost. This meant "lucrative operations" for the mandarins.[87] Although the mandarins mercilessly squeezed the peasants for taxes, the French believed that the Cambodian administration was so corrupt and inefficient that the three million francs it collected in taxes each year ought to have been five million.[88] Aymonier was also concerned that Norodom did not contribute a single piastre to the cost of running the protectorate. He believed that the French had missed the opportunity provided by their suppression of the Pou Kombo revolt to demand radical revision of the Treaty of 1863. Reform was necessary, he wrote, and the Governor at Saigon must impose it. The Minister in Paris agreed with Aymonier and Krantz, yet counseled caution, advising that they should wait until the death of the King before proceeding.[89] Aymonier seems to have been in two minds. He considered that corruption and misery were so extensive that there was a great potential for revolt. He proposed an immediate reduction in taxes; a revised system of *corvée*; the vigorous suppression of banditry (a great source of suffering for the ordinary people); the introduction of strict civil list of stipends for the multifarious members of the royal family; and the reform of the arbitrary justice system.[90] The latter invited corruption, given that magistrates derived their income directly from fines imposed on malefactors.[91] The French considered that in general Cambodian law was contradictory, vague, and redolent of medieval barbarism.[92]

Although a number of the early French administrators made great efforts to understand Khmer culture, many did not comprehend that Cambodians simply saw life differently than did post-Enlightenment Europeans. Many of them learned the language and strove to understand Cambodian customs. Some, such as Moura, Aymonier, and Garnier, wrote informative and thoughtful books about the country they even came to love. They considered it self-evident that their reforms would be very popular with those they considered would benefit from them.[93] Yet, to their bafflement, this was to prove too optimistic an assessment. The French administrators of this period were, in the main, earnest, honest in their desire for reform, and sympathetic to the Cambodians. Yet, they approached the country with "orientalist" notions. Their mission was essentially paternalistic and grounded in the unexamined assumption of European superiority based on legal-rational authority. The Khmers, however, saw their own traditional customs and laws as legitimated by many hundreds, perhaps thousands, of years of practice. Buddhism, with its emphasis on merit, also taught them resignation and held out the hope for a better lot in a later life. The French perhaps forgot that their own rationalist ideals were of recent vintage and that Europeans had long been just as resigned to life as "nasty, brutish and short"; an interlude on the way to heaven or hell.

The pact with Prince Sisowath

Many official reports written in this period betray a note of mounting exasperation, sometimes of anger and disgust, directed at the King in particular. Krantz's successor, Baron Duperré, deplored the "bad administration of the kingdom...[and] the complete incapacity of the King, and above all, the impossibility of obtaining the least reform from this sovereign..." He clearly wished for Norodom's decease, or at least his abdication, but was gloomy about the caliber of the candidates available for the succession. Surveying the field, he noted that Norodom's eldest son was "not very intelligent" and thus unacceptable. The others were either too young, or did not take their responsibilities seriously. Therefore, he continued, "I have cast an eye on the Second King", (Sisowath). He ordered the French *Résident*, Jean Moura,[94] to arrange a discreet interview to ascertain Sisowath's reliability and his attitude to reform.[95] While the French had been impressed with Sisowath's good showing in the suppression of the Pou Kombo revolt, they had still had doubts about his ability and character. Aymonier had thought him "false and underhand as his brother" and doubted he would be any more favorably disposed to reform.[96] Moreover, if he had acquitted himself well against Pou Kombo, the French would not have forgotten that he had also led a revolt against Norodom himself, and spent five years in exile at Saigon for it. Yet, Duperré had a limited field from which to choose. If Moura found Sisowath reasonably satisfactory, he was to present him with a secret convention which would commit him to reform. In theory, the five members of the Council of Ministers would choose the next king.[97] This time, when the King died or abdicated, the French *Résident* was to attend the Council. He was to impose France's candidate on the Council after reading a forceful statement that continuation of a "detestable" administration was intolerable.[98] Sisowath was eager for the crown. He told the skeptical Moura that if the French made him king, he would do France's bidding and give his assent to modifications to the 1863 Treaty.[99] In fact, Sisowath would prove to be a loyal friend to France for the remainder of his days: many would say he was a French puppet. The knowledge that they had such a reliable backstop probably gave the French the confidence to press the wily Norodom harder for reforms.

For his part, Norodom had a very different political agenda to his half-brother. His reasons for inviting the French into his kingdom were ambiguous in the first place, although he most certainly did so in order to strengthen, rather than diminish Cambodian sovereignty. There is evidence that he was unhappy with the failure of the French to return all or part of the Mekong delta region from Cochinchina.[100] He was often indirect, however. His preferred approach to French demands was passive resistance. While hastening to assure the French of his good will, he would smile and assure them of his friendship, yet give away nothing, and change nothing. Although he agreed to some major reforms, particularly against slavery, in 1877 (and earlier in 1872), the ink of his signature faded as things went on as before.[101] The following year, Norodom appeared to agree with the *Résident* that the new laws should be enforced, and, moreover, that the buying of justice should cease, that there ought to be a drive against administrative corruption, and that money should be made available to fund useful public works.[102] Two years later, when again pressed to implement the new laws, Norodom reproached the French for not giving him enough time. He claimed, slyly, that in 1863, all of the mandarins of the kingdom had been opposed to the new protectorate because it would overthrow the customs of the country. "I alone in the kingdom did not take their advice," he argued. "Would you have me believe that they were right?"[103]

Such sophistry irritated the French. It must have seemed like arguing with the Sphinx. Le Myre de Vilers reported that, "The political, administrative and economic situation in Cambodia is still the worst... The financial disorder surpasses all bounds and the King takes all revenues for his own personal use." In 1881, the Colonial Minister issued instructions to the protectorate to take firm steps to take over the public finances of the kingdom.[104] In particular, the French demanded directly that Norodom contribute 66,000 piastres (around 333,000 francs) annually towards the expenses of the Protectorate. Norodom, stung by the demands, wrote to the French President, complaining of the "rudeness" of the French officials. They had trampled on his rights, he protested, and were forcing him to do things that were contrary to the Treaty of 1863. The situation was "intolerable" and if the President did not heed his plea, he would compromise the "sincere and deep affection" that he and his people felt for France.[105] In the meantime, he refused to budge. Two years later, the French had still not received any money and Norodom avoided any discussion of it[106] while continuing to profess his loyalty and gratitude to France. Governor Thomson considered that the King's intellectual faculties were rapidly deteriorating and that he had fallen under the bad influence of anti-French mandarins. He hinted darkly, too, of the alleged influence on the King of francophobic Chinese residents belonging to the Society of Heaven and Earth.[107] While he claimed that Norodom's consumption of alcohol and opium had affected his intellectual capacities, another contemporary observer describes him as "intelligent and wise".[108] There is a growing personal antipathy in Thomson's words, but they also reflect shifts in French policy towards the colonies.

There were few French people in Cambodia during this period—perhaps one hundred administrative personnel besides the military garrison and a smattering of private citizens.[109] Although would-be settlers had tried to obtain land, Norodom had blocked almost all such projects. Article Five of the 1863 Treaty *did* appear to give the French the right to acquire land, but this provision conflicted with the crown land system. Apart from some land occupied by administrative, naval and military facilities at Phnom Penh, and some religious buildings, the French occupied very little of the country's soil. In 1882, however, a certain M. Caraman applied for a grant of land in order to set up a plantation. The application was blocked and this contributed to the growing dissatisfaction of the French. The Governor complained that no one in France understood that the Treaty was to the sole advantage of the Cambodian crown.[110] Hobson's "economic taproot"[111] of colonialism had not taken hold in Cambodian soil at this stage, but the French clearly believed that it ought to. As Hobson and other writers have argued, the 1880s saw a radical shift in the extent and direction of European imperialism. Not only did the European powers seize enormous swathes of territory across Africa and Asia, but also, according to Hobson, they developed a "conscious policy of Imperialism"[112] that aimed to harness the colonies for European economic advantage. Hobson observes that in the early 1880s in France, "a great revival of the old colonial spirit took place". France seized Senegal and vast tracts of the Sahara in 1880 and the following year she marched into Tunisia. By 1900, the French overseas empire amounted to over 3.5 million square miles, and almost all of the lands seized since 1880 were in tropical or subtropical regions held to be unsuitable for white settlers.[113] The chief French theoretician of this "new imperialism" was the influential economist, Paul Leroy-Beaulieu, and its foremost political exponent was Jules Ferry—*"Le Tonkinois"*—Prime Minister of France between 1879-1881 and 1883-1885. Although Ferry was a relatively late convert to the imperialist cause, by 1883 he supported an aggressive and "forward" policy in Indochina and elsewhere. Such a policy meant a sharp clash with Norodom and traditionalism in Cambodia. Another factor was that the opening of the Suez Canal in 1869 had shortened the sea route from Europe to the Orient by many thousands of miles. Cambodia was not so remote as it had been and it was no longer a case of "out of sight, out of mind".

Late in 1883, Thomson prevailed upon Norodom to sign yet another agreement. The French administration of Cochinchina would collect duties on opium and spirituous liquors sold in Cambodia and subtract

66,000 piastres annually from them for the expenses of the protectorate. A new constitution would establish landed property and abolish slavery. Justice and the administration would be reorganized along liberal lines.[114] French exasperation had also led them to toy secretly with the idea of incorporating Cambodia directly into Cochinchina,[115] although they did not pursue this, perhaps because they still believed Norodom's death to be imminent. In addition, they had already made a secret agreement some years before to put the pliable Sisowath on the throne after Norodom's death.

The French demand a new treaty

Norodom's political method could be summed up as a self-fulfilling prophecy of *"plus ça change, plus ça même chose"*.[116] The reforms he had agreed to in 1883 and the preceding decade remained a dead letter. On the surface, relations with the French remained cordial. Early in March 1884, Norodom welcomed Governor Thomson to Phnom Penh. Clad in the uniform of a French divisional general, the King staged a spectacular fête for his visitor. There were races of the traditional long Khmer pirogues on the Quatre Bras, where Thomson's corvette, the *Alouette*, lay at anchor. There were banquets, flowers and fireworks. Norodom assured Thomson of his undying fidelity to France. Unmoved by the pageantry, Thomson, a career civil servant of the Third Republic, did not lose sight of his goal, even as he dispensed the customary presents to the royal retinue he privately held in contempt. The former *Préfet* of the Loire had come not to make polite conversation nor to watch the royal dancers, but to enforce reform on a stubborn opponent. He had a number of private audiences with the King and his secretary-cum-translator, Col de Monteiro, at which he presented the King with a list of demands for a new treaty. The next day the *Alouette* marked the King's apparent agreement with a 21-gun salute.[117] The shots were blanks, but the more thoughtful *Phnompenhnois* and palace officials might have ruminated on French power. Norodom, as usual, equivocated. He wrote to Thomson advising him that his translation of the proposals was unclear on several points and that he would submit them later to the Council of Ministers.[118] Such delaying tactics did not work this time. Thomson left for Saigon, but two months later he returned on what he admitted privately was a pretext. A large fire had destroyed a whole district in Phnom Penh adjoining the French concession, causing 140,000 francs worth of damage and killing two Chinese, but Thomson was more interested in forcing Norodom to comply with reform than visiting the ruins.[119] The French demands, if implemented, would lead to a massive diminution of Cambodian sovereignty and royal power. Article 1 would give *carte blanche* to the French to do *whatever they wished*. It stated that, "His Majesty the King of Cambodia accepts all the administrative, judicial, financial and commercial reforms which the government of the French Republic deems useful in future to facilitate the work of the protectorate."[120] Cambodian officials would continue in their jobs, but under French supervision. The French would have control over customs and taxes, public works and other services affecting Europeans. They insisted that the Cambodian budget would pay the expenses of the Protectorate. Moreover, they were to regulate the finances of the royal household and a civil list would apply to the King and princes. They again demanded the abolition of slavery and insisted on the creation of private property in land.[121] In addition, the 57 provinces would shrink to eight, each under the supervision of a French official. Judges and magistrates would receive fixed salaries. They would create a Phnom Penh municipal council under the permanent presidency of a French *Résident-Maire* (mayor). The French would directly appoint a majority of councilors and provide the King with a list from which to choose the remainder.[122]

The demands were the most radical so far and fully in accord with Jules Ferry's aggressive colonial policy. Norodom protested that the proposed new treaty would diminish his personal prestige and authority, and that of the Cambodian authorities. The government and the people, he lamented, were not accustomed to such departures from the ancient ways.[123] Norodom Sihanouk has claimed that King Norodom's private secretary told his master that the French proposed his abdication, not a treaty.[124] On 11 June, the Council of Ministers rejected the proposals and demanded a French guarantee that they would not weaken royal authority.[125] Perhaps they believed that they could continue to stone wall, but Thomson, fully backed up by the Minister in Paris, was determined to succeed. He complained of the King's bad will and refused to believe the King's claim that he could not see him because "I am sick, very tired and I cannot walk."[126] "I have proof, Your Majesty," thundered Thomson, "that in spite of your state of health, you have not suspended your official entertainments and that your ministers are meeting day and night under your presidency." He concluded by warning that if he had not heard from Norodom by midday of the day following, June 14, that he would take steps to ensure what he felt was the respect due to France.[127] Some days later, the Minister at Paris received a telegram from Thomson stating that he had resolved to achieve his ends by force if necessary.[128]

Thomson's gunboat diplomacy

In fact, Thomson had already taken steps to assemble what amounted to a small expeditionary force. On 14 June, the corvette *Alouette* again dropped anchor in the Quatre Bras. Apart from her regular crew, she was carrying 120 French marines, 150 Vietnamese *tirailleurs* (sharpshooters) and 7 officers from Mytho and Vinhlong, to augment the French garrison. Three days later, at 4.45 a.m. as the city still slept in the humid wet season darkness, the French troops surrounded the royal palace that stands just 100 meters from the riverbank. At 5.30 in the morning, accompanied by staff officers and a detachment of twelve marines,[129] Thomson barged into the royal chambers, pushing aside a courtier who tried to block the way,[130] and rudely awoke the sleeping king. Thomson emerged at 9.15 a.m. to announce that Norodom had signed the new Treaty and agreed to all of its points.[131] Although Havas, the official French news agency, trumpeted that Norodom had signed the new treaty voluntarily, some of the French metropolitan newspapers were skeptical. The Paris *Télégraphe* noted that Havas had neglected to tell of the veritable "expeditionary force" that Thomson had used to obtain King Norodom's "voluntary abandonment of his rights of sovereignty and of three quarters of his revenues."[132] In truth, Norodom, his palace surrounded by heavily armed troops, and with the guns of the *Alouette* within point blank range, had signed because he had no choice. Branda states bluntly that Norodom was told, "You must choose: accept the treaty or abdicate" and adds that Thomson threatened to take the King aboard the *Alouette* if he would not sign.[133] Later generations of Cambodians were in no doubt about the circumstances. Prince Areno Yukanthor told the French President in the late 1930s that Thomson had imposed the treaty at bayonet point.[134] Indeed, he had.

Afterwards, for all of Thomson's reports of "perfect order and absolute calm",[135] a powerful insurrectionary spirit was growing, fed by the blows and insults the French had delivered to Cambodian pride and by popular attachment to the ancient Khmer traditions. Even before Norodom signed, there were rumors of insurrectionary movements and of mandarins dispatching their families and precious belongings to the provinces to avoid danger.[136] However, in a triumphal mood, the French seemed unaware of this. A deceptive calm reigned. At the year's end, Thomson reported to Paris that the "new order of the day is welcomed here with unanimous satisfaction."[137] In its own way, bearing in mind the scale of the consequences for Cambodia, this was as inept a reading of the situation as Neville

Chamberlain's later forecast of "peace in our time" for Europe on the brink of World War II. Indeed, the French felt so confident that they again thought seriously of annexing the Protectorate to their colony in Cochinchina.[138] They pushed ahead rapidly with their reforms as soon as the French President ratified the new Treaty in late October. Before the year was out, they had set up posts and *Résidences* throughout Cambodia and had inaugurated the Phnom Penh municipal council.[139] They would have done well to remember that a tiger is silent when it is about to spring.

Notes

[1] Charles Meyer, (1971) *Derrière le Sourire Khmer*, Plon, Paris, p.72.

[2] Frank Vincent Jnr., (1873*)*, *The Land of the White Elephant. Sights and Scenes in South-Eastern Asia. A personal narrative of travel and adventure in Farther India embracing the countries of Burma, Cambodia, and Cochin-China (1871-2)*, Sampson, Low, Marston, Low, and Searle, London, p.285.

[3] Milton Osborne, (1994), *Sihanouk. Prince of Light, Prince of Darkness*, University of Hawaii Press, Honolulu, p.15.

[4] Milton Osborne, (1969), *The French Presence in Cochinchina and Cambodia. Rule and Response (1859-1905)*, Cornell University Press, Ithaca, New York, p.204.

[5] Jean Moura, (1883), *Le Royaume du Cambodge*, Vol. I, Librairie de la Société Asiatique de l'École des Langues Orientales Vivantes, Paris, p.226.

[6] Huy Kanthoul, *Mémoires*, unpublished French-language typescript, p.18. Chandler Papers, Monash University.

[7] AOM FM, Carton 1, A00 (9) French Consul at Bangkok to M. Rémusat, Min, Foreign Affairs, Paris, 16 September 1872.

[8] AOM Indochine AF 13 Dossier A30 (22). Cambodge 1874-1875.

[9] Paul Branda, (1892), *Ça et La. Cochinchine et Cambodge. L'Âme Khmère. Ang-Kor*, Librairie Fischbacher, Paris, p.5.

[10] For a discussion of the Buddhist doctrine of merit, see Moura, op.cit., p.158.

[11] AOM Indochine AF 13 Dossier A30 (22) Cambodge 1874-1875. J. Moura, Note on the modifications necessary to the Treaty of 1863.

[12] Osborne (*Rule and Response*) op.cit. p.175.

[13] Anonymous, (1893), "Le Cambodge en 1893", *Revue Indo-Chinoise Illustrée*, Hanoi, September, p.158.

[14] Max Weber's typology of traditional, charismatic and legal-rational authority is useful here. For a discussion of this, see Max Weber, (trans. A.M. Henderson and Talcott Parsons), (1947), *Theory of Social and Economic Organization*, Free Press, New York.

[15] Moura, op.cit., Vol. II, p.126.

[16] Justin J. Corfield, (1990), *The Royal Family of Cambodia*, Khmer Language and Cultural Centre, Melbourne, p.12.

[17] Osborne, op.cit., pp.179-180.

[18] Louis de Carné, (1872), *Travels in Indo-China and the Chinese Empire*, Chapman and Hill, London, p.32.

[19] The British traveler J. Thomson records that Norodom received him "with great courtesy" and lodged him in a house in the royal compound. [J. Thomson, (1875), *The Straits of Malacca, Indo-China and China or Ten Years' Travels, Adventures and Residence Abroad*, Sampson, Low, Marston, Low and Searle, London, p.156.]

[20] Osborne, op.cit. p.191.

[21] De Carné, op.cit. One wonders if the pun was intentional, given his appetite for cognac, Marsala, whisky and champagne.

[22] Edgar Boulangier, (1887), *Un Hiver au Cambodge*, Alfred Mame, Tours, p.72.

[23] Ibid. p.128.

[24] De Carné, op.cit. p.31.

[25] Vincent, op.cit. p.277.

[26] De Carné, op.cit.

[27] Ibid. p.47.

[28] Vincent, op.cit. p.285.

[29] De Carné, op.cit.

[30] Vincent, op.cit, p.273. I have not found any other reference to this intriguing character. The higher figure of *Tagals* is given in A. Bouinais and A. Paulus, (1884), *Le Royaume du Cambodge*, Berger-Lévrault, Paris, p.15.

[31] Ibid p.276.

[32] De Carné, op.cit.

[33] AOM RSC 258, Affaires politiques indigènes, 1867-1890. Letter from Governor of Cochinchina to *Résident Général* at Phnom Penh, 26 May 1886.

[34] Osborne, op.cit. p.190.

[35] Prince Areno Yukanthor drew attention to Norodom's contribution in a long letter to the President of the French Republic in 1938. See AOM FM INDO. NF Carton 47, Dossier 568.

[36] Vincent, op.cit. pp.279-283.

[37] Adolphe Belot, (1889), *500 femmes pour un homme*, (Sixteenth edition), E. Dentu, Paris, p.61.

[38] Vincent, op.cit. p.285.

[39] De Carné op.cit. p.32.

[40] Branda, op.cit. p.58.

[41] B. Marrot, (1894), *Exposition de Lyon 1894. Section Cambodgienne. Notes et souvenirs sur le Cambodge*, Forézienne P. Rousten, Roanne, p.38.

[42] Bouinais and Paulus, op.cit. p.42.

[43] Vincent, op.cit. p.287.

[44] In the late 1880s, the price of opium varied from 455 to 540 piastres per picul in the Hong Kong markets. (*Le Courrier d'Haiphong*, 12 June 1887, Hanoi.) One picul was the equivalent of 60 kilograms. One piastre was worth roughly 5 francs.

[45] Branda, op.cit. p.5.

[46] J. MacGregor, (1896), *Through the Buffer State. A record of recent travels through Borneo, Siam and Cambodia*, F.V. White, London, p.205.

[47] AOM Indochine AF 13 Dossier A30 (22). Governor of Cochinchina to the Minister of the Navy, 25 August 1874. Branda (op.cit. p.58) says the establishment was at Kompong Chhnang.

[48] J. Thomson, op.cit. pp. 156-157.

[49] From the practice of passing money in a handshake.

[50] Francis Garnier, (trans. Walter E.J. Tips), (1996), *Travels in Cambodia and Part of Laos. The Mekong Exploration Commission report (1866-1868)*, Vol. I, White Lotus, Bangkok, pp.50-51.

[51] AOM RSC 258. Affaires politiques indigènes, 1867-1890. Letter from M. Hardie, Hongkong and Shanghai Banking Corporation, Saigon, 5 April 1873.

[52] AOM RSC 258, Affaires politiques indigenes, 1867-1890. Letter to *Résident*, 14 October 1882.

[53] Belot, op.cit., p.137. Sometimes rendered as *bacouin*. Belot, who visited Phnom Penh in the late 1880s, records that the *Résident Maire*, M. Orsini, told him that it was difficult to see Norodom because "He is tired. He plays a lot of *Ba-Quan* these days..."

[54] AOM RSC 258, Affaires politiques indigènes, 1867-1890. Letter from Ohier, Governor of Cochinchina, to the Commandant at Phnom Penh, 5 September 1869.

[55] De Carné, op.cit.

[56] AOM RSC 258. Affaires politiques indigènes, 1867-1890. Letter from Governor of Cochinchina to the *Résident* at Phnom Penh, 10 March, 1882. Contains clipping of article by "Trois Étoiles" from the *Siam Weekly*, Bangkok, undated. Given that French officials knew Norodom had kidnapped girls, allegations of such behavior on the part of his mandarins should not surprise us.

[57] Anonymous, (1894), "Cambodge", *Le Mékong*, Hanoi, 29 June.

[58] AOM Indochine AF Carton 14, Dossier A 30 (28) Esclavage au Cambodge, 1877-1880. Aymonier, *Résident* at Phnom Penh to the Governor of Cochinchina, 18 March 1880.

[59] Belot, op.cit. pp. 61-63.

[60] Ibid.

[61] Branda, op.cit. p.287.

[62] M. Le Faucheur in Georges Taboulet, (1955), *La Geste Française en Indochine. Histoire par les textes de la France en Indochine des origines à 1914*, Librairie d'Amérique et d'Orient, Paris, Tome II, p.659.

[63] Boulangier, op.cit. p.93.

[64] Belot, op.cit. pp.61-63.

[65] *Siam Free Press*, (1895), J.J. Lillie, Bangkok, 22 July.

[66] William Augustus Collins, "An investigation into the division of the Chams into two regions", Unpublished MA thesis, University of California, Berkeley, 1966, pp.49-51.

[67] Belot, op.cit. pp.72-73.

[68] Bouinais and Paulus, op.cit. p.36.

[69] Belot, op.cit. pp.75-76.

[70] See Christine Sparks, (1980), *The Elephant Man*, Futura Publications, London, for a fictionalized account of Merrick's life.

[71] Branda, op.cit. p.289.

[72] AOM Indochine AF 13, Dossier A30 (22) Cambodge 1874-1875. Rapport confidentiel sur le Cambodge, 24 August 1874, by Aymonier.

[73] AOM Indochine AF Carton 15, Dossier A30 (44) Au sujet des femmes du roi du Cambodge (1880).

[74] AOM Indochine AF Carton 14 Dossier A30 (28) Esclavage au Cambodge. Aymonier, *Résident* at Phnom Penh, to the Governor of Cochinchina, 18 March 1880. The article is "Une Colonie Esclavage", *La Lanterne. Journal Politique*, (1880), 14 January, Paris.

[75] AOM Indochine AF Carton 18, Dossier A30 (68) Meurtre d'une jeune fille. Complicité du fils du 2ème roi, 1884. One presumes that Duong Chakr's lover was his half-sister because such relationships were common among the members of the royal family.

[76] Belot, op.cit. pp.92-95.

[77] Ibid. pp.77-79. Identical twins were regarded as unnatural monsters.

[78] AOM Indochine, AF Carton 17 Dossier A30 (66) Cambodge. Correspondance, rapports du Gouverneur Thomson, 1883-1884. Letter to the Colonial Minister, 27 July 1883.

[79] AOM Indochine AF 13 Dossier A30 (22) Cambodge 1874-1875. Letter from Governor Krantz to the Minister of Colonies, Paris, 3 June 1874.

[80] Ibid, letters from Krantz to the Minister, 30 June 1874 and 14 July 1874.

[81] Ibid, Letter from Krantz to the Minister, 3 June 1874.

[82] Alain Forest, (1980), *Le Cambodge et la Colonisation Française. Histoire d'une colonisation sans heurts (1897-1920)*, Éditions L'Harmattan, Paris, p.10. Si Votha, it will be recalled, was a half-brother of both Norodom and Sisowath.

[83] Moura, op.cit., Vol. II, pp.174-175, 181.

[84] Unsigned article, (1893), *Siam Free Press*, J.J. Lillie, Bangkok, 17 October. Given Norodom's flight from rebels in 1861, this claim rings true.

[85] Édouard Testoin, (1886), *Le Cambodge, Passé, Présent, Avenir*, Ernest Mazereau, Tours, p.83 and Moura, op.cit. Vol. I, p.253.

[86] AOM Indochine AF 13 Dossier A30 (22) Cambodge 1874-1875, op.cit. Letter from Krantz to the Minister, 3 June 1874.

[87] Ibid. Letter from Krantz to the Minister, 25 August 1874. *Corvée* is a system of compulsory labor on public projects, often with tools and beasts of burden thrown in by the laborers. The distinction between public works and the private projects of the rulers was often blurred.

[88] Ibid. Most of the taxes maintained the royal family.

[89] Ibid, Letter from the Minister to Krantz, 30 July 1874.

[90] Ibid.

[91] Testoin, op.cit. p.84.

[92] For an account of the code, see Moura, op.cit. pp. 268-297.

[93] Letter from the Minister to Krantz, 30 July 1874, op.cit.

[94] Moura was also the writer of a history of Cambodia, frequently cited in the present work. Diligent and intelligent, he is a good representative of the early French officials in the kingdom. Moura was born at Moissac on 3 April 1827 and educated at the École des Arts et Métiers in Aix-en-Provence. (See Taboulet, op.cit. p.661.)

[95] AOM Indochine AF Carton A30, Dossier 26. Cambodge, Rapports, correspondences de l'Amiral Duperré et du Bessant, 1875-1877. Duperré to the Minister, 22 October 1875.

[96] Aymonier, Rapport confidential sur le Cambodge, 24 August 1874, op.cit.

[97] In fact, the courts of Annam and Bangkok had for many years claimed the right to nominate Cambodia's kings and the Council merely rubber-stamped their candidates.

[98] Duperré to the Minister, 22 October 1875, op.cit.

[99] AOM Indochine AF Carton A30, Dossier 26. ibid. Letter from J. Moura to Admiral Duperré, 13 May 1875. Also text of the secret convention between Sisowath and Victor Auguste Baron Duperré.

[100] AOM HCC 33 Frontières 1873-1949. Correspondence regarding delineation of the frontier between Cambodia and Tay Ninh province. Letters from Governor of Cochinchina to the French Representative (Moura) at Phnom Penh, 6 and 11 February and 12 July 1873.

[101] AOM Indochine AF Carton 14 Dossier A30 (28) Esclavage au Cambodge, 1877-1880. *Résident* at Phnom Penh to the Governor at Saigon, 18 March 1880. (The decree abolished all categories of slaves except debt slaves and gave hereditary slaves the right to buy their freedom. Also, in theory, it abolished the trade in *Montagnard* slaves.) The abortive 1872 reforms are discussed in Moura, op.cit. Vol. II, pp.178-180.

[102] AOM Indochine AF Carton 14, Dossier A30 (34) Governor at Saigon to the Minister, 7 August 1878.

[103] AOM Indochine AF Carton 14 Dossier A30 (28) Esclavage au Cambodge, 1877-1880. *Résident* at Phnom Penh to the Governor at Saigon, 18 March 1880.

[104] AOM Indochine AF Carton 15 Dossier A30 (52) Situation au Cambodge. Rapports de le Myre de Vilers, 1880-1882. De Vilers to the Minister, 19 November 1881.

[105] Ibid. Letter from Norodom to the President of the French Republic, 1881.

[106] AOM Indochine AF Carton 17 Dossier A30 (66) Cambodge. Correspondance, rapports du Gouverneur Thomson, 1883-1884. Letter from the Minister to Thomson, 16 March 1883.

[107] Ibid. Letter from Thomson to the Minister, 30 July 1883.

[108] Testoin, op.cit. p.88.

[109] AOM Fonds Ministeriels. Indochine Ancien Série, Carton 2, Dossier AA00 (25) Rapport par M. Blancsubé, 1886.

[110] AOM RSC 258. Affaires politiques indigènes, 1867-1890. Governor at Saigon to the *Résident* at Phnom Penh, 10 May 1882.

[111] J.A. Hobson, (1965), *Imperialism: A Study*, Ann Arbor Paperbacks, University of Michigan, p.71.

[112] Ibid. p.19.

[113] Ibid. pp.19-21.

[114] Cambodge. Correspondance, Rapports du Gouverneur Thomson, 1883-1884. op.cit. Letters exchanged between Thomson and the Minister, 23 September, 9 October, 11 October, 21 December and 30 December 1883. The convention was signed on 19 September 1883.

[115] AOM Fonds Ministeriels, Indochine, Ancien Série, Carton 2, AA00 (25). Report by M. Blancsubé, 1886, op.cit.

[116] That is, "the more things change, the more they remain the same", which does not have the same ring in English.

[117] AOM Indochine AF Carton 17 Dossier A30 (66). Cambodge. Correspondance, rapports du Gouverneur Thomson, 1883-1884. Letter from Thomson to the Minister, 20 March 1884. Col de Monteiro was a member of a leading family of Portuguese descent.

[118] Ibid. Letter from Norodom to Thomson, 20 March 1884.

[119] Ibid. Thomson to the Minister of Colonies, 30 May 1884.

[120] Cited in Bouinais and Paulus, op.cit. p.21.

[121] AOM Indochine AF Carton 18 A30 (67). Cambodge. Convention de 17 juin 1884. Texte, annexes et correspondences et ratification du 8 Juin au 31 Décembre 1884. Thomson to the Minister of Colonies, 18 June 1884.

[122] *Organisation du Cambodge*, op.cit. pp.8, 20-21. The first city administration, under *Résident Maire* Ernest Morin, included six French, three Cambodians, one Vietnamese, two Chinese, one Indian and one "Malay", i.e. Cham. See Denis Nardin, (1964), "Phnom-Penh: naissance et croissance d'une administration urbain". Mémoire en vue du diplôme d'études superièures de droit public. Faculté de Droit et des Sciences Économiques de Phnom Penh, pp. 7, 19, 188.

[123] Cambodge. Convention de 17 Juin 1884. op.cit. Letter from Norodom to Thomson, 7 June 1884.

[124] John P. Armstrong, (1964), *Sihanouk Speaks,* Walker, New York, p.37.

[125] Cambodge. Convention de 17 Juin, op.cit. Norodom to Thomson, 11 June 1884.

[126] Ibid. Norodom to Thomson's Chef du Cabinet, Klobuwkowski, 12 June 1884, and Klobuwkowski to Norodom, 12 June 1884.

[127] Ibid. Thomson to Norodom, 13 June 1884.

[128] Ibid. Thomson to Minister, 17 June 1884.

[129] Ibid. Lt. Colonel Miramond to Thomson, 20 June 1884. Rapport sur les dispositions militaires prises pendant le séjour des troupes à Phnom-Penh.

[130] David P. Chandler, (1993), *A History of Cambodia*, Second Edition, Allen and Unwin, St. Leonards, NSW, p.257n.

[131] Miramond, op.cit.

[132] *Télégraphe*, 24 June 1884. Paris. Quoted in Cambodge. Convention de 17 Juin 1884. op.cit.

[133] Branda, op.cit., p.8.

[134] Letter from Areno Yukanthor to the President of the Republic, op.cit.

[135] Cambodge. Convention de 17 Juin 1884. op.cit. Thomson to the Colonial Minister, 2 August 1884.

[136] Ibid. Thomson to the Minister, 17 June 1884.

[137] Ibid. Thomson to the Minister, 1 December 1884.

[138] AOM FM, Indochine, Ancien Série, Carton 2, AA00 (25) Note on the establishment of a protectorate in Cambodia. Report by Blancsubé, 1886. See also Cambodge. Convention de 17 Juin 1884. op.cit. Letter from Thomson to the Minister, 10 January 1885. Blancsubé disapproved of the plan on the pragmatic grounds that it would backfire on the French.

[139] Ibid. Thomson to the Minister, 3 November 1884.

Chapter 5

The Great Rebellion

Khla krap kom tha khla sampeah—If the tiger lies down quietly before you, don't say it respects you.

—Khmer proverb.[1]

On 9 January 1885, armed rebels stormed a remote French military post at Sambor, upstream of Kratié on the Mekong River. The surprise attack was almost certainly organized by Si Votha, Norodom's half-brother, although the French claimed that "Chinese bandits" were also involved.[2] Thus began a general insurrection that was to drown the country in blood and fight the French to a standstill, albeit with melancholy consequences for the Khmers themselves. The effects of the war were disastrous. When it was over, large swathes of the countryside were ruined, famine stalked the land, and the population was in decline. For the French, it was a costly lesson in the futility of waging war against guerrillas operating on their own terrain, with natural refuge provided by forest, marsh and mountain, and with the support (tacit or otherwise) of the general population. Not even 4000 heavily armed French troops, equipped with artillery, gunboats and quick-firing guns, could quell the rebellion. What began as an intra-dynastic struggle, coordinated by mandarins with different material interests to those of the peasantry, ended as a quasi-national-liberation war supported by most Cambodians. However, it is doubtful that the Khmers had a developed national consciousness at the time.[3] Milton Osborne's characterization of the rebellion as essentially traditionalist in inspiration is accurate.[4] As is explained below, it only ended when Norodom threw the prestige of his royal office behind moves for peace.

The French were quite unprepared for the insurrection, which spread from Sambor in the north to the length and breadth of the kingdom. Although, as David Chandler has argued, the rebellion was led by a number of independent chieftains,[5] and there were perhaps four principle "foci" of revolt,[6] the simultaneous unfolding of events suggests that the leaders had decided to make common cause via communication channels that were invisible to the French. This suggests a degree of organizational cohesion and logistical sophistication. We should not underestimate the scope and importance of the uprising, although the French tried to do so. Perhaps wanting to put the best spin on it for his superiors at Paris, Governor Thomson claimed that the revolt was not as serious as that of Pou Kombo, or the uprising of the mid-1870s.[7] This was understandable, given that he had so singularly failed to foresee the insurrection and had basked in the glow of the "success" of the 1884 Treaty. He was probably also anxious to scotch the alarming rumors circulating in the foreign press. The *New York Times*, for instance, claimed that the rebels had overrun several posts and massacred the garrisons.[8] His superiors were alarmed, however. They removed Thomson from his post at Saigon shortly after the outbreak of the insurrection and replaced him with the more cautious Filippini.

Si Votha, a formidable opponent

The French faced a formidable opponent in Si Votha. When the uprising began, the Prince was already a veteran guerrilla chieftain. He had spent much of his adult life in the remote northeast, where he maintained a court in the jungle, and even levied customs duties on trade.[9] Like subsequent rebels—most notably the *Khmers Rouges* in the 1960s[10]—he had formed close ties with the local hill tribes, who acted as his eyes and ears for the approach of enemies. Si Votha was 43 years old at the outbreak of the insurrection, five years younger than his half-brother Norodom, whom he feared and detested. Although cynics claimed that he had originally taken up arms against his older brother because of a squabble over a woman,[11] this demeans a redoubtable and persistent man. The squabble might well have happened, but it alone cannot explain why Si Votha was willing to sacrifice the luxuries of Phnom Penh for the rigors of life in the jungle. His life was hard and his privations must have contributed to his early death. He was committed to his cause and driven by a visceral hatred of the French interlopers as much as by his desire for the crown. A more objective French account recognized that Si Votha had enormous prestige among the Khmers and acknowledged him as a foe worthy of respect and a person of "intelligence and energy".[12] The contrast between this dedicated, even driven man and the King is striking. Yet, we should be wary of casting him as a modern nationalist. His was a traditionalist revolt. If he had won his long battle to oust his brother and drive out the French, he would have been a king in the same general mold as Norodom, certainly more dynamic, and less sybaritic perhaps, but equally despotic.[13]

Although peace had never completely returned to Cambodia after the death of Pou Kombo, the sporadic rebellions that flared in the provinces from time to time had been contained. Banditry, too, had waxed and waned with the seasons and the cycle of poor and abundant harvests, but it did not often directly affect the French; generally, the peasants were the victims and they inhabited a world remote from that of their "protectors", who could afford to regard it as routine. The Great Rebellion was different. It caught the French off guard and was some time before they recognized, or admitted, how serious it was. As we have seen, they had moved quickly to implement reforms after the President of the Republic ratified the Treaty in late October 1884. Any fear they might have felt in the immediate aftermath of the treaty forced on Norodom had abated in the apparent calm that lay over the countryside. They were also preoccupied with the bloody pacification of Annam and Tonkin at the time. Yet, as Governor Thomson's replacement, M. Filippini, put it, the "quiet" period was actually one during which the revolt was incubating.[14] While French attention was elsewhere, the mandarins and members of the royal family were assiduously preparing the ground for revolt, taking their version of the issues to the people in the remotest hamlets of the land. Their message was simple. They might have said, "the French want to take over our country and force their alien customs on us. Their unequal new treaty gives them the right to do whatever they see fit. None of our ancient customs is safe. To arms!" The mandarins might have been ruthless oppressors, concerned above all with maintaining their rights to exploit the peasantry, but they were Khmers and did share some joint interests, and a common culture, religion and language, with the ordinary people. The French, in contrast, were foreigners. They were Christians. They had insulted the King. They had not bothered to consult the Khmers about the reforms they wished to introduce. The French assumed the reforms would be popular with the Khmer people because they appeared so self-evidently rational and necessary. The French were making an error common to those who seek to impose reform "from above"; that is they were indifferent or deaf to the opinions of those "below". Thomson behaved as a severe Victorian paterfamilias determined to administer a dose of castor oil to a resentful child; significantly, the colonialists often wrote of their *protégés* as children. The French were largely ignorant of what went on in the peasant villages. Even in the best of times, much of what went on in the country was invisible to the French. Now, they were positively blind, the victims of their own sense of European superiority. Charles Thomson might have considered the Khmers as a passive mass, a "savage race" used to rulers who would "mete and dole unequal laws", but he made a colossal blunder when he assumed that they would obey him as they obeyed their traditional rulers. A letter written by a French officer in November 1886, almost two years after the revolt broke out, conveys the isolation of the French. He described how:

> Almost every Cambodian is an enemy of the French, and would be a rebel if he had a gun, or if his interests did not bid him to be quiet. A French officer's life is not safe. You cannot go four kilometres beyond the town without arms and great precautions...I have been out to hunt three times since I have been at Penompein, [*sic*] and yet I have heard a ball whistling close to my ear.[15]

His words could have been written 60 or 70 years later in the Mekong delta, the Red River Valley, or even 80 years later in Afghanistan, by similar bewildered and lonely soldiers speaking French, English or Russian in strange lands.[16] It was the eternal lament of the colonial infantryman caught in a war that made little sense to him, and which he could not win by the textbook tactics of Saint-Cyr or West Point. For the foreign mercenaries who fought alongside the old French *marsouins*, the war must have been even more bewildering, for they could not fall back on patriotism as justification for their presence. The French commanders responded to the situation with brutal contempt, terrorizing the "inscrutable" natives, as official reports were later to admit.

The military post at Sambor was home to 40 such mercenaries, Vietnamese *tirailleurs* officered by a handful of French. The post was stormed, doubtless under cover of darkness, by a larger force of

Cambodian partisans of Prince Si Votha, armed with rifles. The irregulars fled, apparently with heavy losses, but not before they had burned down some houses and the telegraph post and killed the French commander and quartermaster, and four *tirailleurs* besides.[17] According to reports in the international press, the rebels actually overran government positions and murdered their garrisons.[18] Two days after the initial attack, some hundreds of miles away at Pursat, rebels, employing elephants stormed another French post, forcing a clearly nervous Thomson to put 200 soldiers on standby on gunboats in Cochinchina. The authorities also arrested a Sino-Khmer *métis* in Phnom Penh for circulating a letter from Si Votha announcing the start of the insurrection.[19] The letter was dated 1 January, that is *before* the attack on Sambor, and indicates that the uprising was not spontaneous. Two hundred soldiers under the command of the energetic Lieutenant-Colonel Miramond traveled up the Mekong to reinforce the post at Sambor and were said to have pursued an 800-strong band of rebels.[20] The assurance with which Governor Thomson reported the conclusion of that skirmish is illustrative of the military mindset which regarded a guerrilla withdrawal as defeat, and not as part of an "unorthodox" irregular strategy of short, sharp attack and withdrawal: the war of the flea and the elephant. Over the next few days, reports flowed in from the provinces, further revealing the national scope of the rebellion as the newly appointed French *Résidents* at country centers reported on the incessant activities of the rebels. Kampot was "in turmoil", reported the *Résident* there.[21] Rebels were also active in Takeo[22] and Kompong Thom. As the revolt spread, French reinforcements were sent up the Mekong. Extra troops arrived aboard the *Alouette* shortly before a force of up to 500 rebels stormed the city of Phnom Penh in May 1885, and drove the irregulars off after a fierce battle.[23] There were reports, too, of the evacuation of European residents from the city.[24] From Pursat, Lieutenant Lafargue reported rebel attacks on five consecutive days.[25] Kompong Thom province, to the north of Phnom Penh and east of the Tonlé Sap Lake, was a hotbed of the rebellion and early on passed into rebel hands. The French *Résident* bemoaned the fact that although Si Votha's emissaries were active, he was unable to seize them because of the complicity of the general population. Murders of pro-French officials and armed attacks grew ever more ferocious and frequent.[26] The rebels themselves sometimes operated from strong fortresses hidden in the jungles. Captain de Jarnowski, a French commander in Takeo, reported destroying one such fort, a sophisticated structure with two *enceintes*, outworks and palisades. He said that the rebel bands around Banteay-Méas, east of Kampot, were "warlike, well-armed and audacious." Some of them contained almost one thousand armed men and were under the overall command of the *Okhna* Heng.[27]

In fact, there were tens of thousands of armed insurgents, enjoying the support of the overwhelming mass of the population. Si Votha probably commanded the largest of the rebel forces, but elsewhere they were sizeable, as in the eastern provinces of Svay Rieng and Prey Veng where some 9000 insurgents operated close to the border with Cochinchina.[28] There is also evidence to suggest that the struggle drew in elements of the Chinese and Vietnamese minorities. This was true in Takeo, where followers of the "chief Annamite", Doc Bo Thuan, joined the insurrection.[29] At Sambor, Chinese joined the first battle of the insurrection.[30] In the Pursat region, bands of Chinese rebels roamed under the command of one Puo-Luc-Ké.[31] Such inter-ethnic solidarity must have alarmed the French, who later pursued a policy of divide and rule with considerable success for their cause, with melancholy effects on Khmer-Vietnamese relations that continue to this day. The French did not start ethnic hatred in Cambodia, but they certainly profited from it and intermittently encouraged it, just as the British did with Hindu-Muslim rivalry in India. As we shall see in subsequent chapters, it put a definite stamp on Khmer nationalism of all stripes, from the *Nagaravatta* group to the *Khmers Rouges*.[32]

Royal complicity in the revolt

Even as early as the attack on the post at Sambor, the French suspected Norodom and other members his family of complicity in the revolt.[33] The evidence, however, was not conclusive. Mandarins in Phnom Penh assured the French that Norodom was not in league with his half-brother, but information received in late March indicated that rebel leaders claimed they were acting on Norodom's orders.[34] The same message came from Kampot province, where rebels claimed that the King had ordered them to drive out the French and cut off their heads.[35] The French must have directly raised their suspicions with the King, because he sent a long letter to Governor Thomson protesting his loyalty to France.[36] In the absence of conclusive proof, Thomson had to conclude that the stories were not true, but he ordered strict surveillance of the royal family as the rumors of their duplicity kept filtering in from the countryside. The French arrested a number of high mandarins for treason[37] and over the next couple of years, a number of Norodom's sons and nephews, including Phanavong and Duong Chakr, the King's favorite, were strongly suspected of treason and some even rode with the rebel columns. Only with difficulty were the French able to restrain themselves from arraigning a number of princes in court for their actions.[38] They suspected the Queen Mother, an arch-traditionalist who lived largely in seclusion at Udong, of sympathy for the anti-French cause.[39] Sisowath subsequently claimed that another of Norodom's sons, Prince Yukanthor, was involved in the plot. This seems likely, despite Sisowath's bias against the Norodom wing of the royal family and his personal hatred of Yukanthor.[40] Other Khmer officials were ambivalent. Governor Filippini wrote that even the rare Khmer provincial governors who had remained loyal to the crown had good relations with the rebels.[41] Even Sisowath, who was firmly on France's side, and who later played a vigorous part in military operations against the rebels, allowed Si Votha to escape into the jungles.

An intractable colonial war

By the time the revolt was over, the French had committed 4000 troops[42] to an "un-winnable" colonial war. They built blockhouses and military posts in many places across the country,[43] a method they were to employ 60 or so years later against Vietnamese revolutionaries with equally indifferent results. By adopting the method of static fortresses, they were tacitly admitting that they were under permanent siege and that rebels had the upper hand. In mid-1886, Governor Filippini lamented that few parts of Cambodia were pacified. In fact, the only completely pacified provinces were Banam and Kratié. Everywhere else, the country was subject to the "incessant raids" of Si Votha's men.[44] Kompong Thom province was almost completely in rebel hands; the French *Résident* of that province was confined to a fort on the banks of the Stung Seng even after hostilities had ceased in most other areas of the country. At night, the rebels would come up close and throw burning brands into the compound.[45] Even close to Phnom Penh, rebels imposed taxes on the population. The French stopped all public works schemes and suspended the recruitment of the Cambodian militia because the force had proven itself unreliable.[46]

The war also cost the French dear. Although it seems that the rebels sustained large losses of life, French casualties also mounted. If "General Winter" had driven Napoleon I from the gates of Moscow in 1812, the Cambodian rebels had an equally effective ally in "General Dysentery".[47] Many French soldiers succumbed to malaria, cholera and other water-born diseases that are endemic in Cambodia, struck down as effectively as if by enemy bullets, their vital organs cooked by mosquito-born protozoa. A letter dated 14 July 1885 reported that 112 French soldiers had been hospitalized through sickness;[48] a melancholy note for Bastille Day. It was a small fraction of the total. Given the conditions of warfare in malarial swamp and jungle, it would be difficult to overestimate the rate of death and sickness among European troops. Even in peacetime conditions, the rates of death and sickness for Europeans in Indochina were strikingly high: the economic historian Charles Robequain claims that before 1884, European death rates sometimes exceeded 100 per 1000, and rates of sickness 500 per 1000.[49] Osborne cites a French physician, Dr. Maurel, who found the scale of disease among the troops to have been "extraordinary".[50] The rebels' bacteriological and amoebic allies must have thoroughly demoralized the hapless marines and *tirailleurs*. The rebels were often invisible, yet, like the ubiquitous bacteria, their effects were felt everywhere. The war in Cambodia was nothing like "glorious" Solferino or Marengo, of infantry "squares" and magnificent cavalry charges. It was a hell of sudden squalls of rifle balls, of scrabbling for food in the plots of resentful peasants, of thick mud, leeches and snakes, of razor-toothed saurians on jungle riverbanks, of festering tropical ulcers and the cramps of dysentery, of hookworm, of dust and spiders, of frustrating pursuits into unmapped and paludal jungles.[51] Reports tell of how the French soldiers suffered from the enervating heat and the fatigue of the endless marches and counter-marches.[52] The French commanders would have understood the lament of a Chinese general who had invaded Indochina 1800 years earlier: "Rain fell, vapors rose, there were pestilential emanations, and the heat was unbearable; I even saw a sparrowhawk fall into the water and drown".[53]

The French were hampered by the long wet season, which inundated much of the countryside and left seas of stinking mud behind at the start of the dry season. The French officer quoted earlier complained that, "At present no expedition can be attempted, for it is the rainy season. The whole countryside is under water...Our only amusement is the chase, and it is dangerous in the first place because it is necessary to walk in water nearly up to the waist, and because the pirates are constantly on the watch for Europeans." He was "anxiously waiting for the end of the rainy season to re-commence the use of gunpowder." The wet season did not deter the rebels however, for he reported that just a week before, they had surrounded a French military base just four kilometers from the town.[54]

It is small wonder that the French troops resorted to atrocities against their opponents and civilians, sometimes on the orders of their commanders. When J-L de Lanessan became Governor General of French Indochina in 1891, he was horrified by the "acts of incredible brutality" committed against Vietnamese irregulars and civilians. He wrote of the "the burning of villages, the mass shootings, the bayonet slaughters, and the executions of notables"[55] and he was shocked by the practice of decapitating notables "who either did not know or refused to say which way had been taken by a group of rebels that had gone through their village".[56] It would be naïve to think that similar brutality did not mark the conduct of military operations against the Cambodian rebels. As the *Revue Indochinoise Illustrée* of September 1893 admitted, the methods adopted by the French in the Cambodia rising were "brutal, vexatious, [and] tyrannical". It could not be otherwise, the writer claimed, because the entire population had risen against the French.[57] Milton Osborne records that the troopers perpetrated rapes, executions, thefts and assassinations on the civilian population.[58] While he praised the valor of the French troops, Governor Filippini was critical of the way they conducted themselves, using violence against the population and "exasperating" those who had not taken part in the revolts.[59] Many of the French officers were headstrong men who despised civilian authority; a common enough type in French colonial wars right up to the end of the Algerian war of independence in the 1950s and early 1960s.[60] The gung-ho behavior of the French commander in Cambodia, Lieutenant Colonel Badens, verged on insubordination. He was clearly contemptuous of a negotiated settlement and resisted orders to confine French troops to barracks after the civilian authorities came to an understanding with Norodom to end the rebellion.[61] Owing to his "bad attitude" toward the civil authorities, Lieutenant Colonel Chevallier was sent to replace him as commander in October 1886.[62] One suspects that Badens stopped just short of mutiny. One result of French heavy-handedness was the mass emigration of civilians to Siamese-controlled Battambang. Over 40,000 peasants left from the Pursat area, seriously depopulating the region they had fled.[63]

A negotiated solution involving the King

The French Government at Paris was deeply unhappy about the rebellion, and as it wore on, and the costs in men and money mounted, the realization dawned that a negotiated settlement of some kind would be needed to halt the war. The French came to understand that short of mass butchery, the only way to pacify the country was to enlist the active support of the King. That would involve a tactical retreat from the demands made in the 1884 Treaty. The French were eager to develop their commercial and national interests in Cambodia, and this was clearly impossible without an understanding with Norodom. In mid-1886, they talked with the King, promising that the French would not try to impose their authority over the indigenous administration. In particular, they promised to restrict the number of *Résidents* to four, in Kompong Svay, Kampot, Pursat and Kratié.[64]

Accordingly, the King signed a proclamation calling on his subjects to end the rebellion and promised a general amnesty to those who laid down their arms. He sent out princes and mandarins to the four corners of the kingdom with copies of the proclamation. The French gave them considerable assistance, including military escorts, and allowed "every liberty of action". The idea, explained the *Résident-Général* at Phnom Penh, M. Piquet, was "to show the population the intimate union between the Protectorate and its *protégé*", the King.[65] For his part, Norodom promised the French that he would pacify the entire country by January 1887.

Filippini was not entirely sure of Norodom's good faith. He told the Minister of Colonies that if Norodom were dissimulating, he would not hesitate to depose him and put Sisowath on the throne. However, he rejected the idea of incorporating Cambodia into Cochinchina as contrary to the treaty signed with Siam in 1867.[66] Filippini realized that, for the moment, France could "not dream of imposing the entire provisions of the Treaty of 17 June 1884". They would have to go about it little by little, trying to restrain expenditure where they could.[67]

Norodom keeps his promise

As it turned out, Norodom was not dissimulating. Filippini could report that within six weeks of the release of the proclamation "the situation in the country seems to have improved perceptibly." Although Si Votha did not lay down his arms, a number of other rebel princes surrendered, including Bunnavong and Pong Savat, nephews of the King.[68] Norodom himself toured many of the country districts, often in the company of the French *Résident-Général*, staying away from the capital for weeks at a time. This secured the surrender of Si Votha's principal lieutenant, his adopted son, in October,[69] although the French believed that Prince Duong Chakr, the King's favorite son, was still secretly aiding the rebels.[70] Nevertheless, when the King returned from his perambulations in late December, he had secured the surrender of all the principal mandarins and princes except for Si

Votha himself.[71] The French began to pull troops out, particularly "Annamite" *tirailleurs*, but left a force of 600 marines behind until a Cambodian militia could be trained to replace them.[72] Sisowath led a large force into the forests to capture Si Votha. He failed to do so, however, and the French suspected that he let him go deliberately.[73] Si Votha still had immense prestige among the ordinary people and Sisowath must have known that to capture his half-brother was to invite lasting opprobrium.

The rebel prince was largely a spent force, however, and although local rebellions still flared from time to time, Si Votha was never again a serious threat. In May 1890, he sent a bonze to speak on his behalf with the French *Résident* of Kompong Thom, Paul Collard. Collard sent an emissary, M. Schneider, to negotiate with the rebel leader at Koepea in Santuk province in the far northeastern jungles. Si Votha told Schneider that he wished to surrender and live peacefully. Schneider reported, "The Prince is in the most extreme misery". He was, however, fearful of Norodom and asked if the French would let him live in France.[74] Nothing became of the talks, however, and he died shortly afterwards, aged 50, on New Year's Eve, 1891, in the jungles that had been his home for 30 years.

A devastated and depopulated country

Si Votha's fate was melancholy, but the countryside was devastated. Enormous areas of farmland were destroyed or abandoned. One French writer claimed that after a few months: "the major part of the cultivated areas had been abandoned; the peasants had left with their wives, their children, their buffaloes, to seek refuge either in some corner of the immense forests that covered almost the entirety of the country, or in Siamese territory…" They fled either to escape from the rebel chieftains, who sought to enroll them in their forces, or to avoid the French military columns, which "requisitioned their buffaloes, their carts and their boats; and which didn't always distinguish between peaceful people and the insurgents."[75] As a result, famine broke out in many areas, forcing the French to import rice from Battambang and Cochinchina.[76] Some of the destruction appears to have been a deliberate scorched earth policy. In Kampot, for example, armed bands uprooted many thousands of pepper plants.[77] Although Milton Osborne regards Adhémard Léclère's estimate of 10,000 deaths as a reasonable estimate,[78] this seems far too low. It is of course difficult to arrive at an accurate number, but the ferocity with which both sides fought, and the fact of famine leads one to suspect that the figure was much higher.

Statistical evidence reinforces the suspicion. Figures in the pro-colonial *Quinzaine Coloniale*, which was scarcely likely to inflate the death toll to show the French authorities in a bad light, indicate that Cambodia's population declined from around 945,000 in 1879 to 750,000 in 1888.[79] This is a decrease of 185,000, or *almost 20 per cent of the total population*, in a nine-year period. This figure would include deaths from all causes, such as "natural causes", starvation, disease and violence, and the population decrease caused by the departure of tens of thousands of refugees to Siamese-controlled Battambang. The "normal" birth rate did not compensate for what was a huge net loss of population. If the *Quinzaine Coloniale's* figures are accurate, they point to a *demographic catastrophe*. Even if the estimate is, say, 50 per cent too high, which is unlikely, the loss of even ten per cent of a country's population is still an incalculable disaster. One imagines that a sizeable proportion of those who fled to Siamese territory would have returned to their homes after 1886. This would lift the proportion of those who died during the uprising compared with those who emigrated. Even by 1903, the population had reached little more than 1,200,000, only around 260,000 more than in 1879[80] or 450,000 more than Moura's 1888 estimate. The population grew at a slightly faster rate in the next ten years from 1903 to 1913,[81] even if we subtract the population of the former Siamese provinces of Battambang and Siem Reap, ceded to Cambodia in 1907.[82] After World War I, the population grew at a healthier rate. The census of 29-30 November 1921 counted 2,395,714 inhabitants in Cambodia, an increase of about 700,000 in the eight years from 1913.[83]

The Franco-Cambodian war of 1885-86 is a great, little-known disaster of the colonial era. The scale of the devastation must have been a key reason why Norodom decided to cooperate with France and put an end to the uprising. Autocrat though he was, the suffering of his people must have deeply affected him. It is puzzling that this grievously insulted man so doggedly pursued the surrender of the rebels on France's behalf. While it is true that Filippini had promised to back away from the demands in the 1884 Treaty, the treaty remained in force and Norodom was not so naïve to believe that French would not move by more skillful means to implement them. His health was also failing and he would have known that the French favored his half-brother, the *Obbareach*, the Francophile Sisowath, to succeed him on the throne. Such a succession would give the French what they wanted. If the war was a victory for Norodom, it was both pyrrhic and partial. Two years after the end of the revolt, the Governor General of French Indochina noted that; "Since the events of 1884 and our behavior in

1886, we have done nothing more…than to wait patiently for the death of Norodom."[84]

Notes

[1] Cited in Karen Fisher-Nguyen (1994), "Khmer Proverbs: Images and Rules", in May M. Ebihara, Carol A. Mortland and Judy Legerwood (eds.) (1994), *Cambodian Culture since 1975. Homeland and Exile*, Cornell University Press, Ithaca, New York, p.98.

[2] AOM Indochine AF Carton 18, A30 (67). Cambodge. Convention de 17 Juin 1884. Thomson to the Minister of the Navy, 10 January 1885. The claim of "Chinese intrigue" was also reported in the international press, e.g. *The New York Times*, 13 January 1885.

[3] The ideology of the nation-state is a relatively new, European concept, dating from the breakdown of the old feudal order; a social construct rather than a "natural" organism. For a discussion of these ideas, see, for instance, Benedict Anderson, (1991), *Imagined Communities: Reflections on the Origins and Spread of Nationalism*, Verso, London and Eric Hobsbawm, (1987), *The Age of Empire, 1875-1914*, Abacus, London, (particularly Ch.6).

[4] Milton E. Osborne, (1969), *The French Presence in Cochinchina and Cambodia. Rule and Response (1859-1905)*, Cornell University Press, Ithaca, New York, p.223.

[5] David P. Chandler, (1993), *A History of Cambodia*, Second Edition, Allen and Unwin, St. Leonards, NSW, p.145.

[6] Osborne, op.cit. pp.214-216.

[7] AOM Indochine AF Carton 18, A30 (67). Cambodge. Convention de 17 Juin 1884. Thomson to the Minister, 14 July 1885.

[8] Anonymous, (1885), "A revolt in Cambodia. Several French posts captured by the insurgents. The garrisons massacred – the King's brother heads the uprising – Chinese intrigues suspected", *The New York Times* (13 January). By the end of the month, however, this paper quoted official dispatches claiming "the virtual suppression of the revolt". (*New York Times*, 29 January 1885.)

[9] Osborne, op.cit. p.221.

[10] Saloth Sar—or Pol Pot as he was later known—fled from Sihanouk's persecution to the safety of the same region in the early 1960s. He gathered round him the nucleus of what Sihanouk called, in the context disparagingly, the *Khmers Rouges*—literally "Red Khmers". See Ben Kiernan, (1985), *How Pol Pot Came to Power. A History of Communism in Kampuchea, 1930-1975*, Verso, London and David P. Chandler, (1993), *Brother Number One. A Political Biography of Pol Pot*, Allen and Unwin, St Leonards, NSW.

[11] Paul Branda, (1892), *Ça et La. Cochinchine et Cambodge. L'Âme Khmère. Ang-Kor*, Librairie Fischbacher, Paris, p.290. Branda says that the woman had belonged to Ang Duong's harem. He reduces the whole case to one of *"cherchez la femme"*. (Emphasis in the original.)

[12] AOM Indochine AF Carton 19, A30 Dossier 80. Letter from the Governor of Cochinchina to the Minister of Colonies, 14 January 1887.

[13] Early privations for a cause are no guarantee of subsequent self-denial. The opulent lifestyles of many former *Khmers Rouges* leaders are evidence of this, as is the later life of the Chinese guerrilla chief Mao Zedong, or that of Josip Broz Tito in the former Yugoslavia.

[14] AOM Indochine AF Carton 19 A30 Dossier 80. Situation au Cambodge, 1886-87. Report by Governor Filippini to the Minister of the Navy, 30 July 1886.

[15] *The Times*, (1886), London, (19 November).

[16] The bewilderment and pain of the European foot soldier in a later war in Indochina was brilliantly recorded by Philip Caputo in his *A Rumor of War*, Arrow Books, London, 1977. Despite differences of language and time, Caputo's account could speak for the French marines in Cambodia 80 years previously.

[17] AOM Indochine AF Carton 18, A30 (67). Cambodge. Convention de 17 Juin 1884. Thomson to the Minister of the Navy, 10 January 1885.

[18] See, for example, unsigned articles in *The New York Times*, 13 and 14 January, 1885.

[19] AOM Indochine AF Carton 18, A30 (67). Thomson to the Minister, 12 January 1885. A *métis* (feminine *métisse*) is a person of mixed blood. (French.)

[20] Ibid. Thomson to Minister, 13 and 23 January 1885.

[21] AOM RSC 356. Rapports politiques et économiques, Kampot, 1885-1905. (August 1885.)

[22] Ibid. Rapports périodiques, politiques et économiques, Résidence de Takeo, 1 November 1885.

[23] AOM Indochine AF Carton 18, A30 (67). Thomson to the Minister, 6 May 1885.

[24] Unsigned article, (1885), "Revolt against French rule", *The New York Times*, June 4.

[25] AOM Indochine AF Carton 18 A30 (67) op.cit. Governor to Minister 14 July 1885.

[26] AOM RSC 373. Rapports politiques et économiques mensuels. Résidence de Kompong Thom, 1885-1905. March 1886.

[27] ANC RSC E.03 File No 11211. Box No 981. Correspondance du Sous-Résident de Takeo, Jan – July 1886.

[28] Osborne op.cit. p.213.

[29] See, for instance, ANC RSC E.03, File 11211 Box 981, op.cit.

[30] AOM Indochine AF Carton 18, A30 (67). Cambodge. Convention de 17 Juin 1884. Thomson to the Minister of the Navy, 10 January 1885.

[31] Unsigned article, (1885), *The Times*, London, September 30, based on an article in *Le Saigonnais* of 23 July 1885.

[32] The policy was never codified or consistent, however, and clashed with other imperatives.

[33] A dispatch published in *The New York Times* claimed that "letters from Saigon... state that the Cambodian insurrectionists... have, with the King's secret support, attacked Panomping (*sic*) or Nam Wang (*sic*)..." (4 June 1885).

[34] AOM Indochine AF Carton 18, A30 (67) op.cit. Thomson to the Minister, 29 March 1885.

[35] Ibid. Thomson to the Minister, 24 April 1885.

[36] Ibid. Thomson to the Minister, 5 April 1885.

[37] Ibid. Governor to the Minister, 6 May 1885.

[38] AOM AF Carton 19 A30 Dossier 80. Situation au Cambodge, 1886-87. Governor to the Minister, 23 December 1886 and 14 January 1887.

[39] Ibid. Letter from M. Piquet, *Résident-Général* at Phnom Penh, to Governor Filippini, 17 September 1886.

[40] ANC RSC F451 File 24217 Conseil des Ministres 37e séance du 8 novembre 1900. Letter from Sisowath to the *Résident Supérieur*, 17 novembre 1900. When Sisowath wrote the letter, Yukanthor was his direct rival for the succession to the throne. Furthermore, the Norodom prince had made a number of insulting allegations against him in the course of what became known as the "Yukanthor Affair". (See Chapter 6.) Hence, Sisowath had a stake in painting Yukanthor in the blackest colors.

[41] AOM Indo AF Carton 19 A30 Dossier 80. Situation au Cambodge, 1886-87, op.cit. Report by Governor Filippini to the Minister, 30 July 1886.

[42] Ibid.

[43] Ibid.

[44] Ibid.

[45] AOM RSC 373 Rapports politiques et économiques mensuels, Résidence de Kompong Thom, 1885-1905. Report of 25 July 1887.

[46] Ibid.

[47] Disease has always played a major part in wars. Napoleon's war in Russia was no exception. See, for instance, Hans Zinsser (2000), *Rats, Lice and History*, Penguin Books, Harmondsworth.

[48] AOM Indochine AF Carton 18, A30 (67) op.cit. Governor to the Minister, 14 July 1885.

[49] Charles Robequain (trans. Isabel A. Ward), (1944), *The Economic Development of French Indo-China*, Oxford University Press, London, pp.26-27.

[50] Osborne, op.cit. p.217.

[51] Again, perhaps Philip Caputo provides the most graphic 20th century description of an infantryman's sufferings in the Indochinese jungle. (Caputo, op.cit.) Some of the jungle horrors make the flesh creep. Francis Garnier came across an island in the Mekong near the Khône Falls, which was carpeted with leeches, some of them up to three inches long, and all desperate for human blood. (Anonymous, (2000), *The French in Indochina. With a Narrative of Garnier's Explorations in Cochinchina, Annam and Tonkin*, White Lotus, Bangkok, p.10. This book was originally published in Edinburgh in 1884.)

[52] AOM Fonds Ministeriels Indochine Ancien Série, A00 (7) Lettres sur la situation du Cambodge, 1866-67 (*sic*) Letter dated 25 January 1886, to Aymonier. (This was out of place and may have been properly located since I drew the matter to the attention of the archivists.)

98 *France on the Mekong*

[53] The Chinese general was writing in AD 42, although about the jungles of Vietnam. Cited in Keith W. Taylor, (1993), "Diseases and Disease Ecology in the Modern Period in Southeast Asia", in Kenneth F. Kiple (ed.) *The Cambridge World History of Human Disease,* Cambridge University Press, New York, p.440.

[54] Letter reprinted in *The Times,* op.cit.

[55] J-L de Lanessan, (1895), *La Colonisation Française en Indochine,* Paris, p.30. Cited in Joseph Buttinger, (1958), *The Smaller Dragon. A Political History of Vietnam,* Atlantic Books, London, p.384.

[56] Ibid. (Buttinger), p.422.

[57] Anonymous, (1893), "Le Cambodge en 1893", *Revue Indo-Chinoise Illustrée,* Hanoi, September, p.157. The article clearly reflects de Lanessan's views.

[58] Osborne, op.cit. pp.215-217.

[59] AOM Indochine AF Carton 19 A30 Dossier 80, op.cit. Report by Governor Filippini to the Minister, 30 July 1886.

[60] The type was to reach its apogee—or its nadir—in General Raoul Salan, who had been commander-in-chief of the French forces in Indochina and then Algeria. Salan deserted and went underground as leader of the terrorist O.A.S. See, for instance, Paul Henissart, (1973), *Wolves in the City. The Death of French Algeria,* Paladin, St. Albans, Hertfordshire.

[61] AOM Indochine Ancien Fonds Carton 19. A30 Dossier 80. Situation au Cambodge, 1886-87. Report by Governor Filippini to the Minister of Colonies, 30 July 1886.

[62] Ibid. Governor Filippini to the Minister of Colonies, 9 October 1886.

[63] Osborne, op.cit. p.215.

[64] Governor Filippini to the Minister of Colonies, 9 October 1886, op.cit.

[65] AOM Indochine AF Carton 19 A30 (80). Résident-Général aux Résidents, sous-Résidents et commandants de postes. 27 July 1886.

[66] Ibid. Report by Governor Filippini to the Minister, 30 July 1886.

[67] Ibid.

[68] Ibid. Governor to the Minister, 19 September 1886.

[69] Ibid. Governor to the Minister, 21 October 1886.

[70] Ibid. Governor to Minister. 23 December 1886.

[71] Ibid. Telegram from Governor to the Minister, 28 December 1886.

[72] Ibid. Governor to Minister, 14 January 1887.

[73] Ibid. Governor to Minister 8 April 1887.

[74] ANC RSC. E.03 File 4724. Box 498. Dossier No. 8588. Rapport du Résident de Kg. Thom sur les négociations entamées avec le Prince rebelle SIWOTHA en vue d'obtenir sa soumission. 2 May 1890. (Collard later wrote a book on Cambodia: Paul Collard, (1925), *Cambodge et Cambodgiens,* Société d'Editions Géographiques, Paris.)

[75] Unsigned, (1893), "Le Cambodge en 1893", *Revue Indo-Chinoise Illustrée,* Hanoi, September, p.158.

[76] A Galy, (1899), "La production, la consommation et l'exportation des riz en Cochinchine et au Cambodge" *Bulletin Économique de l'Indochine,* Nr. 17 ancien série, Hanoi, pp.597-612.

[77] Adhémard Léclère, (1899), "Les plantations de poiviers au Cambodge en 1899", *Bulletin Économique de l'Indochine,* Nr 18, ancien série, pp.659-671.

[78] Osborne, op.cit. p.228.

[79] Unsigned, (1903), "La population du Cambodge", *Quinzaine Coloniale,* Paris, deuxième semestre, 25 October. The article cites Jean Moura as the source for the 1879 figure. The 1888 figure is supported in an article by Henri Lamothe, a later *Résident Supérieur.* Lamothe says the population of Cambodia was 750,000 in 1887. See Henri Lamothe, (1903), "La situation du Cambodge', *Revue Indochinoise,* 14 September.

[80] ANC RSC D35, File 2970 Box 333, Rapports Mensuels. (1904 - 1905). Rapport Conseil Supérieure de l'Indochine. Session Ordinaire de 1904, No 9. This report cites the results of the census of late May 1903. A claim of 1,500,000 people in 1902 in the *Bulletin Économique de l'Indochine* is clearly wrong. ("Notice sur le Cambodge", *BEI,* No 2 nouvelle série, p.115.)

[81] AOM RSC 429 Rapport Politique 4ème trimestre, 1913, 25 February 1914.

[82] AOM RSC 254, Report on "Monthon Burapha", 1907.

[83] AOM FO3 64265, Rapport Politique 4ème trimestre, 1921. Ten years later, in 1931, there were slightly more than 2,800,000 people in Cambodia. (Unsigned article, (1936), *L'Echo du Cambodge,* Phnom Penh, 15 September.) By 1936, this had grown to a little more than 3 million. (ANC RSC D35 File 5838 Box 577. Documents et Voeux addressées à la commission d'enquête parlementaire (1937-1938).

[84] AOM Indochine AF Carton 19 A30 (84) Rapports politiques du Gouverneur Général Richaud. Richaud to the Minister of Colonies, 3 November 1888.

Chapter 6

"The King is a mere puppet" [1]

[Norodom] mortgaged his own absolute, threadbare and precarious power in exchange for staying on as a symbolic, well-paid chief of state.
—Historian David Chandler.[2]

Little had changed in Cambodia in the two decades since Admiral de Lagrandière prevailed on Norodom to accept the Protectorate. The French controlled the country's foreign relations and defense, but little else, for the country was stubbornly wedded to the old ways. French frustration had boiled over in 1884, but Governor Thomson's "crash-through" approach had only sparked off the Great Rebellion. The French were back almost where they had started and the country was in ruins. Two parallel administrations, the "native" and that of the Protectorate, still existed side by side, the latter funded primarily from the French public purse. On the face of it, Norodom and the forces of traditionalism had won a great victory over the modernizing French. In reality, the situation was more complex; after the flood tide of 1885, Norodom's power, like his own health and vitality, ebbed with every passing year.

In the aftermath of the great rising, many of the old abuses continued unchecked. Slavery was still largely intact. With the exception of some customs dues, finances were still largely in the hands of the dilapidated and inefficient Khmer administration. The uprising had caused tremendous economic and social dislocation and had proved a tremendous drain on French finances.

The rebellion also provided the anti-colonial opposition in France with effective ammunition against the Government, which partly explains why the Colonial Ministry was so anxious to come to a negotiated solution rather than hold out for military victory. There was never any unity on the colonial question within the French political establishment. One wing, led by the conservative republican politician Jules Ferry (and earlier by Prosper Chasseloup-Laubat under the Second Empire), was in favor of an aggressive colonial policy. Colonies would bring glory and economic betterment for France.[3] Another current of opinion was anti-colonialist in a pragmatic sense because its adherents felt that concentration on "France Overseas" detracted attention from the loss of metropolitan France's eastern provinces. The fierce irredentist Georges Clemenceau, for example, wished to keep the eyes of the public firmly fixed on the "lost provinces" of Alsace and Lorraine beyond what Jules Ferry called the "thin blue line of the Vosges". Clemenceau feared that the public might be consoled if France sought compensation overseas.[4] Another current of opinion, encompassing some socialists and some left-republicans, opposed the growth of the empire on the grounds of anti-imperialist principle. Clemenceau attacked colonial conquest as "domination and exploitation of man by his fellow-man" and a betrayal of republican tradition.[5] In the end, the pro-colonial party was to prove supreme and Clemenceau's own Radical party split on the issue, as for instance, in parliamentary debates over the acquisition of Tonkin in the mid-1880s.[6] Even the socialist movement had no common position; the right wing was considerably more pragmatic in its outlook than the left. France's overseas empire, like those of other European powers, grew at a phenomenal rate in the last decades of the 19th century. By 1914, "France Overseas" was around 20 times the size of metropolitan France.[7] Yet, at the time of the Great Rebellion, the pro-colonial wing of French politics had not completely consolidated its power, and it still had to be careful not to give its domestic opponents grounds for attack. Some of the embarrassing facts of the Great Rebellion and its "diplomatic" prologue had trickled out to the public in France, which had already learned of bloody repression of nationalist rebels in Vietnam. The Colonial Ministry saw that a new tack was necessary. The first Governors-General of Indochina, MM. Richaud and J-L de Lanessan, favored a general policy of co-option and persuasion, rather than coercion. Although the picaresque eccentricities of Huyn de Vernéville (*Résident Supérieur* for much of the 1890s) complicated the picture, the arrival of Richaud and de Lanessan did entrench the new spirit already shown in the approach of such officials as Filippini and Piquet.

"Two steps forward, one step back"

Looking back, the Great Rebellion was a case of "two steps forward, one step back" for France, but that extra step forward for France started a process that was to destroy Norodom's power. The new breed of French administrators were often more subtle and flexible, yet just as determined to achieve French hegemony as Charles Thomson had been. Little by the little, the French tightened the screws, although with a minimum of European personnel. A small number of French officials would supervise a reformed "native" bureaucracy.[8] Cambodia was integrated into the Union Indochinoise in 1887, a step that marked the beginning of a more centralized approach.[9] De Lanessan's methods, in contrast with the more *laisser faire* approach of his predecessors, also favored a large-scale public works program.[10] As we shall see, this was to transform the face of at least Phnom Penh in hitherto medieval Cambodia. Governor General Richaud met with Norodom in 1888[11] to discuss reforms, the most important including the introduction of a land tax. The French had also begun preliminary work for the cadastral survey of the country,[12] a sign that they were determined to create private property in land.

By 1892, the French had taken control of virtually all taxes, following a conference between Governor General de Lanessan and Norodom in 1889. The construction of a "superb" new treasury building in Phnom Penh symbolized the new order. Shortly afterwards, the French were able to balance the budget and slash back on the civil list, which they regarded as largely the "sinecures of useless mandarins."[13] In 1897, the *Résident Supérieur* reported that direct and indirect taxes were flowing in without problem, and that there was general economic improvement throughout the kingdom.[14] Tax receipts for 1896 totaled over two million piastres, up by some 320,000 on 1895. When the Queen Mother died, a decree integrated her apanage into that of the Crown.[15] The increase in the number of provincial *Résidents* from four in 1888 to ten in 1894 is another indication of the shift in power.[16]

Although the same old matters were again on the agenda, it was to prove increasingly difficult for Norodom to resist their implementation. One reason for this was his increasingly poor health. Although the French were sometimes wont to exaggerate the gravity of this, there can be no doubt that ill health made him increasingly unable to deal with his skilful and persistent opponents. In late 1888, he was stricken by a painful infection of the marrow of the spinal cord, which tired him easily and caused the French to scrap plans to take him to the Universal Exposition in Paris the following year.[17] The formerly portly monarch was ageing, shriveling, and losing weight. Branda, who met him during this period, described him as "little, thin, clearly wasted by excesses of all kinds..." but also observed that he had maintained "a certain air of dignity natural to all people born into high rank".[18] There is little evidence to suggest, as the French did occasionally, that he was losing his mental faculties, but he simply did not have the energy to block their plans as effectively as he had once done. Perhaps, wandering in his palace grounds, he pondered the wisdom of having interceded to halt the rising. He would have known, however, that although it had cost the French dear, it had been a disaster for his own people. Another rising was out of the question. Smaller revolts flared from time to time throughout the late 1880s, but the royal forces contained them relatively easily and executed the leaders, among them the Pondicherry Indian Mandgeni. There were reports that Mandgeni had fired his rifle at the *Obbareach*, Prince Sisowath, who was in charge of the government's troops, but his rising was a shadow of the earlier conflagration.[19] The French were sufficiently confident by mid-1889 to reduce their garrison at Phnom Penh to 25-30 soldiers under the command of a warrant officer.[20] The death of Si Votha, on the last day of 1891, removed France's most implacable foe. It is difficult to imagine any other person who would have had the drive, the ability, or the prestige, to replace him as rebel *supremo*. Mandgeni and the others in any case lacked royal blood, an essential attribute for would-be rebel chieftains in this intensely traditional society. The death of the Queen Mother in 1895 would also have sapped the traditionalist defenses. Although she spent much of her time in isolation at her estate at Udong, the Queen Mother was a formidable woman, still vigorous in her sixties, with "sparkling black eyes", "very thick hair...cut short in the fashion of the country,"[21] and "with not a gray hair in her head". She was "intensely Cambodian in her sentiments" and disliked the Siamese.[22] The French also suspected her of supporting the rebels during the uprising. Her death would have deprived Norodom of an astute adviser.

For their part, as the *Résident* at Phnom Penh agreed, the French went back to "waiting patiently for the death of Norodom".[23] In the interim, they accepted him as King *faute de mieux*, and relegated his rival, Sisowath, to the wings. The ferocity of the rising had impressed upon them just how resilient this traditional society was, and that Norodom, for all his faults, was the only person who could have persuaded the rebels to lay down their arms. Their aims had not altered, but they would implement them in a cautious and piecemeal fashion. This pragmatic policy worked. Moreover, the French displayed some skill in playing off the rival Khmer ruling elite factions against one another for their own ends. In August 1888, a curious letter from a group of disgruntled Cambodian mandarins arrived on the French President's desk at the Elysée Palace in Paris. The letter complained that, "All of us, the people and the mandarins, who love the French...are in great vexation..." because of corruption and favoritism and the writers laid the blame at the feet of both King Norodom and the French *Résident Général*, M. de Champeaux.[24] The royal palace and the bureaucracy were hotbeds of intrigue and it is difficult to know precisely which interests were involved here. Possibly the letter was engineered by the Sisowath faction as a way of undermining confidence in the King. Whatever the truth, it must have contributed to the French strategy of divide and rule, in which they sought to drive a wedge between the King and the top mandarins. The strategy was particularly successful after 1897, when relations between Norodom and ministers such as Col de Monteiro and Thiounn openly soured, to the advantage of the French.

If MM. Piquet, de Champeaux and Orsini had a relatively low key approach, M. Huyn de Vernéville, who arrived in May 1889 as the first *Résident Supérieur*,[25] was a man of a different stamp. De Vernéville was autocratic in style and somewhat eccentric in his personal life. He was the kind of man who would have agreed that "power is the ultimate aphrodisiac".[26] He shared the *Résidence* at Phnom Penh with his Cambodian mistress, and gossips claimed that she was able to use the relationship to her own pecuniary advantage. The writer Charles Meyer (a confidante of King Sihanouk in the 20th century) states that de Vernéville considered the country as his personal fief.[27] Some years later, during the Yukanthor Affair, intriguing allegations about the *Résident Supérieur* surfaced in the international press. *The New York Times*, for example, published the following spicy tale:

A.M. de Vernéville and a native woman, his friend – one Mi-Ruong [Neak Ruong, JT] – together have got the upper hand at Phnom-Penh...and they "play old Harry there". They have converted the [illegible] cemetery into a pasturage for fat cattle, and the Prince is made to pay a fine if any of his elephants or camels [*sic*] stray onto their property...An unhappy Governor, Suphea Khuon, having told the King that the French Resident had spoken disrespectfully of his Majesty, was sent to penal servitude, and other persons have been decapitated, in spite of the King's efforts to save them, for equally trivial reasons.[28]

This is no doubt an exaggerated account, especially the claims that de Vernéville had mandarins decapitated. Yet, much of the rest of it has the ring of truth, especially in the light of what *official* documents had to say about Mlle. Ruong's behavior. The French historian Alain Forest agrees that de Vernéville was authoritarian by temperament, that he treated Cambodia as his "private game reserve", and that he jealously protected his turf from real or imagined encroachments by his colleagues in Cochinchina.[29] If Governor General de Lanessan in faraway Hanoi was a relatively diplomatic and humane person, this irascible man cancelled out his influence on the ground in Cambodia. Yet, abrupt and imperious as he undoubtedly was, de Vernéville was also a master of intrigue. By the end of his term in May 1897, Norodom's writ did not run much further than the walls of his palace.

French fears over the succession to the throne

De Vernéville's greatest fear was that Norodom might frustrate France's plan of enthroning Sisowath by abdicating first and putting one of his own sons on the throne.[30] The palace seethed with intrigue. Norodom had at least 30 "legal" male offspring from which to choose and Milton Osborne considers that as late as 1888, he was unsure as to who he would like to succeed him.[31] His favorite was Prince Duong Chakr[32], 26-years-old in 1890, and generally regarded as intelligent and capable. In his adolescence, the prince had displayed a considerable capacity for mischief. According to one account, at the age of 13, he accompanied his father during military operations against rebels during the mid-1870s and earned the soubriquet "*cache-ta-canne*" ("hide-your-cane") from the French soldiers due to his habit of carrying a big stick. The account claims the "young prince amused himself by playing all kinds of tricks upon the men, and often pulled down their tents in the night for which sport he received many vigorous canings."[33] His later activities, however, did not amuse the French. They regarded him as an unacceptable successor to his father because of pro-Siamese sentiments and his likely participation in the great rising of the mid-1880s. Indeed, they claimed that his actions at that time amounted to high treason and warranted the death penalty. They also claimed evidence of his continuing links with old rebel chiefs after the rising, claiming that he received "daily visits of suspicious individuals" from Siam and Cambodia. While some of this might have been slightly paranoid, a French report does supply details of visits by the old rebel commanders Soum, Savat Soc, Sam Rat, Xin and Tam Ray Cuon in 1890.[34] Worse, from the French point of view, Duong Chakr was capable and intelligent. He was ambitious, and claimed to be Norodom's oldest son. The French disputed this claim, which would have bolstered his claim for the throne, and added the quasi-legal quibble that he was not the son of the first Queen.[35] On April 30, 1891, royal agents seized Duong Chakr and put him in irons. One week later, the prince wrote to the Minister of Colonies in Paris, complaining that, "For about a year, without cease, I have been plagued by M. de Vernéville, your *Résident Supérieur.*" Soon after his release, Duong Chakr fled to Bangkok. According to French reports, he traveled to the Cambodian border with the intention of fomenting revolt. Norodom disowned the lad, writing that, "I have renounced Prince Duong Chacr [*sic*] as my son and I cannot any more consider him as anything but a rebel..."[36] One is entitled to wonder how Norodom came to reject his favorite son. It does not seem to have been a simple matter of de Vernéville's bullying. Norodom continued to stand up to the Frenchman on other issues for a number of years afterwards. French reports claim that Duong Chakr fled because he had made two attempts on his father's life.[37] While it is possible that the French cooked up the claim to discredit the prince, the lack of evidence to the contrary, combined with Norodom's rejection of his favorite son, leads us to the gloomy conclusion that it might have been true.

The prince left Bangkok for France in 1893 and for a short while he was a well-known habitué of Paris café society. Described as "small, lively and intelligent", he affected western clothes and bicycled jauntily round the city.[38] Shortly afterwards, the French authorities deported him to Algiers,[39] where he astounded the locals by smashing crockery and glasses in a café because the management could not provide him with Bordeaux.[40] Although he found the Algerian climate congenial, he was shortly afterwards sent to Djelfa, a desolate railhead beyond the Atlas Mountains on the edge of the Sahara, where he died on 25 March 1897 at the age of 33 years.[41] The authorities did not record the cause of death, but we may surmise it was heartbreak, perhaps combined with the effects of high living. The prince vanished without trace from popular Cambodian consciousness and the French were free of a potentially dangerous man. As Milton Osborne tells us, "Today, in modern Cambodia, Duong Chaer's name is almost forgotten."[42]

1897: a turning point in the struggle for control

A real turning point in the struggle for control came in January 1897 when Norodom once again fell ill. Huyn de Vernéville moved swiftly to take advantage of the infirmity. He advised Governor General Paul Doumer that Norodom had stopped eating, that his health was "very bad" and hinted at increasing mental impairment. Perhaps he genuinely believed that Norodom was dying. In what his superiors later described as a *coup d'état*, de Vernéville readied the police to arrest all "dangerous personalities" and maintain order.[43] His apparently exaggerated reports led the Minister of Colonies initially to approve plans to ship troops up from Saigon in anticipation of disorders.[44] Further, the *Résident Supérieur* persuaded the members of the Council of Ministers to meet in Norodom's absence and to decide on policy without his approval.[45] It is a safe bet that de Vernéville did not have to press them too hard. They too must have believed Norodom was dying and, as career bureaucrats, would have wanted to curry favor with the French and their *protégé*, the *Obbareach*, Sisowath, who was lurking in the wings.[46] Regardless of their motivations, making decisions without the King's consent was an unprecedented departure from state protocol. In earlier times, this would have amounted to *lèse-majesté*. The desertion of the political elite was a big defeat for Norodom and traditionalism.

Although Norodom's health *was* poor, it seems that de Vernéville had exaggerated the seriousness of the illness to provide a pretext for strong action. Doumer traveled up to Phnom Penh during the following month and had a long interview with the King. Contrary to his expectations, he did not find him on his deathbed. Nor did his mental faculties seem impaired, in fact he found Norodom to be "completely lucid". Perhaps worried about provoking conflict, he urged caution in case the "delicate situation" led to "grave difficulties",[47] perhaps as had followed Thomson's gunboat diplomacy in 1884.[48] The situation demanded diplomatic skills and de Vernéville was too brusque for that. He was recalled to France shortly afterwards, on 14 May 1897, not without a whiff of scandal. Doumer reported that de Vernéville's co-habitation with his Khmer mistress, Neak Ruong, who was involved in crime and corruption, had diminished the authority of France's representatives "in the eyes of the natives". De Vernéville abandoned the woman, leaving her to face trial on charges of receiving stolen jewels, gold bars, diamonds, rubies and other precious stones, which she had stored at the *Résidence*. There were further allegations of bribery of judges, trafficking in favors, swindling, kidnapping and theft. Doumer suspected a number of French citizens of involvement in the criminal circle. Neak Ruong went to prison for five years.[49]

Regardless of official disapproval of his morals, alleged maladministration, and unsubtle approach, de Vernéville had made a vital breakthrough in the struggle for French control of the Khmer administration. Two months after the *Résident Supérieur* left for France, a beleaguered Norodom decreed the reorganization of the Council of Ministers as part of a general shake-up of the Khmer government and civil service. Shortly afterwards, the Council freed the royal and pagoda slaves.[50] The Council itself was a stripped-down version of its former self, and was under French control. As of 11 July 1897, it would consist of five members only, under the permanent presidency of the French *Résident Supérieur.*[51] Moreover, royal decrees henceforth required the latter official's counter signature before promulgation.[52] Osborne notes Prince Yukanthor's later claim that Norodom signed the decree because de Vernéville had threatened to dethrone him if he refused.[53] Some writers claim that de Vernéville had threatened variously to declare Norodom mad, to behead him, to dethrone him, and deport him to Poulo Condore if he did not do as he was told.[54] Yet, while de Vernéville might have been capable of making such threats, the decree was promulgated two months after de Vernéville's departure for France, probably as result of a less brutal intervention by Doumer. One suspects that Norodom buckled under relentless pressure. The French were insistent. His own mandarins sided more and more with them; in the final years of the century Norodom became embroiled in a number of ugly disputes as he tried to reassert his power over them.[55] His mother, a bulwark of the *ancien régime*, and a trusted confidante, had died in 1894. His health was poor and he tired easily. Morally, too, he must have been in decline. Duong Chakr, his one-time favorite son, had recently died in exile half a world away. Even if he believed the French claims of Duong Chakr's attempted parricide, the death of a child is always a grievous blow, particularly of one who had been so close. For this aging, sick old man, the creeping twilight of Khmer sovereignty was increasingly compounded with the sadness of his own memories and the knowledge of his own approaching end.

In the following years, Norodom sometimes attempted to reassert his authority over the Council. Norodom hated the wily and ubiquitous mandarin Thiounn, and Prime Minister Um, perhaps sensing in them a careerism that owed more to Weber's "legal-rational", European, authority than to traditional loyalties. If so, he was right. Thiounn was to prove a loyal servant of France until his death in 1941 and Um played a crucial role in consolidating French power before his death in 1902.[56] Norodom tried to block Thiounn's appointment as secretary of the Council of Ministers in December 1898. He also attempted to stop the elevation of Col de Monteiro to the post of Minister of Marine in this period.[57] His claim that this particularly well-educated mandarin lacked qualifications for the post was absurd and smacked of the pique of a querulous and impotent old man. As with Thiounn, Norodom's real, but unstated, objection would have been de Monteiro's loyalty to France and perceived treachery to himself. Although Norodom was forced to denounce yet another son, Prince Yukanthor, we know that he shared the latter's hostility to Thiounn and other powerful mandarins. A Scottish visitor claimed that by this stage, Norodom "reigns, but does not govern. He is a mere puppet..."[58]

The Yukanthor Affair

The "Yukanthor Affair" was to be the final indignity in Norodom's life. Coming as it did after he had already disowned one favorite son, one suspects that it broke him. Norodom wished Yukanthor to succeed him on the throne; he described him as his "well-beloved son" and heir in a letter written to the President of the French Republic in June 1900.[59] Yet, he could not be sure that the French would honor his wishes. The French had earlier removed Duong Chakr from the race and Norodom must have known about French support for the succession of his half-brother, Sisowath. He might even have suspected the secret agreement by which Sisowath agreed to do France's bidding in return for the crown, although it is unlikely that he ever saw a copy of it. We can also discount unsubstantiated French claims that Ang Duong had asked Norodom to ensure that Sisowath succeeded him on the throne.[60] All things aside, the two half-brothers were too close in age for such an eventuality to cross Ang Duong's mind. All the evidence shows that in 1900, Norodom expected his 40-year-old son, Prince Aruna Yukanthor, to succeed him.

The facts of the Yukanthor Affair have been related a number of times.[61] The French Government had invited Norodom to visit the Universal Exposition in Paris in 1900. He declined because of poor health, but nominated Yukanthor as his representative and gave him several letters, including one to the President of the Republic.[62] The *Affaire* erupted when someone leaked a copy of a letter brought to France by Yukanthor, addressed to M. Georges Leygues, the President of the French Council of Ministers, to the Parisian daily *Le Matin*. Yukanthor claimed that his father had given him the letter, but the

French denied the claim. The paper published the letter in full on 5 October 1900, with an angry (and probably unauthorized) reply by *Résident Supérieur* Gustave Ducos almost a week later. The Yukanthor letter was highly critical of the French administration in Cambodia.[63] It drew particular attention to Thomson's gunboat diplomacy of 1884, and de Vernéville's "coup d'état" in 1897, and called for the restoration of Norodom's sovereign powers. The letter also attacked the powerful mandarins, Um and Thiounn, accusing them of corruption and abuse of power.[64] It made similar claims against specific French functionaries, including M. Albert Lorin, the French *Résident* at Kompong Cham, *Résidents Supérieurs* de Vernéville and Ducos, and Albert Doumer, the Governor General of Indochina.[65] It also attacked members of the Khmer elite. The *Obbareach*, Prince Sisowath— Yukanthor's direct rival for the succession—claimed that the letter had called him an elephant thief and a "ridiculous personage", derided by all Cambodians.[66] It was impossible for the authorities to stop the spread of this embarrassing material. The Anglo-Saxon press reported that Yukanthor had accused the French officials in Cambodia of "bribery, embezzlement, and systematic insolence."[67] The claims outraged the colonial authorities, especially Governor General Paul Doumer, who demanded Yukanthor's repatriation to Cambodia for punishment. Norodom disclaimed authorship and disinherited his son, who left Paris for Brussels with his secretary, Jean Hess. Yukanthor always maintained that his father wrote the letter. The scandal continued, with French agents keeping the prince under surveillance before his return to France and subsequent embarkation on a ship to Indochina.[68] Police agents seized Yukanthor at Saigon and held him for a time on the prison island of Poulo Condore in the South China Sea.[69] After his release, he went into exile in Bangkok and devoted much of his remaining thirty-odd years to unsuccessful intrigues against the French and their *protégé*, Sisowath, whom they placed on the throne in 1904.

The controversy of the *Affaire* lies in the detail and the interpretation. According to the French authorities, Yukanthor was a troublemaker who had acted on his own account. They disputed his claim to the throne, claiming that for many centuries the crown had been passed down within the same family, but not in strict order of primogeniture. The Great Council of the Kingdom, they argued, had sole power in the choice of a successor.[70] Hence, they could argue that it was perfectly legitimate for the Council to choose the *Obbareach*, Sisowath, to succeed his half brother on the throne. The French were being disingenuous. As Milton Osborne points out,

Whatever ideal rules existed for the designation of a new king in traditional Cambodian practice, the one hundred years preceding the institution of the French protectorate...were so unsettled that it is impossible to speak of an established system having operated with any regularity. Kings, and a queen, were placed on the Cambodian throne according to the wishes of outside powers, Thailand and Viet-Nam, with little, if any, regard for the wishes of court officials who were to serve the new sovereign.[71]

Here we have the nub of the matter. As has been shown, the French had long been dissatisfied with Norodom. They feared that if one of his direct descendents were to succeed him, then they could expect only more of the same passive resistance to the reforms they considered necessary for the kingdom. They had already made a secret agreement with Sisowath, who had promised to cooperate fully with their administration. Significantly, the *Obbareach* put in a rare appearance at a meeting of the Council of Ministers held in early November 1900, which decided to block Yukanthor's succession to the throne. Prime Minister Um stressed that there was no law of royal primogeniture in Cambodia and that the succession was purely for the Council of Ministers to decide. Yukanthor, the Ministers agreed, was no more than a usurper.[72] Yukanthor might not have been as compromised in their eyes as Duong Chakr, who had participated in the 1885 Rising, but he had been a young man of 25 at that time and hence might well be "tainted" with rebellion—certainly, Sisowath accused him of complicity in the rising. Doumer claimed that Yukanthor's allegations were "lies" and "slanders". According to the official version, Norodom had voluntarily disinherited his son when presented with the evidence of his "perfidy" in *Le Matin*, claiming that Yukanthor had acted on his own initiative.[73]

Norodom "has no personal will"

It is difficult to credit the French story. What Yukanthor said was substantially true. We know that Norodom had been deeply angered, hurt and insulted by his treatment at the hands of Thomson, de Vernéville, and their successors. The French had invaded his palace in 1884 and quite probably threatened to dethrone him in 1897. After 1897, they had stripped away his powers, in both a *de jure* and *de facto* sense. He could no longer have any faith even in his own mandarins, who colluded with the French against him, and he spent most of his time closeted with his women in the palace.[74] Although the women devoted considerable energy to feuding with the mandarins, Doumer considered that Norodom now lacked the energy to participate in public affairs, and "had no personal will."[75]

Doumer's assessment says more than he perhaps realized. Norodom was a sick old man and although embittered, he lacked the will and energy to stand up against the French. Jean Hess wrote to the Minister of Colonies that Norodom had claimed the French were persecuting him and that he feared for his life. Hess added that, "The conduct of M. Luce, the threats of this *résident*, are capable of killing the old king."[76] Given French behavior in the past, we cannot dismiss Hess's claims out of hand. There can be little doubt Yukanthor passed on the substance of his father's complaints to the French President and that the French authorities intimidated Norodom into disowning him for doing so. *The minutes of the Council of Ministers plainly show that the Résident Supérieur drafted the text of Norodom's letter condemning his son's behavior.*[77] Signing the document meant a significant moral collapse for the old king. Yukanthor's son Areno claims that Norodom gave financial support to his family after the *Affaire*. Might this indicate that he was stricken with remorse for yielding his signature? Even with a clouded mind, he must have been aware that he had agreed to disinherit his most likely successor, and had therefore strengthened the French hand to appoint their crony, Sisowath, to the throne. For their part, the *Affaire* remained such a touchy subject for the French authorities that almost a quarter of a century later, the police seized documents at the home of a writer in France. He had been in touch with Prince Yukanthor in Bangkok and was considering writing a novel or film script on the *Affaire*.[78]

In the following years, Norodom's health declined even further, and with it, all will to oppose the French. An official report written in early 1903 records his "increasingly complete submission...to the decisions of the French authorities."[79] Ironically, he appears to have been popular with the Cambodian people at this time. At the end of 1902, he opened the new pagoda of Pra Khéo, with vast crowds in attendance. By 1903, however, his health worsened.[80] In January 1904, he made his last public appearance, on his 69th birthday. The following month, doctors diagnosed him as suffering from a tumor of the lower jaw and gave him only a few weeks to live. He made his will on 22 March, witnessed by Dr Philippe Hahn, his personal physician, who doubled as the *Résident Maire* of Phnom Penh.[81] At the same time, the Governor General thought it prudent to send a gunboat and an additional infantry company to Phnom Penh in case disturbances should break out because of what he termed the "intrigues" of Prince

Yukanthor.[82] As it happened, Phnom Penh was calm, although civil disturbances led by old rebels of 1885 did break out in Thbong Khmum province.[83] Norodom died on 24 April at five o'clock in the evening, in the *Salle du Palais*. His spirit had probably died some years earlier.

According to Cambodian custom a grand assembly of the Council of Ministers, plus a number of other high mandarins, met to consider his successor.[84] Although Sisowath was the councilors' unanimous choice, the French had made the decision to appoint him years beforehand and reconfirmed it during the Yukanthor Affair. The Council meeting was a mere formality. Henri Lamothe, the *Résident Supérieur,* chaired the meeting, later understating this significant fact as the "sole modification" to the traditional ceremony.[85] Not surprisingly, the French government ratified the decision soon afterwards.[86] As a journalist wrote in *La Quinzaine Coloniale,* "the new king will reign, but we will continue to govern."[87] The novelist Roland Meyer claims, no doubt accurately, that immediately after Norodom's death, the *Résident Supérieur,* accompanied by his loyal servant Thiounn, entered the palace, where they "opened the coffers of the royal treasury, and for several days appeared as the real masters of the place."[88] Paul Beau, the Governor General of Indochina, crowned Sisowath on 26 April 1904, significantly in the name of the government of the Republic of France.[89]

By dint of ruthless treatment of the now deceased king, France was now free to pursue its full "reform" agenda with a pliable figurehead. Norodom's funeral was held on 21 June. At 9 a.m., in "superb weather", before a huge crowd, Sisowath set fire to his half-brother's remains. Retainers placed the ashes in a golden urn and took them into the interior of the palace.[90] Sisowath had a superstitious dread of his half-brother,[91] but perhaps now, the crown upon his head and his "vaulting ambition" satisfied, he could sleep much easier. One wonders, however, if he ever felt any of the guilt suffered by Macbeth after the murder of Duncan, for although he had not slain Norodom, he surely was complicit with the French in harrying an unhappy old man in the evening of his life.[92]

Notes

[1] John MacGregor, (1896), *Through the Buffer State. A record of recent travels through Borneo, Siam, and Cambodia,* F.V. White, London, p.205.
[2] David Chandler, (1997), "From 'Cambodge' to Kampuchea; State and Revolution in Cambodia, 1863-1979", *Thesis Eleven,* No. 50, August, p.37.

[3] See, for instance Stephen Roberts, (1929), *The History of French Colonial Policy, 1870-1925*, Frank Cass, London, p.15. The Ferry wing wanted Cambodia to be a *colonie d'exploitation*.

[4] John Tully, (1996), *Cambodia Under the Tricolour. King Sisowath and the 'Mission Civilisatrice' 1904-1927*, Monash Asia Institute, Clayton, Victoria, p.21. Alsace and Lorraine were annexed by the newly united Germany in 1871 after their victory over Napoleon III in the Franco-Prussian War. They reverted to France in 1919, after Germany's defeat in World War I.

[5] William B. Cohen, (1972), "The Colonial Policy of the Popular Front", *French Historical Studies*, Vol.VII, No. 3, Spring, p.368. Cohen's article is a very useful discussion of socialist and left-republican attitudes to colonialism. See also Chapter 14 for a survey of the impact of the *Front Populaire* government of the 1930s on Cambodia.

[6] Ibid. p.369.

[7] Roberts, op.cit. p.7.

[8] The germ of this idea is contained in proposals by M. Blancsubé, a lawyer and member of the Colonial Council in Cochinchina, in 1886. AOM Carton 2, AA00 (25).

[9] Sorn Samnang, (1995), "L'Evolution de la Société Cambodgienne entre les deux guerres mondiales (1919-1939)" Thèse pour le doctorat d'histoire, Tome II, Université Paris VII, p.10.

[10] His efforts were not always appreciated by the French in the colonies. See, for example, the unsigned article "Les tripotages de M. de Lanessan", *Le Mékong*, Hanoi, 11 June 1894.

[11] AOM Indochine AF Carton 19 Dossier A30 (84) Rapports Politiques du Gouverneur Général Richaud, 1885. *Gougal* to the Minister of Colonies, 3 November 1888.

[12] AOM Indochine AF Carton A30 (89) *Gougal* to the Under Secretary of State for the Colonies, 4 August 1889.

[13] Unsigned, (1893), "Le Cambodge en 1893", *Revue Indo-Chinoise Illustrée*, September, Hanoi.

[14] ANC RSC D35. File 5884. Box 578. Rapports mensuels sur la situation financière et économique du Cambodge, 1897. Report of 24 June, 1897.

[15] ANC RSC D35 File 5865 Box 578. Rapport de présentation du profit de budget du Cambodge pour l'exercice 1896.

[16] Milton Osborne, (1969), *The French Presence in Cochinchina and Cambodia. Rule and Response (1859-1905)*, Cornell University Press, Ithaca, New York, p.235.

[17] Ibid. *Gougal* to the Minister of Colonies, 14 October 1888.

[18] Paul Branda, (1892), *Ça et La. Cochinchine et Cambodge. L'Âme Khmère. Ang-Kor*, Librairie Fischbacher, Paris, p.242.

[19] AOM Indochine AF Carton 20 Dossier A30 (87) Situation Politique au Cambodge, 1889. Reports by *Gougal* to the Minister of Colonies, 29 December 1888 and 16 January 1889.

[20] AOM Indochine AF Carton 20 A30 (89) Situation au Cambodge. *Gougal* to the Undersecretary of State for Colonies, 4 August 1889.

[21] Branda, op.cit. p.21.

[22] M. Bryois, (1893), "The Queen Mother of Cambodia", *Siam Free Press*, J.J.Lillie, Bangkok, 15 September.

[23] AOM Indochine AF Carton 19 Dossier A30 (84) Rapports Politiques du Gouverneur Général Richaud. *Gougal* to the Minister of Colonies, 3 November 1888.

[24] AOM Indochine AF Carton 2 Dossier A00 (29) Letter from mandarins and inhabitants of Phnom Penh asking the President of the French Republic for protection against the King and the *Résident*, 1 August 1888.

[25] Strictly speaking, the leading French officials at Phnom Penh were called *Répresentats du Protectorat* between April 1863 and 18 October 1895. From 18 October 1885 until May 1889, they were called *Résidents Généraux*. From that time until the end of World War II, they were known as *Résidents Supérieurs*. (See Sorn Samnang, op.cit. Tome III, pp.418-421.)

[26] The phrase is attributed to Henry Kissinger, another man whose destiny brought him into contact with Cambodia.

[27] Charles Meyer, (1971), *Derrière le Sourire Khmer*, Plon, Paris, p.98.

[28] Unsigned article, (1900), *The New York Times*, 30 September.

[29] Alain Forest, (1980), *Le Cambodge et la Colonisation française. Histoire d'une colonisation sans heurts*, Éditions L'Harmattan, Paris, p.15.

[30] Osborne, op.cit. pp.236-237.

[31] Ibid, p.234.

[32] The spelling of the name varies: Chakr, Chacr, Chaer.

[33] Unsigned article, (1893), *Siam Free Press*, Bangkok, 17 October.

[34] AOM RSC 258 Affaires politiques indigènes, 1867-1890. Letter to the *Résident Supérieur*, 3 October 1890.

[35] AOM Indochine AF Carton 20 Dossier A30 (96). Prince Duong Chacr. Fils du roi du Cambodge (Norodom 1er). Under Secretary of State of Colonies to M. Le Myre de Vilers, deputy for Cochinchina, 1891.

[36] AOM Indochine AF Carton 20 Dossier A30 (96). Letter to the *Résident Supérieur*, quoted in a report from *Gougal* to the Under Secretary of State for Colonies, 16 October 1892. See also AOM RSC 258 Affaires politiques indigènes, 1867-1890. Letter from The *Résident Supérieur* to *Gougal*, 19 August 1893.

[37] Ibid. (AOM AF Carton 20 Dossier A30 (96). Letter from the Undersecretary of State for Colonies to M. Le Myre de Vilers.

[38] Ibid. Extract from *Le Libre Parole*, 6 April 1897.

[39] Allegedly with an annual pension of 12,500 francs. (Unsigned article, (1893), "Prince Duong Chaer expatriated", *The New York Times*, 27 August.)

[40] Unsigned article, (1893), *Siam Free Press*, Bangkok, 17 October. The management sent out for a few bottles of the wine.

[41] AOM Indochine AF Carton 20 Dossier A30 (96) op.cit. Extract from the register of deaths for the year 1897, Commune of Djelfa, Algeria.

[42] Osborne, op.cit. p.234.

[43] AOM Indochine NF Dossier 585, Carton 48, Telegram from M. Fourès, Hanoi, to the Minister of Colonies, 3 January 1897.

[44] Ibid. Minister of Colonies to *Gougal*, 4 January 1897.

[45] Osborne, op.cit. p.237.

[46] Ibid. p.238.

[47] Minister of Colonies to *Gougal*, 4 January 1897, op.cit.

[48] Prince Areno Yukanthor claimed in a letter to the President of the French Republic in 1938 that there was a revolt when the conditions were imposed in 1899. See AOM FM NF Carton 47, Dossier 568. Areno wrote that, "In 1899, when Doumer's policy was put into practice, a revolt broke out and threatened to extend over the whole of Cambodia..."

[49] AOM Indochine NF Carton 48 Dossier 585. *Gougal* to Minister of Colonies, 8 July 1897 and telegram from *Résident Supérieur* to *Gougal*, 4 July 1897.

[50] ANC RSC F451 File 24190 Conseil des Ministres, 10e séance du 27 décembre 1897, libération des pols et komlâs corvéables des services de majesté le roi et l'obbarache [*sic*] et des pagodes.

[51] ANC RSC F451, Liste des ordres du jour des séances du Conseil des Ministres, 1897-1937. The five ministers were: the *Okhna Akha Moha Sena* (prime minister, minister of the interior and of religious affairs); the *Okhna Veang* (minister of the palace, finances and fine arts); the Okhna *Youmreach* (minister of justice); the *Ohkna Chakrey* (minister of war, public education and public works); and the *Ohkna Kralahom* (minister of marine, agriculture and commerce). See also Sorn Samnang, October 1995, "L'Evolution de la Société Cambodgienne entre les deux guerres mondiales (1919-1939)." Thèse pour le doctorat d'histoire. Tome I, Université Paris VII, p.35. The French also purged the judiciary of the most corrupt and incompetent officials. (ANC RSC F451 File 24184 Conseil des Ministres, 4e séance du 17 août 1897.)

[52] Osborne, op.cit. p.238.

[53] Ibid.

[54] Wilfred Burchett, (1957), *Mekong Upstream*, Red River Publishing House, Hanoi, p.84. Burchett might well have exaggerated for political effect. The allegations were repeated by Norodom Sihanouk. [John P. Armstrong, (1964), *Sihanouk Speaks,* Walker, New York, p.38].

[55] Osborne, op.cit. pp.240-242.

[56] ANC F451 File 24257, Conseil des Ministres, 77e séance du 31 mai 1902. Um was a career civil servant, born in 1822, who had entered the service of Ang Duong at the age of 16. When he died, he had held most positions on the Council of Ministers over a career spanning 66 years. He had rode with French columns against rebels in 1877 and during the Great Rebellion of 1884-85. (ANC RSC F451, File No 24217, op.cit.)

[57] Osborne, op.cit.

[58] John MacGregor, (1896), *Through the Buffer State. A record of recent travels through Borneo, Siam, and Cambodia,* F.V. White, London, p.205.

[59] AOM FM NF Carton 47, Dossier 570. Letter from Norodom to the Minister of Colonies, 23 June 1900.

[60] *Résident Supérieur* Silvestre made the claim in a letter to the Governor General on 9 November 1934. See AOM FM INDO NF Carton 47, Dossier 568.

[61] See Jean Hess, (1900), *L'Affaire Iukanthor: Les Dessous d'un Protectorat*, Felix Juven, Paris; and Pierre L. Lamant, (1989), *L'Affaire Yukanthor: Autopsie d'un Scandale Colonial*, Société Française d'histoire d'outre-mer, Paris. Yukanthor's private secretary, a Belgian journalist, wrote the former publication. The latter [Lamant] is a more objective account.

[62] Letter from Norodom to the Minister of Colonies, 23 June 1900, op.cit.

[63] ANC RSC F451 File 24216 Conseil des Ministres 36e séance du 3 novembre 1900. Traducion en Cambodgien du mémoire du prince Yukanthor adressé au Gt. de la République Française à Paris contre l'administration française au Cambodge et contre les fonctionnaires français et cambodgiens. Communiqué par M. le Résident Supérieur.

[64] AOM INDO NF Carton 48 Dossier 581. Succession de SM Norodom. Agissements du Prince Yukanthor. Avènement de SM Sisowath.

[65] AOM INDO NF Carton 48 Dossier 581. Letter from Albert Lorin, *Résident* at Kompong Cham, to *Gougal*, 3 November 1900.

[66] ANC F451 File 24217 Conseil des Ministres, 37e séance du 8 novembre 1900. Letter from Sisowath to the *Résident Supérieur*, 17 November 1900.

[67] Unsigned article, (1900), *The New York Times*, 30 September.

[68] See AOM INDO NF, Carton 48 Dossier 581. Also AOM FM INDO NF Carton 47 Dossier 568. Prince Areno Yukanthor, fils de Yukanthor et Malika.

[69] AOM FM INDO NF Carton 47 Dossier 568, letter from Prince Areno Yukanthor to the President of the French Republic, 1938, in 3ème bureau file.

[70] AOM INDO NF Carton 47 Dossier 568. *Résident Supérieur* to *Gougal*, 9 November 1934. The official was commenting on claims by Yukanthor's son that Sisowath was not a legitimate ruler.

[71] Milton Osborne, (1973), "King-making in Cambodia: From Sisowath to Sihanouk", *Journal of Southeast Asian Studies*, Vol. 4, No.3, September, p.169. See also David Chandler, (1971), "Cambodia's relations with Siam in the early Bangkok period: the politics of a tributary state", *Journal of the Siam Society*, Vol. 60, No.1, January, pp.153-169.

[72] ANC RSC F451 File 24217, op.cit. Significantly, a statement by Sisowath detailing his long and loyal service to France and the protectorate is appended to the minutes. Although Sisowath has clearly interpreted events to cast himself in the best possible light, the attachment of his letter without comment suggests official agreement.

[73] AOM INDO NF Carton 47 Dossier 570 *Gougal* to Minister of Colonies, 8 November 1900.

[74] Ibid. *Gougal* to Minister, 17 October 1900.

[75] Ibid. Letter from Doumer to the Minister of Colonies, 17 October 1900.

[76] Ibid. Letter from Jean Hess to the Minister of Colonies, 13 October 1900.

[77] ANC RSC F451 File 24231, 51e séance des Conseil des Ministres du 24 septembre 1901. Norodom Sihanouk claims that his parents held up Yukanthor as an example of how far the French would go to punish members of the royal family who stood up to them. This was in the context of Prince Suramarit persuading Sihanouk not to abdicate in protest at the imposition of Latin script during World War II. Although Sihanouk is not always reliable, this does suggest that there was a belief in the royal family that Yukanthor was not acting on his own. [Norodom Sihanouk, (1972), *L'Indochine vue de Pékin*, Éditions du Seuil, Paris, pp.38-39.]

[78] Unsigned article, (1924), "Une histoire cambodgienne", *Le Echo du Cambodge*, 9 May, Phnom Penh. The documents were handed over to M. Lacomblez, *juge d'Instruction au Parquet de la Seine*.

[79] AOM Indochine FM Indochine Ancien Série, Carton 2, A00 (38). Report by Lefèvre-Pontalis on Indochina to the Minister, 22 April 1903.

[80] AOM RSC 426. Rapports Politiques et Économiques du Cabinet de la Résidence Supérieure, 1905 – 1907. Report on the situation between 1902 and 1907 by *Résident Supérieur* Paul Luce to *Gougal*, 21 August 1907.

[81] AOM RSC 258. Affaires politiques indigènes. Henri Lamothe, Rapport sur la situation du Cambodge (Oct 1903 – July 1904).

[82] AOM Indochine NF Dossier 581, Carton 48, *Gougal* to the Minister of Colonies, 25 February 1904.

[83] ANC RSC D35 File No. 2970, Box 333. Rapport Conseil Supérieure de l'Indochine. Session ordinaire de 1904, No.9 and AOM RSC 258. Doumer's measures were indeed prudent. There is some evidence that of rebellion in Takeo led by an old *Achar*, a veteran of the 1885 Rising, in November 1898. (See AOM RSC 404 Complot contre la sûreté, Takeo, 1898.) It is possible that this disturbance was sparked by the 1897 "settlement". Yukanthor's son refers to armed uprisings in 1899 in his 1938 letter to the French President. (AOM FM NF Carton 47, Dossier 568, op.cit.)

[84] Report by Paul Luce, 21 August 1907, op.cit. See also Osborne, "King-making", op.cit.

[85] AOM RSC 258, Report by Henri Lamothe, op. cit.

[86] ANC RSC D35 File No. 2970, Box 333. Rapport Conseil Supérieure de l'Indochine. Session ordinaire de 1904, No.9. op.cit.

[87] Unsigned, (1904), "La mort de Norodom", *La Quinzaine Coloniale, Organe de l'Union Coloniale*, Paris, 10 May, premier semestre, p.293. This reads better in French: "Le nouveau roi régnera; c'est nous qui continuerons à gouverner."

[88] Roland Meyer, (1922), *Saramani Danseuse Cambodgienne*, E. Fasquelle, Paris, p.99

[89] AOM RSC 426 cited in John Tully, (1996), *Cambodia Under the Tricolour. King Sisowath and the 'Mission Civilisatrice', 1904-1927*, Monash Asia Institute, Clayton, Victoria, p.31.

[90] Thiounn, (1904), "Cérémonie de la remise des Titres Royaux" and "Cérémonie du transfert de la salle Moha Mouti ", *Revue Indochinoise*,

deuxième semestre. Also *La Petite République*, 10 August 1904 found in AOM Indochine NF 590, Carton 48.

[91] David Chandler, (1983*), A History of Cambodia*, First Edition, Westview Press, Boulder, Colorado, p.154.

[92] The allusion is to Shakespeare's play *Macbeth.*

Chapter 7

Economic and Social Development in the Nineteenth Century

The day of small nations has long passed away. The day of Empires has come.
—Joseph Chamberlain, an enthusiast of the "new imperialism",
Birmingham, 13 May 1904.[1]

When Norodom died in 1904, the French had been in Cambodia for over 40 years and although they could not have known it, the Protectorate's time was almost half gone. It is time to pause in our narrative to look back at what the French had achieved in the way of social and economic change in the kingdom. While they had eroded the political power of the monarchy— and could expect the process to accelerate after Norodom's death—most of traditional Khmer society remained intact. To what extent that was due to French indifference, or to a concern to maintain indigenous culture is debatable. Although the Khmers of all classes had resisted change stubbornly, we should not forget the role of official indifference in metropolitan France to what many regarded as a faraway backwater.

Cambodia was of scant importance compared with the rest of the huge overseas empire France had acquired in recent decades. Very few French people lived in Cambodia. Except in times of unrest, when marines came up the Mekong to reinforce the garrisons, there were never more than a few dozen French in the kingdom during most of the 19th century. The European population actually *fell* after the Great Rebellion; by 1894 there were only 30-odd civilians and 20 or so soldiers in Phnom Penh,[2] and perhaps 100 in the country as a whole. The French population rose again by the turn of the century—in 1901 there were 500 Europeans in Cambodia, including 53 settlers and 254 officials.[3] However, the colonial enterprise there was very different to J.S. Mill's description of the Indian Civil Service and military as "a vast system of outdoor relief for the [British] upper classes".[4] Most of the French lived in the relative salubrity of Phnom Penh, but the climate everywhere in the country was harsh for Europeans, and they succumbed easily to tropical diseases. In any case, much of the country was impenetrable jungle and scrub, and there were few roads. For many of the French, the language and customs of the inhabitants were equally impenetrable.

"A state of economic stagnation"

There was little commerce or industry in Cambodia, although the country had traded with the outside world for many centuries before the coming of the French. The American historian Thomas Ennis writes that at the end of the 19th century, "Cambodia was in a state of economic stagnation."[5] Such commerce as did exist was mostly in the hands of the Chinese, Cham and Vietnamese minorities. Most Khmers were peasants, getting by with little. When the French began to establish plantations, public works schemes, and other enterprises dependent on wage labor, they lamented the reluctance of the Khmers to seek and maintain employment. One colonial journalist called for industrial conscription.[6] Usurious interest rates crippled "native" commerce. Without access to banks, primary producers were at the mercy of moneylenders who legally could charge anywhere between 40 and 100 per cent per year.[7] There were two banks in Phnom Penh at the turn of the century; the Banque de l'Indochine and the Hongkong and Shanghai Bank, but these dealt primarily with Chinese merchants and the European minority.[8] We have already noted the discouraging effects of slavery on industry.[9] The crown land system was inimical to commercial agriculture and even urban development, and it was only in 1903 that the French seriously set about preparing for land alienation via a system of "native cadastral brigades".[10] The traditional land system affected the towns as well as the rural areas. Phnom Penh moldered in the sun and rain. A visitor to the town in the late 1880s describes it as consisting of one main street, two kilometers long, with 100 one-story houses, "built of bad bricks and of the same very mediocre design; the king is the owner, and he rents them to Chinese traders."[11] Most of the other buildings were of bamboo and thatch and the road was paved with "broken brick and sand".[12] The problem was that until the late 1880s, Norodom personally owned all land in Phnom Penh and was indifferent to urban development.[13]

French lukewarm about economic change

Yet, the French were themselves lukewarm about establishing industry and commerce. France invested more capital in pre-revolutionary Russia than in its own colonies and much of her colonial investment was in Algeria. Unlike the Dutch in the East Indies, France was also hostile to any encroachment by foreign capital. Although the Second Empire had bowed to the wishes of free traders in 1861, by the 1880s the Third Republic reversed this policy under pressure from French manufacturers. The French government assimilated Indochina into the French *Zollverein* in 1887 and a law of January 1892 enforced protectionism in all of the French overseas possessions.[14] Although by the 1880s they regarded Cambodia as a "colony of exploitation", the French invested little capital there, yet official policy excluded potential rivals. The jealous parochialism of certain officials also contributed to the pattern of economic and social stagnation. Meyer claims that Huyn de Vernéville, the *Résident Supérieur* during much of the 1890s, discouraged both private and public economic development,[15] preferring to rule in a quasi-feudal manner.

A general lack of transport paralyzed the development of industry and commerce including commercial farming. Much of the Cambodian soil is very fertile, and the rivers and lakes teem with fish, yet the country lacked outlets for its primary produce. Simple reforms could yield satisfying results. In 1901, the *Résident Supérieur*, Paul Luce, pointed to the tripling of production of fish oils from the Tonlé Sap following the introduction of a more efficient purchasing system as an example of what could be done for the economy as a whole.[16] With the exception of a building program in Phnom Penh begun in the 1890s, there was a general lack of public works in the kingdom. There was, in any case, no central public works department until 1902. Until then, the provincial authorities were responsible.[17] Cambodia lacked roads; some that existed dated from Angkorean times. Elsewhere the spurt of colonialism in the last decades of the 19th century had coincided with a great railroad construction boom, but this had passed Cambodia by.

There was talk in the small settler community in the early 1890s of a rail line from Stung Treng to Laos, but nothing became of it.[18] Although the French rapidly expanded the railroad system elsewhere in Indochina between 1898 and 1913,[19] it was many years before they laid any track in Cambodia. The peasants used buffalo carts and canoes, and elephants were the main means of carrying heavy loads in the backcountry.[20] The public works department began surveys for a road network in 1903, but the actual construction did not start until after Norodom's death,[21] apart from a road from Phnom Penh to Kampot, and another between the latter center and Giang-Thanh, in Cochinchina.[22]

The French had linked Phnom Penh to the outside world by telegraph soon after their arrival. By the 1880s, they had strung wires between Phnom Penh and Chaudoc; Phnom Penh and Kampot, on the Gulf of Siam; Kampot and Ha Tien (to the east in Cochinchina); and Phnom Penh, Pursat and Battambang via Kompong Chhnang. Other lines connected the capital with Sambor, Kompong Cham, Tayninh and Stung Treng near the border with Laos.[23] The main form of physical transport was the steamship system begun by the Messageries Fluviales firm in the 1880s. The company's steamers plied between Saigon and Phnom Penh, and up to Siem Reap and Battambang, at that stage still in Siam.[24] The steamer voyage from Saigon took 30 hours in the late 1880s,[25] and by 1902, there were three services per week on this route.[26] G. Potel, writing in a cyclostyled newssheet in 1899, claimed that the rivers were the natural routes of communication,[27] but upstream from Phnom Penh, navigation was difficult, and the vast accumulation of silt made dredging necessary even in the *Quatre Bras* at the capital. Navigation was hazardous because of shifting channels, sandbanks, and the huge difference between high and low water (as much as ten meters at Phnom Penh) because of the wet and dry monsoons. Commercial shipping was comparatively rare on the Mekong above the capital. The distances were vast and obstacles so numerous that in 1900 the trip between Saigon and Luang Prabang, in Laos, took 65 days at low water. Navigation was also very difficult in the Tonlé Sap River, leading to the Great Lake.[28]

Little change in trading patterns

Such industry as existed was small-scale, as in the case of the European-owned iron mines in Kompong Svay province, where "coolies" dug out low-grade ore by hand.[29] The ore was smelted in artisans' shops but the small amount of iron produced could not meet the country's modest needs. Most iron and steel came from France. The scope and volume of external trade had changed little over the centuries since the Dutch, Portuguese and English came for the raw silk, rice, lacquer, cardamom, hides, dyestuffs, candlenuts, beeswax, alum, honey, "iron out of the Myne", timber, and the teeth and tusks of the elephant and the "Rhenocerott".[30] In 1887, Cambodia's exports were worth between six and seven million francs. The major imports included: "iron, weapons, gunpowder, lead, ironmongery, tools, cloth, cotton goods, haberdashery, perfumes, [and] alcoholic beverages" from Europe; gold leaf, fruit, jams, medicines, leather goods and lacquered boxes from China; and opium from India.[31]

Rice was by far the principal crop and the staple food of the indigenes, who consumed around 495,000 tonnes of it in 1898.[32] The total production in 1900 was 560,000 tonnes from a total cultivated surface of 400,000 hectares,[33] but output fluctuated markedly due to flood or drought.[34] The surplus was exported to Cochinchina or used in the distilleries to produce alcohol, almost 1.5 million liters of it.[35] Other products included high quality pepper and cardamom (both of which were exported to Europe and China; almost 13,000 kilograms of the latter in 1899[36]), cocoa, peanuts, fish and fish products, coffee, corn, sugar cane and palm sugar, betel nut, coconuts, castor oil plants, pineapples, bananas, tobacco and indigo. Mulberries were grown for silk worms and cotton was cultivated in the High Mekong region. Livestock, including cattle, horses and buffaloes, were reared.[37] Peasants grew much of the country's fruit for their own consumption. There was little plantation agriculture at this stage, and livestock rearing was scarcely along scientific lines. An exception was a horse stud in Kompong Chhnang, established by the Frenchman Michelon around the turn of the century.[38] Kaolin was quarried in the northeast and chalk and saltpeter elsewhere.[39] The country's cotton, which was of good quality, equal to that produced in the Dutch East Indies, Dahomey and the USA, was treated in a cotton gin established at Phnom Penh in 1891,[40] and another at Ksach Kandal, set up by a Frenchman, M. Praire. The latter, subsequently taken over by Chinese entrepreneurs, could treat 1500 piculs of raw cotton per day.[41] Poor weather conditions had led, however, to a decline in production in the late 1890s. The cotton was in constant demand in Japan and Hong Kong.[42]

Perhaps the most visible change in Cambodia was the reconstruction of Phnom Penh, following an agreement between Norodom and de Vernéville in 1889. In return for an annual rent of 30,000 piastres, Norodom agreed to cede control over building and development to the municipal council.[43] The French built some offices, stores, houses and military installations in Phnom Penh in 1864,[44] but a French writer claimed that as late as 1889, the town was still "nothing more than a miserable, straggling village".[45] By the end of Norodom's reign, the French could boast that Phnom Penh was growing and becoming cleaner and more beautiful,[46] a "picturesque town" in "a veritable botanical garden.[47] The population grew to around 40,000 in 1900,[48] when many of the graceful French colonial buildings that exist today, painted lemon yellow, with the details picked out in delicate cream, were already gracing the streets.[49] The reconstruction began in early 1890, when the French administration called for tenders worth 30,000 piastres for the demolition of old buildings,[50] including the run-down Chinese and Indian shops along the riverbank. Modern structures of brick and stone, many of them of two storeys or more, rose in their place. The *Revue Indochinoise* boasted that in the near future, Phnom Penh "would certainly become one of the most beautiful and cleanest" towns in Indochina.　Another writer, who had first arrived in the country in 1874, wrote enthusiastically about the developments for visitors to the Cambodian exhibition in the Lyon Exposition of 1894. It was much grander, he wrote, with imposing European buildings in the rue de Kampot and along the Quai Piquet and Quai de Vernéville.[51] The muddy banks of the Tonlé Sap River were revetted with masonry to prevent scouring and collapse at high water and floods. The decrepit "native" market was pulled down and replaced with "a grand market roofed in iron". Engineers put laborers to work draining the fetid swamps and lagoons behind the town, close to where the railroad station stands today. An impressive canal (named after Huyn de Vernéville) was cut through the center of the town to assist with flood prevention and general drainage and to provide wharves and moorings for small craft. Three bridges spanned the canal, each adorned with sculptures and motifs in the ancient Khmer style.[52] The earth excavated for the canal was used to fill in swamps and ponds.[53] The canal ran along what is today the wide grassy reserve between Streets 106 and 108, which run at a ninety-degree angle from the Tonlé Sap River towards the central railroad station and the lake called Boeng Kak. The French also restored the old pagoda, the Wat Phnom, on its "sacred hill" at the northern end of the town, and transformed the slopes into gardens.[54] A new hospital was built, along with a double-story government printing works, police and militia barracks, banks, a prison, workshops, a magazine, customs offices, housing for French officials, and the "superb treasury building" already noted.[55]

Grim social conditions

Social conditions remained grim throughout the kingdom. Medical facilities did not exist outside of the capital, and public education was sparse and rudimentary. The country was a breeding ground for an array of tropical diseases that periodically struck with astonishing virulence. A host of diseases, including malaria, cholera and typhoid were endemic. Water supplies were often polluted, especially when the annual floodwaters retreated. In late 1904, there were huge floods, the biggest since 1867, which caused the population great suffering and loss of most of their crops. All of the great plain of Cambodia, save for Phnom Penh and a few other centers, was under water. Yet, the peasants' misery did not end when the floods ebbed, for an epidemic of cholera broke out.[56] There was no reticulated water supply even in the towns, and no proper sewage disposal. Europeans complained even in Phnom Penh of the stench of the open drains.[57] The vast mass of the population had no understanding of the causes of disease, which is not surprising, given that medical science was a newcomer even in Europe. The results of ignorance were often disastrous. An example of the virulence of the epidemics was the outbreak of cholera in Battambang and Phnom Penh in April – May 1895, in which 3000 people died in the capital alone.[58] Huy Kanthoul was born in rural Kompong Cham province in 1908. His earliest memory was of his grandmother's death. Like many others, she was the victim of an epidemic at a time when "whole villages were emptied of their inhabitants."[59] A French report from 1904 notes that although cholera took numerous victims every year, and despite the "enormous ravages"[60] of infant mortality, the only medical facilities in the country were in Phnom Penh.[61] One year after Norodom's death, the *Quinzaine Coloniale* was pleased to announce that before the end of 1905, two specialist *médecins de colonisation* would arrive in Cambodia. Plans were made to start public education in hygiene, along with a vaccination campaign and the construction of a "native" maternity hospital in Phnom Penh.[62]

Their record in public health had been lack luster, and the French had not achieved a great deal in the field of public education. To be fair, they had neither the funds nor the personnel to achieve much. Until the 1890s, the French administration had little control over customs and taxation, and there were few trained personnel, either French or indigenous.[63] Nor were they able to build on an established educational base, and the population was indifferent or even hostile to European-style education. There were no printed books or brochures in the Khmer language until the first years of the twentieth century.

Modern printing arrived in 1902 when the French installed a lithographic press, with metallic Khmer characters, at a royal printing works in Phnom Penh.[64] The first printed book in the Khmer language may have been St Luke's Gospel. Alexander Lawrence, an Australian missionary, sent the manuscript to France for printing a decade earlier after translation by a Khmer convert called Vong.[65] Handwritten copies of the work of Cambodian poets circulated informally,[66] often written on dried palm leaves held together with string. In the same period, the French began to introduce the metric system to replace the baffling Cambodian system of weights and measures.[67]

Contrary to the claim of the proverb that "The country of the Khmers will always exist", 19th century Cambodia was in grave danger of a losing its national-cultural identity.[68] The architectural and artistic legacy of Angkorean times was crumbling in the jungles of the Siamese-occupied western provinces and even the ancient arts and crafts were in danger of dying out.[69] Male children often did receive a rudimentary education in the pagoda schools, where the monks drilled them by rote in the *satras*, the Pâli and Khmer sacred texts,[70] but education was not prized in a predominantly peasant society. Almost all women and girls were illiterate. Tradition barred them from the pagoda schools.[71]

Between 1864 and 1869, a few Cambodian boys received bursaries to study in schools in Cochinchina, most often at Soctrang.[72] Norodom set up a palace school in 1867,[73] and two years later requested French help to create a French-language primary school in Phnom Penh. The school opened in 1873 under the headmastership of M. Ferreyrolles, a former infantry corporal, after an outlay of 20,000 francs. Magnant records that Norodom "did not flinch" at his share of the cost.[74] The school shifted to new buildings in the rue Ohier in 1882, with Norodom paying part of the construction expenses.[75] By this stage, there were only around 100 primary pupils in French-language schools, and only eight of them were Khmers.[76] A few years later, in the mid-1880s, a number of Khmers went to France to train as interpreters at the École rue Ampère and the École Coloniale.[77]

The "white man's burden"?

In 1893, the Collège du Protectorat opened its doors, with some provision for junior high school instruction. It was to prove durable, changing its name to the Lycée Sisowath in 1935.[78] Many of the members of the country's future political elite were to pass through its doors. In the year before Norodom's death, the French founded the

École Pratique, later to become the Phnom Penh Technical College and revamped the palace school as the École Norodom with 29 pupils.[79] In 1902, there were only four French-language schools in all of Cambodia. One, in Phnom Penh, had 430 pupils and the others, in Prey Veng, Kampot and Takeo, had 60 each.[80] It was a feeble effort, and mocked the words of the grand theoretician of French colonialism, M. Paul Leroy-Beaulieu. According to his theories, which echoed contemporary British ideas of the "white man's burden", tropical countries such as Cambodia would be developed economically and socially as *colonies d'exploitation*. In 1896, Leroy-Beaulieu had described these colonies as places in which,

> the superior race directs, develops and leads the inferior race, supplies capital, develops the country's natural resources and thanks to the intelligent staff of administrators, engineers, capitalists, merchants, teachers, foremen and workmen, transforms a country which has long remained poor...into a prosperous, wealthy region...[81]

Leroy-Beaulieu's ideas were overly schematic[82], for, as D.K. Fieldhouse has remarked, "the modern empires were not artificially constructed economic machines".[83] Despite this caveat, we can observe that while some of what Leroy-Beaulieu prescribed had happened in French Algeria or British India, there was precious little of it in Cambodia. J.A. Hobson's observation that the British were "incapable of implanting [their] civilization in India by present methods..." and were "only capable of disturbing their civilization"[84] ring even more true of the French in Cambodia at this stage. To be fair, the French had dissipated their energies in a protracted struggle just to begin to modify a traditional socio-economic system that was inimical to commerce and industry. The real test of the *mise-en-valeur* policies associated with Governors-General de Lanessan and Doumer was still to come. The death of Norodom removed a major obstacle in Cambodia to the kind of development proposed by Leroy-Beaulieu and others. Norodom's death also came a few years after the onset of a long economic expansionary wave on a global level. This upswing was mirrored in the social, political and cultural spheres in the phenomenon that came to be known as the *belle époque*.[85] Capitalism had entered into a long upswing following the end of the depression of the mid-1890s and this was to last until World War I. This was also the heyday of the "new Imperialism" identified by John Hobson. French colonialism had now emerged from the uncertain shadows of the Norodom years into its "place in the sun".

Notes

[1] Joseph Chamberlain, speech to Liberal Unionist Association at Birmingham, 12 May 1904. Reported in *The Times*, 13 May 1904.

[2] Charles Meyer, (1971), *Derrière le Sourire Khmer*, Plon, Paris, p.98.

[3] E. Giret, (1901), "L'Emigration française aux colonies", *Revue Indochinoise*, 20 May. See also unsigned article, (1902), "Notice sur le Cambodge", *Bulletin Économique de l'Indochine*, No 2, nouvelle série, p.115. According to the 1902 census, there were 575 Europeans in Cambodia, including 461 French civil servants and businessmen, 112 soldiers and 2 Germans. There were also 176,825 "foreign Asiatics" and 1,080,149 Cambodians. (ANC RSC F451 File 34246 Conseil des Ministres, 66e séance du 13 février 1902, "Avis au conseil des résultats du rencensement de la population du Cambodge".)

[4] Cited in J.A Hobson, (1965), *Imperialism: A Study*, Ann Arbor Paperbacks, University of Michigan, p.51.

[5] Thomas E. Ennis, (1936), *French Policy and Developments in Indochina*, University of Chicago Press, Chicago, p.80.

[6] G. Potel, (1900), "Les travailleurs de la terre", *Le Petit Cambodgien*, 28 January.

[7] Louis de Carné, (1872), *Travels in Indo-China and the Chinese Empire*, Chapman and Hill, London, p.38.

[8] "Notice sur le Cambodge", op.cit. p.121.

[9] See Chapter 3.

[10] ANC RSC D35 File 2970 Box 333. Rapport Conseil Supérieure de l'Indochine. Session ordinaire de 1904, No 9.

[11] Edgar Boulangier, (1887), *Un Hiver au Cambodge*, Alfred Mame, Tours, p.36.

[12] Frank Vincent Jnr, (1873), *The Land of the White Elephant. Sights and Scenes in South-Eastern Asia: A Personal Narrative of Travel and Adventure in Farther India Embracing the Countries of Burma, Siam, Cambodia and Cochin-China (1871-72)*, Sampson, Low, Marston, Low and Searle, London, p.269.

[13] John Tully, (1996), *Cambodia Under the Tricolour. King Sisowath and the "Mission Civilisatrice" 1904-1927*, Monash Asia Institute, Clayton, Victoria, p.72.

[14] Stephen Roberts, (1929), *The History of French Colonial Policy, 1870-1925*, Frank Cass, London, pp.41-44.

[15] Meyer, op.cit.

[16] Unsigned article, (1901), "Les produits du Cambodge et leurs debouchés", *Bulletin Économique de l'Indochine*, No. 38 ancienne série, p.713.

[17] AOM RSC 426. Rapports politiques et économiques du Cabinet de la Résidence Supérieur, 1905-1907. Report on the situation between 1902 and 1907. *Résident Supérieur* Paul Luce to *Gougal*, 21 August 1907.

[18] Article by J. Blancsubé, (1893), *Le Mékong*, No.8, 25 November.

[19] Charles Robequain (trans. Isabel A. Ward), (1944), *The Economic Development of French Indo-China*, Oxford University Press, London, p.90.

[20] Ibid. p.104.

[21] Luce to *Gougal*, 21 August 1907, op.cit.

[22] AOM RSC 257. Rapports politiques, 1897-1906. Rapport sur la situation du Cambodge (octobre 1903-juillet 1904).

[23] Édouard Testoin, (1886), *Le Cambodge, passé, présent, avenir*, Ernest Mazereau, Tours, pp.175-176.

[24] Eugène Lagillière-Beauclerc, (1900), *A Travers l'Indochine. Cochinchine-Cambodge-Annam-Tonkin-Laos*, Librairie Ch. Tallandier, Paris, pp.127-130, also unsigned article, (1887), "Le Cambodge. Commerce. Voies de communication", *Le Courrier d'Haiphong*, 6 March.

[25] Boulangier, op.cit. p.33.

[26] "Notice sur le Cambodge", op.cit. p.115.

[27] G. Potel, (1899), *Le Petit Cambodgien*, 23 novembre.

[28] Robequain, op.cit. pp.114-115.

[29] "Le Cambodge. Commerce. Voies de communication", op.cit.

[30] D.K. Bassett, (1962), "The Trade of the English East India Company in Cambodia", *Journal of the Royal Asiatic Society of Great Britain and Ireland*. Appendix. "A Relacon of the Scituation & Trade of Camboja, also of Syam, Tunkin, Chyna & the Empire of Japan from Q[uarles] B[rowne] in Bantam", pp.58-61.

[31] "Le Cambodge. Commerce. Voies de communication", op.cit.

[32] A. Galy, (1899), "La production, la consommation et l'exportation des riz en Cochinchine et au Cambodge", *Bulletin Économique de l'Indochine*, Nr 17, ancien série, pp.597-612.

[33] Rémy Prud'homme, (1969), *L'Économie du Cambodge*, Presses Universitaires de France, Paris, p.254, Tableau 11.

[34] See, for instance, AOM RSC 257. Rapports politiques, 1897-1906. Rapport sur la situation du Cambodge, octobre 1903-juillet 1904.

[35] Galy, op.cit.

[36] Unsigned, (1900), "Le cardamone au Cambodge et au Laos", *Bulletin Économique de l'Indochine*, Nr 30, ancienne série, pp.675-676.

[37] "Notice sur le Cambodge", op.cit. p.121.

[38] La direction de l'Agriculture et du Commerce de l'Indochine, (1901), "Renseignements," *Bulletin Économique de l'Indochine*, Nr 35, ancienne série, pp.415-416.

[39] Testoin, op.cit. p.28.

[40] "Notice sur le Cambodge", op.cit.

[41] Unsigned, (1901), "Cotons au Cambodge", *Bulletin Économique de l'Indochine*, ancienne série, pp. 918-919.

[42] H. Brenier, (1903), "Note sur le coton du Cambodge", *BEI*, Nr 21, nouvelle série, pp.619-623.

[43] Unsigned article, (1893), "Le Cambodge en 1893", *Revue Indo-Chinoise Illustrée*, septembre, Hanoi, p.174. See also Tully, op.cit. pp.72-73.

[44] AOM AF Carton 10 Dossier A30 (6). Admiral de Lagrandière to the Minister for the Navy and Colonies, 30 June 1864.

[45] "Le Cambodge en 1893", op.cit. p.173.

[46] AOM Indochine Carton 2, Dossier A00 (38) Rapport de Lefèvre-Pontalis sur l'Indochine. 22 April 1903.

[47] Rose Quaintenne, (1909), *Quinze Jours au Pays des Rois Khmers,* Coudurier et Montégout, Saigon, p.33.

[48] Denis Nardin, (1964), "Phnom Penh: Naissance et croissance d'une administration urbaine," Mémoire en vue du diplôme d'études supérieurs de droit public. Faculté de Droit et des Sciences Économiques de Phnom Penh, p.1.

[49] For an illustrated study of the growth of the capital, see Michel Igout (with photographs by Serge Dubuisson), (1993), *Phnom Penh Then and Now,* White Lotus, Bangkok.

[50] AOM NF Carton 48. Letter from *Gougal* to the Undersecretary of State for Colonies, 25 February 1890.

[51] Today, respectively, Pochentong Boulevard and Streets 108 and 106.

[52] B. Marrot, (1894), *Exposition de Lyon 1894. Section Cambodgienne. Notes et souvenirs sur le Cambodge,* Forézienne P. Rousten, Roanne, pp.27-28. A 13th century Chinese visitor noted that the Khmer capital contained a number of large bridges, each decorated with statues, including those of nine-headed serpents. See Jean Pierre Abel-Rémusat, (trans), (1819), *Description du Royaume de Cambodge, par un Voyageur Chinois,* Imprimerie de J. Smith, Paris, p.41.

[53] "Le Cambodge en 1893", op.cit. p.175.

[54] Ibid, p.177.

[55] Ibid, pp.178-181.

[56] ANC D35 RSC File No 2970 Box 333. *Résident Supérieur* to *Gougal,* 1 November 1904 and Rapport Politique, November and December 1904, 8 January 1905.

[57] See, for instance, G. Potel, (1899), "Pnompenh a fait sa toilette" and "Les odeurs de Pnompenh..." *Le Petit Cambodgien,* 15 and 26 octobre.

[58] Unsigned articles, (1895), "Cholera in Battambang. Panic among the natives. 3000 native and 16 European deaths", *Siam Free Press,* 23 April and 20 May, Bangkok.

[59] Huy Kanthoul unpublished French-language typescript, Ch. 2. (Chandler Papers, Monash University.)

[60] Unsigned article, (1905), *La Quinzaine Coloniale. Organe de l'Union Coloniale Française,* 25 August, Paris, p.512.

[61] AOM RSC 426. Rapport sur la situation entre 1902 et 1907. *Résident Supérieur* to *Gougal.* 21 August 1907.

[62] *Quinzaine Coloniale,* op.cit.

[63] M. Magnant, (1913), "Notes sur les débuts de l'enseignement français au Cambodge (1863-1890), *Revue Indochinoise,* premier semestre, p.454.

[64] ANC RSC 451 File 24257 Conseil des Ministres, 77e séance du 31 mai 1902.

[65] William Rainey, (1950), *An Australian Pioneer. From the Diary of the late Mr.. Alexander Lawrence, who served the Bible Society in Indo-China, the Philippines and Japan,* British and Australian Bible Society, Kew, Victoria, p.5.

[66] For instance, the work of the poet Int. See Tauch Chhuong (trans. Sithan Hin), (1974), "Battambang in the Period of the Vassal", unpublished English language mss, original Khmer version published in Battambang, p.17.

[67] ANC RSC F451 File 24221 Conseil des Ministres, séance du 29 mai 1901, "projet d'ordonnance royale fixent les poids et mesures cambodgiens et leur équivalent avec le système métrique français."

[68] Tully, op.cit. p.221.

[69] Virginia Thompson, (1968), *French Indo-China,* Octagon Books, p.355. See Chapter 12 below for a discussion of the restoration program.

[70] Charles Bilodeau, (1955), "Compulsory Education in Cambodia", in Charles Bilodeau, Somlith Pathammavong and Le Quang Hông, *Compulsory Education in Cambodia, Laos and Viet-nam,* UNESCO, Paris, p.16.

[71] Ibid. p.19.

[72] Magnant, op.cit. p.454.

[73] Bilodeau, op.cit. p.16.

[74] Magnant, op.cit.

[75] Ibid, p.457. The rue Ohier is today's Street 13 and runs from the vicinity of the central post office in the north to the royal palace in the south, and behind the Wat Onalom.

[76] AOM RSC 304. M. Humbert-Hesse, "Rapport Général sur l'Enseignement au Cambodge", 10 January 1923.

[77] Magnant, op.cit. and AOM RSC 476, Deuxième Bureau, Affaires indigènes, 1906-1909.

[78] Bilodeau, op.cit.

[79] AOM 426 Rapport sur la situation entre 1902 et 1907. Résident Supérieur Paul Luce à Gougal, 21 août 1907. By the 1920s, the École Norodom had shifted to a site on the Quai de Vernéville—today's Street 106.

[80] Luce, op. cit.

[81] Cited in Henri Brunschwig, (trans. William Glanville Brown), (1964), *French Colonialism 1871-1914: Myths and Realities,* Frederick Praeger, New York, p.61. The other types of colony were those in which banks and other finance and trading institutions were set up ("comptoirs"), and *colonies de peuplement,* for white settlers.

[82] By modern standards, his ideas were also racist. However, Leroy-Beaulieu was a liberal in the tradition of J.S. Mill. His talk of "superior" and "inferior" races was the common wisdom of the Victorian and Edwardian world.

[83] D.K. Fieldhouse, (1966), *The Colonial Empires. A Comparative Survey from the Eighteenth Century,* Weidenfeld and Nicolson, London, p.381.

[84] Hobson, op.cit. p.302.

[85] The Russian Marxist economist Nikolai Kondratiev was one of the first to write about the existence of such "long waves" of capitalist development. Kondratiev (followed by Ernest Mandel) identified long upswings and downswings, lasting perhaps decades. These were separate from the periodic crises of overproduction (the short-term boom/bust business cycle) and owed their existence to a combination of the effects of new technology and conjunctural social and political phenomena. See, for instance, Ernest Mandel, (1973), *An Introduction to Marxist Economic Theory*, Pathfinder Press, New York.

Chapter 8

Sisowath "might almost be a Frenchman"[1]

[Although] just as prodigal and just as given to vice [as Norodom] the
Obbareach lacked a taste for absolute power.
                                    —Admiral Krantz, Governor of Cochinchina.

From 1884 to 1945, our kings were nothing more than what the Khmer
people called 'parrots', trained to say 'Bat, Bat' (yes).
                                    —Norodom Sihanouk, *L'Indochine vue de Pékin,*[2]

Prince Sisowath was 64 when Norodom's death finally left his way to
the throne open. The coronation took place on 26 April 1904, two days
after his half-brother's death.[3] Governor General Paul Beau placed the
royal crown on his head "in the name of the French Republic".[4]
Shortly afterwards, Sisowath "set fire to the immense catafalque on
which rested the last pitiful remnants of a great king."[5] It must have
seemed like an exorcism. Norodom had hated him, considering him
"two-faced".[6] His other half-brother, the warlike Si Votha, had
perished over a decade earlier in the jungles, and so Sisowath could
rest easy in the knowledge that there were no other serious contenders
for the throne. In early May, Sisowath's old comrade-in-arms, Paul
Luce, the newly-appointed *Résident Supérieur,* informed the new king
that the President of the French Republic had ratified his coronation.[7]
The ratification was a mere formality, although the French authorities

had evidently again considered incorporating Cambodia into Cochinchina. They dismissed this option, however, recognizing the important symbolism of the monarchy. They knew that such as step would have caused "discontent among the people", an understatement masking their dread of the specter of the Great Rebellion. Critics claimed that French behind-the-scenes involvement in the coronation meant Sisowath had come to the throne illegitimately. He *was* France's choice; the Council of Ministers had rubber-stamped the decision made in Paris to put him on the throne. If the rules of succession common to most European monarchies had applied, then one of Norodom's sons, preferably his eldest should have succeeded his father. While Norodom had disowned his oldest remaining son, the exiled Yukanthor, and Duong Chakr lay in a dusty Saharan grave, he did have literally scores of other male children from which to choose. According to the Norodom wing of the family, the succession should have gone to Mayura, Phanuvong, Salvan or Chanthalekha, Sutharot or Sathavong. This argument overlooks the fact that a foreign power had put Norodom himself on the throne, and that the succession in Cambodia had seldom been directly from father to son. This had been the pattern since the 18th century. As "protecting power", France had stepped into the shoes of Siam and Vietnam, and could even make a quasi-legal case for its rights. We should record, however, that the palace protocol office had "modified ancient usage" to allow the *Résident Supérieur* to attend, and preside over, the Council's deliberations.[8] In any case, might made right, and France appointed all of the Khmer monarchs of the twentieth century: Sisowath, his son Monivong, and then Norodom's great-grandson, the current incumbent, Norodom Sihanouk. If the final test of royal authenticity is popular acceptance, then all of these kings have been legitimate.

An undercurrent of discontent

There was, however, a strong undercurrent of discontent against Sisowath and/or the French in "Norodomist" circles, and this persisted throughout the reigns of Sisowath and his son, Monivong. While generally confined to palace (and harem) backrooms and corridors, it probably did contribute to the widespread 1916 disturbances during World War I.[9] Norodom's son Mayura was involved in an abortive anti-French uprising in the last years of the nineteenth century[10] and appears to have conspired with Yukanthor and the latter's estranged wife, Malika, in 1916. During the last weeks of Norodom's reign and the succession of Sisowath, disturbances also flared briefly in Thbong-

Khmum province, led by "badly intentioned individuals".[11] Another, and apparently unrelated revolt broke out shortly afterwards in the Porong region, led by "an old defrocked bonze of the An-bach pagoda", a pretender who adopted the name Ang Snguon ("king of the country").[12] Rumors circulated for several years in the international press that Sisowath was not quite *comme il faut*,[13] but the adoring crowds who turned out in the streets of Phnom Penh on the first anniversary of his coronation[14] show that the people accepted the new king easily enough. Certainly, there were no "incidents" during the coronation itself, although French gunboats lay in the Mekong just in case.[15]

Because of the perception of him as a French puppet, Sisowath was easy to underestimate. A Paris newspaperman described him during his 1906 tour of France as "a small yellow man with gray hair".[16] An English traveler wrote of a "stout, squat, kindly old gentleman", who "bows constantly like a mechanical doll" and proffers his European guests "sweet champagne, a speech of some length in the vernacular, and Manilla cigars..."[17] Yet, the advancing years had not dimmed his marked physical vitality and the courteous exterior hid a forceful, even ruthless, personality. Another account describes a "large and square head", topped with "silky white hair", a smooth face, thick lips and "the lively little eyes of an elephant". The same writer describes an incident in which a cudgel-wielding burglar invaded Sisowath's palace. While those around panicked, Sisowath coolly took charge and "armed only with his opium pipes", subdued the prowler and had him decapitated.[18]

The King's early life

Sisowath was born on 7 September 1840, either in Battambang (which at that time was part of Siam) or in Bangkok itself.[19] As with his half-brothers Norodom and Si Votha, he was sent as a hostage to Bangkok when still a child.[20] Named An Sor at birth, he was renamed Sisowath after his traditional hair-cutting ceremony in 1854.[21] Sisowath shared a harsh and lonely, even brutal, childhood[22] with his half-siblings in the foreign capital. In later years, Sisowath had a great hatred of the Siamese,[23] and it seems likely that cruel treatment and enforced exile played a part in this. The Siamese did however appoint him *Prea-Keo-Fea*, in 1856 when he was in his late teens.[24] The three boys were never close, and in adulthood, they came to detest and fear each other. Each coveted the throne and hated the others for blocking his way to it. Norodom did have a legitimate claim to the throne, being named *Obbareach* by the Siamese in 1856.[25] He received help from these overlords against domestic rebellions after his father's death. Sisowath's role during this confused period is contradictory. He claimed to have taken Norodom's side against Cham and Khmer rebels in 1857 and again in 1858, when he played a key part in the defense of Udong. Subsequently, again according to his own testimony written in 1900, he organized the successful defense of Udong in 1861 against Si Votha and his Cham allies. He also claimed that, despite Norodom's precipitate flight to Bangkok at that time, he had resisted advice from the mandarins and French officers and priests to take over as king. "I stayed loyal to my brother," he claimed.[26] It is difficult to evaluate such claims, for although we cannot accuse him of lack of martial valor and ability, his professions of fidelity to Norodom ring false in the light of their subsequent relations. Then again, perhaps he was speaking the truth and was estranged from Norodom by degrees. It is true that the French did not contradict his claims when he made them (in 1900), but this might have been because they were then interested in undermining the Norodom wing's claims to the throne during the Yukanthor Affair. What Sisowath does not say in his account of his role in this period is that he later led an unsuccessful revolt against Norodom and later fled into exile in Saigon.[27] During his exile, he appears to have become convinced that his best chance of supplanting his half-brother lay via gaining French favor. His military skills caught the French eye, and contrasted favorably with Norodom's inept performance, but, fearful of Norodom's wrath, he only returned for Cambodia for good in June 1868,[28] arriving aboard a French warship to fight against the Pou Kombo insurrection.[29] He claims that Admiral de Lagrandière commissioned him to put down the rebels, who had "vanquished all of the troops sent against" them by Norodom.[30] Two years later, at the instigation of the French, he became *Obbareach*.[31]

Sisowath's character and his loyalty to France

Thus, decades before his coronation, Sisowath had thrown in his lot with the pale-skinned intruders, relying on their help to force Norodom from the throne. While this never happened, Sisowath's faith was not entirely misplaced as the French often toyed with the idea of forcing Norodom to abdicate. In the wake of the Pou Kombo revolt in 1867, Admiral de Lagrandière had praised Sisowath's "energy and intelligence", and stated his preference for him over Norodom as king.[32] Adhémard Léclère was not convinced, considering that Sisowath was lazy and just as "false and underhand" as his brother, and that he would oppose serious reform "if ever he ascended the throne."[33] Léclère had a point. Like Norodom, Sisowath was fond of opium, alcohol and the harem. Yet Admiral Krantz did not fully share Léclère's view, opining that although "just as prodigal and just as given to vice" as Norodom, the *Obbareach* lacked "a taste for absolute power".[34] The pro-Sisowath wing won out, to a point. Admiral Duperré ordered Moura to draw up a secret agreement with the prince in which he agreed to act in whatever ways the French saw fit should he ascend the throne.[35] Sisowath strengthened his chances nine or so years later by his energetic role in suppressing the Great Rebellion. From the French point of view, the only blot on his record was his reluctance to chance his popularity with the Cambodian people by capturing Si Votha.[36] Huyn de Vernéville summed up official French opinion when he declared Sisowath the easiest person to handle among the contenders for the throne, also drawing attention to his popularity with both ordinary Cambodians and the elite.[37]

The *Obbareach's* surprisingly honest (or pliable) behavior in an incident involving one of his sons may have convinced the French that he was their man. One day in early September 1884, someone found the decapitated body of a 19-year-old Khmer girl close to the river in the "Catholic Village" (the Vietnamese quarter) of Phnom Penh. Suspicion fell on two of the personal slaves of Sisowath's son, Nuppakau, after they fled the city. The French believed that they had only carried out their master's orders and that the girl's murder resulted from a dispute over women between Nuppakau and a sibling, or half-sibling, Prince Peia. When they raised the matter, Sisowath's first response was to ask his son to hand the slaves over to the authorities for punishment.[38] Had the arbitrary justice of the past continued, the slaves would have been executed and the royal culprit would have got off scot-free. Sisowath vacillated, but the French pressed the case, and he agreed to send his son into exile at Saigon or any other place in Cochinchina chosen by the authorities. Prince Nuppakau languished in chains in a prison cell for a while, and the French intervened to commute the death sentence against the slaves. The French considered that "This judgment will have a resounding echo in all of Cambodia. It is, in effect, the first time that the justice system has dared, not only to act against a member of the royal family, but to condemn a prince to penal servitude."[39]

Little more is recorded about Nuppakau after this time;[40] although he seems to have been rehabilitated after a discreet interval, he was never prominent in public affairs.[41] We can only speculate whether his father's disavowal of him was due to a desire to ingratiate himself with the French—or was due to a genuine belief in legal probity. Whatever the reason, it was a radical departure from arbitrary despotism, and adumbrated the kind of legal reforms that Sisowath would give his royal assent to after 1904. In some ways, however, Sisowath did not break the old molds. He maintained a large and jealously guarded harem—albeit smaller than that of Norodom. When a number of his wives took Chinese lovers in 1919, Sisowath ordered Thiounn to lay charges of adultery and *lèse-majesté* and confined them to the palace jail.[42]

A "pensioner of the protectorate"

Shortly after the coronation and Norodom's cremation, Sisowath sent a telegram via the Governor General to the French President, pledging his loyalty to France and promising to devote his efforts to the progress of his country and the Indochinese Union.[43] After the turbulence of the Norodom years, the protectorate had entered into a new era of Franco-Khmer amity. This was symbolized by the close relationship between Sisowath and the new *Résident Supérieur*, Paul Luce, who wrote that he had traveled with the new king in the interior of Cambodia in 1885, at the time when Sisowath "had been charged with pacification campaigns following the great rebellion".[44] Sisowath never disagreed with the French on any issue of substance over the 23-year period of his reign. In the last years of his reign, the Cambodian branch of the pro-republican League of the Rights of Man and the Citizen sent a damning report of the administration of the protectorate to their head office in Paris. The report, which was probably written by the disgruntled former *Résident* Gabriel Maurel,[45] claimed that the king lacked all financial independence, that except for a restricted civil list, he had no budget to dispose of, and dismissed him as "nothing more than a pensioner of the protectorate". "His docility", Maurel continued, "is extraordinary".[46] Norodom had continued to try, feebly it is true, to block the French right up until the end; certain ordinances lay unsigned at the time of his death.[47] With his death—and with the full cooperation of Sisowath—the French were able to assert full and "almost absolute control" over the protectorate. As Maurel pointed out, the treaty of 1863 as modified by the treaty of 17 June 1884 defined relations between Cambodia and France. "The first article" of this, he continued, "provides in effect that the king of Cambodia 'accepts all the administrative, judicial, financial and commercial reforms which the government of the French Republic judges in future to be useful to facilitate the execution of the tasks of the protectorate.'"[48]

Reforms to the legal system

Immediately after Sisowath's coronation, the French enacted a number of reforms, and heaped generous praise on Sisowath for his cooperation.[49] Among the first reforms were some changes to the idiosyncratic legal system. Although Ang Duong had codified the Cambodian legal code to some extent fifty-odd years previously,[50] it was still chaotic, arbitrary, contradictory and in places cruel—even sadistic—and unjust.[51] It was possible for those with money to buy immunity from prosecution or to otherwise pervert the course of justice. The word of a commoner carried less weight than that of a noble.[52] The system encouraged corruption as "native" magistrates relied on fines levied on real or imagined malefactors for at least part of their income. There were no examinations for judicial officials.

Some of the prescribed punishments were ghoulish. Female adulterers could be partially impaled astride a sharpened bamboo stave; an informant told the writer Belot that he interviewed *"une empalée"* in the 1880s. Male adulterers as a rule were merely fined, although draconian punishments could be imposed if their "accomplices" were high-ranking.[53] Prisoners were routinely chained at the ankle, even at the neck if deemed dangerous, for the duration of their sentences. Corporal punishment was common—the infliction of 100 strokes of the cane was not out of the ordinary—and until 1904, judges could legally use "third degree" measures during the interrogation of suspects.[54] Capital punishment was turned into a drawn-out public spectacle. Paul Branda has left a chilling description of the last days of a condemned man. For three days before his death, the prisoner paraded in chains through the streets, guarded by soldiers with sabers. He was forced to tell the crowds what he had done: "Ladies and gentlemen, I have been condemned to death for [...] don't follow my example." Throughout the ordeal, the executioner walked by the wretch's side, his sword drawn from its scabbard, as a constant reminder of his victim's looming fate. On the third day, the executioner took the prisoner to the appointed public place, marked the spot where the blade would fall on the neck with a quid of wet betel, and severed the head from the trunk with one blow.[55] As in the case of the rebel Pou Kombo, the executioner impaled the head on a spike and hoisted it in a public place.

The new era was marked by a series of humane reforms. Three weeks after he became king, Sisowath signed a decree—his first—abolishing corporal punishment.[56] Norodom had constantly avoided signing the decree, which the French had drawn up some time earlier.[57]

In December of the same year, Sisowath signed a new ordinance that stipulated that officials with judicial functions had to pass special examinations.[58] The following August, the practice of chaining prisoners in their cells was abolished by royal decree.[59] The end of the year saw the abolition of the draconian punishments for adultery, and the introduction of more "humane" methods of capital punishment.[60]

In 1906, judges and all members of tribunals were required to swear an oath before a statue of the Buddha.[61] With Sisowath's blessing, the French set up a special commission on penal reform. The commission deliberated for a number of years, but by 1910, it was ready to make recommendations for sweeping changes to the legal code.[62] In November 1911, Sisowath signed a decree for a new criminal code. The new code provided for respect of the ancient principles of Cambodian law, but torture and corporal punishment were "suppressed as incompatible with the principles of humanity and justice".[63] It was stirring stuff and no doubt meant sincerely, but as we shall see, the French themselves did not always obey humanitarian precepts; the French police were to use almost unbelievably sadistic tortures against political opponents, and "third degree" measures against miscreants were commonplace.[64]

Even before the first wave of legal reforms, Sisowath signed a convention for a restricted civil list,[65] long a French objective, and one that he had secretly agreed to years before. The agreement also bound Sisowath to end the crown land system, and to suppress the system of *apanages*, or "fiefs". Accordingly, by mid-1905, Sisowath decreed the end of the latter system. On the day of his coronation, he proclaimed that he would give proprietorship of the soil to those who cultivated it.[66] A new decree of 29 November 1907 gave free title to landholders, with a system of tribunals to resolve disputes, and Sisowath abandoned his "pre-eminent right to proprietorship of the lands of the kingdom".[67]

Strict control over the Cambodian government

A three-tier system of government replaced the old system of *apanages*. A 1908 decree set up local government bodies, or *khum*; a radical departure from tradition as Cambodia had never previously enjoyed responsible local government. The *khum* consisted of groups of hamlets. The *khum* themselves were grouped into larger administrative units, known as *khet* and *srok*, and these in turn were part of a national system of *circonscriptions residentielles*, under the direct supervision of French *Résidents*.[68] None of these bodies were elected, however. The system was designed to allow the French to control the country by relying on a "native" bureaucracy with a minimum of French personnel. Many Khmer peasants seldom encountered French officials. While this gave the appearance of considerable autonomy, in practice the French exercised tight control over the hierarchy via their *Résidents*. Although a French report from 1911 claims that the Cambodian ministers did not passively obey orders, but would "seek to understand" and "sometimes argue",[69] this does not appear to have been the case at lower levels of government, and at higher levels French control also hardened. The minutes of regional bodies—*Conseils des Résidences*[70]—show that most of the talking was done by French officials, and that the bodies were designed as transmission belts for the wishes of the *Résident Supérieur*, and, ultimately, the Governor General in Hanoi. Some of these sessions appear to have been little more than long monologues by the *Résidents*, with the occasional timid question from a Cambodian official. The flavor is one of gatherings of slightly untrustworthy or recalcitrant recruits harangued by NCOs.[71] A similar situation came about in the Council of Ministers, which was reorganized in 1897 and placed under the permanent presidency of the *Résident Supérieur*. The minutes of the Council reveal the steady tightening of French control. In the early years, the voices of the Ministers are heard—and they sometimes argue—but by the time of François (Henri) Baudoin,[72] the "grand old man" of the French administration, they say little. It has become a ritualized process: the Frenchman discourses—sometimes harangues—at length, occasionally a Minister makes a point, but disagreement is rare and at times the Ministers play the part of a chorus. The phrase "All the Ministers: I agree with the report" crops up repeatedly amidst thick chunks of verbatim reporting of the *Résident Supérieur's* speeches.[73]

The French tightened up the system by a series of decrees issued on 20 October 1911, which defined the powers of the *Résident Supérieur* and his consultative body, the Council of the Protectorate. (This was replaced in 1913 by an Indigenous Consultative Assembly.[74]) According to Gabriel Maurel, the 1911 decrees meant that the *Résident Supérieur's* powers were "close to absolute" in matters of law, the police, the fixing and collection of taxes, the drawing up and execution of budgets, public works and so on. Government was by royal decree, but only with the written consent of the *Résident Supérieur*. Maurel considered that "for many years, the *Résident Supérieur*...has governed the country as an absolute monarch."[75] While the consolidation of power by the French did help weed out corruption and incompetence in the Khmer bureaucracy,[76] it did not break the pattern of despotic control. European ideas of democracy stopped on the dockside at Marseilles and as a result, there was no real way for French officialdom to know what the mass of the population thought of the reform program. Indeed, few French could speak Khmer. The underlying philosophy was that the Khmer peasants were like children and their surrogate parents knew what was best for them. As a result, some of the decisions made in the early Sisowath years would come back to haunt the French, particularly the decree tightening the *corvée* requirements for the peasants in 1906.[77]

Although the French had begun a construction program in Phnom Penh in the 1890s, Cambodia was "backward in respect to public works".[78] The country lacked a regular day-labor force and so the French turned to the peasants as a reservoir of apparently docile labor. The *corvée* system required each peasant to perform a certain number of days of compulsory unpaid or very badly paid work every year—90 days by 1914[79]—on projects such as road construction. Peasant property, such as carts, boats, and beasts of burden might also be subject to requisition by the state. By late 1906, there was a comparative boom in construction work in Cambodia: new roads were under construction to link Phnom Penh with Saigon and other Cambodian towns; the Mekong was being dredged at the Quatre Bras and the Levallois-Perret engineering firm had contracted to build pontoons for the Phnom Penh wharf at a cost of 700,000 piastres.[80] Within a few years, the authorities hoped to have built over 3,300 kilometers of all-weather roads and to have completed the Phnom Penh water supply.[81] An irrigation scheme opened in Kompong Speu province in 1908 along with dikes and canals at Stung Treng, all by conscripted pick and shovel labor.[82] A number of plans were made to construct railroads, but these came to naught at this stage. More impressive was the opening of the new port of Phnom Penh to sea-going traffic in 1908.[83] By 1912, "hundreds of Chinese lighters plied their trade, along with postal launches and river steamers owned by Messageries Fluviales..." and in that year twenty-one ocean-going ships docked in the port.[84] In 1910, the French felt proud enough of their achievements to erect a monument to the architect M. Fabre, "the creator of modern Phnom Penh".[85] Bicycles and motorcycles appeared in the capital around this time[86] and in 1911 the first public bus service ran between Siem Reap and Angkor, reflecting an increase in tourism to the ruins.[87] In the same year, Sisowath was able to travel by a new road that cut across mountainous terrain to Kampot on the Gulf of Siam,[88] despite the predictions of cynics that the road would never be completed.[89] In the years immediately before World War I Phnom

Penh and the major provincial centers were connected to electricity.[90] Infectious diseases carried off thousands of victims every year, even in the towns, and the authorities turned their attention to sanitary services. In 1912, following a study tour in France by the chief engineer of the *circonscription* of Phnom Penh,[91] the city council agreed unanimously to build a sewage treatment plant and other sanitary facilities.[92]

Sisowath's visit to France and the return of the "lost provinces"

Two important events marked the first years of Sisowath's reign: a visit to France by the king in 1906, and the return of the western provinces of Battambang and Angkor to Cambodia less than one year later. Although Norodom had planned to visit France for the Universal Exposition of 1900, ill health kept him at home. Sisowath embarked on the *Amiral-Kersaint* at Saigon on 10 March 1906, accompanied by a retinue of sons, daughters, nephews, senior French and Khmer bureaucrats, some 80 members of the royal ballet, and assorted hangers-on; probably 150 persons in all, at great cost to both the French and Khmer public purses.[93]

This "traveling road show" spent six weeks in France, and almost six months traveling to and from Saigon and Marseilles. According to Virginia Thompson, the sea-voyage took much longer than usual because Sisowath insisted that the captain kept the vessel within sight of land.[94] When the steamer finally docked in Marseilles, an immense crowd swarmed over the waterfront and the flag-bedecked streets leading to the city center. Military bands played the French and Cambodian anthems, cavalry and infantry paraded, and dignitaries stepped forward to welcome the king. The crowds gawked at the squat brown man in his exotic costume, stuck with diamonds. As the *Sisowath Chronicle* suggests, the entourage gawked back at a strange world of huge buildings, locomotives, and factory chimneys belching coal smoke.

The king was reportedly "ecstatic" over the Cambodian pavilion at the Colonial Exposition in Marseilles. It was the start of what was to be a triumphal tour. Wherever he went, the king was besieged by vast crowds of well-wishers and sometimes responded by tossing large denomination coins to the street urchins. He visited Napoleon's tomb, ascended part of the way up the Eiffel Tower, banqueted with the President of the Republic in the Elysée Palace, and joined the official party on the dais at Longchamps racecourse for the annual review of troops on Bastille Day, watched by over 200,000 Parisians. Sisowath and his dancers were the darlings of high society and the masses alike.

Rodin sketched the dancers, who performed at the Colonial Exposition before tens of thousands of spectators and on the lawns of the presidential palace. Sisowath was visiting the center of a vast empire at the height of its power.

With hindsight, it is easy to see that the halcyon days of the *Belle Époque* were already foreshadowed with the war and social and economic uncertainty that marked the "age of extremes"[95] after 1914. At the time, it must have felt like an endless summer afternoon of comparative peace and prosperity. The President was in his palace, French industry and commerce were making giant strides, Paris and Marseilles were large modern cities and the tricolor waved over an empire twenty times the size of France itself, with millions of subjects and *protégés* on five continents and a myriad of islands, tropical and temperate alike. Thirty-five-years earlier, France had been humiliated by Bismarck's armies at Sedan, it is true, but the acquisition of a sprawling empire in the last decades of the 19th century must have compensated to some degree for the loss of Alsace and Lorraine to Germany. It must have tickled Sisowath's vanity to be such a popular figure in this place.

As the present author has written, "The reasons for Sisowath's immense popularity are complex. On the official level France was welcoming a vassal whose loyalty and cooperation were valuable for her cause in Indochina..." On another level, "Cambodia had assumed great importance in the popular French mind, despite or perhaps because of its small size and location on the periphery of empire. The King was a tangible symbol of an irresistibly romantic place. Much of this had to do with the posthumous publication forty years before of an account of a visit to the ruins of Angkor by Henri Mouhot and with the stirring exploits of Garnier and Doudart de Lagrée on the Mekong." Further, Sisowath held up a mirror which reflected the self-image the French craved.[96] For his part, Sisowath would have left France convinced that he had linked his destiny with that of a great power. Although in the final analysis Sisowath was a French puppet, it would seem that he had a genuine affection for France and that this governed his behavior as much as his opportunism did.

The return of Battambang and Siem Reap

Sisowath did make one diplomatic blunder during the visit when he stood up at a banquet and demanded that France should "Give me back my Alsace-Lorraine!"[97] This was a reference to the former Cambodian provinces of Battambang and Siem Reap, which had been under

Siamese control since the late eighteenth century. The French were already engaged in negotiations with Siam, and the provinces reverted to Cambodia by a treaty of 23 March 1907. Even earlier, in 1904, France had secured the return of Stung Treng and other northern districts annexed by Siam between 1810 and 1815. Although the 1907 retrocession sparked off a major revolt against French rule in Battambang and Siem Reap, it completed the restoration of Cambodian national integrity.[98] Not only were the provinces rich in rice, fish, tropical hardwoods and semi-precious stones, all of which brought in considerable export revenues, they were also home to the Angkor ruins, which were of huge symbolic importance to the Khmers and the French alike. While the French negotiators knew that they could call on superior military force if need be, the overwhelmingly Khmer ethnicity of the regions gave them a powerful moral argument. As with many frontier disputes, however, the situation was less clear-cut than it appeared on the surface. Many Khmers backed the fierce anti-French revolt of the hereditary Siamese governor, the *Phya* Kathathorn[99]— himself an ethnic Khmer—and the issue strained relations between France and Siam until 1946. The territories had enjoyed considerable autonomy under Siam, even minting their own coins. The ill-defined border regions—often swamp, jungle or mountain—had also long provided sanctuary for anti-French insurgents, including the grand rebel chieftain Si Votha.[100] The treaty sparked off celebrations in Cambodia and in 1909, Governor General Paul Beau unveiled a sandstone monument marking the retrocession on the Wat Phnom[101] overlooking the northern streets of the capital city.

The retrocession brought the educated Khmer elite, above all the King, closer to the French. It must have convinced them that collaboration was the only road for national unity and development. Sisowath's two half-brothers, Norodom and Si Votha had tried different approaches. Si Votha's great rebellion had failed, at great cost to the country. Norodom's "passive aggression" had also failed. Sisowath's way—that of a "shrewd, ambitious pragmatist"[102]—seemed to be the only realistic response at this stage and on the verge of World War I, there was genuine amity between the king and his protectors. Even the King's cataracts worked to the advantage of the French. An eminent surgeon successfully operated on Sisowath's eyes in 1912 and the population regarded it as something of a miracle.[103]

The Khmers and World War I

The First World War further cemented the pact between France and the Khmer elite. French reports express complete faith in the loyalty of the mandarins and the king.[104] Sisowath cooperated in all French projects, throwing his support behind the launch of the national war loan in 1915, of "patriotic days",[105] and a recruitment campaign for soldiers and workers the following year.[106] The text of Sisowath's declaration exhorting Khmers to volunteer for military service exactly mirrors the words of a speech made by the *Résident Supérieur* at a meeting of the Council of Ministers. He did add the rider that, "Our great age does not allow us to respond personally to the call to the defense of right and justice".[107] Given his martial background, he probably meant it and he did not spare his own family. One of the earliest and most prominent recruits was Sisowath's son Monivong, who had already received his commission in the French army after studying at the military academy of Saint-Maixent.[108] Another son, Leng Sisowath (whose mother was probably a secondary wife or concubine[109]) was killed in action in the very last days of the war after being mentioned in dispatches for gallantry.[110] Another six members of the royal family returned to Cambodia in 1920 after serving in the French forces in Europe.[111] Monivong, however, was not allowed to serve in a war zone. The ordinary people, however, did not share the elite's patriotic fervor, with one *Résident* complaining, "The events in Europe continue to leave the population completely indifferent".[112] This was reflected in the failure to meet recruitment quotas set in Hanoi. The Governor General initially requested 5000 Cambodian recruits, 3000 for the army and 2000 civilian laborers. For once, the docile mandarins of the Council Ministers demurred[113] and the French were forced to scale down their demands to two 1000-man battalions and 500 workers.[114] Even so, it proved difficult to meet quotas. Although around 2000 Cambodians did enlist,[115] and numbers of them saw action on the Western and Balkan fronts, the recruitment quotas were never filled, despite bullying tactics by the authorities.[116] The peasants reacted sullenly to this heavy-handedness and in places discontent boiled over into an active anti-recruitment agitation and desertions that helped fuel the great series of demonstrations and rural disturbances we know as the 1916 Affair. (These events are discussed in more detail in Chapter 10 below.) Huy Kanthoul doubts that those who enlisted did so for patriotic reasons. Rather, "they wished to travel, to cross the seas, see France, the marvels of which they had heard extolled so much."[117] Nevertheless, the young Khmer volunteers made good soldiers, despite the alien surroundings, the cold, and the general hellishness of the Western and Balkan fronts—and in spite of the pessimistic predictions of the French authorities. The experiences of one battalion, the 7th Indochinese, which included a number of Cambodians, will suffice to convey the flavor:

> These troops landed in Marseilles in the winter of 1916-17, when a glacial Mistral was blowing. They fought at Verdun and at St. Dié, in the eastern foothills of the Vosges on the Alsatian border. On 4 April, they left a camp at Darboussières and reached the Verdun front on the night of 15/16 of that month. Their first night in the trenches was marked by a blizzard. Towards dawn, it began to rain and they came under the bombardment of enormous guns. There, in this nightmarishly alien environment, many of them were mentioned in dispatches for heroism. Among those cited were two Cambodians, Prach-Sey and Bou, both tirailleurs of the second class...Bou...was badly wounded in the head but refused to be evacuated...[118]

Tirailleur Bou was awarded the *Croix de Guerre* for his courage[119] and Chhuy, an aviator in the new military air arm, received the same decoration.[120] The general in command of Indochinese troops on the Western Front praised his men in a letter read out the Council of Ministers in September 1917. His troops—including the Khmer 20th battalion and the partly Khmer 7th battalion—had seen a great deal of combat and had received numerous citations for bravery.[121] Their heroism inspired younger members of the elite. In 1933, while a cadet at the Saint-Cyr military academy, Sisowath's grandson Monireth traveled to the site of the great battles that had raged in the *grand ballon* region of southern Alsace. The rows of crosses and the shell-torn mountain soil inspired him to write an eight-stanza poem, "Au Cimitière de Silberloch"[122], which he dedicated to "my compatriots who died during the war of 1914-1918". The first stanza reads:

> Bloodstained clouds covered the sky,
> And under the blinding explosions of the shells
> The Hartmannswillerkopf resisted in the same way as the Alsatian spirit,
> Captured, then recaptured, martyred a hundred times,
> This soil of our ancestors was, day after day,
> Relentlessly reduced to dust by the Prussian bullet.[123]

It was not all mud and angry bullets. Old soldiers told Huy Kanthoul that French civilians gave them a warm welcome and presents of flowers and wine, and some Khmer *poilus* "flattered themselves of having conquered the heart of more than one pretty French girl."

Others had marched singing a song with the "bizarre refrain, Madelon, Madelon, Madelon!" At least some soldiers were assigned to garrison work rather than the front line and could observe European life at first hand.[124]

Fears of subversion

The ordinary Khmer people seem to have remained indifferent to the war until the end, although shortages of some goods did give them some cause to notice it. *Résident Supérieur* François Baudoin noted that the peasants, "ordinarily so apathetic and indifferent to distant events", were "relieved by the announcement of our success."[125] Perhaps they were relieved that the shortages and demands for money and recruits would end. For their part, the French were wary of the peasants, especially after 1916. They were also aware of the presence of exiled oppositionists, such as Prince Yukanthor, in Bangkok and worried that they might make common cause with returned Khmer servicemen after the war. Such fears were not unfounded. There had been armed uprisings in the Vietnamese territories during the war,[126] and returned servicemen are often restless when they return to humdrum civilian life—as is shown by the experience of the German *Freikorps* and Mussolini's *Squadristi* on the one hand, and "red veterans" elsewhere after the war. It is also true that some of the Indochinese soldiers and war workers had encountered radicals in Europe. Ton Duc Thang, president of the Democratic Republic of Vietnam after 1969 was a veteran of the Black Sea mutiny of the French fleet during the Great War.[127] Yet, while the French thought that some of the Khmer returnees had developed "ideas above their station in life",[128] and feared the radical labor movement in France might have influenced them,[129] there were no Cambodian equivalents of Ton Duc Thang. However, at least two of the volunteers, Pach Chhuon and Kim Thit, were leaders of the nationalist *Nagaravatta* ("Angkor Wat") group after 1936 and thereafter in the independence movement. Kim Thit served as a corporal in France and became Prime Minister of independent Cambodia in 1956. Pach Chhuon, like Kim Thit, served in Son Ngoc Thanh's anti-French government in 1945, after editing *Nagaravatta*.[130] There was, therefore, some impact on Khmer national consciousness, but it was not as marked as in Vietnam, and it took some time before it showed. At the conclusion of the war, as French administrative reports always stressed, Cambodia looked set to enter into an era of tranquility based on Franco-Khmer amity. An official report claims that when war hero Marshal Joffre visited in

1921, "vast crowds" turned out to greet him, even in the humblest villages,[131] although one suspects the presence of Sisowath in the cortège was a greater attraction than the foreign soldier. A visitor in the early 1920s wrote that Sisowath was "a very docile and good king...[who] might almost be a Frenchman."[132] When the authorities opened a huge bronze war memorial in Phnom Penh in 1925 (designed by the sculptor Ducuing) speakers claimed that the war had "sealed in blood" the friendship between Gaul and Khmer.[133] The monument honored the names of 50 Khmers who had perished in the war, including Prince Leng Sisowath.[134] Clearly, many of these soldiers had entertained a genuine affection for France. Yet, how deep did this amity run, once one left the elite circles of Phnom Penh and the other large towns? We will turn to this question in the next chapter.

Notes

[1] Stella Benson, (1925), *The Little World: travels in the US and Asia*, London, p.303.

[2] Norodom Sihanouk, (1972), *L'Indochine vue de Pékin*, Éditions du Seuil, Paris, p.27.

[3] AOM, RSC 426 Rapport sur la situation entre 1902 et 1907, 21 August 1907.

[4] Adhémard Léclère, (1914), *Histoire du Cambodge depuis le 1er Siècle de notre era: d'après les inscriptions lapidaires, les annales chinoises et annamites et les documents européens des six derniers siècles*, Librairie Paul Geuthner, Paris, p.467. See also AOM RSC 426, op.cit.

[5] H.W. Ponder, (1936), *Cambodian Glory. The mystery of the deserted Khmer cities and their vanished splendour; and a description of life in Cambodia today*, Thornton Butterworth, London, p.271.

[6] Milton Osborne, (1969), *The French Presence in Cochinchina and Cambodia. Rule and Response (1859-1905)*, Cornell University Press, Ithaca, New York, pp.177-178.

[7] ANC RSC D35 File 2970, Box 333, Rapport du Conseil Supérieur de l'Indochine, Session Ordinaire de 1904, Nr.9. Also AOM RSC 257, Rapport sur la situation du Cambodge, (octobre 1903-juillet 1904).

[8] AOM RSC 426, Rapport sur la situation entre 1902 et 1907, by Paul Luce.

[9] For an account of the "1916 Affair", see Chapters 9 and 10 below.

[10] AOM RSC 485. A clipping, probably from *La Dépêche*, undated, includes an article by Henri Lamagat entitled "La vie intime de SM Monivong, prince royal et souverain". This refers to Prince Mayura leading a revolt in Kompong Chhnang province, apparently in the last years of the 19th century. Another account holds that Mayura conspired with the Governor of Siamese-controlled Battambang and was condemned to death in 1897. The sentence was commuted to life imprisonment. (Justin J. Corfield, (1990), *The Royal Family of Cambodia*, Khmer Language and Culture Centre, Melbourne, p.18.) Mayura was released early. (See below, Chapter 9.)

[11] ANC RSC D35, File 2970, Box 333, Rapport du Conseil Supérieur de l'Indochine, Session Ordinaire de 1904, Nr. 9. AOM RSC 257. Rapport sur la situation du Cambodge (octobre 1903-juillet 1904).

[12] AOM RSC 426. Rapport sur la situation entre 1902 et 1907. Rural disturbances are discussed in Chapter 9 below.

[13] See, John Tully, (1996), *Cambodia Under the Tricolour. King Sisowath and the "Mission Civilisatrice, 1904-1927*, Monash Papers on Asia No.27, Monash Asia Institute, Clayton, Vic. p.32n.

[14] AOM RSC 426, Rapport sur la situation entre 1902 et 1907, 21 August 1907.

[15] *Sisowath Chronicle*, pp.1011-1020. (Microfilm in Khmer loaned by David Chandler.)

[16] Unsigned, (1906), *Le Temps*, Paris, 20 June.

[17] Sir Hugh Clifford, (1910), "In Kambodia", (*sic*), *Blackwood's Magazine*, CLXXXVII, June, London, p.786.

[18] Roland Meyer, (1922), *Saramani Danseuse Cambodgienne*, E. Fasquelle, Paris, p.92.

[19] Corfield, op.cit. p.24. The *Bulletin de l'École Française d'Extrême-Orient* (*BEFEO*) (Tome XXVII, p.519) gives Bangkok as his birthplace.

[20] Ibid. (Corfield).

[21] *BEFEO*, op.cit.

[22] Osborne, op.cit., p.179-180.

[23] Louis de Carné, (1872), *Travels in Indo-China and the Chinese Empire*, Chapman and Hill, London, p.15.

[24] ANC RSC F451 File 24216. Conseil des Ministres, 36e séance du 3 novembre 1900. Letter from Sisowath to the *Résident Supérieur,* 17 November 1900. The *Obbareach* was the heir presumptive, the *Prea-Keo-Fea,* favored son.

[25] De Carné, op.cit. p.6 claims that Ang Duong conferred the title (and that bestowed on Sisowath), but if this is so, it was only by permission of the Siamese.

[26] ANC RSC F451, File 24217, letter from Sisowath to the *Résident Supérieur,* 17 November 1900.

[27] De Carné, op.cit.

[28] Moura, op.cit.

[29] BEFEO Tome XXVII, op.cit.; Jean Moura, (1883), *Le Royaume du Cambodge*, Vol. II Ernest Leroux, Librairie de la Société Asiatique de l'École des Langues Orientales Vivantes, Paris, p.171; Osborne, op. cit. p.188; V.M. Reddi, (1970), *A History of the Cambodian Independence Movement, 1863-1955*, Sri Venkateswara University Press, Tiraputi, pp36-37.

[30] ANC RSC F451, File 24217, Sisowath letter, op.cit.

[31] Moura, op.cit. p.172.

[32] AOM INDO AF 11 A30 (12) De Lagrandière to the Minister of Marine, 29 April 1867.

[33] AOM INDO AF 13. Dossier A30 (22). Cambodge 1874-1875. Rapport Confidentiel sur le Cambodge, 24 August 1874.

[34] Cited in Osborne, op.cit., p.193.

[35] AOM INDO AF Carton A30 Dossier 26. J Moura to Admiral Duperré, Governor of Cochin China, 13 May 1875.

[36] Lt. Batz, (1931), "Conference fait par Lt Batz", *Bulletin de la Société des Études Indochinoises*, Vol. 6, Saigon.

[37] AOM Indochine AF Carton 6, A20 (32). Rapport Trimestriel, January 1891, signed H. De Vernéville.

[38] AOM RSC 256, Letter from the Governor at Saigon to the French *Résident* at Phnom Penh, 12 September 1884.

[39] AOM Indochine AF Carton 18, Dossier A30 (68) Meurtre d'une jeune fille. Complicité du fils du 2ème roi, 1884.

[40] A family tree prepared by the Cambodian historian Sorn Samnang shows Sisowath's male offspring as Essaravong, Monivong, Duong Lakhan, Khanarak, Souphanvuong and Vongkat. Sorn Samnang, (1995), "L'évolution de la société cambodgienne entre les deux guerres mondiales (1919-1939)." Thèse pour le doctorat d'histoire. Université Paris VII. Tome I, p.102. (These were the sons of his "principal" wives only and he would have had more with "lesser wives and concubines.) It would seem that Nuppakau lived in disgrace thereafter.

[41] He is listed as one of Sisowath's sons in Council of Ministers minutes regarding taxation in 1899. (ANC RSC F451 File 24210, Conseil des Ministres, 30e séance du 8 novembre 1899.)

[42] AOM RSC 439. Ministre du Palais Royale, 10 December 1919.

[43] AOM Indochine NF Dossier 581, Carton 48. Dépêche Télégraphique, *Gougal* à Paris, 11 May 1904.

[44] AOM RSC 257 Rapports Politiques 1897-1906. Paul Luce to *Gougal*, 23 January 1906.

[45] Gabriel Pierre Auguste Maurel was a highly qualified administrator. He held a doctorate in law. (See ANC RSC C 01 File 15292, Fiches personelles du personnel européen du protectorate avant 1912.) Maurel feuded with the dictatorial *Résident Supérieur* François (Henri) Baudoin in the early 1920s. (See ANC RSC D45 File 13013 Box 1090. Affaire Maurel, 1926.)

[46] ANC RSC D.03 File 13014 Box 1090. Rapport générale et critique de l'administration du Protectorat, par la section cambodgienne de la Ligue des Droits de l'Homme et des Citoyens à Pnompenh au Comité central de la Ligue...à Paris. My photocopy of the report has "1926?" penciled in the top margin. M. Maurel had an axe to grind, particularly with Baudoin, but the report has the ring of truth to it.

[47] Paul Luce attributed this to Norodom's illness. (AOM RSC 426, Rapport sur la situation entre 1902 et 1907.) This might have been a factor, but one suspects that Norodom was dragging his feet to spite the French.

[48] Ibid.

[49] Rapport sur la situation entre 1902 et 1907, op.cit.

[50] ANC RSC D35. File 2975. Box 333. Rapport sur la situation du Cambodge au mois de septembre 1905.
[51] Moura, op.cit. Vol. I, p.281. See also L. Nicolas, (1943), "L'organisation de la justice Cambodgienne", *La Revue Indochinoise Juridique et Économique,* [Kraus Reprint, Neudeln, Liechtenstein, 1970] No 21, pp1-68.
[52] Ibid (Nicolas) p.8.
[53] Adolphe Belot, (1889), *500 femmes pour un homme,* (seizième édition), E. Dentu, Paris, pp. 80-88.
[54] ANC RSC F451 File 24281, Conseil des Ministres, 101e séance du 20 mai 1904.
[55] Paul Branda , (1892), *Ça et La. Cochinchine et Cambodge. L'Âme Khmère. Ang-Kor,* Librairie Fischbacher, Paris, pp.255-256. Lest we become too smug, we should recall that public execution was common in the west until well into the 19th century. Indeed, there are widespread demands in the USA today that it be televised.
[56] ANC RSC D35 File 2970 Box 333, Rapport du Conseil Supérieur de l'Indochine. Session ordinaire de 1904, Nr.9.
[57] AOM RSC 258 Rapport sur la situation du Cambodge (October 1903-July 1904).
[58] The reforms were earlier approved by the Council of Ministers. (ANC F451 File 24294, Conseil des Ministres, 114e séance du 27 mai 1905.) Doubtless, they were first proposed by the French.
[59] Almost 100 years later, in the year 2000, a three-year-old refugee child was put in leg irons in Australia's Woomera detention camp; a stark reminder of the deep-rootedness of barbarism and a reminder that no people have a monopoly on it.
[60] ANC RSC D23 File 3563 Box 421. Conseil Supérieur de l'Indochine. Session ordinaire de 1905. Situation politique, économique et financière du Cambodge. The "humane" method was probably the guillotine.
[61] ANC RSC D35 File 2975. Box 333. Conseil Supérieur de l'Indochine. Session ordinaire 1906. Situation politique, économique et financière du Cambodge.
[62] ANC RSC D35 File 16958 Box 1517. Situation politique, économique et financière du Cambodge. Rapport à Conseil Supérièure de l'Indochine, 1910.
[63] AOM RSC 429. Conseil de gouvernement de l'Indochine. Session Ordinaire de 1912. Situation politique, économique et financière du Cambodge.
[64] See Chapter 14 below.
[65] ANC RSC D35. File 2970, Box 333, Conseil Supérièure de l'Indochine, op.cit.
[66] AOM RSC 426. Rapport sur la situation entre 1902 et 1907. The minutes of the Council of Ministres for 11 and 25 March 1905 also deal with the matter. (ANC RSC 451 File 24291 Conseil des Ministres, 111e séance du 11 mars 1905 and File 24292, 112e séance du 25 mars 1905.)
[67] ANC RSC D35. File No. 3033, Box 341. Conseil Supérièure de l'Indochine. Session ordinaire de 1908.

[68] Ibid.

[69] AOM RSC 429, Conseil Supérieur de l'Indochine. Session ordinaire de 1911.

[70] Set up by decree on 20 August 1903. See AOM RSC 257. Rapport sur la situation du Cambodge (octobre 1903-juillet 1904).

[71] See, for example, ANC RSC E3. File 4746 Box 498, Procès verbaux des séances du Conseil de Résidence de Kg. Chhnang, 1905-1924; RSC E3 File 4249 Box 476, Conseil de Résidence de Prey Veng, 1904-1924. The latter years of the Prey Veng file are interesting as they give us a glimpse of the authoritarian style of the unfortunate Bardez. See Chapter 15 below.

[72] Baudoin's given name was François, but he was commonly known as Henri in Cambodia, as can be seen on the plaque commemorating the opening of the *Musée* Albert Sarraut—today the National Museum—in Phnom Penh.

[73] The Archives Nationales du Cambodge at Phnom Penh hold a collection of the minutes of the Council from 1897 until 1937, with some lacunae: ANC RSC F451.

[74] AOM RSC 428 Rapports politiques, deuxième et troisième semestres 1913.

[75] Rapport générale et critique de l'administration du Protectorat, par la section cambodgienne de la Ligue des Droits de l'Homme et des Citoyens, op.cit.

[76] See, for instance, Tully, op.cit. pp. 52-54, "Files 'at the mercy of the first gust of wind'" for a discussion of these matters.

[77] ANC RSC D35 File 2975 Box 333, Rapport politique et économique, Novembre-Décembre 1906, 3 February 1907. The questions of taxation and *corvée* are dealt with in detail in Chapters 9, 10 and 15 below.

[78] ANC RSCD23 File 3563 Box 421. Conseil Supérieur de l'Indochine. Session ordinaire de 1905, op.cit.

[79] Tully, op.cit. p.159.

[80] ANC RSC D23 File 3563 Box 421. Plan de campagne pour travaux publics à executer en 1906.

[81] AOM RSC 426, Rapport politique et économique, mai-juin 1907.

[82] ANC RSC D35 File 3033 Box 341. Conseil Supérieur de l'Indochine. Session ordinaire de 1908.

[83] Unsigned, (1908), "Ouverture du port de Phnom-Penh à la navigation maritime", *La Quinzaine Coloniale*, premier semestre, pp.145-146.

[84] Unsigned, (1913), "Le mouvement du port de Phnom Penh en 1912", *Bulletin Économique de l'Indochine*, Nr.101, ns, p.254.

[85] AOM RSC 428. Rapport politique et économique, troisième semestre 1910.

[86] Unsigned, (1912), *La Quinzaine Coloniale*, 10 Mai.

[87] Unsigned, (1911), "Siemréap-Ankor-automobile", *L'Impartial de Phnom-Penh*, 11 November, p.2

[88] AOM RSC 428. Rapport Politique et économique, première trimestre 1911.

[89] Clifford, op.cit.

[90] AOM RSC 429. Rapport politique et économique, première trimestre 1912.

[91] Unsigned, (1912), "Assainissement de la ville de Pnom-Penh", *La Quinzaine Coloniale*, deuxième semestre, 10 Septembre, p.625.

[92] AOM RSC 429. Conseil de gouvernment de l'Indochine, session ordinaire de 1912. See Chapter 12 below for a discussion of public health and sanitation in Cambodia.

[93] AOM RSC 426. Rapports politiques et économiques, 1902-1907; Unsigned, (1906), "Le roi du Cambodge à Paris", *Le Temps*, Paris, 20 juin; *Bulletin Administratif du Cambodge*, 1906; Georges Bois, (1913), "Les danseuses cambodgiennes en France", *Revue Indochinoise*, Hanoi, deuxième semestre, pp.261-277. For a detailed account of the royal visit, see Tully, op.cit. pp.1-23. The following account draws heavily on that work.

[94] Bois, op.cit. Also Virginia Thompson, (1968), *French Indochina*, Octagon Books, New York, p.359.

[95] The phrase is the title of the book by Eric Hobsbawm, (1995*), Age of Extremes. The Short Twentieth Century, 1914-1991*, Abacus, London.

[96] Tully, op.cit. pp.20, 21,23.

[97] Unsigned, (1906), *Pall Mall Gazette*, London, 15 June, and Unsigned, (1906), *Marseille Republicain*, 16 June.

[98] There are still some hundreds of thousands of ethnic Khmers in the Mekong delta region of Vietnam and north of the Dangreks in modern day Thailand.

[99] Kathathorn left command of the revolt to a subordinate, the *Visès* Nheou.

[100] For a detailed account of the revolt and the negotiations leading up to the retrocession, see Tully, op.cit., Chapters Three and Four. The Franco-Siamese war and the provinces' occupation during World War II is discussed in Chapter 22 below.

[101] *Phnom* is Khmer for hill or mountain.

[102] Tully, op.cit. p.38.

[103] *Sisowath Chronicle*, pp.1151-1160; RSC 429, Rapports politiques deuxième et troisième trimestres, 1912.

[104] AOM RSC 430, Rapport politique, troisième semestre, 1914, 20 octobre.

[105] AOM Rapport politique, troisième semestre 1917.

[106] Tully, op.cit. pp.168-173.

[107] ANC RSC F451 File 22418, Conseil des Ministres, 238 séance du 20 janvier 1916.

[108] Tully, op.cit. p.171.

[109] I surmise this because although Leng's death is recorded in the *Sisowath Chronicle*, there is no record of any private grief, or of public mourning.

[110] CMIDOM, 15 H 136. Ordre de Bataillon, Nr. 28, 14 juillet 1918. See also the *Sisowath Chronicle*, pp.1171-1180.

[111] AOM RSC 431 Rapport politique, 1er Trimestre 1920.

[112] AOM RSC 364. Rapport politique 15 mars-15 juin 1915 (Kandal).

[113] ANC RSC F451 File 24417, Conseil des Ministres, 237e séance du 17 janvier 1916.

[114] ANC RSC F451 File 22418, Conseil des Ministres, 238 séance du 20 janvier 1916.

[115] Tully, op.cit. p.170.

[116] Ibid. pp.174-175.

[117] Huy Kanthoul, "Mémoires", unpublished French-language typescript, p.47. (Chandler Papers, Monash University.)

[118] Tully, op.cit. pp. 181-182. The Mistral is a cold, blustery wind that blows off the Alps in southern France. *Tirailleurs* were riflemen or light infantrymen.

[119] Ibid.

[120] AOM Fonds Amiraux FO 3 64267, Rapport politique, première trimestre 1923.

[121] ANC RSC 451 File 24466 Conseil des Ministres, 286e séance du 13 septembre 1917.

[122] "At the Silberloch Cemetery".

[123] Translation by Gina Zajusch. The poem was printed as "Au Cimitière de Sibertoch" *[sic]* in *L'Echo du Cambodge* of Phnom Penh on Tuesday 18 September 1934. Hartmannswillerkopf is the Alsatian name for a peak just east of Thann in southern Alsace and is known in French as Vieil Armand. "Sibertoch" is a Gallic corruption of the feature called the pass of Silberloch— Silver Cave—where a memorial chapel and cemetery still stand today. I have corrected Monireth's spelling from "Hartmannswillerkolp". See *Pages d'Histoire – 1914-1915. L'Atlas-Index de tous les théâtres de la guerre*, published by Ibis, Berger-Levrault, Paris et Nancy in 1915. See also, for example, Ian Robertson, (1984), *Blue Guide. France*, Ernest Benn, London.

[124] Huy Kanthoul, op.cit. p.46.

[125] AOM RSC 431, Rapport politique, troisième semestre, 12 octobre 1918.

[126] See Joseph Buttinger, (1967), *Vietnam: A Dragon Embattled*, Vol. I. *From Colonialism to the Vietminh*, Frederick A. Praeger, New York, pp.152-153; and Buttinger, (1958*), The Smaller Dragon. A Political History of Vietnam*, Frederick A. Praeger, New York, p. 433.

[127] See, for example, Pierre Rousset, (1975*), Le Parti Communiste Vietnamien. Contribution à la étude de la révolution vietnamienne*, (seconde edition), Maspéro, Paris, p.41n.

[128] AOM RSC 244. Extrait du rapport de l'Inspecteur Labbe..." 4 avril 1921.

[129] AOM RSC 431 Rapport Politique 3ème Trimestre 1919.

[130] See, for example, Reddi, op. cit. pp.iii, 67, 72n and 100. See also Martin Herz, (1958), *A Short History of Cambodia from the days of Angkor to the present*, London, p.64.

[131] AOM Fonds Amiraux FO 3 64 265. Rapport politique et économique, 4ème trimestre 1921.

[132] Stella Benson, op.cit.

[133] (1925), *L'Echo du Cambodge*, Phnom Penh, 28 February and 3 March. See also AOM RSC 319, 432 and 10. The *Khmers Rouges* destroyed the monument, which was designed by the sculptor Ducuing. The stone base of the monument and some statures of elephants did however survive. These can be seen in the forecourt of the National Museum in Phnom Penh. Huy Kanthoul observed "an exact replica" of the monument at Chambéry in Savoy. (Huy Kanthoul, op.cit. p.46.)

[134] *L'Echo du Cambodge*, Phnom Penh, 3 March 1925.

Chapter 9

Patterns of Rural Violence and Resistance

The Cambodian is like a buffalo, placid, yet terrible if exasperated.
> —King Norodom.[1]

Civilization has made the peasantry its pack animal.
> —Leon Trotsky.[2]

In early 1916, while France's attentions were concentrated on the bloody stalemate of the Great War, an extraordinary movement of social protest erupted on the streets of Phnom Penh and throughout the villages of the kingdom. The central aim of the movement was the amelioration of what the peasants saw as harsh taxes and unreasonable demands for *corvée* labor. "Robust" methods of recruitment for the war effort and official corruption were added irritants. The French estimated that up to 100,000 peasants trekked to Phnom Penh to present their demands to King Sisowath. Although the movement has retained the name the French gave it—the "1916 Affair"[3]—the blandness of this term belittles its significance. In many cases, the marchers thrust aside local Khmer officials who tried to stop them from leaving. There were instances of attacks on Cambodian government posts and reports of demonstrations, occasionally violent, against the French themselves. One *Résident* claimed the turbulence amounted to insurrection in his district[4] and although *Résident*

Supérieur François Baudoin belittled the claim, it was not complete hyperbole.[5] Huy Kanthoul, whose father was a Khmer governor in Kompong Cham during the period, claims that "revolt" broke out "against the French administration" in that province.[6] Baudoin's response was two-pronged. He did not shrink from using lethal force and jailed the "ringleaders". One report claimed that troops used machine guns to disperse recalcitrants[7] and whatever the truth of this, there were a number of deaths. On the other hand, Baudoin conceded many of the protestors' demands: a case of the iron behind the velvet.

1916 embedded in a wider tradition of unrest

The facts of the Affair suggest the existence of some kind of organization. The marchers came from across the kingdom and could not have known each other. The demands they made varied little, if at all, from district to district, and the protests unfolded with remarkable synchronicity. Although Baudoin later downplayed the scope and significance of the movement, the initial French response was one of bewilderment and fear, bordering at times on panic. The French power in Indochina was vulnerable, with many personnel serving in the armed forces in Europe. Baudoin understandably wanted to re-assure his superiors in Hanoi and France that he had matters under control, but the incident raised worrying questions for French power. How welcome were the French in Cambodia? How much did the French really know about their *protégés*? The historian, too, must ask to what extent was the Affair an isolated incident, or a temporary aberration. This chapter will argue that the Affair was embedded in a wider tradition of quasi-political agrarian dissidence. The 1916 Affair and the later well-known murder of *Résident* Bardez in 1925 were merely the most striking manifestations of rural unrest.[8]

While it is true that some French officials learned Khmer and studied the culture, much of what went on in the villages remained unknown to the administration. Those Khmers with whom the officials came into regular contact tended to come from the elite, and were thus unrepresentative of the people as a whole. Official French reports from throughout the period of the protectorate often reveal a curious mixture of complacency and fear of the ordinary people. Local *Résidents* were anxious to reassure their superiors in Hanoi or Phnom Penh of the passivity and goodwill of the "natives", yet the slightest "effervescence" invoked the lurking specter of the Great Rebellion of 1885. These fears were not without substance.

There is considerable evidence to show that by the turn of the 19th century, the Khmer elite—mandarins, nobles and members of the royal family—had developed a strong loyalty to France. Although some embittered members of the Norodom wing of the royal family formed a small nucleus of discontent, many of the elite had earlier thrown in their lot with the French. A group of mandarins around Prime Minister Um and Palace Minister Thiounn had begun openly to side with the French against the king in the last years of Norodom's rule. Sisowath and his heir, Monivong, shared a common francophilia with Thiounn and many Norodom princes served loyally in the administration after 1904. It is difficult, however, to know what the Khmer peasants and town poor thought of the French; whether they hated foreign colonization and dreamed of independence, or whether they were merely indifferent to the French presence and to politics as a whole. Cambodian society was largely pre-literate, and there were daunting barriers of language and culture between the peasants and the French. A scholar such as Suzanne Karpelès, who spoke the Khmer dialects, was something of a nonpareil in French circles. Much of the information about the attitudes of the ordinary Khmers to the French is either ambiguous, or a case of taking one's wishes for reality. Khmer culture had traditionally stressed resignation to Fate and obedience to Authority, but revolts, nevertheless, regularly recurred. The peasants were certainly aware of the white rulers, even though some of them, particularly in the more remote regions, might never have encountered a French person. A Cambodian official told a foreign correspondent in 1945 that, "There was no colour feeling among Cambodians...we have always worked happily with the whites... no matter what other people in Indo-China may think about it."[9] This claim, however, was made by a member of the elite and might have been deliberately diplomatic. Evidence from European sources about Khmer attitudes to the French is contradictory. The English traveler Harry Hervey observed that Khmers would lapse into silence when Europeans drew near.[10] Whether this was due to bashfulness, wariness, or hostility, he does not say. Another foreign visitor claimed that a young French official was nervous about accompanying him to Angkor in 1933 because "the attitude of the natives to us French officials at the moment is very uncertain."[11] The French themselves eagerly seized upon the slightest sign that might indicate the ordinary people liked them. A Vichy journalist wrote in 1941 that, "the Khmer bards don't hesitate to recognize the immense works accomplished by France in their country"[12], citing as evidence a 1921 translation of "Barang Srao Pua", a Khmer fishermen's song from the Tonlé Sap. The song, however, is gently ironic and humorous, qualities not always readily apparent to servants of dictatorship:

> The French pull the ropes
> As far as they can in the kingdom.
> The French come to protect
> Our peaceful country.
> The French pull the ropes
> At the end of the sampan...
> Oh my master
> You have come, it means happiness.
> We have roads on which to walk.
> Even old people are happy,
> Young ones too.
> We have roads where we can walk,
> Without the trouble of walking in water.[13]

French officials often reported the "loyalty" of the peasants, but perhaps the American travel writer Harry Franck was closer to the mark when he claimed that, "In the eyes of the Cambodians the French are merely a passing phase...and they endure this brief affliction as true fatalists do any other misfortune."[14] Peasants have always endured "warts and boils and governments." The French tended to view the Khmers as children, but the peasants were more knowledgeable and sophisticated than they believed. Endurance is not synonymous with consent. Literacy, too, is not a prerequisite for communication. In 1907, the French discovered that peasants in Prey Veng and Kompong Thom hoped that Japan might come to the assistance of rebels to oust the French,[15] which indicates that news of the recent Japanese victory over Russia—of Asians over Europeans—had percolated down to village level. Such rumors, sensational or not, clearly disturbed the French as they indicated an awareness of the world beyond family, *wat* and village.[16]

There is evidence that the "ordinary" Khmers resented the French presence and were willing to follow their leaders against it when the opportunity arose. Huy Kanthoul remembers that the children of his village often played a game of "patriots" versus the French, armed with toy bamboo rifles, much as small boys elsewhere play Cowboys and Indians. "The remembrance of Siwotha, of Poucombo, of the Achar Sva, of Snang Sor, celebrated warriors who had fought the French soldiers, stayed very much alive in everyone's memories," he recalls.[17] The Great Rebellion of 1885 could not have happened without widespread support from both the elites and the ordinary people. Even after Sisowath's ascension to the throne, rural disorders—often with a pronounced anti-French and/or anti-dynastic tinge—were common, although the authorities subsumed many of them under the rubric of banditry in their reports. Yet, as in many other peasant countries, there was no sharp discontinuity between banditry and politics.

Banditry was in fact ubiquitous in Cambodia. As *La Presse Indochinoise* noted in early 1939, it was the product of social conditions in the countryside.[18] In many respects, Cambodian rural society was static, with little cultural, political, economic or technological change. The peasants' relation to the soil and the monarchy had altered little over the centuries. Yet, this does not necessarily imply there was social equilibrium in the villages. Not even the Buddhist doctrines of obedience could prevent social conditions from breeding dissatisfaction. Cambodia's soil was abundant and fertile—at least in the alluvial plains at the center of the kingdom—but cultural patterns and idiosyncratic Khmer "feudalism" did not encourage improvement of the fields and paddies. Unlike their Vietnamese neighbors, the peasants viewed fertilization of the soil with human or animal manure with abhorrence. Overall, they practiced what one generally sympathetic—even at times willfully blind— observer called a crude and wasteful method of rice cultivation.[19] The Khmers had practiced irrigation on a large scale in Angkorean times, but they later abandoned it; perhaps because the large bodies of stagnant or extremely slow moving *baray* water provided a habitat for malarial mosquitoes, perhaps because it caused soil salting. By the standards of thrifty French *paysans* or Vietnamese rice farmers, the Khmer peasants were remarkably improvident. They put little by for bad seasons, a consequence both of religious-based fatalism and the existence of discouraging revenue system that taxed produce, tools, equipment and utensils, not the land itself. Trade, too, was a more or less "noxious" activity and much of it was in Vietnamese or Chinese hands. The Cambodian businessman was a "rare bird", as one French journalist put it.[20] Writers in the Khmer-language press agreed, notably in the journal *Kampuchea*, which often discussed the need for the Khmers to become more entrepreneurially minded, and railed against "laziness".[21]

Nature exacerbated the resulting poverty. Although some French observers believed that any seed thrown willy-nilly upon the earth would germinate, in reality Nature was not so benevolent. Although plants do thrive in the rich earth, the peasants were always at the mercy of the weather, which could be capricious and not all the land was fertile. The populous parts of the country lie in a great flat bowl of low lying alluvial land, centered on Lake Tonlé Sap and drained by the Mekong. This great river was both a giver and taker of life. Vast floods frequently swept downstream, with disastrous results for the farmers. Often, with a cruel irony, the ebb of the waters only heralded crippling drought and epidemics of disease. In 1904, for example, a spectacular flood inundated almost the entire central plain for some two months. The *Résident* of Kompong Cham estimated a loss of 430,000 *piculs* of rice, or two-thirds of the province's entire crop, along with huge losses of fruit trees. Enormous quantities of topsoil were lost to erosion and the current swept away great numbers of livestock. Whole villages in Takeo province decamped to the high plateaus, the peasants preferring the forest demons to the "vast sheet of water" that covered their fields. Afterwards, there came a terrible heat and drought to shrivel those crops the waters had spared.[22] Over 30 years later, in 1937, another huge flood poured down the Mekong, submerging most of Kandal and Kompong Cham provinces. French officials noted the submersion of over 76,000 hectares of prime land for long enough to destroy all of the crops. The peasants' houses, fruit trees and kitchen gardens were "devastated". The *Résident* of Prey Veng estimated a yield of barely three-tenths of the normal rice crop. Again, severe drought followed the retreating floods.[23]

The human effects of these natural calamities were striking. A Saigon newspaper reported in 1923 the continuing presence in that city of "long lines of Cambodian beggars who seem devoid of all resources and who are practically naked". These poor wretches had walked the hundred or so miles from the parrot's beak of Svay Rieng province, "where misery is very great and where they cannot live".[24] At the height of the Great Depression, the destitute peasants who flooded into Phnom Penh to beg were described as "the plague of the streets" and as a "running sore" by a French journalist [25] and could end up in prison for "vagabondage".[26] The peasants were often reluctant to take up wage labor, but a spate of natural disasters throughout 1905 in Takeo forced many to labor as "coolies" in the pepper plantations. Others went into the forests to subsist on "wild food".[27] Throughout Cambodia, other villagers preferred to take what they lacked by force of arms, rather than beg for alms. Arming themselves with a collection of ancient flintlocks, machetes, the odd Mauser stolen from the militia, cutlasses, and even homemade bamboo muskets that were likely to explode in the firers' hands,[28] they would prey on travelers. These epidemics of banditry fluctuated with the cycle of good and poor harvests, and the French were never able to bring them under control.

Some of the bandits were well-armed professionals, making a living from rustling livestock, particularly on the Siamese border, some may have been young men thirsting for more excitement than could be found behind a plow, but a much greater number were amateurs, driven to banditry by episodic distress. Their victims were usually other peasants, although Chinese merchants were always tempting targets. Sometimes they attacked Khmer officials and much less frequently, French settlers or officials. It would be wrong to romanticize the bandits. The results of their raids on Khmer villages were often horrific. When Huy Kanthoul was a young child, he accidentally stumbled on a bloodstained cart, around which were a number of severed heads, the aftermath of a clash between bandits and villagers.[29]

French reprisals after attacks on their own

Attacks on the French always resulted in much more energetic reprisals than did criminal violence against "natives". Between 1900 and the celebrated quasi-political murder of *Résident* Bardez in 1925, there were half a dozen other fatal attacks on Frenchmen, and a number of other serious non-lethal assaults (exclusive of casualties from the long-running pacification drives against the *Montagnard* tribes[30]). Each murder sparked off a massive police operation. The murder of the Angkor curator, Jean Commaille, in 1916, for example, led to a veritable dragnet in the surrounding countryside. (Commaille was killed for the payroll for laborers working on restoration of the Terrace of the Elephants.) The French executed the murderers and threw scores of their real and alleged accomplices into prison cells. The militia evicted the entire population of a nearby village and burned down their homes in an act of savage overkill that would have drawn gasps of outrage if committed against peasants in Metropolitan France.[31] Other French murder victims included M. Prugna, a brutal French customs agent, killed in 1903 on the Battambang frontier[32] and Charles Michelon, an ex-soldier shot to death in 1909 on his way to Cochinchina from the horse stud where he worked as an accountant.[33] In 1913, during an exceptionally volatile period of rural unrest, there were ferocious, although non-fatal attacks on three more French citizens: MM. Castelin, a military officer, Canavy, a settler, and R.P. David, a priest.[34] These three attacks had a distinctly quasi-political flavor. Another settler, the brutal M. Thomas, was murdered in 1918 and M. Duclos, the commander of the *Garde Indigène* in Stung Treng, was slain in 1919, by a Khmer corporal, but both were cases of personal revenge.[35]

Distress and banditry

The rural distress that bred banditry and other forms of rural revolt resulted partly from social, and partly from natural causes. The French were well aware of the relation between poor harvests and banditry, although this was not automatic. A report prepared for the *Résident Supérieur* in 1905, for example, noted an upsurge of brigandage in Takeo province following drought, flood and a typhoon.[36] There were poor harvests in many areas of the country in 1911 and 1912, combined with a general economic downturn. Initially, it seemed the countryside seemed calm, despite the "extreme misery" of the population, but by September, there was a "disturbing recrudescence" of banditry in all parts of the country. The "timid" ate wild roots from the forests, but "the most resolute" swelled the bands of brigands. In a three-month period in Prey Veng in the same year, there were over 100 reported cases of banditry. In Takeo, there was "great insecurity", with junks pillaged. Bandits burned down government offices and killed Khmer functionaries in a number of provinces. Annamite bandits wounded two French customs agents at a post on the Bassac River. By the end of the year, a measure of prosperity had returned, and with it a relative calm, except for in the "bandit heartlands" of Prey Veng. The calm was only temporary. During the following year, 1913, a great wave of banditry rolled across the countryside, with some 1500 arrests between January and May, and a number of executions.[37] As we shall see, much of this latter disorder had a political tinge. Similarly, the period of poor harvests and economic crisis that immediately followed the end of World War I saw a sharp rise in banditry.[38] As can be expected, the harsh economic climate of the 1930s, combined with unfavorable weather patterns, bred widespread brigandage. As a result, during 1930, before the worst of the Great Depression, but during a period of big floods, the daily average prison population in Prey Veng province alone never fell below 100 and at times was almost twice that number.[39] As the full effect of the depression was felt, the countryside sank into a state of constant pillage. In Siem Reap province between mid-1932 and mid-1933, for example, there were 183 acts of plunder by armed bands (some of them involving between 20-30 individuals, well-armed with Siamese rifles); 13 murders; and 55 cases of rustling involving 846 beasts. Bands destroyed the Cambodian government offices at Anlong Veng, robbed Vietnamese shops at Angkor Wat and murdered a number of officials, forcing the French to send reinforcements for the local militia.[40] During the same period in Battambang province, there were 88 acts of banditry; 128 arrests; and 15 bandits killed, along with one militiaman, Sergeant Rem.[41] In Kompong Cham, the number of acts of banditry increased steady from 102 in 1929-30, to 163 in 1930-31, to 252 in 1931-32, with a fall to 231 in 1932-33. The latter fall was probably due to vigorous police action.[42] There were reports of tranquility in the Great Lake region throughout 1935, due to the efforts of mobile police brigades.[43] However, neither the best efforts of the police, nor the gradual improvement in economic conditions after the mid-1930s could eradicate what was an ingrained social problem. In a speech in 1938, M. Marinetti, the *député* for Cambodia and Cochinchina in the French parliament, said that the problem was inherent in the extreme economic insecurity of the countryside.[44]

Social bandits

If this were the case—and the preceding overview indicates that we may fairly take M. Marinetti's word for it—then this begs the question of the effects of French policy on the countryside. Banditry certainly existed before the arrival of the French in 1863, and it was endemic over the border in the independent kingdom of Siam[45] but the question remains as to whether the French had done anything to ameliorate the conditions that caused the problem. We must also ask to what extent the phenomenon was a reaction to French policies; and in particular to taxation and *corvée*, because at least some of the banditry appears to have been of a "social" nature, and overlapped with other forms of resistance. Although the "high tide" of peasant protest came with the "1916 Affair", when tens of thousands of peasants marched on Phnom Penh to present lists of grievances to the king, this event, while extraordinary because of the sheer numbers involved, should be seen in the context of a longer period of rural discontent. Some of this was funneled into what the English historian Eric Hobsbawm has called "social banditry",[46] but some of it found a more "mass" expression in a kind of "agrarian syndicalism".

Social banditry, as Hobsbawm as shown, has been widespread in pre-industrial, rural societies. It has thrived among peasants as a reaction against the injustices of despotic rule, particularly where that rule has been weak and chaotic. As Hobsbawm wrote, "social banditry is universally found, wherever societies are based on agriculture...and consist largely of peasants and landless labourers ruled, oppressed and exploited by someone else—lords, towns, governments, lawyers, or even banks."[47] Thus, it thrived on the fringes of the Ottoman Empire - in the Balkan mountains and in the remoter parts of Anatolia (where it inspired Yashar Kemal's classic Turkish novel, *Memed, My Hawk*[48]); in Sicily and Sardinia; in Mexico; in the "rapparees" of Ireland; and in such figures as Robin Hood in England, Ned Kelly in Australia and Phoolan Devi, the "bandit queen", in late twentieth-century India. In many cases, foreign rule was an additional cause of resentment. Banditry also flourished best where sympathetic terrain allowed the brigands to melt away into swamps, jungles, mountains, or retreat over national boundaries. As the present writer has written elsewhere: "Such an analysis broadly fits the Cambodian countryside, which was notoriously bandit-prone. Whilst landlessness was not a real problem in Cambodia...the peasantry was squeezed by a corrupt and arbitrary administration backed by French power."[49] The terrain was suitable for bandit hideouts and many areas of Cambodia lacked good roads until well into the 20th century. Where they did exist, they were often flooded during the wet monsoon period, frustrating pursuit.

The Ouch gang and other social bandits

There are numerous examples of the classical social bandit type in Cambodia. One of these "noble robbers" was *Sena* (or commander) Ouch (or Uch), a kind of Khmer Robin Hood, who fought the French and the indigenous authorities in the period of World War I in the Kompong Thom district. Ouch was a former Buddhist monk who raised a band of over 100 followers. There is evidence that he enjoyed the tacit support of many villagers and although some reports branded him a common criminal—as Margaret Thatcher did the IRA in the late 1970s—others conceded that his aim was to drive out the French and restore Cambodian independence. It was Ouch's gang which attacked the Catholic mission at Chhlong in 1913 and wounded Father R. P. David. Although Ouch probably died in the jungles, his exploits sent a *frisson* of fear up the spines of the French and indigenous administrators.[50] A hybrid kind of rebel was the anti-dynastic insurgent, a type exemplified by Pou Kombo (whom we met in Chapter 2) and Ang Snguon. The latter, said by the French to be a defrocked *bonze*, launched a serious revolt in the north of the country in the early years of the 20th century. French forces rapidly dispersed his band following an "ill-planned and ill-executed attack" on the French *Résidence* at Thala-Borivet in the Porong region, but similar armed pretenders and old followers of Si Votha roamed the countryside bent on mayhem.[51] Another important revolt flared in the Kampot region, on the Gulf of Siam littoral, in 1909. The rebels, inspired by a Chinese secret society called the Society of Heaven and Earth, landed rifles on the coast, hid in caves, and launched a rebellion from the jungles of the Elephant Mountains. Although an energetic pacification campaign decimated the band and led to the capture of its leader, crowds of supporters stormed the Kampot *Résidence* and it was some time before the French could restore order. Kampot had a large population of Chinese and Vietnamese and the French were worried that they had made common cause with the local Khmers.[52] The events in Kampot would seem to have contributed to the general upsurge of "insubordination" among peasants across Cambodia in 1909. A report indicates that the revolt had made such an impression that 14 prisoners broke out of jail in Kompong Cham, several hundred kilometers away.[53] There was a resurgence of multi-ethnic rebellion in Kampot in 1915.[54] It is reasonable to see a common thread linking such social banditry with the armed insurrection of the Khmer Issaraks against French rule in the 1940s and 1950s, and with the later agrarian discontent that fed the *Khmers Rouges* revolution against both King Sihanouk and Lon Nol's Khmer Republic.

Taxation, corvée and changes to land tenure

When Sisowath came to the throne in 1904, the French moved definitively to concentrate power in their own hands. Norodom's death allowed them to sweep aside the administrative and political logjam that had blocked their program of reforms for several decades. Insofar as the countryside was concerned, those reforms were mainly concerned with taxation, *corvée* labor and ownership of the soil. Although the French administration might have believed (or hoped) that they were enforcing reforms on a passive mass of individuals, careful study reveals that the peasants were an active figure in the equation. French observers warned early in the new century that the reforms could rebound on the French administration.[55] The year 1905 was a year of poor harvests, with "something of an exodus" from the land. Yet, bad harvests were not their only worry. A French report from that year makes the revealing admission that peasants in Stung Treng province were "continually exasperated" by the requisition of "coolie labor" by the *Messageries Fluviales* steamship line. Local village chiefs often used force against the villagers to satisfy the company's demands for unpaid stevedores.[56] Less than three years later, the so-called "Prasat Affair" showed the resentment of peasants in Kandal province towards the government's land measurement program (promulgated by a royal decree of January 1908). The *Résident Supérieur* reported that "agitators" had stirred up a crowd of more than 200 peasants to demonstrate at the house of the Governor of the province. The crowd declared that they would refuse to allow measurement of their lands. Following a lecture by the Governor, the demonstrators dispersed, with the exception of two men, Mau and Sek, who said they would still take their complaints to Phnom Penh. For this "insubordination", they were arrested, but not before a wild *mêlée* in which the pair assaulted Khmer officials. Sek later fled from custody.[57] From the French point of view, land measurement was a necessary step in the privatization of land. Titles of peasant plots were issued only after cadastral surveys were completed. From the peasant point of view, it was unwarranted interference in a time-honored custom. The king had endorsed it, but it emanated from the French and the more astute would have made the link between private title and the introduction of the *impôt foncier*, or land tax. In its own way, the story is also an illustration of the petty autocracy that characterized dealings between peasants and officials in Cambodia. Such behavior is scarcely criminal; a free society would consider it legitimate social protest. Sek disappears from view at this point, but it is quite possible that as an escapee criminalized by a justice system loaded against his class and kind, he fled to the jungle and joined the bandits.

The early Sisowath years saw the introduction of a wide variety of new taxes, and these contributed to an upsurge in social unrest. There were already a bewildering number of tolls and although the French had promised to simplify the system, in reality they introduced new levies and enforced stricter methods of collection. Balancing the books was always an overriding concern in French governance. Head taxes amounted to 2.50 piastres per year for males between 21 and 50 years, in theory declining afterwards to 0.80 piastres for the over-50s, although in practice all paid the higher sum.[58] In 1907, new taxes were put on *ponteas*,[59]—non-riparian terrains—planted with a variety of crops including cotton, indigo and sesame. Sugar palms attracted a tax of 0.5 piastres per tree exploited and new taxes imposed on the cultivation of capsicums and cardamom.[60]

Shortly after the Prasat Affair, other protests—said to be "very numerous"—broke out in Kandal province, this time over taxes on fishing gear[61] and *corvée*. Although the protests were stifled, the authorities noted that a "certain ill-will" continued in some villages and blamed it on the activities of secret societies. The same report mentions the agitation of secret societies in Takeo, where anti-French posters were stuck up on walls, leading to widespread arrests.[62] Crowds also attacked the French *Résidence* in Kampot and disorders in Pursat led to arrests and deportations.[63] The "effervescence" died down in 1910, although the authorities arraigned a number of Chinese distillery workers at Pursat for "serious insolence" to a Khmer judge (*sophea*) and "categorical refusal to pay taxes."[64] Banditry still raged in many districts, with offices burned down and officials murdered,[65] but things calmed down by the end of the year. Small wonder that a relieved *Résident Supérieur* hailed 1911 as a "year of peace" in Cambodia, because only six murders were recorded, and only three of the accused were ethnic Cambodians.[66] Evidently, the French perceived the downturn in turbulence as a sign that their policies had been accepted, for they made further demands on the peasants. In 1911, the government decreed that peasants must contribute 90 days *corvée* per year and pay heavy new taxes, tightening up on laws dating back to 1906. Although it was possible to buy one's way out of *corvée*, most peasants were too poor to pay. The Cambodian historian Sorn Samnang has noted that the demands worried many provincial *Résidents*, who considered them "heavy and excessive".[67] The criticisms by one *Résident*, Charles Bellan, earned him the lasting enmity of his boss, François Baudoin—later dubbed "the tyrant of Cambodia" by the Saigon press.[68] A later commission of inquiry vindicated some of Bellan's criticisms, although his career in Cambodia ended abruptly in 1916.[69]

We have already remarked on what the French called "the worrying political climate" of 1913, which led to savage attacks on a number of Frenchmen, and the huge wave of arrests in that year. Prince Yukanthor, his estranged wife Malika and other dissident members of the Norodom wing of the royal family joined in the froth of agitation. Prince Norodom Mayura, deemed by François Baudoin to be "a disreputable individual, alcoholic and unbalanced",[70] was an inveterate pamphleteer. A stream of anti-French, anti-Sisowath tracts flowed from his pen, often under the name of "Chum" for a *soi-disant* "Comité Cambodgien" and a "League for Civil Rights". Mayura also sent letters to the French parliament, some of which remain in the Quai d'Orsay archives.[71] He spent much of his life in exile for treason[72] and died unrepentant in Songcau in Vietnam. In 1914, anti-French agitation again broke out. A number of "manifestos", believed to originate in Phnom Penh, appeared in the provinces in late 1914. Translations of two of these, signed by "Sam" and "Khuth", and seized in Svay Rieng, still survive. They would appear to be the handiwork of supporters of the Norodom wing of the royal family, possibly Mayura in Phnom Penh, but it is interesting that they turned up in the distant countryside. The tracts claim that there was no justice in Cambodia and that the people lived in poverty and men even had to sell their wives and children to live. The writers demanded the lowering of all taxes for the "oppressed" Cambodians and claimed that the French had been content to let bad people stay in power. In particular, the writers said that the French allowed Sisowath to do whatever he wanted and that there was great violence against both Khmers and *Montagnards*.[73] The second tract finishes with a naïve threat: unless the French lower taxes, the day will come when they will lose 10,000 piastres a day. How this would happen is not specified.[74] The reader might consider Sam and Khuth's claims in the light of French behavior during an incident soon afterwards in Battambang town. The following January, a peaceful crowd of around 100 people marched on the town center in a protest against taxation levels. The local *Résident* arrested them all and handed out stiff prison terms. Three weeks later, 25 prisoners broke out of the Battambang jail. The militia gave chase, killing 13 and wounding another five escapees.[75] It seems possible that the arrested demonstrators played some part in the breakout, although there is no proof of this. The following year saw the eruption of the great wave of unrest known as the 1916 Affair, which is the subject of the next chapter.

Notes

[1] AOM RSC 430, Rapport Politique, 1èr Trimestre, 1915.

[2] Leon Trotsky, (trans. Max Eastman), (1967), *The History of the Russian Revolution*, Vol. III, Sphere Books, London, p.9.

[3] A number of historians have written about the Affair. David Chandler devotes almost four pages to it in the second edition of his *A History of Cambodia*, (Westview Press, Boulder Colorado, 1993, pp.153-156). Alain Forest contributed the chapter entitled "Les manifestations de 1916 au Cambodge" in Pierre Brocheux (ed.) *Histoire de l'Asie Sud-Est, révoltes, réformes, révolutions* (PUL, Lille, 1981). See also Milton Osborne, (1978), "Peasant Politics in Cambodia", *Modern Asian Studies*, 12 (2), London, pp.217-243 and John Tully, (1996), *Cambodia Under the Tricolour. King Sisowath and the "Mission Civilisatrice", 1904-1927*, pp.187-211.

[4] ANC RSC E 03. File No 21176 Box 2260, Rapport politique de 1er Trimestre 1916 (Prey Veng).

[5] Baudoin frequently fell out with his subordinates and had a long-running feud with the Prey Veng *Résident*, Bellan (see below, Chapter 15).

[6] Huy Kanthoul, "Mémoires", unpublished French-language typescript, p. 6. (Chandler Papers, Monash University.)

[7] L.V.L., (1926), "Les origines de l'affaire Bardez", *La Voix Libre*, 9 January 1926, p.1.

[8] The Bardez Affair is discussed in Chapter 15 below.

[9] Times correspondent, (1945), "Internal autonomy for Cambodia French decision", *The Times*, London, 5 November.

[10] Harry Hervey, (1928), *Travels in French Indo-China*, Thornton Butterworth, London.

[11] H. G. Quaritch Wales, (1943), *Years of Blindness*, Thomas Y. Crowell, New York, p.192. Quaritch Wales claimed that not long before his visit, a French official had been murdered in his bed nearby. He does not state who this was and I have found no other reference to the incident.

[12] In *Indochine. Hebdomadaire Illustré*, (1941), Hanoi, 9 Janvier.

[13] "Barang Srao Pua" ("Français tirent un cable") in Tricon et Bellan, (1921), *Chansons cambodgiennes*, Albert Portail, Saigon. Translated from the French version by Gina Zajusch.

[14] Harry A. Franck, (1926), *East of Siam: Ramblings in the Five Divisions of French Indo-China*, The Century, New York, p.77.

[15] ANC RSC D35 File No 2975, Box 333, Rapport Politique et Économique, January-February 1907.

[16] AOM RSC 426. Rapport politique et économique du Cabinet de la Résidence Supérieure, March-April 1905.

[17] Huy Kanthoul, op. cit.

[18] "Réformes souhaitables. Il faut supprimer l'insécurité dans nos campagnes", (1939), *La Presse Indochinoise, Hebdomadaire illustré, politique, littéraire, économique*, 13 janvier, Saigon.

[19] Wilfred Burchett, (1957), *Mekong Upstream*, Red River Publishing House, Hanoi, p.25. Burchett might have been making an oblique call for collectivized agriculture. He contrasts the shallow plowing of Khmer peasants with the "deep plowing" fostered by the Maoist regime in China. Deep plowing was, in fact, largely a disaster. (See Jasper Becker, (1996), *Hungry Ghosts. China's Secret Famine*, John Murray, London.)

[20] Unsigned, (1936), "Il faudrait orienter les Cambodgiens vers le commerce pour l'avenir", *La Presse Indochinoise*, 23 juillet.

[21] AOM RSC 303, Sûreté. Presse, propaganda 1942-44. Revue de la presse cambodgienne,

[22] ANC RSC D35 File No 2970, Box No 333. Report by *Résident Supérieur* to *Gougal*, 1 November 1904.

[23] AOM RSC 386. Rapports Politiques Annuels, Prey Veng, 1914-1938. Rapport Annuel, 1937-1938.

[24] Unsigned, (1923), "Mendiants cambodgiens", *La Voix Libre*, 15 September, p.1

[25] Unsigned, (1935), *La Presse Indochinoise*, Hanoi, 28 September.

[26] Ibid, 24 July 1936.

[27] AOM RSC 426. Rapports politiques et économiques du Cabinet de la Résidence Supérieure, 1905-1907. 1905.

[28] Followers of a certain Chaum Im, an old insurgent of 1885, were armed with such weapons during attacks in Kompong Cham in 1906, although Chaum Im also had an old cannon. See ANC RSC D35 File 2975 Box 333. Situation politique, économique et financière du Cambodge. Rapport politique et économique, March-April 1906.

[29] Huy Kanthoul, op.cit. p.7.

[30] The *Montagnards*, or hill tribes, were non-state peoples who lived by hunting and swidden farming in the jungles and mountains in the borderlands of Cambodia, Laos and Vietnam. They waged a bitter struggle for many decades against the encroaching French and were never entirely pacified. The history of their relations with the French is an Indochina-wide story and beyond the scope of this book. For a detailed study, see Gerald Cannon Hickey, (1982), *Sons of the Mountains: Ethnohistory of the Vietnamese Central Highlands to 1954*, Yale University Press, New Haven. See also John Tully, (1996), *Cambodia Under the Tricolour. King Sisowath and the "mission civilisatrice", 1904-1927*, Monash Asia Institute, Clayton, Victoria, pp.143-157. A new study is Mathieu Guérin, Andrew Hardy, Stan tan Boon Hwee and Nguyen Van Chinh, *Civilisations de la forêt et états modernes, l'integration nationale des aborigènes des hautes terres du Cambodge et du Vietnam*, IRASEC et L'Harmattan, scheduled for publication in 2002. [Exact title might change.] Other general titles include Hugo and Emmy Bernatzik, (trans. E.W. Dickes), (1958), *The Spirits of the Yellow Leaves*, Robert Hall, London; and Georges Condaminas, (trans. Adrienne Foulke), (1977), *We Have Eaten the Forest: The Story of a Montagnard Village in the Central Highlands of Vietnam*, Hill and Wang, New York.

[31] For details of the Commaille murder, see Tully, op.cit. pp. 161, 208-210, 221. Commaille was buried at Angkor. His grave still exists, surprisingly, having survived the long occupation of the ruins by the *Khmers Rouges*.

[32] AOM RSC 296, Affaires confidentielles. Assassinat de M. Prugna.

[33] AOM RSC 296, Affaire Michelon ou Affaire de Thbong-Khmum and RSC 428.

[34] AOM RSC 429, Rapport Politiques, 1er, 2ème & 3ème trimestres, 1913. The Japanese murdered Father David in 1945.

[35] AOM RSC 432, Rapport Politique, 1er Trimestre 1918.

[36] AOM RSC 426. Rapports économique et politique du Cabinet de la Résidence Supérieure, 1905.

[37] AOM RSC 429. Rapports politiques et économiques, 1911-1912-1913.

[38] AOM RSC 431, Rapport politique, 1er Trimestre.

[39] ANC RSC E 03 File 1815, Box 176. Rapport annuel 1930, Prey Veng.

[40] ANC RSC E03 File 499, Box 38. Rapport annuel, Résidence de Siem Reap, 1 juin 1932-31 mai 1933.

[41] Ibid. Rapport annuel, Résidence de Battambang, juin 1932-May 1933.

[42] Ibid. Rapport annuel, Résidence de Kompong Cham, juin 1932-mai 1933.

[43] Unsigned, (1935), *La Presse Indochinoise*, Hanoi, 5 October.

[44] Ibid, 18 February 1938.

[45] David Johnson, "Bandit, *Nakleng* and Peasant in Rural Thai Society", in C. Wilson et al (eds.), (1980), *Royalty and Commoners: Contributions to Asian Studies*, Vol. 15, pp.90-101.

[46] E.J. Hobsbawm, (1969), *Bandits*, Weidenfeld and Nicolson, London.

[47] Ibid, p.15.

[48] Yashar Kemal, (translated by Edouard Roditi), (1984), *Memed, My Hawk*, Fontana Paperbacks, London.

[49] Tully, op.cit. p.135.

[50] AOM RSC 275, Province de Kratié, Affaires Phnongs, 1914-1915. Telegram to *Résident Supérieur* from *Résident* of Kompong Thom, 1 December 1913. RSC 429 Rapport politique, 4ème Trimestre 1913. RSC 430, Rapports politiques, 1er et 2ème Trimestres 1913, 1er Trimestre 1915. RSC 369 Rapport Trimestriel du 15 mars au 15 juin 1915 (Kompong Cham).

[51] AOM RSC 426, Rapport sur la situation entre 1902 et 1907 and RSC 257, Rapport des mois de novembre et décembre 1906.

[52] AOM Fonds Amiraux, F65, 22325, Rébellion à Kampot 17 mai 1909. RSC 428 Rapports politiques et économiques, 1909.

[53] AOM RSC 428 Rapport politique et économique, avril 1909.

[54] AOM RSC 430 Rapport Politique, 1er et 4èmeTrimestres 1915 et 1er Trimestre 1916.

[55] See, for instance Pierre Quillard, (1905), "L'Indochine en danger", *L'Européen. Courrier International Hebdomadaire, Politique, Droit International, Questions Sociales, Littérature, Art*, No, 24, 28 October 1905.

[56] AOM RSC 426. Rapports politiques et économiques du Cabinet de la Résidence Supérieure, 1905-1907.

[57] AOM RSC 427. Rapport politique et économique, 20 novembre 1908.

[58] AOM RSC 427, Rapport politique et économique, 16 octobre 1908.

[59] Riparian fields are called *chamcars* in Khmer. The tax on *ponteas* had been decreed in December 1903, but not enforced.

[60] ANC RSC D35. File 3033, Box 341. Rapport sur la situation politique, économique et financière du Cambodge, 1908. Conseil Supérieure de la Indochina, Session ordinaire de 1908.

[61] AOM RSC 428. Rapport politique et économique, January 1909.

[62] Ibid, Rapport politique et économique, 2ème Trimestre 1909.

[63] Ibid, Rapport politique et économique, 3ème Trimestre.

[64] Ibid, Rapport politique et économique, 2ème Trimestre 1909.

[65] Ibid. Rapport politique et économique, 1er Trimestre 1910.

[66] AOM RSC 429 Conseil supérieur de l'Indochine, Session Ordinaire de 1911.

[67] Sorn Samnang, (1995), "L'Evolution de la Société Cambodgienne entre les deux guerres mondiales (1919 – 1939)." Thèse pour le doctorat d'histoire, Université Paris VII, Tome II, p.329. The thesis cites annual reports from Kompong Chhnang and Prey Veng (RSC 397).

[68] A. Fontaine Laporte, (1926), "Les origines de l'affaire Bardez", *La Voix Libre*, No. 345, 9 January. (Reprinted from *Le Libre Cochinchine*.)

[69] AOM RSC 482. "Perception de l'impôt après l'ordonnance royale de 19 Février 1916. (Deuxième Bureau).

[70] AOM RSC 430, Rapport politique, 4ème Trimestre, 1916.

[71] There is, for instance, a 1912 letter from "Chum" to the Minister of Foreign Affairs in the French Foreign Office archives at the Quai d'Orsay in Paris. [QO Indochine. Personalités Indochinoises. Prince-Agitateurs, II, 1909-1917, (Vol. 3)].

[72] AOM RSC 430 Rapport Politique, 4ème Trimestre 1916.

[73] The French were waging a campaign to "pacify" the *Montagnards* at this time. In one incident in early 1915, tribesmen killed a French administrator, M. Truffot, along with a number of Khmer militiamen, in Kratié province. See AOM RSC 430. Rapport politique, 1er Trimestre 1915.

[74] ANC RSC E.03 File 868, Box 83, Rapport politiques Décembre 1915, janvier, février 1916, Délégation de Soai-Rieng. Rapport Nr. 173.

[75] AOM RSC 430, Rapport politique, 1er Trimestre, 1915.

Chapter 10

The Great Peasant Strike: The 1916 Affair

[The Affair] had neither any tendency nor preparation of a political kind.
—Résident Supérieur Baudoin, 1916.

The peasants are normally invisible to townsfolk and colonial overlords. Leon Trotsky observed that even "the historian is ordinarily as little interested in...[the peasant] as the dramatic critic is in those grey figures who shift the scenery, carrying the heavens and earth on their backs, and scrub the dressing room floors of the actors."[1] Jean de la Bruyère wrote thus of the French peasants,

> Scattered across the countryside one may observe certain wild animals, male and female, dark, livid and burnt by the sun, attached to the earth which they dig with invincible stubbornness. However, they have something like an articulated voice and when they stand up they reveal a human face. Indeed they are human beings...Thanks to them the other human beings need not sow, labour and harvest in order to live.[2]

Usually absorbed in their daily tasks, the peasants sometimes make their presence known to those who take their existence—and their docility—for granted. One instance of this was the "1916 Affair" in Cambodia.

The year 1916 began with good harvests. The *Résidents* reported to François Baudoin that the population was submissive and immersed in its work in the fields.[3] Baudoin must have had some premonition of looming trouble, however, for one year earlier, he had quoted Norodom's *bon mot* comparing the Cambodian peasant to a buffalo, "placid, yet terrible if exasperated".[4] The buffalo was indeed exasperated, and discontent was general. The authorities continued to squeeze the population for taxes, despite the misgivings of some local *Résidents*. In Prey Veng, for example, total taxes collected rose from just under 11.5 thousand piastres in January 1915, to almost 12.8 thousand in January 1916.[5] The peasants were growing restive, making numerous complaints of corruption against officials and militia.[6] Taxes on dogs and farm animals also came into force in late 1915, further irritating them.[7] In some areas, the peasants were required to collect firewood free of charge for the administration.[8] Some writers have also pointed to the recruitment of soldiers and laborers for Europe as a factor in the general discontent.[9] This view is supported by the words of Palace Minister Thiounn who told the Council of Ministers during the disturbances that "The demonstrators were also protesting against recruitment."[10] The French had always experienced great difficulty in recruitment; even in peacetime, many Khmers regarded it "as a form of slavery".[11] In theory, recruitment was voluntary, but in World War I, quotas were set for districts and officials appear not to have been squeamish in their methods to fill them.[12] A British observer, writing twenty years later, claimed that. "Many, perhaps most, of...[the Indochinese soldiers] had been forcibly recruited by methods of great brutality, and this caused much ill-feeling."[13] The French never fulfilled their recruitment targets in Cambodia. There were high rates of desertion and recruits frequently refused to serve when they arrived in the capital for induction.[14] Perhaps the recruitment drive would have generated greater resentment, but for the fact that more than half of all "volunteers" were turned down because of their poor physical condition.[15] Up to April 1916, for example, the army turned away 500 out 800 recruits in Svay Rieng for poor health.[16]

The 1916 Affair actually began in early November 1915, when a crowd of disgruntled peasants made their way from Ksach Kandal on the Mekong to protest what amounted to illegal demands for *corvée*.[17] It was a brave act, given what had been done to the Battambang protestors shortly before, but Baudoin listened and agreed that they had already fulfilled their obligations. However, when the same villagers returned at the end of the year to demand their legal right to buy their way out of the next installment of *corvée*, Baudoin refused and ordered them to work on a road he deemed economically vital. His actions were high-handed and arbitrary, but the legal situation allowed the authorities to have their cake and eat it. A royal decree of June 1903 stated clearly that peasants "who for any reason whatsoever are not able, *or do not wish* to (emphasis in the original) carry out their *prestations*, are authorized to 'buy back' their obligation for the payment of 3 piastres per day." However, the Government also gave itself the "Catch 22" power to requisition further labor if it deemed it necessary.[18] The villagers returned home frustrated. They met with other peasants—and perhaps with monks—and developed an eight-point program of demands for redress of grievances. The program soon gained popularity throughout the kingdom, passing from village to village via the same kind of channels, unseen to the French, which had existed in 1884-86. It was short and moderate, but amounted to a peasants' charter—"a popular program attacking the endemic corruption, privilege and injustice which could only be addressed by sweeping reform of the Khmer bureaucracy."[19] The eight demands were as follows:

- the right to "buy out" of *corvée*;
- abolition of the tax on fishing gear;
- the right to fish free of charge in certain locations;
- reduction of the tobacco tax;
- simplification of the forestry regulations regarding the right to collect fuel;
- suppression of illegal taxes levied by corrupt *notables*;
- payment for *corvée*;
- the purge of corrupt officials and those guilty of abuse of power.[20]

News of the Ksach Kandal "charter" spread rapidly. Officials from most—but not all—districts reported mass meetings of peasants and the passage of "agitators" through the villages, whipping up support for the charter of demands. The *Résident* of Kompong Cham claimed that young men had fanned out through the villages with the call to "Make your way to Phnom Penh to see His Majesty and present your claims according to the general formula prepared in advance."[21] There is also some evidence of the organizers circulating the call in letters[22] and publicizing it in posters on walls,[23] although Baudoin dismissed the latter claim.[24] Baudoin did believe a network existed, however, telling the Council of Ministers that, "We find ourselves in the presence of a movement which seems to be led by agitators. Information received from the *Résidents* indicates that the word of command came from the capital."[25] This seems likely. The charter of demands and the proposal for action could only have been relayed from village to village across wide areas of the kingdom by some kind of organization. As first-year Psychology undergraduates know, informal methods of transmission of information usually lead very rapidly to gross distortions of the original message. One of the most striking aspects of the 1916 Affair was the uniform nature of the demands across far-flung districts of the country. Predictably, the French claimed that many of the participants in the demonstrations had been intimidated into joining: a common response of rulers to mass action by workers or peasants which belittles those who take part and deflects scrutiny from the causes of discontent. Some probably *were* dragooned into taking part—the Governor of Barai reported that up to 3000 "malcontents" gathered there from surrounding districts, threatening to cut off people's heads and burn down their houses if they did not join in[26]—but it is absurd to claim that most of the tens of thousands of participants were forced to take part. Only state power can generally enforce mass compliance with unpopular demands and besides, there was plenty of combustible material for the spark of the charter to ignite, the French and Khmer officials had seen to that.

Networks of "agitators"

While it seems clear that networks of agitators, some of them at least semi-itinerant, fanned the flames of discontent, their identities remain shadowy. At least some of them were literate, or at least believed in the importance of distributing tracts and posters. However, who had the time and the means to agitate? In Europe before the development of mass literacy and communications (including left-wing newspapers), semi-itinerant journeymen often disseminated news and "subversive" ideas in the villages through which they traveled. There is evidence, for instance, that traveling shoemakers and similar tradesmen acted as itinerant organizers during the "Swing" riots by British agricultural laborers against the introduction of laborsaving machinery.[27] Their less peripatetic colleagues often acted as village intellectuals and propagandists for radical and heterodox ideas.[28] The role of Jacobin, anticlerical village schoolteachers in France and Italy is well known. Yet, if comparable networks did exist in Cambodia before and during the 1916 disturbances, who were the agitators? The nature of Khmer village life was in many respects different to that in Europe at the time. Until 1901, the Khmer peasants were not allowed to circulate freely around the country without an internal passport[29] and even after the restrictions were lifted, it is doubtful that they often wandered far from home except in times of exceptional distress. They made most of what they consumed, with the exception of cloth, salt and some other commodities provided by merchants (many of them Chinese). They made and mended most of their own garments and habitually went barefoot because of the climate. There could have been no equivalent of Europe's "political shoemakers". So who were the young men and *gamins* who were said to have "fanned out" to take word of the "peasants' charter" to the villages? Most of those arrested as "ringleaders" seem to have been peasants, although there are also reports of disgruntled Khmer officials and notables siding with the movement. More importantly, the Government suspected widespread involvement by Buddhist monks. The *Balat* of Komchanea in Prey Veng, for example, claimed that the chief *bonze* of the Snoul pagoda in Pearang province was a central leader of the disturbances, and reported the arrival of "strange monks" during the period.[30] Interestingly, given the tradition of racial communalism in Cambodia, some of the monks named as agitators were Vietnamese. The provincial authorities charged one of these, Huynh Van Dat, with "seditious propaganda" and the selling of magical amulets, and deported him to his native Long Xuyen in Cochinchina.[31] There were also deportations from Cochinchina, as on June 16, when a Khmer *bonze* called Khuon was expelled from Chaudoc, presumably for agitating among the ethnic Khmers in that region.[32] Because of such reports, Baudoin placed restrictions on the movements of monks; the *achars* of pagodas had to inform the authorities of the arrival of new monks within three days, for example. In effect, this was the selective reintroduction of the internal passport system abolished in 1901. Baudoin also prevailed on Sisowath to introduce a registration system whereby they had to furnish proof of good character.[33] Baudoin's suspicions of the monks were well grounded. Although it was (and still is) customary for young men to spend a short time as monks, some men chose to make it their vocation. These latter were generally more literate than the mass of the peasantry and would have had an *esprit de corps* and channels of communication reaching beyond the level of the *khum* and the local wat. In addition, as Baudoin knew, they could move around the countryside without attracting suspicion. They were also unencumbered by families, which tend to root people to their homes and farms. They would have had the moral authority to direct their younger, transient colleagues to carry messages and argue for the charter. All the evidence points to the monks providing the backbone of the organizing networks behind the movement of 1916, although not all monks would have participated. This semi-political involvement in social matters adumbrates the part played by the bonzes in the independence movement from World War II on.

A homegrown affair

Although *Résident Supérieur* Baudoin later wrote that the movement was largely an internal Cambodian affair, at first he suspected that the exiled dissident Prince Yukanthor was behind it. Yukanthor was one of a number of exiled Indochinese in Bangkok. While he certainly seems to have tried to capitalize on the movement after it had begun, the French Legation in the Siamese capital considered that it had taken him by surprise. Baudoin opined that, "inquiries made by the French Legation showed not only that the secret intrigues of the Pretender hadn't penetrated into Cambodia last January, but also that his vague and ill-defined projects had not yet materialized in anything except for the sending to Cambodia of two or three bonzes who were arrested at the frontier last March."[34] This opinion has merit. Although the "intrigues" of Yukanthor, Mayura and Malika might well have helped prepare the ground for the movement, such dissidents were more concerned with redressing wrongs to the Norodom wing of the royal family than with the "mundane" concerns of the peasants. The 1916 Affair was essentially an agrarian syndicalist phenomenon—a strike against oppressive taxation, *corvée*, and corruption—but Baudoin overstates his case when he claims it "had neither any tendency or preparation of a *political* kind".[35] [Emphasis added.]

There are some similarities between patterns of rural revolt and social protest in Ireland, England and Cambodia. If the 19th century Irish peasants had formed secret societies such as the "Ribbonmen" and the "Whiteboys", and the English peasants had launched campaigns of rural Luddism, then why could their Cambodian counterparts not launch a coordinated campaign around a peasants' charter? Such a synchronized movement could not have occurred by osmosis and it is probable that the "ringleaders" were anti-French; just as many Irish agrarian rebel leaders opposed the English crown.

Generally, the crowds were peaceful enough, although there was some looting of Chinese shops[36] for grog, blankets and umbrellas. The crowds also plundered kitchen gardens and stole ducks and chickens for food.[37] When the crowds got to the capital, they pushed aside the gates of the royal palace, but it is unclear whether this was deliberate. Milton Osborne says it was caused by the sheer crush of bodies, but François Baudoin told the Council of Ministers that the gates were forced open and that "large groups penetrated into the first compound, asking to see the King."[38] There were also reports of assaults against Khmer officials, particularly in Ksach Kandal. There were also alarming reports of what verged on insurrection in Prey Veng, where militiamen under the command of Gendarme Guilhem opened fire on angry crowds of up to 2000 people, some of whom were armed with axes, sabers, clubs and cutlasses. Guilhem's men shot dead five peasants and wounded twenty others.[39] M. Angelot, the commander of the Prey Veng *gendarmerie*, later reported that between 2000 and 3000 people had stormed the house of the Governor at Lovea Em. Angelot records personally seeing 16 corpses and one seriously wounded man after the rioters had dispersed. He also claims that some of the rioters had rifles, and proposed the decoration of 12 militiamen for bravery.[40] There were no serious French casualties during the disturbances anywhere in the country, but the *Résident* of Kompong Cham claimed that a mob chanting "Death to the *Résident!*" besieged his offices.[41] Baudoin himself mentioned death threats, although he did not elaborate.[42]

Baudoin orders stern repression

The Affair ended almost as abruptly as it had begun, although stubborn foci of discontent remained in some districts (particularly in Prey Veng and Kompong Cham). François Baudoin claimed that the crowds who had traveled to the capital dispersed after they saw and heard Sisowath, who commanded them to go home.[43] The king's order was probably the most significant reason for the evaporation of the movement, but Baudoin is telling only part of the story. He personally unleashed a wave of repression, ordering the hunting down of "agitators" and muttering about plots fomented by agents in Bangkok on behalf of foreign powers and domestic revolution. Khmer courts sentenced hundreds of people to long prison terms, and scores to death, although the French did step in to commute many of the harsher sentences. Baudoin and his subordinates did not hesitate, either, to use murderous force against the demonstrators, rushing reinforcements from Saigon to stiffen the comparatively small Phnom Penh garrison. Probably we shall never know how many casualties resulted from the military repression. The Saigon newspaper *La Voix Libre*, which hated Baudoin, claimed that the troops had machine-gunned the crowds and tossed the corpses into the Mekong. The smallest estimate is of half a dozen dead, and this is certainly too low; the commander of the *gendarmerie* in Prey Veng claimed to have seen many more corpses in one town alone before the crowds left for the capital. At least scores, but as possibly hundreds of people were slain.

Baudoin knew that force alone could not stamp out a movement that had deep roots in peasant dissatisfaction. The 1885 Rebellion hung like a "fearful hobgoblin" in the collective French mind, and with every man and bullet required for the war in Europe, Baudoin would have been hard pressed to find the means to repress another insurrection; particularly with uprisings raging in the neighboring Vietnamese lands. Hence, even as militiamen hunted down the ringleaders, and jailers awaited the arrival of the *bourreau* with his guillotine, Baudoin granted some of the main demands of the charter. He summoned the Council of Ministers—which always now met under his presidency— and legalized the "buying back" of *corvée*. Daily rates for *corvée* labor and the requisition of draft animals, boats, carts and tools were increased.[44] Early in February, Sisowath issued a proclamation advertising the changes. However, there was a sting in the tail: anyone who organized demonstrations after the publication of the decree would be held to be in revolt against the lawful authorities. The king and French and Khmer officials toured the countryside to reinforce the message.[45] Some of the more controversial taxes were scaled down, including the tax on fishing tackle. Exemptions were granted for certain sizes and types of nets if the fish were for family consumption.[46] Taxes on tobacco production were lowered and restrictions on the collection of fuel and other materials gathered in forests were eased.[47]

Such measures dampened down the agitation. Baudoin set up a high level joint Franco-Khmer commission of inquiry to study the complaints and recommend changes. This handpicked commission sheeted the blame directly on the Khmer administration. The result was a major shake-up of the Khmer administration and judiciary.[48] Three hundred mayors were sacked and replaced. Legal proceedings were started against a large number for corruption and abuse of power. Many other middle level officials were sacked and some were imprisoned. Others preferred to resign.[49] Baudoin took steps to ensure that future civil servants were less likely to succumb to corruption. In November of the following year, Governor General Sarraut signed a new statute of indigenous personnel into law. This provided for wide-ranging reforms, including the separation of judicial and administrative functions. Secondly, the decree abolished the old system by which tax collectors directly paid themselves out of taxes collected. Henceforth, they would be salaried civil servants subject to recruitment procedures and training programs. Finally, efforts were made to "raise the intellectual level" of civil servants; salaries were increased and promotion was to be by merit.

Baudoin: "passing the buck"

While there can be little doubt that there *was* widespread corruption in the Khmer bureaucracy, Baudoin's actions were self-serving and he would have frowned on Harry Truman's famous gesture of placing a sign inscribed "the buck stops here" on his desk in the White House. He told his superiors in Hanoi that, "the popular agitation was due to discontent with the *corvée* system and certain abuses committed by the indigenous authorities."[50] Those abuses had happened, but Baudoin cannot blame the Khmer administration for the *corvée* system. The French, it is true, had not introduced *corvée* into Cambodia, but they had certainly extended and refined the system. They had also engaged in heavy-handed recruitment for the military. We must also ask why, if corrupt Khmer officials were to blame, was the district of Prey Veng one of the principal foci of the Affair. Less than one year previously, a French civil service inspector named M. Pauher had written a glowing report about the local Khmer administration. Never before, he wrote, had he seen offices "in such good order" as those of the *salakhet* of Prey Veng. Governor Yea had evidently profited from a study tour of France, Pauher wrote, and his methods of work could serve as a model for "certain European officials". All of the governors in the district, he went on to report, gave "a good impression". Baudoin noted the report straight afterwards, "without comment".[51] One cannot but be suspicious, either, of Baudoin's parallel attempt to shove some of the blame onto his French subordinates, in particular Charles Bellan, *Résident* of the same district until his demotion and transfer to Cochinchina[52] in the wake of the Affair. Baudoin later claimed that Bellan had lost his head and even lied about the events during January 1916 in the district. Bellan, Baudoin said, had claimed falsely that German agents had plotted against France, that pro-German posters had appeared, and that a Pretender calling himself "the little king of Prey Veng" had been active during the disturbances. Baudoin also disputed chief gendarme Guilhem's claim that armed mobs had appeared during the period at Lovea Em.[53] In his defense, Bellan claimed that Baudoin had manufactured a "tissue of lies". The German influence, he claimed, came via a German settler called Russel who had fled from Battambang to Siam at the outbreak of war. Moreover, said Bellan, he actually had a copy of a poster to hand while he was writing to the Governor General with his version of events.[54] While we might never know the exact truth of what happened, we know that Baudoin was an irascible, dictatorial man. The Affair had suddenly exploded, catching him off guard (and incidentally vindicating Bellan's earlier warnings that the *corvée* and taxes would exasperate the peasants). Baudoin, no doubt, wanted to appear to his superiors in Hanoi and Paris to be in tight control of a worrying situation. The conclusion is that the French officials—and Baudoin in particular—had done at least as much, and probably *more* than their Khmer counterparts to cause the unrest. It was the result of policies enforced against the wishes of Norodom and the Council of Ministers (at least until the last years of Norodom's reign and his replacement with Sisowath). It seems, however, that the peasants blamed the mandarin class for allowing the French to introduce those policies. Upon his return from a tour of inspection of rural districts, Son Diep, the *Kralahom* (Minister of Marine) told his fellow ministers "They reproach us for allowing the imposition of too-heavy tasks."[55] This begs the question of who prevailed on them to allow the imposition.

Baudoin's strategy in 1916 was similar to that used by his predecessors to defuse the Great Rebellion in 1885. He eased some of the most onerous demands on the peasants, but the system of *corvée* and taxation remained in place. Later, the screws could be re-tightened. This was to lead directly to the bloody fate of Baudoin's *protégé*, *Résident* Bardez, in 1925 (which is discussed in a later chapter) and indirectly contributed to the growth of support for Khmer nationalism. Nor did Baudoin's actions in 1916 lead to any appreciable diminution of banditry—that great barometer of rural distress in Cambodia. It remained as entrenched as ever, feeding off what the more prescient French observers realized were the social conditions of life in the countryside. Andrew Graham, a British military attaché who visited Cambodia at the end of French rule, saw a 16th century ceremonial sword in the royal palace at Phnom Penh. The color of the sword was said to foretell the future. Graham was told that red meant war and white meant peace. When he asked the guide what its color had been last time it was unsheathed, the man replied that it had been blackish and that this meant that bandits were active.[56]

After 1916, the peasants remained receptive to calls for an easing of their onerous conditions. Peasant response to the publication of a gospel tract in Khmer by American Protestant missionaries in 1923 bears this out. The missionaries were proud of their "first Cambodian gospel leaflets" which featured a line drawing of a coolie laden down at work, with the biblical caption "Come unto me ye that labor and are heavily laden".[57] Christianity had never made much impression on the peasants, yet numbers of them flocked to the Americans, whose delight turned to horror when they realized that their "converts" had interpreted the tract as a call to make common cause against high taxation. In the end, however, all of this peasant agitation broke as waves on a hard shore, often harnessed by others—Si Votha, Pou Kombo, the *Phya* Kathathorn or Saloth Sar—and seldom, if ever leading to unified action by the peasants in their own common interests. As Eric Hobsbawm has written, the peasantry is not a "class for itself" and is chained to a social order of which its exploiters are part.[58] Nothing bears out this claim more forcefully than the ease with which King Sisowath was able to defuse the powder keg of 1916.

Notes

[1] Leon Trotsky, (trans Max Eastman), (1967), *The History of the Russian Revolution*, Vol. III, Sphere Books, London, p.9

[2] Cited in Eric Hobsbawm, "Peasants and Politics", in *Uncommon People. Resistance, Rebellion and Jazz*, (1999), Abacus, London, p.201.

[3] AOM RSC 369 Rapport politique, du 15 septembre au 15 décembre 1915, Kompong Cham and AOM RSC 383, Rapport politique, septembre, octobre, novembre 1915 et Rapport politique du 1er Trimestre 1916, Prey Veng.

[4] AOM RSC 430, Rapport politique, 1er Trimestre, 1915.

[5] ANC RSC E03 File 15517 Box 1300. Rapports mensuels et trimestriels des gouverneurs des provinces, Résidence de Prey Veng, 1916. Tableau comparatif des recettes de mois de janvier 1915 et 1916.

[6] For instance in September 1915, 20 inhabitants of Preas Damrey sent a letter to the *Résident* of Kompong Thom, complaining about the dishonesty of the local Mesrok and the creaming-off of taxes by the militia. (ANC RSC E03. File 15434 Box 1290. Rapport économique mensuel, statistiques de l'état civil indigène, correspondances avec les gouverneurs, Résidence de Kompong Thom. Letter to the Résident of Kompong Thom, September 1915.)

[7] Ibid. Balat of Chikreng to the Résident at Kompong Thom, 9 October 1915.

[8] ANC F451 File 4421 Conseil des Ministres 241e séance du 4 février 1916.

[9] For example, Manomohan Ghosh, (1960), *A History of Cambodia. From the earliest time to the end of the French Protectorate*, J.K. Gupta, Saigon, p.283. Ghosh overstates the case, however. See also John Tully (1996), *Cambodia Under the Tricolour. King Sisowath and the 'Mission Civilisatrice', 1904-1927*, Monash Asia Institute, Clayton, Victoria, pp. 173-177.

[10] ANC RSC 451 File 24420 Conseil des Ministres 240e séance du 27 janvier 1916.

[11] ANC RSC D35. File No 2975. Box 333. Conseil Supérieur de l'Indochine. Session ordinaire 1906. Situation politique, économique et financière du Cambodge.

[12] See, for instance, ANC RSC E 3, File 255, Box 10, Résidence de Kompong Thom. Procès-Verbaux des séance du Conseil de Résidence. The minutes record a discussion of the problems involved in securing a quota of 300 recruits.

[13] PRO, Kew, FO 474/2, F 5655/5655/86. B. Pearn, French Indo-China: Historical background to 1939.

[14] Tully, op.cit. p.174.

[15] AOM RSC 430, Rapport politique 1er Trimestre 1916. See also Tully, op.cit. p.172n for the staggering rejection rates of Indochinese volunteers because of the effects of malnutrition and disease. Only 100,000 of the 600,000 volunteers in all of Indochina were accepted.

[16] ANC RSC E 3 File No 1640 Box 159. Procès-Verbaux de Conseil de Résidence de Soai Rieng. Letter from *Résident* to the *Résident Supérieur*, 27 April 1916.

[17] ANC RSC E.03 File No 868, Box 83. Rapport du Résident du Kompong Cham à Résident Supérieur, 16 Jan. 1916.

[18] AOM RSC 430, Rapport politique, 1er Trimestre, 1915. *Prestations* are taxes levied either in money or in labor on public works. Extra *corvée* was known as *réquisitions*.

[19] Tully, op.cit. p.189.

[20] AOM RSC 430 Rapport politique 1er Trimestre 1916. According to Milton Osborne, Baudoin elsewhere listed 16 demands. [See Milton Osborne, (1978), "Peasant Politics in Cambodia", *Modern Asian Review*, 12 (2), London, p.232n.]

[21] AOM RSC 369. Rapport politique du 15 Décembre 1915 au 15 mars 1916, Kompong Cham. See also Baudoin's rapport politique, 2ème Trimestre 1916 (AOM RSC 430).

[22] Ibid. (RSC 369).

[23] ANC RSC E03. File 15517, Box 1300, Report of January 1916 from Prey Veng.

[24] AOM RSC 430. Rapport politique, 3ème Trimestre 1916. According to Baudoin, The local Résident claimed that German posters appeared in Prey Veng. This sounds absurd, but there is some evidence to support it.

[25] ANC F451 File 24419 Conseil des Ministres 239 séance du 22 janvier 1916.

[26] ANC E03. File 15434 Box 1290. Letter from the Governor at Barai, to the *Résident* at Kompong Thom, 25 January 1916.

[27] E.J. Hobsbawm and George Rudé, (1969), *Captain Swing*, Lawrence and Wishart, London.

[28] Eric Hobsbawm and Joan W. Scott, "Political Shoemakers", in Hobsbawm, (*Uncommon People*), op.cit. pp.23-58.

[29] ANC RSC F451 Conseil des Ministres, 52e séance du 5 octobre 1901, "Suppression des laissez-passer pour la circulation des habitants dans le royaume".

[30] ANC F65 File No 16064. Correspondances de la Résidence de Prey Veng relatives aux bonzes et leur participation á la rebellion. Translation of letter from *Balat* of Komchanea in Prey Veng, 5 March 1916.

[31] Ibid. Letter from the *Résident* to all governors, 16 March 1916. However, most of the evidence shows that the Chinese and Vietnamese communities remained neutral and were sometimes molested as a result. (AOM RSC 430 Rapport Politique, 3ème Trimestre 1916.)

[32] Ibid. (ANC F65 File No 16064.) Circulaire No. 32 from Résident Supérieur Baudoin to all Résidents, 30 March 1916.

[33] Ibid. (Circulaire No 32). The circular contains a copy of the relevant decree, signed by Sisowath on 17 April 1916.

[34] AOM RSC 430, Rapport politique, 2ème Trimestre 1916.

[35] AOM RSC 430, Rapport politique, 3ème Trimestre 1916.

[36] There had been reports of profiteering by Chinese shopkeepers earlier in the war, so perhaps the looters saw their actions as revenge. (See AOM RSC 366, Rapport d'ensemble, 1914, Résidence de Kandal.)

[37] ANC E03. File 15434 Box 1290. Letter from Governor of Barai to the *Résident* at Kompong Cham, 25 January 1916.

[38] ANC RSC 451 File 24418, Conseil des Ministres, 238 séance du 20 janvier 1916.

[39] ANC RSC G6 File 16501 Box 1430. Dossier générale concernant le gendarmerie de la Résidence de Prey Veng, 1915-1916.

[40] ANC RSC F65 File 16063, 1916. Propositions au faveur du personnel indigène des provinces pour défense courageuse de sala contre les rebelles. Résidence de Prey Veng, 1916. A later report claimed that when arrested, the ringleader Prea Tep and his followers had a number of muskets, rifles, revolvers and ammunition with them. (ANC RSC F65 File 15534, 1916.)

[41] Osborne, "Peasant Politics", op.cit. Baudoin denied this, claiming that the *Résident* had panicked. See below. However, Huy Kanthoul, ("Mémoires", unpublished French language mss. Chandler Papers, Monash University) p.6. claims that the disturbances in that province amounted to an anti-French revolt against *corvée* and conscription.

[42] ANC RSC 451 File 24418, Conseil des Ministres, 238 séance du 20 janvier 1916.

[43] AOM RSC 430, Rapport politique 1er Trimestre 1916.

[44] In Kompong Thom, for example, the rate of pay for coolies was increased from 0.3 piastres per day to 0.5 piastres. Daily rates were set at 2 piastres for elephants, 1.5 for horses, 3 for a buffalo and cart, between 0.3 and 1.5 for a canoe and up to 5 for a junk. (ANC RSC E 3. File No 257, Box 10, Résidence de Pursat. Procés-verbaux des séances du conseil de Résidence. Session d'avril 1916.) The rates were set centrally and differed little between *circonscriptions*. The agendas of the Councils of the *Résidences* were almost identical. (See, for

example, ANC RSC E 3 File No 255 Box 10, Résidence de Kompong Thom. Procès-verbaux des séances du conseil de résidence, Session ordinaire d'avril 1916.)
[45] AOM RSC 430, Rapport politique, 1er Trimestre 1916. The text of the decree was published in the Bulletin Administratif du Cambodge, Phnom Penh, 1916, pp.91-94.
[46] ANC RSC E 3. File No 11559. Box 989. Detaxe de certains engins de pêche, exonérations des droits: extrait du procès-verbal du conseil de Résidence de Soai-Rieng, 1916.
[47] ANC RSC E 3. File 259 Box 10. Résidence de Takeo. Procès-verbaux des séances du conseil de Résidence. Session d'avril 1916.
[48] AOM RSC 430, Rapport politique, 2ème Trimestre 1916; RSC 481, Perception de l'impôt après l'ordonnance royale de 19 février 1916.
[49] AOM RSC 430, Rapports politiques, 2ème Trimestre 1916, 2ème Trimestre 1917; RSC 401, Rapports politiques trimestriels, June-July-August and Sept-Oct-Nov 1916, Soai Rieng. See also the *Bulletin Administratif du Cambodge*, 1916, pp. 269, 276-278, 455-463.
[50] ANC RSC D35 File 4995, Box 520. Conseil de Gouvernement de l'Indochine. Session ordinaire de 1916. Rapport sur la situation générale du Cambodge.
[51] ANC RSC E 03 File 21180. Box 2260. M. Pauher, inspecteur des affaires politiques et administratives. Résidence de Prey Veng. Extrait du rapport d'inspection du 22 février – 10 mars 1915.
[52] ANC RSC F65. File No 7763. Affaire Bellan: documents divers concernants le comportement de M. Bellan, Résident à Prey Veng, et les troubles populaires Prey Veng en janvier et février 1916. Arrête No 2467 en date du 28 Octobre 1916 déférant M. Bellan, Admin. de 2ème classe devant un conseil d'enquête. Bellan was sent to Baclieu in Cochinchina.
[53] Ibid. Letter from Baudoin to *Gougal*, 24 September 1916.
[54] Ibid. (Arrête No 2467).
[55] ANC RSC 451 File 24419 Conseil des Ministres, 239e séance du 22 janvier 1916.
[56] Andrew Graham, (1956), *Interval in Indo-China*, Macmillan, London, pp.96-97.
[57] Unsigned, (1923), "First Cambodian Gospel leaflets", *The Call of French Indo-China*, No. 4, Gospel Press, Hanoi, July-August, p.10.
[58] Hobsbawm, ("Peasants and Politics") op.cit. pp. 200-201.

Chapter 11

"A Kind of *Belle Époque*": The Monarchy and Politics Between the wars

If I have stretched out my account of the years between the wars, it is because this period was for me, as for others of my generation, a kind of 'belle époque', forever gone. Afterwards, Cambodia would never again be the same.

—Huy Kanthoul, Cambodian teacher, writer and politician.

French residents in Cambodia would have seen little to celebrate as New Year's Day dawned in 1918. The war that most people had thought would be over inside six months had dragged on for four bloody years. *Résident Supérieur* François Baudoin reported a certain "lassitude of spirits" due to the prolongation of the war. "Alarmist rumors" circulated in the Chinese and "Annamite" communities, he wrote. There were scarcities of imported goods and steep price rises for most commodities.[1] The unexpected news of the victory in Europe later in the year caused relief and euphoria in French circles in Cambodia. The French presence was stretched thin. Many of the men among the 1000 or so French people who had lived in the country until 1914 had gone home to join the armed forces. The 1916 Affair revealed the vulnerability of the French power in wartime. Save for Sisowath's actions, the Affair might have lead to a serious challenge to French power. The war years had been a gray time, with few luxuries and little in the way of diversion from the war, so news of the victory must have provided color to the settlers' lives. Even the Cambodians, allegedly "so generally apathetic and indifferent to distant events", took notice, or so Baudoin reported. A special edition of the official *Gazette Khmère* appeared and there were government-sponsored parades in the streets.[2] The residents of Phnom Penh, both European and Asian, marked Armistice Day on 11 November with a "spontaneous demonstration of patriotism", and perhaps this was the case,[3] although Baudoin's own reports are contradictory. Later, he said that the Khmers ignored the conclusion of peace. However, he found consolation in their apparent indifference to news of the Bolshevik Revolution in Russia.[4] Sisowath remained staunchly pro-French and a royal proclamation took the news of peace to the villages.[5] One wonders how the peasants knew of the revolution in Russia, if the king had to inform them of the armistice in France.[6] Baudoin supplies no answers, perhaps because he did not need to engage in soul-searching; French power must have seemed secure and he reported shortly afterwards that the victory in Europe had boosted French authority in Cambodia.[7] The French reported that when Marshal Joffre visited in December 1921, "vast crowds" turned out to welcome him, even in the villages[8] where the tour was recorded on film.[9] There is some hyperbole here; the Marshal traveled with Sisowath, always a draw card, but they would have been curious about the great warrior. The historian Robert Aldrich has written that the period between the wars was the zenith of the French Empire—a veritable "golden age."[10] A silent film exists which shows Phnom Penh in those days: elephants lumber in single file outside the royal palace and barefoot Khmer troops march on the palace parade ground, some dressed in khaki, others in dress whites, while a military band plays a tune we can never hear.[11] These are grainy, flickering images from France's colonial heyday. There is no sense of threat. Having seen off their enemies in Europe, the French could devote more attention to their colonies. They could not have known that the golden age would be a coda for their power.

The Cambodians probably *were* impressed to some extent by news of the victory. Most, however, continued their lives as before, plowing and sowing, more concerned about the signs of an impending bad harvest than about distant events. The secret police kept a close watch for signs of disaffection, but reported none. For a small number of families, the news of peace meant that their men would be returning from the battlefields and factories of France. The Governor General promised their speedy repatriation and promised preferential treatment to ensure their reintegration into civilian life.[12] Even the returned servicemen, in the main, seemed happy to merge back into civilian life, although the *Sûreté* opened files on a minority for "intemperance", provoking brawls, showing disrespect to the indigenous authorities and generally acting above their station.[13]

The enduring contract between France and the Khmer elite

King Sisowath was 79-years-old when the war ended, and had been a loyal supporter of France for some 50 years. The American travel writer Harry Franck saw him as a "play king" and a "poor old figurehead" living in dowdy opulence under gilded spires.[14] The English writer H. Churchill Candee thought of him as "a lion with drawn claws", living in a court that was "a sort of shady circus".[15] The octogenarian king's "playthings" included a harem of around 240 girls and women—less than Norodom had kept, but considerable nevertheless—and piles of gold and jewels.[16] The British diplomatic visitor Mr. B.C. Newton considered that, "Although Cambodia is nominally a protectorate...like Tonkin, it is indistinguishable except technically from a French colony."[17] Sisowath *was*, as these writers implied, a French puppet, but they did not fully grasp that he was nevertheless indispensable for France's interests. He had fought with the French against Pou Kombo's men, and again taken up arms for the Protectorate in the Great Rebellion of 1885. He had also sent a number of his sons to fight for France in the Great War. He had defused the potentially explosive peasant movement of 1916 in a way that the French could never have done. He was the traditional head of a traditional society and his subjects obeyed him out of conviction. If they obeyed the French, it was at least partly because Sisowath bade them to do so. Franck observed that because of his sacred authority, "cases containing jewels of great price in the silver temple are not locked, but are protected merely by pasted strips of paper with the name of the guardian written on them." The common folk would never steal his possessions.[18] Except for his failing health, Sisowath appears to have lived out his final years in serenity. Photographs from the time show the bluff, square head to be grizzled with age, yet at ease with the world. One photograph shows him as an 87-year-old in early 1927, dressed in fine European style, with cravat, starched shirt, highly polished shoes, knickerbockers and cane, sitting ramrod straight on an elegant French chair.[19] The "contract" between France and the Khmer kings was to continue almost until the end of the reign of Sisowath's son, Monivong, when it began to break down under the pressures of war, Japanese occupation, and Khmer nationalism.

Sisowath's slow physical decline

The state of Sisowath's health was of increasing concern in the years after the Great War. Like Norodom, he was fond of the pleasures of the flesh, but was possessed of a strong constitution that offset the effects of his excesses. His sight had begun to fail before the war, when cataracts were diagnosed in both eyes. He went to Saigon in 1912, where the celebrated eye surgeon Professor Truc, of Montpellier, successfully operated. The operation was expensive—15,000 francs— but Sisowath's subjects hailed it as a miracle and it and boosted France's prestige in the kingdom.[20] Sisowath remained lucid and in good spirits until well after the war. Official reports from the early 1920s recorded that he was still participating effectively in the country's administration, and that he enjoyed remarkably robust health and physical resistance.[21]   In late 1921, he accompanied Marshal Joffre, the "victor of the Marne" on a grand tour of the country, including a visit to Angkor.[22] The usual Tang Tok festival marked his 84th birthday in September 1923. Vast crowds thronged to the palace grounds in Phnom Penh, where an exposition of Khmer art was on view and there were parades of French and Khmer troops. The royal orchestra played the *Marseillaise* and there were speeches by the *Résident Supérieur* and the King, who praised the "magnificent works" of the French Protectorate.[23] There were similar scenes a year later,[24] but the King's advanced age was beginning to show; even earlier he regularly delegated all questions of secondary importance to his son Monivong, and chose to spend more time resting at his country estate near Kampot.[25] Towards the end of 1924, his eyes began to trouble him again and he was placed in the care of Dr. Vallet, the director of the Cambodian health service, and of the army ophthalmologist Major Marque. This time the diagnosis was glaucoma; an ulceration of the cornea of the left eye, and in 1925, surgery was necessary.[26] He also developed arteriosclerosis at this time[27] and began to worry French officials by a "stubbornly senile" refusal to comply with his doctors' orders.[28] According to Harry Hervey, the old man still smoked 70 pipes of opium a day,[29] although one suspects he did so now more to quell his incessant pain than for pleasure. Death was plainly approaching and the French had to again ponder the question of a suitable successor to the throne. Although the royal offspring were numerous, the French considered that most of them were "insouciant" or "uneducated" and hence unfit for the throne. They were an expensive drain on the kingdom's finances.[30] Ironically, these remarks echoed the sentiments of the disgraced prince, Norodom Mayura, who had died in exile in Cochinchina seven years previously. In 1912, Mayura had written pseudonymously to the French Chamber of Deputies claiming that the Sisowath princes were uneducated and badly thought of by the Cambodian population.[31]

Intrigues for the succession to the throne

The Norodom wing of the royal family had never accepted Sisowath's right to the crown. Prince Norodom Yukanthor spent most of his life agitating against France and Sisowath from his exile and Bangkok. Other members of the Norodom wing, including his estranged wife Princess Malika and Prince Mayura joined him in this, particularly during the effervescence of the 1916 Affair. A number of "Norodomists", including Prince Phatsavath, were kept under police surveillance for many years during this period, although nothing alarming was reported.[32] Yukanthor hated France until the end of his days, but his plotting was ineffectual. French agents kept a close eye on him in Bangkok, and a police report from the mid-1920s claimed that he was "reduced to poverty" and that the ordinary Cambodians never talked about him.[33] The *Sûreté* reported a rekindling of intrigues in 1927, just before Sisowath's death.[34] Other members of the wing had remained aloof from intrigue, but clearly hoped that the French would consider their claims. The rapid deterioration of Sisowath's health would have given them fresh hope. Certainly, many members of the Norodom wing had given proof both of their loyalty to France and of intellectual ability.

Prince Monivong had long been Sisowath's own preferred candidate for the succession (since the death of another son, his favorite, Essaravong in 1907) but the French did not come to agree with him for many years. Sisowath was almost 75-years-old when the Great War began, and the French at that time believed that it would be prudent to revert to one of Norodom's descendants, given the low intellectual caliber or insouciance of many of the Sisowath princes. One of the most likely candidates, Maghavan, died in the year war began, and the French ruled out the otherwise suitable Yuthevong because of his ill health.[35] Another possibility, Sathavong, who had served as Minister for the Interior, was considered committed to the French cause, but he suffered from advanced tuberculosis, and in the event, did not outlive Sisowath.[36] In this period, the Minister for Colonies, advised by

Governor General Albert Sarraut, considered Prince Norodom Sutharot, 46-years-old in 1916, to be the most qualified candidate, despite his apparent lack of ambition. The Minister felt that Monivong would be a poor choice because of his alleged mediocre intelligence and his diffidence about public affairs. Monivong had studied at a French military academy, but the Minister considered that he had not profited by his stay in France. Moreover, he was said to lack popularity among the mandarins and the people.[37]

Sisowath was to stick by the choice of his son until his death. In 1922, according to a French police report, Sisowath had "in effect conferred on Prince Monivong the status of *Préa Kéo fea*." Although only one *Préa Kéo fea* had previously ascended directly to the throne, the title elevated Monivong above other hopefuls and signaled to the people as a whole that Monivong would be the next king.[38] In 1925, the *Sûrêté* considered that, while one could not talk properly about political opinion in the Cambodian population, there were three distinct groups of opinion about who should succeed Sisowath. The first "party" were partisans of Sisowath. The second, the "Norodom party", backed either Sutharot or Phanuvong.[39] The third party consisted of "Those who are indifferent to the two parties, but who fear that Cambodia might become a French colony after the death of Sisowath." The police reporter considered, however, that all three of the parties were loyal to the Protectorate.[40] By this time, official French opinion had shifted against the Norodom party. This seems to be have been especially true of *Résident Supérieur* François Baudoin, who characteristically sided with Sisowath in a dispute between the King and Prince Norodom Ritharasi. Dr Ritharasi, who was perhaps the first Khmer graduate of a French medical school, wished to return to France in order to undertake postgraduate study. In what seems to have been a case of senile cantankerousness, Sisowath refused to allow the young doctor to go. Baudoin backed this arbitrary order and "categorically denied" Ritharasi's request for a bursary. Baudoin got his way over the strenuous objections of the influential Socialist politician Marius Moutet in Paris.[41] In October 1926, Baudoin wrote to the Governor General concluding that Monivong was the best choice for the succession because he had "a less authoritarian personality" than the other contenders, and was, moreover, "more pliable and more open to the direction of the [French] administration".[42] Baudoin's opinion might well have been influenced by bribes from the Sisowath wing.[43] Until six years before Sisowath's death, Baudoin had favored Sutharot.[44] In terms of ability, Sutharot would probably have been the best choice. A police report considered him intelligent and amiable, with a great deal of personal prestige and connections with powerful individuals in the French community. His brother Phanuvong, despite having held high office in the Khmer administration, was out of the race even earlier, as the French considered him to be greedy and without prestige.[45] Baudoin by himself could not have guaranteed that Monivong would succeed his father, but the succession was ensured when the influential colonial official Pierre Pasquier threw his support behind the Sisowath camp. Pasquier, who had served as *Résident Supérieur* of Annam, and who would become Governor General of Indochina in 1928, suspected Sutharot of the cardinal sin of being pro-Siamese, despite being intellectually pre-eminent in the royal family. Pasquier dismissed other possible contenders from the Norodom wing. He ruled out Prince Norodom Chanthalekha as a womanizer who had forfeited all respect in high circles. Others were variously dismissed as corrupt, lacking talent or will, or dissipated and lacking dignity. He declared that Phanuvong was greedy and lacked generosity. Pasquier believed that although Monivong was emotional and lacked the intellect of some of the other contenders, that he was loyal to France and popular among the people. He was, in short, "a real Cambodian" who would never turn towards Bangkok and was "a prince disposed to follow the directions of the French administration."[46]

The death of Sisowath and the succession of Monivong

Even as the intrigues boiled around him, Sisowath's end was fast approaching. He appeared in public for the Bastille Day celebrations in 1926, but thereafter, "enfeebled by age", he spent much of his time in seclusion. In late July 1927, while staying at the home of his son Souphanouvong, the old king suffered a bout of violent diarrhea. He did not recover, and died on 9 August 1927, just a few weeks short of his 88th birthday.[47] Monivong, two French doctors and the *Résident Supérieur* had hurried to his bedside. In Phnom Penh, an artillery unit fired a 21-gun salute and the members of the Council of Ministers assembled to choose a successor. Many Khmers shaved their heads as an expression of grief and respect.[48] The Council of Ministers rubber-stamped a decision made beforehand, for all the claims that the French Government had granted it full freedom of action. Monivong was the unanimous choice of the councilors, with *Résident Supérieur* Le Fol in the chair. The French Government at Paris ratified the decision shortly afterwards.[49] Most Cambodians accepted the choice although Norodom Sihanouk later claimed that the succession of Monivong "caused resentment inside the country because patriotic public opinion supported the Norodom branch."[50] Perhaps this is so and it is possible that Sihanouk heard something at his mother's knee—he was a little boy of four-and-a-half when Sisowath died and his own mother the Princess Kossamak was from the Sisowath branch. The royal palace was a hotbed of intrigue and gossip and the Norodom wing resented the choice of successor. How far that resentment extended beyond the palace walls is another matter and one wonders how "patriotic public opinion" could be gauged in the absence of any democratic method of expressing it.

The semi-official *Echo du Cambodge* listed the major achievements of Sisowath's reign as: the establishment of private property in land, the reform of the penal code and the indigenous justice system, the establishment of the civil state and the foundation of the national library. There have been worse epitaphs and his reign had been one of relative tranquility and reform.[51] According to custom, Sisowath's body lay in state for some seven months before it was cremated. Not surprisingly, the English visitor Eleanor Mordaunt considered that the room containing the body smelled of ferrets,[52] but the royal remains were venerated by the people. When the cremation was finally held at the beginning of March 1928, vast crowds flocked to the capital as the funeral urn was drawn slowly through the streets.[53] The *Sûreté* considered, rightly, that the ordinary people had little interest in the politics of the succession.[54] Soon after Sisowath's death, his uncrowned heir, Monivong,[55] made a grand tour of the kingdom, greeting the thousands of well-wishers who turned out to meet him. He followed this up with a visit to Saigon aboard the royal yacht, the *Khmerac Rithidet*.[56] If there had been any serious opposition to the succession, it melted away.

Monivong could move with equal facility in both societies

According to the Phnom Penh correspondent of the London *Times,* the royal astrologers chose June 22, 1928 as a propitious day for Monivong's coronation. The streets of Phnom Penh echoed with the reverberations of artillery salutes and the strains of brass bands playing the Cambodian and French national anthems. There were banners everywhere in the sparkling sunshine, along with "tall masts supporting nine-storied parasols—the emblem of sovereignty."[57] The people set out offerings of fruit and flowers to ward off the evil spirits of the earth and air from their new sovereign. The coronation was an elaborate affair. At the center of events was Monivong, described by an eyewitness as "a middle-aged man of dark complexion and pleasant countenance, draped in a white and yellow cotton robe".[58] The son of Sisowath and Queen Barombapit,[59] he was 52 years old. He passed over a bridge from the throne hall of the palace and took his place under a gilded canopy on a nine-storied tapering dais. There, surrounded by the high dignitaries of the court and the French administration, splendid in their multi-colored plumage, and by eight high Buddhist monks, he was anointed with "lustral waters" by a series of dignitaries, the first of whom was Alexandre Varenne, the Governor General of Indochina.[60] Although he appears to have been reluctant to accept the crown, Monivong was as staunchly pro-French as his father had been. With his large, square face, short stature and brilliant black eyes under folded eyelids, he closely resembled his father, too.[61] Monivong had visited France in 1906 in his father's entourage, and had stayed on to study at the Saint-Maixent military academy. He graduated as a sub-lieutenant in 1908 and served for a short period afterwards in the 127th Infantry of the Line at Brive, Corrèze, in France.[62] A Siam-based British diplomat considered that Monivong had "a broad outlook and is very much attached to France: it is therefore most probable that he will continue the recent policy of wise reforms and of collaboration with the government of the Protectorate..."[63] He spoke fluent French and could move with equal facility in Cambodian or European society.[64] He could wear the uniform of the French officer or the brocaded *sampot* and tunic of a Khmer king,[65] both of which he was. He was promoted to Brigadier-General in 1934 on the recommendation of Governor General René Robin,[66] although he saw little combat other than during pacification missions with his father in the late 19th century.[67] Although the French would not allow him to volunteer for active service in World War I, his commission was important to him. The contemporary writer Herman Norden claimed that Monivong preferred to be addressed by his army rank rather than his royal title.[68] He was a gorgeous sight in his full dress uniform, ceremonial sword by his side, with cocked hat, sash, medals and gleaming gold braid.[69] Early in his reign, he appears to have astonished the French when he upbraided his subjects for not working hard enough and for being content with subsistence farming. (He had a life-long interest in scientific farming.) In the same period, Monivong also wrote a long article on the need for Cambodia to build a modern army.[70] Yet, for all that, he was by nature a private person, preferring to steal away to his estates whenever possible.

Monivong suited French designs. In him, they had found a king who was perfectly willing to play the part of a loyal figurehead, leaving important decisions to the French. Late in life, he was said to come to

Phnom Penh from his Bokor estates only "to do his ceremonial duties and to keep in touch with the administration, which is carried on by his Ministers under the strict supervision of the French *Résident Supérieur*." The same observer added, that, "He would probably be glad to dispense with the ceremonies", but for the insistence of the French on maintaining the outward formalities.[71] He had little aptitude for politics and the French considered him less intelligent than the Norodom princes,[72] many of whom had played an active part in the administration. He seems to have been "an intensely introspective man"[73] given to quiet pleasures such as chess and writing verse to accompany classical Khmer dances".[74] One of Monivong's verse compositions, written in honor of M. Reynaud, the French Colonial Minister, who visited Cambodia in 1931, has survived.[75] On the other hand, he seems to have shared his father's penchant for the bottle, the opium pipe and the harem.[76] He was also reputed to be a spendthrift. Money slipped through his fingers, especially if there were new cars to buy. His garage was stocked with barely used vehicles, and if he did not have cash, he bought on credit, to the despair of his accountant, who "tore out his hair" trying to find money to pay his master's debts.[77] The royal *seraglio* was, however, a pale shadow of Norodom's vast institution, housing four or five dozen wives and concubines[78] as opposed to hundreds, the result of decades of cost cutting. His uncle and father's harems had been recruited from mandarin families, even from those of the Council of Ministers. It was considered an honor for a daughter to be accepted, especially if she became a favorite, and was a road for advancement. However, by Monivong's reign, the French had stripped the monarchy of much of its power and there was little incentive for mandarin families to offer their daughters. Monivong's girls tended to come from humbler, plebeian backgrounds.[79] One of the first things the French asked Monivong to do following his father's death was to sign a document providing for further cuts to the civil list. The document had been drafted even before Sisowath's death.[80] As he aged, Monivong's interest in state affairs waned still further. His grandson Norodom Sihanouk recalls him as taking no interest at all in the details of the administration, even signing official papers without reading them. Monivong and his predecessors, he continued, "were nothing more than 'parrots' trained by the French to say 'yes'."[81]

The furor over the "invading lepers" of Caodai

Yet, for all the patina of the European gentleman, with elegant drawing room manners and a penchant for Bond Street cigarettes[82],

Monivong was still a traditional king and not entirely powerless. Even before his coronation, he demanded that the French take steps to suppress a new religious movement, Caodai, which was making thousands of converts among his subjects, particularly in the eastern border provinces of Prey Veng and Svay Rieng.[83] The French willingly complied, sensing in the sect an acid that might leach the social cement of the kingdom. Caodaism was a strange new "syncretic" religion that had been founded in the mid-1920s by the mystic Le Van Trung in Cochinchina. It drew on elements from Buddhism and Christianity, and included the Buddha, Christ and Victor Hugo among its pantheon of saints. Le Van Trung had dubbed himself "Pope" of the movement, which he ran from a temple near the Black Mountain in Vietnam's Tay Ninh province. The scholar Khy Phanra, who has outlined the history of Caodaism in Cambodia, considers that the sect's main appeal was to middle class Vietnamese in Cochinchina, who were unable to find a niche for themselves in colonial society, and turned to religion instead.[84] The religion also had a certain appeal for Khmers in the borderlands. Shortly before the wet season began in 1927, thousands of Khmers trekked over the border to the Caodai temple in the Tay Ninh province of Cochinchina. Some were drawn by simple curiosity about the new faith.[85] There had been floods and poor harvests and others were probably tempted by the sect's offer of food and hospitality.[86] Although the *Résident* of Prey Veng considered that Monivong's visit to the province later in the year had somewhat stemmed the exodus, it did not entirely stop the spread of the new faith.[87] Monivong issued a decree banning Caodai as a "false religion" shortly after Sisowath's death—and possibly acting at his father's request—and called on his subjects to remain faithful to their traditional religion.[88]

Two years later, Monivong wrote to M. Lavit, the *Résident Supérieur,* to demand stronger action to repress the sect, comparing its activities to those of "invading lepers". He pointed out that their activities contravened the Treaty of 1863.[89] The Catholics, he wrote, "do not trouble the public order", but the "naïve and credulous spirit of the Cambodian people" made them susceptible to the sect's appeal and menaced the country's "social integrity".[90] He probably acted from the conviction that Caodai was, as he claimed, a false religion. He probably also believed that his subjects relied on him to protect the Buddhist faith. The number of converts to Caodaism was small when compared to the total population, but it was nevertheless probably the most serious threat that Buddhism had faced. Cambodia had been primarily a Buddhist country since the 14th century: other religions were largely confined to ethnic minorities, Islam among the Chams[91] for example. The Khmers had been impervious to the proselytizing of other religions. A king who defected to Islam in the late 17th century was remembered as the "king who left religion".[92] Catholic missionaries had operated in the kingdom since the late 16th century,[93] with a conspicuous lack of success except among the Vietnamese minority.[94] Buddhism and the Catholic brand of Christianity were the only religions recognized by the Treaty between France and Cambodia in 1863. Although the Catholics built churches throughout the kingdom, in practice they were content to leave the Khmers to the monks and to concentrate on their Vietnamese flock. There appears to have been little enmity between the faiths and an Australian Protestant missionary who arrived in the 1890s was initially welcomed by the French administration. He was deported, for his nationality rather than his religion, after tensions arose between Britain and France following the "Fashoda incident" on the Nile.[95] American Protestant missionaries who arrived later were shadowed and harassed by the authorities.[96] One suspects that they were grudgingly tolerated because of their lack of success among the Khmers and because they hailed from a powerful country that was an ally of France.[97] Such religious tension as did exist stemmed from rivalry between the Mohanikay and Thommayuth orders within the Buddhist religion. Until 1864, when the Thommayuth order arrived, there had only been the Mohanikay order in Cambodia. To the non-Buddhist, the differences between them are arcane and are in fact disagreements over rites, not belief,[98] but they did lead on occasion, to disturbances. Of greater importance was the conflict between traditionalists and modernists, as in Battambang in 1937. The traditionalists wished to stick to the old religious texts in the schools, while the latter wanted to use the new publications edited by the École Supérieur de Pali and the Royal Library, and to eliminate Siamese influence from the clergy.[99] The conflict sometimes led to violence, as in Kandal province in 1939, when followers of the two wings clashed over the question of their nominees for the positions of chiefs of the pagodas.[100]

The French acted with alacrity to comply with Monivong's wishes to suppress the Caodai, as they considered it to have an intrinsically anti-French bias. Their constant harassment of the sect had an obsessive flavor, even within the framework of a colonial police state. It was nonsense to believe that the sect would "infect" the Khmers to any large degree, despite the early adherence of tens of thousands to the new religion, and sporadic successes thereafter. Caodai's early successes among the Khmers were in any case largely limited to the eastern provinces of Svay Rieng and Prey Veng.[101] Another royal decree followed in 1928, and afterwards almost all of the religion's Khmer converts left, faithful to their King's command[102] or cowed by the threats of hefty fines and up to five years imprisonment for membership.[103] Caodai did not die out in Cambodia, but its influence was thereafter confined almost exclusively to the Vietnamese minority and the authorities constantly harassed it.[104]

Monivong's humiliations at French hands

Yet, if the French acted swiftly to appease Monivong in the matter of the Caodai, this does not indicate that the King had any real power other than his symbolic value. On occasion, the French would deny him privileges and humiliate him publicly. In 1928, shortly before his coronation, when he was a middle-aged man, he fell in love with an 18-year-old Siamese dancer, the Princess Nangsao Baeng, whom he met during a theatrical performance in Battambang. The pair planned to marry and the affair was discussed at length in the Bangkok press. The colonial authorities considered that the articles were anti-French and perhaps considered the marriage would be a security risk, for they would not allow Monivong to live with the girl.[105] Nevertheless, Monivong remained loyal to his masters. He sent his two eldest sons, Monireth and Monipong to study in France in 1929,[106] mirroring the custom set much earlier of sending royal offspring to the court at Bangkok. Like their father, the two princes graduated as French army officers, albeit from the Saint-Cyr academy, not Monivong's own *alma mater*. Relations between the king and the French authorities were reported as being very cordial up until 1935.[107] A crisis in Franco-Cambodian relations was looming, however. A photograph taken in late 1936 shows Monivong as a thickset man in middle age, with the square head of the Sisowaths, heavy jowls, thick eyebrows, a drooping moustache and hair *en brosse*. The chest of his general's uniform is covered in the "fruit salad" of military ribbons. It is his 61st birthday, but his black eyes are melancholy.[108] Perhaps, in his heart, he was aware that he was a pampered puppet. Perhaps also his air of sadness reflects the increased consciousness of mortality that humans acquire as they age. However, we also know that Monivong had been on very bad terms with M. Achille Silvestre,[109] who served as *Résident Supérieur* until late 1936.[110] Silvestre, a man with a certain dark charisma, had served in Indochina since he arrived as a 23-year-old in 1901.[111] The son of a colonial army officer, he handled power easily and must have terrified his subordinates. He served for many years as François Baudoin's *chef du cabinet* and as mayor of Phnom Penh. In the early 1920s, a journalist described him as Baudoin's *éminence grise* and claimed that King Sisowath had been uneasy in his presence.[112] M. Marinetti, who was Deputy for Cambodia in *the Conseil Supérieur de la France d'outre-mer,* reported in 1936 that he had found a "stormy atmosphere" in Phnom Penh and claimed that Silvestre had "publicly humiliated" the King. Monivong, as a result, was so angry that he refused to live in the capital or to attend official ceremonies and there was serious tension between the Cambodian government and the French administration. Silvestre, evidently, had attempted to bully Monivong into disowning his son, Monireth, who was regarded by the police as being anti-French. Marinetti said that Silvestre had been "vindictive" towards the young prince and that it had taken a considerable effort to repair the rupture with his father.[113] It is significant that the Popular Front government was in office in Paris when Marinetti made this assessment, and that Colonial Minister Marius Moutet readily accepted it. It is difficult to imagine conservative governments taking such a stance. The dispute also spilled out into the open, with the French language paper *Le Khmer* running a "vitriolic campaign" against Silvestre in 1936.[114] Silvestre died soon afterwards at Hanoi.[115] Monireth was a young man of 22 years in 1936,[116] whose offence, in Silvestre's eyes, was to have declared that he believed in democracy and "to expound openly, with the impetuosity of youth, his desire for the social evolution of his country" in the interests of the people. Marinetti considered that the French should foster Monireth, not smother him, and suggested sending him to Laos as Secretary-General of the Kingdom of Cambodia.[117] From all accounts, Monireth was a serious young man. He had graduated as an army officer and volunteered for service in France when war broke out in 1939. He also wrote a number of poems in French and Cambodian publications. The sentiments of his poem on the military graveyard at Silberloch in Alsace[118] leave no doubt that he was intensely loyal to France in this period. His bad experiences with Silvestre must have rankled, for all the placatory efforts of Moutet, Marinetti and the new *Résident Supérieur,* M. Thibaudeau. His good standing with the politicians of the Popular Front would have counted against him with the Vichy administration when his father died in 1941 and Governor General Jean Decoux was casting round for a suitable successor. Ironically, as he aged, he became renowned as the crustiest of Cambodian conservatives.

The twilight of "a kind of belle époque"

The quarrel between Monivong and the French was resolved. Monivong took up his official duties once more. Prince Monireth traveled to Paris to represent his father at the 1937 Paris Intercolonial Exposition,[119] and the French President received him on 20 July of that year.[120] Later that year, his brother Monipong passed his *baccalauréat* at Nice and entered the Saint-Cyr military academy. When Monipong's health deteriorated, he was placed under the protection of François Baudoin, the old *Résident Supérieur*, who had retired to Nice on the Côte d'Azur. Unlike Monireth, who had graduated with a B.A., Monipong was not a diligent student and was said to show a certain ill will towards physical and intellectual activity, despite a robust physique. He had wanted to enter the naval academy at Brest, but had obeyed his father's wishes for him to enter Saint-Cyr.[121]

The old accord between France and Cambodia seemed as strong as ever. As the clouds of war built up in Europe at the time of the Munich crisis, Monivong hastened to assure the French of his continuing loyalty.[122] When the war finally broke out, both Monireth and Monipong immediately volunteered for active service and left for their regiments in France with their father's blessing[123] as proof of his loyalty and regard for France.[124] It is clear that Monireth was Monivong's choice to succeed him as king. A short while earlier, when Monireth was on a grand tour of Europe, Monivong's health had declined and he had requested his son's return.[125] It must have been a major sacrifice to see his favorite son leave again, this time to face possible death on the battlefield. Monivong also made a major public speech of support for the French at this time, standing side by side with the new Governor General, General Catroux, on a podium in Phnom Penh.[126] Even after the fall of France in the summer of 1940, Monivong pledged his loyalty to Marshal Pétain's new Vichy regime,[127] but his health was declining rapidly and he was absent from the Cambodian New Year's festivities in April 1941. *Résident Supérieur* Thibaudeau shared the limelight with Monireth, Monipong and Thiounn instead.[128] The fall of France must have touched Monivong deeply; he was, after all, a high-ranking officer in the French army. The Monivong Chronicle (*bangsavatar*) rarely mentions overseas events, yet it devotes two pages to the defeat.[129] According to King Sihanouk, "the war broke his grandfather's will to live."[130] It was followed by the catastrophe of the Franco-Thai War, which led to the loss of large swathes of Cambodian territory. Monivong's death came swiftly on 23 April 1941[131] when he was resting at his country estate at

Bokor in the company of his two favorite sons and his consort, Saloth Roeung, known as Saroeun, the younger sister of Saloth Sar.[132] The premises were sealed and an inventory made of his considerable possessions and possessions, which included 111 boxes of opium.[133] The French colonial press sang his praises as a good king and an official report claimed that he remained loyal to France until the end.[134] This is debatable. Monivong died a depressed and disillusioned man. Although he had been a French puppet, his loyalty depended on the ability of the French to act as a genuine protecting power.

The Grand Council of the Kingdom met immediately under the chairmanship of the *Résident Supérieur* and voted unanimously to appoint Prince Norodom Sihanouk, from the rival branch of the royal family, as king.[135] It was an astonishing decision. The dead king's choice, Prince Monireth, had been passed over in favor of a teenage greenhorn.[136] Until the last months, Monivong's reign had been largely uneventful. His own palace chronicle, written largely by Palace Minister Thiounn, was wooden, repetitive and pro-French. David Chandler has written that the "dullness" of Monivong's chronicle was deliberate because "they saw the past as something that repeats itself [and] the alternative was chaos."[137] Chaos *was* looming. The colonial edifice that the French had so painstakingly built up since 1863 was crumbling at the edges. Further humiliations lay ahead for France, and growing numbers of Cambodians realized that their self-styled protectors were not invincible.

Old men remember their youth with nostalgic tenderness, glossing over the hard times and bringing the good ones into sharper focus, yet for old Khmers the mellowing influence of time does not completely mislead when they contemplate the inter-war years. The writer and politician Huy Kanthoul is often critical of French rule, yet he remembers the period with affection, as a kind of *"belle époque,* forever gone."[138]

Notes

[1] AOM RSC 431 Rapport Politique 1er Trimestre 1918.
[2] AOM RSC 431 Rapport Politique 3ème Trimestre 1918. The *Gazette* was a government propaganda publication.
[3] AOM RSC 431 Rapport Politique, 4ème Trimestre 1918.
[4] AOM RSC 431 Rapport Politique, 4ème Trimestre 1919.
[5] AOM RSC 431 Rapport Politique 2ème Trimestre 1919.
[6] Perhaps news of the revolution came via the Chinese network, for many of that ethnic group maintained ties with family and friends in their nominally independent homeland.

[7] AOM RSC 431 Rapport Politique, 1er Trimestre 1920.

[8] AOM F0 3 64 265 Gouvernement-Générale de l'Indochine. Rapport Politique 4ème Trimestre 1921. (This document will probably now be located in the AOM RSC files.)

[9] AOM Fonds Amiraux, FO 3 64267 Rapport Politique 1er Trimestre.

[10] Robert Aldrich, (1996), *A History of French Overseas Expansion*, Macmillan, Basingstoke, p.114.

[11] Major E. Alexander Powell made the film, entitled "The Unshod Soldiers of a King", for Goldwyn-Bray studios sometime between 1920 and 1925. A copy can be found in the National Archives of Canada/Archives Nationales du Canada at Ottawa. (35mm, Rack A8, Can 3, Item 1, Cat Mo 1133.) In 1994, the owner of copyright refused to allow it to be copied to videotape even for teaching purposes.

[12] Rapport Politique, 3ème Trimestre, 1918 op.cit.

[13] AOM RSC 431 Rapports Politiques 4ème Trimestre 1919 and 1er Trimestre 1920.

[14] Harry A. Franck, (1926), *East of Siam. Ramblings in the Five Divisions of French Indo-China*, The Century, New York, pp. 35, 39.

[15] H. Churchill Candee, (1925), *Angkor the Magnificent. The Wonder City of Ancient Cambodia*, H.F. and G. Witherby, London, pp. 50-52.

[16] Franck, op.cit. pp. 37-38.

[17] PRO FO 371 12624 W4964/89/17 From Mr. B.C. Newton, Peking, to Western Dept. Foreign Office, 21 March 1927.

[18] Franck, op.cit. p.37.

[19] *L'Echo du Cambodge*, 21 January 1927.

[20] AOM RSC 429 Rapports Politiques, 2ème & 3ème Trimestres 1912. AOM Indochine NF Carton 48, Dossier 580 (1) *Gougal* to Minister of Colonies, 25 October 1912, "Maladie du Roi Sisowath". The illness and treatment is also recorded in the *Sisowath Chronicle*, pp.1151-1160.

[21] AOM RSC 430 Rapports Politiques, 2ème and 4ème Trimestres, 1921.

[22] AOM RSC 430 Rapport Politique, 4ème Trimestre 1921.

[23] "La 84 anniversaire de sa majesté Sisowath", (1923), *Revue du Tourisme Indochinois. Bulletin Officiel du Syndicat d'Initiative de l'Indochine*, No. 21, 26 September, pp.12-16, Saigon.

[24] *L'Echo du Cambodge*, 19 April 1924.

[25] AOM RSC 430 Rapport Politique, 3ème Trimestre 1922.

[26] AOM RSC 432 Rapport Politique, 4ème Trimestre 1924. In addition, AOM Indochine NF Carton 48 Dossier 581 (2) *Gougal* to Minister of Colonies, 23 June 1925. Sisowath was not the only Cambodian to suffer with his eyes. The French opened an ophthalmological clinic in Phnom Penh during this period and this was soon treating between 80 and 100 patients daily, mainly for trachoma and conjunctivitis.

[27] AOM Indochine NF 579 (2) *Gougal* to Minister of Colonies, 2 January 1925.

[28] *Gougal* to Minister of Colonies, 23 June 1925, op.cit.

[29] Harry Hervey, (1927), *King Cobra: An Autobiography of Travel in French Indo-China,* Cosmopolitan Books, New York, p.110. Hervey cites a Frenchman he dubs "The Tired Cavalier" as the source of this information. This person appears to have been the former administrator Roland Meyer, the author of *Saramani Danseuse Cambodgienne* (E. Fasquelle, Paris, 1922).

[30] AOM Indochine NF Carton 48 Dossier 580 (2) *Gougal* to Minister of Colonies, 23 June 1925.

[31] QO Indo-Chine. Personalités Indochinoises. Prince-Agitateurs II. 1909-1917. (Vol. 3). Letter from "Cambodian Committee", signed by "Chum" to the Chamber of Deputies. Forwarded, with accompanying note, by the President of the Chamber to the Minister of Foreign Affairs, 5 January 1912.

[32] AOM Fonds Amiraux, 7 15 (3) Rapport Annuel de la Sûreté, 1924-1925. On Phatsavath see AOM FA 7F 13 (1). Hoeffel, Chef du Service de la Sûreté, Phnom Penh, Note mensuelle, December 1927.

[33] AOM Fonds Amiraux, 7F 15 (2). Chef de la Sûreté au Cambodge à le Directeur des Affaires Politiques et de la Sûreté Générale à Hanoi, 20 August 1924. Yukanthor died in exile on 27 or 29 June 1934. *L'Echo du Cambodge,* 3 July 1934, gives the former date, Sorn Samnang gives the latter. [Sorn Samnang, (1995), "L'Evolution de la Société Cambodgienne entre les deux guerres mondiales (1919-1939)". Thèse pour le doctorat d'histoire. Université Paris VII, Tome I, p.87.]

[34] AOM Fonds Amiraux, 7F 15 (5) Rapport Annuel de la Sûreté, 1 July 1926-30 June 1927.

[35] AOM Indochine NF 579 (2) Carton 48, Trône du Cambodge, Minister of Colonies, Paris, 12 June 1914.

[36] He died in 1926. (AOM Indochine, NF 579 (2) Carton 48, *Résident Supérieur* to *Gougal,* 2 October 1926.)

[37] Ibid. Minister of Colonies to *Gougal,* 23 June 1916.

[38] AOM Fonds Amiraux, 7F 15 (6) Rapport annuel, Sûreté, 31 May 1927-1 June 1928. The title was given to the prince who was closest to the throne after the *Obbareach* or successor.

[39] Phanuvong had served as Minister of the Interior and was for many years a member of the Phnom Penh Municipal Commission. He was considered loyal and wore the Legion of Honor. (AOM RSC 430 Rapport Politique, 1er Trimestre 1918.)

[40] AOM Fonds Amiraux 7F 15 (3) Rapport annuel (Sûreté) 1924-1925.

[41] AOM FM Indo NF Carton 47 Dossier 565. Re: Prince Norodom Ritharasi. Moutet was to become Colonial Minister in the Popular Front Government of the mid-1930s. Ritharasi went to France anyway, and successfully completed his doctoral thesis. This was published in 1929 as *L'Evolution de la Médecine au Cambodge* by the Librairie Louis Arnette in Paris. He later became a country doctor and was accused of performing illegal abortions. ("Un affaire étrange. Un médecin cambodgien est arrêté à Saint-Jean en Royaner", *La Presse Indochinoise,* 14 October 1939.)

[42] AOM Indochine NF 579 (2) Carton 48, Résident Supérieur to *Gougal*, 2 October 1926.

[43] AOM Indo NF Carton 48 Dossier 578, *Les Annales Coloniales*, proceedings of the Commission de l'Algérie des Colonies et des protectorats, 19 November 1927.

[44] Osborne, op.cit. p.171.

[45] AOM Fonds Amiraux, 7F 15 (6) Rapport annuel (Sûreté) 31 May 1927- 1 June 1928. Phanuvong lived from 1871 until 1934. (*L'Echo du Cambodge*, 27 March 1934.)

[46] AOM Indochine NF Carton 48 Dossier 578. Note secrete pour M. le Ministre des Colonies au sujet de la dévolution du trône du Cambodge par Pierre Pasquier, Paris 1927. Pasquier finished on what he confessed was a sentimental note. It would be a kind of betrayal of the memory of Sisowath if his wishes were denied, he wrote. Be that as it may, such sentiment did not sway a later Governor General, Jean Decoux, in favor of Monivong's choice of successor and nor had it stopped them from promoting Sisowath over the Norodom wing in 1904.

[47] AOM FA FO 3 64271. Letter from the *Résident Supérieur* to *Gougal*, 5 August 1927. Also AOM RSC 366 Rapport annuel d'ensemble (Kandal) June 1927-June 1928.

[48] AOM RSC 365 Rapport politique (Kandal) 3ème Trimestre 1927.

[49] AOM FA FO 3 64271 op.cit. Rapport Politique Mensuel, August 1927, dated 6 September 1927.

[50] Norodom Sihanouk with Wilfred Burchett, (1973), *My War with the CIA. Cambodia's Fight for Freedom*, Penguin, Harmondsworth, p.145.

[51] *L'Echo du Cambodge*, 16 August 1927.

[52] Eleanor Mordaunt, (1932), *Purely for Pleasure*, Martin Secker, London, p.276.

[53] *L'Echo du Cambodge*, 3 March 1928; AOM Fonds Amiraux 7F 13 (1) Envoi 368/SS, Sûreté à Résident Supérieur et Chef de Sûreté, Hanoi,, 8 April 1928; Henri Marchal, (1928) "Cambodge. Cérémonies de l'incineration de S.M. Sisowath, *Bulletin de l'École Française d'Extrême-Orient*, Tome XXVIII.

[54] AOM Fonds Amiraux, 7F 15 (6) Rapport Annuel – Sûreté – 31 May 1927 – 1 June 1928.

[55] Lived 1876–1941. Reigned 1927–1941.

[56] AOM RSC 386 Rapport Annuel, June 1927 – June 1928 (Prey Veng); *L'Echo du Cambodge*, 16 September, 1 October 1927.

[57] Phnom Penh Correspondent, (1928), "The King of Cambodia. Coronation Scene", *The Times*, London, September 18. See also "Couronnement de S.M. Sisowath Monivong, *Bulletin de 'École Française d'Extrême-Orient*, Tome XXVIII, 1928.

[58] Ibid (*Times.)*

[59] *L'Echo du Cambodge,* 16 June 1928. The Queen Mother died in September 1930, aged 76 years. She had married Sisowath at the age of 16, in 1872. (*L'Echo du Cambodge,* 20 September 1930.)

[60] *The Times,* London, September 18, op.cit. Lustral waters have passed over a lingam in a Buddhist shrine.

[61] Pierre Billotey, (1929), *L'Indochine en zigzags,* Albin Maurel, Paris, p.227.

[62] Académie des sciences d'outre-mer, (1976), *Hommes et Destins,* Tome VI, *Asie,* Académie des sciences d'outre-mer, Paris, pp.377-378 and "Le trône du Cambodge de SM Sisowath Monivong à SM Norodom Sihanouk", *Indochine Hebdomadaire Illustré,* 15 May 1941.

[63] PRO, FO 371 12515 F 8052/429/61. "The New King of Cambodia".

[64] H.W. Ponder, (1936), *Cambodian Glory: The Mystery of the Deserted Khmer Cities and their Vanished Splendour and a Description of Life in Cambodia Today,* Thornton Butterworth, London, p.154.

[65] Billotey, op.cit.

[66] AOM RSC 435 Relations with royal family 1932-1935. Telegram from *Gougal* to *Résident Supérieur,* 21 July 1934. Also *L'Echo du Cambodge,* 24 July 1934. He was made honorary president of the graduates of Saint-Maixent in Cochinchina and Cambodia in 1935. [*L'Echo du Cambodge* and *La Presse Indochinoise,* 8 October 1935.]

[67] "Le trône du Cambodge, 15 May 1941, op.cit.

[68] Herman Norden, (1931), *A Wanderer in Indo-China. The chronicle of a journey through Annam, Tong-King, Laos and Cambodgia,*[sic] *with some account of their people,* H.F and G Witherby, London, p.275.

[69] A photograph of Monivong in such attire accompanies an article entitled "L'avènement de S.M. Monivong", in *L'Echo du Cambodge,* 13 August 1927. A painting of him in similar garb hangs today in the National Museum at Phnom Penh.

[70] ANC RSC D35 File 2799 Box 288. Rapport sur la situation du Cambodge, 1927-1928. Draft of Rapport sur la situation politique et administrative, June 1928-May 1929. (This box contains a number of apparently unsorted items. Author.)

[71] The Hon. Steven Runciman, (1939), "Indo-China's Toy Capitals. The French Way. An essay in political archaeology", *The Times,* London, March 4.

[72] Milton Osborne, (1973), "King-making in Cambodia: From Sisowath to Sihanouk", *Journal of Southeast Asian Studies,* 4 (3), p.171.

[73] John Tully, (1996), *Cambodia Under the Tricolour. King Sisowath and the "Mission Civilisatrice", 1904-1927,* Monash Asia Institute, Clayton, Victoria, p.299n.

[74] Ponder, op.cit.

[75] Jean Dorsenne, (1931), "Une soirée chez Sisowath", *Journal des Débats,* Vol. 38, Pt. 2, Paris, October 30.

[76] AOM Indochine NF Carton 48 Dossier 577. Note on the succession to Monivong. (Undated, but probably 1936 or 1937.)

[77] Huy Kanthoul, "Mémoires", unpublished French-language typescript, p.75. (David Chandler Papers, Monash University.)

[78] Guy de Pourtalès, (preface by Jean Lacouture), (1990), *Nous, à qui rien n'appartient. Voyage au pays khmer,* Flammarion, Paris, p.143. It was a miserable life, with the wives confined to their rooms: life was killed, claims de Pourtalès. Another estimate is that Monivong had 50 wives plus additional concubines. [Martin Herz, (1958), *A Short History of Cambodia from the Days of Angkor to the Present,* London, p.65.]

[79] Huy Kanthoul, op.cit.

[80] AOM Indochine NF Carton 48 Dossier 580 (2) Enclosure in letter from Gougal to Minister of Colonies, 23 June 1925.

[81] Norodom Sihanouk, (1972), *L'Indochine vue de Pékin,* Éditions du Seuil, Paris, p.27.

[82] Ponder, op.cit. p.154.

[83] Two months before his death, Monivong's father also condemned the new faith. [See Maurice Monribot, (1927), "Caodaisme et Spiritisme. SM Sisowath aurait demandé aux bonzes de rester fidèles au Bouddhisme. Ce serait la condamnation du Caodaisme pour les Cambodgiens", *La Presse Indochinoise,* 19 June.]

[84] Khy Phanra, (1975), "Les origines du Caodaisme au Cambodge (1926-1940)", *Mondes Asiatiques. Revue Française des Problèmes Asiatiques Contemporaines,* No. 3. Automne, Paris, pp.315-316. Donald Lancaster says that the religion began following "psychic experiments" by a circle of Vietnamese clerks in Saigon-Cholon. They claimed to have raised the supreme being, or "Caodai" by the use of a ouija board and a "beaked wicker basket". (Donald Lancaster, (1961), *The Emancipation of French Indochina,* Oxford University Press, London, p.86.)

[85] Ibid. p.323. Some 8000 Khmer pilgrims went to Tay Ninh in November 1927.

[86] AOM RSC 666. Caodaistes. Letter from Le Van Trung, the Caodai Pope, to King Monivong, 24 October 1929. The Pope claimed that even French, Chinese and Indian people had made the pilgrimage from various parts of Indochina.

[87] AOM RSC 386 Rapport Annuel, June 1927 – June 1928.

[88] AOM Fonds Amiraux, FO 64271 Rapports politiques, 1927. Royal edict.

[89] Article 15 of the treaty permitted Catholic missionaries to preach and teach and to set up churches, seminaries, schools, hospitals and convents. Article 13 imposed draconian penalties for proselytizing including confiscation of goods, beheading, reduction to slavery and imprisonment for life. [AOM RSC 227 Notes sur l'activité des Missions Protestants au Cambodge de 1930 à 1940.]

[90] ANC RSC D35 File 2799 Box 288. Copy of letter from Monivong to the Résident Supérieur, 10 April 1929.

[91] The Chams are an ancient people in Indochina. For a discussion, see William Augustus Collins, (1967), "An investigation into the division of the Chams into two regions", M.A. thesis, University of California, Berkeley.

[92] David Chandler in David J. Steinberg et al, (1987), *In Search of Southeast Asia: A Modern History,* revised Edition, Allen and Unwin, Sydney, p.66.

[93] C.R. Boxer, (Ed.), (1953), *South China in the Sixteenth Century. Being the narratives of Galeote Pereira, Fr. Gaspar da Cruz, O.P., Fr. Martin de Rada, O.E.S.A., (1550-1575),* Hakluyt Society, London. Da Cruz wrote that the established religion was "a very great obstacle to the propagation of Christianity in this country". (p.62.)

[94] A fact well recognized by the French and recorded by American Protestant missionaries. See Esther Hammond, (1925), "God's working among the Cambodians at Triton", *The Call of French Indo-China,* No. 11, Gospel Press, Hanoi, April-June. (A complete file of this publication can be found in the Bibliothèque Nationale at Paris.)

[95] William Rainey, (1950), *An Australian Pioneer. Notes from the Diary of the late Mr.. Alexander Lawrence, who served the Bible Society in Indo-China, the Philippines and Japan,* British and Australian Bible Society, Kew, Victoria, pp. 5-7. The Fashoda incident, in Africa, almost sparked war between the two empires and the hapless Lawrence was deported as a spy by Caesar's French servants. The Fashoda incident, which heightened existing tensions between Britain and France, involved French occupation of a remote settlement on the upper Nile in the British "sphere of influence". [See Guy Chapman, (1962), *The Third Republic of France. The First Phase, 1871-1894,* Macmillan, London, pp.345-355 and Christopher M. Andrew and A.S. Kanya-Forstner, (1981), *France Overseas. The Great War and the Climax of French Imperial Expansion,* Thames and Hudson, London, p.24.]

[96] See Tully, op.cit. pp.230-232.

[97] A royal decree of 1 April 1930 stipulated that foreign missionaries must seek authorization from the King to preach in the kingdom. This appears to have been a face saving measure as the missionaries' activities were in clear breach of the 1863 Treaty. [AOM RSC 226 Report by Minister of the Interior and Religion.]

[98] The new order was officially established in Cambodia in 1887. For an explanation, see Sorn Samnang, (1995), "L'Evolution de la Société Cambodgienne entre les deux guerres mondiales (1919-1939)". Thèse pour le doctorat d'histoire. Université Paris VII, Tome II, pp.295-303.

[99] Ibid. p.317.

[100] ANC RSC E03 File 9246 Dossier 814 Rapport annuel, Kandal, 1 June 1928-31 May 1939.

[101] ANC RSC E03 File 9279 Box 818 Rapport politique, 1929, Kompong Cham.

[102] Khy Phanra, op.cit. p.325. ANC RSC E03 File 1815 Box 176 Rapport Politique du 2ème Trimestre 1929, Prey Veng. The *Résident* considered that Caodai propaganda had completely ceased among the Khmer population.

[103] Letter from Monivong to the Résident Supérieur, 10 April 1929, op.cit.

[104] See Chapter 15 below for an account of the repression.

[105] AOM Indochine NF Carton 48 Dossier 577. Letter from *Gougal* to the Minister of Colonies, 20 May 1928. Also "Queen of Cambodia decides to give up", *The New York Times*, 29 April 1928.

[106] *L'Echo du Cambodge*, 30 November 1929.

[107] AOM RSC 422. Rapport annuel, 1934-1935. Cour et Gouvernement Cambodgien.

[108] *La Presse Indochinoise*, 18 December 1936.

[109] AOM INDO NF Carton 48 Dossier 577. Note by Colonial Minister Marius Moutet, 25 June 1936.

[110] Silvestre also served as interim Governor General before the arrival of the new Governor General, Jules Brevié, in that year.

[111] Achille Louis Auguste Silvestre was born on New Year's Day 1879 and died in April 1937. *L'Echo du Cambodge*, 28 April 1937.

[112] *La Voix Libre*, 31 October 1923. Baudoin was himself a formidable autocrat.

[113] AOM INDO NF Carton 48 Dossier 577. Note sur les relations du gouvernement français avec la cour cambodgienne, 13 December 1937. Author M. Marinetti.

[114] David Chandler, (1979), "Cambodian Palace Chronicles (*rajabangsavatar*), 1927-1949: Kingship and Historiography at the end of the Colonial Era", in Anthony Reid and David Marr, *Perceptions of the past in Southeast Asia*, Heinemann Educational Books, Singapore, p.211.

[115] *La Presse Indochinoise*, 24 April 1937, *L'Echo du Cambodge*, 28 April 1937.

[116] Born 25 November 1909 at Phnom Penh.

[117] Ibid.

[118] See Chapter 8 above.

[119] *La Presse Indochinoise*, 5 May 1937.

[120] *L'Echo du Cambodge*, 28 July 1937.

[121] AOM INDO NF Carton 47 Dossier 576. *Gougal* to Minister of Colonies, 18 January 1938. *La Presse Indochinoise*, 28 October 1937. Monipong had wanted to become a naval cadet at Brest, but knuckled under to his father's wishes to enter Saint-Cyr.

[122] *La Presse Indochinoise*, 30 September 1938.

[123] *L'Echo du Cambodge*, 13 September 1939.

[124] "Mort de Sisowath Monivong", *Indochine Hebdomadaire Illustré*, 1 May 1941.

[125] AOM INDO NF Carton 47 Dossier 576, op.cit.

[126] *L'Echo du Cambodge*, 10 October 1939.

[127] Ibid. 31 July 1940.

[128] *Indochine Hebdomadaire Illustré*, 24 April 1941.

[129] Chandler, op.cit. p.211.

[130] "L'Oeuvre de sa Majesté Monivong", *Réalités Cambodgiennes*, 16 August 1958.

[131] ANC RSC F42 File 9069 Box 9069. Succession de sa Majesté Sisowath Monivong. Other reports claim he died on the 24th.

[132] Saloth Sar's family had close connections to the royal palace. A cousin, Meak, became a consort of Monivong and bore him a son, Kossarak, before he became king in 1927. Meak enjoyed the title of *khun preah me neang*—"lady in charge of the women" of the palace. Saloth Sar's sister Saroeun joined the royal ballet sometime in the 1930s and also became a consort. She was at Monivong's bedside when he died and later married a policeman in Kompong Thom. (These details are in David P. Chandler, (1999), *Brother Number One. A Political Biography of Pol Pot,* Revised Edition, Westview Press, Boulder, Colorado, pp.8, 17. Chandler bases his account on an interview conducted with Saroeun by Youk Chhong.)

[133] Succession de sa majesté Sisowath Monivong, op.cit.

[134] AOM RSC 263 Rapport annuel, 1940-41. Minute Livre Vert. Situation politique et administrative.

[135] Ibid.

[136] See Ch. XVIII below.

[137] Chandler, op.cit. p.209.

[138] Huy Kanthoul, "Mémoires", p.67. Unpublished French-language typescript. Chandler Papers, Monash University.

Chapter 12

The "Mission Civilisatrice": Health, Education, and the Restoration of Angkor

We are too imbued with the love of our country to disavow the expansion of French thought and French civilization...We recognize the right and even the duty of superior races to draw unto them those which have not yet arrived at the same level of culture.
—Léon Blum, French Socialist leader 1925[1]

Although there was never any official agreement on the meaning of colonialism, the idea of the *mission civilisatrice* is an important strand in the discourse of modern imperialism. Many influential politicians, journalists and academics believed in the idea, or claimed to. Sometimes this was mere cant to obscure an ugly reality, but we cannot dismiss it out of hand. There were differences, too, between the policies and achievements of the individual colonial powers. It is unquestionable, for example, that the USA contributed more to the social and economic development of the Philippines in the five decades after 1898 than the Spanish colonialists they evicted did in centuries. Shortly after the annexation, the US government sent a shipload of teachers to the Philippines[2] and took steps to improve the general health and welfare of their new subjects. By 1928, almost the entire civil service in the islands was Filipino.[3] This does not mean, however, that the Americans' motives were disinterested. The United States was at the time undergoing industrialization at break neck speed. These were the decades of the "robber baron" capitalists and of Teddy Roosevelt's aggressive imperialist policies overseas. The Americans waged a brutal pacification campaign in the islands[4] and Hobson's "economic taproot" of imperialism sank deep into the soil of the Philippines. The Philippines, in short, is the classical illustration of Karl Marx's view of the dual nature of colonialism, although he did not live to see the American takeover. Each of the other colonial powers falls somewhere along a spectrum, from the brutal plunder of the Congo by Leopold of Belgium, through the Dutch in the East Indies to the British in India.[5] This chapter will examine the effects of the French presence in Cambodia on public health, education and the restoration of the country's archaeological heritage. If there can be any justification in the idea of colonialism as a regenerative force, we must look for it in the legacy of these fields.

The restoration of Angkor and traditional handicrafts

France was tremendously proud of its efforts in the field of cultural resuscitation.[6] The traditional Khmer arts and crafts had gone into serious decline by the time the French arrived and European influence accelerated this decay by flooding the country with cheap mass-produced goods, including knick-knacks and cloth for the traditional *sampot*.[7] Those who made their living from cottage industries in Cambodia could no more compete with the products of the power loom than could those people thrown aside a century earlier in Europe following the advent of steam powered factory machinery. In Europe, the authorities showed scant concern for those who lost their livelihoods and skills in this way; it was "Progress", the way of the capitalist world, which exists by the "constant revolutionizing of production".[8] To their credit, the French authorities in Cambodia were aware of the impact of cheap imports on traditional handicrafts, even though to place any restrictions on such imports contradicted the imperatives of the market. Soon after the turn of the century, they opened a small museum in Phnom Penh, followed shortly afterwards by a school and workshop of indigenous arts and crafts. In 1918, a School of Cambodian Arts was founded, followed two years later by the Albert Sarraut Museum, which exists today as the Cambodian

National Museum adjacent to the royal palace in Phnom Penh. Thousands of items were on display and the museum boasted a well-stocked library.[9] One of the most significant figures in the cultural project at this time was Mlle. Suzanne Karpelès, a scholar who was fluent in Pali, Sanskrit and the Khmer dialects. Karpelès was responsible for the newly founded School of Pali and for the reorganization of the royal library.[10] Ironically, the success of these projects played a part in the gestation of Cambodian nationalism by fostering a sense of pride in Khmer culture, or *khmerité* as it was later known.

The most striking part of this whole restorative project, however, was the refurbishment of the ruins of Angkor and other ancient monuments, which the French recognized as ranking in the forefront of the world's cultural treasures. It is not accidental that models of Angkor occupied pride of place at a number of colonial expositions in Paris and Marseilles from the 1870s until the eve of World War II. The scale of the project was impressive. In 1905, shortly before Battambang and Siem Reap provinces were returned from Siam, Commandant Lunet de Lajonquière traveled over 3000 kilometers throughout Siam and Cambodia, listing over 137 ancient Khmer monuments for restoration, in what was described as a feat of "endurance and exactitude".[11] The phrase could be used of the restoration project as a whole, which involved cutting back the encroaching jungle, building access roads and tracks, shoring up and cleaning stonework, and piecing together and replacing rubble into its original form, rather like a gigantic jigsaw puzzle. Restoration of Angkor Thom began in 1907.[12] The following year, the École Française d'Extrême-Orient appointed the first curator of Angkor, the conscientious, but ill-fated Jean Commaille.[13] His successor, the long-serving Henri Marchal, pioneered a method known as "anastylosis", which involved injecting grout into existing stonework.[14] The work also benefited from a visit made by George Coedès to Java in 1928 to observe the methods of the Dutch Archaeological Service under Dr. Bosch.[15] Marchal founded a society of "Friends of Angkor" in 1915 with the support of the scholar Georges Groslier, who had overall responsibility for the preservation of the Khmer arts.[16] It was an enormous, painstaking work and will probably be, as the writer Quaritch Wales presciently put it the sole permanent reminder of French colonialism in Cambodia.[17] The French archaeologists and scholars had a genuine love for their work that transcended vulgar economic interests or imperialist power politics. Without their efforts, the Angkor ruins would have moldered as they had done for centuries, victim to tree roots, weathering, human vandalism and looting. Moreover, the ruins had lain inside Siam since the late 18th century and were only returned to Cambodian sovereignty in 1907 because of French pressure on the court at Bangkok.[18] When, during the dark days of World War II, Japan brokered an agreement that resulted in the return of the provinces of Siem Reap and Battambang to Siam, the French nevertheless managed to hold on to the area containing the ruins. While Angkor had earlier generated considerable tourist revenue, this fact alone cannot account for such great attachment, particularly as tourism dried up after 1939. Today, Cambodia without Angkor seems unthinkable, so closely are the ruins identified with the Cambodian state and culture. It is significant that the pioneer Khmer nationalists of the 1930s chose to name their magazine after Angkor (*Nagaravatta*), and that, as David Chandler has observed, the towers have appeared on all post-independence flags. France's efforts provided nascent Khmer nationalism with a potent symbol of nationhood.

The effects of literacy

In a broader sense, the renovation of the indigenous education system also contained the seeds of colonialism's own destruction. Cambodia was a largely pre-literate society when the French arrived and there was little change for a number of decades. There were no printing presses in Cambodia prior to the arrival of the French, and before the early 1900s, there had probably only been one booklet printed in Khmer—and that by Europeans, although the translation was done by a Khmer.[19] This is not to say that there was no literary-cultural tradition, but what existed was largely orally based or was painstakingly transcribed onto pages made of palm leaves glued together by hand and held together in one corner with string. Most of this writing was in Pali, not the Khmer vernacular, and was largely of a religious nature. There were some exceptions, including the verse of Int, who was made *Oknha Sotanta* (or "poet laureate") by Sisowath in 1907. Int's work circulated widely in handwritten form.[20] The existence of the new printing presses did not automatically mean that the Khmers would use them and a modern Cambodian literature was slow to emerge. Some Cambodians, including Prince Monireth, did write French verse during the 1930s, including the previously quoted "Au Cimitière de Silberloch".[21] Monireth also published a number of other poems in the French language press in 1934-1935, including "Song de Mâyâ",[22] "Soir funèbre",[23] "Jour de pluie"[24] and "Nostalgie", the latter written in November 1933 at Saint-Cyr.[25] The poems reveal a serious and rather melancholy young man. His father also wrote occasional verse, some of which was read during theatrical performances at Angkor.[26] Published work in the Khmer vernacular was rare. Two books appeared in the mid- 1930s; Nou Hach's *Méaléa Duong Chet,*[27] a love story about a Khmer boy and a Siamese girl, and Rim Kin's *Sophat*. It would be stretching a point, however, to claim this as a literary renaissance.

Part of the problem was that writers need an audience and save for a thin layer of educated people, Khmers did not have the reading habit. In fact, they appear to have read less than the other peoples of Indochina. Rim Kin was inspired to write his novel after noticing that the markets of Phnom Penh were well-stocked with Vietnamese books, but virtually devoid of anything in Khmer.[28] Suzanne Karpelès tried hard to turn the situation round. The Buddhist Institute, of which she was director, opened a bookshop at the Phnom Penh central station in 1933. The shop sold cheap, subsidized editions of Khmer books, many of them printed at a new École Pratique d'Industrie set up in 1932.[29] Two other important cultural events during this period were the opening of the National Library and the central archives. The archives were housed after October 1926 in a new building close to the Wat Phnom and the *Résidence Supérieure*.[30] The library is still housed in a handsome, but crumbling building in front of the National Archives, adjacent to the present-day Hôtel Le Royal on Street 92. In 1927, it held 7,700 volumes and one year later, this had risen to just over 10,000 books, brochures and maps.[31] Progress in promoting literacy and culture was slow, however. In 1944, there were only 636 subscriptions to the Khmer-language weekly magazine *Kampuchea.*[32] Another measurement of functional literacy is the number of letters people write. In November 1942, Cambodian residents of all ethnic groups between them sent 33 letters per 1000 inhabitants, compared with 54 per 1000 in Laos; 65 in Annam, 81 in Tonkin and 166 in Cochinchina.[33] The education system was still rudimentary when Rim Kin and Nou Hach published their books.

Public education in Cambodia under the French

There was no system of mass education in Cambodia when the French arrived in 1863. This should not surprise us, as the idea was very advanced for Europe at the time. (The demand for free, universal, public education was so radical that it was one of the ten chief demands raised in *The Communist Manifesto* in 1848.[34]) Such education as existed in Cambodia was given in the pagodas by monks to male children only and consisted of drill in moral conduct and the sacred Pali and Khmer texts, along with learning some simple carpentry skills.[35] Yet, while there was a considerable expansion of public education in Europe in the latter part of the 19th century, little was done in Cambodia until after Sisowath came to the throne. Twenty years after the formation of the Protectorate, there were only about 100 pupils in French language schools in all of Cambodia, and only eight of these were Cambodian.[36] The first real steps towards a more modern school system were made only after 1911, when Sisowath signed a decree stipulating that Cambodian boys from the age of eight years were to attend "reformed" pagoda schools.[37] The schools were called "reformed" because elements of a European-style curriculum were grafted onto the traditional syllabus. The new material included arithmetic, general knowledge, reading and writing, history, geography and biology. A French teacher fluent in Khmer oversaw the system.[38] There were almost 40,000 pupils in such schools by the 1920s[39] and the 5000th reformed school opened its doors with great fanfare in 1935 at a ceremony attended by Monivong, Governor General René Robin and M. Richomme, the *Résident Supérieur*.[40] It was a modest achievement, but quantity did not translate into quality. The schools suffered from poor teaching methods, lack of resources and funds, ignorant teachers and the reluctance of peasants to allow their children to attend classes when they could be of use in the fields. There was also a clash between the traditional values and beliefs of the monk-teachers, and the post-Enlightenment, European content of the new curriculum, which the monks often considered heretical.[41] A 1921 report noted that, "nothing could be more distressing than the contrast between the wide-awake air of the pupils and the stupid expression of the teacher".[42] There was some talk of teacher training in 1925, but it was not until 1935 that anything was done.[43] Yet, we cannot blame all of the failings of the system on the Khmer teachers. As the present author has written,

> It cannot be denied that the little the French did for the education of the Cambodians was an advance on what had existed before 1863. Despite this qualification, there is little room for French complacency or self-congratulation. Their performance in Cambodia pales in comparison not just with what they did in Vietnam, but also with the achievements of some other colonial powers in Asia.[44]

On the other hand, part of the problem was that the peasants saw little value in education. Truancy was a major problem and although teachers claimed this was largely due to parents keeping their children off school to help with domestic and farm chores, the *Résident* of Prey Veng believed that this was a superficial explanation. Whenever he had been around schools, he had noticed children engaged in other pursuits than schools and fields, he claimed. The problem was, he believed, that instruction was by rote and the pupils were simply bored.[45] From time to time, the French authorities would attempt to force the parents to send their children school. Fines of up to one piastre per offence were introduced as early as 1912, followed in 1916 by provision for jailing the parents of truants for up to five days. Such draconian measures did not work and in the mid-1930s, further decrees were issued to force compliance[46] and school inspectors were very busy in 1939.[47]

In 1918, Governor General Albert Sarraut announced sweeping reforms to education throughout Indochina, including a minimum of thirteen years compulsory schooling for all children in the colonies. All children were to be eligible to sit for the equivalent of the French *baccalauréat* and thus for entry, if successful, to universities.[48] Sarraut meant well, but his vision was never fulfilled in any of the five divisions of French Indochina, above all in Laos and Cambodia. In 1930, the proportion of the budget allocated to education in Cambodia was smaller than in any of the countries of Indochina.[49] French-style education was very restricted. In 1927, there were less than 11,000 primary school students of all races in Cambodia—exclusive of the reformed pagoda schools system—in 154 elementary schools.[50] Although the numbers increased slowly after 1930, it was hardly an impressive effort. The Cambodians themselves made a much greater effort to increase the numbers of schools and students at all levels, as is shown in Table 1 below. It was common for Khmer students to obtain the French (primary) Certificate of Studies at the age of 20. The writer and teacher Huy Kanthoul qualified at 16, an age when French students were beginning their studies for the *baccalauréat*.[51]

If elementary education for children was neglected, so too was the vocational education of adults and teenagers. There was little in the way of industry in the kingdom and Chinese and Vietnamese artisans, some of whom were imported for specific projects, performed most skilled work. Most of the professional engineers and the more highly skilled technicians were French. Although the authorities did set up a kind of technical college, the *École Professionale* in 1912, with instruction by French engineers and Vietnamese fitters, less than half of the students were Cambodian. Most of these were illiterate, and many left in 1917 when a compulsory French course was introduced.[52]

When the French left Cambodia, around 40 years later, there were only 330 students enrolled in five technical education institutions[53] and in 1944 there was only one Cambodian engineer in the whole country.[54] This was scarcely adequate to sustain or build a modern state and economy. Higher education was worse. There was no higher education institution in the country until after World War II when the National Institute of Juridical and Economic Studies was opened for evening classes only. This was the only tertiary education establishment in the country when the French left.[55] Before then, anyone wishing to further his or her academic studies had to go to Hanoi or France. Secondary education was not much better and it was common for members of the royal family to study for the *baccalauréat* in France or at Saigon. In 1935, the Lycée Sisowath was opened on the boulevard Doudart de Lagrée (today's Norodom Boulevard) in Phnom Penh.[56] It was such a special occasion that Prince Norodom Sutharot wrote a commemorative poem in Khmer, which was printed in a French translation in *La Presse Indochinoise.*[57] Many of the future Khmer elite were to study there in the years to come, including Khieu Ponnary, who received a *prix d'excellence* in July 1938.[58] However, little was done in following years to extend secondary education to the rest of the population. When the French left in 1953, there were less than 4000 secondary students of all "races" in Cambodia, out of a total population of just below five million.[59]

Table 1: Number of students in Cambodia, 1930-1960.[60]

Year	Primary	Secondary	Technical	Higher
1930	65,000	310	400	0
1935	56,000	370	260	0
1940	72,000	390	320	0
1945	89,000	680	280	0
1950	183,000	1570	280	240
1955	286,000	3810	330	350
1960	542,000	16840	980	1430

Until the end, the French had a niggardly approach to spending on education in the kingdom. The education of indigenous girls was completely neglected outside of some elite girls' schools where instruction was largely in French. In 1922, there were only 303 "native" girls attending schools in Cambodia, one-third of whom were Cambodian.[61] As the present author has written,

Even if we acknowledge the indifference and hostility of the Cambodians themselves to girls' education, and even if we recognize that feminist consciousness was at a low level in European society at that time...this is still an abysmal record, matched only by that of the Dutch in Indonesia.[62]

The neglect of public health

A similar picture emerges when we examine France's impact on health and illness in Cambodia. When the left wing writer Andrée Viollis visited the Angkor region in the early 1930s, a young French doctor took her on a tour of some villages near Siem Reap. In a sad and angry voice, he denounced the authorities for their neglect of the people's health. In the district, there was only one doctor for 160,000 indigenes. Moreover, essential drugs such as quinine (used in the treatment of malaria) were in short supply, the result of official parsimony, which he contrasted bitterly with the lavish lifestyle of the local *Résident* and his entourage. Each *Résidence,* he noted, had a fleet of expensive cars, yet the medical service lacked ambulances and the doctor claimed that he had to transport serious cases to hospital at his own expense.[63] Few Cambodian doctors were trained throughout the years of the protectorate. If the experience of Dr Norodom Ritharasi is a guide, Khmer doctors could not expect to be treated as equals with their French counterparts. In one instance, a bumptious school inspector called Manipoud tried to overrule Ritharasi's order that a teacher be confined to bed for two days because of chronic dysentery.[64]

While the available figures are contradictory, they are uniformly gloomy. According to the journalist Henri Gourdon, there were only 160 doctors of all races in Indochina in 1931, along with 270 "auxiliary doctors" trained at the Hanoi Medical School.[65] The *Presse Indochinoise* reported in 1937 that of 42 western-trained "native" physicians in all of Indochina, only three were Cambodian,[66] although the following year, a report in *La Dépêche du Cambodge* claimed that there were 17 Cambodian doctors out of 31 "native" doctors in Indochina. No Cambodian had enrolled in medical school since 1930, the latter paper added,[67] and by 1944, there was only one Cambodian doctor in the country.[68] While Gourdon is correct to claim that health had been "completely neglected" by indigenous governments before the French came to Indochina, his figures, proudly paraded during the Paris Exposition of 1931, scarcely reflect well on his country's effort.[69] Nor were French doctors plentiful—according to one report, there was only one in Phnom Penh in 1936.[70] Curiously, the otherwise well-informed economic historian Thomas Ennis considered that medicine was "the high point of French labors in Indochina."[71] One wonders what he considered the low point. In a book published shortly after Cambodia achieved independence, the left wing writer Wilfred Burchett claimed that the French left one qualified dentist[72] two doctors and 110 qualified nurses.[73]

To be fair, the French administration faced a difficult task. The Khmer people themselves had little understanding of the etiology of disease, nor of its prevention. They blamed illness on the activities of demons[74] and were fatalistically resigned to it. Health and education are closely related, but when the French decided that the best—or possibly the cheapest—option for the establishment of a public education system lay via the Buddhist *sangha*, they were trusting to an order whose members were medieval in outlook. The French themselves often despaired about the gross lack of simple hygiene in the Wat Onulom, the principal Buddhist monastery at Phnom Penh, drawing attention to its foul smells and overflowing latrines.[75] The monks, like Khmers in general, believed that malaria and bubonic plague was caused by genies. Cholera was so dreaded by Khmers that they dared not mention it by name. Much of traditional medicine involved spells to ward off the genies and treatment included manioc, tamarind, dew, and a variety of small animals, including the skins and innards of frogs and toads, insects and the ground-up horns of beasts.[76] Dr Norodom Ritharasi believed, however, that by 1931, "almost three-quarters of the population had embraced western medicine."[77] His assessment was optimistic. Even in 2002, aid workers report that knowledge of the causes of disease is rudimentary, especially in the countryside.

Public sanitation was poor, with squalid streets choked with debris the norm. Battambang, for example, was said to be "in a state of indescribable filthiness" in 1915, with animals scavenging among grass and weeds which grew to a height of one-and-a-half meters in the town streets.[78] Over twenty years later, another report drew attention to the atrocious conditions in the poorer quarters of Phnom Penh, where decomposing rubbish stood in tall piles, stinking in the streets.[79] However, the question we must ask is whether the French were prepared to devote the resources to turn the situation round. Many of the endemic diseases resulted from drinking polluted water. There was no clean water at Pursat, for instance, either for natives or Europeans reported the *Résident,* in 1916. The water supply was drawn straight from the river and was contaminated with animal droppings and detritus of all kinds from the banks.[80] How much things improved is a moot point. In 1927, the British diplomat Lord Crewe was of the opinion that "Nowhere...[in Indochina] is there an adequate water supply scheme. In most cases, the foul and polluted water must be used for all purposes. In the big towns, the water is rarely turned on for more than six hours a day in the dry season. Until the towns are provided with adequate water systems, epidemics are bound to occur with annual regularity."[81] Crewe did not exaggerate; the Phnom Penh water supply, which reticulated water pumped from the Tonlé Sap River, began operations only in the year that the Englishman wrote his report.

A grim triumvirate: cholera, plague and smallpox

Cambodia was home to a frightening array of diseases, many of them water-borne or caused by rats, filth and poverty. Infant mortality rates were very high—400 per 1000 in the 1930s—compared to 65 per 1000 in France and 58 per 1000 in Britain at the same time.[82] The grim triumvirate of cholera, bubonic plague and smallpox regularly swept through the country. In 1926, for example—a year chosen at random—there were 124 cases of plague in Cambodia, of whom 49 died; 327 cases of smallpox, of whom 83 died; and 4292 cases of cholera, of whom 1829 died.[83] On average, bubonic plague caused almost 200 deaths per year in the capital alone between the years 1907 and 1930, with a peak of almost 1300 fatalities in 1922-1923.[84] Phnom Penh was considered one of the three permanent foci of the disease in Indochina. The disease was spread by the black rat, of which there were vast numbers in both town and country. The authorities organized periodic rat hunts, offering a bounty of two cents per tail and sending killing teams round the streets and houses. In 1930, almost 46,000 of the rodents were dispatched in this way along with over 7000 killed "voluntarily" by the residents. Stray dogs, too, faced official wrath, for they spread parasitic insects and rabies. Over 3000 *chiens errants* were killed during 1931.[85] Despite these measures, between 1936 and 1940 the *Hôpital Mixte* at Phnom Penh admitted over three thousand patients suffering from either cholera, the plague, or from smallpox, but around one-third of them died, as is shown in Table 2 below.

Other endemic diseases included malaria, leprosy, dengue fever, scrub typhus (particularly among plantation laborers[86]) typhoid, diphtheria, rabies, tuberculosis, beriberi and pernicious anemia, mumps, measles, anthrax and dysentery. On the eve of World War II, up to 17 per cent of the population suffered from hookworm.[87] Forty-three per cent of school age children in Phnom Penh suffered from trachoma in the 1940s.[88] Trachoma, a chronic eye condition associated with poverty, is caused by dust and other particles and can lead to blindness if not treated.

Table 2: Admissions and deaths due to plague, smallpox and cholera, *Hôpital Mixte*, Phnom Penh, 1936-1940[89]

Years	Plague		Smallpox		Cholera	
	Cases	Deaths	Cases	Deaths	Cases	Deaths
1936	22	19	570	107	38	27
1937	15	13	711	374	13	11
1938	4	4	1531	372	0	0
1939	5	5	332	68	0	0
1940	10	10	205	59	0	0
Totals	56	51	3349	980	51	38

Construction of Cambodia's first "mental hospital" was begun at Takmau, 11 kilometers west of Phnom Penh, in 1936,[90] attesting to high rates of psychiatric disorders, particularly depression, among poor Khmers.[91] There were also staggeringly high rates of treponemal infections in some areas of Cambodia (and Indochina as a whole). Andrée Viollis's young doctor claimed that the Siem Reap region was rife with the diseases, including hereditary syphilis—entire villages were "rotten" with it. There was an urgent need, he said, for teams of nurses to treat the sufferers and educate mothers and children because the villagers could not afford to seek treatment in the larger centers. Viollis recorded villages where the population included many with faces eaten away by the disease. The doctor took children by the shoulder and showed her their eyes full of pus. Some were already blind. Others were covered in suppurating sores and nodosities the size of pomegranates. The doctor was in despair; with dressings and salvarsan, he would be able to care for his patients—"these poor buggers"—but he had lost hope of such a program being funded.[92] In fact, treponemal infections—yaws and syphilis—were extraordinarily common in Cambodia and the adjoining Vietnamese portions of the Mekong delta lands. There were particularly high rates of yaws infection (a non-sexually-transmitted sibling of syphilis) in the Kompong Thom and Battambang districts. In 1937, there were close to 100,000 cases of yaws in all of Indochina. Although rarely fatal, the disease often left its victims severely disfigured. "True" syphilis claimed almost as many victims, although without proper diagnostic and treatment facilities, it was difficult to differentiate between the two, and in any case, many sufferers did not present for treatment.

Viollis claims that infection rates near Siem Reap were very high, but does not give any figures, or break them down by type of treponema. It is probable, however, that the overall infection rate rivaled that of Saigon, where 60 per cent of samples of the population tested positive in blood tests for syphilis or yaws. (The test was the same for both.)[93] Yaws was endemic in much of East and Southeast Asia, but it is probable that European sailors brought its deadlier cousin to the region.[94] The very virulence of its symptoms in Cambodia suggests the disease's recent arrival.[95]

Vaccinations: a brighter aspect of French health policy

If France's record of training doctors and other medical professionals was poor, the vaccination program was more successful. The authorities first turned their attentions to inoculation as a way of defeating disease because of the high sickness and mortality rates suffered by French officials, military personnel and settlers in Indochina. Before 1884, the European mortality rate in Indochina often exceeded 100 per 1000. This fell steadily to 10-15 per 1000 between 1913 and 1922, then to just below six per 1000 by 1929. Two hundred and fifty Europeans per 1000 could expect to fall sick before 1884, 2000 per 1000 in 1904 and 150-250 per 1000 between 1905 and 1930.[96] The decrease was in large part due to the vaccination program, which began in Cambodia in the first few years of the 20th century,[97] following the establishment of Pasteur Institutes at Hanoi in the 1890s[98] and later at Phnom Penh.[99] Almost 37,000 vaccinations were carried out, mainly against smallpox, in 1906[100] and the number grew steadily thereafter. There were over 280,000 vaccinations against cholera between early 1926 and mid-1927. By 1927, over 1,600,000 people, or over two-thirds of the population, had been inoculated against smallpox.[101] This was a commendable effort. However, in the end, inoculation, no matter how widespread, was no substitute for clean drinking water and improved sanitation and the success began to flag. An article in *La Presse Indochinoise* in April 1937 attacked the authorities for their failure to provide the indigenes with clean water, particularly during high temperatures, describing the situation as "an insupportable calamity" that caused epidemics of disease among the poor.[102] The onset of the Great Depression caused the authorities to shelve clean water projects until the later years of the decade.

In conclusion, France gravely neglected education and health in Cambodia, both in comparison with her own efforts elsewhere in Indochina and with those of other colonial powers, most noticeably the

United States in the Philippines and Britain in the Indian sub continent. While this neglect might have stemmed at least in part in the field of education from a certain reticence at meddling with an indigenous culture, in the main it was due to an indifference and parsimony that mocks the pretensions of the *mission civilisatrice*. Education and health are the cornerstones of a modern state and economy. It is not drawing too long a bow to attribute many of the failings of the country after independence—perhaps even the tragedies—to the failure of the "protecting power" to foster the development of an educated middle class and a skilled proletariat.

Notes

[1] Cited in Robert Aldrich, (1996), *A History of France Overseas Expansion,* Macmillan, Basingstoke, p.115.

[2] Stuart Creighton Miller, (1982), *"Benevolent Assimilation".* The American Conquest of the Philippines, 1899-1903, Yale University Press, New Haven, Connecticut, p.46.

[3] Alfred McCoy, (1981), "The Philippines: Independence without decolonisation", in Robin Jeffrey, (ed) *Asia – The Winning of Independence,* Macmillan, London, p.43.

[4] See, for instance, Daniel B. Schirmer and Stephen Rosskam (eds.), (1987), *The Philippines Reader: A History of Colonialism, Neo-colonialism, Dictatorship and Resistance,* South End Press, Boston. The downside was the tens of thousands of Filipinos who died resisting the US forces, many of whom had learned their repressive trade in white America's Indian wars.

[5] On India, see, for example, V.V. Oak, (1925), *England's Educational Policy in India,* B.G. Paul, Madras.

[6] Max Weber's observations on the role of intellectuals in the colonial process have already been noted. (Max Weber, (1978), *Economy and Society*, Vol. 2, University of California Press, Berkeley, pp.920-922.)

[7] Thompson, op.cit. p.355.

[8] Karl Marx and Frederick Engels, *Manifesto of the Communist Party,* in *Karl Marx and Frederick Engels,* (1970), Progress Publishers, Moscow, p.38.

[9] *Revue du Tourisme Indochinois. Bulletin Officiel du Syndicat d'Initiative de l'Indochine,* Nr. 72. 19 September 1924, p.18.

[10] AOM RSC 431 Rapport Politique, 1er Trimestre 1920; *Bulletin de l'École Française d'Extreme-Orient,* Tome XXII, Hanoi, 1922, p.377; AOM RSC 432 Rapport Politique 1er Trimestre 1925; Thompson, op.cit. p.352; *Sisowath Chronicle,* p.1210; Guy de Pourtalès, op.cit. p.108.

[11] ANC RSC D23 Rapport sur la Situation de l'École Française d'Extrême-Orient, 1905.

[12] George Coedès, (trans. Emily Floyd Gardiner), (1963), *Angkor. An Introduction,* Oxford University Press, London, p.57 also G. Coedès, (1940),

"Angkor. Les travaux de l'École Française d'Extrême-Orient", *Indochine Hebdomadaire Illustré*, Hanoi, 26 September.

[13] Henri Marchal, (19?), *Angkor. La résurrection de l'art khmer et l'ouevre de l'école française d'extrême-orient*, Office Française d'edition, Paris, p.17. Commaille was murdered near the Angkor Thom ruins in April 1916 and robbed of the payroll for coolies employed on the reconstruction works. It was a tragic and wasteful end. [AOM RSC 355 Rapports périodiques économiques et politiques de la Résidence de Battambang 1907-1916), Rapport Politique 2ème Trimestre 1916 and AOM RSC 295 L'affaire/assassinat de Commaille, 1916.] Commaille was author of *Guide aux ruines d'Angkor*, Librairie Hachette, Paris, 1912. A pen portrait of this erudite, somewhat eccentric, but good-humored man is contained in F. Gas-Faucher, (1922), *En sampan sur les lacs du Cambodge et à Angkor*, Barlatier, Marseille, pp. 71, 91-92, 96. His grave still exists near the Terrace of the Elephants.

[14] Marchal, op.cit. pp.26-27 and Burchett, op.cit., p.61.

[15] Coedès ("Angkor. Les travaux") op.cit.

[16] *Revue du Tourisme Indochinois,* (1924) Saigon, No. 72, 19 September, p.18.

[17] H. G. Quaritch Wales, (1943), *Years of Blindness,* Thomas Y. Crowell, New York, p. 224.

[18] Siam re-annexed the provinces of Battambang and Siem Reap during World War II. Again, only French power assured their return. (See Chapter 22 below.)

[19] William Rainey, (1950), *An Australian Pioneer. Notes from the diary of the late Mr.. Alexander Lawrence, who served the Bible Society in Indo-China, the Philippines and Japan,* British and Australian Bible Society, Kew, Victoria, pp. 5-6.

[20] Tauch Chhuong, (trans. Sithan Hin), (1974), "Battambang in the period of the vassal", (unpublished mss. loaned by David Chandler), p.117. Original Khmer version published in Battambang.

[21] An English translation of the first stanza appears in Chapter 8 above. [Sisowath Monireth, (1934), "Au cimitière de Silberloch. A mes compatriotes morts pendant la guerre 1914-1918", *L'Echo du Cambodge,* 18 September.]

[22] *La Presse Indochinoise,* 25-26 August 1934.

[23] *L'Echo du Cambodge,* 29 January 1935.

[24] Ibid. 30 April 1935.

[25] Ibid. 25 September 1934.

[26] See, for example, Jean Dorsenne, (1931), "Une soirée chez Sisowath", *Journal des Débats,* 38, Pt 2, p.699 and "Grand fêtes d'Angkor", *L'Echo du Cambodge,* 7 May 1935.

[27] "The garland of the heart". See Sorn Samnang, "L'Evolution de la société cambodgienne entre les deux guerres mondiales (1919-1939)". Tome II, Thèse pour doctorat d'histoire Université Paris VII, p.376. Nou Hach lived from 1916 until perhaps 1975, the year the Khmers Rouges took control.

[28] Ibid. Rim Kin lived from 1911 until 1959. We will examine the implications of such "reactive nationalism" in Chapter 13 below. Educated visitors to

Cambodia even today will notice the lack of Khmer-language bookshops and libraries, apart from the National Library in Phnom Penh, which in any case houses many French-language books. The vast majority of bookshops sell only stationery and textbooks for computer and business studies or English classes. However, the murderous anti-intellectualism of the *Khmers Rouges*, followed by years of enforced isolation and poverty did nothing for the cultural advancement of the country.

[29] ANC RSC E03 File 499 Box 38. A.S. Fonctionnement de l'Institut Bouddhique et la Bibliothèque Royale pendant 1932-1933. Suzanne Karpelès au Résident Supérieur, 12 juin 1933.

[30] ANC RSC D35 File 2798, Box 288, Résidence Supérieure au Cambodge, Rapport d'Ensemble sur la situation du Cambodge, 1926-1927.

[31] Ibid and ANC D35 File 2799, Box 288, Rapport sur la situation du Cambodge, 1927-1928. The *Khmers Rouges* vandalized the library's collection between 1975 and 1978 but it was not completely destroyed. According to the archives staff, *Khmers Rouges* lived in the archives building during this time, but comparatively little damage was done to the files. Both institutions suffer today from the apparent indifference of the current government to the national patrimony, but at least steps have been taken to rescue the books and documents from "the gnawing criticism of the mice" thanks to the dedicated staff.

[32] AOM RSC 303. Presse, propagande, 1942-44,

[33] AOM RSC 464 Surveillance de l'Institut Bouddhique, 1943. Cambodians are still reluctant to write letters today, but for different reasons. They believe that the stamps will be removed and their letters consigned to the rubbish bin. It is not unusual for travelers to be asked to post letters abroad.

[34] Marx and Engels, op. cit. p.53.

[35] Magnant, (1913), "Notes sur les débuts de l'enseignement français au Cambodge (1863-1890), *Revue Indochinoise,* 1er Semestre; Direction générale de l'instruction publique, (1931), *La pénétration scolaire en pays cambodgien et laotien,* Ch. 1, Hanoi; Charles Bilodeau, "Compulsory Education in Cambodia", in Bilodeau, Somlith Pathammavong and Le Quang Hong, (1955), *Compulsory Education in Cambodia, Laos and Viet-nam,* UNESCO, Paris; G.H. Monod, (1931), *Le Cambodgien,* Editions Larose, Paris, pp.31-35. See John Tully, (1996), *Cambodia Under the Tricolour. King Sisowath and the 'Mission Civilisatrice, 1904-1927,* Monash Asia Institute, Clayton, Victoria, Ch. Seven, for an extended discussion of "Education, Culture and the Mission Civilisatrice".

[36] AOM RSC 304. M. Humbert-Hesse, Rapport générale sur l'enseignment au Cambodge, 10 January 1923.

[37] Humbert-Hesse, op.cit. Bilodeau, op.cit. p.63.

[38] Henri Russier, (1913), "L'Enseignement élementaire au Cambodge", *Revue Indochinoise,* Premier Semestre.

[39] Humbert-Hesse, op.cit.

[40] *La Presse Indochinoise,* 24 July 1935.

[41] Tully, op.cit.

[42] Cited in Bilodeau, op.cit. p.20.

[43] Ibid. pp.18-19.

[44] Tully, op.cit. p.244.

[45] AOM RSC 648 Extraits rapports politiques trimestriels. Prey Veng 4ème Trimestre 1928.

[46] Tully, op.cit. p.241.

[47] ANC RSC D35 File 8982 Box 789. Préparation du livre vert 1938-1939.

[48] See Bilodeau, op.cit. p.18 and Gail P. Kelly, (1982), *Franco-Vietnamese Schools, 1918-1938: Regional Development and Implications for National Integration,* Center for Southeast Asian Studies, University of Wisconsin-Madison, pp.43-47.

[49] The proportion of the budgets spent on education in the five countries in that year was as follows: Tonkin, 14.23%; Cochinchina, 12.47%; Annam, 14.45%; Laos, 8.76%; and Cambodia, 6.16%. [Direction générale de l'instruction publique, (1930), *Le service de l'instruction publique en Indochine en 1930,* Hanoi, p.12. Report published for the Exposition Coloniale Internationale at Paris, 1931. The Cambodian budget in 1930 was 13 million piastres, of which 800,000 piastres went on education.]

[50] ANC RSC D35 File 2798 Box 288. Rapport sur la situation du Cambodge, 1927.

[51] Huy Kanthoul, "Mémoires", p.49. Unpublished French-language typescript, Chandler Papers, Monash University.

[52] Humbert-Hesse, op.cit. A smaller technical school existed earlier. In 1903, the *Ateliers du Palais du Roi,* gave some technical instruction under a French engineer and some naval mechanics.

[53] Prud'homme, op.cit.

[54] "Il existe seulement au Cambodge, un docteur et un ingénieur de race cambodgien. C'est peu!" *Kampuchea,* No 228. 27 July 1944. In AOM RSC 303. Presse, propagande, 1942-44, op.cit.

[55] Bilodeau, op.cit. p.19.

[56] *L'Echo du Cambodge,* 6 September 1935 and *La Presse Indochinoise,* 12 September 1935.

[57] *La Presse Indochinoise,* 17 September 1935. The poem—at least in translation—lacked Monireth's touch.

[58] Ibid. 15 July 1938. Khieu Ponnary later became the first wife of Saloth Sar, who was more widely known to the world as Pol Pot. She is rumored to have died insane, but the reports might be exaggerated.

[59] Prud'homme, op.cit. pp. 250 and 277.

[60] Based on Rémy Prud'homme, (1969), *L'Economie du Cambodge,* Presses Universitaires de France, Paris, p.277.

[61] Humbert-Hesse, op.cit.

[62] Tully, op.cit. p.243.

[63] Andrée Viollis, (1949), *Indochine S.O.S.,* Editeurs Français Réunis, Paris, pp.72-74.

[64] ANC RSC E03 File 11405 Box 987. Rapport annuel du Dr Ritharasi, Norodom, Médecin des services extérieurs, 19 janvier 1931.

[65] Gourdon, op.cit. p.781.

[66] *La Presse Indochinoise,* 9 November 1937.

[67] *La Dépêche du Cambodge,* 30 August 1938. Clipping in AOM RSC 678. A propos de l'élite cambodgienne.

[68] AOM RSC 303, *Kampuchea,* 27 July 1944. op.cit.

[69] Gourdon, op.cit.

[70] *La Presse Indochinoise,* 20 January 1936.

[71] Ennis, op.cit.p.132.

[72] Burchett, op. cit. p.11.

[73] Ibid. p.73.

[74] See Norodom Ritharasi, (1929), *Évolution de la Médicine au Cambodge,* Librairie Louis Arnette, Paris.

[75] For example, AOM RSC 278. Choléra et peste, Phnom Penh, 1918-1921 and *La Presse Indochinoise,* 13 April 1935 and 30 May 1936.

[76] See Ritharasi, op.cit. See also Guy Porée et Eveline Maspéro, (1938), *Moeurs et coutumes des Khmers,* Payot, Paris.

[77] ANC RSC E03 File 11405 Box 987. Rapport annuel du Dr. Ritharasi, Norodom, Médecin de services extérieurs. 19 January 1931.

[78] Unsigned, (1915), "Au Cambodge", *Humanité Indochinoise,* 17 March, p.2.

[79] Unsigned, (1937), "Cambodge", *La Presse Indochinoise,* 9 April. The writer Harry Franck considered that Phnom Penh was "a calm, well-kept little city, with hardly any of the hubbub of China, and none of its filth..." but added the caveat "at least within sight." [Harry Franck, (1926), *East of Siam. Ramblings in the five divisions of French Indo-China,* The century, New York, p.34.]

[80] ANC RSC E3 File 257 Box 10, Résidence de Pursat. Procès-verbal, Conseil de Résidence, 1ère séance, 20 avril 1916.

[81] PRO 371 12624. w 9882 Lord Crewe to the Foreign Office, 21 October 1927.

[82] Naval Intelligence Division, (1943), *Indo-china,* Geographical Handbook Series, Naval Intelligence Division, London, p.126.

[83] ANC RSC D35 File 2798 Box 288. Rapport sur la situation du Cambodge, 1927.

[84] ANC RSC E03 File 11405 Box 987. Rapport annuel, Ville de Phnom Penh, Service municipal d'hygiene et de prophylaxie, 11 février 1931.

[85] ANC RSC E03 File 1675 Box 162. Rapport sur le fonctionnement des services sanitaires et médicaux et tous services à Phnom Penh et circonscriptions médicales, 1930.

[86] Naval Intelligence Division, op.cit. p.116.

[87] Ibid. pp. 118-119.

[88] Ibid. pp. 120, 123.

[89] AOM, RSC 263. Rapport annuel 1940-41. Minute Livre Vert. Situation Politique et Administrative.

[90] *La Presse Indochinoise,* 4 June 1936.

[91] ANC File 1675 Box 162 Rapport annuel du Dr. Ritharasi, Norodom, médecin des services extérieurs. 19 January 1931.

[92] Viollis, op.cit.

[93] Naval Intelligence Division. op.cit. pp.120-121. Salvarsan was an arsenic-based compound used with varying degrees of success in the treatment of these diseases. Earlier, mercury compounds were used, but these were often more dangerous than the disease. Penicillin was not available until after World War II.

[94] Sheldon Watts, (1997), *Epidemics and History. Disease, Power and Imperialism*, Yale University Press, New Haven, p.162. In the same way, UNTAC personnel contributed to the introduction of the HIV retrovirus in the early 1990s that sparked off the present epidemic of AIDS.

[95] Populations build up resistance to diseases unless the latter are capable of mutating at greater speed. When it first appeared in Europe, syphilis was extraordinarily virulent. With time and natural selection in the human population, the symptoms, while still distressing, were less spectacular. See, for instance, Hans Zinsser, (2000), *Rats, Lice and History*, Penguin Books, Harmondsworth.

[96] Charles Robequain, (trans Isabel A. Ward), (1944), *The Economic Development of French Indo-China*, Oxford University Press, London, pp.26-27

[97] There are references to the new vaccination program in an unsigned article in *La Quinzaine Coloniale* 25 August 1905. There is a report of vaccinations in Kompong Cham, Takeo and Kompong Chhnang provinces in French documents around the same time, e.g. AOM RSC D35 File 2975 Box 333, Rapport politique et économique, novembre – décembre 1906. See also "L'assistance médicale indigène en Indochine", (1908), *Revue Indochinoise*, No 81, 15 May.

[98] Gourdon, op.cit.

[99] Naval Intelligence Division, op.cit. p.110.

[100] "L'assistance médicale indigène" op.cit.

[101] AOM RSC 432 Rapport d'Ensemble 1925-27.

[102] *La Presse Indochinoise*, 9 April 1937.

Chapter 13

Sons of Toil or Sons of Angkor?

Ever since the appearance of their first newspaper in the...1930s, the ideology of Cambodian Nationalists had never gone much beyond the advocacy of Cambodians going into business in order to take control of the country's economic life from the French, Chinese and Vietnamese...

—Historian Michael Vickery.[1]

The 1920s and 1930s are often cast as a politically "dead" period for Cambodia, with little political activity outside of the Chinese and Vietnamese minorities. Overt Khmer nationalism did not make its appearance until World War II and the majority of the population seemed indifferent to politics. Penny Edwards,[2] however, argues that the genesis of modern Cambodian nationalism has deep roots in the overall cultural context.[3] In addition, as argued in Chapter 9 above, much of Cambodia's endemic banditry had a "social" and quasi-political character. This would have contributed to the gradual gestation of nationalism. A number of Khmer language magazines appeared before the better-known publication *Nagaravatta* appeared in 1936. These included *Srok Khmer* in 1926, *Kambuja Surya* in 1927 and *Kampuchea Bodemien* in 1931.[4] None were overtly political, at least not in the nationalist sense[5], but Edwards argues that they "contributed to the homogenizing of Cambodian cultural terrain"[6] and that this was a prerequisite for the development of modern nationalism.

Ironically, the French project of renovation of the Khmer arts, crafts, ancient monuments (especially Angkor) and the Buddhist religion, also contributed to this undermining of French power by providing Cambodians with potent national-cultural symbols. This was not a straightforward development, given that it began as a form of cultural appropriation by France—a striking confirmation of Marx's insight into the contradictory nature of colonialism as both destroyer and renovator.[7] Full-blown nationalist ideas were quicker to take root in the Vietnamese and Chinese milieux than among Khmers and in the former were often mixed together with socialist and communist doctrines, which began to seep slowly into the country in the 1920s.

The Communist movement in Cambodia

The Communist movement in Cambodia remained small until after World War II and until then, its support was largely confined to the Chinese and Vietnamese communities. The origins of Communist activity in Indochina— and therefore Cambodia[8]—can be traced to the attendance of a Vietnamese expatriate, Nguyen Ai Quoc, at the 1919 Congress of the French Socialist Party at Tours. Nguyen Ai Quoc, who was to become famous under the *nom-de-guerre* of Ho Chi Minh, supported the radical wing of the party, which broke away to affiliate to the Third, or Communist International. Thereafter, Ho Chi Minh worked tirelessly for the revolution. He was a founder of the revolutionary newspaper, *La Paria. Tribune du Prolétariat Colonial*, which ran from April 1922 until April 1926.[9] Copies of this paper, along with other left wing material, began to make their way into Cambodia during this time. Although the working class made up a small proportion of the total population and was mainly Vietnamese or Chinese, the French authorities were worried that Khmers who had served as soldiers and workers in France during World War II might have been influenced by radical ideas. There was an upsurge of revolutionary activity in China, Hong Kong and Vietnam in the 1920s[10] and so the *Sûreté* was constantly on the lookout for any signs of labor agitation spilling over into Cambodia. Indeed, a number of trade unions were formed in Phnom Penh the early-1920s, although the police often insisted on calling them "secret societies". In September 1921, a strike of building workers flared in the capital after a meeting between employers and union leaders in a Chinese restaurant failed to reach agreement on a pay claim. Hundreds of workers walked off the job, bringing building work to a standstill. When the workers demonstrated in the streets, a judge ordered the arrest of the "ringleaders", who were assaulted by the police. After serving prison terms of up to six months, the leaders were deported to China. At the same time, the Baudoin administration arranged for a general pay increase[11] and the union collapsed. Police agents redoubled their surveillance of the Chinese quarter of the city.[12] Repression did not always work. Late the following year, there was a general strike of sawmill workers in the capital and this resulted in a small wage increase for the strikers.[13] Again, the strikers were Chinese and Vietnamese. In 1923, the Phnom Penh police chief noted with some satisfaction that there were no Cambodian associations other than an authorized friendly society. There were a number of "subversive Annamite intellectuals", however, who distributed nationalist newspapers such as *La Tribune Indigène* and *L'Echo Annamite*.[14] One year later, the police reported that there were a number of subscriptions to *La Cloche Fêlée* and *La Paria* in Phnom Penh,[15] the latter the Communist journal co-founded by Ho Chi Minh after the split in the French Socialist Party. When Sun Yat Sen, the Chinese nationalist leader, died in 1925 the *Résident Supérieur* let it be known that he would not tolerate any kind of public demonstrations in the country.[16] Baudoin was determined to seal the country off from overseas subversion, which was viewed as contagion. The police opened all mail; often seizing large amounts of literature, including 28 packets of *La Paria* in 1925[17] and material in Chinese characters urging support for strikers in Swatow. By this stage, the authorities were very worried about the spread of socialist and trade union ideas to the rubber plantations in the red earth districts on the eastern bank of the Mekong.[18] In fact, the plantation laborers, many of whom were imported on fixed term contracts from Annam and Tonkin, became renowned for their militancy and formed a bastion of the Indochinese Communist Party.[19] By 1927, the *Sûreté* lamented "a tendency to emancipation", very strong sympathy for the "advanced parties" and a marked hostility to the French among the "Annamite" population of Cambodia. These views were particularly strong among the more highly educated members of the workforce, for instance clerks in the civil service.

By 1927, the police had noted over 40 different "subversive" publications entering the country, including *Cach-Mang-Nhân-Cong (The Revolutionary Workers)* and *Cach-Mang-Thanh-Nien (Revolutionary Youth)*, along with trade union journals, "propaganda for May Day" and material from the Kuomintang.[20] The Kuomintang had organized a General Union in Phnom Penh, with affiliated groups of mechanics, building workers, but also of merchants, which testifies to the cross-class, corporatist ideology that was taking root under Chiang Kai Shek.[21] This did not stop the police from claiming that Chinese employers were at the mercy of their "coolies".[22] At this stage, however, the authorities believed that Communist influence was negligible in the capital, in part due to the tight surveillance of a network of informers and police in the city[23] and along the border with Cochinchina.[24] By the end of the decade, however, the Communists had begun to make headway, at least among the Vietnamese. There were strikes on the rubber plantations, in distilleries and in garages in Phnom Penh in 1929.[25] Activists regularly distributed leaflets at places such as the École Pratique d'Industrie, the Collège Sisowath and the Phnom Penh Garage, preaching strike action for wage increases and the amelioration of workers' conditions. One leaflet protested the death of an electrician named Su, who was killed at the central electricity plant at Russey Keo in March 1931. Communists also substituted red flags with the hammer and sickle for signal flags on road works in Phnom Penh.[26] Communist organizers could expect stiff sentences and brutal interrogation if caught. A certain Nguyen Van Chim, for instance, was arrested in 1930 after he slipped over the border from Chaudoc and organized "suspicious meetings" in Prey Veng province. Chim was charged with sedition and compromising the security of the state and sentenced to 18 months imprisonment, raised after an appeal by the prosecution, to four years.[27]

Another center of discontent was growing among students in the capital. The French complained about the "bad spirit" of students and blamed this on the influence of "certain newspapers", including *Thanh Xuan*. Several young agitators were expelled from school for political activities.[28] Two years earlier, a Vietnamese teacher at the Collège Sisowath had been sacked for importing over 100 copies of revolutionary tracts written specifically for Indochina by the French Communist leader Jacques Doriot.[29] Although the police thereafter kept a close watch on students and teachers, they could not prevent discontent boiling over into what the French writer Marie Martin called a "mutiny"[30] at the Lycée Sisowath in May 1936, less than a year after the school opened.[31] In fact, the incident was somewhat less dramatic than Martin suggests. It happened when 200 school boarders, out on a supervised promenade in the city streets, left the "crocodile" and refused to return in protest at the imposition of personal taxes on those aged 20 and over.[32] Although French newspapers complained about "indiscipline" among the students in following years,[33] a young woman called Khieu Ponnary, who attended the Lycée Sisowath in the late 1930s is unlikely to have been involved. She seems to have been a model student.[34] She later joined the Communist Party and married Saloth Sar (more widely known as Pol Pot).

It is probable that deep-seated ethnic hostility between Vietnamese and Khmers worked to the authorities' advantage and hampered the creation of a united front of students.[35] It was probably a factor in the more general failure of Khmers to involve themselves in leftist agitation in the broader community. However, there were some cases of Khmer participation in Communist activities. The first recorded incident occurred at Phnom Penh one night in August 1930, when the police arrested six young men and boys for distributing illegal tracts under a streetlight at the corner of the avenue de Kampot and boulevard Doudart de Lagrée—today the intersection of Pochentong and Norodom Boulevards. The six Communists had draped a red banner across a wall, inscribed with the hammer and sickle and the words: "Workers, farmers, soldiers, unite to fight against world war, to overthrow French imperialism and create a just government." The police seized over 600 handbills. Three of those arrested were Vietnamese and three were Khmers. The latter were 17-year-old Sau Mel and 13-year-old Prak Sim, both students at the École François Baudoin, and Pen Kraham, a 24-year-old coolie employed at the Phnom Penh power station. The two students broke down under interrogation, supplied the police with names of "ringleaders", and were acquitted, but Pen Kraham was sentenced to one year in jail.[36] We can discount Kraham's plea that he was illiterate and could not understand what he was doing. He naturally was loath to go to prison and "playing stupid" was an astute ploy, given the French tendency to regard Khmers as gormless yokels,[37] although it was unsuccessful in this case. It is significant that Kraham worked at the power station and lived with his Vietnamese wife in the *quartier catholique*; his proletarian occupation and his conjugal arrangements account for his cosmopolitan outlook. However, the Khmer population, most of whom were peasants, remained largely impervious to Communist ideas at this stage, although another Khmer called Thach Choeun, a fisherman from the Tonlé Sap, joined the Communists in 1932 and became leader of the party in Svay Rieng province in 1939. He later adopted the name of Son Ngoc Minh and became the first president of the Communist Party of Kampuchea. He was also involved in an historic demonstration of Buddhist monks in July 1942 under the name of *Achar*[38] Mean. Another Khmer who joined the Communist movement in this period was Tou Samouth, later a "Khmer Viet Minh leader" and an ideological opponent of Pol Pot inside the Cambodian Communist Party in the 1950s and early '60s.[39] The Communist Party began to translate some material from its Vietnamese publication, *International,* into Khmer in the early 1930s.[40] When the effects of the Great Depression began to bite, however, there was a marked falling off in Communist activity and in some areas Communist cells disappeared completely.[41] By 1935, however, there was a resurgence of agitation, with the Communists reorganizing their movement, often by using native doctors and druggists as couriers. A number of other Khmers joined the movement at this time, with the names Ich, Chieu and Sam appearing in police reports.[42] Dissident Trotskyists were also active in Cambodia during this period,[43] distributing a daily newspaper printed in Saigon.[44] Again, their activities were concentrated among the Vietnamese population.

Indifference of the Khmer peasants to Communism

The indifference of the Khmer peasantry to their message must have baffled the Communists, but it stemmed from the material conditions of life; as Marx insisted, consciousness is a reflection of social being. The Khmer peasants had access to land—unlike peasants in the rice deficit regions of Annam and Tonkin where harsh conditions gave the Communists mass support even before World War II. So long as the French did not interfere too much with their lives, the Khmer peasants were content to ignore politics and they often had a marked antipathy for the Vietnamese, who provided the bulk of the Communist cadres in this period. Cambodia was still an intensely traditional society and Cambodians generally carried out their traditional occupations, shunning wage labor. Marxism, on the other hand, was a foreign, modernizing doctrine, pitched primarily at the proletariat (and in Asia at landless and poor peasants) and as such held little appeal for an individualistic Khmer peasantry. Even such Khmer rebellions that had occurred were traditionalist and did not aim at overthrowing "feudalism"[45] as such. There was little industry in any case and hence the soil in which radical socialist ideas might take root was lacking, particularly as far as the Khmers were concerned. This was to change after World War II, but the bastard "Marxism" that triumphed in 1975 under Pol Pot bore little relation to the classical European doctrines of the emancipation of the proletariat and socialist internationalism and was infected both with Stalinism and an ugly, virulent national chauvinism.

The beginnings of Khmer nationalism

Khmer nationalism was even less perceptible than Communism during the interwar period. The writer and politician Huy Kanthoul believes that Khmer nationalism was not very visible up to the end of the 1930s. "The Cambodians," he wrote, "always saw the French as their friends and natural protectors."[46] Like Communism, nationalism did not fall from the sky and nor was it an integral part of the traditional Khmer worldview. Historically speaking, it was of recent vintage, even in Europe. Yet, it did develop throughout an extended gestation period in the 1920s and 1930s. Some of the Khmer recruits who returned home from the trenches after World War I appear to have acquired a political consciousness. Two of these old soldiers were Pach Chhuon and Kim Thit. The former, who was 35 years old when he returned from Europe in 1920, had already been a student in Paris before his enlistment. He had been decorated with the Croix de Guerre for bravery in combat. Kim Thit, who was to become Prime Minister of an independent Cambodia in 1956, had served as a corporal in the French army. Both men became prominent in the proto-nationalist *Nagaravatta* group between 1936 and its suppression in 1942.[47] Neither appears to have been attracted to Communism at any stage of their lives. These men formed part of a small, yet influential layer of intellectuals or semi-intellectuals who were groping their way towards a nationalist consciousness. That consciousness grew in cultural soil provided, inadvertently, by the French. The Cambodian historian Sorn Samnang has written that Cambodian nationalism was boosted by the creation of such institutions as the Buddhist Institute (1930) and the Lycée Sisowath (1935), along with the publication of *Nagaravatta* from 1936. The slow emergence of a Cambodian literature, which included the work of the nationalist poet Kram Ngoy,[48] and the writers Rim Kin and Nou Hach, aided the process.[49] Another novel, entitled *Tonlé Sap* was published in 1938.[50] Such writing was, however, like the small number of Cambodian magazines, restricted to small circles. Before the emergence of *Nagaravatta*, the main Khmer-language magazine was *Kambuja Surya*, published by the Buddhist Institute. The Indian writer Harish Mehta claims that while it was "timid and unchallenging" in its editorial line, it nevertheless made "thickly veiled criticisms of French policy through parable-like, literary short stories, and proverbs soaked with discontent."[51] According to Huy Kanthoul, another proto-nationalist circle existed among former students of the Collège Sisowath. In 1935, they set up an *Amicale des Anciens Elèves* and although the focus of the group was cultural, Huy Kanthoul claims that, "they wished to serve as an instrument of the anti-colonial struggle."[52] This sounds exaggerated, but it probably contains a nub of truth.

The politics of envy

Nagaravatta appeared innocuous to the French when it first appeared in 1936. Its sentiments were pro-Cambodian rather than anti-French and it was strongly antipathetic to the Vietnamese. Although "divide and rule" was never a formal goal or method of French policy, it was certainly part of the quotidian practice of the administration and anti-Vietnamese sentiments would hardly have alarmed the authorities as they diverted discontent from themselves. From its inception, Cambodian nationalism contained a thick strand of envy. The French historian Daniel Hémery has described Khmer nationalism as a "reactive nationalism".[53] Although Wilfred Burchett has claimed that there was no animosity between Khmers and Vietnamese before the arrival of the French,[54] he distorts the facts to score a political point against French imperialism. According to the evidence of Dr. Morice in the 19th century, "the two races detest[ed] each other cordially". The "Annamites", this account continues, regarded themselves as superior because of their lighter complexions and saw the Khmers as little more than savages, with a "radically bad and vicious" nature.[55] On the other side, a Khmer proverb warned that Annamites had hypocrisy in their blood and that it was foolish to try to befriend one.[56] It would be remarkable if such an antipathy had not existed, given that by the 18th century the Vietnamese *Drang nach Süden* had amputated the Mekong delta region from the Cambodian lands. Viscount de Carné visited the country shortly after the establishment of the Protectorate and reported a "mutual dislike" between "Annamites" and Khmers.[57] There is evidence that Khmer judges discriminated against Vietnamese plaintiffs.[58] The Vietnamese formed a highly visible minority in the remainder of the country and by the 1930s Chinese and Vietnamese between them formed over half of the population of Phnom Penh.

Culturally, the Vietnamese and Khmers are quite distinct, speaking utterly different languages and adhering to rival sects of Buddhism. The Vietnamese have an essentially Sinitic civilization; that of the Khmers had emerged from an Indianized tradition. David Chandler considers that, the Vietnamese and Khmers are "perhaps the most sharply contrasted neighbors in Southeast Asia". The differences include "housing, hair styles, clothing (skirt and trousers), writing systems, government organization, methods of carrying things, cuisine, religion, attitudes towards history, armies, land tenure and recording, village administrations."[59] A large minority of the Vietnamese in Cambodia were Christian converts; so many in fact, that the "Annamite" district of the capital was known as the *quartier catholique*. Big cultural differences were also apparent in the attitudes of the two groups towards paid work and to work itself. The Khmers were reluctant to engage in wage labor, whereas the Vietnamese had resigned themselves to it. This was apparent on the rubber plantations where the majority of laborers were imported on fixed term contracts from Annam and Tonkin. It was also true of the urban areas, where Vietnamese and Chinese artisans did most of the skilled work and where Vietnamese were disproportionately represented in government and private clerical work. As discussed in Chapter 3 above, the crown land system, which did not allow the alienation of land, was inimical to the production of large agricultural surpluses for profit. Khmer agriculture tended to the subsistence model, with only small surpluses to pay taxes. The French had introduced private ownership of the land, had carried out cadastral programs and had brought in land taxes (the *impôt foncier*), but the superstructural cultural patterns that had existed on the old material base died hard. They had existed for many hundreds of years and land was fertile and plentiful, at least in the central heartlands of the country. Fish were abundant in the many waterways and an astonishing variety of fruit trees grew, seemingly where their seeds fell on the ground. For many centuries, the king's land could be worked by whoever settled on it.[60]

The Vietnamese attitudes to the land and work could not have been more different. If the Khmers were the Irish or the Scottish Highlanders of Southeast Asia, the Vietnamese were its Lowland Scots or Ulstermen. The analogy is not exact.[61] Nevertheless, the Highlanders shared many attributes with the Khmer peasants. The Lowland "factor", James Loch, described the Highland crofters early in the 19th century as a backward people content with squalor and discomfort, unwilling to change lest this meant abandoning the ways of their forefathers.[62]

Loch had a stake in painting the Highland peasants in the darkest colors as he was busily engaged in evicting them to make room for sheep. Change the bleak Atlantic moors for the paddies of Indochina and his words could be those of an industrious Vietnamese about his Khmer neighbors. The Khmers had never known a feudal system, but the Vietnamese system was based on private property in land (albeit with some communal land). Moreover, particularly in the densely populated northern lands of Annam and Tonkin, land was in short supply and there was always a danger of famine. The land was carefully husbanded and painstakingly spread with manure. The Protestant work ethic was not foreign to these industrious folk who of necessity lived a frugal and orderly life. Nothing was wasted; in a country where so many mouths depended on small parcels of land, to waste was a sin. There was also a tradition of collective effort because drainage and levees were of necessity a communal responsibility.[63] Land was more plentiful in the delta lands of Cochinchina but the age-old cultural patterns remained. In Cambodia, the Vietnamese also made diligent fishermen on the Tonlé Sap or industrious traders in the towns. They also had higher literacy rates than their Khmer neighbors.

It is natural, perhaps, that all of these factors should breed resentment among the Khmers and that as their sense of national identity crystallized that it should be tinged with envy and suspicion of their dynamic neighbors. Whether intentionally or otherwise, the French fed these passions. French newspapers harped on the "Annamite problem".[64] At their crudest, the French could favor Vietnamese in the lower echelons of the bureaucracy as a policy of deliberate divide and rule, but the same effects could flow from myopic pragmatism. Certainly, there was no policy of affirmative action, as we would now call it, to redress the imbalance. A call by a Khmer writer for "positive discrimination" in the civil service was ignored. Probably, the French hired Vietnamese because it was expedient and because staffing the civil service with Khmers would have entailed boosting education spending. This latter course was not something the cheese-paring administration was prepared to do. There is no doubt, either, that the French gave the development of Cambodia a lower priority than for the other sections of Indochina, with the possible exception of Laos.[65] Cambodia was always peripheral to France's main interests in the region.

"Reactive nationalism"

The pages of *Nagaravatta* from 1936 on are full of "reactive nationalism" and this also colors the articles written by Khmers for French-language publications in the same period. In one case, "a group of young Khmers" wrote to M. Marinetti, the parliamentary representative for Cochinchina and Cambodia at Paris, calling for a limit on Chinese and Vietnamese immigration. Marinetti gave the letter to the press and it was published as "The voice of the people".[66] Relations were probably not improved by the publication of a reply from a group of Vietnamese, who asked, "if we didn't come, who would do the jobs we do?"[67] The animosity was to lead to widespread bloodshed after World War II. More constructively, it was a goad for the emergence of Khmer literature, as in the case of the novelist Rim Kin, who noticed the Phnom Penh markets were full of Vietnamese books and was ashamed of his own people's cultural poverty, at least in this field.[68] In the late 1930s, a Khmer called Khémarak Botha (probably a pseudonym[69]) wrote a number of articles for *La Presse Indochinoise* in which he drew attention to the lack of Cambodians in responsible posts in their own country. In one article, Botha advocated a policy of what we would now call "reverse discrimination", calling on the *Résident Supérieur*, M. Thibaudeau, to change the civil service rules of recruitment to reserve jobs for "the sons of Angkor Wat".[70] The phrase is revealing as an example of the "invention of tradition", the creation of potent national symbols.[71] Botha reproached the French for their neglect of education of those "sons",[72] a theme taken up, albeit more diplomatically, by *Nagaravatta*.[73] Although Botha's articles were pro-development and anti-Vietnamese rather than anti-French, he might have trodden on official toes, because after a flurry of letters and articles in the paper in 1938, the paper published nothing more from his pen. Another article, entitled "Administrative bullying" appeared in the same newspaper in late 1935. A group of "Cambodian natives" wrote to protest at the reassignment of "Pacific" class locomotives from Cambodia to Annam. Not without justification, they claimed that the inequality of treatment of the countries of Indochina was "always to the detriment of Cambodia".[74]

The key members of Nagaravatta

Nagaravatta is often hailed as the starting point for modern Khmer nationalism, but in one writer's opinion it was rather "weak kneed" until the arrival of the Japanese in Cambodia in 1940.[75] This was understandable as there was no guaranteed freedom of the press in Cambodia; all publications had to be licensed, the censorship was ubiquitous and press licenses were revocable at will by the government.[76] The Government also ferociously repressed any sign of overt anti-colonialism. (See Chapter 16 below.) The publication of *Nagaravatta* was authorized by government decree of 10 October 1936.[77] Its director, Pach Chhuon was, as we have seen, a World War I veteran who had returned to Cambodia in 1920 with an NCO's rank[78] and become a civil servant. In 1928, aged 32, he became joint owner with a Frenchman of a garage business in Phnom Penh. The magazine's business manager was listed as Ing Vong, a second hand dealer and merchant in the capital; like Pach Chhuon, he was a *rara avis*, a Cambodian entrepreneur. Chhuon's principle collaborators in the project were listed as Ngo Hong (an employee of the Franco-Chinese Bank) and the *Achars* Sen and Them, the latter the secretary of the Royal Library. Another key figure—later the central one—was the French-educated Son Ngoc Thanh, then a 29-year-old magistrate and librarian from an affluent Khmer Krom family.[79] Sihanouk later described Thanh—who was to become his archenemy—as a strong, boundlessly ambitious, dark-skinned young man, who peered out from behind thick spectacles.[80] Another leader of the group was Sim Var, a 30-year-old civil servant from Kompong Cham province, described by Sihanouk as obstinate and passionately attached to his beliefs.[81] According to the French authorities, the paper was run by "a group of Cambodian civil servants with the assistance of teachers from the *École Supérieur de Pali* and of laymen versed in the Buddhist knowledge". Significantly, they were mostly "old boys" of the Collège Sisowath; even Son Ngoc Thanh, who had never attended the school, was a member of the College *Amicale*.[82] One could perhaps describe them as Khmer bourgeois, for a number of them were businessmen, including Tau Mau, an older man of reactionary opinions according to Sihanouk.[83] Given the low literacy rates of the Khmer population, the magazine began with a small print run of one thousand copies per week. This increased to three thousand copies a week in 1938, of which almost one-third was distributed in the capital.[84] The readership was exclusively Khmer; according to the French censors, the paper was hostile to the Siamese and Vietnamese and its political tendency was nationalist. This nationalism did not lead at this stage to criticism of the French in the paper's columns. The censors believed that, although he was vain and a little naïve, Pach Chhuon's loyalty to France was beyond question. Indeed, they described his relations with Prince Monireth as "cold". Monireth, it will be remembered, had fallen foul of *Résident Supérieur* Achille Silvestre because of his support for democracy and social development. Monireth was very involved with the scouting movement in Cambodia, but *Nagaravatta* did not share his enthusiasm. The seeds of the later clash between monarchists and bourgeois republicans are evident in this mutual dislike.[85]

Nagaravatta and Siam

None of the others involved in the paper had come to the attention of the authorities because of their political opinions. *Nagaravatta's* aims, nevertheless, were "to enlighten the Cambodian public [and] to raise its intellectual and moral level" and many of those involved in its publication went on to play prominent roles in the overtly nationalist movement. The paper's nationalism led it quite early into trouble with the French authorities because of a number of strongly anti-Siamese articles. One of these articles accused Siam of coveting Cambodian territory and of wanting to imitate the totalitarian regimes in Europe, specifically Nazi Germany and Mussolini's Italy. *Nagaravatta* was right. The Siamese did indeed wish to retake what they called *Monthon Burapha*, the provinces of Battambang and Siem Reap handed back to Cambodia in 1908 and their government clearly admired Hitler and Mussolini. Within three years of the publication of the offending articles, Siam, by now renamed Thailand because of the revanchist ideology of her rulers, was to go to war with France.[86] At the time the articles were written, however, the French preferred to downplay the threat from Siam and labeled *Nagaravatta's* writers as "maladroit" for raising it.[87] French displeasure must have been tempered, however, by the knowledge that the paper's anti-Siamese line excluded any kind of "pan Asianism". The paper believed that the Siamese authorities had never shown any sympathy for the large Khmer irredenta who lived in their country.[88] *Nagaravatta*, however, saw Cambodia's main enemy as being in the east. The paper was persistently, almost obsessively anti-Vietnamese, claiming that the "Annamites" wished to take over the country via large scale emigration. A mere brawl between Khmers and Vietnamese would provoke a call for the expulsion of the "foreigners"[89] and the paper constantly exhorted its Cambodian readers to reach the level of the "Annamite" population, particularly in business and the professions.

A barrier crossed

Much of what appeared in *Nagaravatta* in the 1930s was harmless from the French point of view. It had a limited circulation among the educated elite and offered no support for Communist subversion. The authorities themselves attest to the loyalty of the paper's staff. *Yet, with its publication, a barrier had been crossed.* Previously unspoken, inchoate thoughts were now being spoken and written and would develop into a full-blown nationalist discourse. Other Khmer publications had appeared since the 1920s, but all been produced under the close guidance of the French; *Nagaravatta* was produced independently and pursued an independent line insofar as possible within the constraints of the censorship. Mehta considers that the importance of *Nagaravatta* lay in its giving a voice to a hitherto silent and fearful Cambodian elite.[90] Now, those views, moderate as they were, were being published openly in the kingdom and the paper had great influence "in the educated Cambodian milieux, particularly in religious circles and among civil servants..."[91] The time for dialogue, however, was nearing an end. The outbreak of war in 1939 and the loss of the western provinces would shatter the old contract that had bound the Khmer elites to the tricolor. The group around *Nagaravatta*— Pach Chhuon, Sim Var and Son Ngoc Thanh most prominently—would soon find themselves at odds with the French empire. A number of them would become active in the post-colonial bourgeois republican movement, which was eventually to overthrow the monarchy in Lon Nol's 1970 *coup d'état*.[92] The Communists, too, would go on to win a much greater share of political support among the Khmers than observers might earlier have thought possible. History sometimes mocks the treasured creed of gradualism and like reefs in apparently calm sea, sharp breaks suddenly rend the pacific social fabric. The seemingly eternal colonial afternoon was about to end, although the sun blazed until the end, if through the gathering clouds of war. To borrow a phrase, the equilibrium was about the be punctuated.[93]

Notes

[1] Unpublished typescript on politics in Cambodia in the 1940s and 1950s. Chandler Papers, Monash University.

[2] Penny Edwards, (1999), "Cambodge: The Cultivation of a Nation, 1860-1945", unpublished Ph.D. thesis, Monash University.

[3] *Nagaravatta* = Angkor Wat.

[4] Edwards, op.cit. p.8. *Srok Khmer* = "Cambodian country", *Kambuja Surya* = "Cambodian Sun", *Kampuchea Bodemien* = "Cambodian News".

[5] The strict censorship would have made the expression of nationalist views difficult (see Chapter 15 below) and these publications were under French control in any case. The *Kambuja Surya*, for example, was a monthly review published under the auspices of the Royal Library and Suzanne Karpelès. [See John Tully, (1996), *Cambodia Under the Tricolour. King Sisowath and the "Mission Civilisatrice", 1904-1927,* Monash Asia Institute, Clayton, Victoria, p.229n and Virginia Thompson, (1968), *French Indo-China,* Octagon Books, New York, p.352.]

[6] Ibid.

[7] See, in particular, Karl Marx, "The Future Results of British Rule in India", in Shlomo Avineri, (ed.), (1969), *Karl Marx on Colonialism and Modernization. His dispatches and other writings on China, India, Mexico, the Middle East and North Africa,* Anchor Books, New York, pp.132-139.

[8] The most comprehensive study of Communism in Cambodia remains Ben Kiernan's groundbreaking *How Pol Pot Came to Power,* Verso, London, 1985.

See also David P. Chandler, (1992), *Brother Number One. A Political Biography of Pol Pot,* Allen and Unwin, St Leonards, NSW, which is crisply written and thoroughly researched.
[9] Daniel Hémery, (1990), *Ho Chi Minh. De l'Indochine au Vietnam,* Découvertes Gallimard, Paris, pp.46-49.
[10] See, for instance, Hémery, op.cit. passim and Harold R. Isaacs, (1961), *The Tragedy of the Chinese Revolution,* (Second Revised Edition), Stanford University Press, Stanford, California.
[11] AOM RSC 234. Révoltes au Cambodge (Agitateurs Chinois). Grèves des ouvriers charpentiers et maçons chinois. Memo septembre 1921.
[12] AOM RSC 234. Rapport confidentiel, Chef de la sûreté au Résident Supérieur, 26 décembre 1921.
[13] John Tully, (1996), *Cambodia Under the Tricolour. King Sisowath and the 'Mission Civilisatrice, 1904-1927,* Monash Asia Institute, Clayton, Victoria, p.290.
[14] AOM Fonds Amiraux, 7F 15 (1) Rapport annuel de la Sûreté, 15 August 1923.
[15] Ibid. 7F 15 (2) Rapport Annuel de la Sûreté, 20 August 1924.
[16] AOM RSC 432. Rapport politique, 2ème Trimestre 1925.
[17] AOM Fonds Amiraux, 7F 15 (3). Rapport annuel de la Sûreté, 27 August 1925.
[18] AOM Fonds Amiraux 7F 15 (4) Rapport annuel de la Sûreté, année 1925-1926.
[19] For a detailed discussion of conditions of work and the workers' response, see Chapter 16 below.
[20] AOM Fonds Amiraux, 7F 15 (5) Rapport annuel de la Sûreté 1er juillet 1926 – 30 juin 1927.
[21] Ibid. 7F 15 (6) Rapport Annuel de la Sûreté, 20 June 1928.
[22] Sûreté, 1926-1927, op.cit.
[23] AOM Fonds Amiraux FO 64271 Letter from Résident Supérieur to *Gougal,* 5 July 1927.
[24] Ibid. Letter from Résident Supérieur to *Gougal,* 29 October 1927.
[25] AOM RSC 218. Sûreté Envoi No 592-SS à Résident Supérieur, Rapport Annuel, 31 mai 1929 – 1er juin 1930.
[26] AOM RSC 225 Surveillance des activités communistes 1930-1931.
[27] ANC E03 File 1815 Box 176. Rapport annuel du 1er juin 1930 au 31 mai 1931. (Prey Veng.)
[28] AOM RSC 218. Sûreté Envoi No 592-SS à Résident Supérieur, Rapport Annuel, 31 mai 1929 – 1er juin 1930.
[29] AOM RSC 240. Communisme, 1929. The tracts included Doriot's "Pour la libération nationale de l'Indochine" and "Appel de Jacques Doriot à la jeunesse révolutionnaire Indo-Chinois". (Doriot later swung to the extreme right and collaborated with the Nazis during the Vichy period in World War II in France.)

[30] Marie Alexandrine Martin, (1989), *Le Mal Cambodgien. Histoire d'un société traditionelle face à ses leaders politiques, 1946-1987*, Hachette, Paris, p.64 and Annexe I, chronologie.

[31] The high school opened in September 1935. ["Inauguration du Lycée Sisowath," *L'Echo du Cambodge*, 6 and 17 September 1935.]

[32] *L'Echo du Cambodge*, 12 May 1936 and *La Presse Indochinoise*, 10 June 1936. It is tempting to see some connection between the strike and the formation of the Popular Front government at Paris, but the strike predated Blum's victory.

[33] For instance, *La Presse Indochinoise*, 10 June 1936.

[34] Ponnary received a *prix d'excellence* in 1938. *La Presse Indochinoise*, 15 July 1938.

[35] The tension between Vietnamese and Khmer students was often noted in official reports. See, for instance, ANC RSC E03 File 499 Box 38. Rapport annuel sur la situation du Collège Sisowath et des écoles annexes (année scolaire 1932-1933).

[36] AOM RSC 433 Révoltes au Cambodge. Note confidentielle, Sûreté, Phnom Penh, 11 August 1930. Lest any reader moralize over the boys' capitulation, the author directs them to Chapter 15 below, where there is a discussion of the methods used by the police on political suspects.

[37] American Blacks, particularly in the "Deep South" also played on white stereotyping. It is a defense mechanism of the powerless. For an imaginative reconstruction of this, see William Styron, (1967), *The Confessions of Nat Turner*, Random House, New York.

[38] A title given to high ranking and respected monks.

[39] It is possible that Tou Samouth was murdered on the orders of the Pol Pot faction. This explanation was adopted by the Vietnamese Communists after 1979, and by Ben Kiernan. See Kiernan, op.cit. pp.197-198. This is unlikely. For an opposing view, see Chandler, op.cit., pp.63-64 and David P. Chandler, (1999), *Brother Number One. A Political Biography of Pol Pot*, Revised Edition, Westview Press, Boulder, Colorado, p.61. Chandler points out that Tou Samouth disappeared during a period of generalized repression of Communists ordered by Sihanouk. It is most likely that Sihanouk's police kidnapped and murdered Tou Samouth and disposed of his body by weighting it with stones and dropping it from a canoe into the Mekong.

[40] Ben Kiernan, (1985), "Les origines du Communisme Khmer", in Camille Scalabrino et al, *Cambodge. Histoire et Enjeux, 1945-1985*, Asie Débat 2, L'Harmattan, Paris, p.76. The monks' demonstration is discussed in Chapter 17 below. Pol Pot (Saloth Sar) was a small child at this time—he was probably born on 25 May 1925. Chandler earlier believed that Pol Pot was born in 1928, but it seems that Pol Pot lied about his age in order to secure a scholarship to study in France. See Chandler, op.cit., p.7.

[41] ANC RSCE03 File 499 Box 38 Rapport Annuel Résidence de Kampot, June 1932-May 1933

[42] AOM RSC 233 Activités communistes, 1934-1936.

[43] ANC RSC F71 D611 16665 Note confidentielle, Surête, 1 July 1939.

[44] AOM RSC 306 Presse, censure, propagande, 1939. The leading Trotskyist was one Le Tan Quoi, also known as Dong Tu, who worked as a clerk for the department of public works.

[45] I use the term in inverted commas as a kind of shorthand, given that no suitable descriptor exists to fit traditional rural civilization in Cambodia. See Chapter 3 above.

[46] Huy Kanthoul, "Mémoires", p.61. Unpublished French language typescript. Chandler Papers, Monash University.

[47] Tully, op.cit. p.218.

[48] Sorn Samnang, (1995), "L'Evolution de la société cambodgienne entre les deux guerres mondiales (1919-1939)", Thèse pour le doctorat d'histoire. Université Paris VII, Tome II, p.369.

[49] Ibid. p.376.

[50] Harish C. Mehta, (1997), *Cambodia Silenced. The Press Under Six Regimes,* White Lotus, Bangkok, p.28.

[51] Ibid. p.242.

[52] Huy Kanthoul, op.cit. p.76.

[53] Cited in Sorn Samnang, op.cit. p.381.

[54] Wilfred Burchett, (1957), *Mekong Upstream,* Red River Publishing House, Hanoi, p.6.

[55] Anonymous, (Preface by Dean Meyers), (2000), *The French in Indochina. With a Narrative of Garnier's Explorations in Cochinchina, Annam and Tonkin,* White Lotus, Bangkok, p.90.

[56] Norodom Sihanouk, (1981) *Souvenirs doux et amers,* Hachette, Paris, p.44.

[57] Louis de Carné, (1872), *Travels in Indo-China and the Chinese Empire,* Chapman and Hill, London, p.11.

[58] AOM RSC 256 Affaires politiques indigènes 1867-1890, letter from Governor of Cochinchina to the French *Résident* at Phnom Penh, 22 June 1881.

[59] David Chandler, unpublished seminar notes, Centre of South East Asian Studies, Monash University, 23 March 1978.

[60] Nature was often harsh, however. See Chapter 9 above.

[61] Highland society was feudal. The peasants were tenants-at-will of the laird.

[62] John Prebble, (1969), *The Highland Clearances,* Penguin Books, Harmondsworth, p.56.

[63] For a discussion of the Sinitic agricultural society of Vietnam, see Pierre Gourou, (1975), *Man and Land in the Far East,* Longmans, London and Pierre Gourou, (1965), *Les Paysans du Delta Tonkinois. Etude de géographie humaine,* Mouton, Le Haye.

[64] See, for instance, *La Presse Indochinoise* of 22 September 1937, which contains one of an interminable series of articles of the "problem".

[65] See Chapter 12 above for some comparisons of education spending.

[66] "La voix du peuple", *La Presse Indochinoise,* 21 November 1938.

[67] Ibid, 5 December 1938.

[68] Sorn Samnang, op.cit. p.376.

[69] It is possible that Botha was Prince Monireth, the blunt-spoken heir apparent to the throne.

[70] Khémarak Botha, (1938), "Cambodge aux Cambodgiens", *La Presse Indochinoise,* 14 February.

[71] For a discussion of the creation of new national symbols, see Eric Hobsbawm and Terence Ranger, (1993), *The Invention of Tradition,* Cambridge University Press, Cambridge.

[72] Khémarak Botha, (1938), "Les établissements scolaires sont nettement insuffisants au Cambodge", *La Presse Indochinoise,* 9 May.

[73] *Nagaravatta,* 19 June 1937. In this issue, the paper called for an increase in the number of places for Khmer students in franco-indigenous schools.

[74] Un groupe de Cambodgiens indigènes, (1935), "Brimades administratives. Le Chemin de fer de Phnom-Penh à Mongkolborey sera-t-il dépouillé de ses locomotives Pacific?" *La Presse Indochinoise,* 20 November.

[75] Mehta, op.cit. p.31

[76] See Chapter 15 below for a discussion of the lack of civil freedoms in Indochina.

[77] Much of the information in the following paragraphs is based on an official report written by a French censorship officer on 1 May 1938 and contained in ANC RSC F71 D611 D610 16665, Articles de presse—notices sur la presse au Cambodge—contrôle des journeaux—Nagaravatta—contrôle de la presse, divers, 1935-1940.

[78] One French source claims he was an interpreter in the military during the war. (AOM Fonds Amiraux 7F 29 (7) Etude sur les mouvements rebelles au Cambodge, 1942-1952.)

[79] Son Ngoc Thanh was born at Ky-La in Travinh province, Cochinchina, on 7 December 1908 of a Khmer father and a Vietnamese mother. He attended primary schools in Travinh, Phnom Penh and Saigon and completed his *baccalauréat* at the Lycée Montpellier in France. Afterwards, he studied law for one year at the Faculté de Droit at Paris. He worked at a bank in Paris and then as a civil servant in Cochinchina and Cambodia. [État-Civil de Reseignements, Son-Ngoc-Thanh (Cambodgien de Cochinchine), contained in Son Ngoc Thanh Papers, in Chandler Papers, Monash University.]

[80] Sihanouk, op.cit. p.73. Sihanouk's work is often tendentious and should be used with caution.

[81] Ibid. p.74.

[82] État-Civil, op.cit.

[83] Sihanouk, op.cit. p.73.

[84] Of the 3000 copies, 1900 were distributed in the Cambodian provinces, 900 in Phnom Penh and 100 in Cochinchina. There were ten subscriptions each in Siam and France and the administration took 20. A one-year subscription cost four piastres and the price per copy was eight cents. (ANC RSC F71 D611 D610 16665 op.cit.)

[85] Post-independence politics in Cambodia has contained three broad strands: the monarchists, the bourgeois republicans of the Son Ngoc Thanh variety, and the Communists, although there has been considerable overlap, the actors have tended to come from the same elite circles and some moved from one "camp" to another.

[86] These matters are discussed in Chapter 17 below.

[87] For a discussion of Franco-Thai relations in the 1930s and World War II, see Chapter 17 below. For a discussion of Franco-Siamese relations up to 1907-08, see Tully, op.cit. Chapters Three and Four.

[88] *Nagaravatta,* 12 August 1939.

[89] Ibid. 12 August 1939.

[90] Mehta, op.cit. p.30.

[91] Articles de presse—notices sur la presse au Cambodge—contrôle des journeaux—Nagaravatta—contrôle de la presse, divers, 1935-1940, op.cit.

[92] Lon Nol, however, was for many years a faithful servant of the king and his right hand man, Sirik Matak, was from the Sisowath wing of the royal family.

[93] The allusion is to the writings of the celebrated—if controversial—American evolutionary theorist Stephen Jay Gould, who postulated that evolution was not a gradual process, but a series of equilibria punctuated by sharp breaks. Whatever the outcome of the debate in biology, the idea has clear relevance for the history of human societies and indeed—as Gould's detractors were quick to point out—has an affinity with Marx's theory of historical materialism. However, the idea need not have any teleological implications in the vulgar Marxist sense. See Stephen Jay Gould, (2002), *The Structure of Evolutionary Theory,* Harvard University Press, Boston.

Chapter 14

Boom, Bust and Social Development Between the Wars

The French are destroying the racial individuality of the people whom they rule, and harnessing them to the plough of their own peculiar form of progress...

—Harry Hervey, American traveler, 1927.[1]

Cambodia emerged from the Great War in poor economic shape, almost in recession. The country's staple exports—rice, maize, pepper and livestock—had slumped, partly due to a shortage of shipping, partly due to demands for the cultivation of crops such as the castor oil plant for the war effort, and partly due to the general and pressing imperatives of France's wartime economy.[2] The slump in trade with France was not compensated for by new trade links. Much of the country's pre-1914 trade had been with France. Government policy discouraged free trade and viewed Cambodia as only another *colonie d'exploitation* that existed to benefit France. Thus, in 1918, neighboring Siam ranked only as Indochina's tenth largest trading partner, despite a long common frontier and the advantages of cross-border commerce.[3]

The war years saw a fall in the production of essential commodities and the stagnation of development projects. Cambodia's rice production fell from around 900,000 tonnes in 1914 to 600,000 in 1915 and rose only to just under 670,000 tonnes in 1917. Maize production plummeted from 14,300 tonnes in 1914 to a low of 2000 tonnes in 1917.[4] Paddy taxes fell from 900,000 piastres to 400,000 piastres in 1919.[5] As a result, the specter of famine cast a shadow over the armistice celebrations. Baudoin averted starvation by importing food grains for sale at subsidized prices and banning the export of rice.[6] The measures effectively disrupted the activities of Cholon merchants, who were hoarding grain to force up prices. Public works and forestry projects were used to create work for the destitute.[7]

Sarraut's mise-en-valeur policy

The economic downturn was short-lived, however. The period between the end of the war and the end of the 1920s was generally one of economic growth in Cambodia. This was punctuated by occasional poor harvests and followed by the devastating slump that affected world trade after 1929. Economic development, however, was not entirely a *laisser faire* process in Indochina, but occurred within the framework of a development (*mise-en-valeur*) plan drawn up by Governor General Albert Sarraut in the post-war years. This was a kind of colonial "corporatism,"[8] that left little to Adam Smith's "invisible hand of the market" and smacked more of the "indicative planning" practiced by French governments for much of the post-World War II period. The state already played a guiding role in the colonial economy, particularly after the incorporation of Indochina into the French customs union in 1887. Since January 1892, protectionism had been legally enforced in all of the French overseas possessions.[9] In 1938, 95 per cent of European business capital, and all capital in government securities in the French colonies was French.[10] French investment in the colonies was boosted when the Bolshevik Revolution in Russia ended investment in what had previously been France's largest capital export destination. We should not overstate the amount, however, and by the mid-1930s, two-thirds of it was invested in North Africa.[11] Cambodia was very much a poor cousin. In many ways, Sarraut's *mise-en-valeur* policy was an attempt to implement Leroy-Beaulieu's grandiose theories of colonial development, but with invisible brakes applied. There was, though, to be state-sponsored development—the planned creation of infrastructure, including roads, railroads and ports, and the stimulation of trade and industry.[12] The state's pre-eminent partner in post-World War I development was the powerful Banque de l'Indochine, set up in 1875 and described by the historian Robert Aldrich as "the architect of colonial monetary policy". The inter-war years marked the apogee of the bank's power, with credits of some 3.5 billion francs in the 1920s. Critics saw the bank as an octopus concerned with its own interests rather than the overall welfare of the colonies. This private bank issued the Indochinese currency, the piastre, and functioned as a loan bank rather than as a savings bank. Small businesses grumbled with some justification that the bank cared only for large corporate projects. The bank also had a controlling interest in distilling, mining, rail and maritime transport, matches and paper in the colonies.[13] Little or no effort was made to set up "native" banks and financial institutions.[14] A further component of the state-corporate conglomerate was the rubber companies. Although rice and maize remained Cambodia's biggest export earners on the eve of World War II, rubber was in third place and rapidly closing the gap.[15] Rice production soared during the 1920s as more land was brought into production; over 800,000 tonnes of paddy were harvested in 1927, compared with 600,000 in 1925.[16] Some of the increase was also due to the introduction of more scientific farming methods, although this should not be overstated and small family plots using traditional methods remained the norm. The new methods included pumping water for irrigation and mechanical harvesting. Tractors, however, were only of use in new fields, as the older paddies were too irregular in size, shape, and configuration of the floor for their use.[17] Such expensive machines were in any case out of the question for the great mass of poor peasants. Peasant rice growing methods remained as they had been for centuries. The farmers did not use fertilizer and were suspicious of change. Much of the soil was naturally fertile and— except in times of flood or drought—assured a living and a surplus for the farmers. The small population meant there was no real competition for the soil, only a small percentage of which was cultivated.[18] The Australian writer Wilfred Burchett relates an anecdote—possibly apocryphal—of a US aid worker in the 1950s who showed peasants how to double their yields of rice, only to find that they planted only half the previous acreage.[19] The French met with similar frustrations.

France's interests always paramount

However, none of this should be taken to mean that the French were industrializing Cambodia. They did not feel it was in their interests to do so, or were indifferent, and they were hostile to foreign investors doing the job for them. There was little industry before World War I, except for artisans' workshops, rice mills, some sawmills and a few

cotton gins.[20] Little else was built between the wars, except for some
distilleries, power stations, railroad workshops, sawmills, a few
agricultural processing plants and latex mills on the rubber plantations.
On the eve of World War II, Cambodia was much less developed than
Vietnam. The problem was that "France's interests were always
paramount".[21] France saw her far eastern colonies primarily as sources
of tropical commodities and dog-in-the-manger regulations prevented
other countries from investing there, with the result that they were
"starved financially,"[22] Cambodia and Laos in particular. Thomas
Ennis considered that, "Cambodia does not show any extensive
colonization activities", a condition he attributed to "the enervating
climate".[23] Behind the protectionist barriers erected by the state, the
French capitalists were free to do as they chose—or chose not to do—
and the economy stagnated despite some early promise.

Cambodia lacked a developed infrastructure in 1918, although as
previously outlined, a network of roads was under construction when
war broke out, and there were regular steamer and telegraph services.
Sarraut's initial plans for Cambodia were to expand and improve the
transportation web. In 1917, he unveiled plans for a major trunk road
to link Saigon and Bangkok via Phnom Penh and Battambang. Other
all-weather roads were to link all the major population centers, and a
blue water port was planned for the gulf coast at Ream, west of
Kampot.[24] Public works projects had continued throughout the war
period, employing *corvée* labor. The rate was accelerated afterwards,
but was hampered by a shortage of engineers and technicians—many
of whom had left for France during the war—and by the Khmers'
entrenched suspicion of wage labor.[25] Finding labor was often a
problem and was often a topic of discussion at *Résidence* council
meetings. The minutes of the Council of the Kompong Thom
Résidence in 1916, for example include a lengthy discussion of the
problem. Governor Hy of Stoung said that there were three possible
solutions: to resort to private contractors; to revert partially to the old
system of compulsory extra *corvée*; or to raise wages. The *Oknha* Ros
said that contractors would be too expensive and could only be funded
by a general increase in taxation. Hy thought that wages should be
raised from 0.30 piastres a day to 0.50, but to be paid on a piecework
basis according to the number of cubic meters of earth shifted.[26] In the
event, the shortfall in available labor throughout the kingdom was
made up by penal labor. M. Maspéro reported that in mid-1920, one
thousand convicts had been transferred from the grand Bokor scheme
in the Elephant Mountains behind Kampot to Route Locale 12 between
Tonlé Bet and Kompong Cham.[27]

The road-building project was ambitious, and received praise from foreign visitors, including Lord Northcliffe, the proprietor of the London *Times*, in 1921,[28] a British diplomat called Mr. Greg in 1926,[29] and the writer Harriet Ponder some years later.[30] The new roads—many of them riding above the flood plains on embankments and topped with concrete—served a number of functions, from improving access of products to markets, to allowing the French to move around the countryside more easily for administrative purposes (including the collection of taxes). Regular car and bus services ran between Phnom Penh and Battambang and to Saigon from the early 1920s. The latter trip took twelve hours. Kampot could be reached from the capital in four to five hours.[31] Buses on the major routes were often comfortable, but Eleanor Mordaunt has left us a vivid account of a hair-raising journey between Ream and Kampot in the late 1920s. After missing the mail bus to Phnom Penh because of laborious passport controls, Ms. Mordaunt found a seat on a Kampot bus. She sat next to the hot engine aboard a bus crammed with peasants, goats, fowls, bags of rice and other cargo under a canvas roof. The bus ambled through scores of villages in hellish heat and the stench of durian, but Mordaunt was struck by the politeness and hospitality of the Khmers. At one point, the passengers had to disembark to allow the bus to travel over an unsafe bridge.[32] Today, the road is an obstacle course of potholes and washouts, some waist deep.

The new roads also allowed easier access to Angkor and other archaeological sites for tourists and restoration work. By 1924-25, following the completion of improved access routes (one incorporating over 23 ancient Angkorean bridges[33]) and the inauguration of Cook's Tours,[34] one thousand visitors per year were visiting the Angkor ruins.[35] The industry proved recession proof, even in the worst years of the Great Depression of the 1930s, with over 3000 visitors in 1933.[36] Nor did steep taxes of up to 30 per cent extra on hotel bills seem to deter them, despite the worries of journalists.[37] The visitors included Charlie Chaplin, then at the height of his fame, in April 1935.[38] Shortly afterwards, the authorities staged a grand Angkor festival, at which a new statue of the Buddha was unveiled, and there were traditional dances and a theatrical performance written in verse by King Monivong.[39] It is not difficult to see why the Angkor ruins were a tourist attraction. Although travel writers have written a great deal of orientalist nonsense about Angkor, the ruins are imposing by any standard. The writer Andrée Viollis likened the vast buildings to the palace of Versailles,[40] but the scale is grander and Versailles has nothing of the magnificent carved friezes that provide a stunning visual record of an ancient civilization. The French restoration project was also impressive. Although we might perhaps charge France with the cultural appropriation of the monuments, there can be no doubt that France saved them from inexorable plunder and decay. Since the Khmers shifted their capital from Angkor around 1450, it had been plundered by, among others, the Siamese. In the late 19th century, the Frenchman Louis Delaporte sent 120 massive boxes of Angkorean stonework to France.[41] In 1924, the writer André Malraux was arrested with 600 kilograms of stonework sawn from the Banteay Srey temple in his possession,[42] a philistine crime for which he never apologized, though he later became Minister for Culture in France. Perhaps the most laughably naïve cultural vandals were the Americans who wanted to buy the Banteay Srey temple and ship it back to the USA, or their Hollywood brethren who wanted to use Angkor as a backdrop in a Tarzan film.[43] Still, the natives could be just as eccentric. The English writer Osbert Sitwell records that the mild-mannered Cambodian chauffeur who drove him to Angkor was driven into a rage at the sight of a dog, and that he would run over the unfortunate beasts without hesitation.[44]

Other public works projects

Drinking water remained a problem throughout Cambodia, although steps were taken to improve the supply of potable water and electricity to Phnom Penh and other centers, including Kampot, Kep, Takeo, Kompong Thom, Siem Reap and Angkor.[45] Phnom Penh's water, pumped from the Tonlé Sap River, was treated in a filtration plant after 1927,[46] which must have lessened the high rates of water-borne infectious diseases. A third pump was installed in 1933 to boost supplies.[47] The telegraph network stretched for over 3500 kilometers by the end of 1926, including almost 780 kilometers in urban districts, and the French could boast the existence of 67 post offices.[48] Siem Reap, Svay Rieng and Kompong Trach were lit by electricity in 1928 and there were new diesel plants in Kompong Cham and Takeo. A high-tension line, the longest in Indochina, terminated at Kampot.[49] The road network was extended throughout the 1920s: by 1925 it was possible to make a circuit of the Great Lake during the dry season[50] and at the end of the following year a road snaked up from Mimot in eastern Cambodia to Melouprey.[51]   The port of Phnom Penh was dredged by the *Claparède* to accommodate vessels of four-meter draught in the same year. Improved docking facilities[52] and a slipway were built in the same period, along with a system of masonry dikes to prevent flooding.[53] Two years later, a large cantilevered steel bridge, 610 meters long and named after King Monivong, spanned the river at Phnom Penh.[54] One year later, Governor General Pierre Pasquier and King Monivong jointly turned the first sod for a railroad line between Phnom Penh and Battambang.[55] The initial estimate was that the line would cost 17 million piastres.[56] Work on an extension of the railroad from Battambang to Mongkolborey was approved in late 1931.[57] The construction of the whole line provided work for between 4000[58] and 6500 laborers.[59] There were numerous difficulties of construction. The way is often barren, but is also subject to flooding.[60] There are a number of raised causeways and almost one hundred steel or reinforced concrete bridges.[61] In the first year of operations, the railroad's 17 locomotives hauled almost 60,000 tonnes of freight.[62] The railroad was extended from Mongkolborey to Aranya in Siam after 1933.[63] The historian Ennis notes, however, that Europeans held all of the responsible posts on the rail system[64] and Vietnamese held many of the others.

Regular air services were introduced around the same time, after two aviators, Paillard and Le Brix made the long flight from France.[65] Phnom Penh was linked to Saigon via an airstrip at Prey Veng in 1928.[66] By the end of the 1920s, tourists were flying to Siem Reap and Angkor by regular seaplane service.[67] As the end of the decade, the old symbol of the French *mission* in Indochina, the "intrepid explorer", was eclipsed by the new symbol of the heroic aviator. Air France opened a regular air service between Saigon and Paris in 1929.[68] This was a startling development at the time, and the unpredictability of the aircraft rather enhanced the romantic allure of air travel.

The bustling city at the Quatre Bras

The development of the country was reflected in the growth of urban centers, particularly Phnom Penh. The population of that city doubled between 1900 and 1930 to 80,000. By 1936, it had expanded to over 100,000.[69] It was a noisy, smelly, hot and vibrant place, with a mix of ethnic groups crowded into the wide, tree-lined boulevards and narrow alleys. The population was divided roughly three ways between Khmers, Vietnamese[70] and Chinese[71] and they tended to live in different quarters of the city; the Chinese around the new market, the Khmers in the *faubourg cambodgien* east of the royal palace and the Vietnamese in the "Catholic village" near the waterfront. Intermarriage between Khmers and "Annamites" was rare, but the presence of thousands of Sino-Khmer *métis*[72] attested to links that stretched back to Angkorean times, when Chinese sailors would jump ship and take Khmer wives.[73] There were sprinklings of Indians—often shopkeepers, textile merchants and moneylenders of the *chetty* or *chettiar* caste[74]— from British India and the French colony of Pondicherry. There were Europeans and *métis* of various racial admixtures. There was also a sizeable minority of Chams, the Islamic descendants of the ancient empire of Champa, and smaller numbers of Malays, Shans, Siamese, Filipinos and Burmans. The Chams were often merchants, although they were famous as makers of the buffalo carts that creaked through the streets of the city from the villages. There were Buddhist wats, Cham mosques and Catholic churches—foremost among them the Sacré Coeur—along with Caodai temples, the latter barely tolerated by the authorities. Curiously, unlike elsewhere in the Muslim world, the Cham faithful were called to prayer not by the cries of a *muezzin*, but by drums and gongs. There were sharp smells of decay, the pungent aromas of durian and spices and the reek of the fermented fish paste called *prahoc* by the Khmers. Buddhist monks in their saffron robes begged for alms in the crush and black-faced charcoal sellers peddled their wares. In the markets and on the streets, peasants sold eggs and chickens, fish from the Tonlé Sap and fruits and vegetables. Luc Durtain wrote that the multi-ethnic crowds were thickest in the markets, where one could buy all kinds of exotic goods.[75] Eleanor Mordaunt admits to being frightened of the crowded streets, clogged with cars, carts, *cyclo pousses* and pedestrians, when she visited shortly after King Sisowath's death in 1927.[76] The occasional elephant lumbered along in the throng. There were also complaints in the newspapers of dangerous driving, a new misdemeanor.[77] New traffic regulations were introduced in 1936; drivers had to obey police instructions; pedestrians would stay on the footpaths and were not to jaywalk, particularly at crossroads. Given the Khmer penchant for blocking the sidewalk with stalls, vehicles, drying rice, piles of vegetables, fish and other goods, it must have been difficult to comply with the regulations. All traffic was exhorted to keep to the right, obey a 30-km/h speed limit, and signal to indicate a change of direction.[78] The royal band would sometimes add to the cacophony; Osbert Sitwell heard it play a cacophonous rendition of the march from *Aida*.[79] Judging by the noisy chaos of the streets today, the French were unsuccessful in their attempt to introduce order.

Phnom Penh lies on the flat delta land and is dominated by the fifty-foot high "mountain" that gives the city its name. A gray stone stupa sat—and still does—at the summit of the *phnom* like a long-handled bell. Trees and gardens cloaked the hillside, partly hiding from view a monument commemorating the return of Battambang and Siem Reap provinces in 1907. The major French offices—including the *Résidence Supérieure*, the *Résidence* of Kandal province, the *Résidence* of the mayor of the city, the National Library, the Banque de l'Indochine, the Customs building and the Post Office—clustered on or near to the circular road that runs around the base of the *phnom*. Many of these buildings were unusually graceful structures, with steep tiled roofs and slightly "oriental" eaves, shuttered windows, the walls rendered and painted in yellows, whites and blues. A few blocks away, the Canal de Vernéville, spanned by half a dozen bridges, still ran from the central railroad station and Boeng Kak Lake to the river. Near its outlet, the steamships of *Messageries Fluviales* tied up at a series of pontoons, which rose and fell with the great fluctuations in the height of the river. Out of sight of the sweating wharf coolies, the native "rookeries" and the smells of the markets, the better-off French residents enjoyed a privileged lifestyle, sipping *apéritifs* on the terraces of their clubs after work or listening to bands such as "Jaky's Jazz" at the Royal Palace Hotel. This establishment boasted "all mod cons", lifts, telephones and multilingual staff.[80] The French had little contact with the natives, except for servants and members of the elite. The leafy European residential precincts were quite separate from the other districts of the city. At the weekends, the French could motor to the hill stations at Bokor—"the Buffalo's Hump" near Kampot—or Kirirom, or else take the sea air at the beach resort of Kep, for Phnom Penh is always warm and the resorts provided relief from the heat and flies. When the diurnal temperature fell to 11 degrees Celsius one day in January 1934, it was as extraordinary an event as a total eclipse and was frigid for the indigenes.[81]

Not all the Europeans were well to do. There were private soldiers, mechanics and lower level civil servants—more of the latter, proportionally, than in the British, Dutch or American colonies, where those jobs were given to the indigenes. The poorer clerks and suchlike drank *vin ordinaire* at zinc-topped bars and lived in modest dwellings, although most had servants, a maid or a Vietnamese "boy". The tree-lined streets provided the illusion of a southern French town for the homesick. Tennis was fashionable in Phnom Penh society, with fierce competition for the Sisowath Monivong Cup.[82] A fencing club was formed in 1935 and a sailing club ventured onto the Tonlé Sap in the same year.[83] Soccer matches were held in the municipal stadium, which opened in late 1938.[84] Cinemas had first appeared in 1913, and theatrical troupes had visited the town since 1909, with performances by Molière and others. Even the occasional circus made the journey upriver from Saigon to perform in the city.[85] Horseracing was very popular, with the *Prix d'Angkor*, the *Prix de Kompong Thom* and the *Prix de Sa Majesté Sisowath* held regularly at the Phnom Penh racecourse. Rugby was a distraction for the energetic and their admirers.[86] Eleanor Mordaunt scoffed at the French for what she saw as their affected social life, with snobbish women teetering on ridiculously high heels,[87] but this might have been traditional English rivalry and upper-middle class *hauteur* at the antics of Gallic colonials. Some British visitors came to Cambodia determined to sneer at their French rivals. One of the more vituperative was the mescaline imbibing Geoffrey Gorer, who derided the Wat Phnom as a wart and dismissed the royal palace (which he believed to be inhabited by an Emperor) as cheap and flashy.[88]

Phnom Penh had its share of vices, too, with "public girls" plying their ancient trade on the streets: a popular Khmer song warning with macho persiflage, "Beautiful woman/You must look after yourself/I have torn down the fence/I have broken the lattice/Look after yourself/I will come this evening."[89] Some punters, however, found that "a night with Venus meant a lifetime with Mercury",[90] for syphilis—like HIV/AIDS in Cambodia today—was rampant. Gambling, too, was deeply entrenched, although the authorities often tried to stamp out the dens in the rue Ohier (today Street 13). The card game of *trente-six-bêtes* and *bacouin*, similar to roulette, were favorites.[91] The vices of the town poor and peasants were largely restricted to betel nut and cheroots made of coarse tobacco rolled up in banana leaves,[92] but the more affluent of all races could indulge their appetites for marijuana, opium, and even absinthe after it was banned in metropolitan France.[93] Opium was used frequently by well-off Khmers, but seldom by the poor. Huy Kanthoul claims that the ranks of French officialdom were "ravaged" by addiction to the drug, which was sold in bales stamped "R.O." (*Régie Opium*).[94] Import and sale of the drug was a highly lucrative state monopoly, with almost three million piastres' worth imported in 1930,[95] much of it from India. Almost a quarter of a million piastres worth was sold in Kampot alone in 1929.[96] The use of the drug was officially restricted to authorized "dens" and these were kept under surveillance to exclude women and children.[97] Sales plummeted during the Depression, but there was a roaring trade again by 1939.[98] There was crime, too, as could be expected in any city—some of it committed by Europeans—although it was hyperbole to compare Phnom Penh to Chicago, as did one over-imaginative journalist.[99] One perennial feature of the city was inter-racial brawls, in which Khmers and Vietnamese[100]—who dismissed each other, respectively, as *Yuon* or "barbarians from the north" and *Thô*, or "men of the earth"[101]— would bash each other senseless on the river banks and other common territory.

The 1931 Intercolonial Exhibition

Public works projects were in full swing during the period leading up to the Great Depression. They included the construction of an 11-kilometer long dike-cum-roadway along the riverbank.[102] An official report noted that the onset of the Depression overseas did not stop essential public works projects from going ahead in the capital, including the surfacing and extension of the road system and the construction of drains, sewers and footpaths. Freight tonnages moving through the port, however, showed a marked decline between 1929 and 1931, revealing that the little city could not hope to escape the effects of the world economic crisis.[103] Elsewhere, as the crisis developed, public works projects were abandoned, as in Siem Reap, where work ceased on over 700 kilometers of roads.[104] Like the construction of the Empire State Building in New York or the Sydney Harbor Bridge in Australia, railroad construction in Cambodia defied the general downward economic trend, triumphs of the will in difficult times.

Mention must also be made of the 1931 Intercolonial Exposition in Paris[105]—held to mark the centenary of the conquest of Algeria—which also appeared to defy the gloomy economic climate. The Exposition was a grand celebration of French colonial power, and while Cambodia was a comparative economic backwater, it was a powerful symbol, nevertheless, and the one chosen by France to represent Indochina as a whole. The French authorities in Cambodia threw themselves vigorously into preparations. The Cambodian pavilion was built in the Khmer style behind the central Indochinese building, which itself was a reproduction of the grand temple of Angkor,[106] rising out of the great park at Vincennes on the banks of Lake Daumesnil. The replica, illuminated at night, became the most familiar face of the exhibition.[107] A contemporary observer wrote that, although Indochina was "predominantly Annamite", the symbol was the "jewel" of Angkor. For the great majority of visitors, the temple would remain synonymous with the exposition as a whole.[108] M. Tetard of Indochine-film, made two films about Cambodia for the exposition.[109] Vast crowds queued to watch the Cambodian royal dancers, who were accompanied on their journey by Palace Minister Thiounn and Princess Vongkath.[110] Monireth and Monipong, two of King Monivong's sons who were studying in France, also visited the displays. They were said to be agreeably "astonished" at the Angkor exhibit.[111] The purpose of the exhibition was to act as "a great propaganda piece for the empire, designed to spark pride and commitment"[112] and to convince the public that colonies were necessary for civilized nations. Exhibits inside the replica extolled the wisdom of French colonial policy in Indochina, and its successes in the fields of education, public health and commerce.[113] Not all French people were convinced. Léon Blum, the Socialist politician who was shortly to lead a Popular Front government in France, attacked the exposition. "Here we have the reconstruction of the marvelous stairway of Angkor and are watching sacred dancers," he said, "but in Indochina they are shooting, deporting and imprisoning."[114] Marius Moutet, who was to become Colonial Minister in Léon Blum's Popular Front government, had long been a critic of the use of forced labor in Indochina. He added his voice to Blum's.[115] The Left organized a counter-exposition, but it could not hope to compete with the lavish official entertainments.

The Great Depression in Cambodia

The Great Depression of the 1930s hit Indochina hard. Neither railroads nor Colonial Expositions could stave off the inevitable slump that descended like a shroud over France and her empire. The depression hit France one or two years later than many other parts of the world, but it lasted longer. As the historian Julian Jackson has observed, by mid-1935, when the rest of the world was starting to emerge from the crisis, France was still in the depths of the trough.[116] Indochina—Cambodia included—was tied tightly to the economy of the *métropole* and could not hope to ride out the storm. The prices of tropical commodities tumbled,[117] many businesses went bankrupt and numbers of French settlers lost their life savings. Development projects were halted.[118] Much of Cambodia's commerce had been in Chinese hands and an exodus of failed traders to China showed the depth of the slump. "Insofar as it was in the hands of Chinese," wrote one observer in 1933, "the whole commercial structure of Cambodia has crashed. There is practically nothing left of it..."[119] Even opium sales fell steeply, with dire consequences for the official coffers.[120] The slump also gravely affected the lives of the peasants, workers and the town poor. Not even French civil servants were spared. In mid-1931, the rate of unemployment rose in Phnom Penh.[121] By the following year, over 1000 workers had been laid off because of the downturn in trade.[122] Civil servants fretted over looming budget cuts. In early 1933, official salaries were slashed by 10 per cent, causing some 150 angry lower echelon bureaucrats to hold a protest meeting in the Festival Hall in Phnom Penh.[123] The cuts were probably closer to 30 per cent when allowances were taken into account.[124] Huy Kanthoul, then a young teacher, observed that the French *fonctionnaires* were so resentful that they did not seem to mourn the death of Governor General Pierre Pasquier in a 'plane crash in 1931, holding him responsible for the austerity measures.[125] A new French-language newspaper promised its readers that "We are going to speak the least possible about the crisis; we will strive, on the contrary, to make you forget it".[126] It was whistling in the dark and the paper itself folded after barely two months. It was desperate times, with the prices of rice, rubber and other commodities plunging as overseas markets dried up. An apparently depressed newspaper correspondent lamented the silence of the night in the unlit streets of the capital during the Depression: "Night falls, Phnompenh is a distressing spectacle, it is silence. It is shadow. It is death."[127] The French government slashed its financial contributions to Indochina by over 30 million piastres and all of the colonies experienced budget deficits,[128] forcing them to cut expenditures from 180 million piastres to just over 100 million in the 1934 budget. Public works projects were shelved indefinitely, services cut, and the ordinary people had to bear a heavier taxation burden.[129] The following year, the French treasurer, M. Pierre Laval, decreed further cuts to salaries, services and pensions, applicable to the colonies as well as France itself.[130] Due to the savage cuts, the Cambodian administration was able to balance its budgets for the first time since 1931[131] and even to announce a 2.56 per cent restoration of salaries by the end of 1935.[132] This was coupled with a slight easing of personal taxation in January 1936.[133] Yet if these measures promised some amelioration of hardship for the French settlers and officials, what of the masses of ordinary Khmers, who had little or no savings with which to cushion the effects of the crisis? The Khmer peasants and town poor were never affluent in the first place. Mordaunt considered them "miserably poor" and described the Phnom Penh boatmen as "skinny men with arms like boys of nine".[134] The rejection rates for Indochinese army recruits during World War I were staggeringly high, attesting to widespread ill health and malnutrition even in "good" times. The authorities rejected half of the Khmers who reported for service at the Phnom Penh barracks in 1916.[135] The pages of *La Presse Indochinoise* provide some inkling of the misery of the poor during the Great Slump. The paper reports that speculators preyed on the people, forcing up the price of salt and other essential commodities.[136] Loan sharks battened on human misery and shady pawnshops proliferated.[137] Unemployed coolies and beggars were said to "haunt the passenger arteries" of the towns, where, desperate for food, they would "compete for the pity" of the more fortunate.[138]

Others used more robust means to feed their families. In July 1933, fifty Cambodians stormed aboard a junk at the Truong Khanh market in Soctrang, just over the border in Cochinchina. Each took a sack of rice in what an inquiry labeled a *jacquerie,* akin to "requisitions" organized by Communists in northern Annam. The miscreants were arraigned at an extraordinary court session, and sentenced to long jail terms. In their defense, they simply said they were hungry.[139] As if these problems were not enough, the huge floods of 1936 inundated the poorer quarters of Phnom Penh[140] and submerged almost all of the nearby provinces of Kandal, Prey Veng, Kompong Cham, causing immense damage to crops and houses.[141] During the following year, drought brought famine to many corners of the countryside. By 1936, the worst of the Depression was over, but these natural catastrophes masked the effects of the generalized economic upturn. Peasants who lived largely by subsistence agriculture might have been insulated to a degree from the effects of the slump,[142] but they could not escape the hunger that followed flood and drought. The city poor suffered too, as shortages forced up the price of rice from 2.50 piastres per picul to four piastres in one month alone in late 1936.[143] *La Presse Indochinoise* reported that King Monivong was so moved by the distress of the villagers in Battambang province that he began to dispense free rice grown on his estates at Trapeang Chong near Pursat. Many peasants walked away from their land and trekked to cities in search of food and work. A later article drew attention to the great misery of pepper growers, whose crops were virtually worthless because of the fall in commodity prices. Bodies were found floating in the river at Phnom Penh, and there was a resurgence of prostitution in rural centers as women sold themselves for the price of a bowl of rice. The French citizens of Phnom Penh held a series of balls and sports events to raise money for flood victims and on one occasion in 1938, there was even a grand ball in Paris to raise funds, attended by Colonial Minister Marius Moutet.[144]

Cambodia and the Popular Front

Moutet[145] was Colonial Minister in the Popular Front government led by the Socialist Léon Blum, which came to power in June 1936.[146] It is reasonable to ask what an avowedly left wing government did for the poor of the colonies and for the general social and economic development of Cambodia. At home, the Popular Front pushed through a number of reforms, including paid holidays, pensions, caps on overtime, the 40-hour-week and restrictions on the almost *seigneurial* powers of the employers. Although mild by later standards, for millions of French workers these reforms afforded the first respite from lives of unremitting drudgery. The Popular Front's effect on the colonies was much less striking, both socially and politically. This was in part because the coalition had no clear or shared colonial policy and because it held power only briefly. The Radicals, who were in favor of the status quo, opposed many proposals for reform and often agitated for increased repression of nationalist dissidents in the colonies. The Socialists were in favor of the eventual independence of the colonies, but in the meantime, they believed that the colonial peoples would benefit from French civilization.[147] The party had drifted steadily rightwards on the colonial question since the time of Jean Jaurès and it is likely that the independence option was no longer taken seriously by most of the party's leaders. Blum supported the idea of France's *mission civilisatrice*, as is shown by his words, "We recognize the right and even the duty of superior races to draw unto them those which have not arrived at the same level of culture".[148] Even the French Communist Party (CPF), which had previously held an anti-imperialist line of support for the independence movements in North Africa and Indochina, adopted an ambivalent position. Party leader Maurice Thorez said, "the right to divorce does not signify the obligation to divorce." (What, one wonders, did M. Thorez think of forced marriage?) The CPF had "turned Jacobin" and even welcomed the repression of nationalist rebels in Algeria, at this time.[149] Although there were fierce anti-colonial critics inside the Socialist Party, the historian Julian Jackson considers that, "Whatever the previous commitment of the Socialists to ultimate self-government, this was not at any stage the objective of Blum's government, nor of any of the ministers concerned with colonial policy."[150]

Aldrich believes that the Socialist Party was committed to "modern colonialism", that is to "fighting [the] abuses of colonialism rather than the system itself."[151] Colonial Minister Moutet was in favor of greater emphasis on the social and economic development of the colonies. He proposed a large-scale program of public works, but with free, rather than *corvée* and penal labor, organized rural credit schemes and spoke in favor of raising living standards and improving health and education.[152] In mid-1937, at Moutet's initiative, provincial offices for native food supply were set up in Cambodia to counter periodic famine.[153] Moutet also proposed a Colonial Fund for Economic Development[154] to supervise augmented investment in the colonies, but the proposal was blocked in parliament, even though his initial request was for only 50 million francs for *all* of France's colonies.[155] Moutet's *petit bourgeois* Radical allies were loath to part with as much as a *sou* more than they had to in order to maintain the Empire that sustained their belief in French superiority. Politically, the Popular Front's only significant reform in Indochina was the release of some political prisoners under a partial amnesty, although this mainly affected Vietnam. Again, the Radicals applied the brakes. The *Presse Indochinoise*—which supported the Radical Party and thus the Popular Front—disapprovingly dubbed Moutet "the minister for clemency" for his part in the amnesty.[156]

Moutet also set up a Commission of Inquiry to determine what reforms were necessary, but it was an ineffectual body[157] and did not deliver a final report. The Commission appointed Justin Goddard, a former Socialist deputy, to report on conditions in Indochina. Goddard visited Cambodia in January 1937,[158] was fêted by the local branch of the League of the Rights of Man and the Citizen,[159] and left shortly afterwards. His impression of the French administration in Indochina was more than favorable. He professed to be "amazed" at France's grand works[160] and singled out progress in public hygiene for praise. Moreover, he believed that social conflicts had been resolved through the "wise application" of the government's social laws and considered that the misery of the rural population had been alleviated,[161] although not ended.[162] Moutet himself was lukewarm about reform. Although he had previously attacked those who ran the colonies as *seigneurs*, he did not attempt to curb their power and Goddard's report must have swayed him further towards the status quo. The colonial service was hostile to the new government and its functionaries in Indochina "dragged their feet" rather than implement policy changes. However, Moutet himself acted as a brake on the plans of his more idealistic colleagues, even conspiring with the reactionary permanent head of his political affairs department at the ministry to "revise the decisions taken by Moutet's socialist collaborators."[163] With such a timid, essentially conservative man as Moutet at the helm, the Popular Front failed even on its own limited terms. The Popular Front had branches in Indochina, including one at Phnom Penh and these were disappointed with the lack of real change. The Socialist Party's southern federation of Indochina publicly attacked the "absolute contradiction" between the Popular Front's program and the "reactionary policies" actually carried out in the region.[164]

Some reforms were promulgated. Under the government's instructions, French officials in Cambodia ordered a number of reforms to working conditions. In late 1936, for instance, the length of the working day was limited, night work was forbidden for females, the *patrons* had to grant their employees one day off each week, and there were to be annual paid holidays.[165] Soon afterwards, a further decree banned the employment of boys under the age of 12 and stipulated that only boys over the age of 16 years could work night shift.[166] Soon after M. Goddard's visit, Monivong signed a decree (probably without reading it) that provided for the arbitration of disputes and for industrial relations inspectors.[167] Strikes and other forms of industrial strife did occur in Cambodia, although by the 1930s they were largely restricted to the Vietnamese contract laborers on the rubber plantations.[168] In the 1920s, Vietnamese and Chinese workers in the capital had set up unions and agitated for better pay and conditions, but by the time of the Popular Front, these organizations had disappeared,[169] partly because of high unemployment during the Depression[170] and partly because of police repression.[171] The *Sûreté* savagely repressed labor agitation by deporting, jailing and torturing the leaders. One survivor was the Vietnamese-dominated Phnom Penh postal workers union, affiliated to AGFALI, the government employees' federation.[172] The Popular Front did little to change the situation; even if Moutet sympathized with the poorly paid indigenous workers, the situation is summed up in Leon Trotsky's *bon mot*, "Governments come and go, but the police remain." Mostly, the Popular Front's reforms, where they directly applied to the indigenes, remained on paper, as the Cambodian correspondent of *La Presse Indochinoise* told his readers. The reporter called on M. Moutet to think about the plight of the day laborers and contract coolies in Cambodia, who had seen nothing of the Popular Front's social reforms, though their conditions were much worse than those of their counterparts in France. Despite the Popular Front, claimed the correspondent, coolies still toiled for "miserable pay"—as low as 1.25 piastres per day—with no days off, no sickness or injury pay and no paid holidays.[173] The old colonial police and civil service apparatus remained in control and it did not favor social or political reform. The *Résident* of Kampot province, for example, considered that unions caused "abnormal" relations between employers and their workers.[174] The new inspection powers were entrusted to such *Résidents*[175] who had little interest in their implementation outside of the small workforce of French and *assimilés,* and even then, grudgingly.[176] This was made clear in late 1937 when M. Marinetti, the deputy for

Cochinchina and Cambodia at Paris, announced that the reforms were not applicable to the indigenes.[177] Paid annual leave was made compulsory in 1938, but only for Europeans and *assimilés*.[178] Although Moutet had announced plans for large-scale public works carried out by free labor, in practice things went on as before with forced labor. In 1938, for example, a four and a half mile long canal for the Takeo water supply was dug by hand, exclusively by penal labor.[179] One can almost hear the French engineers and officials sneering at the edicts of the distant "Red" government.

For most Cambodians, however, the political complexion of the Popular Front was irrelevant. The overwhelming majority of the population were Khmer peasants, subsisting on smallholdings remote from office and factory. The urban working class was tiny and predominantly Vietnamese or Chinese, with a smattering of Europeans in the more highly skilled manual jobs and clerical positions. It is likely, however, that the more politically aware urban residents of all ethnic groups were given heart to demand changes after the movement for a Popular Front government gathered steam and France was swept by a wave of sit-down strikes. In late 1935, for instance, a number of inhabitants of the poorer quarters of Phnom Penh demonstrated against high taxes, for which they said they received little in return in the form of water and electricity supplies, sewerage or flood control. Significantly, a large number of the protestors were Khmers, commented *La Presse Indochinoise*.[180] There are also reports of an increase in strike activity among building workers and printers in Phnom Penh during the Popular Front period, although on a small scale.[181] The Popular Front, however, was too short-lived to realize its modest ambitions for the colonies. In April 1938, the Blum government fell and Daladier took over a cabinet purged of its Socialist members. We can be sure that the French officials in Cambodia believed things had returned to normal. William Cohen's assessment that "the accomplishments of the Popular Front...were limited" and that "the colonial peoples had neither been liberated nor had their lot improved markedly"[182] was true above all of remote Cambodia. The Popular Front had been timid and had relied upon a colonial bureaucracy for whom reform was anathema to implement what little change was proposed. Moutet's choice of Governor General, Jules Brevié,[183] was a comparatively enlightened man, but he inherited an apparatus crammed full of time-servers and reactionaries. Even as Brevié's ship steamed east to take him to his new appointment, an old Cambodia hand, M. Silvestre, was carrying out his duties, *pro tempore*.[184] Silvestre was the former *Résident Supérieur* at

Phnom Penh. The reader might recall that it was Silvestre who had so offended Monivong by his heavy-handed treatment of his son, Prince Monireth, that the king refused to carry out his public duties. Silvestre had been angered by Monireth's moderately progressive views on democracy and the social development of his country.

Slow economic recuperation

The advent of the Popular Front in 1936 coincided with an upturn in the economy. The year before was still a grim time economically for France and its colonies. In Indochina as a whole, rice production had steadily fallen since 1933 and that of maize had only marginally increased. Moreover, between September 1934 and March 1935, the price of rice and other commodities fell sharply.[185] Yet, the sluggish economy began to revive during the following year. Prices for some export commodities, pepper and cocoa in particular, picked up in the first quarter of the year.[186] This was despite the fact that pepper production exceeded consumption in France.[187] The same source noted that while it was difficult to gauge trends based on customs receipts, because much of Cambodia's exports were sent via Saigon, receipts for 1935 in the port of Phnom Penh had substantially increased over 1934, from a little over 90,000 piastres to over 110,000.[188] The French franc was devalued in September 1936,[189] probably to make French exports more competitive, but this would have had little effect in Indochina, which was tied closely to the French economy, with the exception of some specialized products such as cotton and kapok, which were exported to Japan, Hong Kong and the Netherlands. These exports would have benefited by the approximate one-third devaluation of the piastre.[190] Rubber production—heavily subsidized during the black years of the Depression—was reported as being "back to normal". The price of a tonne of rubber rose from around 400 piastres in 1934, to 550 in late 1936, causing a steady increase in production. Cotton prices were also up, although drought had restricted production. The price of kapok also experienced steady growth. Tourism was flourishing, with over 5000 international visitors to Angkor in the financial year ending June 1939.[191] A similar picture emerged in forest products, but the once flourishing cattle trade had almost ceased to exist. The centuries-old trade in lacquers, gums and resins was likewise somnolent, but a writer noted that Cambodia's "economic anemia" was on the mend.[192] This increasing confidence was reflected in a Cambodian budget increase of almost 180,000 piastres for 1937 over 1936.[193] There were some cuts to expenditure, however. In May 1938, the French

Government reportedly refused to ratify the Cambodian budget unless Monivong reduced the size of his harem.[194]

Economic recovery also resulted in many of the suspended public works projects re-opening, along with new schemes. The government was determined to do something about the dangerous alternation of flood and drought, which so often brought ruin to the crops, or at least caused wildly fluctuating yields.[195] Although the ancient Khmers had built large irrigation schemes, the practice had fallen into desuetude long before the arrival of the French.[196] The French themselves had built hydraulic works in the delta region of Cochinchina as early as the 1880s, but had neglected the task in Cambodia, despite the problem of erratic water levels.[197] Wet rice cultivation was the mainstay of the Cambodian diet, and brought in export revenues second only to those generated by maize. Battambang province in particular was an enormous "rice basket" but crops were often spoiled by the vicissitudes of the weather. The French started a moderately ambitious irrigation scheme at Bovel in the mid-1930s. The scheme, which contained over 70 kilometers of canals, irrigated some 30,000 hectares of paddy fields. When the coolies had finished, they had shifted over 200,000 tonnes of earth. *Résident Supérieur* Richomme claimed that the works had resulted in an average increase in crop yields of 40 per cent, and in some cases, of up to 150 per cent. Other hydraulic works were started elsewhere in the country, including at Prey Nop near Kampot, where a 14 kilometer-long dike was equipped with automatic sluices, and at Takeo, where a dam almost one kilometer long impounded nine million cubic meters of water.[198] The Takeo schemes (which continued until the war) only employed convicts, regardless of Marius Moutet's disapproval of forced labor.[199] Mechanized grain silos were also built at the port of Phnom Penh in 1936, capable of handling almost 12 per cent of Cambodia's maize production.[200] Other new projects, including, variously, roads, electricity plants, bridges, sewage systems, navigation locks and potable water works were either begun or completed in a number of centers in 1935-36, including at Prey Veng,[201] Battambang,[202] Takeo,[203] and Kompong Chhnang.[204] By 1937, according to an official report, potable water works, many of them newly built, were supplying piped water to all the major centers of Cambodia.[205] Even some villages in Kandal province were connected to piped water.[206] As discussed above, the importance of a supply of clean drinking water in the prevention of water-borne diseases cannot be underestimated. Unfortunately, modern Cambodia is still heavily dependent on a dilapidated infrastructure built 50, 60 or even 70 years ago by the French, although current construction work on a trunk water main along Monivong Boulevard promises to improve the situation.

Other notable public works projects completed at this time included Route Coloniale 13, the new Phnom Penh market and an airfield for the capital. Route 13 was all-weather road linking Saigon to Luang Prabang in Laos via Cambodia. Work on this ambitious undertaking, 1500 kilometers long, had been suspended in 1931.[207] The new Phnom Penh market, a soaring art deco dome with four projecting wings, still exists today and was important enough to rate a mention in the "Monivong Chronicle".[208] Built of reinforced concrete in 1937, its cool halls were vastly more salubrious than the ramshackle markets they replaced.[209] The pace of new work accelerated as the Depression faded. The 1938 public works budget was up by almost one third over 1937, with most money earmarked for roads, waterworks, electricity generators and distribution networks.[210] There was even money once again for non-utilitarian purposes such as urban beautification, as in Svay Rieng, where gardens and flowers were planted in front of official buildings.[211]

In France itself, the opening of the 1937 Paris Exposition—again with a replica of Angkor in pride of place, but this time in the Bois de Boulogne rather than the Vincennes Park—bore witness to the newfound optimism. *La Presse Indochinoise* ran an enthusiastic article entitled: "Across the colonies —brush fires—the commerce of France and her colonies", which reported a significant resurgence of trade and industry. Indochina's imports from France rose from 104 million francs in 1933 to 1050 million in 1936. Exports from Indochina for the same period rose from 86 million francs to 467 francs. Economic relations were heavily skewed in France's favor, but the overall improvement was undeniable.[212] The total value of Cambodia's exports grew from 79 million piastres in 1937 to 94 million in 1938. The figures for the three leading commodities, maize, rice and rubber jumped from 27 million, 20 million and 10.5 million respectively to 28 million, 24 million and 16 million.[213] By 1937, according to the economic writer Paul Renon, Indochina's overseas trade levels (including to France) were higher than ever before—around 250 million piastres, as compared with a maximum of around 240 million piastres in the "roaring twenties" which preceded the world slump, which saw the total fall to a little over 100 million piastres.[214] By the late 1930s, Cambodia was experiencing a "dizzy" increase in the cost of living.[215] The capitalist business cycle had come full circle. With the Second World War, however, new problems sent the economy back into stagnation.

Notes

[1] Harry Hervey, (1927), *King Cobra: An Autobiography of Travel in French Indo-China,* Cosmopolitan Books, New York, p.1.

[2] AOM RSC 431 Rapport Économique, 1917, dated April 1918. Rapports Politiques, 1er, 2ème, 3ème and 4ème Trimestres, 1918, op.cit.

[3] PRO Kew, FO 628/34. "Economic relations, Siam and France, 1918." Covering letter from British Consul at Saigon to the British Legation at Bangkok, 27 December 1918 and clipping of article by Ernest Outrey from *L'Impartial,* 24 December 1918.

[4] Rapport Économique 1917, op.cit.

[5] AOM RSC 431 Rapport Politique 2ème Trimestre 1919.

[6] AOM RSC 431 Rapport Économique, 3ème Trimestre 1919.

[7] AOM RSC 431 Rapport Politique, 2ème Trimestre 1919.

[8] *Mise-en-valeur* = development. Corporatism was an official dogma of Fascist Italy. There were important differences between what existed there and in Indochina, but I use the term as a kind of shorthand to describe an economic system in which the state played a central role, in collaboration with large private institutions.

[9] Stephen Roberts, (1929), *The History of French Colonial Policy, 1870-1925,* Frank Cass, London, pp.41-44.

[10] D.G.E. Hall, (1968), *A History of South-East Asia,* (Third Edition), Macmillan, London, p.789.

[11] Thomas E. Ennis, (1936), *French Policy and Developments in Indochina,* University of Chicago Press, Chicago, p.4. Ennis wrote that, "France has only about 70,087,000,000 francs invested in the colonies, two-thirds of which is in North Africa."

[12] Robert Aldrich, (1996), *A History of French Overseas Expansion,* Macmillan, Basingstoke, p.115.

[13] Ibid. pp. 179-183.

[14] Ennis pp. 2-3.

[15] The rubber industry is discussed in detail in Chapter 16 below.

[16] ANC RSC D35 File 2799 Box 288. Rapport sur la situation du Cambodge, 1927-1928

[17] ANC D35 File 2444 Box 234 Rapport annuel sur la marche de Service de l'Agriculture en 1929.

[18] According to Ennis, only 1,000,000 hectares out of a total of 17,363,000 were cultivated in the mid-1930s. (Ennis, op.cit., pp.129-130.)

[19] Wilfred Burchett, (1957), *Mekong Upstream,* Red River Publishing House, Hanoi, p.26.

[20] John Tully, (1996), *Cambodia Under the Tricolour. King Sisowath and the 'Mission Civilisatrice', 1904-1927,* Monash Asia Institute, Clayton, Victoria, pp.54-55. There were also some primitive iron mines, quarries, potteries, rope and cordage works, and small textile mills, which produced for the domestic market and export to Singapore.

[21] Ennis, op.cit. p.6.

[22] Ibid. p.4.

[23] Ibid p.129.

[24] AOM RSC 431 Rapport Politique, 3ème Trimestre 1917. Ream is a naval base today and the main cargo port is at Kompong Som or Sihanoukville.

[25] AOM RSC 431 Rapports Politiques 2ème Trimestre 1919, 1er and 2ème Trimestres 1920.

[26] ANC RSC E3 File 255 Box 10. Résidence de Kg Thom. Procès-Verbaux des séances du Conseil du Résidence. Session d'avril 1916.

[27] AOM RSC 431 Rapport Politique 2ème Trimestre 1920.

[28] Alfred Northcliffe, *The Times*, London, 23 December 1921. See also *Revue du Tourisme Indochinois, Bulletin Officiel du Syndicat d'Initiative de l'Indochine*, Nr. 24, 12 octobre 1923, Saigon.

[29] PRO Kew FO 371 11839 (1926) w 953/953/17. Rpt. on visit to Cambodia of H.M. Rep. Mr. R. Greg.

[30] H.W. Ponder, (1936), *Cambodian Glory: The Mystery of the Deserted Khmer Cities and their Vanished Splendour and a Description of Life in Cambodia Today*, Thornton Butterworth, London, pp.140-144.

[31] *Revue du Tourisme*, op.cit. 29 June and 10 August 1923. The trip to Saigon takes about 8 to 9 hours even today.

[32] Eleanor Mordaunt, (1932), *Purely for Pleasure*, Martin Secker, London, pp.266-268

[33] Ponder, op.cit. See also *L'Echo du Cambodge*, 21 March 1925 on the opening of the direct road to Angkor.

[34] *Revue du Tourisme*, op.cit. 4 and 23 May and 15 June 1923. Until 1923, the number of tourists was falling. There were 260 in 1920 and 222 in 1922.

[35] AOM RSC 432 Rapports Politiques 4ème Trimestre 1924 and 2ème Trimestre 1925.

[36] According to the *Sûreté's* figures, there were almost 1200 visitors in 1929-30. (ANC RSC D35 File 2800 Box 288 Rapport sur l'exercice de Protectorate pendant la période 1929-1930. Inspection du Travail. Also AOM RSC 321. Résidence de Siem Reap, Rapport Annuel, 1 juin 1931 – 31 mai 1932, which reports that Angkor tourism had risen from 2300 to at least 2600 during that period. This had risen to over 3000 by mid-1933. (ANC RSC File 499 Box 38. Rapport Annuel, Siem Reap, 1 juin 1932 – 31 mai 1933.)

[37] Unsigned, (1935), "Assassinons le tourisme!" *La Presse Indochinoise*, 3 May.

[38] *L'Echo du Cambodge*, 14 April 1935 and *La Presse Indochinoise*, 18 April 1935. Chaplin, unfortunately, makes no mention of the visit in his autobiography, stating instead that, "Many excellent travel books have already been written about the Orient, so I will not encroach on the reader's patience." (Charles Chaplin, (1966), *My Autobiography*, Penguin Books, Harmondsworth, p.362.)

[39] Unsigned, (1935), "Grand fêtes d'Angkor", *L'Echo du Cambodge*, 7 May.

[40] Andrée Viollis, (1949), *Indochine SOS*, Editeurs Français Réunis, Paris, p.72. Viollis visited in 1932.

[41] H.W. Ponder, (1936), *Cambodian Glory: The Mystery of the Deserted Khmer Cities and their Vanished Splendour, and a description of Life in Cambodia Today*, Thornton Butterworth, London, p.105 and L. Delaporte, (1880), *Voyage au Cambodge. L'Architecture Khmer*, Librairie Ch. Delagrave, Paris.

[42] AOM RSC 208 Affaire Malraux-Chevasson. See also Jean Lacouture, (trans. Alan Sheridan), (1975), *André Malraux*, André Deutsch, London. Malraux and his wife, Clara, have written unreliable accounts of the affair. [Clara Malraux (trans. Patrick O'Brien), (1967), *Memoirs*, Bodley Head, London.] The Banteay Srey, or "women's temple" is celebrated for its unusually deep and exquisite bas-reliefs, carved in hard pink sandstone.

[43] Burchett, op.cit. pp.77-78.

[44] Osbert Sitwell, (1940), *Escape with me! An Oriental Sketchbook*, Macmillan, London, p.79.

[45] AOM RSC 432 Rapport d'Ensemble, 1925-26.

[46] ANC RSC D35 File 2799 Box 288. Rapport sur la situation du Cambodge, 1927-1928.

[47] ANC RSC E03 File 499 Box 38, Rapport annuel, Résident-Maire de Phnom Penh, 1 juin 1932- 31 Mai 1933. The daily average water consumption was 10,517 cubic meters.

[48] ANC RSC D35. File 2798 Box 288 Rapport sur la situation du Cambodge, 1927.

[49] AOM RSC 432 Rapport d'Ensemble, 1925-1926. *Echo du Cambodge*, op. cit. 13 July 1928.

[50] AOM RSC 432 Rapport Politique 1er Trimestre 1925.

[51] *Echo du Cambodge*, 8 January 1927.

[52] ANC RSC D35 File 2798 Box 288. Rapport sur la situation du Cambodge, 1927.

[53] ANC RSC D35 File 2799 Box 288. Rapport sur la situation du Cambodge, 1927-1928.

[54] AOM RSC 658 Travaux publics. Also *Echo du Cambodge*, 3 November 1928. The bridge is mentioned in the "Monivong Chronicle". [David Chandler, (1979), "Cambodian Palace Chronicles (*rajabangsavatar*), 1927-1949: Kingship and Historiography at the End of the Colonial Era", in Anthony Reid and David Marr, *Perceptions of the Past in Southeast Asia*, Heinemann Educational Books, Singapore, p.210. Destroyed during the civil war of the 1970s, it was later replaced by a new structure commonly known as the "Japanese bridge" because of financial support from Tokyo.

[55] *L'Echo du Cambodge*, 6 July 1929. The project was approved by the government at Paris in November 1928. (*L'Echo*, 23 November 1928).

[56] Ibid, 11 January 1930.

[57] Ibid, 2 February 1932.

[58] *La Revue Khmère*, Phnom Penh, 28 June 1932.

[59] *L'Echo du Cambodge*, 5 July 1932,

[60] André Surmer, "La chemin de fer de Phnom-Penh à Mongkolborey", *Indochine Hebdomadaire Illustré*, 20 February 1941.

[61] *L'Echo du Cambodge*, 5 July 1932.

[62] ANC E03, File 499, Box 38, Rapport sur le fonctionnement du Service des Travaux Publics, 1932-33.

[63] *L'Eveil du Cambodge*, 29 August 1933. Also "La voie ferrée Indochine-Thailande", *L'Echo du Cambodge*, 31 January 1940.

[64] Ennis, op.cit. p.123.

[65] *L'Echo du Cambodge*, 9 March 1929.

[66] Ibid, 31 March 1928.

[67] Ibid, 13 April 1929.

[68] Ibid. 23 February 1929.

[69] Denis Nardin, (1964), "Phnom-Penh: Naissance et croissance d'une administration urbaine". Mémoire en vue du diplôme d'études supérieurs de droit public. Faculté de Droit et des Sciences Économiques de Phnom Penh, pp.1 and 231.

[70] There were said to be 150,000 "Annamites" in Cambodia in 1926. (ANC RSC D35 File 2799 Box 288. Rapport sur la situation du Cambodge, 1927-1928. Ch. III.)

[71] There were around 91,000 Chinese in Cambodia in 1921 and 95,000 in 1926. (Ibid.) The number declined during the Depression. By 1942, there were said to be over 83,000 "foreign Asiatics", mostly Chinese. (AOM RSC 675. Rapport annuel du Cambodge, juin 1942-juin 1943.) According to an article by Philippe Devillers in *Le Monde* of 8-9 September 1946, the number had grown to 250,000 by that time, of whom 40,000 were resident in Phnom Penh. (Contained in AOM HCC 10. Relations avec les Cambodgiens, esprit de la population, 1945-1947.) For an extended discussion, see William Willmott, (1967), *The Chinese in Cambodia*, University of British Columbia Publications Centre, Vancouver.

[72] According to Robequain, there were 68,000 Sino-Cambodians in 1921. (Charles Robequain, (trans. Isabel A. Ward), (1944), *The Economic Development of French Indo-China*, Oxford University Press, London, p.27.)

[73] Zhou Daguan (Chou Ta-Kuan), (trans. From Paul Pelliot's French version of the Chinese original by J Gilman and D'Arcy Paul),(1987), *The Customs of Cambodia*, The Siam Society, Bangkok.

[74] The French press often commented unfavorably on Indian moneylenders. An article in *L'Avenir du Cambodge* of 29 May 1912 claimed that some of them charged up to 250% interest. Pierre Brocheux claims that the "chettys" first arrived in southern Indochina at the beginning of the 20th century following French authorization for them to do so. (P. Brocheux, (1972), "Vietnamiens et Minorités en Cochinchine pendant la Période Coloniale", *Modern Asian Studies*, 6, 4, p.445. Their arrival would appear to be a little earlier. An article entitled "De l'hypothèque" in *Le Petit Cambodgien* of 19 December 1899 laments the "legendary rapacity" of the chettys.

[75] Luc Durtain, (1930), *Dieux blancs, hommes jaunes*, Flammarion, Paris, p.238.

[76] Mordaunt, op.cit. p.274. The invention of the *cyclopousse* (rickshaw) by a French mechanic is mentioned in the "Monivong Chronicle". [Chandler, op.cit. p.210.]

[77] *La Voix Libre*, 26 September 1925.

[78] *L'Echo du Cambodge*, 3 March 1936.

[79] Sitwell, op.cit. p.77.

[80] Advertisement in *L'Echo du Cambodge*, 30 June 1931.

[81] Although not as cold as in lowland Tonkin, where snow fell on the same day. (*L'Echo du Cambodge*, 26 January 1934.)

[82] Ibid. 19 July 1930.

[83] *La Presse Indochinoise*, 20 and 25 October 1935.

[84] Ibid. 11 January 1939.

[85] Nardin, op.cit. p.231.

[86] *L'Echo du Cambodge*, 5 and 19 January 1924.

[87] Mordaunt, op.cit. p.277.

[88] Geoffrey Gorer, (1936), *Bali and Angkor or Looking at Life and Death*, Michael Joseph, London, pp.153-154.

[89] A. Tricon et Ch. Bellan, (1921), *Chansons Cambodgiennes*, Société des Etudes Indochinoises, Saigon, 1921.

[90] Before the use of penicillin, compounds of mercury or arsenic were widely used to treat the disease. The cure was often little less horrible than the disease.

[91] The French first tried to ban bacouin and the game known as "trente-six bêtes" in the 19th century, but it flourished illegally. See, for instance, *Le Petit Cambodgien*, Phnom Penh, 18 January 1900 and Fred Abaly, (1910), *Notes et souvenirs d'un ancien marsouin (Cochinchine-Cambodge, 1899-1901)*, A. Leclerc, p.140.

[92] B. Marrot, (1894), *Exposition de Lyon 1894. Section Cambodgienne. Notes et souvenirs sur le Cambodge*, Forézienne P. Rousten, Roanne, p.37-38.

[93] H.G. Quaritch Wales, (1943), *Years of Blindness*, Thomas Y. Crowell, New York, p.227. The growing and use of marijuana had been forbidden by royal decree in 1908. (ANC RSC 451 File 24316 Conseil des Ministres, 136e séance du 12 mai 1908.) This is somewhat remarkable, given the Protectorate's opium monopoly and Sisowath's taste for the latter, stronger drug.

[94] Huy Kanthoul, "Mémoires", p.63. Unpublished French-language typescript. Chandler Papers, Monash University.

[95] ANC D03 File 7973 Box 699. Preparation du livre vert. Rapport annuel. Statistique sur le fonctionnement du protectorat, 1929-1938.

[96] ANC RSC E03 File 499 Box 38. Rapport annuel, Résidence de Kampot, juin 1932-mai 1933.

[97] ANC RSC E03 File 9246 Box 814, Rapport annuel Résidence de Svay Rieng, 1 juin 1938 – 31 mai 1939. The use of opium had been regulated by royal decree in 1907. (ANC RSC F451 File 24312 Conseil des Ministres 132e séance du 23 novembre 1907.)

[98] ANC RSC E03 Rapport Annuel de Kampot, juin 1933-mai 1933 and ANC E03 Rapport Annuel, Svay Rieng, 1 juin 1938-31 mai 1939.

[99] "Phnom-Penh ou Chicago?" *La Presse Indochinoise*, 14 May 1937.

[100] In one case, between 40 and 50 Vietnamese and Khmer boatmen brawled on the riverbank in front of the royal palace, with one death and a number of serious casualties. ("Un mort, sept blessés. Bataille sue la fleuve", *La Presse Indochinoise*, 20 November 1939.)

[101] Louis Malleret, "La minorité cambodgienne de Cochinchine". Conférence d'Information, faite à Saigon, le 17 décembre 1945, sous le patronage du Bureau des Affaires du Service Fédéral de l'Instruction Publique, pour les officiers et fonctionnaires du Corps Expéditionnaire de l'Indochine.

[102] "Unsigned, (1932), "Les grands travaux de la ville", *L'Echo du Cambodge*, 7 June.

[103] AOM RSC 321, Rapport annuel du Résident-Maire de Phnom-Penh. I juin 1931 - 31 mai 1932. Imports and exports through the port rose slightly 109,400 tonnes in 1930, but then dropped to 95,000 in 1931.

[104] AOM RSC 321, Résidence de Siem Reap, Rapport annuel, 1 juin 1931 – 31 mai 1932.

[105] The most detailed account of the exposition is Catherine Hodeir and Michel Pierre, (1991), *L'Exposition Coloniale*, Editions Complexe, Paris. There are very few remains of the great event. The total cost of the enterprise was 318 million francs. Ticket sales and income from other sources recouped 30-35 million francs and there were eight million visitors.

[106] *L'Echo du Cambodge*, 18 January 1930. See also Claude Farrère, (1931), "Angkor et l'Indochine", *L'Illustration*, Paris, May 23. [The latter is a special edition devoted to the Exposition).

[107] Hodeir and Pierre, op.cit. pp.78-79.

[108] Henri Gourdon, (1931), "Les Palais et les Pavillions. L'Indochine", *La Revue des Deux Mondes*, Paris, pp.774-793.

[109] ANC RSC D03 File 7973 Box 699. Rapport sur la fonctionnement du Musée Économique et sur la situation commerciale du Cambodge pour l'année 1930.

[110] *L'Echo du Cambodge*, 31 March 1931.

[111] Ibid, 18 August 1931.

[112] Aldrich, op.cit. p.261.

[113] Gourdon, op.cit.

[114] Cited in Aldrich, op.cit. p.265.

[115] Aldrich, op.cit. p.153. The French made extensive use of convict labor and peasant *corvée*. For a discussion of the contract labor system on the Cambodian rubber plantations, see Ch. XVI below.

[116] Julian Jackson, (1988), *The Popular Front in France. Defending Democracy, 1934-38*, Cambridge University Press, Cambridge, p.9.

[117] The price of paddy, for example, fell from around 1.5 piastres per picul to as low as one piastre. There was, according to an official from Prey Veng province, an "overproduction of tropical commodities". ANC RSC E03 File

1815 Box 176, Rapport générale de la province de Prey-Veng, 1er juin 1930-31 mai 1931,

[118] Aldrich, op.cit. p.118, citing Jacques Marseille, (1984), *Empire Colonial et capitalisme français: histoire d'un divorce*, Paris, Chs. 6 – 7.

[119] M. Ganay in the *Bulletin du Comité de l'Indochine*, June 22 1933, cited in Robequain, op.cit. p.43.

[120] ANC RSC E03 File 499 Box 38 Rapport annuel, Résidence de Kampot, juin 1932-mai 1933. Sales in Kampot province fell from just under 243,000 piastres in 1929, to just over 57,000 piastres in 1933.

[121] "Le chômage à Pnom-Penh", *L'Echo du Cambodge*, 2 June 1931.

[122] ANC RSC D35 File 5905 Box 579 Draft of Annual Report, Inspection du Travail (1931-1932)

[123] *L'Echo du Cambodge*, 7 February 1933.

[124] "The French as colonisers. I. Culture in Indo-China", (1934), *The Times*, London, September 4

[125] Huy Kanthoul, op.cit. p.59.

[126] "Notre but", (1933), *L'Eveil du Cambodge*, 6 July.

[127] *La Presse Indochinoise*, 17 July 1936.

[128] *L'Echo du Cambodge*, 12 December 1933. (Report on meeting of the Commission of Colonies in Paris.)

[129] *The Times*, September 4, 1934, op.cit.

[130] "Les mésures d'économies", *La Presse Indochinoise*, 18 July 1935.

[131] *La Presse Indochinoise*, 1 November 1935 and *L'Echo du Cambodge*, 29 October 1935.

[132] *L'Echo du Cambodge*, 31 December 1935. The partial restoration was decreed by the Governor General.

[133] *La Presse Indochinoise*, 19 October 1935.

[134] Mordaunt, op.cit. pp. 276-277.

[135] By 1 April 1916, 1600 Cambodians had presented at barracks. Half were rejected on health grounds. (See AOM RSC 430, Rapport Politique, 1er Trimestre 1916.) According to another official source, 600,000 men were examined for service in Indochina, but only 100,000 accepted. (AOM Fonds Amiraux, XI, 19991.) The *Bulletin Médical* of 13 March 1920 claims an 80 per cent rejection rate, largely due to the effects of trachoma, cholera and meningitis. (Contained in CMIDOM, 15 H 134.)

[136] *La Presse Indochinoise*, 30 June – I July 1934 and 1 December 1934.

[137] Ibid, 15 July 1936.

[138] Ibid, 28 November 1935.

[139] *La Tribune Indochinoise*, 10 and 19 July 1933.

[140] *La Presse Indochinoise*, 13 February 1936.

[141] AOM RSC 386. Rapport annuel, 1937-1938, Prey Veng. The floods are described in Chapter 9.

[142] They were not entirely disconnected from the market because they had to sell produce to pay taxes.

[143] "En un mois, le prix du picul de riz a haussé de 2$50 à 4$00. La misère des consommateure", *La Presse Indochinoise*, 10 November 1936.

[144] *La Presse Indochinoise*, numerous issues between 1936 and 1938.

[145] Marius Moutet, a barrister by profession, served as parliamentary deputy for Lyons from 1914. A member of the Socialist Party's right wing, he was closely allied with Herriot. (Details from *La Presse Indochinoise*, 2 July 1937.)

[146] The Popular Front formed government under the Matignon Accords of 7 June 1936 as a coalition of the Socialist and Radical Socialist parties. The Communist Party supported the new government in parliament, but did not accept ministries. The Radical Socialist Party—more often known simply as the Radicals—was not socialist and was only mildly radical outside of its traditional anti-clericalism. See, for instance, Julian Jackson, *The Popular Front in France Defending Democracy, 1934-38,* Cambridge University Press, Cambridge, 1988.

[147] This was the position of the "grand old man" of the Socialist Party, Jean Jaurès. See William B. Cohen, (1972), "The Colonial Policy of the Popular Front", *French Historical Studies,* Vol. VII, No. 3, Spring, p.371.

[148] Cited in Aldrich, op.cit., p.115.

[149] Cohen, op.cit.p.392.

[150] Jackson, op.cit. p.155.

[151] Aldrich, op.cit. p.115.

[152] *La Presse Indochinoise*, 12 June 1937. See also Jackson, op.cit. p.156.

[153] Ibid. 25 June 1937. (*La Presse Indochinoise*.).

[154] Ibid.

[155] Cohen, op.cit.p.386.

[156] (*La Presse Indochinoise*, 11 July 1936.)

[157] Jackson, op.cit. pp.156-157.

[158] *L'Echo du Cambodge*, 19 January 1937.

[159] Ibid. 25 January 1937.

[160] Ibid. 14 April 1937.

[161] Ibid. 13 March 1937.

[162] Ibid. 7 April 1937.

[163] Jackson, op.cit. p.157.

[164] *La Presse Indochinoise*, 21 August 1937.

[165] *L'Echo du Cambodge*, 20 October 1936.

[166] ANC RSC D35 File 2420 Box 227. Notice sur le travail au Cambodge, arrête de 30 décembre 1936. See also G.V.V. (1937), "Le lit de procuste. Le paysan paîra – pour changer – l'addition des réformes sociales", *La Presse Indochinoise*, 30 janvier 1937.

[167] *L'Echo du Cambodge*, 9 February 1936.

[168] See Chapter 16 below.

[169] *La Presse Indochinoise*, 28 July 1938. The report noted that although there were some unions for Europeans (primarily civil servants) none existed for Asians at that time.

[170] As in Kampot province by 1933. ANC RSC D35 File 499 Box 38. Rapport annuel, Kampot, juin 1932-mai 1933.

[171] The 1920s economic boom generated a number of jobs in construction, sawmills and light industry. Many of the jobs, particularly the more skilled ones, were filled by Chinese and Vietnamese immigrants. These workers set up a number of trade unions and there were strikes, particularly in the building industry in Phnom Penh. The police did not hesitate to bash, jail and expel the "ringleaders". See John Tully, (1996), *Cambodia Under the Tricolour. King Sisowath and the "mission civilisatrice, 1904-1927"*, Monash Asia Institute, Clayton, Victoria, pp. 286-290. The Depression crippled such organizations.

[172] Ibid. 11 October 1938.

[173] *La Presse Indochinoise,* 5 February 1937.

[174] Kampot, Rapport annuel, op.cit.

[175] Ibid. 7 April 1937.

[176] The *Résident Supérieur,* for example, insisted that the weekly day off would be enforced in all government services, but this would cover only a fraction of the total workforce of the country. [*La Presse Indochinoise,* 5 July 1937.]

[177] Ibid. 17 November 1937.

[178] Ibid. 1 July 1938.

[179] Ibid. 7 March 1938.

[180] Unsigned, (1935), "Les quartiers disinherités", *La Presse Indochinoise,* 30 October.

[181] Ibid. 5 June 1937, 15 and 28 January 1938

[182] Cohen op.cit. p.393.

[183] Brevié was previously Governor of French West Africa.

[184] *La Presse Indochinoise,* 29 August 1936.

[185] "Alerte l'Indochine Rizicole", *L'Echo du Cambodge,* 14 January 1936.

[186] *La Presse Indochinoise,* 26 February 1936.

[187] Ibid. 29 September 1936.

[188] Ibid. 26 September 1936.

[189] *L'Echo du Cambodge,* 29 September 1936.

[190] "Aujourd'hui! Douze millions de piastres", *La Presse Indochinoise,* 6 octobre 1936.

[191] ANC RSC E03 File 9246 Box 814, Rapport annuel, Siem Reap, 1 June 1938- 31 May 1939.

[192] "L'Orientation économique du Cambodge", *La Presse Indochinoise,* 1 and 5 October 1936.

[193] "Longtemps encore, notre pays manquera le pas dans la voie du progrès", *La Presse Indochinoise,* 14 November 1936.

[194] *The New York Times,* 8 May 1938.

[195] *La Presse Indochinoise,* 11 October 1937. The rice harvest in drought prone Takeo province varied between 38,000 and 65,000 tonnes, for example.

[196] Primitive devices such as basket scoops or *norias* were used in some instances. (Naval Intelligence Division, (1943), *Indo-China,* London, p.278.)

[197] Ernest Outrey, Vice President, Commission des Colonies, (1936), "L'Ouevre Coloniale de la France en Indochine", *L'Echo du Cambodge*, 12 May 1936.

[198] Report by *Résident Supérieur* Richomme in *La Presse Indochinoise*, 5 November 1935. Also 14 April 1936 in the same publication.

[199] *La Presse Indochinoise*, 7 March 1938.

[200] AOM RSC 284.

[201] AOM RSC 285 Travaux publics, 1935-1936, *L'Echo du Cambodge*, 21 January 1936 and *La Presse Indochinoise*, 22 June 1936.

[202] *La Presse Indochinoise*, 20 January 1936

[203] Ibid, 25 February and 19 November 1936. Also *L'Echo du Cambodge*, 7 July 1936. The navigation locks at Takeo were the first in Cambodia.

[204] Ibid, 2 June 1936.

[205] AOM RSC 231 Distribution d'eau (1937). The report lists the following centers and amounts of piped water supplied in cubic meters per day: Phnom Penh, 10,000; Stung Treng, 120; Siem Reap, 300; Battambang, 1000; Pursat, 1000; Kampot, 500; Prey Veng, 150; Kratié, 200; Kompong Thom, 300.

[206] *La Presse Indochinoise*, 2 June 1936.

[207] Ibid, 30 June 1937 and 24 January 1938. Also *L'Echo du Cambodge*, 26 January 1938.

[208] Chandler, op.cit. p.210.

[209] *L'Echo du Cambodge*, 17 November 1937.

[210] ANC RSC D35 File 8982 Box 789. Rapport sur l'exercice du protectorat pendant la période 1er juin 1938- 31 mai 1939. The expenditure rose from 2,339,096 piastres to 3,098,985 piastres, the report informs us.

[211] *La Presse Indochinoise*, 12 August 1937.

[212] "A travers les colonies – les feux de brousse – le commerce de la France et ses colonies", *La Presse Indochinoise*, 25 May 1937. Interestingly, Algeria's exports to France outweighed her imports.

[213] ANC RSC D35 File 8982 Box 789. Préparation du livre vert 1938-1939. Livre III Développement économique. Section I Colonisation et mise-en-valeur.

[214] Paul Renon, (1940), "Evolution de l'économie indochinoise", *Indochine Hebdomadaire Illustré*, 12 September, graph on p.9. Overseas trade grew from around 60 million piastres in 1900, to around 140 million in 1920, thence to approximately 210 million in 1925, after which it leveled off at around 240 million until the great slump, when it plummeted to just over 100 million piastres.

[215] AOM RSC 695 Coûte de la vie 1939.

Chapter 15

A Dictatorship of Police and Civil Servants

The Résident Supérieur of Cambodia governs the country as an absolute monarch.

—Phnom Penh lawyer Gabriel Maurel, 1926.

Although the British newspaper tycoon Lord Northcliffe believed that *"la colonisation française [est] la colonisation par la sympathie"*[1], other observers observed a darker side to the spurt of development after World War I. Some saw a colonial police state, lacking the civil and political rights enjoyed in France. At least one Khmer writer has drawn attention to French racism against his people.[2] Some European observers wondered whether development improved the peasants' lives. The road system was an impressive achievement, thought the American writer Harry Franck, but he considered that it had increased the helplessness of the people, as the French officials were able to move around the country quickly to impose their will on them.[3] The French eased taxes after the 1916 Affair, but re-imposed them afterwards. One tragic event, the murder of Félix Bardez, the *Résident* of Kompong Chhnang in 1925, flowed directly from heavy taxation. Two other, much greater tragedies revealed the indifference of the French administration to the human cost of development. The construction of the European pleasure palace at Bokor, and the establishment of the rubber plantations after 1921, caused great suffering to the "coolies" who worked on them.

The Protectorate of Cambodia was a dictatorship of civil servants and police. The King and his Council of Ministers had little real control over the affairs of their country, and although a "native" administration existed parallel with that of the French, it acted only with the *Résident Supérieur's* permission. In normal times, the Council of Ministers rubberstamped decisions already made by the French. Real power had passed to the French even before the coronation of Sisowath, although a number of top ranking mandarins, Palace Minister Thiounn in particular, were key collaborators, essential, even, to the French project. Thiounn was a far more formidable person than his royal superiors. Harry Franck, who could be an astute observer, has described him as a kind of political comprador and as "an intelligent hard worker, supple, well-informed" and who, "speaking French fluently...has made himself indispensable..."[4] A French journalist has left us a vivid portrait of the mandarin in his "severely plain" office. Under a number of photographs affixed to the wall, sat an old man with "lively eyes behind his glasses", possessed of "the exquisite courtesy of a fine old oriental diplomat".[5] An accompanying photograph shows him to have had a stern face, a big moustache and haughty eyes, a man sure of his worth and certain of his position. He had served France loyally since Norodom's reign. In the process, he had made himself much richer than the kings[6] and held more power than any other Khmer. If it was true that Norodom had "mortgaged his own absolute, threadbare and precarious power in exchange for staying on as a symbolic, well-paid chief of state",[7] this was doubly so of Sisowath and his successor, Monivong. In theory, the power of the *Résident Supérieur* was modified by the French parliament, but in practice, faraway Paris could do little to check his power, and the power of this un-elected civil servant was almost absolute. The Colonial Ministry was largely dependent for information on reports from the *Résident Supérieur's* own office—generally filtered via the Governor General's staff in Hanoi. There was no Ombudsman's office to investigate complaints independently. There was no tradition, either, of an independent judiciary. The other check on government power—a free press—was largely absent. The Phnom Penh lawyer Gabriel Maurel considered the sole long-running French-language paper published in Cambodia, *L'Echo du Cambodge*, to be a mouthpiece for the administration. Although technically "free", the *Echo* received a 3000-piastre government subsidy every fortnight,[8] a case of "he who pays the piper calls the tune". Its predecessor, *L'Impartial*, did not live up to its name. The Saigon-based Radical paper *La Voix Libre* claimed to be suppressed in the kingdom.[9] Maurel claimed that Baudoin forbade the Chinese merchant Shy-Chong-See from publishing a rival to the *Echo*.[10] When left wing and nationalist Vietnamese and Chinese papers began to appear in the 1920s, the *Sûreté* repressed those who distributed them. The Post Office regularly sent thousands of letters and packets to the police for "inspection" and many were confiscated. By the mid-1920s, the police had dossiers on over six hundred people.[11] The *Sûreté* even kept watch over the *Echo du Cambodge*. The chief of police in Phnom Penh reported to Hanoi that the paper "seems devoted to the administration's interests",[12] which was hardly surprising given that it was kept afloat by government subsidies. The police also kept a suspicious eye on all visitors. The level of surveillance was extraordinary. Harry Franck claimed that the police kept lengthy dossiers on all foreigners and that Germans and Russians were not admitted to the country. The police subjected his own passport to frequent "studying", stamping and annotation during his time in the kingdom.[13] Eleanor Mordaunt, arriving from Bangkok by Danish steamer at the port of Ream circa 1931, missed her bus to Phnom Penh because the customs authorities amused themselves by inspecting her passport for an inordinate length of time.[14] A Belgian tourist called Simon warranted a note from the police chief to the *Résident Supérieur* after he disembarked at Ream in 1926, although he appears to have been harmless. The police even snooped on Angkor tourists. They rifled through the possessions of an American citizen called Eva Jane Smith while she was out of her hotel room[15] and reported on what others ate for dinner.[16] None of these people was a political threat; the probing was just routine surveillance by a police force obsessed with control. The *agents* might also have been seeking bribes. According to many accounts, corruption was rife in the French administration in Indochina. The British diplomat Lord Crewe considered that,

The blot on the country as a whole is the swarm of *petits fonctionnaires* brought out from France and Corsica and paid very small salaries. Few are paid as well as a good native clerk in Singapore and Hong Kong...Consequent on their poor pay, venality is rife among lower French officials, and rumour pretends it is by no means uncommon in the highest spheres.[17]

The writer H.G. Quaritch Wales has left a vivid pen portrait of one of these functionaries, M. Lorgeau, whom he met at the port of Ream in 1924. Wales described the unfortunate officer as being astoundingly ignorant of Cambodia, despite fifteen years residence in Indochina. The policeman spent his days shuffling, smoking and grumbling on his verandah, sipping cognac and reading old copies of *La Vie Parisienne*.[18] His was the everyday face of *la mission civilisatrice* for the Khmers. Probably, it was Lorgeau who caused Eleanor Mordaunt to miss her bus.

François (Henri) Baudoin, doyen of Résidents Supérieurs

The autocratic personality of François Baudoin, the doyen of French *Résidents Supérieurs,* flourished in such political soil. Baudoin, who filled the top job from 1914 until 1927, retired to the Côte d'Azur with the rank of "Honorary Governor General of the Colonies".[19] Deceptively round faced, with the air of a dandy, this proud possessor of an almost Prussian waxed moustache,[20] was a martinet who bore out Thomas Ennis's observation that republican France's overseas form of government was "aristocratic" rather than democratic[21]— "occidental despotism", perhaps. He was invariably the principal speaker at Council meetings—sometimes the only one—and chaired them at the same time. Very rarely did the ministers dissent from his directions.[22] Rumors of corruption on his part do not seem to have adversely affected his career.[23] He made many enemies, but had friends in high places. Shrewd and intelligent, he surrounded himself with men as hierarchically minded as himself and was intolerant of administrators who showed independence. He promoted followers such as Émile Desenlis and Félix Bardez, hard men who did as he told them and got on with the job without too many scruples (although, as we shall see in Chapter 16 below, Desenlis was capable of compassion). The careers of civil servants who crossed Baudoin ended abruptly. One of these was the veteran administrator Charles Bellan, *Résident* of Prey Veng, who had served in Cambodia since 1899. This man had incurred Baudoin's displeasure early in World War I by criticizing the welter of taxes and demands for *corvée,* although the *Résident Supérieur* made no comment at the time.[24] Bellan warned that these measures were causing great discontent and his predictions were borne out in the 1916 Affair. Bellan also annoyed his superior by allegedly using vehicles and boats without permission, and enjoyed long-running feuds with Baudoin's cronies, Bardez[25] and Desenlis. Bellan alleged that an earlier *Résident Supérieur,* Ernest Outrey, had removed Desenlis from office following a complaint that he had imprisoned around 100 peasants without charge or trial for periods of up to two years. When Baudoin took over the top job, he promoted Desenlis to a high position in the police.[26] Baudoin demoted Bellan after the 1916 Affair, and sent him to Baclieu in Cochinchina, replacing him with Desenlis.[27] While it is true that the repression that followed the 1916 Affair was the heaviest in Prey Veng under Bellan[28], one suspects that Baudoin moved against him to deflect criticism of himself over the Affair, and to remove a gadfly. Certainly, the two men seem to have personally detested each other. They made a number of serious allegations against each other, but it was an unequal contest, for Baudoin had the ear of higher authority. Bellan alleged that Baudoin had covered up in a number of incidents of police brutality during 1918. He claimed that a policeman had fired all the bullets in his pistol at a Khmer soldier who failed to salute him in a Phnom Penh street and that Baudoin had covered up the incident. Bellan also alleged that Baudoin had protected a French militia commander following a massacre of 12 unarmed thieves at a pagoda near Kompong Trabek in Prey Veng province.[29] Another incident in which rank was used to cover up a crime occurred at Kampot in 1927, when a rich and influential member of the French community ran over and killed a 12-year-old Khmer child. The death, alleged *La Tribune Indochinoise,* was due to dangerous driving, but the culprit got off virtually scot-free.[30] Such incidents did not bode well for the independence of the judiciary and the rule of law. The allegations against Baudoin had earlier led to an official enquiry, but the inspectors found that the complaints were groundless. The opposition press in Saigon considered, however, that it was difficult to gather evidence as Baudoin remained at his post throughout the investigations.[31]

Baudoin also ran foul of another administrator, Gabriel Maurel, who had entered the Cambodian administration in 1906[32] and left the service to practice as a barrister in Phnom Penh.[33] Maurel, who held a doctorate in law, was one of Baudoin's most trenchant critics. In 1926, under the auspices of the Cambodian Section of the League for the Rights of Man and the Citizen, he wrote a stinging attack on the political-legal regime in Cambodia. The report claimed that, "the *Résident Supérieur* of Cambodia governs the country as an absolute monarch" and that King Sisowath, who at the age of 86 years was "in a state of mental debility", was incapable of taking any initiative in government. "His docility," claimed Maurel, "is extraordinary". The indigenous population was at the mercy of the autocratic Baudoin,

Maurel wrote. Both the Council of the Kingdom and the Municipal Council of Phnom Penh existed only to rubber stamp Baudoin's decisions. These bodies could make no decision whatsoever without his agreement and he was "absolutely sovereign in financial matters" and held all police powers in his hands. He could expel whoever he liked, particularly Chinese and "Annamites", from Cambodia, without giving any reason. Maurel went on to accuse his former boss of snooping on citizens' private mail. He lambasted the administration of mismanagement and cronyism, verging on corruption, in its handling of government contracts.[34] The administration's newspaper friends hit back, describing Maurel as a speculator and a rogue with an inflated sense of his own worth.[35]

The Cambodian penal code

As Lord Acton said, "Power corrupts. Absolute power corrupts absolutely." The French authorities in Cambodia passed laws that would have been unthinkable in France or any other democracy during normal times. The use of beatings and torture was routine. There was no freedom of speech or assembly. The Phnom Penh barrister Robert Lortat-Jacob, drew the left wing writer Andrée Viollis's attention an article in the Cambodian penal code, added in 1924, which forbade "All injurious criticism of the actions of the French or Cambodian administrations..." Infractions of this law were punishable by imprisonment of three months to one year and a fine of between 10 and 100 piastres.[36] The all-Indochina legal code was just as draconian. A decree of 31 December 1912 stipulated that no association of more than 20 persons, whether intended for "religious, literary, political or other purpose", could exist without official permission. The leaders of illegal organizations could be jailed for up to six months and fined up to 200 francs. All other members could be jailed for up to three months and fined up to 200 francs and persons allowing their premises to be used for meetings could be similarly punished. The regulations applied to "whites, indigenes and *assimilés* of any nationality" and permission was revocable at any time.[37] The laws were amended in Cambodia in 1931 to provide for up to five years imprisonment, to suppress the Caodai religious sect.[38] The Cambodian branch of the League of the Rights of Man and the Citizen regularly demanded, unsuccessfully, that the laws be brought into line with "the great universal laws known to all civilized peoples".[39] Lortat-Jacob gave numerous examples of the denial of rights to prisoners, and of torture inflicted on them. He told Viollis of cases in which French settlers and indigenous functionaries who had murdered Khmers before numerous witnesses went unpunished.[40]

Prison conditions were often appalling. Prince Norodom Ritharasi, who worked for a time as a medical officer in the Phnom Penh prison system, reported treating prisoners whom warders had severely beaten.[41] Surprisingly, the warders were punished in this case, for torture and ill treatment were routine in the prison system. The director of the Central Prison in Phnom Penh reported to the *Résident Supérieur* in 1932 that, "In spite of torture performed by the *Sûreté...*" a Communist prisoner named Ung Buon refused to talk.[42] The director reported the torture dispassionately; it was mere bureaucratic routine. Ung Buon must have been very brave, given the imaginatively sadistic police methods of the time. Andrée Viollis has left a disturbing account of the methods used by the *Sûreté* in Cholon on both male and female prisoners. There is no reason to doubt that the Cambodian *Sûreté* were less brutal or inventive. Beatings, canings, the suspension of prisoners on their toes, and the insertion of needles under finger and toenails were common. The inquisitors denied food and water to prisoners under interrogation. They put young female political offenders into the same cells as rapists. They used pincers to spring eyeballs from their sockets and funneled gasoline into prisoners' stomachs. They slashed the skin of prisoners' legs into long shreds, plaited it with cotton, and set it alight. Perhaps most ghastly of all was the insertion of a corkscrew into the urinary tract, followed by its sharp removal.[43] Such practices mocked French hypocrisy over the Cambodian legal code. As Virginia Thompson noted, the hideous tortures allowed in the traditional Cambodian legal code were often tempered with Buddhist prescriptions of mercy.[44] The French police were merciless.

The persecution of the Caodai sect

The police singled out the Caodai religious sect for constant harassment, despite its protestations of loyalty, following demands for its suppression by Monivong in the late 1920s. Its temples were demolished and there were arbitrary arrests[45] and even torture[46] of adepts and laity.[47] The police deported some followers into the hands of the Saigon *Sûreté*.[48] In May 1931, the *Tribunal Correctionel* in Phnom Penh sentenced the sect's leaders to long prison terms and ordered the dissolution of the society.[49] The Court of Appeal in Saigon upheld the judgment and the Cour de Cassation rejected a further appeal in 1932.[50] The sect proved resilient, however, and it sought and

obtained the support of leading politicians in France, including Albert
Sarraut, the former Governor General of Indochina, and Marius
Moutet, the Socialist Deputy who became Colonial Minister in the
Popular Front government. A party of Caodaists visited France during
the International Colonial Exposition of 1931 to put their case before
the public. The Parisian weekly paper, *La Griffe*, ran a front-page
article in October 1931 blasting "the exorbitant power" of the *Résident
Supérieur* in Phnom Penh and casting the Caodaists as martyrs. The
agitation even spread to the French colony in Madagascar, where the
left wing journal *L'Aurore Malgache* attacked the suppression of the
Caodai.[51] Supporters in metropolitan France raised thousands of francs
for a legal defense fund in Phnom Penh administered by the radical
barrister, Robert Lortat-Jacob.[52] M. Pujol, the Phnom Penh police
chief, claimed to have discovered a link between Caodaism and the
Nazis, who came to power in Germany in 1933, as both movements
used the swastika.[53] In fact, the swastika was an ancient cultural
symbol in Asia and had been incorporated into the eclectic mélange of
Caodai's philosophy before it is likely that its adherents had heard of
Hitler.[54] It does seem, however, that Le Van Trung, the Caodai Pope,
who died in 1935, might have had secret dealings with the Japanese.[55]
The sect also welcomed the World War II Armistice between Marshal
Pétain and Germany. In 1942, the Caodai temple at Phnom Penh
sought Japanese protection.[56] According to one report in 1944, they
believed that the Nazis would take over Indochina and grant them a
privileged status.[57] Such a belief was fantasy, of course, but given
constant repression by the French, one can scarcely blame the
Caodaists for pro-Axis attitudes.

Most of the Caodai faithful were Vietnamese, as were most
Communist militants. Cambodian nationalism was almost invisible
during the 1920s and 1930s and most Khmers were politically
apathetic or loyal to the Protectorate. Despite this, French suspicions
grew. Huy Kanthoul records that by the 1930s, "The settlers felt that
something had changed. They feared the resurgence of nationalist
sentiment among the colonized people..." As a result, "The least
criticism of the colonial authorities would expose you to sanctions out
of all proportion to the offence."[58]

Bokor: "a black hole for public funds"

One project in particular came to symbolize the dark side of French
rule between the wars. The Bokor hill station still stands today, albeit
in ruins, to mock colonial hubris atop the mountain called "the

Buffalo's Hump." At the end of World War I, François Baudoin backed a proposal for a lavish resort complex perched high in the Elephant Mountains, with breathtaking views over steep precipices to the Gulf of Thailand. His enemies alleged that he was jealous of similar establishments in Annam and Tonkin. There would be a luxury hotel, with a sanatorium and leisure facilities, reached by a new road, which would wind up from the lowlands near Kampot to an altitude of over 1000 meters. Guests could chance their luck at the roulette tables in a spacious casino, or nurse their after-dinner drinks before roaring log fires lit to keep out the winter chill. To stand before these fireplaces in the ruins of the complex today is a glum experience indeed. One hears the incessant dripping of the rainwater seeping through the high ceilings. The wind gusts in through the empty window frames and it is difficult to imagine a time when the logs crackled against the cold. At the time, it was an island of Europe in Asia; European-style fruits and vegetables—even strawberries—could be grown, and the cool uplands would provide guests much needed relief from the sweltering climate of the plains below.[59] Like the Ritz in Paris, the hotel would be open to all who could afford to pay: in practice, this meant the well-off French and members of the "native" elite. King Monivong later lived there on a country estate, as did Sihanouk. Ordinary "natives" would act in menial capacities and provide labor for the construction of the roads and other works.

Preliminary works, including surveying and some horse and walking tracks on the plateau, were completed in 1919,[60] but the work dragged on for a number of years due to a shortage of skilled technicians and free labor. Peasants and convicts cut the road with machetes, picks and shovels, aided by requisitioned buffalo carts, through rugged terrain and thick jungle. In some spectacular sections, the road was carved deep into the rock. The cost to the public purse was substantial. In late 1923, *La Voix Libre* described the project as "an endless black hole for public funds", and singled out François Baudoin in particular for blame.[61] The Bokor project smacked of waste and corruption and despite the authorities' characteristic cheeseparing, they were prepared to pour large sums of money into the project. Baudoin had a villa built for his own use, replete with a private electrical power plant, out of public funds.[62] In 1925, a new ten-room extension to the hotel was built at a cost of 335,000 piastres,[63] accounting for some 20 per cent of the annual public works budget.[64] In comparison, the total public expenditure on education throughout the kingdom for 1925 amounted to slightly more than 630,000 piastres.[65] Total government expenditure for 1926 was 10 million piastres[66] and the total public works budget for 1924 was only 1,770,000 piastres.[67]

The complex opened with a glittering ball, described in detail by the *Echo du Cambodge*. Champagne flowed, there was a sumptuous repast, and the guests danced to a jazz band. The official guests included the wife of *Résident* Félix Bardez, said to be "ravishing" in a mauve gown.[68] The *Echo* denounced critics of the scheme as carping malcontents.[69] The opposition was unbowed. A leading "malcontent" thundered: "Bokor! Nine hundred million [francs] sunk into a building! Unbelievable opulence exists side by side with nameless misery...There, the imagination is tormented by the knowledge of how the pangs of hunger and the sweat of all the days are squandered."[70]

Conspicuous consumption of public funds was not the only reason for animadversion. The project was also profligate with human lives. The journalist Fontaine Laporte denounced Baudoin's project as "the grand work of the tyrant of Cambodia", claiming that the Bokor road was "reinforced with human bones"[71] and the writer Marguerite Duras, who spent part of her childhood on a smallholding at Prey Nop, in Kampot province west of Bokor, supports the claim of a tropical Gehenna.[72] Interviewed years later, Duras recalled her mother's horror at the treatment of the convict laborers at Bokor. "The whole road was like the Way of the Cross", she said. "Every kilometer, every two kilometers, you could see holes filled up with people who'd been put there to force them to work, to punish them; they were put in the ground up to their necks, under the sun, as an example." Many of the laborers, according to Duras, were Vietnamese convicts, imprisoned for inability to pay taxes.[73] Ironically, a special "Bokor tax" existed in Cambodia at the time[74] so it was possible to end up in a chain gang on the Bokor road for one's inability to meet the taxes levied to build it! Unofficial estimates of the number of dead on the project vary from 900[75] to 2000.[76] No official figures are available, perhaps as this would amount to an admission of wrongdoing. Alternatively, perhaps officialdom saw the deaths as unavoidable and unexceptional; what later generations would call "collateral damage". No documentation about the working and living conditions of the laborers appears to have survived. If the relatively well-documented conditions of rubber plantation workers are a guide, conditions at Bokor must have been grim and the unofficial estimates of the death toll cited above are plausible. Certainly, the construction work would have been more onerous than plantation labor, as it relied on human muscle to cut the forests, dig the earth, and drill and hammer the stone of the mountainside. For every death attributable to direct physical abuse and accident, there must have been many more due to poor food, neglect and disease—particularly malaria, which was rife in the jungles. Perhaps six or seven laborers died for every few hundred yards of road. The contrast between this brutal squalor and the achingly beautiful sea views over Phu Quoc Island must have tested the Buddhist fatalism of these dragooned peasants.

The Bardez Affair

The French built Bokor for their own benefit, but the peasants paid for it in blood and sweat, both directly and via taxes. Critics claimed, with justification, that the tax burden in Cambodia was disproportionately higher than elsewhere in Indochina.[77] High levels of taxation had often caused discontent and although the French eased some taxes after the 1916 Affair, this was a tactical retreat rather than a permanent concession. Tax yields fell steeply in the last years of World War I, primarily because of the slump in rice production. Paddy taxes fell from 900,000 piastres in 1918 to 400,000 in 1919.[78] By the 1920s, one of the primary, even obsessive, concerns of the French administration was to gather the maximum possible amounts of tax. The barrister M. Gallet claimed that the French administration arbitrarily decided to impose an extra tax bill of 700,000 piastres on the Cambodian people in 1924.[79]

Henri Poiret, the *Résident* of Kompong Chhnang province, reported with some satisfaction that, "in spite of poor weather...the collection of paddy taxes had risen to more than 41,500 piastres in 1922, as against 37,500 in 1921." When all other taxes were included, taxes were up by about 15,000 piastres over the previous year.[80] The following year saw another increase in paddy taxes, again "in spite of very bad atmospheric conditions", to almost 44,000 piastres.[81] One year later, *Résident* Poiret reported another mediocre harvest and warned, somewhat prophetically, that, "The Cambodian of Kompong Chhnang appears to be taxed almost to the limit of his means."[82] The harvests were better in 1925 and paddy taxes leapt again to over 77,000 piastres[83], an increase of over 50 per cent in four years.

The major reason for the abrupt leap in taxes collected in Kompong Chhnang was the arrival of a new *Résident*, Félix Louis Bardez. This official, who was 43 years old in 1925, was a trusted crony of the *Résident Supérieur*, François Baudoin, and had served as his private secretary before the war. The Americans would have called him a "can do" administrator. Born in the XVth arrondissement of Paris, he had come to Cambodia in 1907 as a young civil servant, after serving in the army, where he had risen to the rank of sergeant.[84] Bardez was tough, experienced and hot tempered. The Cambodian historian Sorn Samnang describes him as "vigorous and ambitious". Bardez returned to France in 1916 and served with distinction on the Western Front. He was wounded in action at Soissons, rose to the rank of sub-lieutenant and was awarded the Croix de Guerre for gallantry. Characteristically, he had refused evacuation after suffering a wound to the hand.[85] Baudoin had picked him as a "trouble-shooter" to replace Poiret. The *Résident Supérieur* had introduced a number of new taxes in recent times, and was determined to close any tax loopholes. The minutes of the June 1924 provincial council record, for instance, that Phnom Penh had ordered the collection of dog taxes, which had fallen into disuse.[86] On the same date, *Résident* Bardez addressed the provincial council of Prey Veng, stressing that François Baudoin had recently returned from leave in France and was determined to force the pace of the economic development of Cambodia. The minutes read like a continuous monologue (or possibly harangue) by Bardez. The Khmer councilors said little. Bardez remarked that, "tight control over all taxes was necessary". The administration had resolved to crack down on evasion and corruption, he warned.[87]

The local peasants were unhappy with the drive for increased taxes. On two occasions, several hundred of the poorest people marched in from the Kraang Leav district to present their grievances to Bardez in the provincial capital. Bardez promised to look into their complaints, but when he dispatched an official to investigate, the men fled into the forest and women wielding sticks drove the man away. Bardez consulted with Baudoin, who instructed him to restore order and collect all taxes owed.[88] One morning in the following April, M. Bardez set out with an escort of militiamen to extract unpaid land taxes from the villagers of Kraang Laev,[89] a few miles to the west of the provincial seat of Kompong Chhnang. On the way, he visited several other villages without incident.[90] According to Gabriel Maurel, Bardez left alone, but was later joined by a militia escort.[91] Bardez quickly got down to business. The villagers pleaded that they could not pay, but he chose not to believe them, suspecting that they had hidden part of their crops. He lined them up in the center of the village and delivered an insulting and threatening harangue, even suggesting that the women should prostitute themselves to raise the outstanding money. He demanded to know how the village could have afforded a new pagoda if they were as destitute as they claimed. He tied some of the men up and went to have lunch. In the meantime, the villagers drank palm wine in the hot sun, angry that Bardez had forbidden them to eat. After he had lunched, Bardez resumed work, evidently convinced that the villagers were concealing their wealth. The sun had risen high in the sky. The wine fumes rose to the men's heads as the Frenchman goaded them. The irascible *Résident* appears to have known little Khmer and his ignorance led him to underestimate the seriousness of what was happening.[92] According to Baudoin, tensions rose after the arrival of a number of strangers in the village. The strangers were rude and abusive, causing the crowd to grow restive, whereupon Bardez sent for reinforcements.[93] His escort, the Cambodian militiaman, Leach, nervously cocked his rifle and a ripple of rage spread through the crowd. The villagers wrestled the man's rifle from his hands, someone hit him over the head with a wooden stool (some accounts say an axe was used) and he fell dead. Bardez was a physically courageous man and perhaps emboldened by feelings of racial superiority. He was a Frenchman and a battle-scarred warrior from the mud of Soissons. They were Asian peasants defying lawful authority. He pushed forward to rescue the militiaman, but the crowd surged at him with "the sudden violence of a storm",[94] trampling and bludgeoning him to death with an axe outside the village *sala*. His Khmer interpreter-cum-clerk, Suorn, had sought refuge in the village *wat*, but the mob dragged him outside over the protests of the monks and put him to death. In the *mêlée*, the tax money Bardez had collected went missing.[95] Two or three hundred villagers left the three bodies sprawled in the dust and set off on foot towards the town of Kompong Chhnang, brandishing sticks and machetes, intent on burning down the buildings of the French administration. Somewhere along the road, their resolve began to falter as their rage and the effects of the alcohol wore off, and the bleakness of the future asserted itself in their minds. Although they had brandished sticks and machetes, they surrendered meekly when half a dozen militiamen—the reinforcements Bardez had called earlier—confronted them and fired a single volley of bullets. They confessed readily, incriminating one another, helped when they faltered by the usual "third degree" techniques of the police.

The incident remains an enigma. Khmers had earlier killed a number of other Frenchmen, but, excluding those killed during the uprisings of the 19th century,[96] the deaths resulted from motives of personal gain or private revenge. Although David Chandler called it "a premonition of revolt in colonial Cambodia", it did not ignite overt anti-French sentiment in the kingdom at the time. Once the adrenalin and wine wore off, the villagers themselves were horrified by what they had done.[97] The kingdom was generally quiet at the time, with the exception of some pillage by bandits in the Kraang Leav region. King

Sisowath changed the name of the village to *Derachan*—"bestial" or "village of animals"—because he judged the population collectively guilty.[98] The *Sûreté* reported that the general population of Cambodia did not approve of the killings.[99] Eighteen villagers were arrested in connection with the murders, and of these, five were acquitted for lack of evidence, one went to the guillotine, and the others were sentenced to imprisonment for between seven years and life, mostly at the penal colony on Poulo Condore.[100] Although there appears to be nothing in French law to support the idea of collective guilt, the authorities enforced harsh punishments on the entire village. Sisowath's decree stated that in the old times before the Protectorate, the whole population would have been reduced to slavery and have had all its possessions confiscated. This was no longer possible, but because of the alleged collective guilt of the villagers—or at best their "shameful passivity"—the following measures would be taken:

- There would be a ceremony of expiation at the village wat, with sermons by the highest religious dignitaries in the land. All villagers were compelled to attend and to confess their guilt;
- A monument—*chet dey*—paid for by the villagers, would be erected with a text determined by the Council of Ministers in Khmer and French on a granite plaque;
- Any inhabitant who had left the village since the crime was to return home, on penalty of confiscation of all their property and a prison sentence of up to three years;
- The village was to bear the name *Derachan* for ten years;
- No resident of the village would be permitted to change their place of residence for five years and would carry a special personal taxation card, white in color, with a black border;
- Every year on the 18 April, a special commemorative service would be held in the village wat;
- Local authorities would be relieved of their duties for negligence or bad will and would be fined or jailed as necessary;
- The royal proclamation would be affixed in every village and hamlet throughout the land.[101]

The text, unveiled shortly afterwards on the *chet dey*, read as follows:

In memory of MM Félix Bardez, *Administrateur des Services Civils de l'Indochine, Résident* of France at Kompong Chhnang; Suorn, *Sécretaire des Résidences du Cambodge;* Léach, native guard, odiously murdered in this place on 18 April 1925. This monument was erected at royal command by the inhabitants of the old khum of Kraang Leav, today Khum Dérachan...[102]

A political murder?

Scarcely had the blood soaked into the soil, when a furious debate erupted over the significance of the crime. It is possible that a less abrasive man would have escaped Bardez's fate. Without wishing to lend weight to orientalist stereotype of the "gentle land", we should observe that the Khmers are generally a courteous and hospitable people. Showing one's anger reflects badly on a person in Khmer culture. Other *Résidents* were pushed by the taxation imperatives of the regime to confront the peasants, yet none were murdered. A British diplomat considered that Bardez had provoked his own death by being "over-zealous and very tactless", but still believed that it was a "political murder".[103] Indeed it was. The villagers had killed Bardez while he was on official business, attempting to extract unpopular taxes. If Bardez had been respectful, they would have resented the impost, but probably spared the life of the man who made it. Some of the perpetrators appear to have been drunk,[104] but while this fact has to be taken into account, it cannot itself explain why the murders happened.

Against all reason, the French authorities claimed that the murders lacked any political significance. The semi-official *Avenir du Cambodge* scorned suggestions that the Kraang Leav events amounted to a *jacquerie* against taxes.[105] The *Sûreté* claimed that the murders resulted from a "thirst for personal vengeance" stirred up by low characters.[106] The chief of the cadastral department, Jules Bornet, claimed that taxation levels were well within the ability of the peasants to pay. Bornet admitted that taxes had risen since 1907, but pointed out that, "the surface area planted with paddy had tripled". He also believed—probably correctly—that the peasants underestimated crop yields to pay less tax.[107] However, the situation was not as clear-cut as Bornet claimed. As the present author has written, "the figures show that that cultivated surface [of Cambodia] increased by 250,000 hectares between 1905 and 1925; that the yield per hectare *declined* [emphasis in the original]; and that taxes rose both in absolute terms and in terms of the ratio between total area cultivated and taxes collected." Most importantly, the mode of assessment of taxation changed in 1924. Previously, taxes had been levied on crop yields for a given year. Now, they depended on the amount of land owned, regardless of fluctuations in yield (which could be very great). Harvest taxes had given way to land taxes.[108] The French officials in Cambodia—François Baudoin in particular—would have been eager to convince their superiors in Paris that the murder was an aberration rather than an indicator of discontent.

Although the French officials denied it, there was an enormous reservoir of latent and at times overt ill feeling over high taxation, and this was to last until the end of the protectorate. Corrupt tax collectors were still a problem, too. The traveler Harry Franck alleged in 1926 that some had made great personal fortunes from their chicanery.[109] Eight years after Bardez died, perhaps haunted by his shade, another *Résident* wrote from Kompong Chhnang to his superiors to ask for the lowering of heavy taxes because they were causing "a certain ill will",[110] and some 200 "credulous" peasants in Kompong Thom joined a movement led by a certain Oum to demand the cancellation of debts.[111] In 1934, an opposition newspaper claimed that the Cambodians suffered "fiscal tyranny" and paid the highest taxes in Indochina. Ten thousand peasants had fled to the forest to escape paying onerous taxes, the paper claimed.[112] Taxes on bicycles were 200 per cent higher than in Saigon.[113] It appears that the ill feeling was enormous, because in 1936 King Monivong decreed, over the countersignature of the French *Résident Supérieur*, that all personal taxes owing from before 1935 would be remitted, and that all taxes for 1935 would be cut by 50 per cent.[114] While this reduction might have stemmed in part from pressure from the Popular Front government in Paris, it might also have resulted from memories of the Bardez and 1916 Affairs. By World War II, taxes were as high as ever. In December 1939, a crowd of peasants from the villages of Chamcar Samrong and Prek Tatan walked to Battambang town to protest to the authorities that their land taxes had quadrupled since 1938.[115]

The Cambodian peasants were barely literate, if at all, and they neither owned nor wrote for newspapers. However, if they "could not represent themselves", they most certainly were represented, whether they knew it or not. The murders and the subsequent trial provoked an explosion of anti-establishment anger in opposition circles in Phnom Penh, Saigon, Hanoi, and France itself. The dissident barristers, M. Lortat-Jacob and M. Gallet, defended the accused in court and the Radical press joined the attack on the French administration. François Baudoin's old enemy, Gabriel Maurel, wrote a scathing attack on the administration for the League for the Rights of Man and the Citizen in France.[116] Bardez's murderers were physically in the dock of the Phnom Penh assizes but the dissident barristers and their friends in the

Saigon press succeeded for a while in putting the administration on trial in the court of public opinion.

Bardez and the mission civilisatrice

One doubts, however, that they succeeded in their suit. In the end, the trial was an auto-da-fé. François Baudoin was probably correct in his claim that only "rare" Europeans dissented from the official line on the causes of the assassination.[117] Had the phrase been in vogue, he might have dismissed the dissidents as members of the "chattering classes". According to claims in *Sûrêté* documents, based on reports by police agents and informers, there was popular approval across the ethnic groups for the punishments inflicted on the murderers.[118] This was probably the case, although the French were prone to hear what they wanted to believe and many were remarkably ignorant of the country. The French settlers and officials regarded Bardez as a martyr for many years afterwards, marking the anniversary of his death with graveside orations.[119] He symbolized the aspirations of the *mission civilisatrice;* the affair harked back to the "heroic" early period of the protectorate when gallant naval officers struggled and sometimes died for the nation. The French might have mused, as they pursued their relatively humdrum lives in Phnom Penh, that there was still a bit of the martyr and hero in all of them. Critics of the French mission might have invoked the words of Marlowe in Joseph Conrad's *Heart of Darkness;* "The conquest of the earth, which mostly means the taking it away from those who have a different complexion or slightly flatter noses than ourselves, is not a pretty thing when you look into it too much." Most of the French, however, would have agreed with Marlowe's caveat that, "What redeems it is the idea only. An idea at the back of it; not a sentimental pretence but an idea; and an unselfish belief in the idea..." The settlers and officials, no matter how venal they were, could have identified Bardez—and themselves—with that.[120] As for the killers, over a decade later, eleven of them still languished in the penal colony on Poulo Condore, all but forgotten by their countrymen. The French authorities dismissed out of hand an appeal for clemency by the Vietnamese newspaper *Cong Luan*. "The murder of *Résident* Bardez was never considered as a political crime and the murderers and their accomplices were treated as convicts under the common law", stated a French official in 1938.[121]

This was a profoundly racist age. Although it was possible for Indochinese indigenes to become *assimilés;* that is, brown Frenchmen subject to French law and customs and with the right to vote, for most

Khmers this was only a theoretical possibility. Scarcely sixty years before the foundation of the Protectorate, French slave-owners in the West Indies had divided their "thinking property" into dozens of categories based on the ratio of "white" to "black" blood in their veins. The existence of such *métis* draws attention to the politics of interracial sexual liaison, usually between white slave owners and their female slaves. In Cambodia, it was common for French settlers and officials to take Khmer mistresses. Marriage was much less common and sexual relations between "native" males and Frenchwomen were taboo. This was shown in a case in the late 1930s, in which the son of an important Khmer official in Battambang brought his young white wife back with him after studying in France. Huy Kanthoul sums up the results thus: "'*Mésalliance*', decided the colonial authorities, supported by all of this violently racist French colony...The father and son were threatened with the worst penalties and the young man, with death in his soul, was forced to send his wife back to France."[122] Such racism led the colonialists to squander human lives on the Bokor project and, as we shall see in the next chapter, on the rubber plantations in the east of the country.

Notes

[1] *Revue du Tourisme*, op.cit. 29 June 1923. The magazine used his words as a running footer on most of its pages at this time.

[2] Huy Kanthoul, op.cit. p.62.

[3] Harry A. Franck, (1926), *East of Siam: Ramblings in the Five Divisions of French Indo-China,* The Century, New York, p.12.

[4] Ibid. p.84.

[5] "Autour des rélations siamo-cambodgiennes. Cinq minutes avec S.E. Thiounn premier ministre de Sa Majesté Sisowath Monivong", *La Presse Indochinoise,* 1 July 1937.

[6] Franck, op.cit. Several of Thiounn's descendents were to become high ranking members of Pol Pot's government of Democratic Kampuchea after 1975. Others were prominent under both Sihanouk and the Khmer Republic.

[7] David Chandler, (1997), "From 'Cambodge' to Kampuchea; State and Revolution in Cambodia, 1863-1979", *Thesis Eleven,* No. 50, August, p.37.

[8] ANC RSC D 03. La Section cambodgienne de la Ligue des Droits de l'Homme et des Citoyens à Pnompenh au Comité central de la Ligue des Droits de l'Homme et des Citoyens à Paris. No date, but probably 1926 (penciled in margin).

[9] *La Voix Libre,* Saigon, No 172, 24 November 1923. The French Radical Party was anti-clerical and republican. It was not "radical" in the sense of the "radical left" today, although the party did join the Popular Front governments of the 1930s in Paris.

[10] ANC RSC D 03 op.cit.

[11] AOM Fonds Amiraux, 7F 15 (3) Rapport Annuel (Sûreté) Année 1924-1925.

[12] AOM Fonds Amiraux, 7F 15. Chef de la Sûreté au Cambodge M. le Directeur des Affaires Politiques et de la Sûreté à Hanoi, 15 August 1923.

[13] Franck, op.cit. pp.28-32.

[14] Eleanor Mordaunt, (1932), *Purely for Pleasure,* Martin Secker, London, p.265.

[15] AOM RSC 300. Surveillance des Étrangers.

[16] AOM RSC 218 Sûreté Envoi No. 592-SS à Résident Supérieur. Rapport Annuel 31 mai 1929-1 juin 1930.

[17] PRO FO 371 12624, w 9882 Lord Crewe to the Foreign Office, 21 October 1927.

[18] H.G. Quaritch Wales, (1943), *Years of Blindness,* Thomas Y. Crowell, New York, p.217.

[19] ANC RSC F42 File 9065 (1939-1941). Letter from *Résident Supérieur,* Phnom Penh, to Gougal, 4 December 1940.

[20] Thus, he appears in a photograph that accompanies a valedictory article on the front page of the *Echo du Cambodge,* 21 January 1927.

[21] Thomas E. Ennis, (1936), *French Policy and Development in Indochina,* University of Chicago Press, Chicago, pp.9-10. There was, of course, no hereditary right of succession, so the point should not be taken too far.

[22] The minutes of many of these meetings can be found in the Cambodian National Archives at ANC RSC F451, procès-verbaux, Conseil des Ministres, 1897-1937.

[23] It was possible that Baudoin may have accepted bribes from Sisowath so that he would favor Monivong's claim for the succession to the throne. (AOM INDOCHINE NF Dossier 578 Carton 48, *Les Annales Coloniales,* 19 November 1927.)

[24] ANC RSC E 03 File 21180 Box 2260.

[25] ANC RSC F65 File 7763, Affaire Bellan. Rapport No 169 en date du octobre 1915 au sujet de l'attitude de M. Bellan.

[26] "La justice au Cambodge", *La Voix Libre,* 18 October 1922 and "L'Affaire Bellan-Baudoin", *L'Argus Indochinois,* 27 May 1922.

[27] ANC RSC E03 File 21176 Box 2260. Rapport Politique du 3ème Trimestre 1916, Prey Veng. See also ANC RSC F65, op.cit. Arrête No 2467 en date du 28 octobre 1916 déferent M Bellan, Admin. de 2ème classe, devant un conseil d'enquête.

[28] ANC F65 File 7763, op.cit. Extrait du rapport No 249 30 June 1916. Letter from Baudoin to the Governor General. Thirteen people were sentenced to death in Prey Veng following the Affair, along with 30 life sentences.

[29] ANC F65 op.cit. Extrait du mémoire Bellan, 1924.

[30] *La Tribune Indochinoise,* 13 April 1927.

[31] Ibid. "The Administration de M. Baudoin au Cambodge", 23 September 1927. The inspection took place in 1926. See also AOM RSC 432 Rapport politique 1er Trimestre 1926.

[32] ANC RSC C 01 File 15292. Fiches personelles du personnel européen du protectorat avant 1912.

[33] ANC RSC D45, File 13013 Box 1090. Affaire Maurel, diveres plaintes contre l'administration pour questions de concessions, abus de pouvoir, etc. 1926.

[34] ANC RSC D 03 op.cit.

[35] Maurice Espinet in *Le Petit Cambodgien*, 7 – 11 July 1931.

[36] Andrée Viollis, (1949, orig. published 1936), *Indochine S.O.S.*, Editeurs Réunis, Paris, p.71.

[37] AOM RSC 227. Cultes. "En droit" – summary of the code. No date or author, although it appears to have been written in 1938. The articles of the code that suppressed freedom of assembly were 291, 292 and 294.

[38] Ibid.

[39] For example, AOM RSC 215. Letter from the Vice-President of the Cambodian branch to the *Résident Supérieur,* 29 September 1927.

[40] Viollis, op.cit. pp.71-72.

[41] ANC RSC E 03 File 1675 Box 162. Report on vaccinations at the central prison hospital, Phnom Penh, 19 January 1930, by Dr Norodom Ritharasi.

[42] AOM RSC 433 Révoltes au Cambodge. Director of the central Prison to the *Résident Supérieur,* 4 January 1932.

[43] Viollis, op.cit. pp. 51-53.

[44] Virginia Thompson, (1968), *French Indo-China*, Octagon Books, New York, p.330.

[45] AOM RSC 666. Caodistes, 1931-1934. Résident at Takeo to the Résident Supérieur, 5 January 1929.

[46] AOM RSC 667 Letter of 3 July 1930 from the barrister M. Lortat-Jacob to the Procureur-Général.

[47] Ibid. Letter from Le Van Trung, the Caodai Pope to Monivong, op.cit.

[48] AOM RSC 667, Expulsion of Nguyen Van Tri, 1930.

[49] ANC RSC D35 File 5905 Box 579. Minute du Livre verte, Cambodge. Rapport sur l'exercice du protectorat 1931-1932.

[50] AOM RSC 669. Surveillance Caodaistes. Sureté, 1934.

[51] Clippings in AOM RSC 232 Affaires Religieuses – Caodai.

[52] AOM RSC 669 Surveillance Caodaistes, op.cit. Contains a photograph, taken by the police, of a receipt for 10,000 francs, raised in France, signed by Le Van Bay and sent to Lortat-Jacob.

[53] Ibid. A.S. nouvelle intervention de M. MOUTET en faveur des Caodaistes.

[54] Kipling also used the symbol to illustrate his books until it was adopted by the Nazis.

[55] PRO FO 474/2 F 5655/5655/86 French Indo-China. Historical background to 1939, B. Pearn, Research Dept. Pearn does not reveal the nature of this alleged contact.

[56] André Gaudel, (1947), *L'Indochine Française en face du Japon*, J. Susse, Paris, p.47.

[57] AOM RSC 308 Re: attitudes to France. Sûrêté Interieure, "Tractes alarmistes d'origine caodaiste", 17 October 1944.

[58] Huy Kanthoul, op.cit. pp.60-61.

[59] Dr E.M. Vallet, (1925), "Etude sur la station d'altitude de Bokor", *L'Echo du Cambodge*, 4 April.

[60] AOM RSC 431. Rapport Politique, 1er Trimestre 1920.

[61] Unsigned, (1923), "Bockor le gouffre", *La Voix Libre*, No. 170, p.1, 17 November.

[62] Vallet, op.cit. and "Bockor le gouffre", op.cit.

[63] "La Gouffre de Bockor", *La Voix Libre*, No 280, s January 1925, p.1.

[64] AOM RSC 432, Rapport d'Ensemble, 1925-26.

[65] Direction générale de l'instruction publique, (1930), *Le service de l'instruction publique en Indochine en 1930*, Hanoi, graph facing p.12.

[66] AOM RSC 432, op.cit.

[67] "Réunion de la commission annuelle des travaux publics au Cambodge", *L'Echo du Cambodge*, 10 October 1925.

[68] *L'Echo du Cambodge*, 21 February 1925, p.1.

[69] For instance, *L'Echo du Cambodge*, 13 June and 18 July 1925.

[70] From M. Gallet's speech for the defense at the Bardez trial, reported in *L'Indochine Enchaînée*, No 18, February 1926.

[71] A. Fontaine Laporte, (1926), "Les origines de l'affaire Bardez", reprinted from *Le Libre Indochine*, in *La Voix Libre*, No 345, 9 January.

[72] Alain Vircondelet (trans. Thomas Buckley), (1994), *Duras. A Biography*, Dalkey Archive Press, Illinois, p.15.

[73] Marguerite Duras and Xavière Gauthier, (trans. Katharine A. Jensen), (1987), *Woman to Woman*, University of Nebraska Press, Lincoln, Nebraska, p.99.

[74] David Chandler, op.cit. p.157.

[75] *La Cloche Fêlée*, Saigon, 26 January 1926.

[76] "L'ineffable M. Baudoin", (1927), *L'Argus Indochinois*, Hanoi, 12 March.

[77] M Gallet, in his speech for the defense at the Bardez trial, said that an inspector of colonies had made this claim. (*L'Indochine Enchaînée*, op.cit.)

[78] AOM RSC 431, Rapport Politique 2ème Trimestre 1919.

[79] *L'Indochine Enchaînée*, op.cit.

[80] RSC 397 Rapport d'Ensemble sur la période 1921-1922. Kompong Chhnang. M. Poiret was Félix Bardez's predecessor.)

[81] Ibid, Rapport annuel, Kompong Chhnang, juin 1922 – juin 1923.

[82] Ibid, Situation Politique et économique, Kompong Chhnang, 15 septembre 1924.

[83] Ibid. Rapport annuel 1 juillet 1924 – 1 juin 1925.

[84] ANC RSC C01 File 15292. Fiches personelles du personnel européen du protectorat avant 1912.

[85] Sorn Samnang, (1995), "L'Evolution de la société cambodgienne entre les deux guerres mondiales (1919-1939). Tome II. Thèse pour le doctorat d'histoire. Université Paris VII, pp.333-334.

[86] ANC RSC E03 File 16033 Box 1361 Procès-verbal, Conseil de Résidence de Kompong Chhnang, 16 juin 1924.

[87] ANC RSC E3 File 4249 Box 476. Conseil de Résidence de Prey Veng, 16 juin 1924.

[88] ANC RSC D 03. La Section cambodgienne de la Ligue des Droits de l'Homme et des Citoyens à Pnompenh au Comité central de la Ligue des Droits de l'Homme et des Citoyens à Paris. Probably written by Gabriel Maurel.

[89] Sometimes called Krang Leou.

[90] ANC RSC F451 File 24657 477e séance des Conseil des Ministres du 19 avril 1925.

[91] ANC RSC D 03, (Maurel) op.cit. The following account is based on Maurel; David P. Chandler, (1982), "the Assassination of *Résident* Bardez (1925). A premonition of revolt in colonial Cambodia", *Journal of the Siam Society,* Bangkok, Vol. 70, pp.35-49; on various contemporary accounts in the French-language press in Indochina, including "La tragédie de Kompong-Chhnang", *"Echo du Cambodge,* 25 April 1925; Nguyen Pham Long, (1925), "Mon impression d'ensemble sur l'affaire Bardez, *La Voix Libre,* No 342, 19 December; the *Echo du Cambodge* of 9 May 1925; "Le royaume de Sisowath sous la terreur", *Voix Libre,* No 307, 9 May 1925; "L'Affaire Bardez", *La Voix Libre,* 5 December 1925; AOM RSC 261, "Cour criminelle. Assassinat de M. Bardez, Résident de France à Kompong Chhnang"; and John Tully, (1996), *Cambodia Under the Tricolour. King Sisowath and the 'Mission Civilisatrice',* *1904-1927,* Monash Asia Institute, Clayton, Victoria, pp. 279-284. Although the Saigon Radical press sometimes exaggerated their claims against Baudoin, Long's piece is a measured analysis.

[92] Maurel, op.cit. Very few Frenchmen knew Khmer. Even in 1931, the writer Guy de Pourtalès was told that Mlle Suzanne Karpelès was one of the few French people able to speak the language and converse with the monks. Guy de Pourtalès, (1990, orig. published 1931), *Nous, à qui rien n'appartient.* *Voyage au Pays Khmer,* Flammarion, Paris, p.108.

[93] ANC F451 File 24657 op.cit.

[94] Long, op.cit.

[95] ANC F451 File 24657 op.cit.

[96] A number of others were killed by the hill tribes. See Tully, op.cit. "The revolt of the hill tribes", pp. 143-157 and Gerald Cannon Hickey, (1982), *Sons of the Mountains: Ethnohistory of the Vietnamese Central Highlands to 1954,* Yale University Press, New Haven.

[97] The villagers are still reluctant to discuss the Affair today. A 75-year-old woman called Beum told Martin Lejehan (a nom-de-plume) "It was difficult, miserable to live in a village called *Phum Derachan."* Neither Beum nor other old villagers were prepared to say more, despite the fact that a book called

Phum Derachan, published in 1987, is studied today in all Cambodian schools.
[Martin Lejehan, (1999), "Le villages des bêtes", *Gavroche*, février, p.50.]
[98] AOM RSC 261, op.cit. The Bardez Affair is recorded also in the *Sisowath Chronicle*. The text of the decree was published in *L'Echo du Cambodge*, 9 May 1925.
[99] AOM Fonds Amiraux, 7F 15 (3) Rapport annuel (Sûreté) année 1924-1925.
[100] AOM RSC 261, op.cit.
[101] ANC RSC F451 File 24658, Conseil des Ministres, 478e séance du 23 avril 1925.
[102] ANC F451 File 24660 Conseil des Ministres, 480e séance du 4 juin 1925. It would seem that the French later relented and allowed the village to revert to its old name before the ten-year period was up.
[103] PRO, Kew, FO 371 11839. Report on visit to Cambodia of HM Rep Mr. Greg.
[104] ANC RSC F451File 24673 Conseil des Ministres, 493e séance du 21 janvier 1926.
[105] "Les derniers echos de l'affaire Bardez," *L'Avenir du Cambodge,* 23 January 1926.
[106] AOM Fonds Amiraux 7F 15 (3), op.cit.
[107] AOM RSC 261, op.cit. Rapport par Bornet, le Chef du Service du Cadastre, 23 octobre 1925.
[108] Tully, op.cit. p.282.
[109] Franck, op.cit. p.83.
[110] ANC RSC E03 File 499 Box 38 Rapport Annuel, Kompong Chhnang, juin 1932-mai 1933.
[111] ANC RSC D35 File 499 Box 38. Rapport annuel, Kompong Thom, June 1932-June 1933.
[112] "Tyrannie fiscale. Le Cambodgien est le plus imposé de tous les paysans de l'Indochine", *La Presse Indochinoise*, 25-26 August 1934. An example of the higher taxes was the capitation tax, which averaged 2.50 piastres in Tonkin and Annam, 5.50 piastres in Cochinchina, and 7.75 piastres in Cambodia. (*La Presse Indochinoise*, 20 May 1936.)
[113] Ibid. 22 September 1936.
[114] Ibid. 27 May 1936. A grossly regressive income tax was introduced in Cambodia in February 1938, but this mainly affected Europeans and *assimilés*. The rate of taxation actually decreased the higher the income. Ibid, "L'impôt personnel au Cambodge", 16 February 1938
[115] Unsigned, (1940), "Les malheureux Kkmers protestent", *La Presse Indochinoise*, 4 January 1940.
[116] Maurel, op.cit.
[117] AOM RSC 432 Rapport Politique, 4ème Trimestre 1925.
[118] AOM Fonds Amiraux 7F 15 (4) *Sûreté* report, 1st July 1925-30 June 1926.
[119] Bardez's fellow ex-servicemen held services at his graveside on All Saints Day for many years. The details of one such ceremony are recorded: "Les

Fêtes de la Toussaint à Phnom Penh", *Bulletin Administratif du Cambodge*, No 66, nouvelle serie, Phnom Penh, November 1936.

[120] Marlowe in Joseph Conrad, (1999), *Heart of Darkness and other Stories*, (Revised Edition), Wordsworth, Ware, Herts. p.34.

[121] ANC RSC C01. File No 14331 Surveillance de la presse de langue indigène janvier - avril 1938.

[122] Huy Kanthoul, op.cit. p.62. *Mésalliance* = "bad match" or "misalliance".

Chapter 16

King Rubber

[The coolies are] human livestock, terrorized by the overseers, and they don't dare complain for fear of bullying and cruelty.
—Émile Desenlis, *Résident* of Kompong Cham, 1927.[1]

The boom of the 1920s saw the beginnings of large-scale plantation agriculture in Cambodia. The most important new crop was rubber, which was planted in the *terres rouges* (red earth) region in the east of the country, hitherto inhabited almost solely by *Montagnard* tribes. Rubber quickly became one of the most lucrative export commodities. At last, it seemed the French dreams of *mise-en-valeur* would bear fruit. There was, however, a dark side to this new development, as the rubber companies pushed the hill tribes off their traditional lands and created a new class of super-exploited rural proletarians to work the plantations.

Although westerners had set up some plantations in the 19th century, these were on a relatively small scale, and the main crop was cotton.[2] Cardamom plantations also existed, particularly in the Pursat region west of the Tonlé Sap, but these tended to be in the hands of Chinese and other Asians and were comparatively small. Early in the 20th century, French observers noted the suitability of parts of

Cambodia for rubber, and considered that certain native species might be commercially exploitable.[3] This proved not to be the case, so settlers introduced the Brazilian rubber tree, *hevea brasiliensis,* into Indochina from Ceylon during this period. By 1907, there were a number of rubber plantations in Cochinchina and Annam and one near Kampot in Cambodia, although this was very small.[4] The industry took off sharply after the end of the war in 1918. Rubber prices increased steadily until the mid-1920s,[5] and the depreciation of the French franc and the piastre stimulated exports and investment in Indochina. So great was the demand due to the expansion of industrial, domestic and military uses for rubber that the well established British plantations in Malaya were unable to meet it, further stimulating activity in Indochina.[6] The red earth districts of eastern Cambodia proved very suitable for rubber trees and the industry established itself as a permanent feature of the region.

The first large plantation was set up at Chup in 1921, followed by a second at Thmar Pitt in 1924 and others at Peam Cheang, Stung Trang and Chamcar Loeu after 1925.[7] Two years later, a French consortium carved out a new plantation under Belgian management at Mimot (sometimes rendered as Memot or Memut). In 1922, there were over 1200 hectares planted in rubber. This increased to almost 6000 hectares in 1925, and jumped again to about 23,000 hectares by 1930. When Cambodia secured its independence, there were over 30,000 hectares planted in rubber.[8] The largest plantations were those at Thmar Pitt, Chup, Peam Cheang and Mimot, all owned by French concerns, the largest of which was the Compagnie du Cambodge. The actual concessions of land handed over to the rubber companies were much larger—over 110,000 hectares by 1926.[9] The bulk of production went to France and by the 1930s, rubber was the most important Indochinese export[10] although in terms of value, it ranked third among Cambodian exports.[11] The Cambodian rubber plantations were smaller than their counterparts in Cochinchina, but were much larger than those in Annam.[12] In 1926, Indochinese rubber exports were worth 280 million francs, but this declined to under 200 million in 1927,[13] partly due to the effects of the Stevenson plan in which representatives of the big rubber producers and consumers agreed to cap prices. The Great Depression adversely affected the industry after 1929-30, but it was kept afloat by a government subsidy of 0.20 piastres per kilogram,[14] probably because rubber was of key strategic importance to French industry and to the military. Much of the military transport in World War I was horse-drawn, with wooden wheels. The debacle of trench warfare convinced military thinkers of the need for rapid motorized units, which required rubber for tires and other applications. When war broke out again in 1939, Nazi Germany was chronically short of rubber. They made up the shortfall partly with synthetic rubber and partly, as we shall see, by imports from Vichy Indochina.[15] Rubber was king of Cambodia's exports, and the plantations were the fiefs of the French rubber companies. The companies stayed on after independence and in the late 1950s, Cambodia was still the world's sixth largest producer of natural rubber.[16]

The human costs of the new plantations were high and began even before workers began to clear the forests. Although shareholders might have believed the plantations were set up on *terra nullius*, much of the land selected for rubber was already occupied. At Mimot, for example, several thousand Stiengs—a hill tribe—lived as they had done for perhaps thousands of years by swidden farming.[17] The company was impatient to begin operations, despite the fact that the Stiengs had already planted their usual crops on the land. When the administration at Phnom Penh baulked at demands by the rubber company for the immediate evacuation of the Stiengs, the well-connected company president Colonel Fernand Bernard[18] wrote to Alexandre Varenne, a former Governor General in Paris to try to speed up proceedings. In the event, despite ""furious opposition" from the Stiengs, a compromise was reached: the company would compensate the Stiengs for the loss of their homes and land, and some parcels of land would be reserved for their exclusive use. The deal was, however, heavily weighted in the company's favor, for as Bernard said, the planters would put the land to much more profitable use than the "primitive tribes"[19] who would also lose their ancestral lands and way of life.

Khmer distaste for plantation work

Once the question of access to land had been settled, the rubber companies faced the problem of finding large numbers of coolies at short notice to clear and plant the new concessions. The hill tribes were reluctant to accept such employment, and even if they had been keen to do so, there were not enough of them. Thick jungle and bamboo had first to be cleared: a particularly onerous task with machetes in the sweltering heat. Roads and accommodation had to be built and some provision made to provide clean water. The reluctance of Cambodians to hire themselves out as wage laborers had caused a great deal of comment in French publications and short of a system of industrial conscription, the rubber companies could never hope to recruit sufficient labor from the Cambodian population.[20] The Cambodians were loath to leave their villages for the jungles, which were infested with malarial mosquitoes, and which they saw as the abode of demons. The Dutch in Java had solved the problem by persuading the peasants to grow rubber as a cash crop to supplement that which was produced on plantations, but this does not seem to have occurred to the French.[21] This may have been because the scheme to get Khmers to grow the castor oil plant as a cash crop in World War I does not seem to have been successful.[22] Khmers remained a minority on the plantations throughout the colonial period. By the late 1920s, they comprised no more than 18 per cent of the over 8000-strong plantation work force. They disliked routine tasks such as weeding, tapping and working in the latex mills and were mainly employed as piece workers, or by the task, on jobs such as clearing forest.[23] An official report considered that the straitened economic circumstances of the early 1930s Depression might make the Khmers more reliable, but this did not happen at this stage.[24] Quite simply, the life of a rural wage laborer did not appeal to independent Khmer peasant proprietors, no matter how small or poor their holdings.

The Tonkinese bonded laborers

The solution lay in the densely populated "rice deficit" regions of Tonkin and northern Annam, where the Vietnamese peasants eked out a hard living on tiny plots of land, or as landless laborers. Beginning in 1919,[25] thousands of the poorest Vietnamese peasants were lured from their villages by the prospect of steady work and food. Over 5000 "coolies" arrived on the plantations between 1925 and 1927 and the *Résident Supérieur* at Phnom Penh considered that it would be necessary to bring a further 14,000 each year to keep pace with the growing demand for labor.[26] By World War II, there were almost 16,000 indentured laborers on eight major plantations in Cambodia, mostly on piecework rates. A further 1000 labored on public works projects.[27]

Recruitment was supervised by the General Manpower Office in Hanoi, working in conjunction with the French administration in Cambodia, although they sub-contracted the actual job of organizing volunteers to Vietnamese middlemen in the towns and villages. Some of these recruiting agents appear to have doubled as usurious moneylenders, playing a role akin to that of the *gombeen* men who profited from misery and mass emigration in mid-nineteenth century Ireland. Certainly, many agents were unscrupulous, promising better wages and conditions than actually applied on the plantations.[28] The recruits signed on as bonded laborers legally contracted to work on the distant plantations for three or four years. All too many of them were to exchange the companionable poverty of their village communities for the bleak and regimented distress of rural barracks. Some were to perish of disease and others were to suffer at the hands of sadistic overseers, and while treatment did vary between plantations, life was always hard. The peasants walked to the coast, where they were herded in their hundreds aboard ships such as the "Merlin", the "Compiègne" and the "Claude Chappe" which lay at the Haiphong docks ready to sail to Saigon.[29] Once at the dock, the peasants were no longer their own masters. Should they run away en route, soldiers would hunt them down and deliver them to the plantations. At Saigon, the coolies transferred to river steamships that took them up the Mekong to Kompong Cham province and the plantations that lay at some days walk from the left bank.

The mature plantations were an impressive sight, with long lines of regimented trees growing where once the unkempt jungle had held sway. The workers tapped the trees by cutting grooves in the trunks. The latex flowed, "pale green during the day and whitish towards evening,"[30] into receptacles that were periodically emptied into larger containers. The liquid latex was processed by heat and rollers in mills, from which it emerged as thick, solid slabs for export. The sight of such vast enterprises stunned the visitor Pierre Billotey when he visited in the late 1920s. In Kompong Cham, he wrote, are huge rubber plantations, richer than anywhere else in French Indochina. Only when you had been there could you comprehend the enormity of the concessions and the huge effort that they entailed.[31] Charles Robequain saw something different, noting the "melancholy gloom" of the plantations.[32] Life was certainly gloomy for the Vietnamese laborers who tended the rubber trees and worked in the latex mills. Although they were not slaves in the strict sense since they were not the permanent property of their masters, they must have wondered at the legal distinction. As with many overseas workers employed on contract in the Gulf States today, they were denied liberty of movement as their employers held their travel documents—in this case their ID cards. They were also forbidden to leave the plantations for any reason, even on their unpaid days off, without written permission from the management. According to labor inspector Delamare, wages and conditions were inferior to those paid for comparable work on Dutch plantations in the East Indies and in French enterprises in the New Hebrides and New Caledonia.[33]

Word of the conditions trickled back to Tonkin, where an "Annamite" newspaper cautioned would-be coolies of the life they could expect in the "deadly places" that were the plantations,

> one is really unhappy, o you who read this. It is tiring work, beating and digging ceaselessly, clearing and cutting the forest throughout the day. It thunders and rains in torrents and the grief and pain, too, are relentless. The sweat and the tears don't dry; the blows and exactions render life too hard to endure. Some people, tired of it all, take flight but alas, they are retaken immediately and led to the place of torture... O Tonkinese, don't be seduced or led into leaving...[34]

Rubber planting is a capital-intensive, risky industry, particularly in the early stages, when the land must be cleared and planted with seedlings. Large amounts of capital must be poured into the business. Many years must pass before the trees mature and the plantation comes on stream. The terrain on the *terres rouges* was rugged, thickly vegetated and difficult to access. Shareholders in such ventures are notoriously close-fisted, willing managers to make do with the smallest possible expenditures and to start making profits in the shortest time. These factors combined to produce a particularly insensitive and onerous work-discipline, which, taken in conjunction with poor wages and appalling living conditions made life unhappy for the laborers.

The "human livestock" at Mimot

Probably, the worst of all plantations was that owned by the Société Indochinoise des Plantations de Mimot situated on high ground near the border with Cochinchina at a place known to the Stiengs as Kchéay. From that plateau, on a clear day, it was possible to glimpse the South China Sea at Cape Saint-Jacques. Life, however, was no sylvan idyll. The rain poured in through the straw roofs of the barracks, foodstuffs were dear or unobtainable and human excrement polluted the water supply. Many of the laborers suffered from suppurating sores caused by punctures from the sharp edges of bamboo they were clearing to make way for rubber trees.[35] Here, in the late 1920s, several thousand laborers were crammed into ramshackle huts, living, in the words of *Résident* Desenlis, "as human livestock, terrorized by the overseers" and not daring to complain "for fear of bullying and cruelty."[36] These appalling conditions first came to official notice when labor inspector Delamare visited the plantation to find out why several hundred coolies had staged a "desertion en masse" to complain to the French *Délégué* at Kratié.[37] Delamare observed the unhealed scars of whipping on the workers' bodies and learned that they had been denied medical treatment. Following the inquiry, the manager, a 31-year-old Belgian named Antoine d'Ursel with many years experience as a planter in the East Indies and the Straits Settlements, was fined 100 francs and reprimanded by the *Inspecteur-Général du Travail* at Hanoi. The French administration also banned the recruitment of additional labor until conditions met their satisfaction. More strikingly, the head overseer, another Belgian national called Jacques Verhelst, was found guilty of assault and battery and expelled from Indochina. This sinister young thug had regularly brutalized the coolies under his command. In one instance, he whipped several women, one of whom was pregnant, with telephone wire attached to a cane for fetching drinking water without his permission when they were thirsty. In another, he tied a young man by his wrists round a verandah post throughout the night and afterwards beat him savagely with a frayed whip, a *nerf de bouef*. Verhelst routinely struck the workers with a bamboo cane, fists and boots, regardless of their age or sex. He meted out such treatment if work quotas were not fulfilled, or for the slightest infractions of the rules. Although Verhelst was the worst offender, the brutality did not cease after his expulsion, with one French official stating that he believed the complaints, even taking into account the "tendency of the Red River people to exaggerate". The court ruled that d'Ursel was aware of much of his subordinates' brutality.[38]

In fact, brutality was common on most of the plantations and was an unofficial part of a work-regime designed to extract the maximum profit from each laborer. In addition, a system of fines was imposed for infractions of work discipline and flight was savagely punished. In practice, these conditions applied to men, women and children, despite the passage of a child labor law in Cambodia in 1924,[39] and further paper reforms during the period of the Popular Front in the 1930s.[40] It seems, however, that after the inquiry into conditions at Mimot, the enthusiasm of the French administration to enforce better treatment began to flag. There was a rash of labor disputes in the late-1920s and early 1930s, and officials must have been reluctant to be associated with radicalism. Probably there was behind-the-scenes string pulling by the rubber companies, their shareholders and political supporters.

Labor Inspector Delamare's report

Rubber workers' wages and conditions remained poor. In 1932, the laborers generally worked ten hours a day, sixty hours a week,[41] but this did not include time spent traveling to and from work, which was not paid. In addition, workers were expected to make up for uncompleted tasks in their own time, although by World War II they had won payment for overtime.[42] The average annual wage in Cambodia and Cochinchina in 1931 was 55 piastres, or 550 French francs. The average French wage was then 6200 francs, and a Moroccan laborer could expect 1850 francs.[43] Before 1929, adult men and women were paid 0.40 and 0.30 piastres respectively per day, although generally they carried out similar tasks. Adolescents received half the adult male rate.[44] Rubber workers' wages were cut by half after the crash of 1929 according to one French report,[45] by a third according to others.[46] In 1941, men were paid 0.32 piastres per day—less than a sixth of the average pay of a French laborer a decade earlier—and women 0.25 per day, scarcely more than after the cuts, although the Depression was largely over and profits had risen steadily after 1935.[47] The work could be dangerous: there were 39 serious accidents in 1940, 32 of them fatal.[48] In 1929, Delamare wrote a devastating account of conditions on the plantations, but much of what he had to say never made it into the final reports to the Governor General in Hanoi.[49] According to reports in the Saigon press, plantation laborers suffered a serious calorific deficiency[50] and this was confirmed by internal reports. Inspector Delamare estimated that the daily calorific intake for male coolies at Mimot was 2297, compared with 2907 for a Tonkinese *tirailleur* (the latter augmented to 3582 calories on active service). All the workers were malnourished.[51] All plantations gave a free ration of rice, another report noted, but added that; "no plantation feeds its coolies properly." Meals were generally of rice (usually second grade and often moldy) and dried fish and there was a general insufficiency of fresh foods, including fruit, vegetables, meat and fish. Regarding claims that the coolies were used to it, an inspector countered that it was "an enforced frugality". Most plantations made no effort to establish fruit trees or vegetable gardens, sometimes claiming they would not grow in the red earth. The inspector noted, however, that the French commander of the Native Guards at Mimot had a fine vegetable garden "*en pleine terre rouge*" and that one plantation manager, M. Chollet[52] at Snoul, had, established a "superb" kitchen garden for his laborers. Doctors were critical of the laborers' diet, but management generally ignored their recommendations. Housing conditions were generally inadequate and sometimes unsanitary. Most laborers lived in corrugated iron barracks in groups of two to ten, some on concrete floors, but more often on dirt. All plantations did have running water, however. Medical facilities were usually "poor or bad", with sanitary facilities particularly bad at Mimot, Stung Trang and Kantroy plantations.[53] Even at Thmar Pitt, comparatively well run by a boxer and old Malaya hand called Camus, the lavatories (which served both men and women) consisted of an open concrete drain with a thatched roof over it. Delamare reported that, "The [fecal] matter remains in the gutter, exposed to the air and flies and from time to time is expelled with a jet of water."[54] Because of the general lack of hygiene, outbreaks of cholera, dysentery and other diseases were common. Mortality rates ranged from 0.8 to 3.0 per cent, with "spikes" during epidemics. During one epidemic at Kantroy, the entire European staff fled to Saigon, and the native nurses likewise left their posts.[55] Presumably, the luxury of flight was forbidden the laborers. Malaria was endemic, along with tropical ulcers and trachoma. Psychiatric ailments such as depression were common.[56] Dysentery was widespread; as was nephritis; along with skin diseases such as scabies and mange; respiratory ailments including bronchitis; and diseases due solely to deficient diet, including beriberi and pernicious anemia.[57] The inspector's report was heavily edited and sent to Hanoi with the claim that, "the employers recognize the importance of food for the health of their workers".[58] It should be noted, however, that the work of the Pasteur Institute did much to combat malaria. The simplest solution was better drainage, although the Institute also recommended the more ecologically doubtful measure of spraying with petrol, fuel oil and paris green.[59]

Psychological damage

Yet, even when steps were taken to improve nutrition and hygiene, the quality of life remained poor on the plantations. The laborers and their families were typically housed in barracks, constructed of either corrugated iron or woven bamboo, divided into compartments by wattle-and-daub screens, for smaller groups. These somber edifices each commonly housed anywhere between 40 and 100 coolies, depending on their dimensions. The roofs often leaked—at Mimot, the monsoon rains actually poured in through a gap the width of a hand where the ridge capping ought to have been—and the huts sometimes stood in pools of mud and water. At Mimot, swarms of flies milled ceaselessly. Truly, the laborers were human livestock—beasts of burden. Inspector Delamare, commenting on Mimot—which in fairness he viewed as by far the worst of the plantations—said "The European personnel seem not to want to lower themselves to treat the coolie with kindness...the existence of the Tonkinese coolies is miserable and pitiful..."[60]

This conscientious and humane man also noted something less obvious about even the best of the barracks: the psychological damage they inflicted in their inmates. The Tonkinese peasants, he wrote, were used to private family life and individual liberty in their native villages. On the plantations, in contrast, they were housed in soulless, military-style accommodation, their lives punctuated by the sounds of the "trumpet or whistle". They should have been able, he argued, to retire each evening to the company of their family, or to that of a small group of friends. Where the conditions of their native villages were reproduced, he claimed, the workers were in good spirits, very lively and gay, in well-kept houses with furniture, lamps, photographs and other simple confirmations of their humanity. It would not cost much, given the warm climate of Cambodia, Delamare added, to provide *maisonettes* grouped in villages, in streets and courtyards, with little gardens and wells. The rubber companies, however, retorted that housing in barracks made it easier to keep the workers under surveillance and to ensure cleanliness. It was regrettable, Delamare said, that the Health Service agreed with them.[61] The barracks continued and contributed heavily to the "gloom" noted by Robequain. It was the sorrow of alienated humanity far from home.

"Sons of bitches and starvation wages"

For their part, the laborers bitterly resented the conditions in which they lived and worked. More than two decades after the plantations came on stream, and despite some amelioration of conditions, even highly skilled craftsmen still found numerous grounds for complaint. In 1944, the police intercepted a letter sent by a former employee to a friend still on the Mimot plantation. The writer, who had found better work as a fitter in a Saigon power station, wrote: "Here the wages are very high! Not like the starvation wages at Mimot", adding that the French bosses on the plantation were "sons of bitches" who treated their workers badly.[62] The plantation workers responded to ill treatment and poor conditions in a number of ways, including flight, physical retaliation against particularly brutal overseers, and collective action to win better conditions. The French disapproved of all of them. One of the worst plantations was Kantroy, where coolies attacked a surveyor named Pellen with machetes and rubber tapping knives in 1929.[63] Rates of desertion were always high, although they leveled off somewhat towards World War II. There were 228 desertions from nine plantations during the first trimester of 1929, and of these only 67 were retaken.[64] In the last six months of the previous year, another 365 had fled, many of them the day after arriving. One evening in December 1935, 300 laborers deserted together. The police and militia combed the forests throughout the night, rounding up all but 13 of the escapees.[65] There were also numerous fines and other punishments for "bad will" and infractions of the rules.[66] Brawls and riots were said to be "habitual".[67] In the late 1920s, desertions were so frequent that special surveillance squads patrolled the neighboring Vietnamese provinces of Thudaumot and Tayninh, hoping to intercept fleeing laborers.[68] Under the impact first of the Depression, and later of improving conditions—although not wages—some indentured laborers chose to stay on as free workers, but desertion rates always remained high. Ninety per cent of those who escaped evaded recapture.[69] Out of over 13,000 rubber coolies in 1939, almost 1700, or roughly 13 per cent deserted.[70]

The desertions troubled the authorities, but the bad conditions led early to militant labor action, including strikes, go-slows and work-to-rule protests. The plantations became—and remained—a stronghold of the Indochinese Communist Party. Significantly, however, the Cambodian workers remained largely aloof from the militancy of their Vietnamese counterparts. Industrial action reached a peak around 1930. In July 1930, 100 Tonkinese walked off the job at Chup plantation, claiming breaches of their employment contracts. A few days later 300 workers struck at Thmar Pitt.[71] The *Résident* of Kompong Cham reported that coolies had again walked off the Chup plantation in August in protest over the brutality of a French supervisor, M. Hertel. Although the *Résident* spoke to the workers, the following day they launched a go-slow campaign. In this case, they won. M. Hertel was replaced and legal action instituted against him by the police.[72] Over 200 workers at Peam Cheang repeated the tactic a few days later, complaining of excessive hours of work and inadequate medical facilities. The strikers were jailed for five days for disturbing the peace by marching on Kompong Cham. Thereafter, the strikes, go slows and riots intensified, particularly after the wage cuts of 1929. The authorities kept an eye open for itinerant agitators, two of whom were seized near Kandal Chrum in late 1930 for traveling without identity cards.[73] Other Communist "ringleaders" who came to the attention of the police held responsible posts, such as Phung Dang Khoa, an accounts clerk on the Thmar Pitt plantation.[74] Although industrial action declined as the effects of the crisis took hold, and there were widespread cutbacks to the workforce, it was never entirely absent, despite heavy penalties, such as jail, for putting up placards.[75] The organizers of a demonstration against piecework at Stung Trang in June 1933 were sacked and deported.[76] After the effects of the slump began to ease after 1936, and large numbers of workers were rehired, there was a resurgence of militant activity on the plantations, such as at Chup in May 1936.[77] The *Résident* of Kompong Cham warned that despite the perceptions of economists and newspapermen, strikes were far more common during periods of prosperity than during slumps.[78]

The plantations remained hotbeds of militancy until the last years of French rule, as was shown by a general strike across the plantations in 1950. According to Wilfred Burchett, the strike won a general wage increase, better food, and an end to the assault and detention of workers.[79] By that time, Cambodia and the rest of Indochina were only a few years away from the battle of Dien Bien Phu and King Sihanouk's "royal crusade for independence".[80] Repressive as it was, colonialism also contained the seeds of its own destruction. In 1931, the grand organizer of the Intercolonial Exposition, Marshal Lyautey, sent the writer Guy de Pourtalès to Cambodia to report on what he saw. Lyautey was the doyen of France's old soldiers and had spent much of his life battling rebels in North Africa. He passionately believed in France's *mission civilisatrice* and the Exposition was the culmination of his life's work. In some ways, de Pourtalès was a poor choice of literary emissary. Like Karl Marx before him, he observed the fatal flaw of the colonial project, citing a Vietnamese intellectual who noted that although France oppressed the colonial peoples, the spirit of their liberation also came from France.[81]

Notes

[1] ANC RSC M17/M12 (1267) File 1108. Incidents de plantation de Mimot, 1927. Rapport sur la manifestation de 330 coolies des plantations de Mimot le 19 août 1927, et sur l'état particulièrement mauvais de la main-d'oeuvre tonkinoise employée sur ces plantations à cette date. No 65-C.

[2] See, for example, the article on the success of Cambodian cotton plantations in *Le Mékong*, No. 122, 7 November 1894, Hanoi.

[3] See, for example, the *Bulletin Économique de l'Indochine:* "Une liane à caoutchouc signalée au Cambodge" (1900, No 30 as, p.748); "Notes sur une liane à caoutchouc de la Cochinchine... et le Cambodge" (1901, No 39 as, pp.802-804); "Lianes à caoutchouc du Cambodge" (1901, No 41 as pp.1015-1016).

[4] "Les plantations de caoutchouc en Cochinchine, en Annam et au Cambodge", *Bulletin Économique de l'Indochine*, No 109 ns, 1914, pp.592-593. See also

[5] "La hausse du caoutchouc et l'application du plan Stevenson", *L'Avenir du Cambodge,* 30 January 1926.

[6] See D.G.E. Hall, (1968), *A History of South-East Asia,* Third Edition, Macmillan, London, p.789.

[7] AOM RSC 422 Report of the *Résident* of Kompong Cham, 1924-1935. Stung Trang is not to be confused with the similar sounding Stung Treng.

[8] Rémy Prud'homme, (1969), *L'Economie du Cambodge,* Presses Universitaires de France, Paris, Tableau 14, "Culture de l'hévea, 1920-1965".

[9] AOM RSC 432, Rapport d'Ensemble, 1925-1926.

[10] Robert Aldrich, (1996), *A History of French Overseas Expansion,* Macmillan, Basingstoke. p.190.

[11] ANC RSC D35 File 8982 Box 789. Préparation du Livre Vert, 1938-1929. In 1939, Cambodian rubber exports were worth 16,000,000 piastres, compared with 28,000,000 for corn and 24,000,000 for rice.

[12] Paul Renon, (1940), "Evolution de l'Économie Indochinoise", *Indochine Hebdomadaire Illustré,* Hanoi, 12 September.

[13] CMIDOM, Château de Vincennes, 15 H 10 3 Les troubles d'Indochine.

[14] ANC RSC D35 File 5905 Box 579 Minute du Livre Verte, Cambodge. Rapport sur l'exercice du protectorat, 1931-1932. The price of rubber varied from 0.50 to 0.70 piastres per kilogram before the crash, when it fell to around 0.35 piastres. The government subsidy was 0.20 piastres per kilo.

[15] CMIDOM documents quoted in this chapter show the French military command's keen interest in the Indochinese rubber industry.

[16] Wilfred Burchett, (1957), *Mekong Upstream,* Red River Publishing House, Hanoi, p.50n.

[17] Otherwise known as slash-and-burn or shifting cultivation. The *Montagnards* traditionally had cut clearings from the forest and burned the wood. The ash fertilized the thin jungle soil, enabling the farmers to plant crops for three or four years, after which they would move on. Practiced on a small scale by a small population, it was probably an ecologically sustainable form of farming.

[18] Colonel Bernard was an old colonial hand and was France's chief negotiator in the talks leading to the retrocession of Battambang and Siem Reap from Siam in 1908. He was thus a man of considerable influence. (His experiences as a negotiator are recorded in F.A. Bernard, (1933), *A l'École des Diplomates: La Perte et le Retour dÁngkor,* Les Oeuvres Representatives, Paris.)

[19] ANC RSC M14 File 8226 "Plantation de Mimot: problèmes de développement et de la main d'oeuvre, 1927." Compensation was paid at a rate of 12 piastres per hectare and 6 piastres per dwelling.

[20] See, for instance, M. Potel, (1900), "Les travailleurs de la terre", *Le Petit Cambodgien,* Phnom Penh, 28 January.

[21] The Javanese peasants grew 50 per cent of the island's rubber on their smallholdings. See Hall, op.cit. pp.788-789.

[22] The scheme is discussed in AOM RSC 430 Rapport Économique 1917. Huy Kanthoul recalls a teacher asking her pupils to "Tell your parents to plant castor oil plants. The administration will buy the crop at a price of 5.10 piastres per picul." (Huy Kanthoul, "Mémoires", p.44. Unpublished French-language-typescript. Chandler Papers, Monash University.)
[23] ANC RSC E 03 File 9279 Box 818. Rapports trimestriels et annuels de la Résidence de Kompong Cham, 1929. Rapport Politique 1er Trimestre 1929. The breakdown of the work force by ethnic origin and/or place of origin on the nine plantations was as follows: Cochinchinese, 153; Tonkinese, 6554; Cambodians, 1459; Europeans, 33. The latter were all in managerial or supervisory positions.
[24] ANC D35 File 499 Box 38. Inspection du Travail au Cambodge, Rapport Annuel, 1 July 1932-30 June 1933.
[25] Charles Robequain, (trans. Isabel A. Ward), (1944), *The Economic Development of French Indo-China,* Oxford University Press, London, p.78.
[26] RSC 432 Rapport d'Ensemble, 1925-1927. ANC RSC D35 Rapport d'Ensemble, 1926-1927.
[27] AOM RSC 263 Rapport Annuel 1940-41. Minute Livre Verte. (Contract laborers from Annam and Tonkin, 1 June 1940 – 31 May 1941.)
[28] Labor Inspector Delamare named two agents at Nam Dinh and Haiphong in particular as giving false verbal promises. (ANC RSC M14/M10 File 8218, Part II.)
[29] ANC RSC M14 File 8222. Recrutement de main d'oeuvre la Société des Plantations de Mimot.
[30] Description in *Trung-Hoa-Nhat-Bao,* journal annamite, 16 juillet 1927 in ANC RSC M17/M12 (1267) File 1108 Incidents de plantation de Mimot, 1927.
[31] Pierre Billotey, (1929), *L'Indochine en zigzags,* Albin Michel, Paris, p.223.
[32] Robequain, op.cit. pp. 212-215.
[33] ANC RSC M14/M10 File 8218. Rapport sur la situation matérielle et morale des émigrés tonkinois employés sur les plantations de la Cie du Cambodge et du Syndicat de Mimot, 28 avril 1927, signé Inspecteur du Travail Delamare.
[34] ANC RSC M17/M12 (1267) File 1108 Incidents de plantation de Mimot, 1927. Extrait du *Trung-Hoa-Nhat-Bao,* journal annamite, 16 juillet 1927, op.cit.
[35] ANC RSC M14/M10 File 8218, op.cit.
[36] ANC RSC M17/M12 (1267) File 1108. Incidents de plantation de Mimot, 1927. Rapport sur la manifestation de 330 coolies des plantations de Mimot le 19 août 1927, et sur l'état particulièrement mauvais de la main-d'oeuvre tonkinoise employée sur ces plantations à cette date. No 65-C.
[37] ANC RSC M17/M12 (1267) File 1108. Letter from the *Résident* at Kompong Cham to the *Résident Supérieur,* 30 August 1927.
[38] Information from numerous official letters and reports in ANC M17/M12 (1267) File 1108, Incidents de plantation de Mimot, 1927.

[39] Thomas E. Ennis, (1936), *French Policy and Development in Indochina*, University of Chicago Press, Chicago, p.159.

[40] See Chapter 14 above.

[41] CMIDOM 15 H 10 3. L'organisation du travail en Indochine.

[42] AOM RSC 263 op.cit.

[43] Naval Intelligence Division, (194?), *Indo-China*, London, pp.298-299 and ANC RSC M14/M10 File 8218, op.cit.

[44] ANC RSC D35 File 2799 Box 288. Rapport sur la situation du Cambodge, 1927-1928. Section III, Inspection du Travail. Note, this document was a draft only.

[45] AOM RSC 433 Révoltes au Cambodge. Note confidentielle, Surêté, Phnom Penh to Résident Supérieur, 11 August 1930.

[46] ANC D35 File 499 Box 38. Inspection du Travail au Cambodge, Rapport Annuel, 1 July 1932-30 June 1933, op.cit. and AOM RSC 423 Livre vert du Cambodge, 1935-1936, Chapitre II Inspection du Travail.

[47] Unsigned article, (1936), "L'Orientation Économique du Cambodge. Le Caoutchouc", *La Presse Indochinoise*, 1 October. Cambodian rubber was worth around 400 piastres a tonne in 1935. This rose to 500 piastres, then 550 in 1936.

[48] AOM RSC 263, Rapport Annuel 1940-1941, op.cit.

[49] ANC RSC D35 File 2799 Box 288, op.cit.

[50] "L'offensive contre l'inspection du travail en Indochine", *La Tribune Indochinoise*, 7 March 1930.

[51] ANC RSC M14/M10 File 8218, op.cit. Part II , Visite du groupe des plantations de Mimot.

[52] M. Chollet later published his memoirs: Raoul Chollet, (1981), *Planteurs en Indochine Française,* La Pensée Universelle, Paris. A report from 1939 singled out his plantation for its "numerous desertions". (ANC RSC E 03 File 9246 Box 814. Rapport Annuel de Kompong Cham, 1938-1939.)

[53] ANC RSC D35 File 2799, Box 288 op.cit.

[54] ANC RSC M14/M10, File 8218, Part I, op.cit.

[55] ANC RSC D35 File 2799, Box 288 op.cit.

[56] ANC E 03 File 9729 Box 818. Circonscription médicale de Kompong Cham, Rapport du 2ème Trimestre, 1929.

[57] ANC RSC E 03 File 9279 Box 818, op.cit.

[58] ANC D35 File 2800 Box 288. Rapport sur l'exercice du Protectorat pendant la période 1929-1930.

[59] Robequain, op. cit. p.78. In the longer term, the problem of malaria has seldom been permanently solved anywhere in the world by chemical means alone.

[60] ANC RSC M17/M12 (1267) File 1108, op.cit.

[61] ANC RSC M14/M10 File 8218 op.cit.

[62] AOM RSC 308. Copy of letter sent by De Van Tam at Cholon to Dinh Van Khang at Mimot. Intercepted by the *Surêté* and sent to the Inspector of Labor for Cambodia, 29 August 1944.

[63] ANC RSC D35 File 2799, Box 288 op.cit.

[64] ANC RSC E 03 File 9279 Box 818, op.cit.

[65] AOM RSC 424. Livre Vert, 1935-36. Rapport Annuel, Kompong Cham, 1935-26.

[66] ANC RSC D35 File 2799, Box 288 op.cit

[67] ANC RSC E03 File 9279 Box 818. Rapport Trimestriel (2ème trimestre 1929), Kompong Cham.

[68] Ibid. Rapport Politique Annuel, 1929. This is a draft, and the information has been crossed out.

[69] AOM RSC 422. Annual report of the *Résident* of Kompong Cham, 1934-35. In 1943, there were only 470 "free coolies", including indentured laborers who re-enlisted, and over 17,500 indentured laborers. (AOM RSC 675, Rapport Annuel, June 1942-June 1943.)

[70] ANC RSC D35 File 8982 Box 789, Préparation du Livre Vert, 1938-1939, op.cit.

[71] AOM RSC 218 Surêté Envoi No 592-SS, Rapport Annuel, 31 mai -1er juin 1930.

[72] ANC RSC E03 File 9279 Box 818, Rapport Politique annuel 1929, Kompong Cham.

[73] ANC E03 File 9248 Box 814 Compte-rendu tournée de police, post de Kandal Chrum, 4 – 7 décembre 1930.

[74] AOM RSC 225. Surveillance des activités communistes, 1930-31. *Surêté* to the *Résident Supérieur*, 4 February 1931.

[75] ANC RSC D35 File 499 Box 38 Rapport Annuel, June 1932 – June 1933, Kompong Cham.

[76] Ibid. Inspection du Travail au Cambodge, Rapport annuel, 1 juillet 1932 – 30 juin 1933.

[77] *La Presse Indochinoise,* 18 May 1936.

[78] AOM RSC 424 Livre Vert, 1935-36. Rapport annuel, Kompong Cham.

[79] Burchett, op.cit. p.134.

[80] See Chapter 25 below.

[81] Guy de Pourtalès, op.cit. p.75.

Chapter 17

The Fall of France and the Franco-Thai War

[The Franco-Thai Treaty] is a cornerstone for the establishment of the Greater East Asia prosperity sphere [and] Japan will not tolerate any obstruction of this program.

— Japanese Foreign Ministry, 1941.[1]

The 1920s and 1930s were the halcyon years of the Protectorate. French administrators and the Khmer elite alike must have considered that the future would look very like what they had known during the preceding twenty years. There would be stability, order, and a sense of progress. While the world depression had been an ugly interlude, the economy had picked up by the late-1930s and although one did not need to be clairvoyant to see the approaching war between Germany and the West, national pride insisted that *les Boches* would once again be seen off. During the Munich crisis of late 1938, Monivong pledged his fidelity to France[2] and in the following year his sons Monireth and Monipong volunteered for active service in Europe.[3] The fall of France in the northern summer of 1940 shattered these assumptions. Furthermore, Japanese troops were massing on the northern borders of

French Indochina. Thoughtful Khmers must have wondered if the protecting power could actually protect them.

The fall of France was sudden and swift after the "phony war". The German armies poured through the Ardennes, slicing deep into the heart of France and a generation after the Marne and Verdun, Hitler's men goose-stepped under the Arc de Triomph and sauntered down the boulevards of Paris. On 22 June 1940, Hitler forced France's demoralized leaders to sign the surrender in the same railroad carriage at Compiègne in which Germany had yielded in 1918. France's theoretically powerful army was smashed and a million demoralized *poilus* were herded behind barbed wire in Germany. Worse than the physical defeat was the psychological trauma. Right wing politicians stitched up an armistice with the victors. Half of the country was to be governed from the resort town of Vichy by a geriatric former war hero, Philippe Pétain, while the northern half was ruled directly by the Nazis. The Vichy regime repudiated France's alliance with Britain, its language stridently pro-Axis as it turned its back on "decadent" democracy. Official anti-Semitism poisoned the air of the puppet-state and seeped into the colonial press in Indochina and beyond. The ringing democratic slogans of the Jacobins—"Liberty, Fraternity and Equality"—were jettisoned for the prosaic imperatives of an authoritarian state: "Work, Family, and Fatherland". It was an enormous moral collapse.

Monivong's disillusionment with France

Far away in Cambodia, old King Monivong, already sick from the pampered excesses of his life, slid into terminal depression. In July 1940, the new Governor General, Admiral Decoux, paid him a visit in Phnom Penh. The King received him courteously and assured him of his loyalty to the new head of state, Marshal Pétain.[4] However, within a few months his health declined markedly, Decoux observed. Never the one to interest himself with the routine of state affairs even in happier times, Monivong locked himself away on his country estates at Pursat, Kompong Speu or Kampot with his family, mistress and cronies, and took no further notice of his obligations to protocol. According to Decoux, Monivong's last months were spent in idleness, except for days when his old passions for modern rice farming, furniture making or casting busts of himself in concrete were rekindled. He developed what Decoux tartly calls "a marked difficulty with our language"[5] and refused to meet with French officials or even speak their language. He must have been profoundly disillusioned, for he spoke French fluently. He had graduated proudly from the Saint-Maixent military academy and risen to the rank of brigadier general in the French army. His sons had passed out from haughty Saint-Cyr. In sophisticated circles, he could pass as a "brown Frenchman", a trifle diffident perhaps, but unswervingly loyal. The fall of France was a catastrophe, far worse than the capitulation of Napoleon III at Sedan in 1870, for there were German troops permanently on French soil. How, he must have mused, could this "tiger with broken teeth"[6] protect Cambodia? Many other Cambodians must have shared his fears. Others must have sensed that the road to their own liberation lay in France's powerlessness, an Asian equivalent of the Irish adage that "England's disadvantage is Ireland's opportunity". If so, that view was to be strengthened in the years to come as Siam and Japan moved to take advantage of France's weakness.

Former Governor General Albert Sarraut had once asked himself the same question and concluded that Indochina could not be defended. Sarraut even floated the idea of handing over the French Asian territories to the British Empire in the event of war. The coastline of Indochina is long and France is far away. France did have warships at Tourane and Saigon, but they were antiquated and their admirals had scarcely seen a shot fired in anger.[7] Governor General Decoux himself was described as one of the many French admirals who had not seen battle.[8] The days of the swashbuckling naval officers who had carved out this Asian empire were long gone. The air force was small and relied on old airplanes.[9] It was no better on land. The French garrisons were relatively small[10] and the loyalty of the Vietnamese troops in particular was suspect; there were revolts in Tonkin between 1938 and 1940.[11] Their weapons were old, their commanders bogged in routine, and their ideas of strategy and tactics were still stuck in the trenches of Verdun or the Somme.[12] A French-Australian wool buyer, Pierce Robin, who had served in the French army in Indochina in 1940, described the French forces as "lamentably weak" in an interview with Australian military intelligence.[13] A determined enemy with imaginative commanders would find few obstacles to victory here, for all the bluff that there were around two million men of military age in Indochina and that "the Cambodian *tirailleur* is robust, well-disciplined and of certain loyalty."[14] In 1938, M. Georges Mandel, the Colonial Minister in the Daladier Government, had sought to boost military spending on Indochina, but it was too little too late.[15] The French also launched a recruiting drive for *tirailleurs* in Cambodia, calling for volunteers and, as in 1916, conscripting the recalcitrant if quotas were not met.[16]

During the phony war, French propaganda praised "the invincible alliance" between Britain and France and displayed a photograph in *L'Echo du Cambodge* showing France's Admiral Darlan with Admiral Sir Dudley Pound. "Germany," the article claimed, "is already vanquished on the seas".[17] After the German attack began in Europe, a headline in *La Presse Indochinoise* made the astounding claim of "One million German soldiers killed in the north of France."[18] It was propaganda for consumption by fools. France was incapable of defending itself or Indochina. In 1940, General Raoul Catroux was called from his retirement to become Governor General of Indochina—the first soldier to hold the position in fifty years—but by then, the situation was hopeless.[19]

Two threats: Japan and Thailand

There were two looming threats: the Japanese armies to the north in China, and those of an increasingly truculent Siam, renamed Thailand by her revanchist rulers. By 1939, Japan's armies had fought their way to southern China, impelled by an unshakeable faith in their country's manifest destiny as "the sun over Asia". In the words of the propagandist Ichiro Kudo, the editor of the *Osaka Mainsuchi* in the mid-1930s, "The aggressive movement of Japan south is her oldest mission."[20] The years following the Meiiji Restoration in 1868 had seen Japan develop into a modern military-industrial power with the same imperialist impulse as the western powers. Beyond China lay the sprawling lands of Indochina, Burma, India and the archipelagos and peninsulas ruled by the Dutch, the British and the Americans—full of the wealth Japan coveted for the factories of the crammed Home Islands. To the west, the high mountains and plateaux of Yunnan and Tibet blocked the swift passage of the Japanese armies. Their most convenient land route to the south lay through the deltas, broad valleys and coastal plains of Vietnam and Cambodia. Indochina, it is clear with hindsight, was itself a coveted prize for Japan because of its raw materials. Even before World War II broke out in Europe, the Japanese Government demanded passage for troops and equipment through Tonkin in order to attack the Chinese nationalists from the rear. This was in breach of the Nanking Convention, but "panic stricken", the French Government agreed to the Japanese demands.[21] In contrast with the ill equipped and unreliable French colonial troops, the Japanese were well armed, with motorized infantry and artillery units and excellent discipline.[22] They possessed one submachine gun per three or four soldiers, compared with one light automatic weapon for every dozen French soldiers.[23] Numbers of French indigenous troops immediately deserted to the Japanese.[24]

France was also worried about Thai designs on French territory in Cambodia and Laos. In March 1935, the Siamese King Prajadipok had abdicated and a group of nationalist army officers had taken over the government and put a nine-year-old regent on the throne.[25] Earlier, in 1932, the army had intervened to put an end to the corruption of the Siamese princes. These events did not worry the French; in fact they appear to have had sympathy for the aims of the officers[26] and relations with Siam warmed throughout the 1920s[27] and led to an official visit to Cambodia by the Siamese King and Queen in May 1930.[28] As the decade wore on, however, alarming signals began to emanate from Bangkok. The French writer André Gaudel writes of "perfidious attacks" on France in the Bangkok press in November 1936.[29] In 1937, the Thai Government demanded the re-negotiation of the "unequal" treaty of 1925,[30] which had granted rights of extra-territoriality to French citizens and restricted Siam's rights to impose tariffs on imports from Indochina.[31] France abandoned these privileges in a new treaty signed in early December 1937.[32] Although the treaty defused tensions for a while, alarming rumors of Thailand's growing military strength and new-found bellicosity persisted, along with propaganda in the Bangkok press about the "injustices" of the retrocession of the provinces of Battambang and Siem Reap to Cambodia in 1907. In 1936, the writer H.G. Quaritch Wales saw in some public gardens in Bangkok a flowerbed laid out as a map of Thailand and including the "lost provinces".[33] The following year, French military intelligence noted that militant nationalist propaganda was widespread and that the Thai government had again increased military spending.[34] Moreover, many leading Thai politicians and military men were Nazi sympathizers and "partisans of dictatorship" in their own country, even sending presents to Hitler, Goering and von Blomberg.[35] Even more ominously, Thailand had grown increasingly friendly with the Japanese, with negotiations under way for a new treaty between Bangkok and Tokyo.[36] Some years previously, the friendship had caused the Siamese delegation to the League of Nations to abstain on the Lytton Report, which had condemned Japanese aggression in Manchuria. The Thais, wrote one observer, have "turned their backs on the West and look to Tokyo for guidance." The volume of imports from Japan was growing and increasing numbers of Thais were studying in Japan in preference to Europe. There were rumors, too, of secret treaties that would enable Japan to set up naval and air bases in Thailand.[37]

By 1939, France was a rabbit mesmerized by snakes. In January 1940, fearful of provoking the Thais while France's attention was focused on the European war, the Indochinese authorities forbade the publication of anything likely to offend Bangkok.[38] Cambodian Palace Minister Thiounn dismissed a *Nagaravatta* article that warned of the Siamese threat, advising Khmers to "have confidence in the French Government."[39] On the very eve of World War II, the *Résident* at Battambang reported that the Khmers were "confident in French protection" and that relations with Siam were conducted with "perfect courtesy".[40] In fact, Thailand had been steadily building her military strength and by 1940, her air and ground forces outnumbered those in Indochina.[41] Only her naval forces lagged behind, despite attempts to boost them throughout the 1930s with Japanese and Italian assistance, with orders for submarines, torpedo boats and battleships from Axis shipyards.[42] By 1940, despite the apparent hesitation of Premier Pibul Songkram,[43] Thailand was seething with irredentist sentiment. *Phra* Sarasas, the extreme nationalist and pro-Japanese ex-Minister for Economic Affairs, claimed that,

> the parental stem [of the Thai nation] left in Yunnan still numbers about 26,000,000 people, and the territories annexed by France and Britain contain some 5,000,000 of the Thai people, hence all in all the Thai can boast 46,000,000 souls.[44]

Irredentist frenzy in Thailand

The fall of France in the summer of 1940 removed Thai fears that the French could resist their designs on Cambodian and Lao territory. As early as June 1940, Thai forces began to build up at Aranya, close to the border with Cambodia.[45] They received encouragement from the Japanese, who themselves had taken advantage of France's humiliation to demand the right to station troops, warplanes and naval vessels in Indochina. This was granted after a Japanese attack on Lang Son in Tonkin on 24 September and the mass desertion of France's indigenous troops following the first Japanese shots.[46] Afterwards, the Japanese behaved as an army of occupation.[47] By late 1940, the British Government considered that the Thai nationalists, including the Premier, were in "a frenzy of indignation against Indo China".[48] French residents in Thailand, including priests, were insulted and roughed up in cells and later deported[49] and a pro-French Dutch journalist was murdered.[50] *Luang* Vichitr Vadhakarn (otherwise known as Wichit), a super-nationalist playwright who also served as Director-

General of Fine Arts at Bangkok was instrumental in whipping up the hullabaloo. Wichit had great influence on the Thai Cabinet, despite being "a charlatan and a buffoon, as well as a noisy demagogue", lamented the British Ambassador, Sir Josiah Crosby.[51] Propaganda films played in Bangkok cinemas to enthusiastic crowds. Crowds demonstrated in the streets. The playwright Wichit dramatized the Thai claim to Cambodia in the play *Rajamanu*:

> **Soldier:** The Khmer are surely very similar to us Thais in their appearance?
> **Rajamanu:** Why, what are they too but Thais? Coming by chance into the country of the ancient Khom, they acquired the name "Khmer". The name "Khmer" is an entirely fictitious name for them, in fact they are Thais and our younger brothers.[52]

The Thais distributed pamphlets in Indochina calling for the return of Laos and Cambodia, despite formal diplomatic protests[53] and a so-called "Free Khmer Party" was formed later in Bangkok.[54] Ambassador Crosby believed that "The collapse of France has gone to the heads of the Thais and [the] lure of the lost provinces is now in their blood." Indeed, he believed that the Thais wanted to absorb all of Cambodia.[55] For their part, the French concluded that, "the spilling of blood is inevitable". Following a long series of border "incidents" and allegations of over-flights of each other's territory by both sides, the border between Indochina and Thailand was closed on 20 October 1940.[56] France had no friends. An appeal by Vichy to Berlin that "it was not in the interest of the white races to hand Indo-China over to Japanese, Chinese, and Siamese troops" was ignored in that bastion of "racial purity".[57] British Government documents make it clear that Vichy could expect no help from "perfidious Albion" either. The policy of both Britain and the United States was to try to buy favor with the Thais at the expense of the Japanese, even if that meant the occupation of all, or large portions of Indochina by Thailand. The following month, the Secretary of State for Dominion Affairs informed the Australian Prime Minister that the British would accept such an occupation "without too much protest". The British felt that if Indochina was to "go", then it was preferable that as much of it as possible went to Thailand rather than Japan.[58] At the same time, the British and Americans conspired to prevent a French fleet, including an old aircraft carrier with some aircraft, the *Béarn*, from sailing from Martinique in the Caribbean to reinforce their Indochinese squadrons.[59] The Anglo-Americans were worried that the troops and aircraft might be used for the benefit of the Axis powers,[60] although the US made a half-hearted—and unsuccessful—attempt to get Australia to supply some military aircraft after a Vichy mission to Washington DC.[61] Perhaps at root, too, was the age-old mistrust between the two powers on opposite sides of the English Channel. The British had long considered Thailand to be within their sphere of influence and had previously considered that the Thais had a legitimate claim to "Monthon Burapha". The British Prime Minister Winston Churchill was an avid imperialist and may have been motivated by a desire to punish the "hereditary rival"—even if this meant a shared interest with Japan. As one grandiloquent Briton put it in 1941: "Lord Randolph Churchill once said: 'Ulster will fight and Ulster will be right.' His son has said: 'Thailand will fight, and she will not fight alone'."[62] The British Government went so far as to ask Australia to supply steel for a Thai graving dock in late 1941[63] and to send military advisors and artillery to Bangkok in the same year. The Anglo-Americans also considered sending the Thais military aircraft, despite earlier blocking the departure of the *Béarn*.[64] This "appeasement" policy was not successful, for Thailand declared war on Britain in late 1942.[65] Given the supply of rubber—a crucial war material—by the Vichy authorities in Indochina to Nazi Germany and Japan, this assiduous courting of the Thais was understandable.[66] However, the realization that the Anglo-Americans would not oppose their designs on French territory only encouraged the Thais in their irredentist agenda. The stage was set to let slip the dogs of war.

War on the Thai frontier

The demoralized French probably knew that the game was up even before concerted hostilities broke out. In late September 1940, the *Résident Supérieur* ordered his subordinates at Kompong Thom to prepare to evacuate all archives and munitions to the capital:[67] a remarkably defeatist move, given that the former town lies several hundred kilometers south of the Thai border. From this period onward, reports of small-scale armed incursions over the border from Thailand grew more frequent.[68] The Governor General, Admiral Decoux, visited Phnom Penh in October, presumably to stiffen morale.[69] Shortly after he left, the Siamese Council of Ministers held an extraordinary meeting at Bangkok and decided to step up shipments of arms and ammunition to border zones.[70] There was an armed incursion by Thai regulars at Ream on the Gulf coast a few days later[71] and numerous reports of Thai airplanes violating Indochinese airspace.[72] The Thais also stepped up a propaganda campaign in the Cambodian borderlands, claiming that the Thais and Khmers were the same people.[73] They claimed to have recruited "numerous" Khmers, Laotians and Vietnamese to the Thai army, and promised large bounties to any who followed, according to a Khmer *Balat* in Kompong Thom province.[74] Some militiamen did desert, taking their weapons—including in one case a Hotchkiss machine gun—with them.[75] The Thais encouraged deserters with promises of cash payments. The going rate was 20 piastres per private (with arms and ammunition), rising to 60 for a corporal, 80 for a sergeant and 100 for a junior officer. Administrative staff would receive between 40 and 160 piastres, depending on grade.[76] The Thais also persuaded captured Foreign Legionaries to call on their fellow soldiers to desert.[77]

The fall of France had shocked King Monivong and Siamese propaganda did seduce numbers of Khmers, but there is some evidence that large numbers of his subjects remained loyal to France up to this time. There were a number of demonstrations of loyalty in Phnom Penh and regional centers in late 1940, with crowds of up to 10,000 marching under the tricolor and pledging their support for the king and the French government. [78] Given the size of these gatherings, it is unlikely that all of the demonstrators were forced to participate. There were also reports of delegations of Khmers visiting the *Résident Supérieur* to affirm their loyalty to Monivong and France.[79] This, however, was only part of the story. The Cambodian Minister of the Interior visited Battambang in December 1940 and reported to the *Résident Supérieur* that the situation "frankly, is not good". A number of inhabitants of the province, including two *mekhums*, had immigrated to Thailand, taking quantities of arms and ammunition with them. Perhaps they had believed Siamese claims that the French "eat flesh and drink blood." Others were worried that the French border troops could not repel attackers.[80] The report was disturbing evidence of the ambiguity of the frontier and of the doubtful loyalties of many of the inhabitants. The region had once been Siamese for over a century and had launched a large-scale uprising against French rule after 1907. In another instance, coolies employed on construction work at Preao in Battambang province went on strike, allegedly after Thai incitement.[81] On the other hand, the *Indochine Hebdomadaire Illustré* reported other large pro-French, anti-Siamese demonstrations in Battambang and Siem Reap in December 1940, adding that they were organized "spontaneously" by local notables.[82]

By late-1940, open hostilities had broken out, with artillery fire, aviation attacks and infantry raids in both directions across the border. Tanks and armored personnel vehicles were used on flatter terrain. The

Thais threatened to bomb Saigon and both sides did drop bombs and strafe villages,[83] and later on, major cities.[84] In early December, the Thais bombed two French gunboats.[85] To make up for a lack of bomber planes, the French military requisitioned Air France civilian airplanes to drop grenades and incendiaries. Given French demoralization after the fall of France, and the unreliable nature of many of their "native" troops, the Thais were astonished by the "surprisingly good show put up by the French and Annamites".[86] French resistance seems to have temporarily lifted King Monivong's spirits, for late in December he granted an interview to a United Press correspondent in which he praised the Protectorate for bringing 70 years of progress to his country and avowed that the war marked "a singular moment in history".[87] In the event, he was right, but for the wrong reasons.

A skirmishing war

The land war heated up towards Christmas, but it remained a *guerre d'escarmouches*—a skirmishing war—with casualties in the tens and hundreds. There were perhaps 14,000 French troops on 150 miles of border.[88] They faced a determined enemy. A French soldier said the "Siamese proved good 'bush-fighters'" who would "lurk in trees and fire Tommy guns on troops passing underneath" and would often attack and fall back, even in more conventional warfare.[89] This form of warfare was particularly effective in the heavily forested Dangrek Mountains, which are much steeper on the Cambodian side than in Thailand.[90] Over one hundred European casualties were admitted to hospitals in Phnom Penh in both November and December, with the figure rising to almost 350 in January and declining thereafter. The surgical team at Battambang, closer to the fluid front lines, operated on almost 200 casualties.[91] *Time* magazine, however, reported that there were 600 casualties in one battle in January[92] and one French document claimed that around 1000 Thais had been killed and wounded in the Sisophon region, compared with 200 *légionnaires*. The report also claims that the Thais lost a number of tanks, armored cars and planes.[93] A battalion of Khmer *tirailleurs* saw action in the "duck's beak" salient near Poipet, fighting along a riverbank and in dense bamboo. A number of Cambodians were mentioned in dispatches, including *tirailleur* of the second class Tem Bem, who was shot from the air, yet continued at his post. The Cambodian troops were said to have proved their courage and stamina[94] but sometimes an element of farce emerged. One not completely reliable source told a story about magic soup that would ward off danger. Indochinese troops were said to have requested the same kinds of "magical" amulets that their enemies wore into battle (and indeed many Khmers do believe this). Their French officers did not have any, but "Finally they had tiny clay images made, went through the motions of having them blessed, then threw them into a cauldron of soup. Anyone drinking this soup, they announced, would be protected against danger." In the event, the sector remained calm and the effectiveness of the "magic" was never tested.[95]

Small-scale it might have been, but the war was fought savagely. Both sides bombed towns indiscriminately, with inevitable civilian deaths. Thai bombs fell on Stung Treng, Battambang, Siem Reap, Sisophon, Ream and Mongkolborey. The French bombed Aranya and Oudorn in Thailand on several occasions.[96] The Geneva Convention seems to have been ignored as when a Thai university student who had visited the front "described his amusement…at seeing the nurses from the [French] Red Cross tents scatter in all directions when [their] post was attacked from the air and machine-gunned."[97] Although Thai propaganda leaflets promised European prisoners an easy life,[98] there have been claims of French prisoners being displayed like animals in cages in Bangkok.[99] There is no reason to believe that the French observed the old courtesies of war either.

French victory at the Koh Chang naval battle

The land war was a stalemate, despite the early optimism of the Thais, who had counted on an early capitulation by an apparently demoralized opponent. The most spectacular battle of the war, however, was not fought on land, but at sea towards the end of January 1941. The Battle of Koh Chang was a clear-cut French victory, despite Siamese denials. French Indochina had the edge over the fledgling Thai navy in terms of size and firepower, despite an ongoing armament program by the Thais throughout the latter half of the 1930s. The Thai navy consisted of some fast Italian torpedo boats of the "Montefalcone" type, some armored coast guard vessels and gunboats, plus four elderly submarines. The largest vessels were the *Dhonburi* and the *Sri Ayunthia,* each of around 2200 tons. In all, the Thai Navy consisted of no more than 30 vessels including some auxiliary craft. There was some doubt about the seaworthiness of the submarines. Some weeks before the naval battle, an American correspondent wrote, "Some think they can submerge, some think they cannot. The Navy has never tried. It recently offered to take some newspapermen out to prove the submarines could submerge. The newspapermen demurred. The Navy called the experiment off."[100] The submarines played no part in the battle.

France's far eastern fleet might have spent much of its time in mothballs and its detractors might have sneered that commanders had seen little action, but it was more than a match for its Thai counterpart. On 15 January, the French fleet set sail from Saigon under the command of the veteran Captain Bérenger, who first went to sea in 1906 at the age of 18. Bérenger's flagship was the 9350-ton cruiser, the *Lamotte-Picquet*, armed with eight six-inch guns and capable of 30 knots. Accompanying the cruiser were four gunboats, an armed merchant ship and two sloops of over 2000 tons each. The little fleet rounded the Cape of Camau and steamed towards the labyrinth of islands that lie off the coast of Cambodia and Thailand. On the morning of January 17, Bérenger sent a light spotter plane to investigate the Thai fleet that he expected to find inside or outside the harbor bar of the Chantaboun River. Incredibly, the Thai officers ignored the aircraft and the Thais were "caught napping", some even without steam up. Captain Bérenger was able to sail his ships within range of the enemy near Koh Chang Island. The cruiser opened fire at point blank range, sinking the *Songkhla* and the *Chonburi* and two of the Italian PT boats within ten minutes, and seriously damaging the larger *Dhonburi*. Plumes of smoke rose 400 meters into the sky from the stricken ships. The *Dhonburi's* commander, realizing that his ship was sinking, beached his vessel. The cruiser's guns also silenced some nearby shore batteries manned by Thai marines. According to a Danish merchant navy officer who witnessed the battle and rescued survivors, the *Dhonburi's* sister ship, the *Sri Ayuthia*, ignominiously fled even as the PT boats were resisting to the death. The ship's commander was so frightened of the cruiser's guns that he sailed into the mouth of the Chantaboun River without bothering to navigate through the channels and stuck hard on the harbor bar, opening the vessel's plates as a result. In contrast, the French suffered few, if any, casualties. Eyewitnesses dismissed Thai claims of scoring two direct hits on the *Lamotte-Picquet*. The Koh Chang battle was a serious defeat for Thailand and the loss of life was considerable. The British Ambassador at Bangkok, Sir Josiah Crosby, heard reliably that of the 860 officers and men on the destroyed Thai ships, only 82 survived. The figure was roughly confirmed by other knowledgeable Thai sources, despite the official Thai claims of 100 dead and 300 wounded. Following the battle, Bérenger was promoted to rear admiral, while his Thai counterpart, Vice-Admiral *Luang* Sindhu Songgramjaya, fell under a cloud.[101]

Yet, one week later, when Japan offered to mediate a truce, both sides readily agreed.[102] Thailand was unnerved by the naval battle and feared that the French might return to finish off the rest of her little navy. Nor had the land war gone as smoothly as Bangkok had planned. Although there were desertions to the Thai side, the colonial and foreign legion troops fought better than the Thais had expected. For their part, the French were running low on oil supplies for their navy, although the Thais were probably not aware of it. Overall, the French considered that they had given a good account of themselves and could expect to emerge from the negotiations with honor and territory reasonably intact. Thailand could expect some territorial gains.

Japan the real winner

They were wrong, as it turned out, for although the Thais gained territory in Cambodia and Laos, they were not the real winners. The negotiations confirmed Japan as the pre-eminent power in the region: any peace was to be a *pax japonica* and Thailand was cemented firmly as a satellite in the Nipponese New Order. Indochina, too, would be further drawn into the Greater East Asia Co-Prosperity Sphere, the French allowed to rule only by Tokyo's grace. Two days after the two sides agreed to Tokyo's mediation, the Japanese cruiser *Natori* steamed into Saigon harbor to host peace talks while a fleet of aircraft carriers and cruisers stood offshore. A *Time* correspondent supplied a folksy summary of the situation:

> Asked last week in Washington whether accepting Japanese mediation was not equivalent to letting a fox arbitrate between two rabbits in a cabbage patch, Thai Minister Mom Rajawongse Seni Pramoj replied: 'What would you do if you were a rabbit?'[103]

He could not say that he had not been warned. The American statesman Cordell Hull claims to have told the Minister on January 13, that is before the Battle of Koh Chang, that "Japan would 'swallow up' both countries" and that the Thai Government ought to "compose its differences with Indo-China at once."[104] It is probable that Sir Josiah Crosby gave similar advice: his opinion was that acceptance of Japanese mediation was unfortunate for all except Japan.[105] Delegates from the two sides signed a truce aboard the *Natori* on 31 January and agreed to continue negotiations for a final settlement at Tokyo.[106] Both sides agreed to pull back 10 kilometers from positions occupied on 28 January and to refrain from further hostilities.[107] In reality, the truce meant that they agreed to Japan's terms and the agreement was signed as Japanese military aircraft flew overhead. Commander Yashamura told United Press at Saigon that Vichy had accepted Japan's proposals "in principle" and warned that "stubbornness" could lead to further loss of territory.[108]

Peace was officially restored on 11 March 1941 when Thai and French plenipotentiaries signed a treaty at Tokyo. Although the French made some desperate attempts to wriggle out of the trap,[109] they bowed to *force majeure*. Power grew out of the barrels of the guns of the tens of thousands of disciplined Japanese soldiers in Indochina and their powerful fleet offshore. Although the Thais did not get all they had claimed—there is evidence that a powerful lobby wanted all of Cambodia—they did get back most of the territories ceded to Indochina between 1893 and 1907. This included part of the provinces of Siem Reap, Stung Treng and Pursat and all of Battambang; an area containing some one million people. It was a serious economic blow for France. The lost Cambodian provinces yielded over 250,000 tons of high quality rice per year (or around one-twentieth of the Indochinese total), plus large quantities of corn and pepper. The French also lost control of the Pailin gem mines and part of the Tonlé Sap fisheries. The Thais celebrated with triumphal marches and tolling bells, and their government instructed their subjects to fly Thai and Japanese flags. The Japanese Foreign Office extolled the Treaty as "a cornerstone for the establishment of the Greater East Asia prosperity sphere" and warned that, "Japan will not tolerate any obstruction of this program."[110] Two months later, Japan and French Indochina signed an economic treaty to cement the master and servant relationship. Indochina became part of the "yen bloc" and agreed to accept Japanese imports and capital investment. Japan was given special tariff and navigation rights and was guaranteed supplies of rice, maize, rubber, coal and other minerals at cheaper prices than could be obtained elsewhere.[111] Of a total of 58,000 tons of Indochinese rubber exported per year, 40,000 tons were to go to Germany and Japan, the majority of it to the latter. Only 8000 tons were to go to France, with the balance going to the USA.[112]

By the terms of the treaty between Thailand and French Indochina, the formal delineation of their new border was to be completed by 10 July 1942.[113] The hand-over of the disputed territories took place somewhat sooner, at a ceremony at Battambang 11 August 1941. An ethnic Khmer, *Luang* Kovid Apheuvongs, Director-General of posts and telegraphs and minister without portfolio in the Thai cabinet[114] led the Thai delegation. It must have been an emotional event for him, for 34 years earlier his father, the *Phya* Kathathorn, had quit the citadel in the city, moving slowly to Siam with a huge caravan of ox-carts, elephants, horses and thousands of retainers. This despotic sybarite had also taken the entire treasury from the citadel, amounting to more than five million francs and left behind him a sea of churned mud and "numerous victims of theft, disorder and vengeance."[115] Somewhere in his saddlebags, the *Phya* carried the flag that had flown over the domains over which his family had ruled as hereditary viceroys since 1795. Now, his son brought it back.

Kathathorn had also left behind his trusted lieutenant, the *Visès* Nheou, to lead a stubborn and bloody rebellion against the occupying French forces. Nheou's uprising was eventually defeated and the Siamese government had bowed to French pressure and exiled him to the remote Kra peninsula facing the Indian Ocean. Kathathorn himself was long dead. The Thais had never accepted the spirit of the 1907 Treaty that had cost them the territories they called "Monthon Burapha" and saw the return as long overdue justice. In their propaganda, they claimed that Thais and Khmers were the same people. Borders are often ambiguous and nations are constructs rather than fixed and "natural" entities. In a sense, as the present author has argued elsewhere,[116] the French and the Siamese had partitioned Cambodia in the 18th and 19th centuries. Under the Apheuvongs, Monthon Burapha had its own currency and the *Phya* Kathathorn was as legitimate a ruler as the kings —or viceroys as the Siamese insisted they were—at Phnom Penh and Udong. No plebiscite was ever held to determine the loyalties of the population of the region and their ambiguous loyalties were to be tested again when the territories reverted to Indochina after the defeat of Japan in 1945. In any case, the idea of citizenship would have puzzled people long accustomed to despotic rule.

The day of the hand-over must have been a bitter one for the French delegation. The tricolor and the Cambodian ensign were lowered and in their place, the Thai envoy, *Luang* Kovid Apheuvongs, hoisted his father's old flag.[117] The French *Résident* vacated the official residence at Battambang—a handsome colonial building that still stands today— and a Siamese governor moved in.

The loss stunned the Cambodian people. Norodom Sihanouk later recalled that his fellow Khmer pupils at the Lycée Chasseloup-Laubat in Saigon observed a period of "national mourning."[118] King Monivong was at least spared the pain and indignity of the formal handing over of the western territories. He was inconsolable at the approaching loss, however. Sihanouk recalls that his grandfather withdrew completely into himself. He ate little and "his door was closed to all", including French officials and his close friends and family favorites.[119] He died at his estates at Bokor on 23 April, slightly more than a month after the treaty had signed the western lands away. With him at the end was, as we have seen, his favorite concubine, Saloth Roeung, known as Saroeun, the younger sister of Saloth Sar (the future Pol Pot).

A commission delegated by the Council of Ministers entered his estates to make an inventory of his considerable possessions and to fix the seals on the doors of his sundry palaces and villas.[120] He had turned his back on his country's erstwhile protectors in his last months on earth. In a way, he had outlived his time and he could not face the uncertainties of life in a time of rapidly declining French power. Had he died a year or so sooner, he would have been spared the pain of the new situation. Other Khmers, too, would have felt the same sense of outraged bewilderment that the loss of the territories caused the king. We can also be sure that some of them began to imagine the possibility of life without the French. If the French could not protect them, they may have reasoned, perhaps they too could vanquish the colonial overlords. The Japanese and the Thais had punctured the myth of European invincibility; a lesson that was to be underscored early in the following year when the "impregnable" British fortress of Singapore fell to a smaller Japanese army and the Dutch were vanquished in the East Indies. As Ellen Hammer wrote: "Defeated in Europe in 1940, France was defeated in Asia in 1941. One day the Vietnamese would cite their failure as proof that France had forfeited its right to 'protect' Indochina."[121] The Cambodians would say the same.

Notes

[1] Cited in unsigned article, "Peace restored on Indo-China Thailand frontier, on Japan's terms; French lose 18,000 square miles". *China Weekly Review*, 15 March 1941.

[2] *L'Echo du Cambodge*, 5 October 1938.

[3] Ibid. 13 September 1939.

[4] Jean Decoux, (1949), *A la barre de l'Indochine. Histoire de mon Gouvernement Général (1940-1945)*, Plon, Paris, p.284. *L'Echo du Cambodge*, 31 July 1940.

[5] Ibid. (Decoux).

[6] "The new sovereign and the new government", *Nagaravatta*, 14 May 1941. The article was censored. The phrase referred to Cambodia, preyed on by

savage animals—the implication was that France was powerless to protect the Khmers. Perhaps it was also a hint that France itself was a tiger with broken claws?

[7] According to one military historian, the French had around one dozen warships and 800 personnel in Indochinese waters in 1939. [Claude Hesse d'Alzon, (1985), *La présence militaire française en Indochine, 1940-1945*, Publications du service historique de l'Armée de Terre, Paris, p.25.]

[8] Jacques M. May, (1951), *A Doctor in Siam*, Jonathan Cape, London, p.218.]

[9] Around 80 airplanes of all types and 1500 men, including 500 Europeans according to d'Alzon, op.cit.

[10] D'Alzon claims that the French ground forces in Indochina in 1939 comprised 29 battalions of infantry; seven artillery groups; and two companies of sappers—in all 30,000 men, of whom 12,500 were Europeans. Ibid. Taking into account members of the Garde Indigène, other militias and the police, there were probably between 100,000 and 120,000 armed men in Indochina, but many would have been of dubious worth in battle. [CMIDOM, 15H 106 Deuxième Guerre Mondiale, Stationnement des troupes de l'armée française en Indochine au 16 janvier 1939 and Order de Bataille en Indochine, octobre 1940.]

[11] Gerald L.G. Samson, (1939), "Japanese threats to Indo-China frighten the French", *China Weekly Review*, January 14, pp.214-215; Unsigned, (1938), "La Défense de l'Indochine", *Revue des Deux Mondes*, 15 November; and d'Alzon, op.cit. p.81.

[12] These were the views, if not the words, of the more clear-sighted contemporary observers. See for instance, J.L. Gheerbrandt, (1940), "The French Empire and the War", *Asiatic Review*, n.s. 36, pp.327-334, April.

[13] AAm 22-401-123 Department of the Army. Subject Indo China. Memo for the Secretary, Department of External Affairs, Canberra, 23 November 1940. Interview with Pierce Robin, wool buyer.

[14] *Revue des Deux Mondes*, op.cit.

[15] Mandel asked the French parliament for "440,000,000 francs worth of guns, coastal batteries, [and] harbors..." in Indochina. Special correspondent, (1940), "French peacefully penetrated Indo-China until war peril compelled establishment of Defenses in 1938", *The China Weekly Review*, December 21. The great French naval base at Cam Ranh Bay was still under construction in 1940. [See Ellen J Hammer, (1954), *The Struggle for Indochina*, Stanford University Press, Stanford, California, p.16.]

[16] AOM RSC 266 Résidence de Kampot, Rapport Mensuel March 1940. The *Résident* reported recruiting 175 *tirailleurs* by that month in the *khet*, of whom 22 were taken against their will.

[17] "L'Invincible alliance", *L'Echo du Cambodge*, 14 February 1940. This was a sad irony, given Darlan's subsequent prominence at Vichy.

[18] "Un million de soldats allemands tués dans le nord de la France", *La Presse Indochinoise*, 24 mai 1940. Reports like this are beyond irony.

[19] Hammer, op.cit. p.15.

[20] Cited in John C. Le Clair, (1937), "Siam looks to Tokyo", *National Review*, No. 109, November.

[21] Samson, op.cit.

[22] Interview with Pierce Robin, op.cit.

[23] AAc A981 INDO 7 Part 1 War records – Indochina and Japan. Memo to the Secretary, Dept of External Affairs from J.T. Fitzgerald, 23 November 1940.

[24] Interview with Pierce Robin, op.cit.

[25] Le Clair, op.cit.

[26] ANC RSC F451 File 24809, Conseil des Ministres, 629e séance du 13 juillet 1932. Letter from French military attaché at Bangkok to the *Résident Supérieur* at Phnom Penh.

[27] A British diplomat considered that "friendlier relations...emphasize the fact that Siam has accepted in spirit as well as the letter the existing frontier." (PRO FO 371 11839 w953/953/17 Rpt. Of visit to Cambodia of HM Rep, Mr. R. Greg.) Further evidence of cordial relations included cultural exchanges, the return of arrested Khmer bandits and prison escapees and the opening of the road between Aranya and Battambang province. (AOM RSC 228, Relations avec le Siam, 1927-1935.) Even the old nest of subversive Indochinese exiles at Bangkok had dwindled to a small band, including some bonzes and "the odd fish merchant, jeweler, writer, chauffeur" and some old Siamese functionaries from Monthon Burapha, including the Phya Kathathorn. (AOM RSC 299, French Legation at Bangkok, 1927-1930.)

[28] Reported in *L'Echo du Cambodge*, 10 May 1930.

[29] André Gaudel, (1947), *L'Indochine Française en face du Japon*, J. Susse, Paris, p.29.

[30] The Treaty was signed on 14 February 1925. [CMIDOM, 15H 103, historique des rélations Franco-Siamoises de 1862 à 1940.]

[31] Virginia Thompson, (1941), *Thailand. The New Siam*, Macmillan, New York, pp.195-196.

[32] CMIDOM 15H 103, historique, op.cit.

[33] H.G. Quaritch Wales, (1943), *Years of Blindness*, Thomas Y. Crowell, New York, p.296.

[34] CMIDOM 15H 103 Situation Générale 15 August 1937.

[35] Ibid. Activité allemande au Siam, 15 August 1937.

[36] Ibid. L'activité japonaise au Siam, 15 August 1937.

[37] Le Clair, op.cit.

[38] Thompson, op.cit.

[39] "Cinq minutes avec S.E. Thiounn", *La Presse Indochinoise*, 1 July 1937. The same paper (Ibid. 3 August 1937) scoffed at warnings by Colonel Fernand Bernard, who had been France's negotiator with Siam before the return of the lost provinces in 1907. An anti-Thai article by the Colonel appeared in English the following year: Col. F.A. Bernard, (1938), "The Security of Indo-China and Siamese Imperialism", *The Asiatic Review*, April, pp.305-314.

[40] ANC RSC E03 File 9246 Box 814, Rapports Annuels de tous les Résidences provinciaux du Cambodge, 1938-1939.

[41] D'Alzon, op.cit. pp.89-90. In that year, the Thai forces included 44 battalions of infantry; 13 artillery groups; nine cavalry squadrons; six sapper battalions and three tank companies. See note 4 above for an account of French strength.

[42] See, for instance CMIDOM 15H 103 Bulletin Trimestriel des Renseignements, 1934-1935 and Le Clair, op.cit.

[43] Judith A. Stowe, (1991), *Siam Becomes Thailand. A Story of Intrigue*, Hurst and Co, London, p.143. As Stowe notes, the irredentist plays of Wichit were temporarily banned in 1937 so as "not to imperil the negotiation of the non-aggression pacts with France and Britain." Pibul went so far as to tell the British Ambassador at Bangkok that he preferred to see France in power in Indochina, not Japan. (pp.143-144.)

[44] *Phra* Sarasas, (1940), *My Country Thailand (its history, geography and civilization)*, Maruzen, Tokyo, p.163.

[45] AOM RSC 210 *Résident Supérieur* to *Gougal* 30 June 1940; *Délégué* at Pailin to the *Résident* at Battambang, 27 July 1940.

[46] Paul Baudouin, (trans. Sir Charles Petrie), (1948), *The Private Diaries (March 1940 to January 1941) of Paul Baudouin*, Eyre and Spottiswoode, London, pp.248-251. An American journalist also reported that some Italian and German Foreign Legionaries had swore never to fight the Japanese again. (PRO 371 27759, 9 January 1941.)

[47] AAs C 320 IC 6 The Situation in Indo-China 1941-1941. Letter to G3, Intelligence Section, Eastern Command, Victoria Barracks, Paddington. 31 May 1941. From Lt. G.H.V. Newman, Intelligence section, Eastern Command. Notes from interview with Mr.. Griffin, Shell Oil, recently stationed in Hanoi.

[48] AAc A 59 54/1 553/8 Pacific and Far East Cablegrams relating to Thailand, September 1940 - October 1942. Secretary of State for Dominion Affairs, London, to the Australian Prime Minister, 3 December 1940.

[49] "New madness. Radio Bangkok continues to lie", *La Verité*, 2 December 1940 and *Indochine Hebdomadaire Illustré*, 9 January 1941.

[50] Hubert Hermann, a correspondent for the East Indies paper *Soerabaya Handelsblatt. La Verité*, 13 December 1940.

[51] PRO 371 28108 Indo-China/Siam dispute. Sir Josiah Crosby to the Foreign Office, 9 December 1940.

[52] Cited in Crosby, ibid.

[53] Baudouin, op.cit. p.237.

[54] Scot Barmé, (1993), *Luang Wichit Wathakan and the Creation of a Thai Identity*, Institute of Southeast Asian Studies, Singapore, 1993, p.168. The party, though headed by an ethnic Khmer, was a puppet of the Thai government.

[55] AAc A5954/1 553/8 op.cit. Australian High Commissioner, London, to the Prime Minister's Department, Canberra, 21 August 1940.

[56] CMIDOM, 15H 103, historique, op.cit.

[57] Baudouin, op.cit. p.239.

[58] AAc A981 INDO 7 Part 1 War records, Indochina-Japan. Secretary of State for Dominion Affairs to the Prime Minister, Canberra, 10 November 1940. The historian E. Bruce Reynolds believes that Britain's aim throughout the conflict was to drive a wedge between the Thais and Japan. (E. Bruce Reynolds, (1994), *Thailand and Japan's Southern Advance, 1940-1945*, St Martin's Press, New York.)

[59] AAc A981 INDO 7 Part 1 Secretary of State for Dominion Affairs to the (Australian) Prime Minister, 10 August 1940. The Vichy authorities at Martinique were dependent upon the US for oil supplies and the US almost "closed the tap" (i.e. faucet) except for small quantities for cars and maintenance purposes.

[60] See, for instance, Nicholas Tarling, (1990), "The British and the First Japanese Move into Indo-China", *Journal of South East Asian Studies*, Vol. XXI, No 1 March, pp.35-65.

[61] AAc A 981/1 INDO 4 Indo-China relations with Australia. Casey, Australian Minister at Washington to the Dept. of External Affairs, Canberra, 19 September 1940. See also AAc 5954/1 230/5, 29 October 1940.

[62] A.F. Thanevot, (1941), "Japan and Thailand", *Asiatic Review*, October, pp.849-845.

[63] AAc A5954/1 704/12 Graving dock. Dept of Defence Coordination. War Cabinet Agendum No 391/1941. Secret. Confidential. Memo for Secretary, Dept of External Affairs, Canberra. Minute of War Cabinet, Melbourne, 5 December 1941. The proposal was not approved owing to the demands of Australian war production.

[64] Ibid. Secretary of State for Dominion Affairs to the Australian Prime Minister, 19 November 1941.

[65] This was, opined Sir Josiah Crosby, "an unforgivable sin", but he added that there were "a lot of extenuating circumstances". [AAc A5954/1 553/8 Pacific and Far East Cablegrams relating to Thailand, Sept 1940-October 1942. Cablegram from Australian High Commissioner, London, to the Minister for External Affairs, Canberra, 1 December 1942.]

[66] Numerous rubber cargoes were sent aboard Vichy ships from 1941 onwards, some of which were intercepted by Allied naval patrols. Details can be found at AAm 2060/20/8 MP 1185/8. Department of Defence. Naval Board "N" branch, Navy secretariat. Secret and confidential files multiple number series 1923-1950.

[67] AOM RSC 210. *Résident Supérieur* to *Résident* at Kompong Thom, 28 September 1940.

[68] Ibid. *Résident* at Battambang to the *Résident Supérieur*, 5 October 1940. See also *La Verité*, Saigon, 10 October 1940.

[69] *La Verité*, 17, 19 and 21 October 1940.

[70] *La Verité*, 26 October 1940.

[71] AOM RSC 210 Report from *Patrouiller directeur* Borel, Ream, 31 October 1940.

[72] AOM RSC 163, Report of 9 November 1940 and passim.

[73] Copies of the propaganda leaflets are contained in AOM RSC 322. Surveillance de la propagande siamoise.

[74] AOM RSC 210, letter from the *Résident* of Kompong Thom to the Military Commandant at Phnom Penh, 13 November 1940.

[75] AOM RSC 210, *Résident* at Siem Reap to the *Résident Supérieur*, 21 November 1940. Also AOM RSC 308. Rpt by Inspector Bauche, Chief of Mobile Police to the *Résident* at Kampot, 20 July 1944. The latter concerns the return and arrests of six Khmer militiamen who had deserted in 1940/41.

[76] Ibid. From translation of a Thai propaganda leaflet.

[77] AOM RSC 322. In one case, the *legionnaires* Herman Franzisko and Alexandre Jankowski called on their former comrades to desert, promising good treatment and warning that the Thais were better armed than the French troops.

[78] AOM RSC 163. *Résident* at Battambang to the *Résident Supérieur*, 17 November 1940. Also AOM RSC 163, op.cit. Numerous publications also reported on the demonstrations, some of them publishing photographs. See, for instance, *L'Echo du Cambodge*, 6 and 17 November 1940; *La Verité*, 19 November 1940; *Indochine Hebdomadaire Illustré*, 3 November and 19 December 1940; and *L'Echo du Saigon*, 17 November 1940.

[79] *La Verité*, 27 November 1940.

[80] AOM RSC 210. Frontières avec le Siam. Rapport de tournée effectuée dans le province de Battambang le 12 décembre 1940. 14 décembre 1940.

[81] Ibid. Letter from *Sureté* to *Résident Supérieur*, 27 December 1940.

[82] *Indochine Hebdomadaire Illustré*, 19 décembre 1940.

[83] PRO 371 28108. Indochina/Siam dispute. Military attaché to the War Office, 24 December 1940.

[84] PRO FO 371 28108, Indo-China/Siam dispute, Reuters report, 17 January 1941.

[85] AAc A5954/1 553/8 Pacific and Far East – cablegrams relating to Thailand, Sept. 1940 – Oct. 1942. Crosby to Australian Prime Minister, 2 December 1940.

[86] Ibid. Memo by Anderson, probationer vice-consul at Bangkok, 23 December 1940.

[87] Reported in *La Verité* of 19 December 1940.

[88] Gaudel, op.cit. p.100.

[89] AAs C320 IC10 (Indochina 1941). Intelligence summary (Australian military intelligence). Interview with Mr. Scamps, 5 September 1941. Scamps was a French citizen who had lived in Sydney since he was a child. He rallied to the French colors in December 1939 and saw active service in the border war.

[90] *La Verité*, 15 January 1941.

[91] AOM RSC 263. Rapport Annuel 1940-41. Minute Livre Vert. Situation politique et administrative. D'Alzon, op.cit. pp.92-94 puts the total number of French casualties in "the high hundreds".

[92] "Guns on the Mekong", *Time*, January 27 1941.

[93] AOM RSC 21. Telegrams to *Gougal*, 1939-1942. Telegram sent 23 January 1941.

[94] *Indochine Hebdomadaire Illustré*, 27 March 1941.

[95] "The Postman Say", *Bangkok Post*, 6 August 1946.

[96] *Indochine Hebdomadaire Illustré*, 6, 8, 9, 11 January 1941 and *La Verité*, 7, 9, 10, 21 January 1941 and AOM RSC 163, op.cit.

[97] AAc A981 FRA 4 France – Relations with Thailand. Memo by Mr.. Probationer Vice Consul Anderson, British Consul General, Bangkok, 23 December 1940.

[98] AOM RSC 322 Propagande siamois, 1940-41.

[99] Stowe, op.cit. p.169.

[100] "Affair of the Mekong," *Time*, 30 December 1940.

[101] My account of the Koh Chang battle is based on the following sources: "Le récit d'un temoigne", *La Dépêche d'Indochine*, 21 January 1941; *Indochine Hebdomadaire Illustré*, 23 January 1941; Numéro Spécial, 1 February 1941 and 17 April 1941; "Bataille dans le Golfe de Siam", *La Verité*, 18 January 1941 PRO 371 28111 and 371 28112; AAc A981 FRA 4 France – Relations with Thailand and A981 FRA 81.

[102] "Le Japon offre sa médiation acceptées par les deux parties", *La Verité*, 25 January 1941.

[103] "Mediation: It's wonderful", *Time*, 10 February 1941.

[104] *The Memoirs of Cordell Hull*, (1948), Vol. 2, Hodder and Stoughton, London, 1948, p.985.

[105] AAc A981 FRA 81 France – Relations with Thailand. Crosby to Anthony Eden, Foreign Minister, cablegram received 24 February 1941.

[106] "Le fin d'une agrésion inutile", *Indochine Hebdomadaire Illustré*, 6 February 1941.

[107] *La Dépêche d'Indochine*, 1 February 1941.

[108] "Indo-China capitulates to Japan on Thai demands but Americans and British still hold strong position", *China Weekly Review*, 8 March 1941.

[109] Ibid. "Indo-China joins anti-appeasement group with flat rejection of Tokyo's arbitration on Thai claims". 1 March 1941; "Indochine et la crise extrême-orientale", *Indochine Hebdomadaire Illustré*, 27 January 1941. The latter article was heavily censored, indicating the authorities' fears of offending Japan.

[110] Ibid (*China Weekly Review*)."'Peace restored on Indo-China, Thailand frontier, on Japan's terms; French lose 18,000 square miles". 15 March 1941.

[111] Ibid. "Indo-China moves step nearer to complete Japanese domination as economic treaties are signed." 10 May 1941.

[112] AAc A5954/1 553/8 I.6475.

[113] AAc A981 FRA 81. France – Relations with Thailand. Extract from short wave broadcast, 26 June 1942.

[114] Ibid. Crosby, British Minister at Bangkok to Anthony Eden, Foreign Office, 11 August 1941.

[115] John Tully, (1996), *Cambodia Under the Tricolour. King Sisowath and the 'Mission Civilisatrice' 1904-1927*, Monash Asia Institute, Clayton, Victoria, pp.116-117.

[116] Ibid. Chapters Three and Four.

[117] Crosby to Anthony Eden, 11 August 1941, op.cit.

[118] Norodom Sihanouk, (1981), *Souvenirs doux et amers*, Hachette, Paris, p.49.

[119] Ibid. p.51.

[120] ANC RSC F42 File 9069 Succession de sa Majesté Sisowath Monivong, 1941. His possessions included 111 boxes of opium.

[121] Hammer, op.cit. p.26.

Chapter 18

A Little Tiger on the Throne

This new and gorgeous garment, majesty,
Sits not so easy on me as you think.
—William Shakespeare, *Henry the Fourth Part II,* Act V, Scene II.

On the afternoon of the day King Monivong died—24 April 1941—the Grand Council of the Kingdom met to choose his successor.[1] Monivong had left no testament.[2] The Council unanimously approved France's choice, an 18-year-old princeling called Norodom Sihanouk, overlooking the obvious candidates, Princes Monireth and Suramarit, and a 34-year-old "also ran" called Norodom Norindeth.[3] Sihanouk swore his allegiance to France and her "glorious Marshal", Philippe Pétain. Two days later, the French government ratified the decision and Pétain sent greetings to the new king.[4] For the third time, France had presided over the deliberations of the body charged with responsibility for choosing Cambodia's kings.[5] The choice, however, was so unexpected that it could have succeeded only because France had squeezed every ounce of independent spirit from the Councilors.

The news stunned the two leading contenders, Suramarit, the new king's father and Monireth, the eldest son of Monivong. Shortly before World War II, Colonial Minister Georges Mandel had summoned the pair to Paris to discuss their claims.[6] Although Mandel had made no pronouncement, most observers regarded Monireth as the *prince héritier* and despite rumors of a rift with his father, King Monivong, it is likely that he remained his father's choice. No hard evidence exists to back up the rumor of discord, said to stem from Monireth's decision to marry a young woman called Rosette Poc, the daughter of a rich mandarin, against his father's wishes. The "pretty and seductive" Ms Poc had enjoyed a reputation for taking lovers before she took up with the prince,[7] but Monireth was smitten[8] and refused to give her up. This might have irked his father but it does not mean that he disinherited his stubborn son for it. Monivong's anger may have been softened by the memory of his own anguish when the French had forbidden him to marry a Siamese dancer shortly after he ascended the throne. The rumor might have been a product of backstairs gossip in the royal palace, but the French might have helped it along to justify their surprising, even astounding choice. What we know of Monivong's disillusionment with France makes it unlikely that he would have approved the French choice. On the balance of probabilities, Monireth was his father's preference, as the Sisowath wing of the royal family maintained. Monireth was also France's preferred choice for king as late as 1939[9] and the press commonly referred to him as the heir to the throne.[10]

The choice of the 18-year-old, who was to rule as King Norodom Sihanouk Varman, must have surprised even the docile mandarins of the Grand Council and wider circles of the Khmer elite. Huy Kanthoul, who was a classmate of Sihanouk's in Saigon, was surprised. He says that the prince was little known outside of a small circle.[11] Although *Nagaravatta* announced its support for Sihanouk,[12] the announcement came three weeks after the Council meeting, which might indicate a period of shock or soul-searching for the editors. They favored the Norodom wing, but it is likely that they had backed Suramarit.[13] Sihanouk is contradictory; although at one point he says that the *Nagaravatta* circle welcomed the news of his succession enthusiastically,[14] elsewhere he claims that the group disliked him, but liked his father.[15] It must also have astonished those French residents who were not privy to the inner circles of power and it did cause some mutterings in the French-language press, despite the willingness of the censor to apply the muzzle. *Résident Supérieur* Thibaudeau complained to the Governor of Cochinchina about "fantastic echoes, often unfortunate and sometimes intentionally misleading" in the Saigon press.[16] Lastly, by his own admission, the decision surprised Sihanouk so much that he burst into tears when told the news.[17] Sihanouk was at home for the Easter holidays when word came of Monivong's impending death. He later wrote that he had never imagined that he might be the choice to succeed his grandfather. Nor, he added, had his mother; both had thought the contest was between his father and his uncle.[18]

Sihanouk was born at Phnom Penh on 31 October 1922,[19] the son of Prince Suramarit and Princess Kossamak Nearirak. He was a walking synthesis of the two wings of the royal family, descended on his mother's side from Monivong and Sisowath and on his father's from Prince Sutharot and King Norodom.[20] They named him Sihanouk, which derives from "siha", or lion, at the suggestion of his grandfather, Prince Sutharot. For what it is worth, Sihanouk claims that an astrologer predicted that he was born to occupy the throne.[21] Yet, by his own account, he was an obscure schoolboy when Decoux chose him as king. Donald Lancaster describes him as having "a capacity for short-lived enthusiasm and artless candour."[22] Huy Kanthoul found him "serious and humble", albeit docile.[23] Photographs show him as a shy young man with a winning smile, callow and untried, especially in comparison with his uncle, the stern soldier Prince Monireth. Monireth, a graduate of the prestigious Saint-Cyr military academy, had served the government in a number of capacities and had rallied to his regiment in France before the military collapse of June 1940. Huy Kanthoul describes Monireth as "intelligent and modern", with a reputation for direct speech.[24] Sihanouk's father, Suramarit, also had better credentials, but although intelligent, he had a reputation for laziness in some circles. After leaving the Lycée Chasseloup-Laubat in 1917, he served as aide-de-camp and interpreter to King Sisowath. After Sisowath's death in 1927, he became Monivong's private secretary and later director of the royal chancellery. Since 1939, he had worn the ribbon of the order of *commandeur de la légion d'honneur*. When Monivong died, Suramarit was serving as Minister of the National Economy.[25]

It is difficult to tell what Sihanouk's character was like at the time because of a lack of dispassionate witnesses and documentary evidence. The French were determined to present their young *protégé* in the best possible light and official Khmer opinion was unlikely to demur from their viewpoint. Sihanouk himself has left us with a number of accounts, but we should treat them with caution, for they contain elements of retrospective self-justification mixed in with more candid self-appraisal. He constantly inflates himself. He has insinuated, for example, that soon after ascending to the throne, he had to wrestle with the question of independence,[26] but this is unlikely. He claims elsewhere that such a concern only began in 1945,[27] before which, by his own admission, he was a "playboy" and a "useless young man".[28] However, while some Khmers such as the *Nagaravatta* circle *were* moving rapidly towards nationalism in 1941 and earlier, it is very unlikely that this gauche youngster was a secret sympathizer. In fact, he did not display any enthusiasm for independence until the option was forced on him by events in 1952-53. Already, however, he did not like taking orders. Shortly after his coronation, Sihanouk recorded, the Secretary-General of Indochina, Georges Gautier, moved to marry him off to the daughter of a wealthy mandarin. Sihanouk refused, claiming that he burned with resentment at the impost.[29] This rings true and Sihanouk has probably conflated that personal resentment against Gautier with the development of his later pragmatic nationalism.

Yet, if Sihanouk engaged in retrospective self-dramatization, there has been an opposite tendency to belittle him. After he had led Cambodia to independence and insisted on her neutrality during the Cold War, the US media often treated him with amused disdain. *Time* and *Life*, for example, dubbed him "Snookie" and caricatured him a saxophone-playing buffoon and "tubby" dilettante.[30] We should not fall into this trap, but we should also be wary of the hagiographic accounts common in the French colonial press at the time of his coronation. There was no press freedom during the Vichy dictatorship and the censor's blue pencil was ubiquitous. The Decoux regime played up Khmer culture for its own ends. Norodom Sihanouk was the descendent of the kings of Angkor, especially Jayavarman VII,[31] and France was the protector of this illustrious line. The colonial press cast Sihanouk as a brilliant student who had taken all the prizes for Latin, Greek, History, Mathematics, Physics and English.[32] In this version, the royal paragon rose every morning at five o'clock for a rigorous program of calisthenics before applying himself to his studies; no pallid bookworm, he was a "sporting monarch", who loved horse riding, tennis and basketball.[33] Also—and this was of considerable interest to the Vichy authorities—Sihanouk had an active interest in youth movements. He himself had progressed from Cub Scout to pack leader.[34] Milton Osborne adds the details that he had an aptitude for music and was fond of the cinema, but cautions that there were "varying estimates" of his scholastic ability.[35] Indeed there are *only* estimates. There are no records of his school report cards in the French or Cambodian archives, although those of Lon Nol and other prominent Cambodian political figures are extant.[36] One suspects that Sihanouk's records may have been removed so as not to conflict with the Dionysian image of the perfect scholar and athlete. After leaving school, he received private tuition from the Khmer banker Sonn Sann and René Morizon, a French pedagogue and author. While he may have been the brilliant student the journalists claim, he later suffered from an inferiority complex when in the company of intellectuals, perhaps due to his truncated schooling.[37] However, his subsequent career, for all of its hedonism, theatricality and dilettantism, shows him to be an intelligent and shrewd man capable of bursts of intense hard work—a man of dark shadows and sudden, mercurial flights. Although Sihanouk benefited from the veneration traditionally given to their kings by the Khmer people, he could not have survived politically as a purely traditional ruler during the turmoil of post-independence Cambodia. He was also a genuinely charismatic figure in the sense meant by Max Weber; that is, a leader with "special gifts" that enabled him to develop a rapport with his subjects that went beyond traditional fealty.[38]

Sihanouk seems to have been a lonely child, raised largely by his great aunt, Mme. Chau Khun Pat, in his infant years.[39] His parents were drifting apart and although his mother was affectionate, "his father emerges...as an amiably dedicated womaniser, kindly enough to his son in a distant fashion, but hardly concerned with his day to day development."[40] Such a childhood explains the later emotional lability of the man, how he craved the limelight and sought to dazzle the world with his brilliance. His cinematic career provided an outlet for acting out the traumas of his childhood and youth. It is possible that his father's distance accounts at an unconscious level for Sihanouk's abdication in his favor in 1955. Sihanouk's own explanation was that abdication would allow him a freer hand in politics, but it is possible that he was also subconsciously seeking his distant father's love and attention by an act of self-abnegation that gave Suramarit the crown that had eluded him in 1941. Sihanouk spent much of his childhood away from home, especially after he had completed his primary education at the École François-Baudoin in Phnom Penh. In 1935, like many other members of the Khmer elite at that time, he went to Saigon to continue his studies at the Lycée Chasseloup-Laubat,[41] boarding with the family of a Franco-Indian customs official who was related to an accountant at the royal palace at Phnom Penh.[42] His schoolmates found him to be a pleasant, resourceful, but timid boy.[43] But for his sudden ascension to the throne, he could have expected to go on to study in France, perhaps at a military academy, perhaps at university, and to serve in high administrative positions as his father had done before him.

So why did the French pluck this young man from the sidelines and put him on the throne? Governor General Jean Decoux said that although Monireth had good qualities, Sihanouk was a better choice because he would put an end to the old rivalries between the two wings of the royal family. He was descended from both wings and had been an excellent student at Saigon, Decoux claimed.[44] Mme. Decoux also found the young prince "sweet" and might have lobbied for him on that account, but there were weightier considerations. According to Sihanouk, the French were anxious not to offend moderate Khmer nationalists, particularly those around *Nagaravatta*, who wanted the Norodom wing back on the throne.[45] However, such considerations did not stop the French from putting Monivong on the throne ahead of his rivals in 1927 and Monireth, too, was descended from both wings of the royal family: from the Sisowath side via his father and from the Norodom wing via his mother, Princess Kanviman. Monireth was probably the candidate best qualified to take over from his father and Sihanouk's own father, Suramarit, could also make a reasonable case. It is most likely that Decoux considered that Sihanouk's youth and relative lack of *savoir-faire* would make him malleable. He was intelligent and personable, even charming, but as yet unbent by life into a fixed character—like the Jesuits, Decoux's pedagogic team could "make the man". After he had completed his education, Decoux reasoned, he would show loyalty and understanding to France in precarious times. However, as Sihanouk himself later put it, the French were wrong to believe that he was a lamb, because he was a tiger, if only a little one. [46] He had the name of a close feline cousin, in any case.

If Decoux saw Sihanouk as a lamb, he would have regarded Monireth as a tiger. Monireth loved France, as Sihanouk claims,[47] but he had an independent streak and a caustic tongue, with which he mocked the so-called "National Revolution" and anything else he chose.[48] Huy Kanthoul wrote that Monireth

> openly criticized certain official abuses, the misplaced pretensions of the 'little Frenchmen' who despised the natives. He wrote sensible articles for the papers, but with a tone that was always excessive, freely shooting off arrows against taboos that others did not dare mention. This both and amused and displeased a French colony jealous of its privileges. However, among the young Khmers, he was very popular. As Chief Scout, he traveled through the countryside as the darling of the people.[49]

This could not have pleased Decoux, who was a loyal, sour, and even fanatical Pétainist. There were other disagreeable memories in the collective mind of the old stagers of the administration. Monireth had fallen foul of *Résident Supérieur* Achille Silvestre back in 1936 for his advocacy of "progressive" and mildly democratic views. Monivong had sided with his son against Silvestre, and Marius Moutet, the Colonial Minister in Léon Blum's Popular Front Government, had intervened on the prince's side. Vichy could not entrust the crown to one who had once "passed for a democrat",[50] and who was still so gruffly independent. Decoux, too, was new to Indochina in 1941. He had not yet met Monireth or Suramarit and he relied on "old hands" from the French Administration for advice. He had heard unfavorable things about Monireth from Silvestre, and Thibaudeau was hostile to him too.[51] Decoux would have detested Blum's Popular Front and resented it for taking Monireth's side in the dispute with Silvestre.[52] Just how democratic Monireth's opinions had remained is open to debate. He developed a reputation for authoritarianism as he grew older and for all his glad-handing of the people, he seems to have despised them. He said publicly that he did not believe young Khmers should continue their studies because "the more they learn, the more difficult they are to govern". According to Huy Kanthoul, Monireth had become more arrogant following his marriage. He was smitten with his wife and gradually adopted the elitist attitudes of her family. His wife was the daughter of an unpopular mandarin who had amassed a fortune by shady means and some of this unpopularity rubbed off on Monireth, particularly in intellectual circles.[53] This would not have conflicted with French beliefs, but he was too willful and independent to suit their interests. The diplomatic situation was delicate at the time and Decoux might have been worried that Monireth's bluntness would have jeopardized France's delicate relations with Japan.[54] Finally, there is also some suggestion that bribes might have passed hands to influence the choice. Sihanouk's one-time amanuensis, Charles Meyer, has claimed that the mother of Norindeth, another Norodom prince, gave extravagant gifts in the hope of improving her son's chances.[55] Osborne suggests that Sihanouk's mother, Princess Kossamak, might have done the same.[56] Princess Kossamak was in any case a strong-willed and striking woman quite capable of winning over key players through sheer force of personality. A British Foreign Office report much later summed her up as a "woman of strong character and practiced statecraft who has long exercised considerable political patronage...She has a statuesque beauty reminiscent of the statues of Angkor and much grace and charm of manner."[57] Sihanouk himself was long in her shadow and it is quite possible that her lobbying tilted the balance in favor of her son.

Whatever the exact nature of these machinations, Sihanouk was warmly greeted by the Cambodian population. For the French and the

Khmer elites, his coronation diverted attention from the pain and confusion of the Nazi victory and the amputation of Battambang and Siem Reap. Despite isolated mutterings—and the resentment of Monireth—Sihanouk was as legitimate a king as any of his predecessors and the population accepted him enthusiastically. They had never chosen their rulers, so who were they, they might have reasoned, to question this decision by the Grand Council of the Kingdom? In any case, foreigners, French or Vietnamese and Thai before them, had long chosen Cambodia's kings.

The day of the coronation was set for 22 October 1941, shortly before Sihanouk's 19th birthday. The day dawned "hot but radiant", with the promise of flowers and spectacles for the immense crowds already choking the streets for the pageant. At 8.30am, a guard of honor met *Résident Supérieur* Thibaudeau at the royal palace. The royal band played the *Marseillaise* and the royal fanfare—hopefully in tune by this time—and Sihanouk stepped forward, clad in gleaming white raiment, for the start of a long day's festivities. There was a 21-gun salute, before the new king made a triumphal circuit of the city streets, up boulevard Doudart de Lagrée to the Wat Phnom and back down what is today the Quai Sisowath along the banks of the Tonlé Sap River. In the parade, there were a number of elephants, including a rare "white", or albino, swarms of mandarins, pages, princesses and grand dames, all "sumptuously clad". There were representatives of the hill tribes and the Chams. Sisowath's first rode a horse and then an elephant, just as his grandfather, Monivong, had fourteen years earlier, and Sisowath had done before him. The Khmers sang,

> The King rides on a horse,
> And on an elephant's back,
> In the *réachea sey.*
> In an ornate palanquin. [58]

The detachments of Cambodian *tirailleurs* and French marines were part of the pageantry rather than a precaution against the enthusiastically respectful, even worshipful, but excited crowds. The orange robes of thousands of Buddhist monks lent splashes of color to the darker garments of the throng of peasants and city folk. As the parade filed back into the palace, the boom of another artillery salvo echoed over the *Quatre Bras.* In front of the main gates of the palace some seven hundred students from the Lycée Sisowath, organized by a philosophy student called Iem Kadul, stood in lines, each waving tiny French flags and portraits of Philippe Pétain. The students had also made a long banner inscribed with the words: "Long live the Marshal; long live His Majesty Norodom Sihanouk Varman; for a long and happy reign" and decorated with flowers and motifs of Angkor Wat. At 6.30 pm, in the throne room of the palace, before a crowd of Khmer and French dignitaries, M. Thibaudeau placed the crown of Cambodia on the young man's head. Thus began a public life that has spanned over sixty years of the country's history. Perhaps for a while, lost in the almost medieval pageantry, the French officials could forget their humiliation and imagine they represented a great power. However, Japanese journalists and photographers were out in force to record the event, the popping of their magnesium flares irritating the young king. Their presence at what they saw as an important Asian event was a reminder of France's weakness.[59]

Notes

[1] *Indochine Hebdomadaire Illustré*, 1 May 1941.

[2] Charles Meyer, (1971), *Derrière le Sourire Khmer*, Plon, Paris, p.109. There appears to be no written record of Monivong's thoughts on the matter. Possibly, he was too dispirited to care any more, which might also explain why he died intestate.

[3] Son of Norodom Sathavong and Princess Pindara.

[4] *Indochine Hebdomadaire Illustré*, 8 May 1941.

[5] For an informed discussion of succession to the Cambodian throne, see Milton Osborne, (1973), "King-making in Cambodia: From Sisowath to Sihanouk", *Journal of South-East Asian Studies*, Vol. 4, No. 3, September, pp.169-185.

[6] Milton Osborne, (1994), *Sihanouk. Prince of Light, Prince of Darkness*, University of Hawaii Press, Honolulu, p.23.

[7] Ibid. pp.23-24, Meyer, op.cit. p.109 and Sihanouk himself op.cit. p.85.

[8] Huy Kanthoul, "Mémoires", p.77. Unpublished French-language typescript, Chandler Papers, Monash University. Ms. Poc was the daughter of Poc Hell, a rich mandarin who was related by marriage to the powerful Palace Minister Thiounn and the *Phya* Kathathorn.

[9] Osborne op.cit. ("King-making") p.179. Osborne cites archival evidence for this claim. See also ANC RSC "Correspondance au Départ, 1 September to 31 December 1939. *Résident Supérieur* Thibaudeau to King Monivong, Phnom Penh, 11 September 1939, No 1647, Confidential and Secret."

[10] As, for instance, in the article "Le Prince Monireth, héritier du trône quitte le Cambodge pour aller combatte sur le front français", *La Press Indochinoise*, 2 décembre 1939.

[11] Huy Kanthoul, op.cit. p. 78.

[12] *Nagaravatta*, 14 May 1941.

[13] Sihanouk claims that the *Nagaravatta* people "exulted" when they heard the news of his succession. (Sihanouk, op. cit. pp.60-61.)

[14] Norodom Sihanouk, (1972), *L'Indochine vue de Pékin*, Éditions du Seuil, Paris, p.33.

[15] Sihanouk, (1981), *Souvenirs doux et amers*, Hachette, Paris, p.74. This could well be the case. During his exile after July 1942, Son Ngoc Thanh wrote to Suramarit. [Letter from "Le représentat en chef des bonzes de toutes les pagodes bouddhiques et des bouddhistes khmers de la presqu'île indochinoise" to the Chief Bonze of Cambodia, the Head Bonze of Langka Pagoda and Prince Suramarit. Son Ngoc Thanh Papers, in Chandler Papers, Monash University.]

[16] AOM RSC 485 Censure. Presse et Edition, 1941. Letter from Thibaudeau to the Governor of Cochinchina, 6 May 1941. Thibaudeau named *L'Opinion* of 28 April and 3 May 1941 and *La Dépêche de l'Indochine* of 2 May 1941.

[17] Sihanouk, *L'Indochine vue de Pékin*, op.cit. p.28.

[18] Norodom Sihanouk with Wilfred Burchett, (1973), *My War with the CIA. Cambodia's Fight for Survival*, Penguin, Harmondsworth, p.144. Also Sihanouk, *(Souvenirs)* op.cit. p.53.

[19] Sihanouk, *(Souvenirs)* op.cit., p.23. Some sources give the date as 22 October, but we can expect him to know his own birthday.

[20] *Indochine Hebdomadaire Illustré*, 15 May 1941.

[21] Ibid.

[22] Donald Lancaster, (1961), *The Emancipation of French Indochina*, Oxford University Press, London, p.97.

[23] Huy Kanthoul, op.cit. p.78.

[24] Ibid. p.77.

[25] "Le trône du Cambodge de S.M. Sisowath Monivong à S.M. Norodom Sihanouk", *Indochine Hebdomadaire Illustré*, 8 May 1941.

[26] Sihanouk with Burchett, op.cit. p.144.

[27] John P. Armstrong, (1964), *Sihanouk Speaks*, Walker, New York, p.54.

[28] Sihanouk, *L'Indochine vue de Pékin*, op.cit., p.33.

[29] Sihanouk with Burchett, op.cit. p.146. Meyer, (op.cit. p.111) claims that Gautier was concerned to stop inbreeding in the royal family, but dismisses the danger of this.

[30] For instance, "Cambodia. Trustworthy, Loyal, Helpful, Brave, Clean, Reverent & Snookie", *Time*, 20 November 1964.

[31] David P. Chandler, (1993), *A History of Cambodia*, Second Edition, Allen and Unwin, St. Leonards, NSW, p.195.

[32] *L'Opinion*, 28 April 1941. Clipping in AOM RSC 485. Censure Presse et Edition, 1941.

[33] Jean-Marie Bathernay, "Le jeune roi d'un peuple vénérable", *Indochine Hebdomadaire Illustré*, 6 November 1941.

[34] *Indochine Hebdomadaire Illustré*, 15 May 1941.

[35] Osborne, op.cit. p.22. Sihanouk mentions an early love of the cinema in his *Souvenirs*, op.cit. p.29. The whole family would watch Marlene Dietrich and Maurice Chevalier.

[36] ANC RSC 17673, Lon Nol. Some of Lon Nol's report cards from the Lycée Chasseloup-Laubat have survived. Lon Nol was a mediocre pupil, but used his elite connections to advance his career. He was a loyal Sihanoukist after independence, but broke with the King and staged a coup in 1970 with US backing.

[37] Jean Lacouture, (trans. Patricia Wolf), (1970), *The Demigods: Charismatic Leadership in the Third World*, Alfred A. Knopf, New York, p.221.

[38] Ibid. passim. Weber's ideas are set out in Max Weber, (trans. A.M. Henderson and Talcott Parsons), (1947), *Theory of Social and Economic Organization*, Free Press, New York.

[39] Sihanouk, op.cit. p.27. Mme. Pat, who was of "bourgeois origin", had been married to Prince Hassakan, one of the many sons of King Norodom. See also Sihanouk, *L'Indochine vue de Pékin*, op.cit. pp.21-23.

[40] Osborne, op.cit. p.22. Sihanouk mentions his father's "adventures" in *L'Indochine vue de Pékin*, op.cit. p.23.

[41] *Indochine Hebdomadaire Illustré*, 15 May 1941.

[42] Preface by Penn Nouth, (1959), *L'Action de S.M. Sihanouk pour l'independance du Cambodge, 1941-1955*, Phnom Penh. (Collection of articles from *Réalités Cambodgiennes*, 13 September 1958 to January 1959.) P.2. Also Sihanouk, *L'Indochine vue de Pékin*, op.cit. pp. 20-21.

[43] Meyer, op.cit. p.110.

[44] Jean Decoux, (1949), *A la Barre de l'Indochine. Histoire de mon Gouvernement Général (1940-1945)*, Plon, Paris, p.284.

[45] Sihanouk, op.cit. p.53.

[46] Sihanouk with Burchett, op.cit. p.145.

[47] Sihanouk (*Souvenirs*), op.cit. p.55.

[48] Meyer, op.cit. p.107.

[49] Huy Kanthoul, op.cit. p.77.

[50] Gilbert David, (1994), *Chroniques secrètes d'Indochine (1928-1946)*, Vol. I, Editions L'Harmattan, Paris, p.138.

[51] Sihanouk, op.cit. p.55.

[52] We should not forget that Léon Blum was a Jew. Vichy was stridently anti-Semitic and the sentiment was rife in the French armed forces. As late as the 1990s, official French military historians still claimed that the guilt of Alfred Dreyfus was an open question.

[53] Huy Kanthoul, op.cit. p.77.

[54] Osborne, op. cit. ("King-making") p.180.

[55] Meyer, op.cit.

[56] Osborne, ("King-making") op.cit. p.178n. There was also a suggestion that François Baudoin might have been bribed to improve Monivong's chances back in the 1920s.

[57] PRO FO 474/9. Appendix. Biographical notes. No. 23. Leading Personalities in Cambodia, 1955. Mr. Heppel to Mr. Macmillan. (Received May 16).

[58] Cambodian song, "Journey of the King", in A. Tricon and Ch. Bellan, (1921), *Chansons Cambodgiennes*, Société des Études Indochinoises, Saigon. The *réachea sey* was a kind of palanquin used for riding on an elephant's back.
[59] The above account draws on the following sources: AOM RSC 671 Couronnement de Sihanouk, 25-30 octobre 1941; AOM RSC 672, Couronnement de Sihanouk; *Indochine Hebdomadaire Illustré*, 15 May 1941; *L'Echo du Cambodge*, 30 April 1941; *L'Opinion*, 29 and 31 October 1941; *La Dépêche de l'Indochine*, 22 October and 2 November 1941 and Sihanouk (*Souvenirs*), op.cit. p.69.

Chapter 19

The Vichy Regime: Authoritarianism, *Khmérité* and Revolt

Rudyard Kipling—who we should not forget was English—wrote that "East is East and West is West and never the twain shall meet". The French and the Indochinese, attached together for three quarters of a century, prove the contrary.
—Indochine Hebdomadaire Illustré, 25 December 1941.

The death of Monivong coincided with the start of a new period in Franco-Khmer relations. The nascent Cambodian nationalist movement gained strength and purpose as a whole layer of educated Khmers realized that they might be able to escape the Faustian bargain struck between King Norodom and Admiral de Lagrandière almost 80 years before. Politically and economically, it was a gloomy time for French colonialism. The trappings of the Third Republic were cast aside and replaced by those of Pétain's quasi-fascist, authoritarian *État Français*. Although France was the nominal ruler of Indochina in World War II, the real power lay with Japan, which was at that time using the territory as a staging ground for the southward thrust of her armies.[1] The Japanese soldiers were an army of occupation; egged on by their officers to flaunt the fact, they often humiliated the French. The new Governor General, Admiral Decoux, was terrified of them. Meanwhile, in Europe, Nazi troops occupied northern France and the southern part was governed as a quasi-independent state from a capital at the spa town of Vichy. The presence of Marshal Philippe Pétain, the "hero of Verdun" at the head of the government was reassuring in so bewildering a time. Vichy received the support of a huge slice of the French population, particularly among the peasantry, the numerous middle classes and the Catholic Church. Pétain pledged to set up a corporate state[2] roughly modeled on Franco's Spain.[3] One symbol of the new order was May Day, re-invented as the "festival of work and social cooperation", and celebrated at the church of Sacré Coeur and the Wat Onulom at Phnom Penh.[4]

However, not everyone supported the Marshal. A section of the French army escaped at Dunkirk and formed the nucleus of a government-in-exile at London under the young officer, Charles de Gaulle. Predictably, Pétain declared the pro-Allied Free French movement illegal and put a price on de Gaulle's head. France's overseas empire split between partisans of de Gaulle and Pétain. In Indochina in July 1940, Governor General Raoul Catroux slipped away from his pro-Vichy military colleagues and joined the Gaullists. The French Indochinese administration plumped for Pétain, despite the presence of a substantial number of Gaullists in the territories. An Australian government report estimated Gaullist support at as high as 70 per cent among the French in Indochina in late 1940,[5] but another claim contradicts this, asserting that the majority were "stupefied" by the fall of France, blamed it on Britain and supported Pétain.[6] The *Résident Supérieur* at Phnom Penh claimed that the French population of the city "had rallied with enthusiasm to the policies of the Marshal."[7]

In Catroux's place, Foreign Minister Platon appointed his naval colleague, Admiral Jean Decoux, as Governor General.[8] Decoux proved himself a Vichy zealot. After the war, he was arrested and put on trial in France, but was able to convince the court that he had no alternative but to go through the motions of supporting Vichy. The record casts doubt on this version. Decoux governed Indochina via what a Gaullist engineer, M. Bourgoin considered a layer of "fanatics".[9] Mr. Meiklereid, the acting British Consul at Saigon, described Decoux as a man "small physically as in mental outlook, and irascible to a degree which deprives him of all charm."[10] Bourgoin said, "His most outstanding characteristic is that although usually calm and rather reserved, he literally explodes [*sic*] when the conversation turns to the Fighting French..." Notable Vichy zealots in the French Cambodian administration included the police official Truc and his Alsatian colleague, Ernest Hoeffel.[11]

Savage repression by Decoux

Immediately after his appointment, Decoux unleashed a savage repression[12] against real and potential opponents. A witness said, "The Decoux government has exerted such strong repressive measures that hardly any support for the de Gaulle movement has been organised."[13] The police were omnipresent. Huy Kanthoul writes that they "poked their noses into everything", splitting hairs to try to prove hidden subversion. Political talk could land the unwary in prison.[14] An intelligence officer who interviewed a former Hanoi resident outside of Indochina wrote, "It was noticed that Mr. Griffin frequently glanced over his shoulder during the interview as he has not yet become accustomed to the freer conditions obtaining in Australia."[15] There was a steep rise in the number of prisoners. In 1936, there were 917 prisoners in all the jails of Cambodia.[16] By 1943, this had grown fourfold, with almost 950 prisoners held in the Phnom Penh prison alone.[17] The normal jails were augmented by what police boss Truc himself described as a concentration camp, built in late 1940 to isolate "undesirables" at Pich Nil on Route Locale 7, in a malarial area of Kompong Speu province near the pass between the Kirirom and Elephant Mountains. Elephants and tigers roamed the nearby jungle.[18] In March 1943, the camp housed almost 40 prisoners, 31 of whom were detainees held without trial. However, unlike the camps at Dachau and Drancy,[19] Pich Nil was a ramshackle affair and by 1943, Truc feared a mass break out.[20] There were both Khmer and Vietnamese prisoners in the camp, including a number of Caodaists, who were expelled to Cochinchina after it was judged that they had "learned their lesson".[21] Militiamen under European command guarded the camp. The ordinary French jails in Cambodia were brutal places,[22] so Pich Nil must have been a place of despair. One French guard, a certain Douvrier, was described after a dispute with a colleague as "a malevolent functionary, wicked, with a lunatic character...who readily abuses his authority..."[23]

The regime had all the trappings of Franco's Spain and the other right wing totalitarian states, with a personality cult around the octogenarian Marshal Pétain, whose portraits stared down from public buildings and churches in Cambodia. Slogans such as: "Only one leader: PÉTAIN. Only one duty: OBEY. Only one motto: SERVE"[24] [capitals in the original] were repeated endlessly. Football crowds were required to stand and chant his name before matches began[25] and the fascist salute was adopted at all public events. The limited press freedom that had existed disappeared and all newspapers had to extol the virtues of Pétain and his "National Revolution". Large white spaces attested to the power of the censors, who suspended publication of *Nagaravatta* for a while in 1940 for ridiculous reasons.[26] Later, the French press largely censored itself. Pro-Allied propaganda disappeared overnight from the pages of *L'Echo du Cambodge* and other publications, replaced by sour xenophobia and visceral anti-Semitism, with a stream of articles denigrating Britain and extolling collaboration with Germany.[27] Decoux's main mouthpieces in Cambodia were the heavily subsidized color magazine *Indochine Hebdomadaire Illustré*[28] and the old establishment stalwart, *L'Echo du Cambodge*. When the British fortress of Singapore fell, the press crowed at their ex-ally's humiliation. Pro-Axis broadcasts by Indochinese Vichy Radio caused "a considerable amount of indignation..." in the French Pacific colonies[29] and the press gloated over the early Nazi victories over the "Bolshevik anti-Christ",[30] and played up Pope Pius XII's praise for Italian soldiers on the Eastern Front.[31] Another widely read paper in Indochina was *L'Impartial*; edited by "a very doubtful character called Bernard,"[32] "a man of amazing violence".[33]

The regime was so obsessively anti-British that officials at Phnom Penh banned such films as *Gunga Din* and the *Bengal Lancers* for exalting "the courage and *esprit de corps* of the English army in India"[34] and prohibited screenings of *Entente Cordiale* because it "glorified Franco-English friendship".[35] Nor was there to be any frivolity; shortly after the Armistice with Germany, the crusty old *Résident Supérieur* Thibaudeau banned public dancing on pain of imprisonment for the second offence.[36] A number of Khmers, including the businessman Sonn Sann, Sihanouk's father Prince Suramarit, Education Minister Meas Nal, the journalist Kim Hak and former *Lycée* prizewinner Mlle. Khieu Ponnary,[37] worked with Vichy journalists on the directorate of the zealously pro-Axis *Radio Bulletin du Cambodge*.[38]

The anti-Jewish laws in Cambodia

The cruelest Vichy crusade was against the Jews, who were persecuted despite their small numbers in Indochina. The official media blamed the fall of France on the alleged intrigues of Jews,

Marxists and democrats. *Indochine* even invented a new category of ideological error, adding "Judeo-Gaullist propaganda"[39] to the usual Axis abuse of "pluto-judeo-freemasonry".[40] In October 1940, Pétain promulgated a Statute of the Jews, modeled on Hitler's Nuremberg Laws, which banned Jews from state employment and public life.[41] Admiral Decoux swiftly enforced the law in Indochina. He instructed his subordinates to bar Jews as a matter of "urgency" from a range of jobs including governors, teachers, employees in the mines and public works departments. The judiciary, police and armed forces were to sack all Jews.[42] In later years, the regime extended the provisions of the Statute; all public figures, even in private industry and commerce, and including Asians, had to obtain a "certificate of Aryan nationality".[43] Thus, M. Charles Lambert declared at Phnom Penh on 14 December 1940 that he was not a Jew. In a ceremony beyond farce, M. Tan Mau, a Khmer businessman and member of the *Nagaravatta* group, wrote, "I, the undersigned, a member of the Chamber of Commerce and Agriculture swear on oath that the law of 3 October 1940 does not apply to me"—i.e. he swore he was Aryan and not Jewish.[44] Suspicion of "cosmopolitans" extended to the Chinese population, many hundreds, even thousands of whom were expelled from Cambodia during the Vichy years, ostensibly for non-payment of taxes,[45] but really as a means of "ethnic cleansing." In late 1941, Decoux stopped all telegraphic communication with the USA and the British Empire and announced that all foreigners were to report weekly to the police. He directed this in particular against British residents but it was something of a dead letter in Cambodia where the sole British subject was already serving a prison term in Phnom Penh.[46]

One essential feature of European fascism, the single mass party, was lacking in Cambodia. Indeed, there were no legal parties; Pétain had dissolved *all* the existing parties in June 1940. However, the Vichy old soldiers' legion (*Légion Française des Combattants*) functioned as the *de facto* single party in Indochina. Admiral Decoux claimed that the Legion was "neither a political party nor a combat association", but he added, "It is an instrument—the best instrument—of French unity."[47] The Cambodian magazine of the Legion, with contributions from Pétain, Laval, Decoux and Darlan, was one long howl against "degenerate" democracy, Perfidious Albion and the Jews.[48] The Legion's activists bullied all Frenchmen to join and "only very few had the courage to abstain."[49] Civil servants could not expect promotion unless they joined.[50] Gaullists referred to it as "the local Gestapo" and British Consul Meiklereid claims that it maintained a network of paid informers and that "any indiscreet remark was duly reported to them with serious consequences for the person concerned."[51]

Mass organization and the Khmers

It is a paradox that although totalitarian states are strictly oligarchic, they need to legitimize and strengthen themselves through mass participation. Both the Nazis and the Italian Fascists came to power as mass movements of the petty bourgeoisie, as "counter-revolutions" against the "Reds", and maintained a number of mass organizations after they seized power.[52] Although Vichy claimed to have come to power after a "National Revolution", the Nazis had in fact installed Pétain in office without any of the civil disturbances that had marked the fascist takeovers elsewhere in Europe. Nevertheless, Vichy consciously set out to stabilize and extend its social base via the construction of controlled mass organizations that aped those of the established fascist states. There were not enough French people or *assimilés* in Cambodia to sustain such organizations. Bunchan Mul later wrote that in "some provinces there were only one or two Frenchmen left; others had four or five. In Kompong Speu province there were none..."[53] The French were isolated from France and at the mercy of the Japanese. Many French citizens in the colony were ambivalent about the Marshal and some were secret supporters of the Free French. The presence of the Japanese had broken down ideas of European superiority among the "natives". Thus, probably from fear as much as ideological orthodoxy, Decoux decided to launch the Yuvan, a mass organization for Khmer youth, and to turn the Boy Scouts (led by Prince Monireth) into an organ of the state. The existing youth movements in Cambodia were placed under the control of a Vichy functionary, M. J. Lébas, the *président du comité central des oeuvres de jeunesse*.[54] The most significant Vichy mass movement, the Yuvan, was set up in 1941 with King Sihanouk as "the leading Yuvan in the Kingdom", but under the actual direction of the Khmer businessman, Sonn Sann (not to be confused with later *Khmers Rouges* leader Son Sen). Sonn Sann, who had studied in France, worked closely on the project with Meas Nal, the Education Minister.[55] As in other such movements overseas, strong emphasis was placed on the importance of "healthy minds in healthy bodies," with a fanatical Pétainist naval officer called Ducuroy coordinating youth sports.[56] Ironically, these organizations were to provide the Khmers with their first taste of mass politics—a vivid example of Marx's point about the contradictory nature of colonialism, albeit it in a form he did not foresee. The organizers of these movements were able to mobilize tens of thousands of Khmer youths in a variety of activities. The experience of the Yuvan in particular was invaluable for the growing nationalist movement. Alas, it was to provide a top-down, undemocratic model of political organization for Sihanouk and other post-independence political figures.

Bringing young Khmers out of the home: the Yuvan

Decoux was eager to foster Khmer national pride if he could harness it for the Vichyite cause. The Yuvan deliberately sought to bring spectacles and pageantry into the lives of Khmer youth to inspire them with Vichy and Angkorean ideals. The memory of Joan of Arc was impressed into state service as a model of heroic self-sacrifice. Young people trained in youth cadre schools and camps, where they marched, sang and competed in sports competitions as a way of building an *esprit de corps* and loyalty to Pétain. In one case, reminiscent of Olympic pageantry, relays of runners carried a flaming torch around Cambodia, cheered on by enthusiastic crowds.[57] Most importantly, the Yuvan had what *Indochine* called "a purely Cambodian character"—or *khmérité.* For thousands of young Khmers, it was their first taste of disciplined, quasi-political activity, even, as David Chandler has pointed out, their first experience of extra-familial organization of any kind.[58] Over 15,000 fascist-saluting Yuvan marched past Sihanouk at the royal palace, on 6 November 1943.[59] Another 15,000 had celebrated his birthday on 22 October 1944.[60] Some 500 Yuvan camped at Angkor in September 1942 to carry out restoration work on the ruins.[61] In late 1944, a girls' section, the Yuvani, appeared,[62] an oriental version of the League of German Girls, the *Bund Deutscher Mädel.*

This encouragement of *khmérité* extended to other areas of life and although not directly political, it contributed to the subtle changes of consciousness that were spreading through Khmer society. Decoux oversaw the renovation of the royal palace, built schools and sports stadiums and increased the budget for the restoration of Angkor.[63] The regime idealized the ancient Angkorean period—the reign of Jayavarman VII in particular[64]—and raised the salaries of "native" functionaries, partly to cement their loyalty, partly to bolster their self-esteem. Officially-sponsored Khmer publications such as *Kampuchea* continued many of the themes previously raised by *Nagaravatta*, encouraging Khmers to struggle against "laziness" and to involve themselves in commerce, the professions and skilled trades so as to develop the country and compete with the Vietnamese and Chinese.[65] Contemporary Khmer high culture was encouraged, as when a number of Khmer writers were honored at Sihanouk's 20th birthday in 1942. The writers included Huy Kanthoul, a magistrate and later a leading Democrat politician, who had published a translation of La Fontaine's *Fables* into Khmer. Others, included Chet Chim Tap, who had written a drama called *The Glorious Soldier*; Khem Penn and Banteng, the co-authors of a poem about Joan of Arc[66]; Kan who had written a poem entitled "The Legend of Teao Ek"; and Yeng Sai, who had published a novel entitled *Blooming Flower, Wilted Flower.*[67] Sihanouk, doubtless encouraged by the French, also introduced a number of new Cambodian decorations in this period. These included the *Khemara Kalarit* (Order of Sporting Merit), in August 1944 and a female order of merit, the *Satrei Vattana,* in late 1943.[68]

Romanization and austerity

Yet, if Decoux deliberately encouraged *khmérité* to harness it to Vichy's needs, his "autocratic temperament and purblind insensitivity"[69] stirred up massive resentment. He was particularly ham-fisted in his approach to reform of the Khmer alphabet and the Buddhist calendar, seeking to romanize the script and bring in the Gregorian calendar regardless of Khmer feelings. The Buddhist monks, who are greatly esteemed by the people, spearheaded opposition to the changes. Norodom Sihanouk has claimed that he considered abdicating in protest against the changes, but that his parents persuaded him not to[70] and perhaps such a whim did cross his mind. The French were used to seeing the Khmer people as a passive, apolitical mass. The fact that some members of the Khmer elite, including the journalist Kim Hak, publicly praised the new script added to the complacency of French officials.[71] Members of the elite, who often looked down on the ordinary people for their lack of French[72] were out of touch and their advice to the French was of dubious merit. It is possible, although by no means certain, that a more patient administration might have changed the people's minds about the new *quoc ngu khmer* script, but the drama unfolded against a background of increasing resentment against the wartime austerity, which was exacerbated by the regime's economic policies. Bunchan Mul, who was a young nationalist activist in 1942, claims that taxes grew heavier and heavier and that "The Khmer people had no rights or liberty at all; [the French]...took away all our rights and we could not protest." Some families had so few clothes that they were forced to take it in turns to venture outside, or else bought cheap shorts made out of plaited grass.[73] The war had seriously disrupted shipping and the treaty with Japan forced Indochina to sell agricultural and mineral commodities at very low prices. In fact, Japan became almost the sole trading partner, supplying small quantities of manufactured goods and taking almost all of the country's exports, much of which were obtained on credit. As they gained the upper hand, the Allies also steadily tightened their naval blockade on the countries of the "Greater East Asia Co-Prosperity Sphere". Rubber production was cut back and the cotton industry declined to 25 per cent of its pre-war levels. The Government introduced strict rationing of foodstuffs, petrol and oil, and cars were adapted to run on wood alcohol or charcoal. Exotic lubricants appeared, made of copra, fish, peanut and castor oil for industrial machinery and cars.[74] Salt, which is essential for the production of the Khmer staple *prahoc*, was virtually unobtainable. Some people added wood ashes to give their food the salty taste Khmers crave.[75] Before the war, Cambodia had exported rice and although Japan took some of this, it did not make up for what had been lost when other markets disappeared. This caused great bitterness, as did the compulsory sale of oils, rice, firewood and kapok to the government at low prices for the Japanese war effort—or for resale by the Government at inflated prices to the public. The people also resented Japanese demands for *corvée* labor for military purposes. The government also continued with a number of pre-war public works and irrigation schemes, such as the reconstruction of the western *baray* at Angkor and dams and canals in Kandal province.[76] As usual, *corvée* and convict labor was widely used and this was a continuing source of discord, despite the very real benefits of irrigation. By the end of the war, according to Sihanouk, the Japanese had even stripped the windows and doors out of the schools for firewood.[77] In 1942, however, the French were the most visible target for public anger.

The Khmer population had been politically dormant since the great demonstrations of 1916, but this was about to change. The *quoc ngu khmer* issue sparked off the most direct anti-French movement since the Great Rebellion of the mid-1880s. Until 1942, anti-French feeling had been muted, even timid, outside of the small and illegal Communist circles,[78] which were largely confined to the Vietnamese community. The politics of *Nagaravatta*, the Khmer-language weekly founded in 1936 by Son Ngoc Thanh, Sim Var and Pach Chhuon, illustrate this timidity. Although at times the magazine spoke in subversive parables, the censors found little fault with it.[79] Its nationalism was relatively unsophisticated and attacked the

Vietnamese rather than the French. After the territorial losses following the Franco-Thai war, however, the magazine grew bolder, with evidence that the Japanese encouraged more openly anti-French positions. According to the French writer Gilbert David, the Japanese stirred up opposition to romanization from behind the scenes to weaken the administration.[80] Son Ngoc Thanh secretly contacted the Japanese military commanders soon after they moved into Cambodia in 1941 and they appear to have encouraged the anti-French demonstration of 20 July 1942.[81] Son Ngoc Thanh claims to have submitted plans for independence to the Japanese commanders.[82] The *Nagaravatta* edition of 14 May 1941 was heavily censored because it had indirectly criticized French weakness by portraying Cambodia as a rabbit preyed upon by savage animals.[83] After this, the censors struck out large sections of more than 30 issues, including a dozen editorials before the paper was closed down after the disturbances of July 1942.[84] The process was uneven, however, for as late as January 1942, an issue of the paper considered that "so far Pétain's policy seems good for us."[85]

The "Revolt of the Parasols"

It is likely, however, that the editors were circumspect in order to avoid unpleasant consequences, perhaps acting on Japanese advice. The letters of Son Ngoc Thanh, the central nationalist leader, reveal that he was already secretly negotiating with the Japanese to secure independence for Cambodia. Thanh claims to have contacted the Japanese Gendarmerie shortly after they moved into Cambodia in 1941.[86] Events soon took a more radical turn. In July 1942,[87] a leading monk and teacher of Pali at the Buddhist Institute, the 45-year-old *Achar* Hem Chieu[88] delivered a series of inflammatory anti-French sermons in Phnom Penh. His closest friend and supporter was a 23-year-old Phnom Penh bicycle merchant called Nuon Duong.[89] Their militancy illustrates the increasing resolve of the *Nagaravatta* group as a whole.[90] Hem Chieu was associated with a "modernist group" at the School of Pali,[91] which included the *Achars* Pang Kat, So Hasy, Khieu Chum and Uk Chea. The opportunity to put their revolutionary nationalist principles into practice came from an unexpected quarter. The French were concerned about brawling between Cambodian *tirailleurs* and militiamen (or "red boots" and "black boots" as they were called by the Khmers) and asked Hem Chieu to chastise the miscreants during the course of a sermon. Instead, he seized the opportunity to deliver a revolutionary harangue. He called on all the monks to boycott the romanization of the Khmer script and the introduction of the Gregorian calendar. More broadly, he condemned the French administration as arbitrary and dictatorial and asked the soldiers if they would serve Cambodia or the foreign masters, and denounced "the abuses of power by our self-styled French protectors who are themselves today under Japanese domination." Unfortunately for the monks, some pro-French soldiers were present and they told the authorities of the revolutionary diatribes. The authorities arrested fifteen other soldiers and lured Hem Chieu to visit the government offices, where he was seized and defrocked of his *Achar's* robes. Nuon Duong was also arrested at his home and it looked as if the agitation had been quelled.

However, news of the arrests incensed many people in the capital. Early on the morning of 20 July 1942, following a decision by the *Nagaravatta* leaders, several thousand angry Khmers began to congregate in the streets close by the Wat Phnom and the adjacent *Résidence Supérieure*, demanding the release of the arrested *achar.* According to Bunchan Mul, who acted as a bicycle courier for the nationalists, the Japanese police approved of the demonstration, but insisted that it had to remain peaceful and orderly. Many of the marchers were monks and because they carried their traditional sunshades, the event became known as the "Revolt of the Parasols". Prominent among them was the *Achar* Mean, another teacher of Pali. He later adopted the alias of Son Ngoc Minh and became the first president of the Communist Party of Kampuchea. A number of Khmer Caodaists (who had their own complaints against French intolerance) and lay nationalists joined the monks. The central leader of the demonstration was the old soldier Pach Chhuon, an editor of *Nagaravatta*, who marched in the front ranks of the demonstration, charged with presenting the grievances of the crowd to the authorities at the *Résidence*. Significantly, although some of the demonstrators met by the walls of the royal palace before making their way up the Boulevard Doudart de Lagrée to the Wat Phnom, they did not make any representations to King Sihanouk; unlike in 1916, when the crowds had presented their grievances to King Sisowath. The authorities were at first content to keep the demonstrators under surveillance, but the police spies were "pale and scared", wrote Bunchan Mul. A large crowd with a banner filed into the street between the Hôtel Le Royal, past the National Library, to the Wat Phnom and the *Résidence* while large numbers of bystanders looked on from the footpaths.

The riot at the French Résidence

Accounts vary as to what happened next. According to Son Ngoc Thanh, who had taken refuge with the Japanese police, Pach Chhuon was allowed into the *Résidence*, only to be arrested and bundled out by the back door.[92] Thanh claimed that police inspector Brocheton said publicly to Pach Chhuon, "It isn't Japan, it isn't the Japanese gendarmerie who give the orders here. It's me, it's France."[93] Bunchan Mul, who was among the demonstrators, says that the pressure of bodies forced Pach Chhuon through the doors and into the arms of the police, who snatched him away. According to Osborne, Pach Chhuon led part of the crowd into the *Résidence*, where they attacked officials and broke furniture. Sihanouk claims that violence broke out when a monk struck a French official with his parasol, breaking his nose. These last accounts telescope events. What is certain is that a confused mêlée broke out in which the demonstrators fought back with sticks, stones, sunshade handles and *kaun tang* against several hundred riot police. One of these *kaun tang*—large rivets tied to long pieces of strong elastic—struck Inspector Brocheton on the head and blood poured over his shirt. Bunchan Mul threw a bicycle at the policemen. Many others on both sides were hurt before the police drove the crowd from the street. Two truckloads of Japanese police arrived and stood by. They did not intervene, but Son Ngoc Thanh's claim that their presence prevented the French police from opening fire on the demonstrators[94] has the ring of truth. Given the ruthless intolerance of French for the slightest criticism of their rule, it is likely that the Japanese presence prevented a bloodbath. The police and the military arrested Pach Chhuon and between thirty and two hundred other demonstrators, depending on the account. There were numerous arrests at the time and others were picked up later after the police developed photographs of offenders. Bunchan Mul was arrested as he set up his coffee and noodle stall the following morning.

The clash was savage and the use of *kaun tang* suggests a degree of premeditation by some of the demonstrators, but the response of the French authorities was draconian. The following December, a special tribunal at Saigon sentenced Pach Chhuon, Hem Chieu and Nuon Duong to death. Many others were given long sentences; Bunchan Mul, for instance, was given five years hard labor plus fifteen years of exile from Cambodia on completion of his sentence. The Government in France later commuted the death sentences to life imprisonment at Poulo Condore—Tralach Island to the Khmers—the penal colony in the South China Sea. The Government feared that executions might inflame Cambodian opinion.[95] It is also possible that the Japanese secretly made representations on the prisoners' behalf.[96] Hem Chieu fell sick and died at the end of 1943, but Pach Chhuon and dozens of others worked on the chain gangs until freed by the Japanese in 1945. The prisons served as political universities where the somewhat unsophisticated Khmer rebels learned from Viet Minh and other Vietnamese revolutionaries. Bunchan Mul tells us that Vietnamese prisoners welcomed the Khmers and were very kind to them. They "understood the idea of rebellion with a common interest before we did", he wrote. The Viet Minh prisoners used their time to educate themselves in politics, history and foreign languages and the Khmers learned a lot from them.[97]

Not all of the leaders of the Parasol Affair were captured. The Japanese military police, the *Kempetei*, smuggled Son Ngoc Thanh to Siamese-occupied Battambang, from whence he traveled to exile at Bangkok and Tokyo. Other prominent figures fled to the countryside. *Achar* Mean, for example, is believed to have spent two years at Yeay Tep in Kompong Chhnang province.[98] *Nagaravatta* was banned and its assets were liquidated,[99] but Pach Chhuon, Son Ngoc Thanh and Bunchan Mul went on to play prominent roles both in the struggle for independence and in the subsequent politics of post-colonial Cambodia. Meanwhile, in the aftermath of the Revolt of the Parasols, the French police rounded up hundreds of suspects and placed the Buddhist Institute under surveillance, warning the director to keep politics out of religion.[100] The Caodai sect was savagely repressed although the Caodaist temple in Phnom Penh had sought protection from the Japanese.[101] By a peculiar train of logic, the Caodaists believed that the Japanese were their allies because of the sect's adoption of the swastika, itself the symbol of Japan's German ally.[102]

The significance of the Parasol Affair

Although the Revolt of the Parasols failed, it was an important milestone in the development of Khmer nationalism. Interestingly, as Milton Osborne and others have pointed out, King Sihanouk has always downplayed the affair. Bunchan Mul's account was not published until after the anti-Sihanouk coup in 1970; David Chandler believes that the book could not have been published earlier because it "successfully corrects the myth that Sihanouk alone was responsible for Cambodia's independence."[103] At the time of the demonstration, Sihanouk was a docile instrument of the French and preoccupied with pleasure. He devotes a scant three paragraphs to the affair in his memoirs before moving on to what he clearly regards as the more important matters of his love life.[104] Not surprisingly, the future relationship between Sihanouk, Son Ngoc Thanh and the other members of the former *Nagaravatta* group was to prove stormy. In the meantime, Thanh's circle bided their time, but grew more implacable in their desire to evict the "white vultures" from their country.[105] In exile, Thanh began signing himself the "Representative of the Khmer Nationalist Party for the Independence of Cambodia".[106] Thanh raged that although the French "always pretended to be the protector of Cambodia", they had done virtually nothing for the social, intellectual or economic development of the country. Moreover, they were incapable of defending the country from its enemies.[107]

For the time being, the French had crushed overt opposition to their rule. The Japanese had encouraged the demonstration, but remained cautious. As we have seen, Son Ngoc Thanh had approached the Japanese police commander at Phnom Penh with a plan for a coup against the French. The commander was sympathetic, but in the event, he took no steps to put the plan into practice. Bunchan Mul claims that the Japanese approved the demonstration but insisted on passive resistance to any use of force by the French.[108] The Japanese commander was in a delicate situation as Japan and Vichy France were allies. Japan's attentions were in any case focused on the unfolding war in the Pacific. It is most likely that the Japanese decided on a "wait and see" policy, although they could have crushed the French garrison had they wished. The French troops in Indochina were unreliable and the Japanese had 26,000 disciplined troops there in May 1942, including 7,000 in Cambodia.[109] However, staging an anti-French putsch would have been a messy diversion at this stage. Indochina was important to Japan as a source of raw materials and so long as they kept coming, coups were out of the question, at least until military victory was achieved in the Pacific. It is likely, too, that the Japanese had decided that Son Ngoc Thanh's plotters were too politically unsophisticated to back at that stage. The 20 July demonstration was militant, but most of the population remained bystanders and the French were able to quell the riot without recourse to armed soldiers. David Chandler has argued that the Japanese did not see Son Ngoc Thanh as a skilled political leader.[110] Openly backing a grab for power by Son Ngoc Thanh would have been a leap into the dark. Thanh himself appears to have decided that the best course of action lay in working for a Japanese victory, after which the French could be overthrown and a "national socialist monarchy" installed in Cambodia.[111] Although with hindsight this seems a foolish dream, it seemed realistic at the time. Japan encouraged Asian nationalism, if only for her own imperialist ends, but for Son Ngoc Thanh and others like him, Japan was "the sun over Asia". The Japanese army, battle-hardened by a decade of fighting in China, seemed invincible. In December 1941, Japanese planes destroyed much of the American Pacific fleet as it lay at anchor at Pearl Harbor. In February 1942, the Japanese had sunk the British battleships "Repulse" and "Prince of Wales", overwhelmed a larger British army at Singapore and afterwards occupied the Netherlands East Indies. The Philippines fell in January 1942 and amphibious troops fanned out north to the Aleutians and southeast across the Pacific islands. As we now realize, Japan's supply lines were over-extended and once the United States entered the war, Japan could not hope to win against such a military-industrial colossus. As early as May and June 1942, the battles of Midway and the Coral Sea had blunted the Japanese attack. By the next year the "island-hopping" offensive of Admiral Nimitz and General MacArthur was well under way, with American landings on Guadacanal, New Georgia, Vella-Lavella and joint operations in New Guinea, Bougainville and New Britain driving the Japanese back. When the Japanese did act to install an "independent" Cambodian government, it was already too late.

Growing resentment against French rule

None of this was clear in 1942, however, and a head of resentment was building up against the French among the population. The French had originally set up the Buddhist Institute and the School of Pali as a way of controlling the Buddhist *sangha*, but a rift had opened between the monks and the "protectors". Given the esteem in which the people held the monks, the rift could not but expand. Wiser heads might have chosen the methods used by France after the 1885 Rebellion and the 1916 Affair, and granted concessions, even if only to buy time. This time, the administration did not back away from the measures that had directly sparked off the discontent. Shortly after the revolt of the parasols, they ordered the romanization of Khmer in a royal decree, or *kram*.[112] In July 1944, another *kram* replaced the Buddhist calendar with the Gregorian.[113] The mandarins accepted the measures readily, but the monks remained irreconcilably opposed.[114] Sihanouk later claimed that he had protested to the French about the measures and had even considered abdicating.[115] There is no way of verifying the claim, but Sihanouk must have been aware of the bitterness that was building up against the French. Although he had not identified himself with the

20 July movement, as nationalist feeling grew he could not afford to be seen as having opposed it at the time. Simmering nationalist sentiments occasionally broke out into the open in the following years. An alleged sorcerer called Chea Keo was arrested in Kompong Thom in August 1944, and charged with membership of a "nationalist party", the Society of Heaven and Earth. Surprisingly, given Vichy ruthlessness, the court acquitted him for lack of evidence.[116] The fact of his arrest, however, attests to the administration's fears. Other Khmers had left for Siamese-occupied Battambang as early as 1941. There, under the leadership of Poc Khun, they set up a Khmer Issarak (Free Khmer) committee dedicated to driving the French from their homeland.[117] This movement-in-exile was to form the basis of an anti-French guerrilla army. (See Chapter 25 below.)

Meanwhile, the French administration settled down to an uneasy coexistence with the Japanese. Even as the Allies pushed back the Nazi troops in Russia and North Africa and advanced up through the leg of Italy, Decoux's men continued their pro-Axis course. The lead article in the edition of *Indochine* in April 1944 praised Marshal Pétain on his 88th birthday as a blue-eyed exemplar of the "Nordic race".[118] Shortly afterwards, the paper raged against the D Day landings in Normandy and exaggerated the damage inflicted by the Nazis on the Allied armies.[119] The fascist saluting, parading and chanting in praise of the "National Revolution" continued even after the liberation of Paris in September 1944.

Decoux reads the signs of Axis defeat

The war, however, was coming closer to an end. It was clear to all except the most fanatical fascists that the Axis was doomed. In June 1944, the French army commander in Indochina, General Mordant, secretly agreed to cooperate with the de Gaulle government in Paris.[120] By March 1945, Zhukov's Red Army divisions had fought their way through East Prussia, deep into Poland and even into Silesia. Marshal Rokossovsky's armies had encircled Danzig, where the guns of the German Navy had shattered the Polish defenses on the Westerplatte in the opening days of the war. In the West, all of France was free bar an area of Alsace near Haguenau and Allied armies had driven into the Rhineland, where General Patton stood before Coblenz. In the Pacific, General MacArthur had returned to the Philippines, British "tommies" and Gurkhas had regained most of Burma and the US Marines had hoisted the stars and stripes over Iwo Jima after three weeks of intense hand-to-hand combat. The war came closer when American aircraft bombed Phnom Penh on 7 February 1945, causing widespread damage, killing one hundred people and wounding another 250 in the crowded "native" precincts.[121] The Japanese complained that French anti-aircraft crews refrained from firing on the airplanes; by this stage, the French authorities feared compromising their future relationship with the Allies. One wonders how such an act of random terror against defenseless Asian civilians was supposed to advance the war effort. It was less than ten years since the Nazi attack on the city of Guernica in the Basque country had shocked world opinion, but terror against civilians had become routine. Shortly afterwards, Dresden perished in a ghastly firestorm. The Phnom Penh raid was small in comparison, but it was a portent of the massive aerial attacks on Cambodia ordered by Kissinger and Nixon during the Second Indochina War.

Meanwhile, Decoux quietly dropped the pro-Axis rhetoric; *Indochine* now referred to the "liberation" of France and not to its invasion by "Judeo-Gaullists" and other "criminals". The Pétainist slogans disappeared; the typewritten words "République Française" replaced "État Français", which was scored out on official letterheads.[122] The new tilt, however, exposed the French to great danger. On the surface, Cambodia was calm, but the Japanese had read the all-too-visible signs that their erstwhile ally was about to defect. The Japanese were becoming increasingly truculent; on 5 February, they seized land at Kompong Chhnang for military purposes and repeated this at Pochentong, on the outskirts of Phnom Penh, three weeks later.[123] Around the same time, they refused to hand back Vietnamese deserters from the French army in Cambodia.[124]

On 17 February 1945, the Japanese Foreign Ministry informed its ambassador at Moscow, Mr. Sato, that Admiral Decoux had said that he wished to continue to cooperate with Japan. Decoux said he believed that "a legitimate government would one day be set up by popular vote in France in place of de Gaulle's regime..." "However", the report continued, "the Governor General has gradually abandoned his Pétain leanings and is pandering to de Gaulle." The ubiquitous portraits of the Marshal vanished, the Legion was abolished and the anti-Jewish laws rescinded. While Decoux continued "on the surface to be friendly" to the Japanese and complied with their demands, he stood "in great fear lest the fact of his having complied should reach the ears of the British and Americans." The report stated that "the views of Decoux and Cosme...have reached their government by telegraph and other means through the French Chargé d'Affaires in Switzerland, but so far Paris has not replied, though it is pretty certain that the views of the two officials named explain the absence in de Gaulle's speeches, of any violent references to France's relations with Japan."[125]

According to Japanese short wave broadcasts, Decoux was in secret contact with the US air force and navy, and had begun troop deployments for attacks on Japanese forces. Moreover, the French soldiers had failed to fire on Allied planes during air attacks on Saigon and Phnom Penh, the Japanese complained. Decoux had tried to hold a prayer meeting for France's liberation and he had said in a broadcast that, "Last year our motherland was liberated and the year is one which promises to bring hopes for those of us living in French Indo-China." Hard-line Pétainists—or suitable scapegoats—were purged.[126] Sensing imminent Allied victory, "the French in Cambodia began to lift their heads and adopt a more and more arrogant attitude," Huy Kanthoul later recalled.[127] For the Japanese, these actions and attitudes were intolerable. Their military security was threatened and the time had come to dispose of a regime they had tolerated only so long as it cooperated with them.

Notes

[1] Such was the opinion of the French Chargé d'Affaires at Bangkok in an intercepted message to the Vichy Foreign Minister. On 6 December 1941, he reported that Japanese troops at Pursat and other places were regrouping, probably in order to stage a rapid southwards advance. (PRO HW/1/307.)

[2] Paul Raynal, "Principes du régime corporatif", and "Caractéristiques essentielles du corporatisme", *Indochine Hebdomadaire Illustré*, 14 August 1941.

[3] For a discussion of Vichyite ideology, see Zeev Sternhell, (trans. David Maisel), (1986), *Neither Right nor Left. Fascist Ideology in France*, Princeton University Press, Princeton, New Jersey. For a collection of the writings of the ideologues who inspired Vichy, see J.S. McClelland (ed. and introduced), (1970), *The French Right (from de Maistre to Maurras)*, Jonathan Cape, London. Closer to Franco's Catholic authoritarianism than to Mussolini's fascism or Hitler's pagan Nazism, Vichy's ideas were embedded in a tradition stretching back to the anti-Enlightenment dogmas of Joseph de Maistre (1753-1821), who regarded the French Revolution as a rebellion against God. Anti-Semitism was an integral part of this ideological stew, spiced up by the writings of, among others, Gustave Le Bon (1841-1931), Édouard Drumont (1844-1917) and Charles Maurras (1868-1952).

[4] *Indochine Hebdomadaire Illustré*, 8 May 1941.

[5] AAc A 981 INDO 7 Part 1 War Records – Indochina, Japan. Memo to the Secretary of the (Australian) Dept of External Affairs from J. T. Fitzgerald, 23 November 1940.

[6] PRO FO 371 27759. Letter from Mr. P.M. Panfield to W.R. Cockburn, 16 December 1940. This is itself contradicted by other reports, one of which claimed "The majority of French residents are pro-de Gaulle." (AAs C320 IC 9 [Japanese in Indo-China.] Rpt by G.H.V. Newman, 25 July 1941 to G3, Intelligence Section, Eastern Command. Interview with George Noellat at Euroa Court, Randwick.)

[7] AOM RSC 263. Rapport Annuel, 1940-1941. Minute Livre Vert, Situation Politique et Administrative.

[8] Jacques Michel (ed.), (19?) *La Marine Française en Indochine de 1939 à 1955*, Tome I, *septembre 1939 - août 1945*, État-Major de la Marine, Service Historique, Paris, p.39.

[9] PRO FO 371 35915 Notes and extracts from report on conditions in Indo-China prepared by Capt. J.C. Bourgoin, 4 March 1943. Bourgoin had been an engineer for 19 years in Indochina before being sacked by the Vichy authorities for his politics.

[10] AAc A981/1 INDO 2 Part 2 Indochina. Report on conditions in Indo-China from E. W. Meiklereid, British Consul-General, Saigon, 11 July 1941.

[11] PRO FO 371 35915 op.cit. Ernest Hoeffel was born at Strasbourg in 1900. He was a career civil servant in Cambodia from 1923, taking up posts as *Résident* at Takeo, Kratié and Kompong Cham, then as chief of the *Sûreté* in Cambodia. He was promoted to Governor of Cochinchina in 1942. (*Indochine Hebdomadaire Illustré*, 3 December 1942.)

[12] David, op.cit. p.108.

[13] AAs C320 IC6 The Situation in Indo-China 1941-1941. Letter to G.3, Intelligence Section, Eastern Command, Victoria Barracks, Paddington 31 May 1941 from Lt. G.H.V. Newman, Intelligence Section, Eastern Command. Notes from interview with Mr. Griffin, Shell Oil, recently stationed in Hanoi.

[14] Huy Kanthoul, "Mémoires", p.60. Unpublished French-language typescript, Chandler Papers, Monash University.

[15] Ibid.

[16] AOM RSC 423 Livre Vert du Cambodge, 1935-36. API file appended to top of Chapter I of the report.

[17] AOM RSC 675 Rapports Annuels du Cambodge, 1942-43. Rapport Annuel sur l'exercice du Protectorat pendant la période du 1er juin 1942 au 31 mai 1943. Signé Barrault, inspecteur délégué du Protectorat.

[18] Claude Fillieux, (1962), *Merveilleux Cambodge*, Société Continentale d'Éditions Modernes-Illustrées, Paris, p.30.

[19] French Jews were rounded up by the French police and incarcerated in the Drancy stadium in the Paris suburbs before deportation to the gas chambers in the East.

[20] AOM RSC 336. Inspection of prisoners, 1943-44. Report by Police Chief Truc, 1 March 1943.

[21] AOM RSC 308. Report from *Sûreté* to the *Résident Supérieur*, 20 December 1944.

[22] Cambodian prisons seem to have been worse than those elsewhere in Indochina. The Khmer revolutionary Bunchan Mul attests that "Conditions in Prey Nokor [Saigon] Prison were much better than in Phnom Penh." (Bunchan Mul, (trans. Chanthou Boua), "The Umbrella War of 1942", extract from *Kuk Niyobay (Political Prisoner)*, in Ben Kiernan and Chanthou Boua (eds.) (1982), *Peasants and Politics in Kampuchea, 1942-1981*, Zed Press, London, p.123. [Note, "umbrella" is a mistranslation of the French word "ombrelle", which actually means a sunshade or parasol.]

[23] AOM RSC 487 *Résident* at Kompong Speu to the *Résident Supérieur*, 5 June 1944.

[24] Cited in numerous publications, including *Indochine Hebdomadaire Illustré*, 1 January 1942.

[25] Norodom Sihanouk, (1981), *Souvenirs Doux et Amers*, Hachette, Paris, p.96. The athletes chanted "Maréchal, nous voilà. Devant toi, le sauveur de France, nous jurons, nous tes gars" etc.

[26] Huy Kanthoul, op.cit.

[27] In, for instance, *L'Echo du Cambodge*, of 20 and 27 November 1941.

[28] PRO FO 371 35915 op.cit. *Indochine* was edited by Jean Saumont with a government subsidy of 60,000 piastres per year

[29] AAc A 981/1 Indo 3. Use of Saigon Broadcasting Station, short wave messages from Saigon on Nov 26 1942 to Noumea etc.

[30] See, for instance, *La Dépêche de l'Indochine*, 22 October 1941.

[31] *Indochine Hebdomadaire Illustré*, 27 September 1942, citing *Légionnaire du Tonkin* of 1 September 1942.

[32] AAc A981/1 Indo 9. Indo-China – US. Visit of M Louis Castex to USA. Australian Legation Washington DC to the Dept of External Affairs, Canberra, July 25 1941.

[33] PRO FO 371 35915 op.cit.

[34] AOM RSC 655. Censure cinématographique 1941. Sûrêté, 31 July 1941.

[35] Ibid. 3 October 1940.

[36] Royal decree number 1909, reported in *La Presse Indochinoise*, 2 July 1940.

[37] Khieu Ponnary later became the first wife of Saloth Sar, alias Pol Pot.

[38] AOM RSC 303. Presse, Propagande 1942-44.

[39] As in, for instance, the *Indochine Hebdomadaire Illustré* of 8 October 1942.

[40] Ibid. 26 November 1942.

[41] AOM RSC 650 Deuxième Bureau, 1940-1941. Statut des Juifs: application de la loi du 3 octobre 1940 – aux assemblies élus du Cambodge. Interestingly, access to this file is still restricted.

[42] Ibid. Circulaire du Gougal - v-421/P1 – du 6 novembre 1940. Marked "circulaire très urgent".

[43] Ibid. Circular from Decoux to chiefs of local administration, 13 March 1942. The later measures were noted by the British. (PRO WO/208/636 Cambodia. Gendarmerie. Feb. 1939-Nov 1945. Items extracted from the *Journal Officiel de l'Indochine* 4 July 1942. *"Anti-Jewish measures"* (emphasis in original.)

[44] AOM RSC 650, op.cit. Declaration signed by Tan Mau at Phnom Penh on 22 December 1940. Khmer schoolchildren read of *nos ancêtres les Gauls*, but it was absurd to have them swear *nos ancêtres n'étaient pas les Juifs!*

[45] AOM RSC 203. Expulsions of Chinese for non-payment of taxes.

[46] AOM RSC 453 Conflit du Pacifique. Action Française. Telegram from *Gougal* to *Résident Supérieur*. 10 December 1941. The unfortunate Briton, Frederick Stubbs, 44, was serving a two-year sentence for fraud.

[47] *Indochine Hebdomadaire Illustré*, 9 September 1943.

[48] *Légion Française des Combattants. Union Locale du Cambodge*, No. 5, September-October 1941.

[49] PRO FO 371 35926 British Nationals in Indo-China, 1943. Report by Meiklereid to the British Foreign Office, 3 December 1942.

[50] Bourgoin, op.cit.

[51] Meiklereid to the Foreign Office, 3 December 1942, op.cit.

[52] See, for instance, Daniel Guérin, (trans. Frances and Mason Merrill), (1973), *Fascism and Big Business*, Monad, New York.

[53] Bunchan Mul, op.cit. p.119.

[54] *Indochine Hebdomadaire Illustré*, 15 May 1941.

[55] J. Desjardins, (1944), "A l'ombre de la révolution maréchalienne. Le Cambodge et sa jeunesse", *Indochine Hebdomadaire Illustré*, 17 August 1944.

[56] *Kampuchea*, No 258, 12 October 1944, in AOM RSC 303, op.cit. Also Sihanouk, op. cit. p.96.

[57] "En suivant la course du flambeau", *Indochine Hebdomadaire Illustré*, 1 January 1942.

[58] Chandler, op.cit. p.195.

[59] Desjardins, op. cit.

[60] *Indochine Hebdomadaire Illustré*, 7 December 1944.

[61] "Visite au camp de jeunesse d'Angkor Vat. *Indochine Hebdomadaire Illustré*, October 1942. Also "Des camps de jeunesse en Indochine", *L'Echo du Cambodge*, 21 May 1941.

[62] Kim Hak, "Réflexions du juge lièvre sur le mouvement de jeunesse féminine," in *Kampuchea*, No 296, 20 January 1945. In AOM RSC 303, op.cit.

[63] David, op.cit. p.139.

[64] Chandler, op.cit.

[65] The headlines of *Kampuchea* included: "Cambodians must struggle against laziness—it is very harmful" (No 304, 10 February 1945); "Few Cambodians are merchants—why commerce is useful" (No 303, 8 February 1945); "To build Angkor, the old Cambodians became masons, carpenters, architects...let us imitate them!" (No 291, 9 January 1945); "Learn all the professions that the country needs. This is the duty of all Cambodians!" (No 276, 30 November 1944); and "It is wrong to believe that manual work is dishonorable!" (No 271, 18 November 1944).

[66] Vichy invented a cult around the "maid of Orleans".

[67] *Indochine Hebdomadaire Illustré*, 24 December 1942.

[68] Ibid. 28 September and 2 November 1944.

[69] Donald Lancaster, (1961), *The Emancipation of French Indochina*, Oxford University Press, London, p.97.

[70] Norodom Sihanouk, (1972), *L'Indochine vue de Pékin*, Éditions du Seuil, Paris, p.38.

[71] See, for instance, *Kampuchea*, No. 288, 30 December 1944. Meas Nal, the Education Minister, also extolled the Gregorian calendar in an interview with the paper (No 230) on 1 August 1944.

[72] Bunchan Mul, op.cit. p.116.

[73] Ibid. pp. 115-116.

[74] M.D. "La situation économique de l'Indochine", *Indochine Hebdomadaire Illustré*, 19 November 1942 and "L'Indochine et les produits de substitution. Où en sommes-nous?" 15 July 1943.

[75] Bunchan Mul, op.cit. p.116. *Prahoc*, or fermented fish paste, is an important source of protein in the Khmer diet and salt is essential in its production.

[76] Decoux, op.cit. p.453 and, for example, the *Indochine Hebdomadaire Illustré* of 28 January 1943. The western *baray* had been in disrepair since Angkorean times. It is still in use today.

[77] Sihanouk, *Souvenirs Doux et Amers*, op.cit. p.94.

[78] Communist activity had been banned by royal decree on 11 November 1939. ("Contre les communistes", *La Presse Indochinoise*, 24 November 1939.)

[79] AOM RSC 462, Presse surveillance, December 1941.

[80] Ibid. This is an educated guess, for David cites no documentary sources for his claim.

[81] Bunchan Mul, op.cit. pp. 118-120.

[82] Son Ngoc Thanh, "Mémoire sur l'entretien avec la Gendarmerie", August 1941. Son Ngoc Thanh Papers, in Chandler Papers, Monash University.

[83] AOM RSC 485 Censure Presse et Edition 1941. Contains text of the censored article entitled "The new sovereign and the new government", from *Nagaravatta,* 14 May 1941.

[84] Harish C. Mehta, (1997), *Cambodia Silenced. The Press Under Six Regimes*, White Lotus, Bangkok, p.31.

[85] Michael Vickery, "Cambodia: The Present Situation and its Background", unpublished typescript, Chandler Papers, Monash University.

[86] Son Ngoc Thanh, "Mémoire sur l'entretien avec la Gendarmerie", op.cit.

[87] The following account draws on a number of sources, including Bunchan Mul, op.cit., David, op.cit. pp. 141-142; Mehta, op. cit. p. 33, Osborne, op.cit. pp. 31-33; Ben Kiernan, (1985), *How Pol Pot Came to Power. A History of Communism in Kampuchea, 1930-1975*, Verso, London, pp. 43-45; Sihanouk, op.cit. pp.75-76 and the Son Ngoc Thanh Papers held at Monash University.

[88] Born at Tumnup, Kandal province, in 1897. Died 2 January 1943 at Poulo Condore. (AOM 7F 29 (7) Etude sur les mouvements rebelles au Cambodge, 1942-1952.)

[89] Ibid.

[90] Sihanouk believed that the monks were members of the group (Sihanouk, op.cit. p.74.) and this is borne out in Bunchan Mul's book.

[91] AOM RSC 464 Surveillance de l'Institut Bouddhique, 1943. *Résident Supérieur* Gautier to the Secretary-General of the Institute, 22 June 1943.

[92] Son Ngoc Thanh, "Entretien", op.cit.

[93] Letter from Son Ngoc Thanh to the General *État-Major* of the Imperial Japanese army in Indochina, not dated, but written apparently shortly after 20 July 1942. Son Ngoc Thanh Papers, op.cit.

[94] Son Ngoc Thanh, "Mémoire", op.cit.

[95] As the British found to their cost when they executed the leaders of the 1916 Rising in Ireland.

[96] Son Ngoc Thanh hints at this possibility in his "Mémoire", op.cit.

[97] Bunchan Mul op.cit. pp.123-124.

[98] Chandara Mohapatey, "A Khmer Issarak Leader's Story", (trans. Timothy Carney), cited in Ben Kiernan, "Les origines du communisme khmer", in Camille Scalabrino et al, (1985), *Cambodge. Histoire et Enjeux, 1945-1985*, Asie Débat 2, L'Harmattan, Paris, p. 77.

[99] AOM RSC 303 Presse, propagande 1942-44. Annexe à l'envoi No 313 Ip du 9 février 1944. Sûreté Activités nationalistes (no 5) Société D'Édition Nagaravatta, 23 juin 1943.

[100] AOM RSC 464, letter from Gautier to the Secretary General of the Buddhist Institute, 22 June 1943, op.cit.

[101] André Gaudel, (1947), *L'Indochine française en face du Japon*, J. Susse, Paris, p.47.

[102] AOM RSC 208. Report by s/brigadier Nguyen-Van-Anh and Le Phung Yen to the *Résident* at Takeo, 21 October 1944.

[103] David Chandler, cited in Ben Kiernan and Chanthou Boua, op.cit. p.115.

[104] Sihanouk, op.cit. pp.75-76. Immediately after this cursory treatment, he moves on to Chapter XI, "Mes aventures et mes amours".

[105] Letter from "Le représentat en chef des bonzes et toutes les pagodes bouddhiques et des bouddhistes khmers de la presqu'île indochinoise" addressed to the Chief of Bonzes in Cambodia, the Head of the Langka Pagoda at Phnom Penh and to Prince Suramarit. Son Ngoc Thanh Papers, op.cit.

[106] For example, letter to the Director of Dainankoosi at Saigon, 1 October 1942. Ibid.

[107] Ibid. Letter to Chin, 28 July 1942.

[108] Bunchan Mul, op.cit. p.120.

[109] PRO FO 371 31766. Axis influence in FIC, 1942. Report from Chungking to the Foreign Office, 21 May 1942.

[110] David P. Chandler, (1986), "The Kingdom of Kampuchea, March-October 1945: Japanese-sponsored Independence in Cambodia in World War II", *Journal of South East Asian Studies*, Vol. XVII, No 1, March, p.84.

[111] Son Ngoc Thanh, letter to his supporters, Tokyo 10 April 1943. Son Ngoc Thanh Papers.

[112] Sorn Samnang, "'Evolution de la société cambodgienne entre les deux guerres mondiales (1919-1939)", Thèse pour le doctorat d'histoire. Université Paris VII, Tome II, p.372.

[113] *Indochine Hebdomadaire Illustré*, 10 August 1944.

[114] Sihanouk, op.cit. p.86.

[115] Osborne, op.cit. pp.33-34.

[116] AOM RSC 308, *Sûreté* at Phnom Penh to the *Résident* at Kompong Thom and the *Résident Supérieur*, 1 August 1944.

[117] Kiernan, op.cit. p.78.

[118] *Indochine Hebdomadaire Illustré*, 20 April 1944.

[119] Ibid. 15 June 1944.

[120] Ralph B. Smith, (1978), "The Japanese Period in Indochina and the Coup of 9 March 1945", *Journal of South East Asian Studies*, IX, 2, p.276. Lancaster, op.cit. p.103.

[121] *Indochine Hebdomadaire Illustré*, 20 February 1945.

[122] As in, for example, AOM RSC 301, *Résidence Supérieure*, correspondence, Jan-March 1945. Decoux's switch of allegiance saved him from long imprisonment or worse. Along with Bérenger and others, he was put on trial after the war for collaboration, but was acquitted. A few lower ranking scapegoats "took the rap", as the Americans would say. See, for instance, *The New York Times*, 18 February 1949. See also the Admiral's own account in Jean Decoux, (1949), *À la barre de l'Indochine. Histoire de mon Gouvernment Général (1940-1945)*, Plon, Paris.

[123] Ibid.

[124] AOM RSC 308, "Annamites pro-Japonais, 21 February 1945.

[125] PRO HW/1/3536 Decoux's shift from Pétain to de Gaulle in 1945. Intercepted message from FO Tokyo to the Japanese Ambassador, Moscow. Sent 17 February 1945, transcription in English 22 February.

[126] PRO FO 371 46305. DOMEI broadcasts in English to Europe, 9 and 10 March 1945.

[127] Huy Kanthoul, op.cit. p.95.

Chapter 20

The Japanese Coup, the Kingdom of Kampuchea and the Return of the French

*The Kingdom of Cambodia no longer feels the need for French protection
and hereby declares that the treaty of protectorate with France is null and
void.*

—Norodom Sihanouk, 13 March 1945.[1]

*The Cambodian people had always loved France and the pro-French
feelings of his people were evident to all.*

—Norodom Sihanouk, reported by Agence France Presse, 13
November 1945.

At sunset on 9 March 1945, sirens wailed and shots echoed in the
streets of Phnom Penh.[2] A Japanese *coup de force* was in progress. As
the Japanese had planned, the *Phnompenhois* dispersed, fearing
another Allied air raid. Thousands of heavily armed Japanese troops
moved quickly through the dying light to take over the important
buildings in the city. They stopped all traffic and scoured the streets,
arresting the French in their homes.[3] The Japanese soldiers opened fire
with heavy machine-guns on the Beylie and Doudart de Lagrée

barracks, prompting some desultory rifle fire in return. The coup was over in half an hour, but not before the corpses of four or five Khmer militiamen sprawled in the orange dust outside the *Résidence Supérieure*.[4] Their masters, however, were reluctant to make the same sacrifice; after firing a few shots to save their honor, the French garrisons filed out of their barracks, led by their commander, Colonel Bellon.[5] The same process had occurred simultaneously throughout the five regions of French Indochina. General Noël, the commander of southern Indochina at Saigon, surrendered at the first hint of force, but there was some serious resistance in Tonkin,[6] and some provincial garrisons, including those at Kompong Thom and Siem Reap, fled to the Cambodian jungle to set up a *maquis*. One band of around forty men traversed almost the whole country, from north to south, and tried to escape by boat on the Gulf. Others retreated into the mountains southwest of Pursat and waged guerrilla war. Other Cambodian garrisons resisted for hours or days before surrendering to superior force,[7] although one Cambodian source close to the Japanese later said that the French resistance nowhere lasted more than 24 hours.[8]

Far away in Hanoi, the printers were working on the 9 March edition of *Indochine Hebdomadaire Illustré* when a detachment of Japanese soldiers burst in and stopped the presses. They forced the compositors to break up the type and the next day, a special (and final) edition of the magazine appeared, carrying a proclamation by the Japanese commander-in-chief in Indochina. The proclamation declared that the Japanese actions were necessary because of the "lack of sincerity of the French authorities…in the execution of the accord for the joint defense of the country." The Japanese wished to assume responsibility for defense, the proclamation continued, "in collaboration with the Indochinese peoples". Public order would be restored and indigenous functionaries were requested to resume their functions. The lives, goods, rights and interests of the general population would be protected as part of "the reconstruction of a new Indochina".[9] They were brave words, but the Japanese "sun over Asia" was setting even as the Khmer dusk shrouded the bodies of the dead militiamen in Phnom Penh.

The proclamation hinted at the kind of political future Japan envisaged for Indochina. The French Administration was abolished. A sunset to sunrise curfew was imposed, along with martial law throughout the five regions of Indochina. Admiral Decoux and his top aides were held in "protective custody" at Locninh[10] and the disarmed French soldiers were interned in concentration camps, often in brutal and unsanitary conditions. Meanwhile, the previously cocksure French civilians[11] resident in Cambodia soon had cause for dismay. On 24 March, mobs attacked French citizens in the streets and Phnom Penh and Saigon and besieged their houses following false news spread by the Japanese Domei Press Agency. The Japanese authorities used the incidents as a pretext to intern the French, allegedly for their own safety. Men, women and children were imprisoned in what one French writer later described as "camps of slow death", where, abused by brutal guards, they suffered from lack of food and water and endured vermin and disease.[12] A number of Frenchmen were murdered after or soon before the Japanese surrender. The *Kempetai* (military police) executed Father R.P. David and a *métis* called Sère in a ditch at Kratié as night fell on 22 August.[13] David, who had served as a priest for many years in Cambodia, had survived an attack on his life by the bandit *Sena* Ouch back in 1913. Three other high-ranking French officials, M. Haelewyn, the *Résident Supérieur* of Annam, Édouard Delsalle, an *Inspecteur des Affaires Politiques*, and Abel Desalle, the commander-in-chief of the *Garde Indochinoise*, were murdered at the same time near Stung Treng. Afterwards, their killers paraded with bloody swords and clothing to advertise the event.[14]

Sihanouk asked to declare independence

Khmer dignitaries were spared such an ordeal. Immediately after the *coup de force*, King Sihanouk's Uncle Buor Horng—a man of strongly anti-French opinions—and some Japanese officers arrived at the royal palace. They took Sihanouk's French aide-de-camp, de Boysson, into custody, along with the *Résident Supérieur*, André Berjoan, who had assumed his duties less than a month before. To the young king's great surprise, the Japanese special advisor to Cambodia, M. Kubota, asked him to declare his country's independence from France.[15] Sihanouk was not the only surprised Khmer that day. There is little evidence that even hard line pro-Japanese nationalists knew in advance of the *coup de force*.[16] The Japanese told the nationalist Chandara Mohaptey, then living at Stung Treng, to ready himself for an announcement, but did not tell him what it was about until after the coup.[17] Sihanouk had little choice but to comply with Kubota's wishes. He asked the royal astrologer to nominate a propitious date and on 13 March, he broadcast the proclamation of the independent Kingdom of Kampuchea,[18] telling the world, "Cambodia no longer feels the need for French protection.[19]

Sihanouk also decreed the country's change of name to Kampuchea.[20] Shortly afterwards, further *kram* abolished the use of the Gregorian calendar and the romanized *quoc nhu khmer* script.[21] The declaration of independence was a momentous event and was the start of a grim time for the French in the country, but little changed for the Khmers as far as their daily lives were concerned. The Japanese had held the real power since 1941 and now they had moved to the front of the political stage. None of Sihanouk's cabinet ministers at this time were anti-French nationalists. On the contrary, they had always been loyal to France and the King. Now, faced with new masters, they responded cautiously, unsure of the extent of their powers.[22] Perhaps they were also wary of offending the French and their British and American allies at this late stage in the war. Certainly, the wording of Sihanouk's declaration of independence was almost apologetic and eschewed nationalist rhetoric.

Sihanouk ignores the returning nationalist prisoners

Nor did Sihanouk encourage militant nationalism in others, as the surviving participants in the "Revolt of the Parasols" of 1942 found when they arrived home. Liberated from Poulo Condore by the Japanese, Nuon Duong, Bunchan Mul and their friends arrived back in Phnom Penh in Japanese military trucks, hopeful of a triumphal welcome. Sihanouk ignored them. Nuon Duong died in poverty soon afterwards and the king excluded the others from public life. According to Bunchan Mul, "Those of us who were alive did not have jobs, partly because the group who were slaves to the French still hated us, and partly because Sihanouk was at that time pleasing the French, since he saw that they now had the Allies to help them defeat the Japanese; he did not care, think about or assist us in any way at all. He even oppressed us further..."[23] It is also very likely that Sihanouk was already jealous of anyone who might steal his limelight. Later, he presented himself as the sole author of his country's independence, glossing over the role of the *Nagaravatta* group and the "parasols" and claiming that his travels in the countryside during the Vichy period led him to "detest the iniquities of colonial rule".[24] Perhaps the latter part of his claim is true, but Nuon Duong and his comrades had suffered for Cambodia's independence while Sihanouk, "horny as a rabbit" by his own account, was chasing girls, watching films, playing sport and collaborating with the French.[25] One doubts the depth of his nationalist fervor during the period of the independent kingdom and in the following period when the French restored their power. He was motivated by more immediately pragmatic and personal considerations.

For all of his foppery, however, Sihanouk was learning the political ropes. He had some astutely pragmatic advisors who must have known that although the Japanese forces were intact in Indochina, Allied victory was inevitable. Sihanouk had nothing to gain by exaggerated anti-French or pro-Japanese nationalist displays. The appointment of the eccentric Admiral Thierry d'Argenlieu as the new Governor General of Indochina on 12 August pending the inevitable return of Allied troops underlined the precarious nature of Cambodian "independence".[26] It was by no means certain, however, that Allied victory would mean a return to the pre-war colonial status quo. Shortly before the Japanese *coup de force*, the French government in liberated Paris promised to grant "home rule" to Indochina after the war.[27] This was public knowledge in the West and it is possible that Sihanouk knew of it too. The French position was in large part a response to the anti-colonial bellicosity of US President Roosevelt, who scorned France's colonial record and proposed a UN trusteeship for the Indochinese colonies after the war.[28] France and Britain resented what they considered Roosevelt's "ill-conceived and typically American-woolly views on the future of other people's possessions",[29] but they were in no position to challenge his authority and realized that some change was inevitable. Some sections of French opinion, including *Combat*, the former *Maquisard* publication, agreed with Roosevelt's assessment, describing France's past colonial policy as "a scandal".[30] Thus, at the time of the *coup de force*, Sihanouk's interests were best served by a policy of *attentisme*—"wait and see". He would avoid giving offence to the Japanese, but would ignore the pro-Japanese nationalists. Thus, although he claimed to have "begged" the Japanese authorities to bring back the nationalist leader Son Ngoc Thanh,[31] this seems unlikely. He had already spurned the pioneer nationalists of July 1942 when they returned from Poulo Condore, and too close an association with Thanh could jeopardize his future relations with the Allies. On the other hand, Son Ngoc Thanh was a well-known figure in Cambodia and Sihanouk might have decided that he needed to appease Thanh's supporters. However, on balance, one wonders why he would encourage the return of a nationalist firebrand at such a delicate conjuncture. Again, it is likely that Sihanouk is attempting retrospectively to enhance his nationalist credentials.

The return of Son Ngoc Thanh

Son Ngoc Thanh returned in May 1945 aboard a Japanese bomber, to a triumphant welcome by his followers at the Pochentong aerodrome.[32] Sihanouk named him as his Foreign Minister, probably at the suggestion of the Japanese ambassador, Mr. Matsumoto. Although the French writer Gilbert David claims that the peripatetic nationalist displayed a "mistrustful patriotism that worried his Japanese mentors",[33] the truth seems rather more banal. Son Ngoc Thanh, too, seems to have succumbed to the general atmosphere of "wait and see" at this stage. David Chandler notes wryly that his presence did not appear to have "galvanized" the government's timid behavior.[34] Son Ngoc Thanh, too, had grown accustomed to waiting for his Japanese mentors to act and he did not have much of a political program beyond driving out the French. His political philosophy was a mixture of *Khmérité* with Japanese ideas of a "familial" state and pan-Asianism.[35] He declared himself in favor of a "national socialist monarchy", but at other times, he excluded the King from the Khmer nation. This semi-fascist, semi-mystical mélange was topped off with vague anti-Semitism,[36] which probably derived from the general outlook of Vichy and the Axis powers, although he might have picked some of it up during his pre-war sojourn in a Paris bank. Sihanouk subsequently mocked Thanh as the Japanese *Gauleiter* of Cambodia[37] and scorned him as an opportunist interested only in personal power.[38] This is overly harsh and self-serving. Whatever his faults, Son Ngoc Thanh was a consistent and sincere nationalist. The most constant part of his outlook was his francophobia, although, curiously—perhaps with an eye on posterity—he chose to write in the French language in his letters to supporters during his Japanese exile. The French, he complained, had trained no Cambodian engineers, politicians, men of letters or savants, economists, journalists, or captains of industry, despite their claim to be his country's protectors.[39] In this he was, largely, correct, but he was short on solutions, save for a belief in Japan as the "Mother of Yellow Asia".[40] Sihanouk says that Thanh distinguished himself during the period mainly by his exaggeratedly pro-Japanese stance, by requisitioning lorries, carts, compressors and other machinery for their use.[41] He was extraordinarily naïve in other ways, as was shown a little later in his career when he proposed an alliance with the Viet Minh, little realizing that collaboration with the Japanese was anathema to the Communists. Whatever his merits, Thanh was not a nationalist leader of the stature of Sukarno, Ho Chi Minh, Ba Maw, or Chandra Bose, which explains in part why the Japanese were earlier reluctant to give full backing to his anti-French schemes.

The new government concentrated on keeping the administrative apparatus ticking over, but it did take some initiatives, such as declaring July 20—the anniversary of the parasol revolt—as the new national day. The government also called on the Khmers to overcome the sense of inferiority inculcated by the French and decided to phase out French as the language of instruction in schools, although this was more a declamatory pose than a concrete proposal for many of the schools were requisitioned as barracks by the Japanese at the time. The government also turned its attention to history in order to provide a legal gloss for the declaration of independence. Echoing Prince Yukanthor, Sihanouk described the Treaty of 1863 as an alliance and its subsequent revisions imposed by Charles Thomson in 1884 as "usurpation".[42]

The government also set up its own militia, the *Corps des Volontaires Cambodgiens*, more commonly known as the Greenshirts, which reached a peak of several thousand members by the time of the Japanese capitulation. The Greenshirts were a paramilitary-cum-police force, created by Defense Minister Kim Thit on 11 July, apparently on the recommendation of Son Ngoc Thanh and with the full backing of the Japanese authorities. The government entrusted overall command to Captain Chum Muong,[43] evidently on the basis of nationalist rather than military credentials, as he had been a civil servant in the Ministry of Religious Affairs after his return from exile at Bangkok, where he went to escape the French crackdown after the parasol revolt. Training, however, was in the hands of Japanese instructors and NCOs. By early August, 520 men had enrolled. Three days after the A-bomb fell on Hiroshima, the Japanese army commander, Marada, advised the Cambodian government to dissolve the formation into the *Garde Nationale* and *Garde Royale*. The government officially decreed the disbandment of the force on 15 August. According to British military intelligence sources, many recruits had already deserted and the force was down to 250 men. However, the Greenshirts were not completely disbanded, but were re-dubbed the *Corps Nationaux*. The numbers swelled to over 800 by September, mainly because of the incorporation of men and NCOs from the *Garde Indochinoise*. In the same month, Kim Thit planned to boost the strength of the force to 2000 men, despite the capitulation of Japan, in order to resist the return of the French.[44] For all of his apparent nationalist ardor, however, the Defense Minister was to play a duplicitous role, conspiring with the French, the British, and possibly Sihanouk's mother, to oust Son Ngoc Thanh from office and ensure his own political survival.

The nationalist coup of 9 August

The defeat of Japan was imminent even in the early days following the Japanese *coup de force* of 9 March 1945, yet pro-Japanese nationalists still believed in the final victory of their mentors. Up to 30,000 people turned out in Phnom Penh to celebrate independence on the new national day of 20 July. Such misplaced confidence was understandable, given the paucity of hard news and the tangible signs of undiminished Japanese power on the ground in Indochina. Yet, Japan could not hope to win, and the faith of the Thanhists was misplaced. The US air force had been bombarding Japanese cities and factories since 1943 and marines had stormed ashore at Iwo Jima on 19 February 1945. The first atomic bomb fell over Hiroshima on 6 August, followed three days later by another on Nagasaki. The USSR formally declared war on Japan on 8 August and moved immediately to occupy the Kurile Islands and Sakhalin.

Such a backdrop gives a slightly surreal tinge to what came next in Cambodia. During the night of 9/10 August, while the Japanese ruling elites were already locked in bitter debate over the question of surrender, Greenshirt diehards stormed into the royal palace at Phnom Penh, brandishing a pistol and demanding to see the king. It made little logical sense to stage such a desperate act so late in the war and perhaps the men had put their faith in astrology rather than reason, for, according to Sihanouk, the plotters chose the date because nine is considered a lucky number in Cambodia.[45] They put the Prime Minister, Ung Hy, under arrest. Scuffles broke out and Sihanouk's loyal aide, Nong Kimny was shot and wounded by one of the rebels. Sihanouk afterwards claimed that the shooting was deliberate because the "Thanhists" regarded Nong Kimny as a French stooge.[46] Huy Kanthoul, on the other hand, says that the shooting was "maladroit" but not intentional.[47] One suspects Sihanouk put the worst possible spin on it to blacken the name of his archenemy, Son Ngoc Thanh. In the event, Nong Kimny was rushed to hospital, where doctors saved his life in an emergency operation. He went on to serve Sihanouk in a number of high positions in the government and diplomatic corps.

The subsequent fate of the somewhat befuddled gunmen is testimony to the truth of the adage that "those who live by the sword die by the sword". At least five of their number died violently, caught up in the tragic wars and revolutions of post-war Cambodia. Four of them, Hem Savang, Mey Pho and Neth Laing Say, joined the Issaraks. Hem met his death at the hands of the arch political turncoat, the warlord Dap Chhuon, in July 1949. Mey Pho, who became a "Khmer

Viet Minh" allied with the Vietnamese Communists, spent many years in Hanoi after the conclusion of the First Indochina War. He returned to his homeland in 1970, only to be executed by Pol Pot's men in 1975. Neth Laing Say, who was secretary to the Japanese official Kubota at the time of the coup, joined the Issaraks and died in an ambush in Kompong Speu in late 1946. Mao Sarouth became a political commissar in the Khmer Issaraks before falling victim to Dap Chhuon in July 1949. Another of Kubota's secretaries, Thach Sary, survived to become a brigadier general. He sided with Lon Nol after the coup against Sihanouk in 1970 and was executed by the Khmers Rouges in April 1975.[48]

It is unclear who ordered the putsch. Huy Kanthoul claims that it had Japanese backing.[49] Sihanouk says that the gunmen acted on Son Ngoc Thanh's orders and while this is probably true, there are some discrepancies. Son Ngoc Thanh, for example, did not accept the post of Prime Minister for five days after the coup and he had the plotters imprisoned.[50] Perhaps he did this to smooth Sihanouk's ruffled feathers, for he also included a number of old guard royalists in his cabinet, alongside more predictable choices from his own political current. The Sihanoukist Ung Hy, for example, stayed on as Finance Minister, sitting next to Thanhists such as Pach Chhuon. Thanh was also quick to announce his support for the monarchy, specifically naming it as one of the central pillars of the state, along with the Buddhist religion, independence and improved education. The new Prime Minister added a bizarre note by insisting on the centrality of the Japanese alliance at a time when the Tojo regime was literally in its last days. Less than a fortnight after the coup, Allied aircraft circled over Phnom Penh, dropping leaflets promising that the French would soon be back and on August 30 a number of French officers parachuted into Cambodia to carry out military and political reconnaissance.[51] Another source claims that a British officer flew to Phnom Penh with a French officer, Captain Gallois, on 8 September.[52] This is possible. Clandestine British and American units were present in Indochina some time before General Gracey's 14th Army troops arrived at Saigon in mid September, and the (British) Royal Air Force began regular flights between Saigon and Bengal from late August.[53]

Murder at Pich Nil

If the shooting of Nong Kimny was accidental, there is evidence of more systematic violence by the new government's officials. The new regime inherited the French concentration camp at Pich Nil and used it to detain pro-French opponents without trial. The Minister of the Interior, Sum Hieng, also exiled officials he believed to be pro-French to remote areas.[54] Sum Hieng could cut his cloth to suit any political occasion. A career bureaucrat, he was the Cambodian delegate to the 1931 Colonial Exhibition in Paris. He was anti-French under Son Ngoc Thanh then joined Prince Monireth's pro-French administration in late 1945.[55] He had a hand in the disappearance of other opponents, one of whom, Pen Kamcak, was arrested on suspicion of being a French police spy and taken to the Pich Nil camp. Sihanouk claims that Sum Hieng's men shot Kamcak in the forest outside of the camp and left the body for the tigers to eat.[56] A recently declassified French document backs Sihanouk's claim, revealing that Sum Hieng sought Son Ngoc Thanh's permission to take the unfortunate man to Pich Nil. The most startling revelation in the report is the claim that "Lon Nol, the chief of the national police appears to have been one of the murderers of Pen Kamcak." The politically durable Lon Nol is one of the central figures of post-independence Cambodian politics and military affairs. He served the French, then the Independent Kingdom (both before and after the Greenshirt coup), and then the Monireth and other governments after 1945. He went on to serve in high positions in Sihanouk's army and police after independence before staging a coup against the king in 1970. Afterwards, he served as President of the increasingly corrupt Khmer Republic until its overthrow in 1975, when he fled to the USA.

According to the French document, Lon Nol and others appeared at the camp on the night of 30 September and dragged Pen Kamcak from his sleep. Another policeman, Ngo Suy Chay, told the victim that he was free and was to follow him from the camp. The prisoner followed the policeman to a car, in which Lon Nol was waiting. There he was shot three times at point blank range. Afterwards, Lon Nol reported that his victim lay dead in the forest. The report claims that Lon Nol's driver and guards from the camp witnessed the murder.[57] The unfortunate Pen Kamcak met his death only a fortnight before the British and French ousted Son Ngoc Thanh from power. Significantly, the French document does not attempt to link Son Ngoc Thanh with the murder. Another French report claims that another unnamed Khmer was murdered around the same time, although it does not speculate as to who carried out or ordered the deed.[58]

Son Ngoc Thanh's referendum

Earlier, Son Ngoc Thanh had sworn to resist the French if they dared return. He also organized a five-question referendum on the question of independence and the legitimacy of his government on September 3, 1945. Although it was the first time adult male Khmers had been asked to vote on anything, this Stalinist style operation was scarcely a good omen for Cambodian democracy. According to Sihanouk, each citizen had to vote in public and sign his voting slip very visibly with his name and address. Not surprisingly, when the results were declared on 3 October, out of a total over 541,000 voters (men aged between 18 and 60), there were only two or three "invalid" votes.[59] The figure of 99.999 per cent for Son Ngoc Thanh was ludicrous and the ballot was scarcely secret, but this should not obscure the fact of a widespread yearning for independence. Thanh must have realized that, with Japan's defeat, it was only a matter of time before the French came back to claim their colony and the referendum was an attempt to bolster his authority. Shortly after the announcement of the results of the plebiscite, he sent an envoy, Pann Yun (or Pan Ying) to Bangkok to try to negotiate a military pact. According to Sihanouk, Son Ngoc Thanh was willing to recognize continued Thai sovereignty over Battambang and the other territories ceded in 1941 in return for military assistance against the French.[60] The Thais were reluctant to commit themselves. They were doubtless engaged in their own soul searching as to what the Allied victory meant, given their recent alliance with Japan. Thanh was no more successful in his bid to ally himself with the Viet Minh. Although Chandler puts this down to poor communications,[61] the fact that the Viet Minh had waged a guerrilla war against the Japanese makes it unlikely that they would ally themselves with someone they would have regarded as a fascist puppet and a liability besides.[62] The Viet Minh stood at the head of a powerful mass movement. They had occupied large swathes of Vietnamese territory following the Japanese collapse and they saw themselves as being on the verge of independence. They were in fact a long way from it; the arrival of Major-General Douglas Gracey's crack British and Indian troops at Saigon in mid September provided a beachhead for the return of the French. Shortly after Gracey's arrival, armed conflict broke out and the Viet Minh would have been even less inclined to bolster Son Ngoc Thanh's regime. The closest Thanh came to forging an alliance was with the pro-Japanese and short-lived Tran Trong Kim government in Saigon, and this was of no practical value to either group.[63] Son Ngoc Thanh was powerless to prevent the return of the French.

On 8 October, the first detachment of British soldiers—40 Gurkha mercenaries—flew into Pochentong airport aboard a Japanese military aircraft piloted by a member of the *Kempetei*, the military police. Their commander was Colonel E.D. "Moke" Murray, a lanky, tough and seasoned officer who had fought in Burma and more recently against Viet Minh insurgents at Saigon. Murray, who had the complete confidence of the British commander at Saigon, General Gracey, was sometimes clear about his role. "We were holding the fort for the French," he recollected thirty years later, before trying to fudge what he had said. After spending a night in a "tacky little room" at the Royal Hotel, Murray moved into the French *Résidence*, as befitted his rank and mission, he felt, and set about preparing the ground for the return of the French. He enjoyed cordial relations with Defense Minister Kim Thit, who told him that although he was a nationalist, he was pro-Sihanouk and anti-Son Ngoc Thanh. Murray met with King Sihanouk soon after his arrival at Thit's suggestion, but did not attempt to call on the head of government, Son Ngoc Thanh. He had heard from intelligence sources, Murray said later, that the Prime Minister was "fanatically nationalist", "anti-King" and even "pro-Communist". It is probable that Kim Thit told him the same story. Murray also believed that the Japanese continued to play a role in political affairs. This information—such as it was—was enough to seal Son Ngoc Thanh's fate. Murray flew back to Saigon, where he reported to Gracey and the newly arrived French commander, General Jacques Leclerc, on the situation at Phnom Penh. According to Sihanouk and the British, Kim Thit was also in Saigon at the same time. Land and river communications between the two cities were closed at the time due to the activities of the Viet Minh, so Kim Thit must have flown to Saigon with Allied permission. It seems unlikely that Sihanouk played any conscious part in the unfolding conspiracy against his Prime Minister. In fact, he categorically denies it.[64] Murray states specifically that the king was not involved, regarding him as young playboy who was "under the thumb of Mum", that is the Queen Mother, the Princess Kossamak. Kossamak was, however, close to the Defense Minister, Kim Thit and it is clear that the pair were involved in Murray's schemes. A British Foreign Office report states that Kim Thit arranged the arrest of Son Ngoc Thanh in Saigon, because he was convinced that his erstwhile ally "aimed at the abolition of the monarchy."[65] It is also almost certain that Prince Monireth was involved. Monireth was a powerful pro-French figure in the Khmer elite and would have had little time for Thanh's nationalist posturing. After Sihanouk appointed him Prime Minister the day after Son Ngoc Thanh's arrest, Monireth secretly set up a committee to negotiate with the returning French. The result was a *modus vivendi*, signed the following January, which granted Cambodia a measure of autonomy.[66]

Murray reported to Gracey and Leclerc that Son Ngoc Thanh "had to go". Leclerc replied bluntly, "Well, arrest him". Murray demurred, claiming disingenuously that he was a British officer and could not meddle in Cambodian political affairs, so Leclerc volunteered to do the job himself. The three officers formulated a plan, which "had to be fixed, very carefully and very secretly", said Murray. Murray had learned that Sihanouk would shortly be out of town on a religious pilgrimage and suggested this as the best time to make the arrest. After flying back up to Phnom Penh, Murray invited the Prime Minister to his headquarters for the first time on October 17. Thanh seems to have had no inkling of what was about to happen. He was "all smiley" and "most friendly", recalls Murray, dismissing him as "a silly little man". After drinking some tea, Murray made an excuse and left Thanh making plans with another British officer for a tiger hunt. He raced out to the airport and returned to the headquarters with General Leclerc and a French NCO. "It was like a comic opera," said Murray. "There was the Prime Minister with David Wenham, [the other British officer] chitter chattering about elephant shoots, and General Leclerc strode in, pushing me aside, with his gunman...[The] poor little Prime Minister thought Leclerc was welcoming him and got up to sort of say 'How lovely!' He was taken by the scruff of the neck by the gunman, bundled into a car and off." Murray never saw Son Ngoc Thanh or Leclerc again.[67]

The "Cambodian people had always loved France"

An Allied military communiqué announced a few days later that "The ex Cambodian first minister Song [sic] Ngoc Thanh was brought recently to Saigon *on the orders of the Allied commander.* [Emphasis added.] The reason for his removal...is that his activity in Cambodia threatened the security of the Allied forces and he was working against Cambodian interests."[68] One wonders if Kim Thit and the Queen Mother defined those interests. According to E.W. Meiklereid, the British Consul at Saigon, the Queen Mother "still wields considerable power" and that as a result, the incoming French representative, General Alessandri, "appreciates the necessity of obtaining her support." For his part, said Meiklereid, Sihanouk accepted the arrest as

a "fait acompli" [*sic*]. This is likely, as Sihanouk's personal relations
with the *Nagaravatta* group had never been warm. Although Colonel
Murray did not recall any disturbances following the arrests, Consul
Meiklereid reported that subsequent arrests of pro-Thanhist officials
resulted in a protest strike by Cambodian railroad workers.[69] Apart
from this, however, the public response was muted. Sihanouk
appointed Prince Monireth Prime Minister in Son Ngoc Thanh's place
and the French moved in subsequent months to consolidate their
position in the kingdom. Sihanouk officially welcomed them at his
birthday celebrations on 13 November. He told an Agence France
Presse representative that, "he had no anxiety as to the future as France
would be Cambodia's guide and counselor." He added that the
"Cambodian people had always loved France and the pro-French
feelings of his people were evident to all." He did point, however, to
"certain disadvantages of the previous Protectorate regime" and
expressed the desire for greater autonomy.[70] He later claimed to have
used more muscular language—"General Leclerc spoke to me of
autonomy, my response to him was: independence,"[71] but the facts
speak otherwise. While Son Ngoc Thanh traveled into prison and exile,
Sihanouk was drinking champagne from silver goblets with the French
and British officers at the Phnom Penh water festival. Murray recalls
that the King kept jumping up to try to kiss him when bestowing
medals on the Allied officers at the birthday celebrations.[72]

For his part, Murray seems to have thoroughly enjoyed his stay in
Cambodia. He traveled to Angkor by jeep and was the guest of honor
at balls and receptions. Perhaps this hectic social whirl anaesthetized
the small nub of guilt he felt over his part in the abduction of Son Ngoc
Thanh, although he said much later that he and Colonel David
Wenham "felt terrible about it."[73]   Murray was a competent career
soldier. He had fought his way through 1000 miles of mountain and
jungle in the Burma campaign, but he was politically naïve and in any
case used to carrying out the orders of his superiors. He disliked the
French and believed that they made poor colonialists and contrasted
their "patronizing" and arrogant treatment of the "Annamites" and
Cambodians with British behavior in India. He was unimpressed by the
senior French army commander in Cambodia, General Alessandri, and
scorned French military ability. Like many of his caste and kind,
Murray already suspected that independence was inevitable for India,
but believed that the French were firmly opposed to granting
independence to their Indochinese subjects.[74] Orders, however, were
orders and Murray was trained to obey, regardless of how squeamish

he felt about matters such as the arrest of Son Ngoc Thanh and the return of the French.

Another British officer did not smother his doubts. Robert Williams, a young officer with the Indian soldiers at Saigon, excoriated the French role in Indochina and bitterly lamented the British role in their reinstatement. He wrote to his father to say, "We are blind or wicked, one or the other—God forbid the latter. We are denying the people the right of liberty for which we have fought...The French have no justification for staying here." He added that the return of the French "denied the ordinary rights of justice, a living wage, équalité (*sic*), fraternité, liberté..." and predicted, "Oh! We will rue the day we set foot in FIC..."[75] His sentiments echoed those voiced at Hot Springs by US President Roosevelt in 1943.[76] While Williams referred specifically to Gracey's suppression of the Viet Minh in Saigon, the British had achieved the same ends in Cambodia, although without bloodshed. In the light of the subsequent catastrophes visited upon the peoples of Indochina, Williams' words should give us pause for thought. The French were back and it would not prove easy to winkle them out.

On 20 October, Murray met with three senior French officers in Phnom Penh to discuss an outbreak of cholera and spraying the city with DDT. Murray also raised concerns about French plans for the future of the kingdom. It was necessary for the maintenance of public tranquility, he said, to inform the population as quickly as possible whether Cambodia was to enjoy independence or revert to its former status as a dependency of France. There are reports of the countryside falling into disorder, with "theft and banditry on a grand scale" and "frequent collusion between the thieves and the police force" in Kompong Thom province, for instance.[77] Murray believed that any statement that Cambodia was to revert to its old status was likely to "cause great unrest and possibly active resistance in the country." In that case, he warned, it would be necessary to make the statement before the removal of Japanese troops, as they would be needed to maintain order. Lt. Colonel Huard replied that it was almost certain that Cambodia would stay a French dependency.[78] Soon afterwards, Murray recalls, "the French started to move out of Saigon, and they arrived in Phnom Penh without so much as a by-your-leave".[79]

After a short while, the French authorities announced that they had decided to grant internal autonomy to Cambodia. According to the London *Times*, there would be "relatively few French officials in administrative posts, but [Cambodia]...will welcome assistance from French advisors." The country would remain an integral part of the French Union, with France in charge of her external affairs. King

Sihanouk expressed his satisfaction with the proposals.[80] The new Cambodian Prime Minister, Prince Monireth, declared that he was in favor of the "purification" of the "Annamite" population of Cambodia of its pro-Viet Minh elements. He was initially reluctant to involve himself in any large-scale purge of Thanhists from the administration as this might provoke discontent in the population,[81] but changed his mind a fortnight later and ordered a *razzia* against them.[82] Meanwhile, French troops were pouring back into southern Indochina via Saigon. They suppressed the Viet Minh in the Cochinchinese border province of Travinh, probably with the support of the large Khmer Krom population,[83] and on 27 December Alessandri reported to General Leclerc that French troops had secured "strict control" over traffic between Phnom Penh and Saigon.[84] Although there was a reservoir of bitterness against Sihanouk and the French over the arrest of Son Ngoc Thanh and a spirit of belligerent nationalism in some quarters, the French had secured control of the country without sparking the bloody unrest feared by Colonel Murray. They were probably helped by the relatively abundant harvests of the time. Whereas there were rice shortages in Cochinchina and famine in Tonkin, Cambodia produced a surplus of over 100,000 tons of rice—much more if Battambang province, still occupied by Thailand, were included.[85] The political status quo was provisionally endorsed in a *modus vivendi* signed between Prince Monireth and General Alessandri at Phnom Penh on 7 January 1946.[86] The French realized that they could not force a reversion to the system that had existed before the Japanese coup. Too much had changed since 1939. French prestige had been battered by the Nazi victory in 1940, by their subservience to Japan and their humiliation at the hands of the Thais in 1941. Cambodia had enjoyed a kind of independence under Japanese auspices. Many thousands of Cambodians had heard nationalist orators and joined mass organizations, first under the Vichy regime and then during the Kingdom of Kampuchea.

The January 1946 modus vivendi between France and Cambodia

The *modus vivendi* promised a measure of autonomy for Cambodia; the old almost seigneurial powers of the *Résidence Supérieure* were over. Henceforth, France's representative would be known as the High Commissioner. He was the accredited representative of France and the Indochinese Federation in Cambodia, and would act as permanent advisor to the king. He would attend all sessions of the Council of Ministers and ten French advisors would assist the seven Cambodian

Ministers to ensure the smooth workings of the administration. The agreement stated that they had to be consulted in certain situations while in others they would offer suggestions. Technical advisors and experts would assist the heads of departments. On a regional level, the old system of fourteen French *Résidences* was abolished. There would be seven provincial governments, including the city of Phnom Penh, with a French advisor and deputy nominated by the High Commissioner in each. Financial decisions could not be made without their advice.

The French also allowed most of the laws and decrees promulgated during the Kingdom of Kampuchea to remain. As David Chandler has observed,

> Those they rescinded included the one that had proclaimed Cambodia's independence and others that had set up offices for a prime minister and a minister of foreign affairs. The French also rescinded those that had given Cambodian names to streets and institutions in Phnom Penh; and they replaced two holidays that celebrated independence—March 12 and July 20...—with holidays from metropolitan France. Finally, the French cancelled two laws enacted in October that may well have struck them as impertinent. These decreed that income and property taxes should be collected, for the first time, from Europeans as well as from Asian residents.[87]

Real power back in French hands

The accord did mean a greater degree of autonomy than had existed under the protectorate, *but real power still lay in French hands*. Most importantly, the High Commissioner was charged with overall responsibility for the maintenance of public order via his control over the French armed forces in the country. France was responsible, too, for external affairs and French citizens would continue to enjoy legal extra-territoriality through the system of French courts. French "experts" would supervise the Cambodian police and justice system, the health services, public works and so forth. Certain government services would remain under the sole jurisdiction of the High Commissioner, including the Treasury, customs and excise, posts and telegraphs, railroads and industry. A French advisor would assist the Cambodian Defense Minister and would be responsible for the reorganization and instruction of the Cambodian Army. Overall, there was not a hint of independence, eventual or otherwise, in the document.[88] A French journalist, writing in *Le Monde*, summed up French attitudes thus, "The colonial era is now a closed chapter. A new form of imperial cooperation is now opening, and Cambodia is the first branch of the Empire to benefit by this evolution. The main problem is the aptitude of the Cambodians to govern themselves."[89] Prime Minister Monireth would have agreed with this assessment. The consolidation of French power was completed at midnight on 4/5 March 1946, when Indochina ceased to be under the Allied military command and full powers reverted to France.[90]

Notes

[1] PO FO 371 46305. Declaration of Independence by the Cambodian Government. Intercept of Domei broadcast in English for Europe, 13 March 1945.

[2] Norodom Sihanouk, (1981), *Souvenirs doux et amers,* Hachette, Paris, p.100. Eveline Porée-Maspero, who was in Phnom Penh at the time, considers that the purpose of the sirens was to lure the French from their homes. [Cited in David P. Chandler, (1986), "The Kingdom of Kampuchea, March-October 1945: Japanese-sponsored Independence in Cambodia in World War II," *Journal of South East Asian Studies,* XVII, 1, March, p.81.] One wonders about this. The most probable effect would be to clear the streets, as people would seek shelter. This would enable the Japanese troops to move round unhindered.

[3] Huy Kanthoul, *Mémoires,* unpublished typescript, Chandler Papers, Monash University, p.95.

[4] Eveline Porée-Maspero, cited in Chandler, op.cit.

[5] Claude Hesse d'Alzon, (1985), *La présence militaire française en Indochine 1940-1945,* Publications du service historique de l'Armée de Terre, pp.224-225 and Gilbert David, (1994), *Chroniques secrètes d'Indochine (1928-1946),* Vol. II, Editions l'Harmattan, Paris, pp.514-515.

[6] Donald Lancaster, (1961), *The Emancipation of French Indochina,* Oxford University Press, London, p.105. General Sabattier felt that Japanese action was imminent and numbers of his soldiers were able to take to the mountains.

[7] André Gaudel, (1947), *L'Indochine en face du Japon,* J. Susse, Paris, pp.161-162 and d'Alzon, op.cit. pp.226-229. Lancaster, (op.cit. p.106) claims that those who escaped were all "soon rounded up" but this appears to be wrong.

[8] Chandara Mohaphtey, "A Khmer Issarak leader's story", edited by Timothy Carney, 24 January 1976. Unpublished typescript, Chandler Papers, Monash University.

[9] "Proclamation", *Indochine Hebdomadaire Illustré,* 10 March 1945.

[10] "Japanese control in Indo-China. Reported arrest of Governor General", *The Times,* London, 12 March 1945 and État-Major de la Marine, Service Historique, *La Marine Française en Indochine de 1939 à 1955,* Tome I, *Septembre 1939 – Août 1945.* Travail dirigé par le Capitaine de Vaisseau (R), Michel, Jacques, du Service Historique de la Marine, p.52.

[11] Huy Kanthoul, op.cit. p.95, claims that as Allied victory seemed surer, "The French in Cambodia lifted up their heads once more and adopted a more and more arrogant attitude."

[12] Gaudel, op.cit. pp. 186-188 and G.H.P., (c.1945), *La "Kempetai".* Saigon, Hanoi, Haiphong, Nhatrang, Huê, Vinh, Phnom-Penh, Vientiane, Mars-Septembre 1945, Imprimerie Français d'Outre-Mer, Saigon.

[13] AOM HCC 11. Inspector Magniadis to Chief of *Sûrêté*, 29 May 1946. The Kempetei were the Japanese military police. A number were executed after the war.

[14] Gaudel, op.cit. p.188.

[15] Sihanouk, op.cit. pp.100-101. The king claimed he was almost as surprised by the Japanese plans as he had been when the French put him on the throne. (Norodom Sihanouk with Wilfred Burchett, (1973), *My War with the CIA. Cambodia's Fight for Survival*, Penguin, Harmondsworth, p.146.)

[16] Chandler, op.cit. p.81.

[17] Chandara, who had taken part in the "revolt of the parasols" in 1942, later became a high-ranking Issarak. Chandara, op.cit.

[18] Sihanouk, (*Souvenirs*) op.cit. pp100-101.

[19] PRO FO 371 46305. Declaration of Independence by the Cambodian Government, op.cit.

[20] There is perhaps no exact transliteration of the Khmer word for their kingdom, although "Cambodia" and "Kampuchea" are closer than the French "Cambodge".

[21] Chandler, op.cit. pp.80-81.

[22] Chandler, op.cit.

[23] Bunchan Mul, "The Umbrella War of 1942" [extract from *Kuk Niyoba*, trans. Chanthou Boua], in Ben Kiernan and Chanthou Boua (eds.), (1982), *Peasants and Politics in Kampuchea*, 1942-1981, Zed Press, London, p.126.

[24] Sihanouk and Burchett, op.cit. p.146.

[25] Norodom Sihanouk, (1972), *L'Indochine vue de Pékin*, Éditions du Seuil, Paris, p.33. In French, Sihanouk said he was *un chaud lapin*, literally a "hot rabbit".

[26] PRO FO 371/46307. F52/11/61 App. Of Admiral Thierry d'Argenlieu as *GOUGAL*.

[27] PRO FO 371/46304 Situation in FIC. F 730/11/61. Press release. French Press and Information Bureau, New York, January 19, 1945. The French plans were discussed in the English-language press. See, for instance, "Home Rule for Indo-China", *The Manchester Guardian*, 26 March 1945.

[28] Speaking at a Pacific Relations Conference at Hot Springs, Virginia, in March 1943, Roosevelt "referred to Indo-China and said that although it had been in French hands for 100 years the population was no better off" and that "So far as he was concerned the restoration of that country to France was out". AAc A989 43/735/302 The Far East and French Indo-China. Rpt. from Washington Legation to War Cabinet, Aust. 18 March 1943; PRO FO 371/46304 Situation in FIC. F 730/11/6, British Consul Paris; FO 371/3592

Future of French I.C. (1943), Foreign Office Minute of 8 Sept. 1943 by Mr. Strang; and PRO FO 371/35930 Future of FIC – French Views, 1943.

[29] Foreign Office Minute of 8 Sept 1943 by Mr. Strang, op.cit.

[30] *Combat*, Paris, 21 January 1945. Cited in PRO FO 371/46304, F 730/11/6 op.cit.

[31] Sihanouk, *(Souvenirs)*, op.cit. pp. 99-105.

[32] Ibid. p.104.

[33] David op.cit. p. Vol. II, p.642.

[34] Chandler, op.cit. p.83.

[35] Ibid, p.84 and Son Ngoc Thanh, letter of 10 April 1943, in Son Ngoc Thanh Papers, in Chandler Papers, Monash University.

[36] Ibid. (Son Ngoc Thanh.)

[37] Sihanouk *(Souvenirs)*, p.109.

[38] Sihanouk with Burchett, op.cit. p.147.

[39] Son Ngoc Thanh, op.cit., Letter to Chin, 28 July 1942.

[40] Ibid. Letter from Thanh, styling himself "Le représentat en chef des bonzes de toutes les pagodas bouddhiques et des bouddhistes khmers de la presqu'ile indochinoise".

[41] Sihanouk *(Souvenirs)*, op.cit. pp.104-105. Sihanouk formed a good opinion of the Japanese, whatever his public statements to the contrary. In fact, in 1955, he seriously considered inviting up to 5000 Japanese settlers to take up land in Stung Treng and Kompong Cham provinces. [CANCOM. Arnold Smith, Canadian ICC delegate to the Secretary of State for External Affairs, Ottawa, 15 November 1955 in Arnold Smith papers, Canadian National Archives/Archives National du Canada, Ottawa. (Accessed by kind permission of Mr. A.C. Smith, Toronto.)]

[42] Chandler, op.cit. p.85.

[43] The Issarak Chandara claims that Chum Muong "disappeared" shortly after the return of the French. Chandara, op.cit.

[44] Information on the Greenshirts is from a number of sources. One of the most important is PRO WO/208/636 Cambodia Gendarmerie, February 1939 - November 1945. Cx FB/IV/814 30.11.45. "French Indochina: Corps volontaires cambodgiens." Rpt No 4569 12 Nov 1945. Chandler, op.cit. p.86, considers that the total strength of the Greenshirts was around 1000 at the end of the war, but perhaps as high as 3000.

[45] Sihanouk, op.cit. p.107. For a discussion of the symbolism of numbers in Cambodia see Eveline Porée-Maspero, (1958), *Cérémonies Privées des Cambodgiens*, Éditions de l'Institut Bouddhique, Phnom Penh, p.22.

[46] Sihanouk *(Souvenirs)*, op.cit. p. 107.

[47] Huy Kanthoul, op.cit. p.96.

[48] Ben Kiernan, "The Seven Young Coup Makers of 9 August 1945", unpublished and undated typescript based on French intelligence archives, various interviews with Khmer, Thai and Vietnamese informants and Bunchan Mul's *Charit Khmaer*. In Chandler Papers, Monash University.

[49] Huy Kanthoul, op.cit. p.97.

[50] Chandler, op.cit. p.88. Sihanouk claimed that Son Ngoc Thanh was "imposed upon me as the Prime Minister." (Sihanouk with Burchett, op.cit. p.147.)

[51] Chandler, op.cit. pp.88-89.

[52] Yves Gras, (1979), *Histoire de la Guerre d'Indochine*, Plon, Paris, p.54.

[53] See George Rosie, (1970), *The British in Vietnam. How the twenty-five year war began*, Panther, London, p.50. The clandestine units included the British Force 136 E Group and elements of the American OSS. E Group was charged with the repatriation of the thousands of Allied POWs in southern Indochina; the RAPWI program (Repatriation of Allied Prisoners of War and Internees). Colonel E.D. Murray referred to the existence of RAPWI elements in Phnom Penh after his arrival there in September. (Interview with Anthony Barnett, 1982. Typescript in Chandler Papers, Monash University.) Some of the Allied POWs in Cambodia were Australians.

[54] AOM. HCC 10, Esprit de la population, Rapport Politique, 7 juillet 1947.

[55] PRO FO 474/9. Appendix. Biographical notes. No 23. Leading personalities in Cambodia, 1955. Mr. Heppel to Mr. Macmillan (Received May 16). In 1942, when Sum Hieng was *Chauvaikhet* of Prey Veng, the French awarded him the rank of *Chevalier de la Légion d'Honneur*. (*Indochine Hebdomadaire Illustré*, 24 December 1942.)

[56] Sihanouk (*Souvenirs*), op.cit. p.111.

[57] Rapport Politique, 7 Juillet 1947, op.cit.

[58] AOM HCC 11. Sûreté fédérale. Letter from Lt. Colonel Huard to Prince Monireth, 22 October 1945.

[59] Sihanouk, op.cit. pp.111-112; Chandler, op.cit. p.89; and Philippe Preschez (1961), "La Démocratie Cambodgienne", Thèse pour Diplôme de l'I.E.P., Paris, p.12.

[60] Ibid, Sihanouk, also Chandler, pp.89-90).

[61] Chandler, p.90. Communications were poor and there was an acute shortage of fuel, but the main reason for the breakdown was that the Viet Minh controlled the countryside of Cochinchina. (See Barnett interview with E.D. Murray, op.cit.)

[62] Such a case is argued by Gilbert David, (1994), *Chroniques Secretes d'Indochine (1928-1946)*, Vol. II, Éditions L'Harmattan, Paris, p.642.

[63] Ibid, p.643. The Japanese installed the Tran Trong Kim government after the 9 March coup. See also Masaya Shiraishi, "La presence japonaise en Indochine (1940-1945) in Pierre Brocheux, William J. Duiker, Claude Hesse d'Alzon, Paul Isoart and Masaya Shiraishi, (1982), *Indochine Française 1940-1945*, Presses Universitaires de France, Paris; and Ralph B. Smith, (1978), "The Japanese Period in Indochina and the Coup of 9 March 1945", *Journal of South East Asian Studies*, Vol. IX, No 2.

[64] Sihanouk (*L'Indochine vue de Pékin*), p.43. "I swear on my honor that it is false," wrote Sihanouk, adding that although he had no sympathy for Son Ngoc Thanh, that he would not hand over a Cambodian to a foreign general. As usual, Sihanouk probably exaggerates for effect. Later, in June 1952, he

had no compunction in using French troops to back a *coup d'état* against the Democrats. It is likely that he was busy entertaining himself while the conspiracy against Thanh unfolded.

[65] PRO FO 474/9. op.cit.

[66] On the secret cabinet meeting which set up a negotiating committee, see David P. Chandler, (1991), *The Tragedy of Cambodian History. Politics, War and Revolution since 1945*, Silkworm Books, Bangkok, p.27.

[67] The above paragraphs either are direct quotes, or are otherwise based on information from the Barnett interview with Murray, op.cit.

[68] PRO. FO 959/4. SACSEA Communiqué No 14, "Premier of Cambodia is detained", *Times of Saigon*, 22 October 1945. (*The Times* was a roneoed publication produced by the Allied Military Command.)

[69] PRO FO 371/46311. Situation in FIC as of 24 October 1945. By E.W. Meiklereid, British Consul at Saigon.

[70] PRO FO 371/46311. Celebrations on Sihanouk's birthday, November 13 1945. Meiklereid, Saigon, to the Foreign Office, 20 November 1945

[71] Sihanouk (*Souvenirs)* op.cit. p.115.

[72] Barnett Interview, op.cit.

[73] Ibid.

[74] Ibid.

[75] PRO FO 371/46311. "Letter from Mr. R.G. Williams to the Sec. of State endorsing letter from his son, young officer in the Indian Army at Saigon, who has been in the East for four and a half years." 4 December 1945. (FIC = French Indochina.)

[76] General MacArthur also disapproved the way things were done. He said in Tokyo, "If there is anything that makes my blood boil...it is to see our allies in Indo-China...deploying Japanese troops to reconquer the little people we promised to liberate. It is the most ignoble kind of betrayal." Cited in Rosie, op.cit. p.94.

[77] AOM HCC 10. Esprit de la population, 1945-1947. Handwritten note by M. Galaraneau, former *Résident* of Kompong Thom. Galarneau says that an Annamite Catholic priest, Father Tol, believed that the local Khmer population wanted either a speedy return of the French Administration, or the English or the Americans to come; anything to be freed from the "yoke of the Cambodian administration." There might be truth in this, although as a Catholic priest, Father Tol would probably have been close to the French.

[78] AOM HCC 11. Sûreté Fédérale. Minutes of conference held at Phnom Penh at ALF HQ Phnom Penh at 1100 hours, 20 December 1945. Present, Brig. E. D. Murray, Lt Cols Huard and Duwenham (*sic*) and Comdt Besson. [General Gracey allowed Murray, whose rank was Colonel, to promote himself (but not to full general) so that General Alessandri would not be his superior officer! Barnett Interview, op.cit.)

[79] Barnett interview, op.cit.

[80] *The Times*, 5 November 1945 and PRO FO 371/46309.

[81] AOM HCC 11, op.cit., French police chief at Phnom Penh to the Representative of the High Commission, 5 November 1945.

[82] Ibid. Internal Cambodian Sûreté Memo, 19 November 1945.

[83] PRO FO 959/4. *Times of Saigon*, December 18 1945.

[84] AOM HCC 11, op.cit. Communication from General Alessandri to General Leclerc, 27 December 1945.

[85] PRO FO 371/46309. Mr. Brain, SACSEA, Saigon, to the Foreign Office. Received 6 November 1945.

[86] ANC RSC FO1 File No 15571, 7 January 1946. Accord fixent le modus vivendi provisoire entre la France et le Cambodge, 07 janvier 1946, signé par S.M. Monireth et Alessandri.

[87] Chandler (*Tragedy*), op.cit. p.17.

[88] Ibid.

[89] Philippe Devillers, (1946), "The Franco-Cambodian Agreement," *Le Monde*, 20 February.

[90] PRO FO 959/6. Handover of responsibility to the French.

Chapter 21

The Parliamentary Experiment

Our political program was in no way subversive by today's standards but for the times, it was almost a revolution.
—Huy Kanthoul, a leader of the Democratic Party.

When the French returned to Cambodia in late 1945, they took control of a country and an economy dilapidated by the long years of war. While there had been little in the way of real fighting in Cambodia, at least since the border war with Thailand in 1940-41, the economic needs of the country had been subordinated to Japanese military considerations. The war had also disrupted overseas trade and even the Mekong downstream to Saigon was closed by Viet Minh activities. The French and their friends in the Monireth government faced a battle to reopen moribund lines of communication, restart public works schemes and restore services interrupted by the war. They also needed to neutralize the nationalist sentiment that had grown enormously since 1939. Although the French army did not face anything so powerful as the Viet Minh insurgency in neighboring Vietnam, they had to reckon with the pro-independence Khmer Issarak guerrilla forces in a number of rural areas. There were disturbing reports of the Issaraks making common cause with the Viet Minh, at least in some districts, and French policy was geared towards convincing large numbers of Cambodians that their interests would be best served by the political settlement negotiated with Prince Monireth. Within a year or so,

Cambodia developed a parliamentary political system, complete with parties and adult male suffrage. Although this was largely a public relations exercise as far as the French were concerned, it took on a life of its own. Another pressing task was to obtain the return of the lands lost to Thailand in 1941. If the French could achieve this, then they might be able to regain the population's confidence in their "protectors".

A country in disrepair

Colonel "Moke" Murray found the French soldiers at Saigon to be "demoralized" when he met them in September 1945.[1] They were poor material with which to re-conquer an empire, so the French must have been relieved by the contrast between the guerrilla-infested countryside of Cochinchina and the relative peace of Cambodia. As the French journalist Philippe Devillers wrote in early 1946:

> Phnom Penh presents a striking contrast to Saigon. Saigon is a European town, its narrow streets filled with soldiers. Phnom Penh is a modern Oriental town with wide avenues bordered by fine villas, their roofs hidden under the coconut trees. What strikes you on coming from Cochin China is the calm atmosphere, the patriarchal life and the cordiality of the population.[2]

Yet, this told only part of the story, as Devillers himself pointed out. The country's roads, railroads and telegraphs were broken down. Traffic still moved slowly on the railroads, but there were practically no cars or trucks, and gasoline and oil were unobtainable. Although the Mekong reopened for shipping down to Saigon in late 1945, it was still a hazardous business, given both the activities of guerrillas and the neglect of dredging. No new public works had been undertaken for some time and no maintenance had been carried out on the old ones. Industry was starved of raw materials, prices had tripled over the past year and the government's coffers were depleted and even empty in some areas.[3] Most schools were closed, public buildings were in disrepair and the Japanese army had requisitioned much of the country's plant and machinery for its own use. There were food shortages, despite the country having a surplus of rice and some other commodities. Rice production had steadily fallen since 1942-43, although nowhere near as steeply as in other parts of French Indochina.[4] The problem was distribution. The rubber plantations east of the Mekong were, however, in good repair, given the demand for rubber as strategically important war *materiel*, and there were large stockpiles awaiting shipment. Forests, though, had been recklessly exploited, at least in part for fuel to replace scarce coal and oil.[5]

Politically, too, the situation was not as rosy for French interests as some reporters claimed. Devillers, for example, believed that the "young folk are Francophiles. They understand that their country must march with France in order to become a modern state."[6] The *Sûreté* claimed in March 1946 that, "calm continues to reign in all of the country"[7] and that nationalist agitation by Pach Chhuon on the frontiers of Takeo and Kampot provinces had completely stopped in the month preceding.[8] However, nationalist sentiment was deeply embedded in the population. The *Sûreté* reported that "a certain bitterness against the King and Prince Monireth" still existed in March 1946 because of the arrest of Son Ngoc Thanh.[9] The *Sûreté* observed that many Cambodian civil servants were "partisans" of Son Ngoc Thanh and wanted them "progressively cleansed" from government employment.[10] A French officer reported that civil servants at Kampot were "very agitated" at what they saw as the "treason" of Prince Monireth for allowing government jobs to go to returning Frenchmen.[11] In fact, it was true that most of the old French officials got their jobs back. Even the most compromised Vichyites, such as the policeman Maurice Pujol, found that their careers were not harmed by their Axis era indiscretions. A politically motivated brawl broke out between Cambodian *tirailleurs* and the police in the O Russey quarter of Phnom Penh in January 1946. Up to 120 policemen arrived to teach the soldiers "a severe lesson".[12] When Cambodian soldiers were sent to Saigon to bolster the French garrison, Lon Nol, now chief of the Cambodian National Police, reported that the general population disapproved. The people, he added however, were skeptical about the reality of autonomy.[13] A policeman called Thierry reported that when a French official visited the *Chauvaikhet* of Kandal in his office, a clerk called Roth Vann said to his colleagues, "What's this Frenchman doing here? We need to kick him in the head and put him outside."[14] There were also a number of strikes in Phnom Penh around this time, sometimes over wages and conditions,[15] but also in protest at the arrest of supporters of Son Ngoc Thanh.[16] An active nucleus of discontent existed among the railroad, although French claims that a cell of the pro-Issarak "Black Star" secret society was active on the railroads should be taken with caution.[17]

Meanwhile, the French were putting the elements of a new political system into place. Under US pressure and the demands of the United Nations Charter, the French were "obliged to play the game of democracy".[18] This involved the creation of an elected parliament and a whole range of civil and political rights previously denied in the kingdom. The French regarded the business somewhat cynically, but the Khmer elites threw themselves into it with varying degrees of enthusiasm. The elite character of the emerging system needs emphasis. As the genealogist and historian Justin Corfield has observed, a small number of extended family networks controlled politics, business, the police, the army and the civil services from 1945 until 1970. Many of the elite had been to exclusive schools together in Saigon, Phnom Penh or France. Corfield has compiled detailed family trees showing the family relationships of this ruling class. One extended family network includes a branch of the Apheuvongs, offspring of the *Phya* Kathathorn, the former hereditary ruler of Siamese Battambang; the Poc family, which included Poc Hell, Monireth's rich father-in-law; and the Thiounns who descended from the long-serving palace minister under Norodom, Sisowath and Monivong. Nestling in the branches of the tree are former Issaraks such as Bunchan Mul, *Khmers Rouges* such as Thiounn Mum and Prasith, royalists and members of the royal family, Democrats, bankers, and Sangkum ministers.[19] A more distant relative of this family was Prime Minister of Thailand in 1945. The family networks controlled the political parties, as Sihanouk noted when he told the French military commander Paul Ely in 1954 that, "those favoring democracy in Cambodia are either bourgeois or princes..."[20]

A number of interest groups began to crystallize into political parties willing to operate within the framework of the *modus vivendi* between Monireth and the French. This was a new development in the colony. French political parties had set up colonial branches before World War II, but apart from the clandestine Indochinese Communist Party, which had mainly attracted Vietnamese, there had been no "native" parties in Cambodia. *Nagaravatta*, it is true, had been a political grouping, but it had not aimed at a mass membership and in any case there were never any elections for it to contest. This was to change in 1946. One faction of moderate nationalists formed around Sonn Sann and Sonn Vennsai. Another group, somewhat fancifully described by a French policeman as "socialist", coalesced around Kim Thit and Neak Tioulong. A cabal of powerful mandarins around Prince Norindeth dubbed itself the Liberal Party.[21] By May, three parties had emerged: Norindeth's Liberals, the *Kana Seri Pheap*; the Progressive Democratic Party, or *Krom Chamrouen Chiet Khmer*; and the Democratic Party, or *Krom Pracheathippetay*. Of these, the two most important were the Liberals and the Democrats and together they were to dominate Cambodian parliamentary politics until independence.

The Liberals were a conservative, royalist, pro-French grouping based on elite layers of functionaries, landed proprietors, Sino-Cambodian merchants and some religious milieux. Most importantly, in the years to come, King Sihanouk came to favor this party, although when the parties first emerged, his father, Prince Suramarit, supported the Democrats. In this early period, the young king began to emerge as an autonomous political actor, although reports from 1946 still saw him as devoting "a considerable amount of his time to personal amusement".[22] He had long been under the influence of others, in particular his strong-minded mother, Princess Kossamak, whom many observers saw as the *éminence grise* behind the throne, and of his uncle, the austere and somewhat authoritarian Prince Monireth. Sihanouk had been a compromise candidate for the throne in 1941 in order to heal the rift between the Norodom and Sisowath wings of the royal family. However, relations between the two wings of the royal family worsened after the war, particularly after Sihanouk and Prime Minister Monireth left for a visit to France on 18 April 1946. Power passed temporarily into the hands of a Regency composed of Suramarit, Norindeth and the old political comprador, Thiounn. Suramarit, Sihanouk's father, was reluctant to hand back control to Monireth, alleging that the Prime Minister was maneuvering for the crown, which he (Monireth) thought was rightfully his.[23] Whatever the truth of the allegation, the feud allowed Sihanouk to move out of his uncle's shadow. Gradually, Sihanouk developed the political style that was to characterize his role in post-colonial Cambodia. Believing that he ruled by divine right, he was impatient with the constraints imposed by constitutional monarchy and intervened increasingly openly in the political process. Until independence, his chosen vehicle was the Liberal Party and the gaggle of smaller right wing parties led by men such as Lon Nol, Dap Chhuon, Yem Sambaur and Nhiek Tioulong.

Prince Yuthevong and the Democrats

The Democrats were a more radical grouping under the leadership of Prince Yuthevong, a genuine intellectual who had recently arrived back from studying at Montpellier, Vichy and Paris, where he studied higher mathematics and astronomy, and married a Frenchwoman.[24] Yuthevong and a group of friends in Paris, including Thonn Ouk and Ngin Karet, had discussed forming the party before their return to Cambodia.[25] Formed in April 1946, the Democrats rapidly became the best-organized political force, with a propaganda apparatus covering most of the country. The party was a magnet for former supporters of

Nagaravatta—including men like Sim Var—and although it did not aim at immediate independence, the French considered it anti-colonialist. It wished to detach Cambodia from the Indochinese Federation, but to remain part of the French Union with representation in the French parliament. Yuthevong's ideas were strongly influenced by the colonial policies of the French Socialist Party. "Our political program was in no way subversive by today's standards," wrote a former leader of the party, Huy Kanthoul. "But for the times, it was almost a revolution." The party campaigned for a constitutional monarchy, a bicameral parliament and universal suffrage. In effect, the party wanted Cambodia to enjoy dominion status along the lines of Australia or Canada in the British Empire. "It was," writes Huy Kanthoul, "too much to ask of the protecting power."[26] Moreover, the party was ambiguous about the Issaraks, considering them patriots, albeit misguided ones. Numbers of supporters of the exiled Son Ngoc Thanh found their way into the party. Electorally, the Democrats became the most successful party in the country, but they suffered the enmity of Monireth, Sihanouk and the French alike.

The Progressive Democrats tried to straddle both camps. Led by Prince Norodom Montana, the Minister for National Economy and Agriculture, the party attracted middle ranking civil servants, merchants and "old clients of the prince". Its platform resembled that of the Democrats, but it wished to work closely with the French administration. It was never very successful, but it was a model of political sophistication compared with the eccentric proposal of M. Poc Hell, Prince Monireth's rich father-in-law, for another party that would be simultaneously conservative, royalist, social democratic and loyal to the Prime Minister. Mercifully, Poc abandoned the project "after critiques by Cambodian intellectuals".[27]

The post-war period also saw the emergence of a French and Cambodian press on an unprecedented scale in the kingdom. Before the war, there had been few newspapers or magazines, except for the Khmer-language proto-nationalist *Nagaravatta*, and French publications such as *L'Echo du Cambodge*, which was pitched primarily at French expatriates and *assimilés*.[28] The new French-language papers included *Le Cambodge*, a semi-official sheet published by the Sutharot Association; *La Liberté*, published by the politician and businessman M. Marinetti, who had sat as the member for Cochinchina and Cambodia[29] in the French parliament; and *Le Democrate*, which was the official organ of the Democratic Party. The Progressive Democrats also began publication of a newspaper called *Le Progrès* from August 16 1946, but this ceased publication the following month following a decree issued by Sihanouk countermanding previous declarations of press freedom. There were also a number of Khmer-language publications, including *Kampuchea*, which replicated *Cambodge*; *Pracheathippatey*, published by the Democrats; and *Pradipa Khmer*, the Liberal Party organ. In addition, there were a number of legal publications in Vietnamese and Chinese, together with clandestine Communist newspapers.[30]

Papers, prisons and bodies of armed men

Such a flowering of parties and papers had its roots both in long term changes in Khmer society and in the relatively liberal approach of the French High Commission. The pre-war *Résidents Supérieurs* had ruled in an authoritarian fashion that precluded independent political organization or expression of opinion. Paradoxically, Admiral Decoux's semi-fascist Vichy regime had drawn large numbers of Khmers out of isolated family and village life, thus contributing to the emergence of the tentative post-war civil society. Finally, the brief period of quasi-independence in 1945 had given many Khmers a thirst for public life and repression alone could not ensure the stability the French craved. The existence of the Issaraks was a permanent reminder of the need for change, with the 1885 Rebellion as a specter reminding what might happen if the French ruled too oppressively. However, we should not overstate the depth of these changes. This was very much a period of flux. Cambodians had no experience of parties or of voting, save for Son Ngoc Thanh's farcical referendum of September 1945. Cambodians had always been subjects rather than citizens, and if the powerful had their way, they would remain so. Even before full independence in 1953, Norodom Sihanouk demonstrated that he would never hesitate to dissolve parliaments and move against basic freedoms if he could not get what he wanted via the ballot box. Paradoxically, Sihanouk was initially a strong supporter of the transformation of his country into a constitutional monarchy. His liberalism did not last. Cambodian politics was to develop into a struggle between the king and his supporters on the one hand and the Democrats on the other. The king eventually won, and the ultimate loser was Cambodian democracy. Real authority, too, remained in the hands of the French until the end of the protectorate, for they controlled the "prisons and bodies of armed men" at the core of state power and they put these at the disposal of the royalists. Although the first Cambodian constitution guaranteed political liberties, the *Sûreté* often flouted them in the years to come.

Cambodia's first general election

On 13 April 1946, Sihanouk announced that he wished to "give autonomous Cambodia a constitution of her own", replete with freedom of speech and association. Final responsibility for the task would be charged to an elected constituent assembly. It was to be a bold departure from the autocratic past. Immediately, a joint Franco-Khmer committee set to work on the task of running the first national elections the country had ever seen.[31] When nominations closed on 28 June 1946, there were 198 candidates, including 63 from the Democrats, 67 from the Liberals, 5 from the Progressive Democrats and 63 independents.[32] Alas, intrigue marred the election campaign. Prince Monireth, acting with covert French support, was determined to block the advance of the Democrats, seeing them as a subversive force, despite their explicit support for the monarchy. He initially banned civil servants from joining political parties and supplied the Liberals and scores of bogus "independents" with petrol and newsprint at public expense. The French police shadowed Democrat leaders.[33] Another problem was that much of the electorate was illiterate and was voting for the first time. An Australian source cited the belief of a British army officer, Major P.L. Sweet that,

> The elections could hardly have been described as having been held under secret ballot. A large percentage of the population is illiterate and the election papers consisted of a disc showing a different design for each party, an elephant for the Democrats, for example: a pagoda and crossed arrows for other parties. The voters had to place one of these in the voting box. They were given considerable assistance in doing this by the Democratic Party whips who, in explaining the different discs to the illiterate, stated that the arrows were dangerous things and should be thrown away; the pagodas were sacred things and should be kept close to the heart by placing in the pockets—voters could then "stable the elephant in the box". *[Punctuation in original.]*[34]

There is probably truth in this, although one suspects that the French authorities gave Sweet biased information, and that any chicanery by the Democrats was balanced out by their own intrigues. Those machinations were unsuccessful, for the elections of 1 September 1946 gave an outright majority of seats to the Democrats: 50 seats as compared with 14 for the Liberals and three independents.[35] Yet, it was more than three months before the Democrats were able to take up their mandate. Monireth refused to step down as Prime Minister, claiming that there was no suitable successor. Eventually, he gave way after receiving a "lecture" from his nephew, Sihanouk, "on the mechanics of constitutional government".[36] This is very interesting, given Sihanouk's later disregard for those principles. The Democrats' leader, Prince Yuthevong, formed a 12-member cabinet in mid-December 1946.[37] Monireth, although increasingly authoritarian and contemptuous of the intellectual caliber of his people, did achieve a certain level of stability for the country during his period in office. Major Sweet reported after a visit in late 1946 that Cambodia gave "the appearance of complete calm. There is no shortage of food. The people look well fed and the price of food is less than half that at Saigon. The people are working as usual and, in contrast to the Annamites of Cochinchina, welcome the French with smiles and salutes in all the villages."[38] Late 1946 also saw the return of the large swathe of Cambodian territory lost to Siam in 1941. (These events are the subject of Chapter 22 below.)

Yuthevong's time in office had been relatively brief but he had worked very hard to modify the draft of a new constitution for the country. The draft was originally the handiwork of Monireth and the French, but Sihanouk had insisted that the constituent assembly should write the final version. The results were very different from those Monireth or the French would have wished. As Michael Vickery recalls, "After lengthy, often stormy, discussion of the draft...which the Democrats considered insufficiently democratic, the assembly produced a revised text which was accepted by the king..."[39] Sihanouk signed the draft document into law on 6 May 1947. Stretching to 107 articles, the constitution laid down the framework for Cambodia as a constitutional monarchy within the French Union, with Khmer as the official language and Buddhism as the official religion. Power emanated from the monarchy but that power was circumscribed by the constitution. The rule of law was to be respected, along with *habeus corpus*. Accused persons were held to be not guilty until proven so. Torture and ill treatment were forbidden. Article 9 guaranteed freedom of speech and publication and rights of association were enshrined in Article 10.[40]

The "Black Star conspiracy"

The new constitution was a brave document and it cannot have pleased the French, who, annoyed by Yuthevong's political style, had conspired with Monireth to prevent a Democratic victory. Worse still, Yuthevong seemed determined to act as if he were the head of a real government. Shortly after Yuthevong formed his cabinet, he offered an amnesty to any Issarak who defected to the government side.[41] A French police report also noted that Yuthevong was leading a movement for the liberation of political prisoners, including Prince Thon Norodom. The party openly canvassed the question in its newspaper, *Pracheathippatey*.[42] In late February or March 1947, perhaps to send a warning that they would not tolerate such independent initiatives, the French police arrested dozens of members of the Democratic Party in the so-called "Black Star" (*Étoile Noire*) Affair. The Black Star, according to the police, was a secret organization dedicated to exterminating the French that had been set up by Thanhist policemen in May 1946. Its members allegedly had black stars or Buddhas tattooed on their bodies. Those arrested included the *Nagaravatta* veteran, Sim Var, along with merchants, civil servants, Khmer policemen and at least one magistrate. The *Sûreté* also arrested twenty Phnom Penh railroad workers on charges of freighting munitions to the Issaraks in the northwestern provinces. Many of those arrested, including Chhim Phonn, were tortured in Saigon jails. Sim Var was accused of being a Japanese stooge, but was not tortured. In fact, there is no evidence that Black Star existed, or that Sim Var was secretly working with the Issaraks. It is, of course, possible that the Issaraks did have agents in the cities and in the Democratic Party, but Sim Var and his co-accused were moderate nationalists committed to working for modest change via the established political order. The arrests coincided with the sentencing of Son Ngoc Thanh to 20 years hard labor by a Saigon court and so it is possible that the Black Star *razzia* was a pre-emptive measure. The "ringleaders", most of whom had served in Son Ngoc Thanh's short-lived government in 1945, were quietly released without being brought to trial.[43] Still, the rumors poisoned the political air and allegations of complicity between Democrats and the Issaraks were to become a stock-in-trade of conservative politicians and French policemen until the end of the colony in 1953. Shortly after the Black Star affair, a letter purporting to be from "the inhabitants of the *srok* of Saang, in Kandal" denounced a leading Democrat politician, Chhean Vam, to the French High Commissioner. Vam, the letter claimed, had levied sums of money from students and sent it to Kim Ann, an Issarak chief at Battambang.[44] Chhean Vam's political opponents had probably fabricated the allegations.

The death of Yuthevong

Yuthevong remained at his post until his death, from malaria, on 18 July 1947. Shortly before, he had spent a brief holiday in a villa owned by Sihanouk at Kep on the Gulf coast, a region notorious for its deadly mosquitoes. Huy Kanthoul, who served as Information Minister in the government, remembers Yuthevong's death as "an almost irreparable loss" to the party.[45] Yuthevong, who some rank-conscious opponents claimed had a right only to the title of viscount rather than prince, was the first Cambodian to graduate with a doctorate in science and he had four other degrees. He had long suffered ill health; in 1933, he had contracted tuberculosis and almost died in a sanatorium in France.[46] Yuthevong's death was a loss for more than the Democratic Party. He stood out as an honest, independent-minded and dedicated man in a system already infected with corruption and careerism. Significantly, Sihanouk did not mourn his passing and even admits unapologetically in his memoirs that when he heard in 1952 that a school in Battambang still bore Yuthevong's name, he told the education authorities to change it.[47] Sisowath Watchhayavong, the former Minister of Justice, succeeded Yuthevong as Prime Minister, and voters went to the polls in December 1947 to elect the country's first National Assembly. The fragile Cambodian democracy was out of the chrysalis stage, although political intrigues already threatened to stunt its growth. On the positive side, Cambodia's first elected assembly had ratified a relatively free constitution and the French had secured the return of the lost provinces. In retrospect, this was the high water mark of the post-war democratic experiment.

Notes

[1] Anthony Barnett, interview with Colonel E.D. Murray. Unpublished typescript, 1982. Chandler Papers, Monash University.
[2] Philippe Devillers, (1946), "The Franco-Cambodian Agreement", Le Monde, 20 February.
[3] Ibid.
[4] PRO FO 371/46309. Mr. Brain, SACSEA, Saigon to the Foreign Office. Received 6 November 1945.
[5] Devillers, op.cit.
[6] Ibid.
[7] AOM HCC 10. Rélations avec les cambodgiens. Esprit de la population, 1945-1947. Sûreté Fédérale, Rapport Mensuel, mars 1946.
[8] Ibid. Rapport mensuel, février 1946.
[9] Ibid. Report from Sûrêté to the director of police, 17 March 1945.

[10] Ibid. Rapport mensuel, janvier 1946.

[11] AOM HCC 10. Sub-lieutenant Fauveau, Kampot, to the High Commissioner at Phnom Penh, 11 January 1946.

[12] Ibid. "Incidents provoqués par des tirailleurs cambodgiens contre la surêté française." French police chief to the High Commissioner, 14 January 1946.

[13] Ibid. Lon Nol, chief of the National Police, to the Minister of the Interior, 18 January 1946.

[14] Ibid. Surêté, note d'information, 5 février 1946.

[15] Ibid. *Surêté* report, 7 February 1946.

[16] PRO FO 371/46311, Situation in FIC as of 24 October 1945. E.W. Meiklereid, British Consul at Saigon to the Foreign Office.

[17] Marie Alexandrine Martin, (1989), *Le Mal Cambodgien. Histoire d'une société traditionelle face à ses leaders politiques, 1946-1987*, Hachette, Paris, p.64.

[18] Huy Kanthoul, op.cit. p.100.

[19] Justin J. Corfield, (1994), *Khmers Stand Up! A History of the Cambodian Government, 1970-1975*, Centre of Southeast Asian Studies, Monash University, Clayton, Victoria, pp.xii-xiii.

[20] David P. Chandler, (1991), *The Tragedy of Cambodian History. Politics, War and Revolution since 1945*, Silkworm Press, Bangkok, p.72.

[21] AOM HCC 11 op.cit. Surêté Fédérale, Rapports Mensuels, février et mars 1946.

[22] PRO FO 959/17. Cambodia Political. E.W. Meiklereid, H.M. Consul at Saigon to the Foreign Office, London. 22 December 1946.

[23] AOM HCC 10, op.cit. Surêté Fédérale, Rapports Mensuels, avril et juillet 1946.

[24] PRO FO 959/14. "Cambodian, Cochin Chinese personalities." 13 February 1947.

[25] Philippe Preschez, (1961), "La Démocratie Cambodgienne", thèse pour le Diplôme de l'I.E.P., Paris, p.18.

[26] Huy Kanthoul, op.cit. pp.101-102.

[27] AOM HCC 11, op.cit. Surêté Fédérale, Rapport Mensuel, mai 1946.

[28] The *Echo* did, however, have a Khmer-language section.

[29] The suffrage was restricted to French residents and *assimilés*.

[30] Information for this paragraph is primarily from AOM HCC 10, op.cit., Monthly Report, September 1946, covering letter of 14 November 1946 from the *Police Nationale*.

[31] AAc A 1838/253 "Political evolution in Cambodia since 1946."

[32] AOM HCC 10, op.cit., Monthly Report, September 1946, covering letter of 14 November 1946 from the *Police Nationale*.

[33] Chandler, op.cit. p.31.

[34] AAc A 1838/253. APLO memorandum No 18. "A report on a visit to Cambodgia *[sic]*, made at the end of September by Major P.L. Sweet, RA, of ALFSEA Liaison Detachment in French Indo-China..." H. G. Stokes, Australian political liaison officer, SEA, Office of the Special Commissioner

in South East Asia, Singapore, 20th October 1946 to the Secretary, Department of External Affairs, Canberra.

[35] Ibid. Some sources give a lower figure for the Democrats. See, for instance, Philippe Devillers, (1946), "Le Cambodge et l'aube de la democratie. Le peuple khmer a vote pour le première fois", *Le Monde*, 8-9 septembre. Devillers claims the Democrats won 30 seats out of 67, compared to the Liberals 14, with the Progressive Democrats failing to win a single seat. Chandler's version is supported by documents in the Australian Archives, including "Political evolution in Cambodia since 1946", op.cit., which is itself a précis of a longer French-language document entitled "Evolution politique du Cambodge depuis 1946".

[36] Chandler, op.cit. p.32. See also Reddi.

[37] The cabinet consisted of eight ministers: Yuthevong (President of the Council of Ministers and Minister of the Interior); Watchhayavong (Justice); Son Voeunsai (Defense); Sonn Sann (Finance); Penn Sam El (National Economy); Chheam Vau (Education); Prak Sarinn (Public Works, Communications and Health); Penn Nouth (State); and four secretaries of state: Huy Kanthoul (Information and Propaganda); Hak Mong Sheng (Finances); Au Chheun (Religion and Fine Arts); and Ouk Thoutch (Provisions). [ANC RSC F42 File No. 18765. Dossier Personnel indigène. Sisowath Youtevong, fils de Comte Chamroeunvong et de la comtesse Yuphiphan. Ordonnance royal de 15 décembre 1946. See also Preschez, op.cit. p.21.]

[38] Sweet, cited by Stokes, op.cit.

[39] Vickery, op.cit.

[40] AAc A1838/280 3016/1/3 PT 1. Constitution of the Kingdom of Cambodia, English translation.

[41] PRO FO 371 69657. Saigon Military Intelligence Report, 10 August 1948.

[42] AOM HCC 10. Sûreté to Comm. Rep, 14 November 1946.

[43] AOM HCC 10. Sûreté Fédérale, Rapports Mensuels, janvier-février et mars 1947; Martin, op.cit.; Chandler, op.cit. p.32. Those arrested included Hem Chamrouen and Sim Var; Houth Smonh, a magistrate; Phlong Taleng a civil servant; Ung Sieu You, a merchant; Kim Kuy, a timber merchant; and two policemen, Norn Troeung and Yin Var.

[44] AOM HCC 10, Letter from the inhabitants of the *srok* of Saang, Kandal province, to the Commissioner, 15 April 1947.

[45] Huy Kanthoul, op.cit. p.105.

[46] Youtevong dossier, op.cit.

[47] Norodom Sihanouk, (1981), *Souvenirs Doux et Amers*, Hachette, Paris, p.139.

Chapter 22

An Asian Alsace-Lorraine

It is not too much to say that to the Siamese the question assumes as great importance as that of Alsace Lorraine did for so long for the French.
—Mr. Thompson, British Ambassador at Bangkok, 7 June 1946.[1]

Give me back my Alsace Lorraine!
—King Sisowath, Paris, 1906.[2]

In December 1946, Thailand reluctantly handed back Battambang and the disputed parts of Siem Reap province to the French authorities in Cambodia. All things being equal, the retrocession ought to have re-cemented French power. The provinces were an important test of French ability to guarantee Cambodian national integrity. Almost forty years earlier, the original return of the provinces to Cambodia had bonded the Khmer elite to France; no one was as delighted as King Sisowath and his Council of Ministers by the provinces' return in 1907. The subsequent loss of the territories to Siam in 1941 had been too much for King Monivong to bear and he had died, sick and disillusioned, on his estates at Bokor. When the French troops marched into Battambang town and raised the tricolor over the Governor's residence in 1946, they could claim, with some justification, to have redeemed their pledge to act as the country's protector. However, it was not to prove sufficient to save their grip on the country. Too much had changed since 1939. The age of European colonialism was fading, and this was as true of Cambodia as of China, India, Indonesia, Burma or Vietnam.

Both sides—France/Cambodia and Thailand—felt that they were in the right in a dispute that had its roots in border adjustments stretching back over 150 years.[3] Both sides were disinclined to compromise, although borders are often more ambiguous things than nationalist ideology will admit and nation-states are often artificial creations. Borders are lines on maps, social constructions rather than "natural" barriers marking off discrete socio-cultural entities. Alsace and Lorraine, the long-disputed provinces on the borders of France and Germany, are a case in point, and both sides used them as a reference point in this Asian quarrel. King Sisowath's comparison of his own "lost provinces" with those lost by France to Germany in 1871[4] was politically astute, but it ignored the deeper social and political issues. The return of Alsace and Lorraine was a French obsession after 1871, but Strasbourg, or Straßburg—the "fortress of the roads"—had long been a German city when it was annexed to France in 1689 after the Peace of Westphalia.[5] When the *Straßburger* Sebastien Brant wrote his classic satire, *The Ship of Fools*,[6] in 1494, it never crossed his mind to use any other language than his own Alsatian German. On the other hand, ambiguous Strasbourg also saw the first public performance of Rouget de Lisle's *Marseillaise*, before the city's mayor, M. Dietrich in 1792. It also bred the fierce (even grotesque) French patriotism of the children's writer Jean-Jacques Waltz, alias "Uncle Hansi". Two more details, plucked almost at random from this socio-cultural stew, highlight the ethnic ambiguity of the place: the detention of Albert Schweitzer as an enemy alien in a French concentration camp in 1914, and the anti-French agitation of Eugen Ricklin's *Heimatbund* [7] during the inter-war years.

The Asian equivalent of this quarrel involved the two fertile provinces of Battambang and Siem Reap, situated south of the Dangrek Mountains and at the western end of the Great Lake. To the south, the thickly forested peaks of the Cardamom and Elephant ranges cut off these inland plains from the sea. Battambang sits astride the Sang Ke River in the richest agricultural district of the Khmer lands, almost 300 kilometers by narrow gauge rail from Phnom Penh, and separated from the Tonlé Sap by an immense reedy marsh. Known as Phratabong to the Thais, it is a quiet town set on high clay riverbanks, with lines of French shophouses in the main streets and the suspicion of mountains on the horizon. Neighboring Siem Reap province is the site of the ruins of the old Cambodian capital of Angkor and is cut off from Thailand by the jungle-clad scarp of the Dangreks. The name Siem Reap—"Siam Defeated"—bears witness to the tension between the two countries. Although predominantly peopled by Khmer-speakers, the provinces were home to minorities of Vietnamese, Thais, Shans, Malays, Chinese and Lao. They were originally incorporated into Siam in 1795, after a Khmer official named Ben usurped power from the weakened court at Udong.[8] The Cambodian crown was powerless to resist and over the next twenty years, the Siamese seized three more provinces in the north of the country. In 1810, a Khmer family, the Apheuvongs, were given the title of hereditary rulers, with their seat of government at Battambang. Although they were Siamese territories, the provinces enjoyed considerable political and cultural autonomy, even circulating their own coins.[9] The majority of government officials were ethnic Cambodians and Khmer was the common tongue, both in everyday life and in much of the government's affairs. In effect, the provinces were "semi-independent principalities", although they were required to acknowledge their status as Siamese vassals and send tribute to the court at Bangkok. The political situation paralleled that which existed in Cambodia-proper, whose kings, (or viceroys as the Siamese insisted they were) were chosen by the Siamese rulers and educated at Bangkok. As the present author has written elsewhere, "Cambodia had been *partitioned*"[10] into two tributary states. [Emphasis in the original.] When the French set up their protectorate in Cambodia in 1863, the western provinces had been detached from the rest of the country for almost seventy years and over forty more were to pass before France negotiated their retrocession. In all, the Siamese had controlled the lands they called *Monthon Burapha* for over a century. In comparison, when the Prussians annexed Alsace and Lorraine in 1871, those provinces had been French for a shorter period than Siem Reap and Battambang had been Siamese. The Siamese could argue with some justification that time and custom had legitimated their claim to the territories. They were Khmer speaking lands, it is true, but then did not the French claim a European territory where the majority of the people spoke Alsatian German and read *Hochdeutsch*? The ruler of the lands, the *Phya* Kathathorn,[11] patriarch of the Apheuvongs family, was 45 years old when the French took over the provinces in 1907. As the French were quick to point out, Kathathorn had many faults. He was a fierce despot who ruled in an arbitrary manner. He loved luxury and maintained a substantial harem. He could be brutal to his subordinates and kept a large retinue of slaves. He was said to be greedy and did not easily differentiate between his own fortunes and those of the government. He even levied the peasants from the fields to act as beaters on his hunts.[12] Exactly the same criticisms had been made of his counterparts in Phnom Penh, especially of King Norodom.

A history of insurrection

When the French marched into the territories in 1907 they might have expected to be welcomed as liberators. Were they not reuniting the "lost provinces" with Cambodia? Did they not bring Cambodian administrators with them? Did they not abolish slavery and attempt to rationalize the web of taxes and *corvée*? Yet, they were met with a revolt that lasted several years and cost many hundreds of lives. The *Phya* Kathathorn himself left for Bangkok with a huge caravan of slaves, elephants, ox-carts, horses, dogs and gold, but he left a network of faithful retainers behind to organize guerrilla warfare against the French. The guerrillas, commanded by an old official called the *Visès* Nheou, cut telegraph lines, burned down French barracks and ambushed French military columns with great audacity. They enjoyed the advantages of knowledge of the local terrain (often trackless swamp and jungle) and could slip over the border into Siam if necessary. Most importantly, they enjoyed the support of a substantial slice of the local population, many of whom immigrated to Siam to escape French rule. The revolt only faded when the French threatened the Siamese government with unpleasant consequences if they continued to aid the rebels. The *Visès* Nheou was arrested by the Siamese gendarmerie and exiled far away to the Indian Ocean coast of the Malay Peninsula.[13]

By 1909, the revolt was over, but the Siamese government never abandoned the belief that the provinces were rightfully theirs. In 1941, with Japanese assistance, they regained control of all of Battambang province and of part of Siem Reap, leaving the French in control of the Angkor ruins and Siem Reap town and its immediate lacustrine hinterland.[14] In their view, they had reclaimed *their* Alsace-Lorraine. A member of the Apheuvongs family moved into the Governor's palace and the rich rice harvests were diverted to the west along a railroad line built by the French to Aranya in Thailand. It is difficult to know what the inhabitants thought of their new political status, because they were not asked to ratify the annexation, although they did vote for Thai parties in the all-Thailand elections of January and August 1946.[15]

A French report quoted an American source's estimate of Battambang as a hotbed of anti-French nationalism, swept by a "wave of discontent" when it became known that the French would return in late 1946.[16] The French themselves feared their return would spark off a revolt as in 1907. After 1942, the provinces had sheltered an assortment of political refugees from Indochina. These included Cambodian army deserters from the border war of 1940-41; Khmer monks and lay people fleeing in the aftermath of the failed "revolt of the parasols"; bandits and adventurers of indeterminate origin; and a variety of Vietnamese rebels, both Communist and nationalist, including veterans of the Yen Bay uprising. There were even cosmopolitan deserters from the Foreign Legion, and, after the capitulation of Japan, absconders from the Imperial Army whose anti-western rancor and fear of capture led them to side with the Issaraks. These elements were potent yeast in a population drenched with anti-French propaganda by the Japanese and Thais, and there were thousands of them, many well armed and trained by Siamese and Japanese drill instructors.[17] Some of the Issarak commanders held officers' rank in the Thai army.[18] Although these refugees had sought sanctuary in Thai-controlled lands as an expedient, many of them preferred any Asian rule to the tricolor. However, the British Minister at Bangkok believed that the fugitive rebels who attacked Siem Reap cared "nothing for the Siamese authorities".[19] They were above all else, Cambodian patriots. As such, they would have resented attempts by the Thai authorities to assimilate the Khmer populations.[20]

French demands for the provinces' return

World opinion was running strongly against the Thais because of their alliance with Japan during the war. By mid-1945—even before the Japanese capitulation—General de Gaulle had secured Anglo-American agreement for the provinces' return.[21] The US supported the *status quo ante bellum* because the territories "acquired by Siam in 1941 were secured with Japanese support after the course of Japanese aggression had commenced".[22] Not even the Russians rallied to Thailand's support, in fact they blocked Thailand's bid for UN membership because of it.[23] Immediately after his installation as French High Commissioner at Saigon in November 1945, Thierry d'Argenlieu demanded the immediate transfer of the territories to General Douglas Gracey's command. He accused the Thais of procrastination on the issue and dispatched military observers to the disputed territories without informing them.[24] Yet, when negotiations began between France and Thailand in January 1946, the Thais were reluctant to concede any territory, desperately trying to save face and to placate domestic public opinion, which was strongly against any concessions. Even after the Siamese delegation to the United Nations Security Council had conceded that the 1941 treaty was invalid, they tried to hang on to Battambang, claiming that it "belongs to Siam and is a Siamese town."[25] They also proposed a plebiscite under UN supervision in the disputed areas to determine their future, but the proposal lapsed for want of support.[26] Their view was not due purely to the desire for territorial aggrandisement, for they appear to have believed sincerely in the pan-Thai ideal, which saw the Khmers as their ethnic kin. Even today, there are large enclaves of Khmer speakers inside Thailand, some situated west of Bangkok, and there is no reported history of official mistreatment of this minority. In 1945, the Thai Prime Minister was an ethnic Khmer, an Apheuvongs, descended from the line of governors of Battambang, and many of the ratings and officers in the Thai navy were ethnic Khmers.

As the year 1946 unfolded, there was little progress towards the return of the territories and the French army began to consider the possibility of military action to secure their return. Although the Thai garrisons were reasonably strong—with up to 4000 regular troops on the Siem Reap border alone[27]—a French officer who visited the area believed that "only a few days military action by the French" would be sufficient to oust them.[28] This is probably true, for the French had recovered from the demoralization that followed the fall of France in 1940. The approach of the monsoon hastened their impatience. The British Ambassador at Bangkok considered that the "French could hardly wait indefinitely. By July, the rains would be pouring down and military operations would then be impossible for several months, during which time the Siamese would have ample opportunity to continue their present policy of infiltration consolidation."[29] Sporadic firefights broke out between French and Thai forces in several places along the long border. In September, for instance, the *Bangkok Post* claimed that a French gunboat on the Tonlé Sap Lake had fired over 50 shells at Thai positions near Svay Donkeo, while searchlights lit up the night sky.[30] The Issarak raid on Siem Reap heightened French indignation and there were reports of French commanders "wearied by politics" and taking matters into their own hands. "Their one idea is to apply to Siam methods successfully employed...in the Atlas Mountains," Ambassador Thompson wrote in June.[31] M. Picot, the French Foreign Minister, shared his concern.[32] Rumors that the Siamese were "pulling out" of Battambang and handing over power to the Issaraks further exacerbated French fears.[33] Full scale war was probably only averted by the opening of a fresh round of negotiations between the two sides at Paris in September, with Prince Monireth representing Cambodian interests.[34]

The border pact of 17 November 1946

The result of the talks was a foregone conclusion. In October, the Thai government earmarked over four million baht to pay for the expected mass evacuation of the territories.[35] Later in the month, a mission arrived at Battambang to begin organizing the departure of the refugees and was met by a crowd of over 2000 people, including Vietnamese (probably Viet Minh supporters) with banners reading: "We support Siam's stand" and "Long live Viet Nam – Siamese Friendship".[36] According to Siamese sources, half of Battambang's 15,000-strong Vietnamese population expressed the wish to move to Thailand, and 3000 of them had already gone at the end of October.[37] The French, fearing disorders when they retook the town, probably heartily wished them gone. A British report claimed that there were "at least several thousand dissident Annamites and Free Cambodians..." in the territories, "rebellious fugitives from French rule, who are well-armed, and in most cases desperate and who are to some extent...led by Japanese deserters."[38] Thereafter, the provinces seem to have degenerated into chaos, with law and order breaking down and refugees clamoring for places on overcrowded trains leaving Battambang for Thailand-proper. There were reports of thousands of refugees camping at the stations for days in hope of finding space aboard the trains. Others were "obliged to 'tramp it' day and night, carrying their belongings with them" to the new frontier.[39] Ill feeling ran high against the French and the Siamese authorities claimed that they could not guarantee the safety of French military observers and civilians at Battambang in this "effervescence".[40] Shortly afterwards, Murray Ellison, an American Protestant missionary, claimed that a "native" who had been distributing a French proclamation was "shot dead" and that there had been a "massacre" of French and Cambodian Christians at Battambang.[41]

The dispute officially ended on 17 November 1946, with the signing of a five-clause border pact between France and Thailand at Washington D.C. Ironically, one of the Thai signatories was Nai Khuang Apheuvongs, a close relative of the former Siamese governor the Phya Kathathorn.[42] The news was greeted with disbelief and anger on the streets of Bangkok and the government almost fell.[43] In fact, the Thais had no choice but to comply, for, as a Thai newspaperman wrote when the government signalled that it must capitulate, the 1941 treaty was not "recognized by any single power of the post-war world. That is the most overriding consideration of all".[44]

After the pact was signed, conditions further deteriorated in the disputed territories and for over a fortnight before the French arrived, the only forces capable of maintaining some degree of law and order were detachments of British troops under General Brunskill, sent in earlier to disarm the Japanese army, and some demoralized Thai gendarmes.[45] Although an advance guard of the French army arrived at Battambang on 25 November without incident, the ordinary people seemed full of sullen resentment. In early December, two French officers were stabbed at the Battambang market and bridges were burned. Elsewhere in the province, Khmers burned down a Vietnamese Catholic village, allegedly because of the pro-French politics of its inhabitants.[46] French sources claim the Issaraks massacred the Vietnamese and this is entirely possible, given the strong anti-Vietnamese bias of Cambodian nationalism.[47] Serious disorders continued even after the arrival of the main body of French troops in early December, with reports of sabotage at the Battambang water works and power station,[48] railroad lines damaged, bridges destroyed and trees cut down over roads.[49] A British officer reported that, "as soon as the French column arrived under Brigadier General de Jonquières, snapping and snarling developed between the French soldiers and civilians, the former generally reflecting a desire to get tough in handling the local population". Another French report claims that the soldiers first entered a deserted town and that the streets were empty to make a political point.[50] A few days later, however, there was a 1000-strong anti-French demonstration, allegedly organized by Communists.[51]

Thereafter, the dispute changed character. With the Thais gone, the Issarak activity merged with that in the rest of Cambodia. France dropped its opposition to Thailand's membership of the United Nations and since that time, the frontier has generally been a peaceful one except for the perennial marauding of bandits, and the incursions of the anti-Vietnamese coalition during the 1980s. The local population accepted their reincorporation into French-dominated Cambodia with sullen resignation, although the Issaraks and Viet Minh remained strong in the region until the Geneva Conference in 1954 freed Indochina from French rule. As for the Cambodian people as a whole, they appeared indifferent, at least to outsiders. The French *Sûreté* held that their perceived attitude "proves that national sentiment among the people is still little developed" and that the retrocession had not generated the kind of enthusiasm that similar events caused overseas, even in other Asian countries.[52] In fact, there had been a sea change in political consciousness since the beginning of the war, and it is likely that the Khmers were tight-lipped in the presence of French policemen. Despite this alleged indifference, French power had less than seven years left to run in the country.

Notes

[1] PRO FO 371 54386. Mr. Thompson to the Foreign Office, 7 June 1946.

[2] King Sisowath, quoted in the *Pall Mall Gazette*, London, 15 June 1906 and *Marseille Republicain*, Marseilles, 16 June 1906.

[3] Years after France regained the territories and Cambodia had gained independence, older Thais still saw them as part of their country. See, for instance, M.L. Manich Jumsai, (1970), *History of Thailand and Cambodia. (From the days of Angkor to the present)*, Chalermnit, Bangkok.

[4] The provinces reverted to France in 1919 and were reoccupied by Germany between 1940 and 1945.

[5] The southern Alsatian city of Mulhouse/Mülhausen did not become French until 1793.

[6] In (Alsatian) German, *Das Narrenschiff*.

[7] Roughly translates as "Homeland League".

[8] For information on the Siamese period and the negotiations for the return of the territories, see Lawrence Palmer Briggs, (1942), "The Treaty of 23 March 1907 between France and Siam and the return of Battambang and Angkor to Cambodia", *Far Eastern Quarterly*, Vol. V, No 4, August; P. de la Brosse, "Le territoire de Battambang. Aperçus politiques", *Revue Indochinoise*, deuxième semester 1907; F.A. Bernard, (1933), *À l'École des Diplomates. La perte et le retour d'Angkor*, Les Oeuvres Représentatives, Paris; David Porter Chandler, (1974), "Cambodia before the French: Politics in a Tributary Kingdom, 1794-1848", Ph.D. thesis, University of Michigan, University Microfilms International, Ann Arbor; Tauch Chhong, (trans Sithan Hin), "Battambang in the period of the vassal", unpublished manuscript, originally published in Khmer at Battambang in 1974; John Tully, (1996), *Cambodia Under the Tricolour. King Sisowath and the 'Mission Civilisatrice, 1904-1927*, Monash Asia Institute, Clayton, Victoria, in particular Chapter Three; George N. Curzon, "The Siamese boundary question", *The Nineteenth Century: A Monthly Review*, Vol. XXXIV pp. 34-55; and J.R.V. Prescott, (1985), *A Study of the Delineation of the Thai-Cambodian Boundary*, Office of National Assessments, Canberra.

[9] The currency was known as the *prak pae*. Tauch Chhong, op.cit. pp.78-80 and Étienne Aymonier, (1901), *Le Cambodge*, Vol. II, *Les Provinces Siamoises*, Ernest Leroux, Paris, p.281. See also Tully, op.cit. p.98.

[10] Tully, op.cit. p.99.

[11] *Phya* was a title, meaning "Lordship". Kathathorn lived from around 1849 until 1922. He succeeded his father in 1888. (Tully, op.cit. p.82.)

[12] Ibid. pp. 100-105.

[13] Ibid. Chapter Four, "Uprising in Battambang".

[14] See Chapter 17 above.

[15] David K. Wyatt, (1982), *Thailand. A Short History*, Yale University Press, New Haven, Connecticut, p.262. It is unlikely, however, that the Thais would have allowed parties favoring a return to Cambodia to run.

[16] AOM HCC 10, Sûreté report, "Source américain, a/s mentalité 'révolutionnaire' des 'intellectuels' cambodgiens de la capitale" [et Battambang.] The source was probably Colonel Law.

[17] AOM HCC 10, Surété Fédérale, rapport mensuel février 1946; PRO FO 371 54385, Franco-Siamese Relations, Thompson to the Foreign Office, 29 May 1946; PRO 371 54392, Thompson to the Foreign Office, 30 October 1946.

[18] AOM HCC 10, Rapport mensuel de septembre 1946, Police Nationale, 14 novembre 1946.

[19] PRO FO 371 54392, Thompson to Foreign Office, 30 October 1946.

[20] According to Huy Kanthoul, the authorities insisted on instruction in Thai in the schools and banned the wearing of certain items of Khmer clothing. [Huy Kanthoul, "Mémoires", French-language typescript, Chandler Papers, Monash University, p.104.]

[21] PRO WO 106 4820. De Gaulle and Siam in 1945.

[22] PRO FO 371 46566. Siam File No 1196. Text of the State Department oral statement to the French Embassy, Washington, 13 October 1945.

[23] "France and Russia oppose Siam's UN membership bid", *Bangkok Post,* 15 August 1946.

[24] PRO FO 371 46311. General FIC. "Celebrations at Sihanouk's birthday. Nov 13 1945." Meiklereid at Saigon to the Foreign Office, 20 November 1945; PRO FO 371 46311, Political situation in French Indo-China, 6 December 1945, telegram from SACSEA to Labour Office, 2 December 1945.

[25] PRO FO 371 54391. Siamese delegation to the Security Council to Mr. Allen, 9 October 1946.

[26] De Gaulle and Siam in 1945, op.cit.

[27] AOM RSC 443. *Sûreté* to *Résident Supérieur*, 8 March 1945; AOM HCC 10. Rapport mensuel de septembre 1946, Police Nationale.

[28] PRO FO 371 54384. Thompson at Bangkok to the Foreign Office 4 May 1946 after conversation with Colonel St. Mleu.

[29] Ibid.

[30] "Residents quit town on border," *Bangkok Post,* 10 September 1946.

[31] PRO FO 371 54386, Thompson to Foreign Office, 10 June 1946.

[32] PRO FO 371 54390. Duff Cooper at Paris to the Foreign Office, 26 September 1946.

[33] PRO FO 371 54390. Thompson to the Foreign Office, 28 August 1946; PRO FO 371 54391, Meiklereid to Foreign Office 23 October 1946.

[34] PRO FO 371 54390. Meiklereid to the Foreign Office, 3 September 1946.

[35] "Plans for mass evacuation from provinces made", *Bangkok Post,* October 19 1946.

[36] Ibid. October 25 1946.

[37] Ibid. "7,500 Annamites plan to evacuate Phratabong", October 28 1946.

[38] PRO 371 54392, Thompson to Foreign Office, 30 October 1946.

[39] "Great trek from border areas into Siam continues", *Democracy*, Bangkok, November 27 1946, also December 4 1946.

[40] PRO FO 371 54392. Thompson to Foreign Office, 28 October 1946.

[41] PRO FO 371 54392, Thompson to Foreign Office, 29 October 1946.

[42] "5 clause border pact signed", *Democracy*, Bangkok, November 19 1946; FO 371 54394. The agreement of 17 November 1946.

[43] PRO FO 371 54393. Thompson to Foreign Office, 26 November 1946.

[44] Editorial, "The Franco-Siam Dispute", *Thai Newsmagazine*, October 20 1946.

[45] PRO FO 371 54393, Foreign Office to French Ambassador, 30 October 1946.

[46] AOM HCC 32. Retrocession des provinces par le Siam, 1946. Materials sent to the Comm. Rep. at Phnom Penh from the Délégation du Haut Commission aux provinces rétrocedés. British observers also reported acts of sabotage. (PRO FO 371 54394. Thompson to Foreign Office, 2 December 1946.)

[47] AOM HCC 10. Sûreté Fédérale. Rapport mensuel, décembre 1946.

[48] PRO FO 371 54394, Thompson to Foreign Office 17 December 1946.

[49] AOM HCC 10, Sûreté fédérale, rapport mensuel, décembre 1946, op.cit.

[50] Sûreté fédérale rapport, op.cit.

[51] PRO FO 371 54394, Thompson to Foreign Office, based on report by Colonel Cowper, who visited Battambang during the retrocession.

[52] AOM HCC 10, Sûreté Fédérale, rapport mensuel, janvier-février 1947.

Chapter 23

Absolutism Versus Parliamentary Democracy

French imperialism and the absolute monarchy is the source of the suffering of the Khmer people.
—Open letter from Khmer students in Paris to King Sihanouk, 1952.

I am not only the giver of the Constitution, but also the giver of elections.
—Norodom Sihanouk, 1952.

The early promise of Cambodia's European-style constitutional parliamentary system was to prove illusory. Even during 1946 and 1947, there were ominous signs presaging its doom in an incipient struggle for supremacy between Sihanouk and the Democratic Party. The Democrats, as the largest party, expected the right to govern within the constraints imposed by the *modus vivendi* and subsequent treaties with the French. For all of his earlier democratic enthusiasm, Sihanouk had revealed that he was willing to play the part of constitutional monarch only up to a point. Cambodian kings had hitherto been absolute rulers[1] and he had already acquired the taste for personal power. These tendencies soon hardened. Several times during the coming years, he intervened directly in political affairs, finally suspending parliament and concentrating executive and legislative power in his own hands. The French, for their part, were happy to let the Cambodians play act at democracy so long as the High Commission and Paris made the important decisions. Ironically, as the servants of the Fourth Republic, they were happy to back up the king in his battles with parliament. The situation was compounded by the Issarak-Viet Minh insurrection, which raged in the jungles and rural areas until 1954. This is not to say that the parliamentary system proved ideal. Sihanouk's taste for power was also matched by a taste for personal enrichment on the part of the many placemen in the National Assembly. Yet, despite such a gloomy political landscape, Sihanouk was able to guide the country towards full independence in late 1953. Although we should not accept his claim to be the sole architect of Cambodian freedom, it was not mere braggadocio. His "royal crusade" secured independence for Cambodia *before* the Battle of Dien Bien Phu forced the French to quit Vietnam and Laos.[2]

The elections of December 1947

The elections of December 1947 returned an absolute majority for the Democrats, who received 73 per cent of all votes cast[3] after a "feverish" campaign during which many "virulent" articles and speeches were printed and delivered.[4] This vote translated into 44 seats out of 75, compared with 21 won by their closest rivals, the Liberals. Two new parties, Nhiek Tioulong and Lon Nol's Khmer Renewal and Kim Thit's National Cambodian Union, failed to win a single seat, despite full coffers and backing in high places. (Both parties were pro-French, but the latter supported membership of the Indochinese Union, whereas Nhiek Tioulong was opposed.[5]) In theory, the National Assembly, which convened in January 1948, was entitled to a four-year term. It ought also have been a time for celebrations, given the return of Battambang and the occupied parts of Siem Reap to Cambodia. However, it quickly became apparent that the Assembly was sliding into the grip of a "profound malaise". Part of the problem was that the huge Democratic majority reduced their opponents to impotence.[6] If they chose—and at times, they did choose—they could gag opponents and guillotine through legislation.

The situation was exacerbated by petty personal squabbles, horse-trading and corruption. A scandal erupted in mid-1948 when a number of deputies, including Sam Nhean, the vice-president of the National Assembly, were implicated in the illegal sale of rationed cotton thread. Prime Minister Chhean Vam's proposal for an investigation was blocked by a narrow vote in the Democratic Party caucus. To ensure the immunity of the culprits, Yem Sambaur, a deputy who doubled as police commissioner, ordered the destruction of the evidence. Chhean Vam resigned in disgust.[7] The French police cited the opinion of Prince Virija, a nephew of Prince Monireth, who justified not voting in the elections by claiming that, "All the parties made use of the election campaign to deceive the people and serve their own personal interests."[8] In fact, the ruling elite was deeply infected with sleaze, and believed that every man had his price. Other French police reports drew attention to the continuing problem of illegal gambling dens in Phnom Penh. These lucrative operations were run by members of the elite, including the politician Sim Var and members of the royal family and enjoyed the protection and active participation of Lon Nol, the chief of the Cambodian police.[9] Lon Nol, who was to head up Sihanouk's political police and who became President of the Khmer Republic in 1970, was a man with a past. As we have seen, he was directly involved in political murder at Pich Nil concentration camp in 1945. Another factor contributing to political instability was that the opposition parties were vehicles for the interests of elite circles who were used to getting their way and resented being denied their share of power and its concomitant perks and privileges.

"An assembly of demagogues"?

The parliamentary experiment was also very new and many of its problems are attributable to simple inexperience. A British observer believed that, "The fear of responsibility and of public opinion, and the lack of executive competence, create an assembly of demagogues who, having no understanding of the spirit of the party system, become all-powerful, while the executive itself is reduced to impotence."[10] The intrigues festered on throughout 1947 and 1948, poisoning the atmosphere within the Assembly. Prince Monireth added to the rancor. He despised the democratic experiment and did not believe that the Cambodians could govern themselves. He founded a newspaper entitled *Krabey Prei* (*Wild Buffalo*), and savagely attacked the Democrats. He also contributed vitriolic articles to a pro-colonialist review called *Sud Mékong*.[11] Truth was a relative term. The right wing parties alleged that the Democrats were in league with the Issaraks and conspired to block legislation introduced by the King[12] despite the insistence of the governing party that they were monarchists. The allegations—like the earlier "Black Star" *canard*—were largely baseless. Although Sihanouk and the Democrats later became bitter enemies, at this stage he remained aloof from the factional feud, recognizing that the Democrats supported the constitutional monarchy.[13] Another problem was the continual meddling of the French in matters that, in theory, they had handed over to Cambodian control. This even incensed Sihanouk. In one incident in November 1948, the Acting French High Commissioner, M. Loubet, sharply criticized the government for its intention of levying a profit tax on large companies, in practice French-owned firms, as there were no Khmer industrialists. Sihanouk, irritated by the Frenchman's presumption, used the occasion of his 26th birthday celebrations to criticize French interference.[14]

Matters came to a head in early 1949 when the ambitious schemer Yem Sambaur quit the Democratic Party and formed a dissident group of 12 in the Assembly. The defection cost the Democrats their majority and Yem Sambaur pounced on his weakened foes. He moved a censure motion and the government fell.[15] On January 24, with the King's consent, Yem Sambaur cobbled together a coalition government with the Liberals, which was approved by a small minority of deputies, including some Democrats.[16] Initially, Yem Sambaur acted like a new broom, sweeping out the most flagrant examples of corruption (at least among his opponents) and negotiating some concessions from the French. One wonders at how much of his newfound zeal was genuine, given his shady role in the cotton thread affair. His coalition, too, was precarious and he could never be certain of majority support within the Assembly. Parties abhor renegades and naturally the Democrats feared and mistrusted the man they had once thought of as one of their own and sought to thwart him whenever they could in what Preschez calls "the politics of obstruction". Inevitably, Sambaur's camp repeated the allegations of Issarak influence inside the Democrats.[17]

Meanwhile, the economic situation continued to deteriorate. Prices rose, imported goods were scarce and the insecurity in the countryside damaged trade and prevented the collection of taxes. Sambaur, who had not yet braved the polls under his own banner, became increasingly unpopular. Democrat supporters marched in the streets and the students at the Lycée Sisowath went on strike, probably egged on by a young student called Ieng Sary.[18] Sambaur, who was developing an openly authoritarian streak, responded by arresting many of those involved in extra-parliamentary agitation and throwing them in jail.[19] He fanned the flames of the crisis by broadcasting his allegations on radio. He threatened to ask Sihanouk to dissolve parliament if he could not govern. It was a fair point, but it lost some of its moral weight given the intrigues that had brought him to power and his authoritarianism. Meanwhile, in the same month as the parliamentary crisis unfolded, a leading Issarak figure, the warlord Dap

Chhuon, had rallied to the government[20] and there were fears of a coup. By this stage, Sambaur had lost control of the parliamentary numbers and even some of his original 12 "disciples" had deserted him. In mid-September 1949, the Assembly approved a censure motion against him by 54 votes to seven.[21]

Sihanouk emboldened

Sihanouk, who had grown impatient with the parliamentary hurly-burly, stepped in to dissolve parliament in what the Opposition regarded as an "arbitrary and unconstitutional move". It is possible that by this stage Sihanouk had decided that adversarial parliamentary politics was an intrinsically unstable form of government. His metamorphosis from a "humble and respectful boy"[22] into a confident political player was almost complete and he had acquired the taste for personal power that was to be his hallmark over the coming decades. Sihanouk declared that fresh elections were out of the question because of the poor security in much of the countryside due to Issarak and Viet Minh operations.[23] While the security situation was a problem, it is also likely that Sihanouk was wearying of the democratic game and was hankering after a government of national union that would put an end to the horse-trading. Significantly, even the Liberals protested against his decision.[24] On 29 September, he installed a new Yem Sambaur cabinet, despite the fact that parliament had been dissolved and fresh elections had not been called.[25] Although the 1947 Constitution did say that power emanated from the monarchy, Sihanouk's actions violated the spirit of that document. For the time being, he might have put a lid on the cauldron of disaffection, but it would only boil over again.

The wily Sambaur enjoyed a new lease of political life. Soon after he formed his new government, he announced that Sihanouk had signed a new treaty at Paris on 8 November 1949 to supersede the *modus vivendi* of 1946. The new treaty granted Cambodia "independence" within the French Union, rather like that granted to the Vietnamese Emperor Bao Dai by the Élysée Agreement of March 1949. The Treaty was widely recognized by France's allies at the time as genuine independence and Cambodia sent legations to a number of countries.[26] Sambaur might have expected to gain prestige as a result, given the widespread nationalist sentiment. However, rather than granting genuine independence, the new treaty merely added to Cambodia's existing autonomy. Most economic, financial, police and juridical powers stayed under French control. If, as Mao Zedong famously insisted, "power grows out of the barrel of a gun", real control stayed in French hands, as they maintained a sizeable well-equipped army in the country and crossed the border with Cochinchina at will. Moreover, in practice they were reluctant to concede any of the additional powers stipulated in the Paris agreement. As the months went by, Sihanouk himself became impatient with French procrastination and was more forthright in his dealings with their officials. British diplomats believed that the King told M. Letourneau, a visiting French Government minister, "quite frankly, that what he wanted in Cambodia was fewer French administrators and more advisors".[27]

The murder of Ieu Koeus

Meanwhile, the new government, without an Opposition to worry about, quickly degenerated towards autocracy. Corruption and the abuse of power were rife and political opponents were subjected to strong-arm tactics. An important leader of the Democrats, Ieu Koeus, was murdered and there was an attempt on the life of another leader, Khuon Nay.[28] Ieu Koeus, the former President of the dissolved National Assembly, was assassinated during a grenade attack on Democratic Party headquarters in Phnom Penh on 14 January 1950.[29] The police charged an illiterate peasant with the crime, but the suspicion of Government complicity generated a wave of popular anger and sorrow, with an enormous crowd following Koeus's funeral cortège through the streets of the capital. The accused man initially claimed he was a member of the Liberal Party, causing a nervous Prince Norindeth to slip away into exile. The French blamed the Issaraks. Some observers blamed the French. Others wondered if Sihanouk was involved, but many eyes turned towards Sambaur,[30] who sank further in public esteem. The government creaked along until early May, when Sambaur presented his resignation to the King. Sihanouk took over personal direction of the Government before handing over to yet another un-elected government under Prince Monipong, which included "apolitical" individuals and members of the smaller parties. Monipong resigned on 26 February 1951, but not before signing new accords with France in June 1950 and putting the administration in better order.[31] However, the downside of the situation was that the minor parties, which were incapable of mounting a serious challenge to the Democrats in open elections, had become comfortable with un-elected power. According to Huy Kanthoul, Monipong was frustrated by their refusal to countenance fresh elections, despite his sincere attempts to reach an understanding with the main political players.[32] It was a murky period, with politicians jockeying for positions. The "differences" between the players in the minor parties were more related to personal feuds and dividing up spoils than principle. There were rumors that a mutiny in the Royal Khmer Army had been narrowly averted after the semi-autonomous warlord Dap Chhuon pledged his allegiance to the King.[33] With Yem Sambaur deeply unpopular and with no parliament from which to form a new cabinet, Sihanouk again took personal control before appointing an interim government charged with calling fresh elections. Although he was soon to embrace unfettered personal power with gusto, at this stage Sihanouk felt obliged to make concessions to constitutional sentiment and perhaps was still in half a mind about it.

Sihanouk's abdication ploy

One curious incident during this period points to the development of Sihanouk's highly idiosyncratic and personalized approach to power. Sihanouk let it be known in October 1950 that he was thinking of abdicating because of the unseemly political wrangling racking the kingdom. Immediately afterwards, a 3000-strong demonstration of Buddhist monks "persuaded" him to change his mind. Although the British Consul, Frank Gibbs, believed that the incident showed that Sihanouk was "young and inexperienced and not a strong character",[34] the reality was that Sihanouk was flexing his political muscles and appealing directly to the people over the heads of politicians and administrators. It was a kind of plebiscite by threat, crude, but effective when dealing with the politically untutored. Gibbs was not the last person to underestimate the diminutive and tubby monarch. Sihanouk had come a long way since, as a tearful teenager, he learned of his accession to the throne. He was now a forceful young man, increasingly sure of his abilities and his place in the world. He also adopted a martial persona, by taking charge of military operations against Issarak rebels in the Siem Reap and Kompong Thom regions. In this way, he doubtless hoped to show that he was the true descendent of warrior-kings such as Sisowath. [35]

The September 1951 elections

Perhaps Sihanouk also judged that support for the Democrats had been eroded since the parliamentary crisis brought on by Yem Sambaur's defection, and that the people might elect a more compliant

National Assembly. He backed the conservative forces against the Democrats during the election campaign[36] held before the new elections on 9 September 1951.[37] However, if Sihanouk thought that the Democrats' following had dwindled, he was very wrong. Although the French strongly supported the Liberals[38] with ink, paper and funds, the Democrats had maintained a well-organized political machine right down to grassroots level that none of the other parties could match. Their opponents, in the main, moved only in elite circles of society. Although Yem Sambaur had repressed his more vocal critics on the streets, his government had not been totalitarian and the Democrats' machine was intact. Furthermore, the bulk of the voters clearly identified the Democrats as the nationalist party, whereas their opponents were close to the colonial power. The election result was a landslide to the Democrats, although the voter turnout was lower than in the past.[39] The Democrats increased their numbers to 54 seats out of 78. The Liberals were down marginally to 18 seats; Dap Chhuon's regional pro-monarchist and anti-communist party, North East Victorious,[40] won 4 seats out of 61 contested; and Nhiek Tioulong and Lon Nol's Khmer Renewal managed two this time round. The people also delivered a devastating judgment on Yem Sambaur's parliamentary maneuvers and questionable extra-parliamentary methods. His newly formed National Reform Party was not short of funds, but it failed to win a single seat, despite fielding candidates in all 78 constituencies.[41] A number of other parties, including the left wing Peoples Party and the Kampuchea Serei Party made their appearance around this time, but they had little support.[42]

Huy Kanthoul's government

Sambaur's old enemies in the Democratic Party formed a new government on 12 October 1951 under the leadership of Huy Kanthoul, a former teacher and cabinet minister in previous administrations. Although Huy Kanthoul claims that Sihanouk told him that "he wished to play the role of a constitutional monarch",[43] and despite an overwhelming electoral mandate, the government lasted scarcely longer than eight months before Sihanouk dismissed it in a *coup d'état*. The old battle lines quickly reformed during Huy Kanthoul's time in office. The placemen resumed their self-interested intrigues and the minor parties put their heads together to work out ways of undermining the government. The French *Sûreté* recorded how Yem Sambaur, Sam Sary and Lon Nol met in early January 1952 at Sam Nhean's house to work out a plan of campaign against the "dictatorship" of the Democratic Party and to demand fresh elections.[44] They were a seasoned band of intriguers, united in their hatred of Huy Kanthoul's government and their disrespect for the ballot box. All three were personally corrupt and unscrupulous in their political methods. They associated with men for whom giving and taking bribes was a natural part of life, as was illustrated in a letter to Lon Nol from a friend in Paris in mid-1952. After remarking on what he had heard of the "dictatorial" tendencies of the Huy Kanthoul Government, the writer, a certain Keo Kimsan, turned to the vexed question of the radical Khmer students at Paris. He sincerely believed that young men such as Saloth Sar and Hou Yuon would change their pro-Communist politics "if given a little more money.[45] The allegation that Huy Kanthoul was a dictator was ridiculous,[46] but it fuelled a bonfire of paranoia and intrigue. Sihanouk, who appears to have been angered by the crushing defeat handed out to his favorite, was reluctant to stay out of politics and the French were alarmed by what they saw as an insidious increase of republican and anti-French sentiment in the Democratic Party. The rumors of collaboration with the Issaraks resurfaced. Lon Nol in particular behaved like a political chameleon, attending meetings of the right or the left as it suited him.[47] Another problem facing the government was that its writ did not run in large swathes of the countryside. This was, of course, true of the areas under Issarak and/or Viet Minh control, but in addition much of northern Cambodia was under the autonomous control of the warlord Dap Chhuon and his ally, Mao Chhay, of the Victorious North East Party.[48]

Social and economic decay

At the same time as the political crisis unfolded, the country was beset by economic troubles and heightened insecurity in the countryside. Phnom Penh was drab and dowdy, with rubbish in the streets and weeds sprouting from the gutters and footpaths. A foreign correspondent told his readers back home in Scotland that "Because the French have officially gone, [*sic*] most of the peasants believe they need pay no more taxes," and that as a consequence, "Roads are seldom repaired and bridges off the main road are beginning to sag." Further, "The Government cannot impose its authority. The capital, once as clean and swept as a French housewife's kitchen, is now sinking into dusty oriental squalor."[49] It is easy to fall back on racial stereotypes, but a more satisfactory explanation for the decay is that the country was desperately poor and weary. No sooner had the Second World War ended, than the countryside was plunged into insecurity because of the Issarak insurgency. The economy, which had atrophied during the war, further decayed as roads were cut and trade declined. The perennial reluctance of the peasants to pay taxes was exacerbated by the difficulty of collecting them. There was little money for public works and large sums of money were diverted to the war with the Issaraks and Viet Minh (although it must be said that corrupt politicians and civil servants creamed off public revenues). Prices rose and commodities became scarce. By 1952, supplies of rice were running short due to the war and black marketeering, and the Government was forced to ban its export.[50] Even the royal palace fell into a state of sloth and apathy, reported a British diplomat who visited for the King's New Year celebrations in April 1952. "The sloppiness of the arrangements and the general apathy of the place were symptoms of the political deterioration..." he sniffed. "The Palace Guard—usually a colorful and smart body of soldiers—used their rifles as resting props and failed to give salutes to any of us. There was no traffic control and the attentions usually given to the diplomatic body on these occasions were absent." An official told the diplomat that the lack of color at the reception was due to the absence of the King on a "cinematographic excursion". Sihanouk still had time to play, despite the crisis.[51]

The "gravedigger of the Democratic Party"

The gathering crisis was aggravated by the return of the man Huy Kanthoul was to call "the gravedigger of the Democratic Party"[52] from exile in France in late October 1951. Son Ngoc Thanh, the veteran nationalist, had written a series of "humble" letters to Sihanouk, begging him to use his influence to allow him to return. Sihanouk, who was reportedly "touched" (and probably flattered) by the letters from his old rival, agreed to help. Thanh's return was rather more dignified than his exit six years earlier, when General Leclerc's gunman had frogmarched him into custody. A huge crowd assembled to meet him, with up to 100,000 Khmers milling around to catch a glimpse of the legendary leader,[53] some from curiosity, others from genuine respect. On the same day—perhaps by design, but more likely by coincidence—the French High Commissioner, M. de Raymond, was murdered by his houseboy, a Viet Minh agent, and terror struck the French community in the capital. The enormous reception must have stroked Son Ngoc Thanh's ego as much as it bruised Sihanouk's. In effect, the reception was a mass anti-colonial demonstration and whatever Thanh's intentions were before his return, it must have convinced him that he should return to the nationalist fray, despite his pledge to Sihanouk and the French that he would refrain from anti-French politics. Shortly afterwards, he made a speech at Takeo, calling for full independence and the withdrawal of all French troops and began publication of a vehemently anti-colonialist newspaper called *Khmer Krauk* (*Cambodian Awakening*). After a short period, the Huy Kanthoul government, embarrassed by Thanh's strident rhetoric, and goaded by the French, banned the paper.[54] This was an interesting move, given the Opposition's claims that the Government was pro-Issarak. Thanh was intransigent. A British observer labeled him a "rabid nationalist" and "a constant source of trouble" who had been behind demonstrations against [French Minister] Monsieur Letourneau's visit. Further, he was even credited with inspiring a number of "injudicious" speeches by the King, and although this does not ring true, perhaps Sihanouk was goaded into making more extreme remarks in order to avoid being upstaged. The same source alleged that Son Ngoc Thanh's presence had galvanized Pach Chhuon and other Democrats into a more bellicose anti-French stance.[55]

A few weeks later—symbolically on 9 March, the seventh anniversary of the Japanese *coup de force*, which had ushered in the "independent" Kingdom of Kampuchea—Son Ngoc Thanh and his deputy, the austere Marxist-inclined nationalist Ea Sichau, rallied to the Issaraks near the border with Thailand. Thereafter, paranoia sprouted on all sides and the provinces were swept by a wave of lawlessness. The French imagined Huy Kanthoul's government to be in league with the Issaraks and relations between the government and Sihanouk became openly hostile. According to British sources, Huy Kanthoul was reluctant to condemn Son Ngoc Thanh's defection. The Prime Minister in turn "blamed the French for making the position such that well-meaning Cambodians felt that they were under the heel of the Colonial administrator." He added that, although he was loyal to the French Union, he wanted Cambodia's independence "recognized, not whittled away."

An interesting feature of the period was Sihanouk's ambivalence towards Son Ngoc Thanh. Although in his later autobiographical writings the King mocked and belittled his opponent, like Huy Kanthoul he was initially reluctant to condemn him outright, considering him a misguided patriot rather than a renegade.[56] Sihanouk told a British diplomat that Thanh was "not a bad man". He recalled his "pleasant boyhood association" with him and noted that he was a "natural leader" who had "always been the one to say 'follow me.'"[57] Yet Sihanouk's attitude to his opponents was hardening. He told the

Englishman that Huy Kanthoul's government was "unsatisfactory" and said that the elections had given the Democrats "too much power". However, the King also insisted that the French High Commissioner was behaving like an old colonial administrator and that this made it difficult for him to come out against the Government "without appearing as a mouthpiece for the French".[58] British diplomats considered that the political situation was "deteriorating". The assassination of Commissioner de Raymond had removed a relatively diplomatic man from the situation. His temporary replacement, the bluff and plainspoken Breton General Dio, did little to calm matters down. According to the British, Dio said "he had found the Cambodians untrustworthy, their Government corrupt and the King incapable of either self-assertion or of sustained attention to affairs of State."[59] Even pro-French Cambodians found it difficult to work with him at this crucial juncture.[60] His successor, M. Risterucci, was said to be an improvement, although he lacked "the elegance of manners which the Cambodians like to see in distinguished visitors".[61]

By mid-1952, the political situation was dangerously volatile. The Government's opponents lost all restraint and one day Dap Chhuon's supporters drove round Phnom Penh in an army jeep, openly calling for a coup against the government.[62] Dap Chhuon's ally, the political policeman Lon Nol railed against what he called the dictatorship of the Democratic Party, likening Huy Kanthoul to Hitler and Mussolini.[63] Eventually, exasperated, Huy Kanthoul responded by arresting a clutch of oppositionists including Dap Chhuon, Yem Sambaur, Sam Nhean and Lon Nol.[64] Most of the cabal were kept in detention for a few hours only, but Yem Sambaur spent the night behind bars as Huy Kanthoul suspected him of involvement in the murder of Ieu Koeus. Lon Nol in particular was angry at his treatment, which is ironic given his prior involvement in murder, his corruption and his subsequent role as Sihanouk's chief political policeman. Moreover, for all the claims of dictatorship, the Democrats allowed the opposition press to continue and even answered the charges in their own newspaper.[65]

Sihanouk's coup d'état of 15 June 1952

For Sihanouk, this "outrage" was the final straw. Instead of rallying to the side of the elected Government against the subversion of the right wing parties, he sacked Huy Kanthoul, on the pretext that the Government had ignored his advice given on June 3 about calming the situation and restoring order. Further, he fumed that the Government had violated constitutional guarantees against search without warrant and detention without trial. Had the restoration of law and order been his intention, one wonders why he did not try to restrain the Yem Sambaur camarilla and Lon Nol's noisy *claqueurs*—after all the Democrats were the legally elected Government. Sihanouk was scarcely acting in good faith and in effect, he was acting as if the leaders of the right wing minority parties were above the law. In fact, Sihanouk's real agenda was to put an end to the parliamentary game and to deliver a knock out blow to the Democrats. With his high-pitched voice choking with indignation, he accused the Government of "inaction, misconduct, disloyalty and abuse of its majority for party ends." The French chimed in, claiming that Huy Kanthoul had taken no real steps to bring the Issarak insurrection under control. It was an old refrain; the French Minister M. Letourneau had earlier expressed his dissatisfaction with the "incapacity" of the Government. Rumors spread that "extremist elements" among the Democrats sought to replace the King with his uncle, "reputedly a weaker figure, to the ultimate end of transforming Cambodia into a republic."[66]

Acting with great secrecy, Sihanouk plotted to bring down the Government in a new coup. Although the new French Commissioner, M. Risterucci denied all knowledge of the King's plans until after Huy Kanthoul had been sacked, there are strong grounds to suspect that Sihanouk solicited French military assistance. Although British diplomats took the word of the King and the French that there was no collusion between them, they could not satisfactorily explain the coincidence of the arrival of two extra battalions in the capital on the day of Sihanouk's coup.[67] Commissioner Risterucci admitted that "he had of course expected something to happen as a result of the King's admonition of the 3rd of June and the arrest of Yem Sambaur on the 8th June", but insisted that, "no hint had been given to him that the Monarch had decided to assume control of the Administration."[68] On the morning of 15 June 1952, French tanks surrounded the National Assembly building and Moroccan troops occupied the square where Ducuing's statue to the dead of the war of 1914-18 stood.[69] He had summoned the extra troops and armor, Risterucci claimed subsequently, because he had "reliable information" that a huge anti-French demonstration was planned for June 15, the anniversary of the Franco-Khmer accords. He feared "a repetition of the Cairo riots", reported the British Consul at Saigon, and "allowed a couple of tanks to rumble along the main boulevards" in a show of force on the day of the King's coup. It was an improbable tale, but the British chose to believe it.[70] Sihanouk dismissed the government and Huy Kanthoul left for France, exiled according to one source,[71] on a "prolonged holiday" according to another.[72] Sihanouk took over the government himself and appointed a supposedly "apolitical" cabinet,[73] which, except for the inclusion of the old *Nagaravatta* man Sim Var, represented the old right wing oligarchs. He temporarily banned all political meetings and demonstrations. The Democrats, dispirited, closed down their party and press. Some of the provincial governors dismissed by the Democrats were re-instated[74] and for the time being, Sihanouk allowed the National Assembly to continue to sit. Although some Democrats cooperated, and took positions in the administration, Sihanouk's old teacher, Sonn Sann, resigned his post as President of the National Assembly in protest.

A storm of protest

Sihanouk's actions sparked a storm of extra-parliamentary protest; with strikes of civil servants, and students, monks and even army officers defying the bans on political activity. In Paris, a group of overseas students addressed an open letter of protest to the King, accusing him of many crimes and declaring that, along with French imperialism, "the absolute monarchy is the source of the suffering of the Khmer people." Among the signatories was a young student technician called Saloth Sar, who later came to the attention of the world under the *nom-de-guerre* of Pol Pot, the leader of the Maoist-inspired *Khmers Rouges*.[75] Until this time, Saloth Sar and his circle had supported the Democrats and the constitutional monarchy. Sihanouk rode out the storm, promising to clean up corruption, iron out the country's finances, and to obtain independence within three years.[76] Sihanouk's diplomats also applied for membership of the United Nations, but the USSR vetoed the move.[77] The National Assembly remained sullen. When, in January 1953, the Assembly refused to approve Sihanouk's budget (originally prepared by the Democrats), he dissolved it and declared a state of emergency, initially for a six month period, but renewable thereafter at his own discretion.[78] A bomb explosion at the Lycée Sisowath provided Sihanouk with further justification. Although the British Legation repeated allegations that the bomb outrage was the work of "student members of the Democratic Party", they offered no proof. The most likely culprits were either the Issaraks or ex-Issaraks around Puth Chhay, who had rallied to the Government in May 1953. Puth Chhay's band, which operated in the Phnom Penh region, was never properly integrated into the Government's forces and was believed responsible for another bomb attack in the capital in August 1953, which killed one European and seriously injured several others.[79] Like the Reichstag Fire, the Lycée Sisowath incident was a convenient excuse for repression. Sihanouk gave his government sweeping powers to arrest and detain people without trial, to search any premises, to banish opponents to exile in the country and to restrict freedom of speech, assembly and publication. There was a wave of arrests of Democrat politicians and party officials, including Sok Chhong, former Minister for National Economy.[80] In contrast to the mild restraints placed for a few hours on Yem Sambaur and his plotters—and Sihanouk's indignation at the breaches of their rights—many of the Democrats were imprisoned for terms of up to 18 months. Lon Nol had pointed the finger at the arrested deputies, claiming that, "There was clear proof that they were following the orders of Son Ngoc Thanh and Ea Sichau who are certainly communists and who are allied with the Viet Minh."[81] With parliament dissolved, the opposition press closed and its deputies behind bars, there was no one to demand that he produce this "proof".

The King giveth and the King taketh away...

Sihanouk formed a new cabinet shortly after the coup. His grip on power was complete. He had vanquished the Democrats and although the party was re-created after independence, it never again enjoyed the power it had briefly exercised during this period. The experiment in constitutional monarchy was over, crushed beneath the tracks of French tanks and Sihanouk's implacable will. Henceforth Sihanouk would run the kingdom as he saw fit. As he told an American diplomat, in a chilling, if unwitting parody of the words of the Christian God, he "was not only the giver of the Constitution, he was the giver of elections." Although Sihanouk echoed the minor parties' complaints about the "dictatorial" behavior of the Democrats, David Chandler's assessment that "his real objection was that the elected government had been attempting to govern the country" rings true.[82] There is also no doubt, however, that, despite the wave of protest strikes and demonstrations against the coup, he was extremely popular with the rural masses. This was underlined when, shortly after seizing power, he made a tour of Battambang to inspect the Franco-Khmer troops who were fighting the Issaraks there. When he returned to the capital,

> he discovered an assembly of over 200,000 Cambodians, subjects who had drifted in from all parts of the country to do honour to some relics of Buddha, but partly also to register their devotion to his person. A people

so devoutly Buddhist saw a happy omen in the arrival of these relics in Cambodia at the time when the King was striving to restore peace in a troubled land.[83]

He had set a pattern of populist absolutism in Cambodian politics, in which he would short-circuit political parties and appeal directly to the people. After independence, he set up a highly personalized system of rule via the Sangkum Party, which was stuffed with yes-men and sycophants eager to do his bidding—foremost among them the durable political policeman Lon Nol. The nascent system wedded traditional absolutism with modern mass politics—the best or the worst of both worlds. Pluralism was out of the question. One model for this system was Vichy, with its mass, top-down organizations in Cambodia during World War II and Sihanouk reviewing the fascist-saluting Yuvan. Instead of "Maréchal, nous voilà",[84] the masses would chant Sihanouk's name. However, Sihanouk would have one advantage that the pious Catholic Marshal would never have; he was widely regarded as *devaraj* or god-king with supernatural powers.

With the parliament and the Democrats out of the way, Sihanouk, now just thirty-years-old and coming to the period of his maximum powers, could concentrate on the issue uppermost in his mind; the winning of independence. The Khmer Issaraks were going from strength to strength and only the proof that he was not a French puppet, as they claimed, would be for him to lead the country to real independence. Sihanouk had seized power from the National Assembly with French assistance, but it was a pragmatic alliance. The pliable youngster they had set on the throne in 1941 had grown into a ruthless political operator determined to seize and hold absolute power.

Notes

[1] Their powers were circumscribed, however, by their subservience to the courts of Annam and Siam and during the Protectorate, to France.

[2] The process was not simple, however. The strength of the Khmer Issarak rebels and their role in the independence struggle is evaluated in Chapter 24 below.

[3] Philippe Preschez, (1961), "La Démocratie Cambodgienne", thèse pour Diplôme de l'I.E.P. de Paris, p.33. Although a detailed and valuable source, Preschez's thesis is strongly biased in favor of King Sihanouk and against his Democratic Party opponents.

[4] AOM HCC 11. M. Pujol, Sûreté fédérale, Rapport Mensuel, novembre 1947.

[5] Ibid.

[6] Preschez, op.cit.

[7] David P. Chandler, (1993), *The Tragedy of Cambodian History. Politics, War, and Revolution since 1945*, Silkworm Press, Chiang Mai, p.39.

[8] AOM HCC 10. Report by Pujol, Chief of Police at Phnom Penh, 18 December 1947. If Virija shared his uncle's views, however, he needed little excuse to condemn the Assembly.

[9] AOM HCC 10. Relations avec les Cambodgiens, esprit de la population, 1945-1947. Sûreté reports of 14 March and 13 September 1946.

[10] PRO FO 371 75962. F6978/1015/88. Mr. F.S. Gibbs, British Consul General at Saigon to FO, 19 April 1949.

[11] Huy Kanthoul, "Mémoires", unpublished French language typescript, Chandler Papers, Monash University, p.107.

[12] Preschez, op.cit, repeats the latter allegation.

[13] Huy Kanthoul, op.cit. p.108.

[14] [14] PRO FO 371 75962. F6978/1015/88. Mr. F.S. Gibbs, British Consul General at Saigon to FO, 19 April 1949, op.cit.

[15] PRO FO 371 75963. F6836/1015/86. Mr. Frank Gibbs, British Consul General at Saigon to the Foreign Office. Enclosure – French government document, "Crise ministerielle khmère".

[16] Preschez, op.cit. p.37.

[17] A claim repeated by Preschez, op.cit. p.38.

[18] According to David Chandler, [op.cit. p.43] Ieng Sary led another strike at the high school later in the year, so it is probable that he was involved in the earlier walkout. Sary later became a central leader of the *Khmers Rouges*.

[19] Huy Kanthoul, op.cit. p.109.

[20] Sambaur's government conducted secret negotiations with Dap Chhuon. [Chandler, op.cit. p.43]. These matters are discussed in more detail in Chapter 24 below.

[21] Preschez, op.cit.

[22] Huy Kanthoul, op.cit. p.109.

[23] Preschez, op.cit.

[24] Huy Kanthoul, op.cit. p.109.

[25] Preschez, op.cit. p.39.

[26] AAc 18398/283. 3016/2/1 Part 3. IndoChina *[sic]*. Cambodia, political general. Copy of treaty between France and Cambodia signed at Paris 8 Nov 1949. See also *The Times*, 21 an 25 January 1950, London. See also Donald Lancaster (1961), *The Emancipation of French Indochina*, Oxford University Press, London, p.238. The British Commonwealth, including Australia, recognized Cambodia's status. AAc A 1838/278. 461/3/1/3. Minister Foreign Office to the Minister of External Affairs, Canberra, 10 February 1950.

[27] PRO FO 959/60 Political Cambodia 1950. British Consul General at Saigon to the Foreign Office, 9 November 1950.

[28] Michael Vickery, unpublished typescript, Chandler Papers, Monash University, p.10.

[29] PRO FO 959/60, op.cit., British Consul at Saigon to the Foreign Office, 23 January 1950. Also *The New York Times*, 16 January 1950.

[30] Chandler, op.cit. pp.44-45. Sihanouk attended the funeral, but as Chandler points out, he typically did not mention the 50,000-strong crowd or the murder in his autobiographical writings.

[31] Preschez, op.cit. pp.39-41.

[32] Huy Kanthoul, op.cit. p.117.

[33] AAc 1838/283. 3016/2/1 Part 3, op.cit. Clipping from *Times of Burma*, 30 August 1950.

[34] Ibid. (AAc 1838/283.) Indo-China Monthly Political Summary, No 10 for October 1950. Frank Gibbs, British Consul General at Saigon to the Foreign Office, November 3 1950.

[35] AAc A 1838/283. 463/2/5/1, op.cit. AFP Morse in English from Saigon, 27/8/49. It must be admitted, however, that his ancestor Norodom was an incompetent military commander.

[36] Vickery, op.cit.

[37] PRO FO 371 92408/79295. FF 1015/134. Mr. Graves to Mr. Younger, "Elections in Cambodia". 1 October 1951.

[38] Huy Kanthoul, op.cit. p.119.

[39] This was due to the insecurity in the countryside, but might have also reflected voter disillusion with the slow pace towards independence—or perhaps also just weariness.

[40] This party, sometimes also called Eisan Meanchhay, was a front for Dap Chhuon, the ex-sergeant who defected from the French army during World War II and became a leader of the Khmer Issaraks before "rallying" to the government. The party's Secretary General was Mao Chhay, an ex-Democrat deputy and an old assistant to Dap Chhuon. [AOM HCC 26 "Parti Nord-Est Victorieux."]

[41] Preschez, op.cit. p.44 and Vickery, op.cit..

[42] AOM HCC 26, Francsécur, Phnom Penh, 12 juin 1950 & 1951.

[43] Huy Kanthoul, op.cit. p.121.

[44] AOM HCC 26, French *Sûreté* note, 27 April 1952 with extract of *BQR du Cambodge*, 25 January 1952.

[45] AOM HCC 77. Surveillance politique des partis. Sûreté, 1946-1954. Letter sent by Keo Kimsan, 66 rue Corentin, Paris 14e to Lon Nol, 267 avenue de Verdun, Phnom Penh, 17 June 1952. Intercepted by French *Sûreté*, 23 June 1952. These were young men, it should be remembered, who were to spend decades in the maquis, shunning material goods.

[46] Vickery, op.cit.

[47] AOM HCC 26, French *Sûreté* note, 27 April 1952, op.cit. general information from file.

[48] Vickery, op.cit. p.12.

[49] Patrick Donovan, (1949), "Plunder and Persecution in 'Paradise' of Cambodia", *Scotsman*, 16 June, clipping contained in PRO FO 371 75964 F 8988/1015/86.

[50] PRO FO 371 101050 1015/81, 130 3/10. British Consul at Saigon to the Foreign Office, June 1952.

[51] PRO FO 371 101048. FF 1015/24, 1012/55/52. British Consul at Saigon to the Foreign Office, 4 April 1952.

[52] Huy Kanthoul, op.cit. p.127.

[53] Lancaster, op.cit. p.138 and Huy Kanthoul, op.cit. p.128.

[54] Huy Kanthoul, op.cit. p.128.

[55] PRO FO 371 101048. FF 1015/22. Mr. Graves at Saigon to the Foreign Office on the defection of Son Ngoc Thanh.

[56] Ibid.

[57] PRO FO 371 101049. FF 1015/63.

[58] Ibid.

[59] PRO FO 371 101048. FF1015/26. Mr. Graves at Saigon to the Foreign Office, No 51. (101114/18/52, 18 April 1952.

[60] PRO FO 371 101172. FS 10386/4. Mr. Wallinger, British Consul at Bangkok to the Mr. Graves Foreign Office, 26 November 1952.

[61] PRO FO 371 101049. FF 1015/63, op.cit.

[62] Vickery, op.cit.

[63] Ibid.

[64] AAc A 1838/283. 463/2/5/1. Indo China, Kingdom of Cambodia – politicians, general. DEA, South-East Asian S/Section, CN/KC, Confidential report, "The assumption of power by the King of Cambodia".

[65] Vickery, op.cit. p.13.

[66] "The assumption of power by the King of Cambodia", op.cit.

[67] Ibid.

[68] PRO FO 371 101049. FF 1015/55. Mr. Graves at Saigon to the Foreign Office, 94 30/60, June 1952.

[69] Huy Kanthoul, op.cit. p.129.

[70] PRO FO 371 101049. FF 1015/55. Mr. Graves at Saigon to the Foreign Office, 94 30/60, June 1952. French documents might shed more light, but much of the official documentation from this period has not been released by the French Archives at Aix.

[71] Lancaster, op.cit. p.272.

[72] Chandler, op.cit. p.64. No doubt Sihanouk made Huy Kanthoul the proverbial offer that he could not refuse.

[73] Preschez, op.cit. p.48.

[74] PRO FO 371 101050. FF 1015/81. British Consul at Saigon to the Foreign Office, 139, 3/10, June 1952.

[75] Lettre de l'Association des Étudiants Khmers en France à Sa Majesté Norodom Syhanouk *[sic]* Roi du Cambodge, Paris le 6 juillet 1952. Copy of text in Chandler Papers, Monash University.

[76] Lancaster, op.cit. p.272.

[77] *The Times*, London, 20 September 1952.

[78] AAc A 1838/283. 3016/2/10 Part 1. Kingdom of Cambodia. Cabinet and senior government officials. DEA Summary of world broadcasts, dissolution of assembly and promulgation of state of emergency. See also Vickery, op.cit. and *The Times*, London, 16 January 1953.

[79] PRO FO 371 112022. British Legation at Phnom Penh to the Foreign Office, 24 January 1954. While the involvement of Democrat supporters cannot be ruled out, more likely perpetrators include the Issaraks, Puth Chhay's men, the French, the Viet Minh, or even Lon Nol's police.

[80] Preschez, op.cit. pp.51-52.

[81] Vickery, op.cit. p.14.

[82] Chandler, op.cit. pp.63-64.

[83] PRO FO 371 101050. FF 1015/82.

[84] Sihanouk himself reports that football crowds in Phnom Penh were required to chant this praise of Marshal Pétain during the Vichy years. [Norodom Sihanouk, (1972), *L'Indochine vue de Pékin*, Editions du Seuil, Paris, p.33.]

Chapter 24

The Khmer Issarak Insurrection

We founded a struggle organization called "Rumdoh Cheat" (Liberate the Nation). The French created confusion and oppressed us. They put us in jail and tortured us with electric wires.
—Chandara Mohaphtey, former Issarak leader.[1]

The constitutional drama in Phnom Penh took place against a background of insurrection and guerrilla warfare across Indochina. Although the war in Cambodia was of relatively low intensity compared with that in Vietnam, it was just as intractable. When the French returned to Cambodia on the coat tails of the British in late 1945, the political landscape had changed forever. Nationalism, hitherto mainly a concern of elite circles of lay people and monks, had spread to the broader population. Much of the urban nationalist sentiment took expression in the Democratic Party, but in the country areas, it often took the form of armed uprisings against the French and those whom the Issaraks saw as French puppets. On one side were the Khmer Issaraks ("Free Khmers") and their sometime allies, the Viet Minh. On the other were the French and their allies in the Royal Khmer Army.[2] From 1945 onwards, thousands of guerrillas, some of them heavily-armed and disciplined, frustrated every attempt by the French and their Phnom Penh Government allies to defeat them. In

1953, a British diplomat observed that, "the French forces in Cambodia have never been able to quell the rebel bands or defeat the Vietminh [*sic*] although together they do not amount to more than about 4,000 men."[3] It is difficult to arrive at an accurate figure of Issarak numbers. The Issarak leader Chandara Mohaphtey claimed to have over 5600 men under arms in 1945/46 in eastern Cambodia, although this sounds too high.[4] The French estimated Issarak strength in the western regions and occupied territories at over 3500 in September 1946,[5] and by 1949 claimed there were 10,600 Khmer rebels throughout Cambodia.[6] The French underestimate Viet Minh strength in Cambodia, however. According to a confidential report written by the Australian Department of External Affairs, there were 3000 Issaraks and 9000 Viet Minh in late 1952. The latter were, however, mainly concentrated along the southwest border with Cochinchina.[7]

How serious a threat were the Issaraks?

The question arises as to whether the rebel bands could ever have mounted a real threat to Sihanouk and the French. Bearing in mind that they controlled up to one-third of the area of the country by the 1950s,[8] we cannot rule out the possibility that they might have seized power at some point. Krot Theam, a former Issarak fighter, later told the Australian historian Ben Kiernan that if the French had not handed over full power to Sihanouk in 1953-54, the King "would have been in serious trouble within two years" as a result of the growing power of the guerrillas.[9] Sihanouk himself more or less admitted this when he told the Thai Foreign Minister, Prince Naradhip, that had he not embarked on the "royal crusade" for independence in 1953, the country would have erupted into full-scale revolt against the French[10] and, by implication, against the monarchy. In the end, the insurrection of the Issaraks and their occasional allies, the Viet Minh, only ended because of the royal crusade for independence in 1953 and the Geneva peace agreement of 1954. Afterwards, the Issaraks went back to their villages, and the Viet Minh and their "Khmer Viet Minh" allies made the long trek to exile in Hanoi. In the absence of a commitment by France to back him with sufficient the troops and munitions, Sihanouk was forced to take the road to independence to head off his nationalist and Communist opponents on the left. By the 1950s, with the onset of the Cold War, the bulk of French war materiel came from the USA. The metropolitan French population was wearying of the endless war and the stream of French corpses it generated. Already there were signs that the tide of colonialism was strongly on the ebb. India had obtained its freedom from Britain with a relative lack of bloodshed and the Indonesians had forced out the Dutch. By 1953, Sihanouk's language indicates that he felt the Indochina conflict would end in victory for Ho Chi Minh's forces, although the great French defeat at Dien Bien Phu was yet to come.

Strength of the Franco-Khmer forces

The French forces in Cambodia were chronically short of men. Occasionally, the commanders spared troops on a temporary basis,[11] but Viet Minh guerrillas kept the bulk of the French Expeditionary Force pinned down in Vietnam, and the bulk of the Cambodian fighting fell to the Royal Khmer Army. In 1948, the Franco-Khmer forces could count no more than 5,600 men, including three battalions of Royal Army regulars and three "mixed" infantry battalions, plus some sappers, medical personnel, a transport section and one section of cavalry. In addition, there were 1200 National Guardsmen—garrison troops in the main—plus 800 armed police.[12] By 1952-53, the Franco-Khmer forces had grown to 8000 regulars and 5000 auxiliaries, often led by French officers and NCOs.[13] It was an improvement, but quantity did not always translate into quality and had the Viet Minh wished, they could have made things much worse than they were for the Government. Although a French commander described the Royal Khmer soldiers as "good and loyal", and "rather better than the average 'Annamite' soldier", they often performed indifferently when up against a determined foe. Sihanouk realized that his men were at a disadvantage and soon after his 1953 *coup d'état* he spoke of raising the army's strength to between 30,000 and 50,000 men within one year. He also set his supporters to work to train a village militia, although this drilled with bamboo poles and any available weapons were distributed to students, who were seen as potential military cadres.[14]

The Issarak war was part civil conflict and part anti-colonial liberation war. Both sides committed atrocities. There is evidence of whole villages burned and their inhabitants put to death. In 1953, in an echo of complaints made against *marsouins* and *tirailleurs* during the Great Rebellion of the 1880s, King Sihanouk lamented that French soldiers were not always able to distinguish between peaceful peasants and insurgents,[15] a perennial problem for colonial infantrymen. Nor should we idealize the Issaraks' conduct. Michael Vickery recalls how some of them regularly tortured and killed their prisoners. The daughter of a Battambang Issarak leader told Vickery how her father kept "his prisoners chained up beneath the house without food or water and then executed them on his own firing range a few hundred yards beyond the back yard." Nobody, least of all himself, regarded the man as a sadist. If the executioners were not in a hurry, they might use "other methods really revolting to observe. One of them had a special name, *srangae pen*, literally 'a field crab crawling round in circles.' " [16] As Vickery insists, the facts of the Issarak war mock the stereotype of Cambodia as a "gentle land" whose innocence was violated only after the *Khmers Rouges* seizure of power in 1975.[17] On the other hand, Chandara claims to have forbidden the killing of any Khmer, "even if the offender had committed a grievous wrong such as working for the French" and to have argued successfully for clemency in a mass trial of prisoners.[18] We should treat the claim with caution, as it is virtually impossible to assess the truth of Chandara's words. Timothy Carney, who edited the former Issarak's manuscript, wisely does not try to do so. Lon Nol's police arrested Chandara and jailed him for three years during the early 1960s.[19] Chandara would scarcely want to give such ruthless enemies the excuse for further persecution.

The origins of the Issaraks

The Issarak movement seems to have arisen independently in a number of locations around the perimeter of the country in late 1945 and early 1946, although a headquarters of sorts existed at Bangkok. Krot Theam claimed that the guerrillas began training in Battambang as early as 1944.[20] One focus of guerrilla activity was in the southeastern provinces of Prey Veng and Kandal. Here, Chandara Mohaphtey, a man in his mid-thirties who had participated in the revolt of the parasols took the lead in organizing the Issaraks. After the 1942 revolt, Chandara had fled north up the Mekong to the remote Kratié and Stung Treng provinces, where sympathetic Japanese officers gave him military instruction. Chandara rose to become commander of the Issarak army and Minister of the Interior, Information and Economy in the Issarak National Central Executive Committee before making his peace with Sihanouk in 1952.[21]

Until late 1946, however, the focus of Issarak activity was in the Siamese-occupied territories, where up to 5000 guerrillas were stationed with their headquarters at Battambang. Bunchan Mul, another veteran of the "revolt of the sunshades" of 1942, who the Japanese had freed from Poulo Condore after the *coup de force* of March 1945, commanded a band of 1000 of these men, who carried submachine guns and rifles of Japanese origin.[22] A British report claimed that the bands were "generally better armed than the French forces, each man having at least a machine carbine and pistol", often of British or US manufacture, donated by the Thais.[23] The northwestern Issarak commanders included a former sergeant of *tirailleurs*, Dap Chhuon, who had deserted to the Thais a year or so after the border war of 1940-41. A domineering and brutal man, he was to play a central role in the Issarak political and military organization before defecting to the Government in 1949. He maintained a guerrilla band in the Kulen Mountains, north of Siem Reap. Another prominent western Issarak at this stage was Hun Apheuyvongs (or Aphaiwong), a descendent of the *Phya* Kathathorn, the ethnic Khmer who had been hereditary governor of the provinces before the French takeover in 1907.[24] The Issaraks had formed a political party under Ros Yoeun at Battambang in February 1946. Soon afterwards, they set up the "Provisional Government of Cambodia" under the presidency of Pan Yung and this enjoyed Thai recognition for a time.[25] The Viet Minh were also active in the region, with a stronghold in the area of the Vietnamese floating fishing village at the northwest tip of the Tonlé Sap Lake.[26]

The Issaraks were heirs to a long tradition of rural insurrection and banditry—some of the latter taking the form of what Eric Hobsbawm had called "social banditry". It is not difficult to recognize Chandara, Dap Chhuon and Ros Yoeun's bands as the descendents of *Sena* Ouch, Pou Kombo and Si Votha's men.[27] There was never a single centralized command over the Issaraks and although there were attempts to unify them, they remained a heterogeneous force until the end. One wing, led by two ex-monks who called themselves Son Ngoc Minh and Tou Samouth, was strongly pro-Communist. These guerrillas collaborated closely with the Viet Minh, and were sometimes known as the "Khmer Viet Minh". Son Ngoc Minh, formerly the *Achar* Mean, a teacher of Pali, had taken part in the revolt of the parasols in 1942 before fleeing to the countryside.[28] He became first president of the Communist Party of Kampuchea and died in exile in Hanoi in the early 1970s. Other Viet Minh-aligned Issaraks in the early stages of the liberation war included the Sino-Khmer Sieu Heng and Long Bunruot, his relative by marriage, who later achieved prominence under the *nom-de-guerre* of Nuon Chea, as "Brother Number Two" in "Democratic Kampuchea" in the 1970s.[29]

Although other Issarak leaders such as Chandara and Dap Chhuon cooperated for a time with the Viet Minh, their prime motivation was a visceral nationalism that was as much anti-Vietnamese as anti-French.

Ideologically, they had progressed little since the revolt of the parasols and they were poorly educated to boot. An extract from an autobiographical piece by Chandara gives the flavor of their thinking: "the Khmer Issarak proclaimed that all Khmer should rise up and arm themselves, unite with the Khmer Issarak to fight and kill all Vietnamese and drive them back to Vietnam," he wrote. He admitted that this was done in the *phum* of Phe and other places and added that "No Vietnamese were permitted to live in Kampuchea territory any more..."[30] The French reported that Issaraks had massacred Vietnamese Catholic villagers in Battambang province in late 1946, allegedly because of their pro-French sentiments.[31] On the other hand, there were reports of the massacre of several hundred Khmer Krom peasants at the hands of the Viet Minh in Chaudoc province of Cochinchina in January 1947.[32] This followed earlier reports of enthusiastic support by Khmer Krom villagers for French repression of the Viet Minh revolutionaries in the province in 1945.[33]

The Siem Reap uprising of August 1946

The first serious uprising occurred on 7 August 1946, at Siem Reap, close to the still-disputed border with Thailand. Two columns of guerrillas totaling up to 500 men emerged from the forest and overwhelmed the Cambodian National Guard garrison. They laid siege to the Grand Hotel, but French soldiers convalescing inside kept them at bay. After fierce gun battles, the Issaraks retreated towards the Angkor ruins, leaving behind thirty dead according to French sources.[34] According to the *Bangkok Post,* there were dozens of casualties on both sides.[35] The British consul at Saigon hinted at Thai collusion and the French High Commissioner at Dalat went further, claiming that there was "irrefutable proof" that Thai officers had led the attack. From all accounts, the rebels gave a good account of themselves. After retreating from the Grand Hotel, they dug in at the Angkor ruins, where, according to an American military attaché, Colonel Law, they "maintained their defense against air bombing and strafing, and attacks by French infantry..." and withdrew only when their ammunition was exhausted. Law was impressed with their use of light machine guns to pin down their opponents with intersecting arcs of fire. The Issaraks wore a distinctive uniform, consisting of a "red vest marked with Buddhist charms against bullets, a traditional peasant fighting costume," and "some wore red head cloths and arm bands." Some of them melted back over the frontier into Siamese territory, but the majority went deeper into Cambodia. The Thai authorities denied involvement, but the incident spurred French determination to reclaim the lost provinces.[36] After speaking with locals, Colonel Law concluded that although some Vietnamese and Japanese might have been involved, the bulk of the guerrillas were Khmers and that Siamese troops were not involved. The Issarak commanders had been preparing for the attack for nine months beforehand. The guerrillas slipped over the border in small groups to shelter with villagers near Angkor until the attack.[37] Nevertheless, it is likely, as a British military observer claimed, that the Thais had supplied the guerrillas with arms, ammunition and ex-army instructors. It is also possible that deserters from the Japanese army fought in their ranks. The British observer believed that the rebels had planned to seize control of Siem Reap, Kompong Cham and Kompong Thom and that the attack on Siem Reap had failed only because some guerrillas had opened fire prematurely at the Grand Hotel and allowed the French to rush in reinforcements.[38] Afterwards, French spitfires patrolled the skies above Angkor.[39]

A serious threat until 1954

Although French and British sources report that the Issaraks were quiet by late 1946,[40] they were far from beaten, and were to pose a serious threat to the French and royal Cambodian forces right up until independence. In late 1946 and early 1947, a serious rebellion flared in eastern Cambodia, with up to 3000 guerrillas marauding through the countryside before their defeat by superior French firepower.[41] Thereafter, the focus shifted to the northwest. In September 1947, the Communist Vietnam radio reported that the "Provisional Government of Free Cambodia" had been set up in the Issarak zones near Siem Reap.[42] According the French, this "government" was a Thai creation and first announced in the Bangkok media. Its first president, said the French police, was an "illiterate and incompetent" guerrilla leader named Hull. Hull might have been politically incompetent, but this did not stop him from launching audacious attacks on his enemies, often in conjunction with Dap Chhuon's men. There were numerous ambushes, with guerrillas attacking government posts and official buildings and lobbing mortar rounds into the power station at Siem Reap. Again, the guerrillas were well armed, with submachine guns, mortars, machine guns and bazookas.[43]

In May 1948, Issaraks and Viet Minh cooperated to hold up the Phnom Penh-Battambang train. It was an ominous sign for the Franco-Khmer forces. A British observer noted that the attack caused the

French great unease because it "was the first instance of co-operation between these two resistance movements..." who were normally "uneasy bedfellows". It was a "gloomy tale of French military weakness", the source continued. By this time the "very dangerous" Issaraks in Battambang and Siem Reap provinces outnumbered the Royal Cambodian forces. One spin-off of the closer relations between Issaraks and Viet Minh was that the latter's flow of arms across the border from Thailand was freed up and they could count on the cooperation of Khmer guides "who know the country intimately." [44]

At this stage, Dap Chhuon emerged as the most powerful figure among the Issaraks, elected in 1948 as president and military commander of the Liberation Committee of the Khmer People.[45] His alliance with the Viet Minh boosted their cause and he even exchanged friendly telegrams with Ho Chi Minh.[46] Elsewhere in Cambodia, the same picture emerged. On 5 December 1948, there was an important gathering of 3000 Viet Minh and left-wing Issarak guerrillas in the "liberated zone" of Peam Chhor in Prey Veng province, close to the border with Cochinchina. The guerrillas raised the flags of their respective liberation movements and presented arms to high-ranking leaders, including the Communist Tou Samouth and the non-Communist Chandara, the deputy president and president, respectively, of the Committee for the Liberation of the People in southeastern Cambodia.[47] Soon afterwards a provisional central committee of the Issarak National Unity Front was formed. It included the Communists Son Ngoc Minh and Tou Samouth, along with non-Communists such as Chandara and Naisarel.[48] In November 1950, Issaraks took part in a meeting of representatives of the three anti-colonial movements in Laos, Vietnam and Cambodia to discuss joint activity.[49] Sieu Heng, the Cambodian delegate, also attended the Second National Congress of the Indochinese Communist Party, held in February 1951, at which it was decided to split the party into three national organizations, including the Khmer People's Revolutionary Party. The latter party was launched formally in June of the same year.[50]

The Viet Minh in Cambodia

The Viet Minh were a far more formidable force than the Issaraks, both politically and militarily. There were over 9000 of them in Cambodia in 1953 and they were well disciplined and motivated by a coherent political philosophy. Although some Viet Minh units in Cambodia were composed of "local" Vietnamese, particularly in the Siem Reap and Battambang region, most of their forces were engaged in operations against the French along the eastern border and came from Vietnam. Their major aim was the liberation of their own homeland. To them, Cambodia was—as was also the case during the American War in Indochina—a sideshow to the main event. They saw the Cambodians as a relatively backward people who would be pulled along and modernized in the backwash of the Vietnamese Revolution.

There is a common belief among Khmers that the Vietnamese Communists sought to take over their country. According to a British report, Sihanouk claimed that, "a Viet Minh success would mark the end of Cambodia as an independent state." At best, said Sihanouk, "Even if the Kingdom were not purely and simply erased from the list of nations, it would witness the disappearance of all its liberties and traditions, which are incompatible with Communist ideology and the Viet Minh will to domination."[51] Monireth said the same thing in 1953: "the paramount enemy was...Vietnam" and "if Cambodia had complete independence now, with not a single French soldier in her territory, she would be 'swallowed up' by Vietnam and Siam within three years."[52] The former Issarak Chandara claims that he defected to the Government following Sihanouk's coup because "Vietnamese communist doctrine clearly aimed to destroy Laos and Cambodia."[53] There is no evidence to support these claims, but they characterized Cambodian political thinking under Sihanouk and successive regimes.[54] Although understandable given the dismemberment of Cambodia by its neighbors before the Protectorate, post-colonial history has proved Sihanouk wrong and the consequences of the belief have been grim for Cambodia and Vietnam alike. Lon Nol made similar claims after his *coup d'état* against Sihanouk in 1970, during which there was a terrible pogrom against Vietnamese civilians living in Cambodia.[55] Pol Pot alleged against all evidence that Vietnam wished to conquer Cambodia. The *Khmers Rouges* launched murderous raids over the border, sustained by the paranoid delusion that they could militarily defeat the Vietnamese. In fact, had the Vietnamese Communists wished to absorb Cambodia and assimilate or eliminate the Khmers, they could have done so after occupying the country following their lightning war against Pol Pot in 1978-1979. The decision to launch the Indochinese Communist Party in 1931 is often cited as proof that the Vietnamese Communists wished to subjugate Cambodia and Laos, but this claim does not bear scrutiny. As Gareth Porter has argued, the Vietnamese party leadership was lukewarm about the project, questioning whether the two countries were ripe for the socialist project, and only agreed with reluctance to form the all-Indochina party after the Comintern insisted it must be done.[56]

In truth, what Sihanouk feared was that if the Viet Minh and their Cambodian allies won, *it would have meant the end of the monarchy.* Sihanouk had collaborated with the French against the Issaraks and Viet Minh. The Viet Minh described him at this stage as a "stooge" and a "lackey" who had "successively served the French colonialists and the Japanese fascists..."[57] Sihanouk earlier told the press in New York that there was a real danger that his people would join the Viet Minh unless France gave Cambodia "real freedom".[58] Of course, he made the claim to gain political advantage against the French, but there was truth in it nevertheless. While the Vietnamese revolutionaries sought wherever possible to "raise the national and social consciousness" of the Khmers they worked with, that is to turn them into Communists, they realized that the liberation of Cambodia had to be work of the Khmers themselves. Not even the worst excesses of Stalinism had dislodged this Leninist "truth"[59] from their thinking, no matter how patronizing their attitudes to the Khmers. However, the attitudes of the Vietnamese Communist leadership to Cambodia did fluctuate because they "always made decisions about Cambodia in the context of its struggle against more powerful outside foes."[60] In the First Indochina War, as in the Second, eastern Cambodia provided a relatively safe haven in which Viet Minh units could rest and regroup before going into action in the Cochinchinese delta. Another major consideration in both wars was to keep Cambodia "open" as a pipeline for supplies and munitions to the guerrillas in the delta. After Mao Zedong's victory in 1949, the Viet Minh in Tonkin were able to transport supplies directly over the border from China, but it was difficult to get these down the narrow length of Annam to the South as the Ho Chi Minh trail did not exist at the time. It was therefore strategically important to ensure that an alternative route was always open from Thailand. Relations with the Issaraks in the western borderlands of Cambodia were subject to pragmatic considerations, regardless of the politics of the bands involved. If possible, the Viet Minh would maintain friendly relations with Issarak bands and seek to recruit Khmers to the Communist cause. At times, they launched major military major military operations to open routes to the Thai border. The *Washington Post* reported one such operation in May 1950, in which 3000 Viet Minh regulars cleared a corridor through to the border.[61] Generally, attacking the Franco-Khmer forces was not a major priority. When they did fight pitched battles, the French and Royal forces found them a deadly foe, as on 14 March 1953, when two

Franco-Khmer companies were attacked in eastern Cambodia by a large force of Viet Minh regulars. The Franco-Khmers managed to escape only by bringing up artillery to shell their opponents.[62]

The Viet Minh had an enormous prestige in Vietnam that the Issaraks in Cambodia could not match. Although there were "bourgeois nationalists" in Vietnam, many of whom had consistently opposed the French, the Viet Minh were able to present themselves as the patriots *par excellence* and to unite disparate sections and social classes in a protracted war of liberation. They owed this to their talent for organization, their ruthlessness and their genuine commitment to driving out the French. Much of the population held the Vietnamese Emperor, Bao Dai, in contempt as a French puppet. It was very different in Cambodia, where the Issaraks were a constant nuisance to the authorities, but were essentially a minority. Most Cambodians, tacitly or otherwise, supported the King, and the monarchy was an integral part of Khmer culture. In the end, Sihanouk was able to win over or marginalize his opponents in a way Bao Dai could not do. This was partly due to the enormous prestige of the Khmer monarchy, but also because of Sihanouk's political skill. It was also because Sihanouk faced an enemy who was, in the main, much less politically and generally educated and disciplined than the Vietnamese revolutionaries. The Communist element was smaller in the Issarak movement because Communism had never caught on among the Khmers in the way it had among the Vietnamese. This was not surprising, given the lack of a Khmer proletariat or any rural communal tradition. As David Chandler has noted, these factors were to set Cambodian Communism on a "disastrous trajectory...whereby a small intellectual elite pulled the poorest peasants not only into class warfare directed against the remainder of Cambodian society, but also toward an autarchic set of policies that led to a full-scale confrontation with Vietnam that was impossible to win."[63] In short, they set Pol Pot and his circle on the path to the catastrophe of Democratic Kampuchea. In the meantime, back in the 1940s, the political level of some Issaraks was so low that they were indistinguishable from simple bandits, let alone social bandits. This was scarcely promising soil for a movement that claimed to stand for human emancipation.

Banditry and the Issaraks

The northern Issarak leader Dap Chhuon was often dismissed as a bandit. This assessment is a trifle cavalier, but there seems little doubt that patriotism played a secondary role to ambition and greed in the motivation of this ruthless warlord. His early alliance with the Viet Minh and his overall commitment to the struggle against the French and Sihanouk was not to last. He appears to have been removed from his high Issarak posts in 1949 because of his brutal individualism and generally authoritarian behavior, which had earlier caused the veteran nationalist Bunchan Mul to quit the Issaraks in disgust.[64] Shortly afterwards, Dap Chhuon rallied to the King in an elaborately staged pantomime at Angkor Thom.[65] In theory, his fighters were absorbed into the Royal Khmer Army, but he continued to run the large parts of the north of the country as his personal fief. This serial turncoat's career lasted until 1959, when Lon Nol's men killed him for leading an alleged anti-Government plot. His 1950 defection, regardless of his unsympathetic character, was a serious blow to the Issaraks and Viet Minh alike. Unrest continued, but it was less coordinated. A Radio Australia broadcast in April 1950 announced that there was great unrest in the southwestern region,[66] but the British Consul at Saigon reported in October that the Issaraks were in disarray. Some had gone over to the Phnom Penh Government, others were fighting alongside the Viet Minh and "even loyal sections are apt, in outlying districts, to indulge in simple banditry when not fighting the Vietminh."[67] This banditry was a serious problem,[68] particularly for the long-suffering peasants. Vickery considers that "Often the vocation of Issarak was no more than a device to give a patriotic cover to banditry...and the bandit 'charisma' may have been as strong a motive as nationalism in attracting men to Issarak life".[69] One of the most notorious offenders was Puth Chhay, the "scourge of Cambodia", who operated in rural districts north of the capital. Puth Chhay led a notoriously ill-disciplined and brutal band of 400 men and hated both the French and the Vietnamese with equal vigor, although he had collaborated for a time with the Viet Minh. Bibulous, superstitious, ignorant, licentious and cruel, he had done time as a common criminal at Poulo Condore. Yet, he was a skillful guerrilla commander. Contemptuously avoiding traps set by his enemies, he led the Franco-Cambodian forces "a long and breathless chase and they never managed to run him to earth."[70] After his break with the Viet Minh in 1949, he was said to "work for his own profit". One day in April 1951, his men attacked the village of Phnhea Lu, north of the capital, and reportedly butchered the entire population.[71] However, Government forces inflicted "considerable damage" on his band in late 1952 and shortly afterwards, he rallied to the Crown.[72] Even then, his men were unreliable and were probably responsible for terrorist murders of French civilians in Phnom Penh.[73] This did not stop Sihanouk's mother, the Princess Kossamak, from adopting Puth Chhay as a favorite,[74] or the King himself from using the former guerrilla's men as a praetorian guard during the royal crusade for independence.[75]

The final years of the insurrection

In late 1951, the Government launched an offensive against the guerrillas. Dap Chhuon threw his men into action against the Issaraks on the Thai border during "Operation Fidelity" in September. In one attack on Issaraks guarding Son Ngoc Thanh's clandestine radio station near the border, Dap Chhuon's men charged their former allies crying "Death to the traitors!"[76] Although the Government forces scored some local successes in Battambang and in Svay Rieng near the Vietnamese border, the general situation remained poor and there was evidence that the Viet Minh were reinforcing their strength in the latter region. The situation sobered the Government, which began to "think seriously of taking firm measures," a British observer reported. The Government summoned all provincial governors to a conference in Phnom Penh on 26 March 1951 to discuss increased security measures.[77] These were of little avail, despite an amnesty proclamation issued by the King in September 1952 after his coup against the Democrats.[78] Individuals and small groups of Issaraks rallied to Sihanouk, but no major formations came across. One important leader who did, however, was Chandara Mohaphtey, although he declined to take part in politics or fighting and went back to farming.[79] Because of the overall lack of success, the Government launched a further offensive in Siem Reap and other provinces and Sihanouk spoke of turning the palace guard into an elite force of shock troops. There were also plans for a village-based self-defense force, but it was unsuccessful, allegedly because of "Buddhist individualism and pacifism", and the "essentially lazy natures" of the villagers.[80] It might well also have been due to sympathy with, or fear of, the guerrillas. The military operations petered out. "Nests of Vietminh" continued to plague the Franco-Khmer forces in Battambang and the British believed that the Cambodian police and military forces were "not up to the required standard" to clear them out.[81] By July 1953, some units of the Royal Khmer Army under French command were disintegrating.[82] By this stage, Sihanouk was speaking openly about the need for Cambodian independence. He complained that Son Ngoc Thanh and the Issaraks "spoke big about expelling the French but directed their activities against the Cambodians." He added that, "If they went into the maquis in French controlled areas and attacked the French troops...they might be considered as true patriots..."[83] He also repeated his claims that the Cambodian people would rise up, and even go over to the Viet Minh if the French did not leave. With great skill—and luck—Sihanouk was about to upstage the French, the Issaraks and the Viet Minh. He even managed to turn round the military situation to some degree,[84] but he would resolve the war by diplomatic and political measures, the former at the negotiating table at Geneva and the latter in his highly idiosyncratic "royal crusade for independence".

Notes

[1] Chandara Mohaphtey, "A Khmer Issarak leader's story", unpublished typescript edited by Timothy Carney, 24 January 1976, written 11 June 1974. Chandler Papers. Monash University. Chandara added the name Mohaphtey, "Interior", during his time in the Issarak provisional government.

[2] For detailed accounts of the Issarak rebellion, see, for instance, Ben Kiernan, (1985), *How Pol Pot Came to Power. A History of Communism in Kampuchea, 1930-1975*, Verso, London, Chapters 2 and 3 and V.M. Reddi, (1970), *A History of the Cambodian Independence Movement, 1863-1955*, Sri Venkateswara University Press, Tiraputi.

[3] PRO FO 371 106746. 79852.

[4] Chandara, op.cit. Chandara claims that there were a further 2000 Khmer Krom Issarak just over the border in Cochinchina.

[5] AOM HCC 32. Retrocession des provinces par le Siam, 1946. Étude sur l'armée siamoise, Saigon, 7 octobre 1946.

[6] Kiernan, op.cit. p.68.

[7] AAc A 1838/283 3016/2/10 Part 1. Kingdom of Cambodia. For Cabinet and senior government officials. DEA, Canberra. Extract from confidential report on Indochina, 17 March 1953.

[8] PRO FO 371 112028. DF 1015/1762. "Survey of the situation in Cambodia", Mr. Littlejohn Cook to Sir Hubert Graves (Saigon), October 9 1954.

[9] Krot Theam, a former Issarak from the Samlaut district of northwestern Cambodia, cited in Ben Kiernan, "Resisting the French, 1946-54: The Khmer Issarak", in Ben Kiernan and Chanthou Boua (eds.), (1982), *Peasants and Politics in Kampuchea, 1942-1981*, Zed Press, London, p.129.

[10] PRO FO 628/89. Cambodia (1-50). British Minister at Bangkok, Mr. G.C. Whitteridge to the Foreign Office, 19 June 1953. "Notes on conversation with the [Thai] Minister for Foreign Affairs, 18 June 1953."

[11] AAc A 4529/1 Cambodia political. – 28 August 1953.

[12] PRO FO 371 69657 F11390/255/86. British Consul at Saigon to the Foreign Office. Military Intelligence Report 15, 10 August 1948.

[13] AAc A 1838/280 3016/12 Part 1 Kingdom of Cambodia – armed forces. DEA summary of world broadcasts. 14 July1953.

[14] AAc A 4529/1 Cambodia political. 28 August 1953, op.cit. The 'Annamite' soldiers in question were the Bao Dai troops, who often made unreliable allies for the French.

[15] PRO FO 371 1067 FF 10317/97. Declaration by Norodom Sihanouk.

[16] Michael Vickery, (1984), *Cambodia: 1975-1982*, Allen and Unwin, North Sydney, NSW, pp.7 and 5.

[17] Ibid. Chapter 1.

[18] Chandara, op.cit.

[19] Kiernan (*Pol Pot*), op.cit. p.188.

[20] Kiernan, op.cit. p.127.

[21] Chandara Mohaphtey, op.cit.

[22] AOM HCC 11. Sûreté Fédérale, rapport mensuel, janvier 1946.

[23] AAc A 1838/253. APLO memorandum No 18, op.cit.

[24] Yat Hwaidi, (trans. Charnvit Kaset-siri), "Norodom Sihanouk and the Khmer Issarak", *The Bangkok Democrat*, typescript in Chandler Papers, Monash University.

[25] AOM HCC 32, Dossier securité. Organisation rebelle en zone cedée.

[26] AAc A 1838/253. APLO memorandum No 18, op.cit. The fishing village still exists today.

[27] See chapters 5, 9 and 10 above for discussions of the Great Rebellion of the 1880s and social banditry.

[28] Chandler says that he took on the name both to capitalize on Son Ngoc Thanh's name and to associate himself with Ho Chi Minh. Son Ngoc Minh, like Thanh, was of mixed Vietnamese and Khmer parentage and hailed from the delta lands of Vietnam. Tou Samouth, the former *Achar* Sok, was another Khmer Vietnamese.

[29] Ibid. p.33. At the time of writing, Nuon Chea, now 76 years old, still lives in the former *Khmers Rouges* stronghold of Pailin in western Cambodia. It seems unlikely that he will ever face trial for his part in the brutality of "Democratic Kampuchea".

[30] Chandara, op.cit. These admissions cast doubt on Chandara's claims of his humane treatment of enemies. Prisoners were treated savagely, although Chandara might have been personally innocent.

[31] AOM HCC 11. Sûreté Fédérale, rapport mensuel, décembre 1946. The village was Keiey Puoy and 100 people were murdered by the Issaraks. [Reddi, op.cit. p.122.]

[32] Ibid. Rapport mensuel, janvier-février 1947.

[33] PRO FO 959/4, extract from *Times of Saigon*, 18 December 1945.

[34] AOM HCC 10. Sûreté Fédérale, Rapport Mensuel, août 1946.

[35] "Cambodians stage uprising at Siem Reap." *Bangkok Post*, August 12 1946.

[36] PRO FO 371 54389. Meiklereid to the Foreign Office, 9 August 1946 and Thompson at Bangkok to the Foreign Office, 15 August 1946. According to a report in the Australian Archives, French soldiers had heard commands given in the Siamese language. (AAc A1838/283. 3016/2/1 Part 3. Indochina. Cambodia- political general. Report No P46/48/6. Colonel Law was skeptical,

but did think that Japanese officers were involved. (PRO FO 371 54390. US Legation at Bangkok: rpt by Military Attaché Law and Vice Consul Buckley, recently at Battambang. 17 September 1946. Contained in report from Duff Cooper at Paris to the Foreign Office, 26 September 1946.)

[37] Law and Buckley, op.cit.

[38] [38] AAc A 1838/253. APLO memorandum No 18. "A report on a visit to Cambodgia *[sic]*, made at the end of September by Major P.L. Sweet, RA, of ALFSEA Liaison Detachment in French Indo-China..." H. G. Stokes, Australian political liaison officer, SEA, Office of the Special Commissioner in South East Asia, Singapore, 20th October 1946 to the Secretary, Department of External Affairs, Canberra.

[39] Report No P46/48/6, op.cit.

[40] AOM HCC 10, op.cit. Sûreté Fédérale, Rapport Mensuel, janvier 1946. op cit Rapport mensuel de septembre 1946; AAc A 1838/253. APLO memorandum No 18, op.cit.

[41] AAc A 1838/283. 3016/2/1 Part 3. IndoChina *[sic]* Cambodia – political. Clipping, "rebellion in Eastern Cambodia follows arrival of French", *Canberra Times*, 3 January 1947.

[42] Ibid. Extract from FARELF communiqué No 12821.INT (SD/4100), 23 September 1947.

[43] AOM HCC 11, Sûreté fédérale, rapport mensuel novembre 1947.

[44] PRO FO 69657. F11390/255/86. Mr. Gibbs, Consul General at Saigon to the Foreign Office, August 1946. Appendix to Saigon Military Intelligence report No 15, of 10.8.48, "The military situation in Cambodgia, [sic] August 1948".

[45] PRO FO 474/9. DF 1012/4. Appendix No 23, 16 May 1955. Also "The anti-imperialist struggle in Cambodia. Early years." Undated typescript, Chandler Papers, Monash University.

[46] Kiernan, *(Pol Pot)*, op.cit. p.58.

[47] Appendix to Saigon Military Intelligence Report, op.cit.

[48] PRO FO 474/9. Appendix No 23. op.cit. Also "The anti-imperialist struggle in Cambodia. Early years," op.cit.

[49] Vietnam News Agency (DRV) Morse, in English broadcast to SE Asia, Nov 1950. The Cambodian representative was Sieu Heng from northwest Cambodia. Transcript in AAc A 1838/2 3020/2/1/1 Part 1. Viet Minh relations with resistance movements in Laos and Cambodia, DEA Canberra.

[50] Chandler, op.cit. p.50 and Kiernan, *(Pol Pot)*, op.cit. pp.82-85. The ICP was formed in October 1930. (Daniel Hémery, (1990), *Ho Chi Minh de l'Indochine au Vietnam*, Découvertes Gallimard, Paris, p.70.)

[51] PRO FO 371 101048. FF 1015/22, British Consul at Saigon to the Foreign Office, 29 March 1952.

[52] PRO FO 371 10150. FF 1015/82. Enclosure with Saigon dispatch no 145 of 22nd October 1952 to Foreign Office. Cited in "Conversations in Cambodia during the visit of Mr. Graves and Sir John Sterndale Bennett, 10th October 1952", op.cit.

[53] Chandara, op.cit.

[54] For an analysis of Vietnamese Communist policy that challenges such simple-minded (or devious) thinking, see Gareth Porter, "Vietnamese Communist Policy toward Kampuchea, 1930-1970", in David P. Chandler and Ben Kiernan, (eds.). (1983), *Revolution and its Aftermath in Kampuchea: Eight Essays*, Yale University Southeast Asia Studies, New Haven, Connecticut, pp. 57-98.

[55] John A. Tully, (1990), " 'Certain and Inevitable Misfortune': War and Politics in Lon Nol's Cambodia, March 1970 – December 1971", unpublished MA thesis, Monash University, pp.32-37.

[56] Porter, op.cit. p.58.

[57] AAc. A 1838/2. 3020/2/1/1 Part 1. Viet Minh relations with resistance movements in Laos and Cambodia. Summary of Viet Minh broadcast 24 June 1953.

[58] AAc A 1838/283. 3016/2/10 Part 1. Kingdom of Cambodia, DEA. Memo for DEA Secretary from SE Asia sub-section 2 July 1953.

[59] The classical "Leninist" position on the national question is contained in, for example, V.I. Lenin, (1971), "The Socialist Revolution and the Right of Nations to Self-Determination", in *V.I. Lenin, Selected Works*, Progress Publishers, Moscow, pp.157-168. Vietnam did invade Cambodia on Christmas Day, 1978, but only after failing to persuade the *Khmers Rouges* to settle differences by peaceful means. Although the invasion does appear to transgress the principle of national self-determination, it was in reality a liberation for the Cambodian people.

[60] Ibid. p.86.

[61] AAc A 1838/283 463/2/5/1 op.cit. Clipping from *Washington Post*, 22 May 1950.

[62] *La Dépêche Franco-Khmère. Hebdomadaire de défense de l'intérêt public*, 14 March 1953. Summary in AAc A 1838/280 3016/12 Part 1 Kingdom of Cambodia – armed forces. 14 July 1953.

[63] Chandler, op.cit. p.49.

[64] Ibid. AAc A 1838/280 3016/12 Part 1. Also Kiernan (*Pol Pot*), p.60. Dap Chhuon did not hesitate to murder even his allies if he deemed it fit. His victims at the time included Mao Sarouth and Hem Savang, who had participated in Son Ngoc Thanh's coup of 9 August 1945. [See also Ben Kiernan, "The Seven Young Coup Makers of 9 August 1945", unpublished typescript, based on French intelligence archives, various interviews with Khmer, Thai and Vietnamese informants and Bunchan Mul's *Charit Khmaer*, Chandler Papers, Monash University.]

[65] Chandler, (*Tragedy*) op.cit. p.43.

[66] Radio Australia broadcast, 5 April 1950. Transcript in AAc A 1838/283 463/2/5/1 Indo China, Kingdom of Cambodia – politics, general.

[67] PRO FO 959/ 60. Political, Cambodia, 1950. British Consul General at Saigon to the Foreign Office, 26 October 1950.

[68] Michael Vickery, unpublished typescript on Cambodia in the 1940s and 50s. Chandler Papers, Monash University; Huy Kanthoul, "Mémoires",

unpublished French-language typescript in Chandler Papers, Monash University, p.106. See also Chapter 9 above on patterns of rural violence in Cambodia.

[69] Vickery (*Cambodia: 1975-1982*) op.cit. p.7.

[70] PRO FO 371 106446. FF 1092/79, *Journal d'Extrême Orient*, 5 May 1953.

[71] Japan News, 5 April 1951 in AAc A 1838/283 463/2/5/1 Indo China, Kingdom of Cambodia – politics general. See also Chandler, op.cit. p.34 for an account of Puth Chhay's character. Chandler says there were 1000 men in Puth Chhay's band.

[72] AAc A 1838/283 3016/2/10 Part 1 Kingdom of Cambodia. Extract of confidential DEA report on Indochina 17 March 1953 for cabinet ministers and senior government officials.

[73] See Chapter 23 above.

[74] PRO FO 474/9, op.cit.

[75] AOM HCC 77. Surveillance politique des partis, Sûreté, 1946-1954. N.Q. 131, 9 juin 1953.

[76] AOM HCC 18. Presse Censure 1951-1952. AFP reports, September 1951 by M. Barré. One wonders what his insurgents would have cried as they attacked Sihanouk's forces in 1959 as he allegedly planned for them to do.

[77] PRO FO 101048. FF 1015/22. British Consul at Saigon to the Foreign Office, March 1951.

[78] "Proclamation royale aux Issarak", in PRO FO 371 101-50. FF 1015/74 September 1952.

[79] Chandara, op.cit.

[80] PRO FO 371 10150. FF 1015/82. Enclosure with Saigon dispatch no 145 of 22nd October 1952 to Foreign Office. "Conversations in Cambodia during the visit of Mr. Graves and Sir John Sterndale Bennett, 10th October 1952", op.cit.

[81] PRO FO 371 101048. FF 1015/24. Secret report, British Consul at Saigon to the Foreign Office, 4 April 1952.

[82] AAc A 1838/280 3016/12 Part 1 Kingdom of Cambodia – armed forces. 14 July 1953. DEA summary of world broadcasts.

[83] "Conversations in Cambodia during the visit of Mr. Graves and Sir John Sterndale Bennett," op.cit.

[84] See Chapter 25 below.

Chapter 25

Sihanouk Triumphant: The "Royal Crusade for Independence"

By our unity alone, with wooden rifles which could not be fired, the very symbol of non-violence, we were the first nation in Indo-China to obtain independence.

—Norodom Sihanouk to India's *Pandit* Nehru, late 1954.[1]

Sihanouk exaggerated for the benefit of his quasi-pacifist friend, Jawaharlal Nehru, when he claimed to have won independence with wooden rifles, but there is a grain of truth in his vainglory. There is no doubt that he snatched independence from a position of apparent weakness. In a sense, circumstances forced the independence option upon him, but once he made up his mind to take it, he maneuvered with brilliance. Some observers, perplexed by his late conversion to the cause of independence, thought him mad, but the more astute realized that he was taking a calculated gamble. In fact, there is every chance that had Sihanouk waited, the French, who by 1953 were weary of their endless war in Indochina, might have granted independence of their own accord. Sihanouk could not afford to wait. Leadership of the liberated nation may well have fallen into the hands of the Issaraks, in which case he would have joined the ranks of the toppled monarchs languishing in faded splendor in some cold city. For a man who believed that *l'état,* or even *la nation, c'est moi,* this was an unbearable thought.

Sihanouk vanquished his domestic parliamentary foes in June 1952 and pledged that he would win complete independence within three years.[2] It was an ambitious promise, but he was to achieve it in a third of the time. He was acutely aware of the attraction of the Issaraks for many of his subjects, and even more so of the growing power of the Viet Minh, whose star waxed as that of the French waned. French public opinion was turning against what had turned into an intractable colonial war. By this stage, even Albert Sarraut, the doyen of French Governors-General of Indochina, was urging that France should disengage.[3] By July 1953, the Laniel Government had decided to get out of the war.[4] (The victory of the Chinese Revolution in 1949 had given the Viet Minh an important ally who could directly supply them with munitions and provide safe haven where necessary.) Official US opinion had swung behind France. Cold Warriors such as Vice President Richard Nixon floated the idea of using "tactical" nuclear weapons against the Viet Minh and the US was providing much of the French army's weaponry, but France was on the ropes, and although the zealots still held out hope of victory, it was increasingly unlikely. Sihanouk risked leaving himself exposed as a French collaborator in the event of a Viet Minh/Issarak victory. Although the French had granted Cambodia autonomy within the French Union, it was not real independence and Sihanouk knew it. A British report summarized the situation thus:

> the King could no longer ignore the dilemma in which his position placed him. He had to choose between calling upon the French for the fullest support in subduing those of his compatriots who were in rebellion against his authority or, by placing himself at the head of a crusade against the French, seeking to win over the rebels to his side.[5]

Soon after his *coup d'état,* Sihanouk and his loyal courtier, Penn Nouth, entered into negotiations with France, and these resulted in the Franco-Khmer Protocol of 9 May 1953. The Protocol granted further concessions and raised Sihanouk's prestige among the Issaraks. A number of important Issarak formations surrendered and joined the Royal Army. One of these was the band led by the former "cheap hoodlum"[6] Puth Chhay, who claimed to have discovered the threat posed to the Cambodian way of life by his former allies, the Viet Minh. Although other important non-Communist bands, including those led by Savangvong and Prince Norodom Chantaraingsay, remained at large, it was a promising start. However, the behavior of the French threatened to undermine these gains when they baulked at implementing the concessions granted in the Protocol. Soon afterwards, on 14 March 1953, Sihanouk left for Paris—allegedly for health reasons, but with trunks of documents relating to his claim for independence. He wrote to the aging French President, M. Auriol, asking for his country's freedom. M. Auriol declined and Sihanouk later claimed that the French Government kept him at a distance,[7] although he lunched with the President on one occasion.[8]

Sihanouk, however, was only getting into his stride. Afterwards, he left on an extended overseas trip to Europe, North America and Japan, ostensibly for a holiday, but really to draw world attention to his claim for independence[9] in what was the beginning of his "royal crusade for independence". He told the *New York Times* that unless the French granted independence, there was a real danger of a general insurrection in which the Khmer people would make common cause with the Viet Minh.[10] Speaking in Montreal in April 1953, he played on the anti-Communist fears that had intensified in the West since the onset of the Cold War, by appealing for French help against the Viet Minh.[11] It was an astute move, and not entirely empty propaganda, given his real fear of Viet Minh success. It also planted the idea that an independent Cambodia under the monarchy was preferable to a Communist satellite state. This was the era of the domino theory and this would have appealed to official thinking. A British Foreign Office report considered that Sihanouk had scored a "propaganda triumph...in America."[12] Still, he had apparently concluded from "French behaviour and tergiversations" that France would never grant Cambodia real independence, an Australian external report later concluded.[13]

Sihanouk's peregrinations continue

The overseas tour electrified the Cambodian population. On 14 May 1953, Sihanouk arrived back in the capital at 8 o'clock in the morning. Despite the comparatively early hour, immense crowds, estimated at several hundred thousand people, turned out to welcome him back.[14] It was an impressive display and mocked French, and his own subsequent claims, that most Khmers did not care about politics or independence.[15] He stayed at the royal palace for less than three weeks before making another dramatic demonstration against the French, probably on the spur of the moment. On 5 June, he left for Siem Reap, escorted by Puth Chhay and his battalion of former Issaraks,[16] as if a US President had suddenly sworn in Al Capone's mobsters as bodyguards and gone on tour in Nebraska or Oregon. His intentions were unclear. He had left "apparently without any intention of leaving the country" according to an Australian report.[17] It was something of a triumphal tour, especially as two further Issarak leaders, Oum and Ouch, personally surrendered to him after his arrival at Siem Reap[18] and he was constantly in the company of the former Issarak chieftains Puth Chhay and Dap Chhuon. Next, in a move that bewildered French and foreign observers and even Cambodian diplomats stationed in Thailand, he suddenly slipped over the border and arrived at Bangkok on 13 June.[19] The Thai Foreign Minister, Prince Naradhip, told the British Ambassador that he had no idea what Sihanouk was doing there.[20] Mr. Stanton, the US Ambassador, said that the move had taken the diplomatic community by surprise and that Sihanouk's decision "appeared to be sudden in as much that the party arrived with very little luggage." His presence embarrassed the Thai Government, which asked him to refrain from political comment and suggested that he move on to another country, such as Switzerland. Sihanouk agreed to refrain from public statements, but issued them anyway, using the Cambodian Legation as his mouthpiece.[21]

Sihanouk "is completely mad"

The British Ambassador repeated French speculation that perhaps "the King's known infirmity of purpose and his readiness to give way to escapism might have led him to baulk at the prospect of the detailed negotiations he knew must await him in the capital" and mused at the possible effects of the death of his favorite daughter six months previously.[22] The French publicly scoffed at what they saw as Sihanouk's "delusions" and asserted that most Khmers were "indifferent" to the question of independence.[23] However, according to an Australian diplomatic report, the French Commissioner, M. Risterucci, "gave the impression he was almost at his wit's end"[24] with the situation. To complicate the picture, a high French official told a British diplomat at Paris that Sihanouk was "completely mad".[25] The Viet Minh, too, scorned Sihanouk's behavior, alleging, among other things, that he had gone to Thailand to stitch up a deal with the "US imperialists". As proof, they drew attention to his history of collaboration.[26] Sihanouk, though volatile, had not gone mad. He was determined to force France to grant the same kind of independence enjoyed by Britain's former colonies. "The entire Cambodian nation is astonished," he wrote, "that India and Pakistan, for instance, do not, as a result of their adherence to the British Commonwealth, have to lose the essential attributes of their independence which are those of military command, police, justice, finance, diplomacy...etc."[27] He warned that, "Cambodians, disappointed and exasperated by the French refusal to accord real independence to their country have informed the King that the only way to obtain independence is to fight the French".[28]

On 20 June, he sent Prince Sisowath Sirik Matak, who had accompanied him on his journey to Bangkok, to Aranya near the Cambodian border, charged with arranging for the passage of the royal party. Two days later, Sihanouk himself crossed over into Cambodia, arriving at Battambang late on the morning of 22 June. He announced that he would stay there, in what was a semi-autonomous zone devoid of French troops. There, he made a number of broadcasts on *Radio Cambodge*, which the French believed fell just short of inciting his people to mutiny against them. A few days later, he sent Sirik Matak back to Phnom Penh to resume his duties as Defense Minister, but Prince Monipong told a press conference that Sihanouk would not return to the capital until he had secured independence.[29] The situation in the capital looked serious. On 26 June, French military reinforcements arrived, supposedly to guard the airport and French civilians and property, but as an Australian reporter noted, the move "was not calculated to calm the Cambodians". Three days later, French troops set up an "inner circle" defense ring in Phnom Penh and units of the Cambodian army under French officers took over all the official buildings, warning Europeans to shelter there behind the bayonets in an emergency.[30] As the tension grew, there were mass desertions of colonial troops to Battambang and numerous brawls and murders involving ex-Issaraks and French troops in Phnom Penh. Puth Chhay's men sought out black African troops in particular for pugilistic attention.[31] Meanwhile, the economy plunged further into crisis. There were shortages of rice and panic buying as farmers refused to sell their crops at new prices stipulated by the Government. Millers stopped buying rice, so troops and police occupied the mills.[32]

The French capitulate

On 28 July 1953, Sihanouk appointed Penn Nouth as Prime Minister of a new government and charged him with re-opening negotiations with the French. Meanwhile, Sihanouk kept up the pressure, organizing a vast parade of soldiers, police and militia, over 30,000 strong, through the streets of Battambang on 23 August.[33] The negotiations and pressure bore fruit one month later with the handing over of all police and judicial functions to Cambodia and on 17

October the French capitulated and agreed to grant the Cambodians full military sovereignty. Sihanouk returned to a triumphant welcome in Phnom Penh, with hundreds of thousands of people again turning out to greet him.[34]

This time, the French did not renege on their promises and on 9 November 1953, the last French soldiers hauled down the tricolor and left for Saigon after a ceremony in the capital,[35] leaving behind only a few units east of the Mekong to ensure the security of their troops in southern Vietnam. Essentially, Cambodia was now an independent country after 90 years of French "protection" and Sihanouk had wiped out the humiliation of the 1884 treaty. The French still controlled much of economic life of country including the import-export trade and the rubber plantations,[36] but political control had passed into Sihanouk's hands.

Flushed with success, he launched "Operation Samakki" in December against Viet Minh irregulars and the following April he took command for a while in Stung Treng and Kratié, where his army engaged Viet Minh regulars who had come down the Mekong from Laos.[37] To say that these were not major battles is an understatement. Some years later, Sihanouk admitted that "Samakki" had been a public relations exercise, with one casualty.[38] It served its purpose, however. The British diplomatic service was taken in[39] and the flow of deserters from the Issaraks accelerated. In February 1954, two of the last remaining non-Communist Issarak bands, those of Savangvong and Prince Chantaraingsay, laid down their arms, leaving only the increasingly isolated Son Ngoc Thanh in bitter opposition.[40] Sihanouk's prestige grew and Lon Nol painted a glowing picture of the King's alleged military skills.[41]

However, perhaps one sixth of the country remained under Communist Issarak control and as much as one half of the kingdom was unsafe at night.[42] On 28 April 1954, the Geneva Conference opened, convened by the USSR and Great Britain in order to extricate France from the Indochinese quagmire. Just over one week later, on 7 May 1954, the French fortress at Dien Bien Phu fell to the Viet Minh, sealing the end of French power in Indochina. The Cambodian delegation stubbornly refused to allow the Issaraks to participate in the Geneva negotiations and the Viet Minh was not keen to allow what they regarded as a side issue to damage their chances. Several thousand "Khmer Viet Minh" afterwards left for Hanoi and the sole remaining non-Communist nationalist leader of any stature, Son Ngoc Thanh, was isolated. Sihanouk was triumphant.

Independence, but at what cost?

Thus closed a chapter in Cambodia's history begun ninety years earlier when Admiral de Lagrandière steamed up the Mekong to impose a treaty on King Norodom. Sihanouk's triumph was to cement his status as the country's supreme leader and reduce his domestic opponents to a long impotence. The rigged elections of 1955 confirmed his triumph. The right wing parties coalesced under Sihanouk's leadership into the Sangkum Reastr Niyum, or "Popular Socialist Community". Despite its name, it ruled in the interests of the rich and powerful. As Michael Vickery wrote of the Sangkum,

> In the first issues of its newspaper, which began publication in June [1955], it set forth an authoritarian philosophy according to which natural leaders should rule and those less fortunate should not envy them. The natural leaders were the rich and powerful who enjoyed such a situation in the present because of virtuous conduct in previous lives (a common belief in popular Southeast Asian Buddhism). The poor and unfortunate should accept their lot and try for an improved situation in the next through virtuous conduct in the present.[43]

This was the Cambodian equivalent of "Podsnappery", the self-serving doctrine lampooned by the English writer Charles Dickens in his novel *Our Mutual Friend*. Mr. Podsnap justifies his indifference to the plight of the poor by wrenching the words of the Bible out of context to prove that "you shall have the poor always with you."[44] If the problem of wealth and poverty is "natural" and even divinely ordained, one can even feel virtuous in one's greed. Hence, just what Sihanouk's victory meant for the "ordinary" people of Cambodia, peasants in the main, is a moot point. Unlike many other Third World leaders who led their people to independence after World War II, Sihanouk had no reforming or democratic social vision. The post-colonial Governments he dominated [and that of his erstwhile crony Lon Nol during the first half of the 1970s] were corrupt and autocratic. Sihanouk had won independence, but in the process, he had trampled the principles of representative government and the rule of law and abused the trust of the people. As David Chandler has eloquently observed "After ninety years of protecting Cambodians from their neighbors, from autonomy, and from enlightenment, the French had every reason to be proud of this particular pupil."[45]

Notes

[1] Cited in PRO FO 474/9. Further correspondence respecting Indo-China (Cambodia, Laos and Vietnam), Part 9, January to December 1955. Cambodia: Annual Review for 1954. Mr. Heppel to Sir Anthony Eden, Foreign Ministry. Received 14 February 1955.

[2] Donald Lancaster, (1961), *The Emancipation of French Indochina*, Oxford University Press, London, p.272.

[3] Stanley Karnow, (1984), *Vietnam. A History*, Penguin Books, Harmondsworth, p.191.

[4] David P. Chandler, (1993), *The Tragedy of Cambodian History. Politics, War and Revolution since 1945*, Silkworm Books, Chiang Mai, p.70.

[5] PRO FO 371 112022, British Legation, Phnom Penh to the Foreign Office, 24 January 1954.

[6] A description by the French *Sûreté*, cited in Ben Kiernan, (1985), *How Pol Pot Came to Power. A History of Communism in Kampuchea, 1930-1975*, Verso, London, p.66.

[7] AAc. A 1838/283. 3016/2/10 Part 1. Kingdom of Cambodia, DEA. Memo for DEA Secretary from SE Asian Sub-section, 2 July 1953.

[8] Chandler, (*Tragedy*), op.cit. p.67.

[9] Lancaster, op.cit. p.273.

[10] *New York Times*, 19 April 1953.

[11] Lancaster, op.cit. p.273.

[12] PRO FO 628/89. Cambodia (1-50). Mr. G.C. Whitteridge, British Minister at Bangkok, to the Foreign Office, "Record of conversation with the American Ambassador on 17th June 1953", sent 20 June 1953.

[13] AAc A 1838/283. 3016/2/10 Part 1. Kingdom of Cambodia. DEA. Memo for DEA Secretary from SE Asia sub-section, 2 July 1953.

[14] Ibid.

[15] In June 1954 he told French commander in Indochina, General Paul Gen Ely, that "those favoring democracy in Cambodia are either bourgeois or princes...the Cambodian people are children. They know nothing about politics and they care even less." Cited in Chandler (*Tragedy*) op.cit. p.72.

[16] AOM HCC 77. Surveillance politique des partis. Sûreté, 1946-1954. NQ 131 de 9 juin 1953.

[17] AAc A 1838/280. 3016/1/3 Part 1. South East Asia. Cambodia – the Monarchy, DEA. Memo from Consul, Saigon to the DEA, 23 June 1953.

[18] Memo for DEA Secretary from SE Asia sub-section, 2 July 1953, op.cit.

[19] PRO FO 474/9. DF 1012/4 Appendix No 23. 16 May 1955 and Memo from Consul, Saigon to the DEA, 23 June 1953, op.cit.

[20] PRO FO 628/89. op.cit. Whitteridge to the Foreign Office, 19 June 1953.

[21] "Record of conversation with the American Ambassador on 17th June 1953", op.cit.

[22] PRO FO 371 10672. FF 10317/97, Whitteridge to the Foreign Office, 17 June 1953.

[23] Memo for DEA Secretary from SE Asia sub-section, 2 July 1953, op.cit.

[24] AAc A 1838/283. 3016/2/10 Part 1. Kingdom of Cambodia, DEA. Australian Legation at Saigon to the DEA. 16 June 1953.

[25] PRO FO 371 112022, British Legation, Phnom Penh to the Foreign Office, 24 January 1954, op.cit.

[26] Memo for DEA Secretary from SE Asia sub-section, 2 July 1953, op.cit. and AAc A 1838/2 3020/2/1/1 Part 1. Viet Minh relations with resistance movements in Laos and Cambodia, DEA. Transcript of broadcasts by "Voice of Nam Bo", 23 and 24 June 1953.

[27] Statement of His Majesty Norodom Sihanouk Varman, King of Cambodia, 12 June 1953, contained in AAc A 1838/238 3016/2/10 Part 1.

[28] *Figaro*, Paris,18 June 1953. See also AOM HCC 77 Surveillance politique, op.cit. Securité, Saigon, 25 juin 1953, which contains reports of similar threats.

[29] AOM HCC 77, op.cit. Commission Générale de France en Indochine. Securité, Saigon, 25 juin 1953.

[30] AAc Memo for DEA Secretary from SE Asian Sub-section, 2 July 1953, op.cit.

[31] Kiernan, op.cit. p.p.131-132.

[32] AAc A 1838/2 750/2 Part 1 Cambodia: reports on economic development. Australian Legation at Saigon to the DEA, 25 August 1953.

[33] Kiernan, op.cit. p.p.131-132.

[34] David P. Chandler, (1993), *A History of Cambodia*, (Second Edition), Allen and Unwin, St. Leonards, NSW, p.186.

[35] Kiernan, op.cit. p.132.

[36] Chandler (*History*), op.cit. p.186

[37] PRO FO 474/9 DF 1012/4. Appendix No 23, 16 May 1955.

[38] Chandler (*Tragedy*), op.cit. p.71.

[39] PRO FO 474/9 DF 1012/4. Appendix No 23, op.cit. and FO 371 12025 DF 1015713. British Legation at Phnom Penh to Sir Hubert Graves, Saigon, 14 January 1954.

[40] PRO FO 371 112025. G.S. Littlejohn Cook, British Legation at Phnom Penh, to Sir Hubert Graves at Saigon, 12 June 1954.

[41] Chandler (*Tragedy*), op.cit.

[42] Ibid.

[43] Michael Vickery, unpublished typescript on Cambodian politics in the 1940s and 1950s in the Chandler Papers, Monash University.

[44] Charles Dickens, (ed. Adrian Poole), (1997), *Our Mutual Friend*, Penguin Books, Harmondsworth, p.144. This is a self-interested corruption of Jesus's rebuke to his disciples; "For ye shall have the poor always with you; but me ye have not always". (Matthew 26.11).

[45] Chandler (*Tragedy*), op.cit. p.72. A more sympathetic, but not uncritical account is contained in Milton Osborne, (1994), *Sihanouk. Prince of light, prince of darkness*, University of Hawaii Press, Honolulu, Ch 6, " A madman of genius".

Conclusion

In the Image of France?

The evil that men do lives after them,
The good is oft interred with their bones.
　　—William Shakespeare, *Julius Caesar,* Act III, Scene II.

Men make their own history, but they do not make it just as they please;
they do not make it under circumstances chosen by themselves, but under
circumstances directly encountered, given and transmitted from the past.
The tradition of all the dead generations weighs like a nightmare on the
brain of the living.
　　—Karl Marx, *The Eighteenth Brumaire of Louis Bonaparte.*

By 1954, the last French soldiers had pulled out of Cambodia, bringing
to an end the ninety years of the protectorate on the middle Mekong.
Since then the country has maintained its integrity, despite the earlier
worries of overseas observers that the lack of trained military
personnel would jeopardize Cambodia's independence,[1] and regardless
of Khmer fears of absorption by their Vietnamese neighbors. The
Geneva Conference broadly endorsed what the Viet Minh guerrillas
had achieved on the battlefield, and what Sihanouk had won by his
"royal crusade for independence" in Cambodia. We must now ask
what the protectorate had achieved for those it aimed, ostensibly, to

protect. A related question is how deeply the French presence affected the country in the long term.

The material foundations for a western society?

The colonial project was never systematic and had a number of sometimes contradictory aims. One of these was the *mission civilisatrice*, which informed the thinking of European social theorists, administrators, settlers and politicians. The grand 19th century theorist of French colonialism, M. Paul Leroy-Beaulieu, had written that the "superior race" would transform the economies of the underdeveloped colonies and "lift up" their peoples.[2] In the 1850s, Karl Marx expressed similar ideas, although without the racist cant so ingrained in 19th century social thought. Marx had written that "England has to fulfill a double mission in India [and so, presumably, France in Cambodia, JT]: one destructive, the other regenerating – the annihilation of old Asiatic society, and the laying of the material foundations of Western society in Asia." Marx went on to say that political unity was "the first condition of...regeneration" and that this unity, imposed at bayonet point, "will now be strengthened and perpetuated by the electric telegraph." A "native army" would be the "*sine qua non* of...self-emancipation" and the growth of a free press would be "a new and powerful instrument of reconstruction." Marx also claimed that an indigenous middle class would spring up, "endowed with the requirements for government and imbued with European science." Furthermore, he believed it was a given that "Modern industry, resulting from the railroad system, will dissolve the hereditary divisions of labor".[3] Although Marx scorned the colonialist powers as being "actuated only by the vilest interests", he nevertheless felt that colonialism would act as an "unconscious tool" in bringing about "a fundamental revolution in the social state of Asia".[4] Some argue that later in life, Marx changed his views on colonialism. Suniti Kumar Ghosh is one who does. He writes, "Speaking of Ireland, Britain's oldest colony, Marx wrote in 1867: 'Every time Ireland was just about to develop herself industrially, she was 'smashed down' and forced back into a mere 'agricultural country'." As for Ireland, Ghosh implies, so for the "dominated" countries as a whole. Ghosh opines that by the late 1860s, "Marx had outgrown his earlier optimism about the revolutionary role of British colonial rule. He came to believe that far from laying down the material premises of a capitalist society, colonial rule destroyed much of the existing productive forces, flung the country backward, and laid the basis of its underdevelopment."

Even the railways—heralded as a means of transformation and the forerunner of modern industry—proved to be a means of converting the colonies into agricultural appendages of the *metropole*.[5] While Marx did come to question whether the destruction and turmoil could be justified by colonialism's "creative" role, Ghosh overstates his case. He also over-generalizes when he cites Marx's views on Ireland as broadly applicable to the Third World. In fact, Marx's views on colonialism were sometimes internally contradictory, and he never left a fully worked-out theory of imperialism.[6]

The Marxist Leon Trotsky never doubted that his mentor had viewed colonialism as having a "double mission"—and he was critical of the idea. Trotsky questioned Marx's idea that, "The industrially more developed country shows the less developed only the image of its own future". "This statement of Marx," wrote Trotsky, "which takes its departure methodologically not from world economy as a whole but from the single capitalist country as a type, has become less applicable in proportion as capitalist evolution has embraced all countries regardless of their previous fate and industrial level." Trotsky concluded that, "England in her day revealed the future of France, considerably less of Germany, but not in the least of Russia and not of India."[7] It was even less the case in Cambodia than in India.

Some positive achievements of the Protectorate

However, the French *did* achieve some worthwhile things during their ninety years, and these achievements confirm Marx's early Hegelian optimism to a limited degree. The French preserved Cambodian political unity, and indeed restored the lost northern and northwestern provinces to the Khmer nation. Before 1863, Cambodia was at the mercy of her neighbors and there is every chance that she would have joined the ranks of the stateless nations of the world, of which the Chams of Cambodia and Vietnam are a constant reminder. France's second great achievement was the restoration of aspects of Khmer culture—most importantly, the restoration of Angkor, the very symbol of Khmer nationhood. Although it is true that in doing so, Angkor's glory rubbed off on France, it was a genuinely selfless project of benefit to the Khmer nation and to all of humanity. It is also entirely possible that many of the ancient Khmer arts and crafts would have died out but for French efforts to preserve them, although it is also true that these had fallen victim to cheap, mass-produced European commodities in the first place. The efforts of Suzanne Karpelès and other French scholars contributed to something of a

Buddhist renaissance. They built libraries and published the classical texts in cheap editions. Thirdly, the French gave Cambodia a protracted period of peace and stability, which was in stark contrast to the chaos of the Dark Age that had preceded their arrival. Fourthly, they built roads and other communications and built Phnom Penh into a modern metropolis. As a British writer wrote of the French communications effort in Indochina,

> Out of the 30,000 kilometers of roads the French have built…20,000 are open and can be used by cars at all seasons of the year. The length is enormous if one compares it with any other of the countries in the Far East except the Dutch East Indies. I never struck a really bad patch of road in the whole of Indo-China, nothing half as bad as some even of the routes nationals were in France up to ten years ago."[8]

We should compare this effort with what existed beforehand. Cambodian roads were little more than tracks and a French proposal for a new road baffled Norodom because, in his royal egotism, as he himself never went to its destination, he could see no use for it. Finally, although the French built few hospitals and trained only a handful of doctors, their mass vaccination programs, clean water and sanitation schemes did much to ameliorate endemic diseases such as smallpox, cholera, dysentery and the plague.

The authoritarian tradition

Yet, in other crucial respects, France short-changed its *protégés* and left behind a dismal legacy that contributed to the later tragedies that befell Cambodian society. The separation of powers, representative government, a free press, and the rule of law are important parts of European political theory and practice. French colonialism did not leave behind representative government, an independent judiciary, still less a guaranteed free press. On balance, colonialism probably strengthened the existing tendencies in traditional Cambodian society towards autocracy and the exclusion of the general population from decision-making.

Recent examples of Cambodian legal practice show that the legacy lingers. In June 2001, almost fifty years after the French left Cambodia, 32 suspected members of a group called the Cambodian Freedom Fighters (CFF) went on trial in the Supreme Court in Phnom Penh for their participation in the November 2000 street fighting in the capital that left eight people dead and at least 14 people injured.[9] Although there is strong evidence against at least some of the accused, and exiled leader Chhun Yasith admits his involvement, the trial and pre-trial process drew strong criticism from the Cambodian Human Rights Action Committee (CHRAC) and international human rights bodies. CHRAC alleged legal irregularities including arrest without warrant, restrictions on access to legal counsel, forced confessions, violations of pre-trial detention limitations and "an intimidating [court] atmosphere which included heavily-armed police, soldiers and police officers with dogs". A number of defense lawyers walked out of the trial in protest. Another attorney, wearying of the constant interventions of Judge Sok Sithamony on the side of the prosecution, told him: "You are playing the role of prosecutor. You always look for evidence against the accused."[10] What is at stake here is not the right of a Government to put alleged "terrorists" on trial, but the right of citizens to a fair trial. Clearly, the lines between government and judiciary are as blurred as they were in 1953, when an Australian Department of External Affairs report drew attention to the dearth of "incorruptible judges" in Cambodia.[11]

The CFF trial was not an aberration. Amnesty International has drawn attention to the widespread use of torture and ill-treatment of prisoners, to the existence of arbitrary detention and widespread judicial irregularities. Prime Minister Hun Sen has ordered the re-arrest of hundreds of people freed by the courts. A former *Khmers Rouges* commander, Nuon Paet, was convicted of the murder of three westerners after a one-day trial. He was arraigned on a mass of charges, some under laws which were no longer in force, or which breached commonly recognized international standards. The judgment in the Nuon Paet case referred to facts and evidence that were not presented in court.[12]

However, the current government is not the worst administration Cambodia has had. Nor are the CFF trial practices solely a hangover from Hun Sen's ruling Cambodian People's Party's Stalinist past. *All* Cambodian governments since independence have violated human rights and since Sihanouk's *coup d'état* of June 1952, none have been elected in fully free and fair elections—although some have been fairer than others. Sihanouk's arbitrary behavior set the standard for all subsequent governments. When governments did not like election results, they simply ignored them, much as Sihanouk did in 1952 when he dismissed the Huy Kanthoul Government in a *coup d'état* backed by French bayonets and armor, and as did Hun Sen after the victory of Prince Ranariddh in 1993, and more recently in 1997. Except for the brief blossoming of limited democracy after 1945, Cambodians have never known anything but authoritarian government, and official corruption and abuse of power have been endemic. After World War II, under international pressure, the French paid lip service to the need to establish democratic institutions in Cambodia, but in practice they colluded with Sihanouk to undermine them. While it is true that there was no tradition of representative or participatory government in pre-colonial Cambodia, the French took care not to plant the seeds. Except in theory, power has never emanated from the people.

Sihanouk boasted that he was the giver and taker of elections and constitutions and surrounded himself with sycophants and brutal enforcers to ensure his pre-eminence during the years between independence and Lon Nol's seizure of power in March 1970. Sihanouk abdicated in 1955, passing the throne to his father, Suramarit, so that he could have more room to maneuver politically. After independence, he amalgamated most of the right-wing parties into the Sangkum Party, the "Popular Socialist Community", which he used as a vehicle for a personalized style of authoritarian populism. Although Sihanouk tolerated opposition parties to some degree, in practice he dominated an authoritarian state and believed it was his birthright to rule. Tragically, this absolutism was to undercut what was arguably Sihanouk's finest achievement—his country's neutrality during the conflict in Vietnam in the 1960s. When that neutrality came to an end with Lon Nol's March 1970 coup, Cambodia entered into a Dark Age of war and genocide. History moves on, indifferent to *ex post facto* speculation, but one cannot help but wonder if a more open and pluralist post-independence system might have spared Cambodia the holocaust.

Until 1946, the French did not allow elections,[13] and they were unknown in traditional Khmer society. The first time the masses of the Khmer people (or at least adult males) voted for anything was in Son Ngoc Thanh's dubious plebiscite during the Japanese-sponsored "Independent Kingdom of Kampuchea". The fragile flame lit by Prince Yuthevong and Sihanouk in 1946 perished when Sihanouk turned his back on his earlier liberalism. Political systems are seldom entirely new and their architects construct them on existing models. Sihanouk was a willing pupil of his French colonial masters, who, despite some early zeal to abolish unjust laws and stamp out corruption, ruled the Protectorate as a dictatorship of police and civil servants. Freedom of speech, of assembly, and of publication did not exist and any newspapers that did circulate legally were subject to strict surveillance and censorship. Despite abolishing traditional Khmer slavery, the French introduced new forms of bondage on the plantations and on the public works schemes. Dissidents were arbitrarily detained and torture and ill treatment of prisoners were routine. Like Sihanouk, the French regarded the Khmers as children incapable of governing themselves, and punished them if they aspired to adult status. Sihanouk emasculated the parliamentary system and erected a travesty of popular government in its place. The French left a model of government that was authoritarian and repressive. If the traditional legal system had been medieval, with venal judges, the French did not replace it with an independent judiciary and respect for the rule of law. If the French had tut-tutted at the "oriental despotism" of Khmer kings and mandarins, their own methods were no antidote. The Rights of Man and the Citizen were not for export and absolutism was only further entrenched.

Corruption was widespread in Sihanouk's kingdom during the 1950s and '60s. After Sihanouk's henchman Lon Nol rebelled against his master in 1970, he presided over a Khmer Republic in which corruption reached astonishing levels. While their soldiers fought and died in battles with Vietnamese and GRUNK[14] troops, Lon Nol's generals sold weapons to the enemy and padded the rolls of their battalions with "phantom soldiers", diverting their pay into their own pockets.[15] This was a real "kleptocracy", but considering that Lon Nol engaged in murder and graft as early as 1945, we should not be surprised at its extent when he became the country's strongman. Corruption thrives under autocratic forms of rule because the general lack of accountability gives dictators the opportunity to keep their hands in the public till, and followers must be rewarded.

The French administrators never regarded themselves as accountable to the Khmer people and thus did nothing to replace the assumptions of Cambodian administrators, for all the distaste of early French officials such as Ernest Brière d'Isle and Francis Garnier for the tax-farming mentality of the indigenous officials. Corruption, too, was often present in the French administration. There were allegations of bribe taking during the successions to Sisowath and Monivong, and Ernest Outrey, the French parliamentary deputy for Cochinchina and Cambodia, claimed that graft was prevalent in the Varenne administration.[16]

Lon Nol was never committed to democracy and had been instrumental in its downfall in 1952. In October 1971, in a move eerily reminiscent of Sihanouk's coup of June 1952, he shut down the parliament of the Khmer Republic, declaring that he would no longer "continue this sterile game of outmoded liberal democracy".[17] The US Ambassador commented that Lon Nol preferred "to rule by consensus, but like all Khmer he instinctively distrusts any opposition".[18] He might have been referring to Sihanouk and the words could apply to Hun Sen. By 1975, the Khmer Republic was morally bankrupt. The rancid flavor is conveyed brilliantly in the diary of William Harben, who was a US diplomat in the country at the time. Even when shells were falling in the outer suburbs, Harben recorded that soldiers guarded an opulent ball where "fops...with their flared trousers and coattails, 20-carat topaz cufflinks, violet ruffled throat pieces and lacquered curls" cavorted.[19] Such conspicuous consumption by a parasitic elite, taken in conjunction with the horrors of US carpet-bombing in the countryside, helps explain the ferocity of the *Khmers Rouges* peasant soldiers.

At the beginning of the 21st century, King Sihanouk is little more than a figurehead—the kind of constitutional monarch that Huy Kanthoul and Prince Yuthevong would have liked him to be back in the 1940s and '50s. His portraits adorn the walls of government offices, street corner buildings, private homes and businesses, but real power has passed him by. Power, however, has not devolved to the people, but to a new strongman, Hun Sen,[20] and his Cambodian Peoples' Party.

Nor was the legacy any better in other spheres of life, where France disturbed the foundations of traditional Khmer society, but did not replace them.[21] The French left Cambodia as an economically backward state with a tiny indigenous middle class. They tended to give administrative positions to Vietnamese, partly from expediency and indifference—there was no conception of affirmative action—and partly from a policy of divide and rule. As Son Ngoc Thanh complained, there were no Cambodian capitalists and few Khmer businessmen, still less an intelligentsia. There was little debate about political theory and power gravitated to the King and few oligarchic families, many of whom had no vision beyond their own enrichment and no conception of the common weal. France also bequeathed a stunted health and education system. There was not one university and only a smattering of high schools for the Khmer elite. The French did introduce a widespread vaccination program—partly because of their own high levels of mortality—but they trained only a handful of doctors and there was one western-trained Cambodian dentist when they left.

Underdevelopment and the Khmers Rouges

The French did not provide Cambodia with the economic "image of its own future". Contrary to Marx's early predictions and Leroy-

Beaulieu's prescriptions, they did not industrialize Cambodia. This was partly due to indifference, but also because they feared competition and saw the colonies as closed markets and sources of raw materials. Cambodia lacked an indigenous proletariat and a native labor movement, and this, combined with the lack of a democratic tradition, was to contribute to the catastrophe of the Pol Pot regime in the 1970s, *although the French could not have foreseen that disaster.* Even where French interests did require the creation of a working class, such as on the rubber plantations, the owners preferred to hire Vietnamese rather than Khmers. Nor was there any policy of affirmative action on the part of small employers of labor in mills and workshops. The country had been wrenched into the orbit of the world market economy, yet much of it still practiced subsistence agriculture. This bred an inwards-looking mentality. Khmer communism, far from being internationalist, adopted the politics of envy common to Khmer nationalism.[22] This travesty of the liberating vision of Marx was to drag Cambodia into a new Dark Age. This was hardly surprising given that such a proletariat as existed was overwhelmingly Vietnamese and that the cultural level of the Khmer movement as a whole was very low. In Cambodia, as David Chandler has pointed out, "a small intellectual elite pulled the poorest peasants not only into class warfare directed against the remainder of Cambodian society, but also toward an autarchic set of policies that led to a full-scale confrontation with Vietnam that was impossible to win."[23] The extreme autarchy during the period eclipsed anything under Stalin in the USSR, although it did derive in part from the Stalinist theory of "socialism in one country". The poorest peasants, we should add, formed a relatively small stratum of Cambodian society in comparison with neighboring Vietnam. Classical Marxist theory holds that there can be no new society until the productive forces of the old are fully developed. Hence, the Mensheviks opposed the Bolshevik Revolution in Russia on the grounds of the country's backwardness. Marxists, they averred, should content themselves with the struggle for a democratic republic until the material conditions for socialism matured. Trotsky retorted that the Russian working class, though small on a national scale, was well organized and had much greater weight in the cities than the countryside. The Russian bourgeoisie, on the other hand, he argued, was weak and incapable of successfully carrying through the struggle for a democratic republic. Hence, the working class could either suffer Tsarist autocracy and war, or link hands with the peasantry to skip over the bourgeois republic and capitalism, directly to the socialist revolution. This was the theory of permanent revolution.[24] As we have seen, there is evidence that Marx came, late in life, to a similar, although not identical position.[25]

Drifting off into pure fantasies

However, given the lack of an indigenous proletariat, it is difficult to see how the theory could apply to Cambodia. Marx and Trotsky's ideas were, in any case, anathema to the *Khmers Rouges*, who derived their ideology from Stalinism via the French and Chinese Communist parties, and coupled it with extreme nationalism. In a sense, the *Khmers Rouges'* vision resembles that which Engels characterized as "utopian socialism", although they gave it a savage twist unforeseen in the gentler nostrums of Fourier or Thomas More. "These new social systems", Engels wrote, in words which might have described the voluntarist schemas of Pol Pot and Khieu Samphan, "were foredoomed as Utopian; the more completely they were worked out in detail, the more they could not avoid drifting off into pure fantasies."[26] Fantasy it was, with a reversion to primitive barter, dams built in some cases without spillways, experts killed as a matter of course, schools largely closed, the cities emptied, machinery trashed, technology scorned, and the people herded into the countryside at gunpoint. The wild delusions of bloodthirsty grandeur in which Pol Pot plotted genocide, imagining that if each Khmer killed 30 Vietnamese, the "historic enemy" could be vanquished, were fantasies too, and not even noble ones. One image sums up the phantasmagoria of the Pol Pot years: in one instance, the empty streets from Pochentong airport into the city were lined with red flags to welcome back Pol Pot from a trip to Beijing. Did the *Khmers Rouges* imagine the applause of invisible crowds? They had trumped Bertolt Brecht's satirical words and abolished the people, without electing a new one.

What kind of society was Democratic Kampuchea?

What kind of society was Democratic Kampuchea? Was it a particularly pure and austere brand of "socialism" as some contend?[27] This version is difficult to credit. Michael Vickery argues convincingly that it was a modern approximation of Marx's Asiatic Mode of Production. Far from abolishing or over-leaping capitalism, the *Khmers Rouges* modeled their brutally dystopic state on the distant past. This was not socialism, nor even a "workers' state" on the road to socialism. In the end, it was a vast exercise in the socialization of poverty in which the wheel of history was turned back to the

Angkorean past in the illusion of building the socialist future.[28] It was a regimented hell that fits August Bebel's sardonic phrase, "barracks socialism". Pol Pot eliminated the urban working class and turned ferociously on the intelligentsia and anyone else who threatened, or was perceived to threaten, his grip on power. Basing themselves on a thin layer of the poorest peasants, the *Khmers Rouges* turned Cambodia into a gigantic rural work camp, after emptying the cities— an operation that smacks of the destructive fury of the barbarians towards the cities of Rome and eclipses even the anti-Western, medievalist fury of the Taliban. There was no conception of democracy. A secretive minority would impose its will implacably on the majority and if the *Khmers Rouges* had even heard of Rosa Luxemburg's warning that socialism must be the will of the majority, they would have scorned it, along with Marx's assumption that, "the proletarian movement is the self-conscious, independent movement of the immense majority, in the interests of the immense majority".[29] In this respect, the *Khmers Rouges* inherited the autocratic methods of the French, of Sihanouk and Lon Nol and coupled them to a barbarous ideology that placed no value on human life. The French were not responsible for what Pol Pot did, and could not have foreseen the horror he unleashed, but they did contribute to the social, political and economic underdevelopment that helped to create him.

How visible is the French legacy today?

Fifty years after independence, how visible is the colonialist past in Cambodia today? The influence of French colonialism is still very tangible in many of France's former African colonies. French is widely spoken and understood from Algeria to the Republic of the Congo, and it is often the *lingua franca* where there are competing tribal languages. One finds similar patterns in Britain's former colonies, particularly India, and the influence of the USA is readily apparent in the Philippines. It is not so clear-cut in Cambodia, particularly outside of the major towns. The signs of western influence are certainly visible everywhere, even in the villages, which often sport gaudy advertisements for world brands of toothpaste, soft drink and cigarettes. This, however, stems more from the more general—and recent—"globalization" than from French colonialism, and few of the brands are French. It is, however, true that French influence lingers, particularly in the cities. The street signs in Phnom Penh are still in French and Khmer, French bread and pastries are widely consumed, and school children still wear uniforms styled after those of their

French counterparts. Large institutions such as the Calmette Hospital and the Alliance Française at Phnom Penh attest to continuing links between the two countries. Many of the prominent buildings in Phnom Penh date from the French era, including the royal palace (still replete with an absurdly flattering equestrian statue of King Norodom), the National (formerly the Albert Sarraut) Museum, the central post office, and the cluster of former *Résidences* around the Wat Phnom. The railroad station, too, dates from the time of the French, along with the narrow gauge tracks stretching away to Battambang and Sihanoukville (Kompong Som). The French-built central market, an art deco secular cathedral consecrated to Mammon, is still the hub of the city's petty commerce and a striking landmark on the low skyline. Architecturally, all cities are palimpsests, yet there is little visible trace here of Phnom Penh's pre-French days, when the city was a straggle of jerry-built shops and thatched huts along the river on what is today the busy Quai Sisowath. Even the street plan dates from the Protectorate and below the crumbling asphalt the French-built drains and water pipes struggle to cope with the needs of a greatly expanded population.

Educated older people usually speak French and many still hold France in nostalgic affection. Yet, there is a yawning gulf between the generations. Cambodia today is a "young" country, with a high birth rate, and teems with children and teenagers as Nature compensates for the demographic catastrophe of the 1970s and the brutal isolation that followed. Few of these youngsters speak French and many are only dimly aware of the colonial past. Phnom Penh, Siem Reap and Sihanoukville boast good French restaurants, but their prices are beyond the pockets of most Cambodians and they cater mainly for tourists and European expatriates. Here and there, the fine old French buildings are falling into ruin and much of Phnom Penh dates from the 1950s and 1960s. Despite the best efforts of the Alliance Française to maintain linguistic and cultural links, English is now the second language of choice for young Cambodians, and EFL schools abound in the capital. The ubiquitous American-style business schools attest that English is the language of globalization, and a ticket—perhaps—out of poverty for young Khmers. Apart from on the street signs, fading advertisements and the facades of some government departmental buildings, French is less and less visible. The old Bokor hill station is a potent symbol of the decayed French connection. Crouched atop a steep scarp overlooking the Gulf of Thailand, it is a dismal sight, with its rooms open to the rain and sun, its walls smoke-blackened and shrapnel-scarred, and its stairs and pathways choked with weeds. Cobras slither across a weed-choked tennis court and the rain murmurs in an overgrown garden. The Catholic church is a burnt hulk on the skyline, but Buddhist monks have established a monastery close by.

The tenacity of tradition

Nevertheless, the weeds and monks at Bokor symbolize the tenacity of tradition and the Khmer people, as in the adage, *Srok Khmer mün del soun*—"the country of the Khmers will never perish". The Cambodian people remain and that is ground for optimism, given the tumultuous events of past decades. The country still has major problems. It is desperately poor—although the wealthy Khmers would be rich even in the First World. An ecological crisis is looming, with clear cutting and illegal logging on watersheds threatening to silt up the country's principal ecosystem, the Tonlé Sap. A strongman, Hun Sen, rules via a form of "guided democracy", and has not hesitated to modify election results with tanks and bayonets. In this, he is a true heir of Sihanouk, Lon Nol and their French teachers. Corruption is endemic at many levels. The police at Kampot, for instance, sit at the entrance to the bridge at the edge of town with hands permanently outstretched for an unofficial "tax" on travelers. They are the lowest tier in a pyramid of graft. The rich can buy "justice" like any other commodity. In the shantytowns on the outskirts of Phnom Penh, HIV/AIDS infection rates are colossal, affecting up to 80 per cent of the adult population—as bad or worse than the most AIDS-stricken South African townships. Landlessness is growing, despite a population density much lower than other South East Asian countries.

It is debatable whether the peasants, who still make up the mass of Cambodia's population, are any better off today than they were before the French introduced the alienation of land. Under the traditional crown land system—a form of usufruct—peasants did not need title to work the land. They were free to occupy it so long as they worked it. The system had its downsides. The peasants were reluctant to produce more than for their own needs and as a result, trade was stunted. This was exacerbated by high taxes on produce rather than the land itself and these taxes were seldom used for the benefit of the country as a whole. Yet, despite widespread misery in times of poor harvests, floods and droughts, there was little social stratification in the countryside and little danger of peasants losing their land. The French cadastral program, however, which created private property in land, inevitably led to growing inequality and even to a problem of landlessness.[30] Today, on most days at dawn, hordes of poor folk huddle in the chill at the Independence Monument in a park on

Sihanouk Boulevard. They are landless rural laborers or small peasants whose holdings cannot provide them with a living. In many cases, rich local notables have driven them off their land by force, or have used the corrupt legal system to deprive them of it. These rural poor and dispossessed are forced to trek to Phnom Penh hoping to secure work. Usually, this takes the form of underpaid casual labor on construction sites and in factories, often in dangerous and unhealthy conditions. Others ply the streets as *cyclo* drivers,[31] or drift into prostitution. Average life expectancy is 53 years,[32] but the poor are old by forty. These people remain "civilization's pack animals".

The "social revolution" that never was

Cambodia desperately needs what the developed countries take for granted—a civil society, balanced economic development, democracy, an independent judiciary, honest officials, and autonomous political and social organizations including peasant and trade unions with independent political representation. Democracy is not a luxury; it is the only corrective to the selfish use of power of elites. Now, almost fifty years after the "royal crusade", it would be churlish and unfair to blame France alone for all of Cambodia's post-independence shortcomings, even less for the horrors that befell the country in the 1970s. The Great Powers—the USA and China in particular—bear a great deal of responsibility too. The US bombing was near genocidal; it contributed to what hard-boiled American political scientists called "forced draft urbanization", and delivered massive blows against the structure of traditional rural society. Before US intervention— undertaken for the most cynical motives[33]—the *Khmers Rouges* were an insignificant force. The blockade of the 1980s, which benefited only Sihanouk and the *Khmers Rouges*, kept the country desperately poor and underdeveloped. At the time of writing, it is only ten years since the end of the Cold War caused the West to abandon their erstwhile *Khmers Rouges* allies and to intervene directly in Cambodian affairs via UNTAC.[34] It is too early to evaluate the results of that intervention, but they have been, to say the least, patchy. It is also too soon to say what economic globalization will mean for Cambodia, but it is unlikely that the siren song of the West will bring the bounty it promises. Francis Fukuyama's Hegelian prediction that the world will be recast in the image of the USA rings false,[35] given the failure of the earlier prescriptions of Leroy-Beaulieu and the *mission civilisatrice*. Cambodia is a desperately poor country in a world increasingly dominated by transnational corporations—any one of which has a greater GNP than most Third World countries—and by economic superpowers that are busily restructuring the world's economy for their own interests. The Cambodian people will be expendable in this calculus of power and wealth: as Benjamin Disraeli once observed, "Colonies do not cease to be colonies because they are independent." Traditional society, too, will be further battered as globalization causes "all that is solid [to melt] into air".[36]

Not everything can be blamed on outside forces. As a Khmer friend, a civil servant, mused in 2001, "We are still so poor and so corrupt. The Government has not paid our salaries for three months, so perhaps some official has put the money in his pocket. But whom should we blame? Why are we still so underdeveloped? Pol Pot has been gone for many years and it is a decade since the blockade ended." The corruption is blatant. One afternoon in 1999, the electricity suddenly cut out—not for the first time—at a major cultural institution in Phnom Penh. The part-privatized electricity company had turned off the power because the Government had not paid the institution's bills. One can imagine the scandal if this happened in, say, Paris, Melbourne or New York—if the power suddenly cut out in London's Public Record Office or Washington's Library of Congress and the staff were forced to bribe a technician to have it illegally restored. However, at the same time, Cambodian Government ministers and high officials enjoy a lifestyle far in excess of what they should be able to afford on their salaries. France is not to blame for this. Yet, on balance, there is no doubt that the French legacy was insufficient to prepare the country for the modern world and that the "social revolution" Marx once predicted is yet to come. Indeed, far from seeing France—or the current globalizers—as disinterested agents of a *mission civilisatrice,* we should ponder Mohandas Gandhi's pithy riposte to the question of what he thought of Western civilization. "I think it would be a good idea," he replied.

Notes

[1] AAc A 1838/283. 3016/2/10 Part 1. Kingdom of Cambodia, DEA reports to Cabinet and Senior Government officials. Australian Legation at Saigon to the DEA, Canberra, 16 June 1953.

[2] Cited in Henri Brunschwig, (trans. William Glanville Brown), (1964*), French Colonialism 1871-1914: Myths and Realities*, Frederick Praeger, New York, p.61.

[3] Karl Marx, "The Future Results of British Rule in India", in Shlomo Averini (ed.), (1969), *Karl Marx on Colonialism and Modernization. His Dispatches*

and Other Writings on China, India, Mexico, the Middle East and North Africa, Anchor Books, New York, pp.132-139.

[4] Karl Marx, "The British Rule in India", in Averini, op.cit. p.94.

[5] Suniti Kumar Ghosh, (1984), "Marx on India", *Monthly Review*, Vol. 35, January.

[6] Marx never used the term "imperialism" in its later "Marxist" usage, as found in the writings of Rosa Luxemburg, Lenin and Rudolf Hilferding—or those of the non-Marxist J.A. Hobson. When he did use the term, it was in the narrower and specific sense of the policies and practices of emperors such as Napoleon III.

[7] Leon Trotsky, (trans. Max Eastman), (1967), *The History of the Russian Revolution*, Vol. III, Sphere Books, London, p.349.

[8] A.H. Broderick, cited in AAc A989 43/735/302 The Far East and French Indo-China. British Foreign Office Research Dept. Report, "The Record of the French Administration in Indo-China", 8 January 1944.

[9] Phelim Kyne, (2001), "Seven days of Cambodian Justice: A CFF Trial Diary", *Phnom Penh Post*, June 22-July 5, 2001.

[10] Kyne, op.cit. Again, the special anti-terrorist measures of the US and other governments raise interesting questions here.

[11] Australian Legation at Saigon to the DEA, Canberra, 16 June 1953, op.cit.

[12] Amnesty International *Annual Report, 2000*. Contained in the *New International World Guide, 2001-2002. An Alternative Guide to the Countries of Our Planet*, CD Rom, New Internationalist, Adelaide/Institut de Tercer Mundo.

[13] A limited roll of French citizens and *assimilés* could vote for colonial deputies in the French parliament.

[14] GRUNK was the French acronym for the anti-Lon Nol coalition between 1970 and 1975, the Royal Khmer Government of National Unity. In theory, Sihanouk led the coalition, but real power lay with Pol Pot and the *Khmers Rouges*.

[15] For accounts of the Lon Nol period, see Chandler, op.cit. pp.192-235; Justin J. Corfield, (1994), *Khmers Stand Up! A History of the Cambodian Government, 1970-1975*, Centre of Southeast Asian Studies, Monash University, Clayton; and John A. Tully, (1990), " 'Certain and Inevitable Misfortune': War and Politics in Lon Nol's Cambodia, March 1970-December 1971", unpublished MA thesis, Institute for Contemporary Asian Studies, Monash University, Clayton. See pp.81-83 for information on corruption in Lon Nol's armed forces.

[16] *The New York Times*, 19 March 1927.

[17] US State Department document released under Freedom of Information to David Chandler. Memo from Ambassador Emory Swank at Phnom Penh to the Secretary of State, Washington DC, 21 October 1971.

[18] Ibid. 26 October 1971. Swank ought to have inserted the word "politician" between "Most" and "Khmers". In fact, most Khmers have never shared power, let alone had the luxury of distrusting opposition.

[19] William Harben's unpublished Cambodian diary, undated entry. Courtesy of David Chandler.

[20] So-called in Harish and Julie Mehta's biography. [Harish C. Mehta and Julie B. Mehta, (1999), *Hun Sen. Strongman of Cambodia*, Graham Brash, Singapore.]

[21] J.A. Hobson made this point about British colonialism in India and it is even more pertinent to the role of the French in Cambodia. [J.A Hobson, (1965), *Imperialism: A Study*, Ann Arbor Paperbacks, University of Michigan, p.302.]

[22] The racism of the *Khmers Rouges* is an equivalent to the anti-Semitism that August Bebel, the 19th century German socialist leader, characterized as the "socialism of fools" and the "syphilis of the workers' movement".

[23] David P. Chandler, (1993), *The Tragedy of Cambodian History. Politics, War and Revolution since 1945*, Silkworm Books, Chiang Mai, p.49.

[24] See Leon Trotsky, (1969), *The Permanent Revolution and Results and Prospects*, Merit Publishers, New York.

[25] See, for instance, Robert Bideleux, (1985), *Communism and Development*, Methuen, London and Teodor Shanin (ed.), (1983), *Late Marx and the Russian Road, Marx and 'the peripheries of capitalism'*, Routledge and Kegan Paul, London.

[26] Frederick Engels, *Socialism; Utopian and Scientific*, in Karl Marx and Frederick Engels, (1970), *Selected Works*, Progress Publishers, Moscow, p.398.

[27] A belief held in common by apologists for Stalinism and capitalism, incidentally.

[28] There is a striking parallel between such modeling (conscious or unconscious) and Mao Zedong's thinking. Mao was fascinated by the ancient Chinese emperors and consciously modeled himself upon them. There was no room for democracy in such an approach. [See, for instance, Harrison E. Salisbury, (1992), *The New Emperors: Mao and Deng. A Dual Biography*, Harper Collins, London.]

[29] Karl Marx and Frederick Engels, *The Communist Manifesto*, in Selected Works, op.cit. p.45.

[30] See, for example, Hou Yuon, "The peasantry of Kampuchea: Colonialism and Modernization", and Hu Nim, "Land Tenure and Social Structure in Kampuchea", in Ben Kiernan and Chanthou Boua (eds.), (1982), *Peasants and Politics in Kampuchea, 1942-1981*, Zed Press, London, pp.34-68 and pp.69-86.

[31] Bicycle taxis, known in other parts of Asia as rickshaws.

[32] *World Guide, 2001-2002*, op.cit.

[33] Cambodia was embroiled in the war at the very time Kissinger and Nixon were seeking to disengage from it. Firstly, the US backed the Lon Nol coup and secondly they invaded Cambodia in "Operation Shoemaker", which drove the Vietnamese Communists deep into Cambodian territory. This was, said the U.S. President, "the Nixon doctrine in its purest form".

[34] The United Nations Transitional Authority in Cambodia.

[35] Francis Fukuyama, (1992), *The End of History and the Last Man*, Penguin Books, Harmondsworth.
[36] Karl Marx and Frederick Engels, (1970), *The Manifesto of the Communist Party*, in *Selected Works*, Progress Publishers, Moscow, p.38.

Glossary

E = English; *Fr* = French; *G.* = German; *J* = Japanese; *Kh* = Khmer; *L* = Latin; *T* = Thai; *V* = Vietnamese.

Abbé	Catholic priest (sometimes abbot). *Fr*
Achar	leading monk in a Buddhist wat. *Kh*
Amicale	friendly society *Fr*
Annam	Central region of Vietnam. Administered separately as a protectorate under a Résident Supérieur at Hué.
Annamite	archaic word for Vietnamese. *Fr*
Apanage	portion of royal domain leased or granted to a follower in France and England. The same practice occurred in Cambodia on a much more systematic basis as there was no landed property in Cambodia before the French. *F* and *E*

Asiatic Mode of Production	In Marx's theory of historical materialism, European society passed through a number of distinct historical stages, including feudalism, capitalism and socialism. Realizing that these categories did not fit Asian societies, Marx formulated the category of the Asiatic Mode of Production, which was characterized by a despotic state and large-scale hydraulic works. Marx based the category on his reading of secondary sources. Unfortunately, it made no allowance for the great diversity of Asian societies and has been sharply criticized by a number of Marxist scholars. However, it does seem to fit the Angkorean society of ancient Cambodia.
Assimilé(e)	A "brown Frenchman" (or woman); a colonial subject who had been assimilated into French culture and granted rights of French citizenship. *Fr*
Baccalauréat	Final year examinations in French high schools. *Fr.*
Baht	Unit of Thai currency. *T*
Balat	provincial official. *Kh*
Ba-Quan (bacouin)	kind of roulette game. *V*
Baray	Artificial lake or irrigation basin in Angkorean times. The Western Baray still exists after restoration by the French during World War II. *Kh*
Belle époque	literally "beautiful epoch", period from around 1890 until the outbreak of war in 1914. *Fr*
Boche	contemptuous term for a German *Fr*

Bonze	Buddhist monk. *Fr*
Cambodge	French name for Cambodia.
Cham	member of a minority ethnic group in Cambodia and Vietnam, with own language, Islamic in religion and descended from the ancient empire of Champa.
Chamcars	riparian fields. *Kh*
Chauvaikhet	local official (see Khet) *Kh*
Chetty	Indian moneylender (member of caste).
Circonscription	administrative unit in Cambodia, supervised by a Résident. *Fr*
Cochinchina	The southern provinces of Vietnam, roughly the Mekong delta region. Administered as a separate colony by the French under a Governor at Saigon.
Corvée	compulsory labor on public works. *Fr*
Cyclo (pousse)	bicycle taxi, rickshaw *Fr*
Délégué	French official in charge of part of a circonscription, reporting to the Résident. *Fr*
Drang nach Süden	Pull to the south *G*
État	State *Fr*
Garde indigène	native militia. *Fr*
Gauleiter	Nazi district leader. *G*
Hochdeutsch	Standard "High" German as opposed to dialects such as those of Alsace. *G*
Impôt foncier	land tax. *Fr*

Indochina	French Indochina was composed of the Protectorates of Tonkin, Annam, Laos and Cambodia, plus the colony of Cochinchina. More rarely, the name applies to all of the Southeast Asian countries between China and India.
Jacquerie	peasant revolt *Fr*
Kampuchea	Cambodia. *Kh*
Kampuchea Krom	Lower Cambodia, the lower Mekong delta region now part of Vietnam. *Kh*
Kempetei	Japanese military police in World War II. *J*
Khand	administrative division. *Kh*
Khet	smaller administrative division. *Kh*
Khmer	Cambodian person, Cambodian language or adjective. *Kh*
Khmer Issarak	"Free Khmer", anti-French guerrilla after 1945. *Kh*
Khmérité	"Khmer-ness", alleged Khmer qualities encouraged by Vichy in World War II. *Fr*
Khmer Krom	Khmer from the Mekong delta region Vietnam. *Kh*
Khmers Rouges	"Red Khmers", Maoist Cambodian Communist Party, followers of Pol Pot. *Fr*
Khum	village administrative unit. *Kh*
Khnhom	debt slavery. *Kh*
Krama(h)	brightly colored and checkered head-cloth/neckerchief worn by most Khmers. *Kh*

Kram	law or royal decree. *Kh*
Li	Old Chinese measurement, about half a kilometer.
Maquis	resistance movement, lit. Mediterranean scrub. *F*
Marseillaise	French Republican national anthem. *F*
Marsouin	French colonial infantryman (lit. white dolphin). Corruption of Swedish and Danish word. *Fr*
Mesrok	village headman. *Kh*
Métis(sse)	person of mixed Asian and European parentage. *Fr*
Mise-en-valeur	economic development *Fr*
Mission civilisatrice	"civilizing mission". *Fr*
Mohanikay	Oldest of the two Buddhist orders in Cambodia. (See also Thommayuth.)
Montagnard	hill tribesman, mountaineer. *Fr*
Monthon Burapha	Thai name for the provinces of Battambang and Siem Reap. *T*
Nagaravatta	Khmer for Angkor Wat and name of mildly nationalist magazine published from mid-1930s and name of the circle, which published it. The group adopted stronger nationalist positions after 1941-42. *Kh*
Neakh ngear	hereditary slavery in Cambodia *Kh*
Nuoc mam	fish sauce *V*
Obbareach	heir apparent to Khmer throne. *Kh*

Ohkna	Governor of a province. *Kh*
Paddy	unmilled rice
Patron	boss, employer *Fr*
Phum	hamlet. *Kh*
Phya	"Lordship" *T*
Phnom	hill. *Kh*
Piastre	unit of currency in French Indochina issued by the Banque de l'Indochine and worth around five francs. *Fr* (orig. Arabic)
Picul	sixty kilograms.
Pirogue	canoe *Fr*
Poilu	French infantryman, equivalent of British "Tommy". *Fr*
Ponteas	fields at a distance from a waterway. *Kh*
Poulo Condore	Prison island in South China Sea. (Con Son to Vietnamese, Tralach Island to the Khmers.)
Prahoc	fermented salt fish paste, a staple of the Cambodian diet *Kh*
Prea-Keo-Fea	title given by Khmer king to favored son. *Kh*
Prak pae	currency in Battambang and Siem Reap before 1907. *Kh* or *T*
Préfet	chief regional administrator in France. *Fr*
Prestation	tax in money or labor on public works. *Fr*

Prey Nokor	Khmer name for Saigon/Ho Chi Minh City. *Kh*
Quoc nhu	Romanized Vietnamese script *V*
Quoc nhu khmer	Romanized Khmer script *V*
Réquisitions	discretionary corvée. *Fr*
Résident	French official in circonscription, roughly equivalent to British Resident or Australian District Commissioner. *Fr*
Résident Supérieur	highest French official in the protectorates of Cambodia, Laos, Tonkin and Annam. (Cochinchina was a colony with a Governor) Subordinate to the Governor General at Hanoi. *Fr*
Saint-Cyr	prestigious French military academy
Saint-Maixent	famous French military academy
Salakhet	village hall. *Kh*
Sampot	traditional Cambodian dress. *Kh*
Sangha	Buddhist clergy *Kh*
Seigneur	feudal landlord, sometimes used as a derogatory term for an authoritarian individual with a belief that he is "born to rule". *Fr*
Siam	Old name for Thailand.
Srok	country or land. *Kh*
Stupa	Spire surmounting a burial place, particularly of a king or other high dignitary. *Kh*

Sui generis	of a special kind. *L*
Surêté	security police. *Fr*
Tagal	Filipino palace guard in Cambodia.
Terra nullius	Empty land, or land held to be so. *L*.
Terres rouges	red earth (laterite) districts on the upper left bank of the Mekong in Cambodia. Ideal for rubber plantations. *Fr*
Thommayuth	Buddhist order, arrived in Cambodia in 1864 from Thailand. (See Mohanikay.)
Tical	unit of Siamese currency – there were fifteen ticaux to the pound sterling. *T*
Tirailleur	sharpshooter or light infantryman. *Fr*
Tonkin	Northern districts of Vietnam, roughly the Red River region. Administered separately as a Protectorate by the French under a Résident Supérieur at Hanoi. Hanoi was also the site of the office of the Governor-General, who was in overall charge of the French administration in Indochina.
Tonlé Sap	Refers either to the Great Lake of Central Cambodia, or to the river that drains from the lake into the Mekong.
Trente-six-bêtes	card game popular in illegal gambling dens. *Fr*
Treponemas	group of diseases including syphilis and yaws. *E*
Udong	Old capital of Cambodia, upstream of Phnom Penh on the Tonlé Sap River.
Usufruct	Right to enjoy the use of land and its produce.

Yunnan	Mountainous region in southern China adjacent to Tibet and Burma, where the Mekong rises.
Yuvan	Cambodian youth movement in Vichy years of World War II. *Kh*
Yuvani	Female equivalent of the Yuvan. *Kh*
Wat	Buddhist temple. *Kh*
Zollverein	Customs union *G.*

Bibliography

1. Archival and library sources

The *ARCHIVES NATIONALES - ARCHIVES D'OUTRE-ME*R at Les Fenouillières, Aix-en-Provence, in France, contain a vast amount of material from the French colonial administration and include letters and reports on administrative, political, economic, financial, public works, educational, health, police and other matters. The French administration sent back much of the material from Phnom Penh to France after independence. The archives also contain an extensive collection of photographs, maps and books. Archival material on Cambodia is located in the general INDOCHINE files, the Fonds Amiraux files, the RSC files, and the HCC files. RSC refers to files from the Résidence Supérieure au Cambodge, which covers the period from 1863 until the Japanese seizure of power on 9 March 1945. HCC refers to documents from the Haute Commission au Cambodge, which replaced the Résidence Supérieure following the return of the French in late 1945. Material from the INDOCHINE files is from the Gouvernement-Général de l'Indochine at Hanoi. This includes copies of reports, letters and telegrams between the central administration and Cambodia, generally via the Résidence Supérieure, and between the central administration and the French Colonial Ministry at Paris. They are listed as either AF or NF – old or new files. The archives have been reorganized in recent years and the few files listed in notes as being from the Fonds Amiraux might have been reclassified, generally as RSC. I have listed documents from Aix in the text as INDOCHINE, AOM RSC, Fonds Amiraux, or HCC, followed by the file number and description of the document, including date, and the letters AOM before the file names indicates they are from Aix. Most of the material dealing with Cambodia is in French, although some documents are in Khmer and a sprinkling of other languages. Unfortunately, many of the documents from World War II and afterwards are not available to the public under the 50 and 60 year rules, ostensibly to protect the anonymity of innocent people. This is also the case in other archives, particularly at the Public Record Office at Kew, London.

The *ARCHIVES NATIONALES DU CAMBODGE* are a very valuable source of information and it is gratifying to see the progress made in cataloging files in recent years. Although the French took much of their archival material back to France after independence, they did leave a surprisingly large amount behind. Some of the material duplicates that at Aix, but many documents can only be found here. For instance, the archives contain files of the minutes of the Cambodian Council of Ministers between 1897 and 1937, although there are some lacunae. The archives also hold maps and photographs. The archives staff say that the building was used as servants' quarters under the Pol Pot regime. Regardless of whether this was so, the archives were largely spared the depredations wreaked on the nearby National Library during this period. The archives were difficult to access during much of the post-DK period, but are now open to the public on a regular basis. The dedicated staff are systematically cataloging and storing what is a priceless part of Cambodia's patrimony. The system is now computerized. I have listed documents in the text as ANC, plus RSC followed by the file numbers, titles or descriptions and dates. The archives' own numbering system is not the same as that used at Aix. The archivists' work was not complete at the time of writing and more documents thus await exploration by researchers. The material available tends to come from the middle years of the Protectorate, with a smaller amount from the nineteenth century and the post World War II years.

The *CENTRE MILITAIRE D'INFORMATION ET DOCUMENTATION SUR L'OUTRE-MER (ARCHIVES DE L'ARMÉE DE TERRE)* or *CMIDOM* at the Château de Vincennes in Paris contain material pertinent to the role of the Khmer soldiers in World War I and to French military operations in Indochina during World War II. Most of the material is on microfilm. I have listed documents in the text as CMIDOM, plus the accession numbers and titles or descriptions and dates.

The *PUBLIC RECORD OFFICE* at Kew, London, contains a great deal of material relevant to Cambodia. Much of this is located in the Foreign Office (FO) files, but some is in the War Office (WO) and the Colonial Office (CO) files. Much of the relevant material originated from the British Legations at Bangkok, Saigon and Phnom Penh. Documents relevant to the entire span of the protectorate, from 1863 to 1953 and beyond are available. Some material, particularly from the post World War II era, is subject to 50 and 60 year rules and hence not yet accessible. Documents are listed in the text as FO, or CO, or WO, plus the relevant numbers, description or title, and date, prefixed by my own code *PRO*, indicating they are kept by the Public Record Office.

The *AUSTRALIAN ARCHIVES* contain a surprising amount of valuable information, especially for the period from 1939 onwards. There is interesting material on the arrival of the Japanese in Indochina, the Franco-Thai War, the Vichy regime and the post-war years. Some of the photographic material is excellent. There is material from the (former) Department of External Affairs, and some from military intelligence. Some files came from the British Government. Files are located in three locations: Melbourne, Sydney and Canberra, although the computer catalogues cover all three locations. I have listed files in the text as *AAm, AAc or AAs*, plus the relevant archive file numbers, followed by titles or descriptions and dates. My own prefixes indicate whether documents are located at Melbourne, Canberra or Sydney.

Another source of documentation is the *ARCHIVES OF THE FRENCH MINISTRY OF FOREIGN AFFAIRS* at the Quai d'Orsay in Paris. The reading room of the Ministry archives is open to researchers after obtaining written permission. These archives contain a considerable amount of material useful to the researcher on Cambodia. I have listed documents from this source as QO, followed by file numbers, titles of contents and dates.

Another valuable source of material is the *BRITISH LIBRARY NEWSPAPER ARCHIVES* at Colindale in London. This location contains very large holdings of major newspapers from around the world, including some from French Indochina and Bangkok.

The *MONASH UNIVERSITY LIBRARY* in Melbourne contains a great deal of material on microfilm, including almost complete runs of

La Presse Indochinoise and other newspapers from French Indochina. The rare book section contains some interesting material, including an almost complete set of *Indochine Hebdomadaire Illustré*. The general library has an excellent stock of books on Cambodia, which reflect the university's emphasis on Asian Studies and the presence of Professor David Chandler in the History Department and the Centre of Southeast Asian Studies for many years. The Asian Studies Research Library located in the basement of the main library at Clayton contains Professor Chandler's research papers. These are a very valuable source of information, and include an original collection of Son Ngoc Thanh's letters to supporters and the French administration, and declassified US State Department documents. There are also unpublished typescripts of interviews with Khmer Issarak leaders, an unpublished French-language manuscript of Huy Kanthoul's memoirs, and a copy of Anthony Barnett's 1982 interview with Colonel E.D. Murray.

The *CANADIAN NATIONAL ARCHIVES/ARCHIVES NATIONALES DU CANADA* contain some documents from the period of the International Control Commission in Cambodia and some black and white silent films from Cambodia in the 1920s. Researchers must seek permission for access to the files of Canadian ICC member Mr. Arnold Smith from his family at Toronto. There are some old films from colonial Cambodia in the archives, but the owners of copyright (not related to the Smith family) refuse to allow their reproduction even for personal teaching use. This is not a major source of material, however.

The *BIBLIOTHÈQUE NATIONALE DE FRANCE* recently moved from its old site on the right bank to a futuristic complex of towers and courtyards upstream on the left bank of the Seine. Unfortunately, the system was not functioning smoothly in 1999, and the staff could not locate a large amount of material, including newspapers previously easily accessible in the old newspaper archives. It is to be hoped that these were "teething problems". Researchers can gain access to the library after an interview. The library contains a vast amount of relevant material, including books and periodicals (many of them rare), maps, posters and photographs. The newspaper annex, formerly at Versailles, is now located in the new building at Paris.

The *STATE LIBRARY OF VICTORIA* at Melbourne and the *AUSTRALIAN NATIONAL LIBRARY* at Canberra contain vast collections of books and periodicals, including a surprising number of rare books on Southeast Asia. Their general periodical sections stock a variety of Australian and overseas newspapers and magazines. Likewise, the library of the *SCHOOL OF ORIENTAL AND AFRICAN*

STUDIES in London has a large collection of books on Southeast Asia, including Indochina. Some of the books on the latter are rare.

2. *Periodicals other than academic journals*

Affiches Saigonnais, Les, Saigon.
Annuaire Générale de l'Indochine, Hanoi.
Argus Indochinoise, L', Hanoi.
Asiatic Review, The, London.
Avenir du Cambodge, L', Phnom Penh.
Bangkok Democrat, The, Bangkok.
Bangkok Post, The, Bangkok.
Blackwood's Magazine, London.
Bulletin Administratif du Cambodge, Phnom Penh.
Bulletin de l'Amicale Cambodgienne des Anciens Combattants, Phnom Penh.
Bulletin de la Société des Études Indochinoises, Saigon.
Bulletin Économique de l'Indochine, Hanoi.
Call of French Indo-China, The, Hanoi.
China Weekly Review, Shanghai.
Cloche Fêlée, La, Saigon.
Courrier d'Haiphong, Le, Haiphong.
Democracy, Bangkok.
Dépêche d'Indochine, La, Saigon.
Dépêche du Cambodge, La, Phnom Penh.
Echo Annamite, L', Saigon.
Echo du Cambodge, L', Phnom Penh.
Européen, L', Paris.
Eveil du Cambodge, L', Phnom Penh.
Figaro, Paris.
France-Asie, Saigon.
Gavroche, Phnom Penh/Vientiane.
Humanité,L', Paris.
Humanité Indochinoise, Saigon.
Illustration, L', Paris.
Impartial de Pnom Penh, L', Phnom Penh.
Indochine Enchaînée, L', Saigon.
Indochine Hebdomadaire Illustré, Hanoi.
Jeune Asie, L', Saigon.
Journal des Débats, Paris.
Kampuchea, Phnom Penh.

Lanterne, La, Paris.
Légion Française des Combattants. Union Locale du Cambodge, Phnom Penh.
Manchester Guardian, The, Manchester.
Marseille Republicain, Marseilles.
Matin, Le, Paris.
Mékong, Le, Saigon.
Monde, Le, Paris.
Moslem World, The, New York.
Nagaravatta, Phnom Penh.
National Review, London.
New York Times, The, New York.
Nineteenth Century, The. A Monthly Review, London.
Observer, The, London.
Opinion, L', Saigon.
Pall Mall Gazette, London.
Petit Cambodgien, Le, Phnom Penh.
Phnom Penh Post, Phnom Penh.
Presse Indochinoise, La, Hanoi.
Quinzaine Coloniale, La, Paris.
Réalités Cambodgiennes, Phnom Penh.
Revue des Deux Mondes, La, Paris..
Revue du Tourisme Indochinoise, Hanoi.
Revue Indochinoise, and *Revue Indochinoise Illustrée*, Hanoi.
Revue Khmère, La, Phnom Penh.
Scientific Monthly, New York.
Siam Free Press, Bangkok.
Siam Weekly, Bangkok.
Straits Times, The, Singapore.
Temps, Le, Paris.
Thai Newsmagazine, Bangkok.
Time, New York.
Times, The, London.
Tribune Indochinoise, La, Saigon.
Verité, La, Saigon.
Voix Libre, La, Saigon.

3. Books, theses and academic journal articles

Abaly, Fred, (1910), *Notes et souvenirs d'un ancien marsouin (Cochinchine-Cambodge, 1899-1901)*, A. Leclerc, Paris.

Abel-Rémusat, Jean Pierre, (trans.), (1819), *Description du Royaume de Cambodge, par un voyageur chinois qui a visité cette contrée à la fin du XIIIe siècle; précédée d'une notice chronologique sur le même pays, extraite des annales de la Chine*, Imprimerie J. Smith, Paris.

Académie des sciences d'outre-mer, (1976), *Hommes et Destins*, Tome VI, Asie, Académie des sciences d'outre-mer, Paris, pp.377-378.

Aldrich, Robert, (1996), *A History of French Overseas Expansion*, Macmillan, Basingstoke.

Alzon, Claude Hesse d', (1985), *La présence militaire française en Indochine 1940-1945*, Publications du service historique de l'Armée de Terre, Paris.

Amnesty International, *Annual Report, 2000*. Contained in the *New International World Guide, 2001-2002. An Alternative Guide to the Countries of Our Planet*, CD Rom, New Internationalist, Adelaide/Institut de Tercer Mundo.

Anderson, Benedict, (1991), *Imagined Communities: Reflections on the Origins and Spread of Nationalism*, Verso, London.

Anderson, Perry, (1974), *Lineages of the Absolutist State*, New Left Books, London, Note B, "The 'Asiatic Mode of Production'", pp.462-549.

Andrew Christopher M., and Kanya-Forstner, A.S., (1981), *France Overseas. The Great War and the Climax of French Imperial Expansion*, Thames and Hudson, London.

Anonymous, (Preface by Dean Meyers), (2000), *The French in Indochina. With a Narrative of Garnier's Explorations in Cochinchina, Annam and Tonkin*, White Lotus, Bangkok.

Armstrong, John P., (1964), *Sihanouk Speaks*, Walker, New York.

Averini, Shlomo, (ed.), (1969), *Karl Marx on Colonialism and Modernization: His Dispatches and Other Writings on China,*

India, Mexico, the Middle East and North Africa, Anchor Books, New York.

Aymonier, Étienne, (1901), *Le Cambodge*, Three Vols., Ernest Leroux, Paris.

Barmé, Scot, (1993), *Luang Wichit Wathakan and the Creation of a Thai Identity*, Institute of Southeast Asian Studies, Singapore.

Bassett, D.K., (1962), "The trade of the English East India Company in Cambodia," *Journal of the Royal Asiatic Society of Great Britain and Ireland*, London, pp.35-61. Appendix, "A Relacon of the Scituation & Trade of Camboja, alsoe of Syam, Tunkin, Chyna & the Empire of Japan from Q[uarles] B[browne] in Bantam".

Baudouin, Paul, (trans. Sir Charles Petrie), (1948), *The Private Diaries (March 1940 to January 1941) of Paul Baudouin*, Eyre and Spottiswoode, London.

Beaucé, Thierry de, (1967), "Le Cambodge. Bouddhisme et développement", *Ésprit*, Vol. 35, Nr. 9, septembre.

Beauvais, René de, (1931), *La Vie de Louis Delaporte, Explorateur, 1842-1925; Les ruines d'Angkor*, Imprimerie des Orphelins d'Auteuil, Paris.

Belot, Adolphe, (1889), *500 femmes pour un homme*, (seizième édition), E. Dentu, Paris.

Benson, Stella, (1925), *The Little World: travels in the US and Asia*, London.

Bernard, F.A., (1933), *A l'École des Diplomates: La Perte et le Retour dÁngkor*, Les Oeuvres Representatives, Paris.

Best, Geoffrey, (ed), (1988), *The Permanent Revolution: The French Revolution and its Legacy, 1789-1989*, Fontana, London.

Bideleux, Robert, (1985), *Communism and Development*, Methuen, London.

Bierman, John, (1990), *Napoleon III and His Carnival Empire*, Sphere Books, London.

Billotey, Pierre, (1929), *L'Indochine en zigzags*, Albin Maurel, Paris.

Bilodeau, Charles, (1995), "Compulsory Education in Cambodia", Part One, in Somlith Pathammavong and Lê Quang Hông, *Compulsory Education in Cambodia, Laos and Viet-nam*, UNESCO, Paris, p.15.

Bouillevaux, V., (1850) *Ma visite aux ruines cambodgiennes*, Imprimerie J. Monceau, St. Quentin.

——— (1874), *L'Annam et le Cambodge*, V. Palme, Paris.

Bouinais, A., and Paulus, A., (1884), *Le Royaume du Cambodge*, Berger-Lévrault, Paris.

Boulangier, Edgar, (1887), *Un Hiver au Cambodge*, Alfred Mame, Tours.

Boxer, C.R., (Ed.), (1953), *South China in the Sixteenth Century. Being the narratives of Galeote Pereira, Fr. Gaspar da Cruz, O.P., Fr. Martín de Rada, O.E.S.A., (1550-1575)*, Hakluyt Society, London.

Branda, Paul, (1892), *Ça et La. Cochinchine et Cambodge. L'Âme Khmère*, Ang-Kor, Librairie Fischbacher, Paris, p.9.

Bréboin, Antoine, (1910), *Livre d'Or du Cambodge, de la Cochinchine et du Annam, 1625-1910*, Burt Franklin, New York, (reprint 1971).]

Brewer, Anthony, (1980), *Marxist Theories of Imperialism. A Critical Survey*, Routledge and Kegan Paul, London and Boston.

Briggs, L.P., (1947), "A sketch of Cambodian history", *Far Eastern Quarterly*, August, pp.356-357.

——— (1948), "Siamese attacks on Angkor before 1430", *Far Eastern Quarterly*, VIII (1), pp.3-133.

———— (1942), "The Treaty of 23 March 1907 between France and Siam and the return of Battambang and Angkor to Cambodia", *Far Eastern Quarterly*, Vol. V, No 4, August.

Brocheux, Pierre, (1972), "Vietnamiens et Minorités en Cochinchine Pendant la Période Coloniale", *Modern Asian Studies*, 6, 4.

Brunschwig, Henri, (trans. William Glanville Brown), (1964), *French Colonialism 1871-1914: Myths and Realities*, Frederick Praeger, New York.

Burchett, Wilfred, (1957), *Mekong Upstream*, Red River Publishing House, Hanoi.

Buttinger, Joseph, (1958), *The Smaller Dragon. A Political History of Vietnam*, Atlantic Books, London.

———— (1967), *Vietnam: A Dragon Embattled. Vol. I., From Colonialism to the Vietminh*, Frederick A. Praeger, New York.

Cady, John F., (1954), *The Roots of French Imperialism in Eastern Asia,* Cornell University Press, Ithaca, New York.

Camoens, Luis Vas de, (trans. William C. Atkinson), (1952), *Lusiads*), Penguin Books, Harmondsworth.

Candee, H. Churchill, (1925), *Angkor the Magnificent. The Wonder City of Ancient Cambodia*, H.F. and G. Witherby, London.

Caputo, Philip, (1977), *A Rumor of War*, Arrow Books, London.

Carné, Louis de, (1872), *Travels in Indo-China and the Chinese Empire*, Chapman and Hill, London.

Chandler, David P., (1984), "Normative Poems (Chbap) and Pre-Colonial Cambodian Society", *Journal of South East Asian Studies*, Vol. XV, No. 2.

———— (1991), *The Tragedy of Cambodian History. Politics, War and Revolution since 1945*, Silkworm Books, Bangkok.

—— (1993), *A History of Cambodia*, Second Edition, Allen and Unwin, St. Leonards, NSW.

—— (1993), *Brother Number One. A Political Biography of Pol Pot,* Allen and Unwin, St Leonards, NSW.

—— (1999), *Brother Number One. A Political Biography of Pol Pot,* Revised Edition, Westview Press, Boulder, Colorado.

—— (1974), "Cambodia before the French: Politics in a Tributary Kingdom, 1794-1848", Ph.D. thesis, University of Michigan, University Microfilms International, Ann Arbor.

—— (1971), "Cambodia's relations with Siam in the early Bangkok period: the politics of a tributary state", *Journal of the Siam Society*, Vol. 60, No.1, January, pp.153-169.

—— "Cambodian Palace Chronicles (rajabangsavatar), 1927-1949: Kingship and Historiography at the end of the Colonial Era", in Anthony Reid and David Marr, *Perceptions of the past in Southeast Asia*, Heinemann Educational Books, Singapore.

—— (1997), "From 'Cambodge' to Kampuchea; State and Revolution in Cambodia, 1863-1979", *Thesis Eleven*, No. 50, August.

—— (1982), "The assassination of Résident Bardez (1925): A premonition of revolt in Colonial Cambodia", *Journal of the Siam Society*, 70, pp.35-49, Bangkok.

—— (1986), "The Kingdom of Kampuchea, March-October 1945: Japanese-sponsored Independence in Cambodia in World War II", *Journal of South East Asian Studies*, Vol. XVII, No 1, March, pp.80-93.

Chapman, Guy, (1962), *The Third Republic of France. The First Phase, 1871-1894,* Macmillan, London.

Chhuong, Tauch, (trans. Sithan Hin), (1974), "Battambang in the Period of the Vassal", unpublished English language mss, original Khmer version published in Battambang.

Chassigneux, Edmond, (1932), *L'Indochine. Histoire des Colonies Françaises et l'Expansion de la France dans le Monde*, G. Hanoteaux & A. Martineau, Librarie Plon, Paris.

Chollet, Raoul, (1981), *Planteurs en Indochine Française*, La Pensée Universelle, Paris.

Clifford, Hugh, (1910), "In Kambodia", (*sic*), *Blackwood's Magazine*, CLXXXVII, June, London.

Coedès, George, (trans. Emily Floyd Gardiner), (1963), *Angkor. An Introduction*, Oxford University Press, London.

Cohen, William B., (1972), "The Colonial Policy of the Popular Front", *French Historical Studies*, Vol.VII, No. 3, Spring.

Collard, Paul, (1925), *Cambodge et Cambodgiens*, Société d'Éditions Géographiques, Paris.

Collins, William Augustus, "An investigation into the division of the Chams into two regions", Unpublished MA thesis, University of California, Berkeley, 1966.

Commaille, Jean, (1912), *Guide aux ruines d'Angkor*, Hachette, Paris.

Conrad, Joseph, (1999), *Heart of Darkness and other Stories*, (Revised Edition), Wordsworth, Ware, Herts.

Corfield, Justin J., (1990), *The Royal Family of Cambodia*, Khmer Language and Culture Centre, Melbourne.

—— (1994), *Khmers Stand Up! A History of the Cambodian Government, 1970-1975*, Centre of Southeast Asian Studies, Monash University, Clayton, Victoria.

Daguan, Zhou, (Chou Ta-Kuan), (trans. from Paul Pelliot's French version of the Chinese original by J. Gilman and D'Arcy Paul), (1987), *The Customs of Cambodia*, The Siam Society, Bangkok.

Dauphin-Meunier, Achille, (1968), *Histoire du Cambodge*, P.U.F., Paris.

David, Gilbert, (1994), *Chroniques secrètes d'Indochine (1928-1946)*, Vols. I and II, Editions L'Harmattan, Paris.

Davis, Horace B., (1967), *Nationalism and Socialism*, Monthly Review Press, New York.

Decoux, Jean, (1949), *À la barre de l'Indochine. Histoire de mon Gouvernement Général (1940-1945)*, Plon, Paris.

Delaporte, L., (1880), *Voyage au Cambodge. L'Architecture Khmer*, Librairie Ch. Delagrave, Paris.

Delvert, Jean, (1961), *Le Paysan Cambodgien*, Mouton, Paris.

Dickens, Charles, (ed. Adrian Poole), (1997), *Our Mutual Friend*, Penguin Books, Harmondsworth,

Dictionnaires Le Robert, (1994), *Le Robert pour tous. Dictionnaire de la langue française*, Paris.

Direction générale de l'instruction publique, (1930), *Le service de l'instruction publique en Indochine en 1930*, Hanoi.

———— (1931), *La pénétration scolaire en pays cambodgien et laotien*, Hanoi.

Duras, Marguerite and Gauthier, Xavière, (trans. Katharine A. Jensen), (1987), *Woman to Woman*, University of Nebraska Press, Lincoln, Nebraska.

Durtain, Luc, (1930), *Dieux blancs, hommes jaunes*, Flammarion, Paris.

Edwards, Penny, (1999), "Cambodge: The Cultivation of a Nation, 1860-1945", unpublished Ph.D. thesis, Monash University. Clayton, Victoria.

Elvins, Harold E., (1961), *Avenue to the Door of the Dead*, Anthony Blond, London.

Engels, Frederick, *Socialism; Utopian and Scientific*, in Karl Marx and Frederick Engels, (1970), *Selected Works*, Progress Publishers, Moscow.

Ennis, Thomas E., (1936), *French Policy and Developments in Indochina*, University of Chicago Press, Chicago.

Fallaize, Elizabeth, (1982), *Malraux: La Voie Royale*, Grant and Cutler, London.

Ferrar, H., et al, (1980), *The Concise Oxford French Dictionary*, Second Edition, Clarendon Press, Oxford.

Fieldhouse, D.K., (1966), *The Colonial Empires. A Comparative Survey from the Eighteenth Century*, Weidenfeld and Nicolson, London.

Fillieux, Claude, (1962), *Merveilleux Cambodge*, Société Continentale d'Éditions Modernes-Illustrées, Paris.

Fisher-Nguyen, Karen, (1994), "Khmer Proverbs: Images and Rules", in May M. Ebihara, Carol A. Mortland and Judy Ledgerwood, (1994) *Cambodian Culture Since 1975. Homeland and Exile*, Cornell University Press, Ithaca, New York.

Forest, Alain, (1980), *Le Cambodge et la Colonisation Française: Histoire d'une Colonisation sans heurts (1897-1920)*, Éditions L'Harmattan, Paris.

——— (1981) "Les manifestations de 1916 au Cambodge" in Pierre Brocheux (ed.) *Histoire de l'Asie Sud-Est, révoltes, réformes, révolutions*, PUL, Lille.

Foster, John Bellamy, (2000), "Marx and Internationalism", *Monthly Review*, Vol. 52, No. 3, July.

Franck, Harry A., (1926), *East of Siam: Ramblings in the Five Divisions of French Indo-China*, The Century, New York.

Fukuyama, Francis, (1992), *The End of History and the Last Man*, Penguin Books, Harmondsworth.

G.H.P., (c.1945), *La "Kempetai"*. *Saigon, Hanoi, Haiphong, Nhatrang, Huê, Vinh, Phnom-Penh, Vientiane, Mars-Septembre 1945*, Imprimerie Français d'Outre-Mer, Saigon.

Garnier, Francis, (translated Walter E.J. Tips), (1996), *Travels in Cambodia and Part of Laos. The Mekong Exploration Commission Report (1866-1868)*, White Lotus, Bangkok.

Gas-Faucher, F., (1922), *En sampan sur les lacs du Cambodge et à Angkor,* Barlatier, Marseille.

Gaudel, André, (1947), *L'Indochine Française en face du Japon*, J. Susse, Paris.

Ghosh, Manomohan, (1960), *A History of Cambodia. From the earliest time to the end of the French Protectorate*, J.K. Gupta, Saigon.

Ghosh, Suniti Kumar, (1984), "Marx on India", *Monthly Review*, Vol. 35, No. 8, January.

Giteau, Madeleine, (1957), *Histoire du Cambodge*, Didier, Paris.

Goloubew, Victor, (1940), "L'hydraulique urbaine et agricole à l'époque des rois d'Angkor", *Cahiers de L'École Française d'Extrême-Orient*, No 24, 18.

Gorer, Geoffrey, (1936), *Bali and Angkor or Looking at Life and Death*, Michael Joseph, London.

Gourou, Pierre, (1965), *Les Paysans du Delta Tonkinois. Étude de géographie humaine*, Mouton, Le Haye.

——— (1975), *Man and Land in the Far East*, Longman, London.

——— (1966), *The Tropical World*, Fourth Edition, Longmans, London.

Graham, Andrew, (1956), *Interval in Indo-China*, Macmillan, London.

Gras, Yves, (1979), *Histoire de la Guerre d'Indochine*, Plon, Paris.

Groslier, Bernard P., (avec la collaboration de C.R. Boxer), (1958), *Angkor et le Cambodge au XVI siècle. D'après les sources portugaises et espagnoles*, Presses Universitaires de France, Paris.

Groslier, Bernard P., (1974), "Agriculture et religion dans l'empire angkorien", *Études Rurales*, No 53-56, (Jan-Dec.)

————— (trans James Hogarth), (1970), *Indochina*, Barrie and Jenkins, London.

Guérin, Daniel, (trans. Frances and Mason Merrill), (1973), *Fascism and Big Business*, Monad, New York.

Hall, D.G.E., (1968), *A History of South-East Asia*, (Third Edition), Macmillan, London.

Halstead, John P. and Porcari, S., (1974), *Modern European Imperialism: A Bibliography of Books and Articles, 2, French and Other Empires*, G.K. Hall, Boston, Massachusetts.

Hamilton, Captain Alexander, (1744), *A New Account of the East Indies*, Vol. II, C. Hitch and A. Millar, London.

Hammer, Eileen, (1964), "The French Empire Today", in E. Meas Searle, (ed.), *Modern France: Problems of the Third and Fourth Republics*, Russell and Russell, New York.

Hammer, Ellen. J., (1954), *The Struggle for Indochina*, Stanford University Press, Stanford, California.

Hanna, A.C., (1931), "The Chams of French Indo-China", *The Moslem World. A Christian Quarterly Review of Current Events, Literature, and Thought among Mohammedans*, Missionary Review Publishing, New York, July.

Hémery, Daniel, (1990), *Ho Chi Minh de l'Indochine au Vietnam*, Découvertes Gallimard, Paris.

Henissart, Paul, (1973), *Wolves in the City. The Death of French Algeria*, Paladin, St. Albans, Hertfordshire.

Hervey, Harry, (1927), *King Cobra: An Autobiography of Travel in French Indo-China*, Cosmopolitan Books, New York.

——— (1928), *Travels in French Indo-China*, Thornton Butterworth, London.

Herz, Martin, (1958), *A Short History of Cambodia from the Days of Angkor to the Present*, London.

Hess, Jean, (1900), *L'Affaire Iukanthor: Les Dessous d'un Protectorat*, Felix Juven, Paris.

Hickey, Gerald Cannon, (1982*), Sons of the Mountains: Ethnohistory of the Vietnamese Central Highlands to 1954*, Yale University Press, New Haven, Connecticut.

Hobbs, Cecil et al, (1950), *Indochina: A Bibliography of its Land and People*, Library of Congress, Washington D.C.

Hobsbawm, E.J., (1969), *Bandits*, Weidenfeld and Nicolson, London.

Hobsbawm, Eric, and Ranger, Terence, (1993), *The Invention of Tradition*, Cambridge University Press, Cambridge.

Hobsbawm, Eric, (1987) *The Age of Empire, 1875-1914*, Abacus, London.

——— (1995), *Age of Extremes. The Short Twentieth Century, 1914-1991*, Abacus, London.

——— (1999), *Uncommon People. Resistance, Rebellion and Jazz*, Abacus, London.

Hobson, J.A., (1965), *Imperialism: A Study*, Ann Arbor Paperbacks, University of Michigan.

Hodeir, Catherine and Pierre, Michel, (1991), *L'Exposition Coloniale*, Editions Complexe, Paris.

Hull, Cordell, (1948), *Memoirs*, Vol. 2, Hodder and Stoughton, London.

Hwaidi, Yat, (trans. Charnvit Kaset-siri), "Norodom Sihanouk and the Khmer Issarak", *The Bangkok Democrat*, typescript in Chandler Papers, Monash University.

Igout, Michel, (with photographs by Serge Dubuisson), (1993), *Phnom Penh Then and Now*, White Lotus, Bangkok.

Imbert, Jean, (1961), *Histoire des Institutions Khmères*, (Vol. II), Faculté de Droit et des Sciences Économiques, Phnom Penh.

Isaacs, Harold R., (1961), *The Tragedy of the Chinese Revolution*, (Second Revised Edition), Stanford University Press, Stanford, California.

Jackson, Julian, (1988), *The Popular Front in France. Defending Democracy, 1934-38*, Cambridge University Press, Cambridge.

James, C.L.R., (1980), *The Black Jacobins. Toussaint L'Ouverture and the Santo Domingo Revolution*, New Edition, Allison and Busby, London.

Jarvis, Helen, (1997), *Cambodia*, Clio Press, Oxford.

Jeffrey, Robin, (ed.), (1981), *Asia: The Winning of Independence*, Macmillan, Basingstoke,

Johnson, David, "Bandit, Nakleng and Peasant in Rural Thai Society", in C. Wilson et al (eds.), (1980), *Royalty and Commoners: Contributions to Asian Studies*, Vol. 15, pp.90-101.

Jumsai, Manich, (1970), *History of Thailand and Cambodia. (From the days of Angkor to the present)*, Chalermnit, Bangkok.

Kanthoul, Huy, *Mémoires*, unpublished French-language typescript, Chandler Papers, Monash University.

Karnow, Stanley, (1984), *Vietnam. A History, Penguin Books*, Harmondsworth.

Keast, John, (ed.), (1984), *The Travels of Peter Mundy, 1597-1667*, Dyllansow Truran, Redruth.

Kelly, Gail P., (1982), *Franco-Vietnamese Schools, 1918-1938: Regional Development and Implications for National Integration*, Center for Southeast Asian Studies, University of Wisconsin-Madison.

Kemal, Yashar, (translated by Edouard Roditi), (1984), *Memed, My Hawk*, Fontana Paperbacks, London.

Kiernan, Ben and Boua, Chanthou, (eds.), (1982), *Peasants and Politics in Kampuchea, 1942-1981*, Zed Press, London.

Kiernan, Ben, (1985), "Les origines du Communisme Khmer", in Camille Scalabrino et al, *Cambodge. Histoire et Enjeux, 1945-1985, Asie Débat 2,* L'Harmattan, Paris, p.76.

———— (1985), *How Pol Pot Came to Power. A History of Communism in Kampuchea, 1930-1975*, Verso, London.

———— "The Seven Young Coup Makers of 9 August 1945", unpublished and undated typescript based on French intelligence archives, various interviews with Khmer, Thai and Vietnamese informants and Bunchan Mul's Charit Khmaer, Chandler Papers, Monash University.

Kiernan, V.G., (1974), *Marxism and Imperialism*, Edward Arnold, London.

Kinder, Hermann and Hiligemann, Werner, (trans. Ernest A. Menze), (1974), *The Anchor Atlas of World History*, Two Vols., Anchor Books, New York.

Kleinpeter, Roger, (1935), *Le Problème Foncier au Cambodge*, Editions Domat-Montchrestien, Paris.

Lacouture, Jean, (trans. Alan Sheridan), (1975), *André Malraux*, André Deutsch, London.

———— (trans. Patricia Wolf), (1970), *The Demigods: Charismatic Leadership in the Third World*, Alfred A. Knopf, New York.

Lagillière-Beauclerc, Eugène, (1900), *A Travers l'Indochine.
Cochinchine-Cambodge-Annam-Tonkin-Laos*, Librairie Ch.
Tallandier, Paris.

Lamant, Pierre L., (1989), *L'Affaire Yukanthor: Autopsie d'un
Scandale Colonial*, Société Française d'Histoire d'Outre-
Mer, Paris.

Lancaster, Donald, (1961), *The Emancipation of French Indochina*,
Oxford University Press, London.

Lanessan, J-L., de (1895), *La Colonisation Française en Indochine*,
Paris.

Langlois, Walter, (1966), *André Malraux: The Indochina Adventure*,
Pall Mall Press, London.

Léclère, Adhémard, (1914), *Histoire du Cambodge depuis le 1er
Siècle de notre era: d'après les inscriptions lapidaires, les
annales chinoises et annamites et les documents européens
des six derniers siècles*, Librairie Paul Geuthner, Paris.

Le Grauclaude, Henri, (1935), *Le Réveil du Peuple Khmer. Notes en
marge d'un voyage au Cambodge de M. Robin, Gouverneur
Général de l'Indochine*, Éditions de la Presse Populaire de
l'Empire d'Annam, Hanoi.

Lenin, V.I., (1971), *Selected Works*, Progress Publishers, Moscow.

Longley, P.R., (1974), *French Periodicals in Victorian Universities
and the State Library of Victoria*, La Trobe University,
Bundoora, Victoria.

MacGregor, J., (1896), *Through the Buffer State. A record of recent
travels through Borneo, Siam and Cambodia*, F.V. White,
London.

McKay, Donald Vernon, (1943), "Colonialism in the French
Geographical Movement, 1871-1881", *Geographical Review*,
XXXIII, pp.214-232.

Malleret, Louis, "La minorité cambodgienne de Cochinchine". Conférence d'Information, faite à Saigon, le 17 décembre 1945, sous le patronage du Bureau des Affaires du Service Fédéral de l'Instruction Publique, pour les officiers et fonctionnaires du Corps Expéditionnaire de l'Indochine.

Malraux, Clara, (trans. Patrick O'Brien), (1967), *Memoirs*, Bodley Head, London.

Mandel, Ernest, (1973), *An Introduction to Marxist Economic Theory*, Pathfinder Press, New York.

Marchal, Henri, (19?), *Angkor. La Resurrection de l'Art Khmer et l'Oeuvre de l'École Française d'Extrême-Orient*, Office Française d'Edition, Paris.

Marrot, B., (1894), *Exposition de Lyon 1894. Section Cambodgienne. Notes et souvenirs sur le Cambodge*, Forézienne P. Roustan, Roanne.

Marston, John, (1987), *An Annotated Bibliography of Cambodia and Cambodian Refugees*, University of Minnesota, Minneapolis.

Martin, Marie Alexandrine, (1989), *Le Mal Cambodgien. Histoire d'un société traditionelle face à ses leaders politiques, 1946-1987*, Hachette, Paris.

Marx, Karl, (trans. Eden and Cedar Paul), (1972), *Capital*, Vol. I, Everyman's Library, London.

Marx, Karl and Engels, Friedrich, (1971), *On Ireland*, Lawrence and Wishart, London.

Marx, Karl and Engels, Friedrich, (1959), *On Colonialism,* Foreign Languages Publishing House, Moscow.

Marx, Karl and Engels, Frederick, (1970), *Selected Works*, Vol. I, Progress Publishers, Moscow.

May, Jacques M., (1951), *A Doctor in Siam*, Jonathan Cape, London.

McClelland, J.S., (edited with an introduction), (1970), *The French Right (from de Maistre to Maurras)*, Jonathan Cape, London.

McCoy, Alfred, (1981), "The Philippines: Independence without Decolonisation", in Robin Jeffrey, (ed) *Asia – The Winning of Independence*, Macmillan, London.

Mehta, Harish and Mehta, Julie, (1999), *Hun Sen. Strongman of Cambodia*, Graham Brash, Singapore.

Mehta, Harish, (1997), *Cambodia Silenced. The Press Under Six Regimes*, White Lotus, Bangkok.

Melotti, Umberto, (1972), *Marx and the Third World*, Macmillan, London.

Meyer, Charles, (1971), *Derrière le Sourire Khmer*, Plon, Paris.

Meyer, Roland, (1922), *Saramani Danseuse Cambodgienne*, E. Fasquelle, Paris.

Michel, Jacques, (ed.), (19?) *La Marine Française en Indochine de 1939 à 1955*, Tome I, *septembre 1939 - août 1945*, Etat-Major de la Marine, Service Historique, Paris.

Migot, André, (1960), *Les Khmers: Des origines d'Angkor au Cambodge d'aujourd'hui*, Le Livre Contemporain, Paris.

Miller, Stuart Creighton, (1982), *"Benevolent Assimilation". The American Conquest of the Philippines, 1899-1903*, Yale University Press, New Haven, Connecticut.

Mohaphtey, Chandara, "A Khmer Issarak leader's story", unpublished typescript edited by Timothy Carney, 24 January 1976, written 11 June 1974. Chandler Papers. Monash University.

Mohri, Kenzo, (1979), "Marx and 'Underdevelopment' ", *Monthly Review*, Vol. 30, No. 11, April.

Mommsen, Wolfgang J., (trans. P.S. Falla), (1981), *Theories of Imperialism*, Weidenfeld and Nicolson, London.

Monod, G.H., (1931), *Le Cambodgien*, Editions Larose, Paris.

Moon, Brenda E., (1979), *Periodicals for South-East Asian Studies: A Union Catalogue of Holdings in British and Selected European Libraries*, Mansell, London.

Mordaunt, Eleanor, (1932), *Purely for Pleasure*, Martin Secker, London.

Mouhot, Henri, (1864), *Travels in the Central Parts of Indo-China (Siam), Cambodia and Laos during the years 1858, 1859 and 1860*, Two Vols. John Murray, London.

Moura, Jean, (1883,) *Le Royaume du Cambodge*, Two Vols., Ernest Leroux, Librairie de la Société Asiatique de l'École des Langues Orientales Vivantes, Paris.

Nardin, Denis, (1964), "Phnom-Penh: naissance et croissance d'une administration urbain". Mémoire en vue du diplôme d'études superièures de droit public. Faculté de Droit et des Sciences Économiques de Phnom Penh. (Unpublished thesis).

Naval Intelligence Division, (1943), *Indo-china*, Geographical Handbook Series, Naval Intelligence Division, London.

Nicolas, L., (1943), "L'organisation de la justice Cambodgienne", *La Revue Indochinoise Juridique et Économique,* [Kraus Reprint, Neudeln, Liechtenstein, 1970] No 21.

Nicot, Jean, (1987), *Inventaire des Archives du Centre Militaire d'Information et de Documentation sur l'Outre-Mer*, Ministère de la Défense, Paris.

Norden, Herman, (1931), *A Wanderer in Indo-China. The chronicle of a journey through Annam, Tong-King, Laos and Cambodgia,[sic] with some account of their people*, H.F and G Witherby, London.

Norodom, Ritharasi, (1929), *L'Évolution de la Médecine au Cambodge*, Librairie Louis Arnette, Paris.

Nouth, Penn, preface by, (1959), *L'Action de S.M. Sihanouk pour l'independence du Cambodge, 1941-1955*, Phnom Penh. (Collection of articles from *Réalités Cambodgiennes*, 13 September 1958 to January 1959.

Oak, V.V., (1925), *England's Educational Policy in India*, B.G. Paul, Madras.

Osborne, Milton E., (1969), *The French Presence in Cochinchina and Cambodia. Rule and Response (1859-1905)*, Cornell University Press, Ithaca, New York.

―――― (1975), *River Road to China. The Mekong River Expedition, 1866-1873*, George Allen and Unwin, London.

―――― (1978), "Peasant Politics in Cambodia", *Modern Asian Studies*, 12 (2), London, pp.217-243.

―――― (1994), *Sihanouk. Prince of Light, Prince of Darkness*, University of Hawaii Press, Honolulu.

―――― (1973), "King-making in Cambodia: From Sisowath to Sihanouk", *Journal of Southeast Asian Studies*, Vol. 4, No.3, September.

Pages d'Histoire – 1914-1915. L'Atlas-Index de tous les théâtres de la guerre, Ibis, Berger-Levrault, Paris et Nancy, 1915.

Pannatier, A., (1923), *Notes Cambodgiennes: Au Coeur du Pays Khmer*, Centre de Documentation et de la Récherche sir la Civilisation Khmère, Paris.

Persell, Stuart Michael, (1983), *The French Colonial Lobby, 1889-1938*, Hoover Institution Press, Stanford, California.

Phanra, Khy, (1975), "Les Origines du Caodaisme au Cambodge (1926-1940), *Mondes Asiatiques*, Nr 3, Paris, Automne.

Pluvier, Jan M., (1995), *Historical Atlas of South-East Asia*, E.J. Brill, Leiden.

Ponder, H.W., (1936), *Cambodian Glory. The mystery of the deserted Khmer cities and their vanished splendour; and a description of life in Cambodia today*, Thornton Butterworth, London.

Porée-Maspero, Eveline, (1958), *Cérémonies Privées des Cambodgiens*, Éditions de l'Institut Bouddhique, Phnom Penh.

Porée, Guy et Maspero, Eveline, (1938), *Moeurs et Coutumes des Khmers*, Payot, Paris.

Porter, Gareth, "Vietnamese Communist Policy toward Kampuchea, 1930-1970", in David P. Chandler and Ben Kiernan, (eds.). (1983), *Revolution and its Aftermath in Kampuchea: Eight Essays*, Yale University Southeast Asia Studies, New Haven, Connecticut, pp. 57-98.

Pourtalès, Guy de, (1990, orig. published 1931), *Nous, à qui rien n'appartient. Voyage au Pays Khmer*, Flammarion, Paris.

Powell, E. Alexander, (c.1920), "The Unshod Soldiers of a King", Goldwyn-Bray Studios (film).

Prebble, John, (1969), *The Highland Clearances*, Penguin Books, Harmondsworth.

Preschez, Philippe, (1961), "La Démocratie Cambodgienne", thèse pour Diplôme de l'I.E.P., Paris.

Prescott, J.R.V. (1985), *A Study of the Delineation of the Thai-Cambodian Boundary*, Office of National Assessments, Canberra.

Prud'homme, Rémy, (1969), *L'Économie du Cambodge*, Presses Universitaires de France, Paris.

Quaintenne, Rose, (1909), *Quinze Jours au Pays des Rois Khmers*, Coudurier et Montégout, Saigon.

Quaritch Wales, H.G., (1943), *Years of Blindness*, Thomas Y. Crowell, New York.

Rainey, William, (1950), *An Australian Pioneer. From the Diary of the late Mr. Alexander Lawrence, who served the Bible Society in Indo-China, the Philippines and Japan*, British and Australian Bible Society, Kew, Victoria.

Reddi, V.M., (1970), *A History of the Cambodian Independence Movement, 1863-1955*, Sri Venkateswara University Press, Tiraputi.

Reynolds, E. Bruce, (1994), *Thailand and Japan's Southern Advance, 1940-1945*, St Martin's Press, New York.

Robequain, Charles, (trans. Isabel A. Ward), (1944), *The Economic Development of French Indo-China*, Oxford University Press, London.

Roberts, Stephen, (1929), *The History of French Colonial Policy, 1870-1925*, Frank Cass, London.

Robertson, Ian, (1984), *Blue Guide. France*, Ernest Benn, London.

Rosie, George, (1970), *The British in Vietnam. How the twenty-five year war began*, Panther, London.

Pierre Rousset, (1975*), Le Parti Communiste Vietnamien. Contribution à la étude de la révolution vietnamienne*, (seconde edition), Maspéro, Paris.

Said, Edward, (1991), *Orientalism*, Penguin Books, Harmondsworth.

Salisbury, Harrison E., (1992), *The New Emperors: Mao and Deng. A Dual Biography,* Harper Collins, London.

Samnang, Sorn, (1995), "L'Évolution de la Société Cambodgienne entre les deux guerres mondiales (1919-1939)." Trois Tomes. Thèse pour le doctorat d'histoire, Université Paris VII. Unpublished.)

Sarasas, Phra, (1940), *My Country Thailand (its history, geography and civilization)*, Maruzen, Tokyo.

Schirmer Daniel B., and Rosskam, Stephen, (eds.), (1987), *The Philippines Reader: A History of Colonialism, Neo-colonialism, Dictatorship and Resistance*, South End Press, Boston.

Seymour, Michael, (ed.), (1980), *The Travels of Sir John Mandeville, Facsimile of Pynson's Edition of 1496*, University of Exeter Press, Exeter.

Shanin, Teodor (ed.), (1983), *Late Marx and the Russian Road. Marx and 'the peripheries of capitalism'*, Routledge and Kegan Paul, London.

Sheehy Skeffington, F., (1908), *Michael Davitt. Revolutionary, agitator and labour leader*, T. Fisher Unwin, London.

Shiraishi, Masaya, "La presence japonaise en Indochine (1940-1945) in Pierre Brocheux, William J. Duiker, Claude Hesse d'Alzon, Paul Isoart and Masaya Shiraishi, (1982), *Indochine Française 1940-1945*, Presses Universitaires de France, Paris.

Sihanouk, Norodom with Burchett, Wilfred, (1973), *My War with the CIA. Cambodia's Fight for Freedom*, Penguin, Harmondsworth.

Sihanouk, Norodom, (1972), *L'Indochine vue de Pékin*, Éditions du Seuil, Paris.

——— (1981), *Souvenirs doux et amers*, Hachette, Paris.

Silvestre, A., (1924), *Le Cambodge Administratif*, Phnom Penh.

Sisowath Chronicle, pp.1011-1020. (Microfilm in Khmer loaned by David Chandler.)

Sitwell, Osbert, (1940), *Escape with me! An Oriental Sketchbook*, Macmillan, London.

Smith, Ralph B., (1978), "The Japanese Period in Indochina and the Coup of 9 March 1945", *Journal of South East Asian Studies*, IX, 2.

Sok, Khin, (1991), *Le Cambodge entre le Siam et le Vietnam (de 1775 à 1860)*, École Française d'Extrême-Orient, Paris.

Souyris-Rolland, A., (1950), "Les Pirates au Cambodge", *Bulletin de la Société des Études Indochinoises*, 25 (4), pp.307-313.

Steinberg, David J., (1959), *Cambodia: Its People, Its Society, Its Culture*, Hraf Press, New Haven, Connecticut.

————— et al, (1987), *In Search of Southeast Asia: A Modern History*, revised Edition, Allen and Unwin, Sydney.

Sternhell, Zeev, (1986), *Neither Right Nor Left. Fascist Ideology in France,* Princeton University Press, Princeton, New Jersey.

Stowe, Judith A., (1991), *Siam Becomes Thailand. A Story of Intrigue*, Hurst and Co, London.

Taboulet, Georges, (1955), "Le Père Bouillevaux à Angkor (1850)," in *La Geste Française en Indochine. Histoire par les textes de la France en Indochine des origines à 1914*, Tome II, Librairie d'Amérique et d'Orient, Paris.

Tarling, Nicholas, (1990), "The British and the First Japanese Move into Indo-China", *Journal of South East Asian Studies*, Vol. XXI, No 1 March, pp.35-65.

Taylor, Keith W., (1993), "Diseases and Disease Ecology in the Modern Period in Southeast Asia", in Kenneth F. Kiple (ed.) *The Cambridge World History of Human Disease*, Cambridge University Press, New York.

Terweil, Bruce, (1983), *A History of Modern Thailand, 1767-1942*, University of Queensland Press, St. Lucia.

Testoin, Edouard, (1886), *Le Cambodge, Passé, Présent, Avenir*, Ernest Mazereau, Tours.

Thion, Serge, (1994), *Explaining Cambodia: A Review Essay*, ANU Research School of Pacific and International Relations, Canberra.

Thompson, Virginia, (1941), *Thailand. The New Siam*, Macmillan, New York.

——— (1968), *French Indo-China*, Octagon Books, New York.

Thomson, J., (1875), *The Straits of Malacca, Indo-China and China or Ten Years' Travels, Adventures and Residence Abroad*, Sampson, Low, Marston, Low and Searle, London.

Tooze, Ruth, (1962), *Cambodia: Land of Contrasts*, Viking Press, New York.

Tricon, A., et Bellan, Ch., (1921), *Chansons Cambodgiennes, Société des Etudes Indochinoises*, Saigon, 1921.

Trotsky, Leon, (trans. Max Eastman), (1967), *The History of the Russian Revolution*, Vol. III, Sphere Books, London.

Tully, John, (1990), "Certain and Inevitable Misfortune: War and Politics in Lon Nol's Cambodia, March 1970 – December 1971." Unpublished MA thesis, Institute for Contemporary Asian Studies, Monash University.

——— (1996), *Cambodia Under the Tricolour. King Sisowath and the 'Mission Civilisatrice' 1904-1927*, Monash Asia Institute, Clayton, Victoria.

Vercel, Roger, (1952), *Garnier à l'assaut des fleuves*, Paris.

Vickery, Michael, (19?), Unpublished typescript on politics in Cambodia in the 1940s and 1950s. Chandler Papers, Monash University.

——— (1984), *Cambodia: 1975-1982*, Allen and Unwin, North Sydney.

Vincent, Frank Jnr, (1873), *The Land of the White Elephant. Sights and Scenes in South-Eastern Asia. A personal narrative of travel and adventure in Farther India embracing the countries of Burma, Siam, Cambodia, and Cochin-China (1871-2)*, Sampson, Low, Marston, Low and Searle, London.

Viollis, Andrée, (1949), *Indochine S.O.S.*, Editeurs Français Réunis, Paris.

Vircondelet, Alain, (trans. Thomas Buckley), (1994), *Duras. A Biography*, Dalkey Archive Press, Illinois.

Watts, Sheldon, (1997), *Epidemics and History. Disease, Power and Imperialism*, Yale University Press, New Haven.

Weber, Max, (1978), *Economy and Society*, Volume 2, University of California Press, Berkeley.

———— (trans. A.M. Henderson and Talcott Parsons), (1947), *Theory of Social and Economic Organization*, Free Press, New York.

Wheatcroft, Rachel, (1928), *Siam and Cambodia in Pen and Pastel, with excursions in China and Burma*, Constable, London.

Willmott, William, (1967), *The Chinese in Cambodia*, University of British Columbia Publications Centre, Vancouver.

Wyatt, David. K., (1982), *Thailand. A Short History*, Yale University Press, New Haven, Connecticut.

Yule, Henry, (trans. and ed.), (1903), *The Book of Ser Marco Polo the Venetian concerning the kingdoms and marvels of the East*, Third Edition, 2 Vols. John Murray, London.

Zinsser, Hans, (2000), *Rats, Lice and History*, Penguin Books, Harmondsworth.

Index

absinthe, 287
abuse of power, 44, 120, 194, 199, 479, 530
affirmative action, 265, 533
Africa, xix, 49, 53, 79, 230, 270, 278, 293, 301, 309, 350, 410, 541
Age of Reason, xix
Air France, 284, 364
air services, 284
Albert Sarraut (National) Museum, 235, 537
alcohol, 68, 69, 73, 78, 134, 149, 326, 402
Aldrich, Robert, 208, 279, 293
Algeria, xix, 99, 106, 116, 126, 132, 139, 288, 293, 310, 536
Alsace, 110, 124, 158, 161, 169, 222, 369, 410, 461, 462, 464, 465
Andaman Sea, xviii, xix

Ang Chan, King, 14, 26, 51, 59
Ang Duong, King, xix, 3, 4, 8, 9, 12, 14, 15, 16, 17, 19, 25, 26, 50, 59, 71, 104, 119, 127, 152, 165
Ang Eng, King, 26
Ang Mey, Queen, 14, 26
Ang Snguon, Pretender, 147
Ang Vodey, King 2, 65
Angkor, xviii, xix, xxii, 6, 9, 10, 12, 13, 15, 22, 25, 28, 33, 34, 36, 56, 65, 156, 158, 159, 162, 170, 175, 179, 180, 188, 210, 225, 228, 233, 234, 235, 237, 242, 248, 249, 255, 256, 266, 270, 282, 283, 284, 287, 289, 298, 300, 302, 305, 306, 314, 384, 387, 389, 400, 402, 415, 433, 463, 465, 470, 501, 507, 527
Anlong Veng, 180

About the Author

John Andrew Tully lives with his family in Melbourne, Australia, and teaches in the Faculty of Arts at Victoria University. He was awarded his Ph.D. and M.A. degrees by Monash University, and his B.A. and teaching diploma by the University of Tasmania. He is also the author of *Cambodia Under The Tricolour* (Monash Asia Institute, Melbourne 1996) and of a novel, *Death Is The Cool Night* (Papyrus Publishing, Melbourne, 1999), which is set in Germany during the rise of the Nazis and in post-war Australia. Tully has also written a number of short stories and book reviews for Australian literary magazines.